Psychology: An Introduction

third edition

Psychology: An Introduction

Jerome Kagan
HARVARD UNIVERSITY

Ernest Havemann

third edition

HBJ **Harcourt Brace Jovanovich, Inc.**● New York●Chicago●San Francisco●Atlanta

Acknowledgments and copyrights for textual material and for illustrations begin on page 567.

ISBN: 0-15-572617-X

Library of Congress Catalog Card Number: 76-282

Printed in the United States of America

Opening pages of the eight Parts by Bill Greer.

Figure illustrations by EH Technical Services.

Cover: Frank Stella, *Sinjerli Variation I*, 1968. Harry N. Abrams Family Collection, New York.

Preface

The 1970s have turned into an especially exciting decade for instructors and textbook writers. The introductory psychology course continues to enjoy immense popularity among students— which can only mean that the word is being passed along, from one year's students to the next, that psychology has much to offer in both scholarship and relevance. At the same time the frontiers of the science are advancing at such a rapid rate that there is always something new to stimulate the imagination. Those who teach psychology, either in the classroom or in print, do not appear in any danger of suffering either from lack of an enthusiastic audience or from the boredom that might arise in a field that has reached its limits and become static.

Yet what makes the teaching of psychology so exciting also makes it enormously difficult. The students who take the introductory course today find a subject matter that differs considerably from the subject matter taught only a few years ago. The course and the textbook must change as the science continues its forward progress; else they fail in their duty to reflect the best of contemporary thinking and to reject older ideas that have been found wanting. The problem is how to make the subject matter thoroughly contemporary while still preserving the framework of the course that has been found so attractive and useful by students of the past.

This third edition of *Psychology: An Introduction* has been reorganized and rewritten to a considerable extent as dictated by new experimental findings and new trends in theory. At the same time, however, we have attempted to retain the features of the earlier editions that seem to have been found most helpful by instructors and students. As before, the book is especially intended for courses in which a brief text is most useful. Indeed the new edition is shorter than the previous edition and the number of chapters has been reduced, in line with the suggestion of many users that the ideal size for a brief textbook is fourteen chapters, each of a length that can be studied adequately in a single week.

We have also held to another of our original aims—which is to cover all topics traditionally considered essential to a solid basic foundation in psychology. We have kept the book short not by omitting any matters of importance but by striving, as before, for strict economy in organization and language. *Psychology: An Introduction* is designed to provide a thoroughly adequate preparation for students who go on to advanced courses. At the same time, however, it has been written in full realization of the fact that many students will have no further exposure to psychology and will profit most from a book that 1) omits unnecessary and confusing detail and 2) applies psychological knowledge to real-life situations. Previous editions appear to have been found useful by both types of students, and we have again attempted to serve both of them through careful attention not only to completeness but also to clarity, interest, and relevance.

Though the book as a whole is short, some sections have been considerably expanded in keeping with current trends in psychological thinking and student interests. For example, Chapter 13 ("Developmental Psychology") has been enlarged to include developmental processes in adolescence and adulthood—which have taken on new importance in recent years because of findings that the human personality is much more resilient and capable of change (presumably throughout life) than had previously been thought.

Chapter 14 ("Social Psychology") has been not only expanded but also almost completely rewritten in an attempt to place it in the shifting mainstream of contemporary social psychological thinking. The chapter has been restructured around what now appears to be the overriding message of social psychology—which is that all of us behave in a way that is often determined to a greater extent by the situation in which we find ourselves (the people around us, who they are, and how *they* behave) than by any immutable traits we may think we possess. The chapter is now focused sharply on the theme of how strongly other people influence our everyday behavior (particularly as shown in attitude formation, attitude change, and conformity) and of how we choose the people who will have the greatest influence (as determined by the principles of interpersonal attraction). Fortunately, a good deal of the scope of modern social psychology can be covered by using the unifying and integrating qualities of such theories as cognitive dissonance, attribution, self-perception, and social comparison—all of which, moreover, are important, interesting in their own right, and essential for the many students who now go on to advanced courses in social psychology.

New topics, not discussed in previous editions, have been added. To provide an overview of the science and a unifying theme for the book, a new section has been added to the introductory chapter describing the major overall problems and issues to which psychology is currently addressing itself. Chapter 5 ("The Senses") now includes the pattern theory of how the senses operate and Chapter 7 ("Heredity,

Glands, and Nervous System") includes altered states of consciousness. Chapter 9 ("Drives and Motives") contains new materials on the hunger drive and its relation to obesity, also on sex as a combination of drive and motive in human beings. Because of the current though hardly unanimous interest in ESP, a section on this topic has been added to Chapter 6 ("Perception").

The reduction in number of chapters has been made possible chiefly by new findings that have helped clarify and consolidate psychology's knowledge of learning processes and memory—to the point where these topics can now be covered adequately in two chapters instead of the three chapters found necessary in earlier editions. In addition, in line with current trends in teaching, the second edition's chapter on statistics has been eliminated—though for the sake of completeness, the topic is covered in an appendix. Omitting the subject from the body of the book raised one potential difficulty. Without some knowledge of psychological statistics, it is impossible to understand how intelligence and other tests are scored or what is meant by correlations between scores. Rather than ignore this problem, or try to solve it in a brief and elliptical footnote, we have included in Chapter 12 ("Tests of Intelligence and Personality") boxed discussions of the curve of normal distribution and of the meaning of correlation. Though these boxes are brief, students without previous knowledge of statistics should find them sufficient for a full understanding of test scoring and interpretations.

Instructors who used the previous edition will find other changes—for, as has been said, a psychology textbook can no longer be merely "revised," like a house getting a coat of paint, but must be rebuilt from the ground up. Psychology in the late 1970s is an ever-changing, important, and exciting science. We have tried to convey the changes, the importance, and the excitement.

Jerome Kagan
Ernest Havemann

Acknowledgments

In preparing this third edition of the book, our greatest asset was the help of a large number of distinguished scholars who—because of their devotion to their specialties and their desire to help beginning students —gave liberally of their time and effort to serve as our reviewers. Some of them provided us with careful critiques of the second edition chapters and suggestions for additions and improvements. Some reviewed the preliminary drafts of the new chapters, and some did both. The authors, of course, take full responsibility for any scholarly defects in the book.

Mark Appelbaum, University of North Carolina at Chapel Hill

Ellen Berscheid, University of Minnesota

Boit Brannen, Western Connecticut State College

Isidor Chein, New York University

John Darley, Princeton University

Greta Fein, Merrill-Palmer Institute

David A. Gershaw, Arizona Western College

Julian Hochberg, Columbia University

Robert R. Holt, New York University

Walter Kintsch, University of Colorado

Robert B. McCall, Fels Research Institute

Daniel McGillis, Williams College

Salvatore Maddi, University of Chicago

Allan F. Mirsky, Boston University Medical Center

E. Neil Murray, Jr., State University of New York at Buffalo

Edward J. Murray, University of Miami

Richard Nisbett, University of Michigan

Theodore H. Sarbin, University of California at Santa Cruz

Sandra Scarr-Salapatek, University of Minnesota

Gary E. Schwartz, Yale University

Jerome L. Singer, Yale University

John Staddon, Duke University

Leon Swartzendruber, University of New Hampshire

Timothy J. Teyler, Harvard University

Elliot S. Valenstein, University of Michigan

Richard A. Weinberg, University of Minnesota

Wayne Wickelgren, University of Oregon at Eugene

Also of inestimable help were the comments of a number of instructors who had been using the second edition and gave us the benefit of their experience by pointing out its assets and liabilities as a teaching tool. We are indebted to these psychologists for many useful suggestions on organization, content, and presentation.

Susan Alt, Lasell Junior College

Isabel Beck, formerly of Santa Barbara City College

Elliott Benay, formerly of Kingsborough Community College

Alva Calfee, College of San Mateo

Michael Ceddia, Massachusetts Bay Community College

William Coggan, Massasoit Community College

Rubye Del Rowan, Lurleen B. Wallace State Junior College

Elliot Entin, Ohio University

Robert Gibson, Centralia College

Mary Hamilton, Highline Community College

Roy K. Heintz, California State University

Katherine Heinz, Mount San Antonio College

John E. Hoffman, East Los Angeles College

Charlton Lee, Cypress Junior College

Don Low, Orange Coast College

Virginia Pfiffner, El Camino College

David L. Quinby, Youngstown State University

Frank Rosekrans, Eastern Washington State College

Joel Rosevelt, Golden West College

David M. Sawyer, Monterey Peninsula College

Jack P. Shilkret, Anne Arundel Community College

David Skinner, Valencia Community College

Russell M. Stoker, College of San Mateo

Our thanks also go to the following psychologists who served as our advisers on the second edition — and whose comments and suggestions continued to play an important part in this new revision.

Carl W. Backman, University of Nevada at Reno

Dean Burchett, Orange Coast College

Thomas N. Cornsweet, Baylor College of Medicine

James Croxton, Santa Monica City College

Elton Davis, Pasadena City College

James Deese, University of Virginia

Charles Dicken, San Diego State College

Peter Dodwell, Queen's University

Dan J. Ehrlich, La Guardia Community College

Donald W. Fiske, University of Chicago

Lois H. Flint, Glendale College

Wallace S. High, Glendale College

William A. Hunt, Loyola University, Chicago

Glenn C. Martin, Santa Monica City College

Hyman Meltzer, Washington University

Edward O'Day, San Diego State College

Jerry Richards, Orange Coast College

Lillian Robbins, Rutgers University

Carol Roberts, San Diego Mesa College

Gerald Sjule, Orange Coast College

Norman J. Slamecka, University of Toronto

Donovan Swanson, El Camino College

William C. Ward, Educational Testing Service

Carl N. Zimet, University of Colorado Medical Center

We have also been assisted in invaluable ways by Ruth Havemann, Doris Simpson, Carole Lawton, and Mark Szpak.

Contents

x

ONE

WHAT IS PSYCHOLOGY?

Psychology can perhaps best be described as a modern attempt to deal with a subject that has interested and puzzled humanity since the dawn of time—namely, what human beings do and think and the reasons for their behavior.

To our ancestors, the subject seemed hopelessly enmeshed in unanswerable questions. Are human beings just another form of animal life, closely related to the beasts of the jungle and especially to the apes? Or do they possess some quality that makes them unique? And how is one to explain all the differences that exist within the human species? Why are some people so quick to learn, others so slow to learn? Why are some people generally cheerful, others generally glum; some hot-tempered, others easy-going?

The questions are endless. Why are some people driven to become world leaders, others content to listen to music and contemplate the beauties of nature? Why do some people appear to be perfectly "normal" and others to behave in ways that are labeled as strange or neurotic or even "crazy"? Are we destined from birth to behave as we do—or do we have a choice?

Until very recently in human history, there were no real answers to the questions. Philosophers debated them. All sorts of answers were proposed. But the answers were a matter of personal opinion—and what one philosopher considered to be gospel truth was considered by another philosopher to be nonsense.

A hundred years ago, the influence of the natural sciences—chemistry, physics, biology, and the like—suggested a new and very different kind of approach. Psychology was born. For the first time, the factual and unprejudiced methods of science were applied to humanity's study of human behavior. For the first time, some of the questions began to be answered not with mere opinions but with fact.

Today, a century later, many questions still remain. Perhaps some of them will never be answered, for human behavior is so complex that it may forever defy any full and complete analysis. But psychologists do have the answers to many of the questions and clues to some of the others, and they are making new discoveries almost every day.

Because psychology is such a new science, and because so many of the old opinions of human behavior persist, there is still a widespread misunderstanding of what psychologists do, what they know, and what they suspect to be true. An introductory textbook must begin, therefore, with a discussion of how the science began and how it now approaches the problems — in other words, an explanation of what the science is and what it is not.

Chapter 1, "The Scope and Goals of Psychology," suggests the wide range of the subject matter: the great variety of observable activity called *behavior* and also of the *mental activity* that goes on unseen and helps influence and explain behavior. The chapter describes the aims and methods of psychology and includes a section on the history of the science. Also discussed are some of the most important problems and issues to which today's psychologists are addressing themselves.

Outline

The scope and goals of psychology

The number of psychologists in the United States has been growing by leaps and bounds. So has the number of college and university students who take the introductory psychology course and often go on to advanced courses. So has the number of books, magazine articles, and television shows built around psychological themes. And so has the number of people who pride themselves on being "good psychologists" who can see through all the camouflage to the very core of human nature—their own as well as other people's.

Oddly enough, this very popularity of psychology is something of a handicap to the student who embarks on the introductory course. The fact of the matter is that the science of psychology is quite different from what people who have never seriously studied it usually believe it to be. The topics in which it is interested cover a much wider range than is generally thought. Its methods are different. And many of its findings have been almost the exact opposite of what people have generally taken for granted about human nature.

What psychology is and is not

Many people believe that psychology provides some magic answers that will enable them to solve their own personal problems, get along better with their families and friends, and perhaps even help others find the road to personal happiness. This view of psychology has been influenced by the widespread publicity given to the psychoanalyst's couch (see Figure 1-1 on the following page) and to such more recent experiments in self-fulfillment as the encounter group (see Figure 1-2).

It is very true that many psychologists—nearly half of them—are engaged in one way or another in trying to help people overcome personality problems or function better in their jobs and personal relationships. These psychologists do sometimes use psychoanalysis or serve as leaders of encounter groups, as well as practice many less publicized techniques. It is also true that psychology in general has learned a great deal about the human personality; it has come to under-

5

1-1

The first psychoanalyst's couch

This is the office in Vienna in which the first person to undergo psychoanalysis first lay down on a couch and began talking out personality problems. The photograph was made in the office of the founder of psychoanalysis, Sigmund Freud (see pages 26–27), about 1895.

stand many of the factors that influence behavior and how behavior can often be changed by varying these factors.

Yet even the best-trained psychologists, after many years of study and experience, do not claim to perform any magic. Indeed one of psychology's most solid findings is that human behavior springs from so many complicated sources that it is very difficult for any of us to understand why we ourselves behave as we do, much less to understand or influence the behavior of anyone else.

Another popular view of psychology is based on its interest in testing. By the time students arrive at college they have usually been tested and retested in numerous ways—for intelligence, mathematical ability, mechanical skill, and various kinds of vocational aptitude. They have also seen many other tests in newspapers and magazines; they have been invited to score themselves as introverts or extroverts, optimists or

1-2

A contemporary "couch"—the encounter group

A new and currently popular form of treatment for personality disorders—or of just plain striving toward greater self-expression—is the encounter group. Whether Freud or encounter groups have more to offer is one of the controversial issues in modern psychology, as explained on page 35.

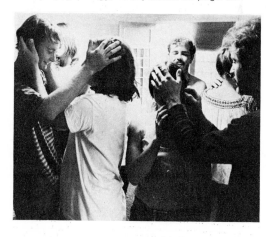

pessimists, good or bad marriage prospects. Thus many students think of psychology as being primarily the source of tests.

Again, this view of psychology is partly true, for tests have been devised by psychologists that are good predictors of school grades, musical performance, ability to work efficiently as an accountant or an electronics engineer or a hospital nurse, and many other matters. But testing is only one small part of psychology. And many of the tests seen in newspapers and magazines have no scientific value at all; they are merely parlor games. Psychologists would want to know a lot more than can be revealed by a few true-false questions before they would attempt to assess your personality or try to predict how you might succeed at such a complicated human relationship as marriage.

Some students take the introductory course because of a fascination with what might be called behavior control, or mind control. Much publicity has been given the idea that psychological discoveries might be used some day to change and manipulate human nature. By dosing people with drugs that affect the brain, or by electrical stimulation of the brain, or even by just applying some of the principles through which animals can be trained, it might be possible to mold people into any form one desired. A "good" dictator, using psychological methods, might wipe out the aggressive impulses that have produced wars. A "bad" dictator might turn humanity into vicious robots that would obey commands automatically and without question.

Again there is some truth to this view of psychology. Psychologists have learned a great deal about how drugs and electrical stimulation can affect the brain and can therefore change behavior. (One of the most spectacular examples is illustrated in Figure 1-3.) But perhaps the most important discovery made along this line is that the brain is so complex, so capable of performing its functions by calling on alternate circuits when the main circuit is blocked, that the whole idea of mind control seems to be just a fantasy of the science fiction writers.

1-3

"Fighting" a bull with brain stimulation

The animal in these photographs is different from any other ferocious bull only in that there are some electrodes carefully implanted in particular spots of its brain. The scientist who implanted them is Dr. José M. R. Delgado of the Faculty of Medicine of the University of Autonoma in Spain, shown here "fighting" the bull with the protection only of a small radio transmitter. At left, the bull charges. At right, Dr. Delgado presses a button on the transmitter, a mild electric current passes through the electrodes in the bull's brain—and the animal stops short, raising clouds of dust. This is one of the most famous demonstrations of how behavior can be controlled by electrical stimulation of the brain.

A definition of psychology

All in all, psychology is both more and less than the popular view of the science would have one believe. It is less in that it is not a new form of magic. (On the one hand, it cannot offer a sure-fire remedy for all the problems that plague mankind. On the other hand, it is not the threat that people fearful of mind control sometimes imagine it to be.) It is more in that it studies a much wider range of topics, and has learned more about more different kinds of human activity, than is generally known.

What then is psychology really like? One way to start defining it is in the words of the poet Alexander Pope, who wrote, "The proper study of mankind is man." (This was in the days before the women's liberation movement pointed out the fallacy of speaking of all people as being of the male sex. Today a poet would more likely write, "the proper study of humanity is humanity.") His words are an excellent clue to the meaning of psychology but only a partial definition. Psychology also studies lower animals; it is interested in the behavior of all living creatures, which it designates by the scientific term *organisms*. Indeed comparative psychology, which is the study of lower organisms in an effort to find comparisons with human behavior, is a flourishing branch of the science — partly because the psychologist can perform experiments with lower animals that it would be unethical to attempt with human beings (for example, the removal of parts of the brain to discover what role these brain structures play in behavior). Moreover, in the case of human beings, psychology is interested not only in observable behavior but also in such inner activities as thinking and feelings.

Perhaps the best possible definition of psychology is this: *Psychology is the science that systematically studies and attempts to explain observable behavior and its relationship 1) to the unseen processes, mental and physical, that go on inside the organism and 2) to external events in the environment.*

Human behavior and the computer

Rothco Original   Bo Brown

"It's really very simple, Edith. Inside is a very tiny mathematician."

The definition of psychology covers an almost breathtaking range of subject matter. To demonstrate the great variety of human behavior and mental processes — and at the same time to introduce some of the major topics covered in this book — let us think of human beings for a moment in terms of comparison with a computer. What will emerge from the discussion is the fact that no electronic machine, however brilliant its accomplishments, has as yet even begun to approach the complexity, skill, and versatility of the human machine.

Consider just the matter of "inputs." Both the computer and the human organism can function only when they receive a flow of information or "inputs." But how much more flexible the human organism is!

To feed information into a computer, the programer ordinarily has to use a typewriter keyboard. The keys produce electronic impulses that the computer can "understand." In a sense the computer also has

⌐О8 ⌐ ОО69О ⌐ 7

208   00690   7

208   00690   7

208   00690   7

Two hundred eight million
six thousand nine hundred and seven

Two hundred eight million
six thousand nine hundred
and seven

Two hundred eight million
six thousand nine
hundred and seven

"eyes." It can scan the numbers on a check, for example, and recognize them. But its scanning powers are limited. The numbers on the check have to be printed in magnetic ink and in a definite pattern. The machine can spot the numbers 208 00690 7 as they are shown at the top left—but it cannot deal with them in all the various other forms that are immediately recognized by the human eye.

As for the spoken word, it has proved very difficult to design a computer that can respond at all to the human voice. To design one that could respond to words as readily as the human ear would perhaps be impossible—for the ear can recognize words whether they are spoken by a high voice or a low voice, in a Boston or a Southern accent, even by someone with a bad cold or laryngitis. Compared with the computer, the human ability to receive inputs through the eyes and ears and make sense of them (the subject of Chapter 5 on "The Senses" and Chapter 6 on "Perception") is a marvel of versatility.

Computers can be said to "learn." That is, they have memories. They can store information. When asked the right question, they can find this information and print it out. But again human beings are much more flexible. Chapter 2 ("The Principles of Learning and Memory") makes clear how intricate is the process of human learning—and how beautifully filed away and cross-indexed is the information in our memories, so that we can find it in all sorts of different ways. We do not have to ask ourselves the "right question." We can usually dredge up the information we have stored away no matter how we go about it.

Computers are good at "information processing." Even the popular little hand-held calculator does a fine job of adding, subtracting, multiplying, dividing, and even finding square roots. More elaborate machines can perform such complex tasks as guiding astronauts through space. But the human organism is also very good at information processing—in ways that most people do not even realize or appreciate but that will be made clear in Chapter 4 ("Language, Thinking, and Problem Solving").

The unique aspects of human behavior

Like the computer, we have our inputs; we learn and store information in memory; we process this information and use it to solve problems.

Even if this were the entire range of human behavior and mental activity, psychology would be a large and significant field of study. But the senses, perception, learning, and problem solving are only a part of psychology's interests. There is much, much more to the science. For human beings display many interesting and important forms of behavior that go far beyond anything exhibited by a mere machine.

As a start toward examining some of the factors that make human life far richer than anything electronic or mechanical, note the students in Figure 1-4 on the following page. In many ways they are alike. They are the same age. They come from similar families and went to the very same high school. On their College Boards, which are a kind of in-

	Student A.	BACKGROUND	Student B.
Age	18		18
Health	Excellent		Excellent
Physical defects	None		None
Father	Mechanic		T.V. repairman
Mother	Nurse		Store clerk
High school	San Pedro H.S.		San Pedro H.S.
		COLLEGE BOARD SCORES	
Verbal	542		545
Math	521		519
		RECORD IN COLLEGE	
Grades	C's		A's and B's
Activities	Few		Many
		LIFESTYLE	
Tendency to be hot-tempered?	No		Yes
Tendency to rely on others?	Yes		No
Ambition	Marriage		Law career
Tendency to get "down in the dumps"?	No		Yes

1-4

Two students—alike yet different

In age, background, and College Board scores, these two students are very much alike. In their present behavior in college, they are very different. Why? For a possible answer, see the text.

telligence test that measures ability to succeed in college, they made about the same scores. Yet there the resemblance ends. In such matters as grades, ambitions, and temperament, they are very different. Why?

Here we get into a whole new area of psychological interests. To understand human beings, we must understand the source and operation of such powerful emotions as anger and fear (the subject of Chapter 8). We must understand something about people's motives, such as the desire to rely on others or to be independent, and their ambitions (the subject of Chapter 9). We must know something about the frustrations and conflicts they experience—and the abnormal behavior, such as a pronounced tendency to be "down in the dumps," that their frustrations sometimes produce (the subject of Chapter 10). We must understand something about the entire human personality (the subject of Chapter 11), which depends on the interaction of all these and many other distinctly human characteristics.

Psychology is also interested in how people grow, mature, and change from birth to adulthood. This is the field of the specialists in *developmental psychology*, whose findings, especially concerning the crucial period from infancy to about the age of ten, are discussed in Chapter 13. And, finally, psychology is interested in how people interact with one another and with their society as a whole. This important field is *social psychology*, discussed in Chapter 14.

The goals of psychology

Thus the scope of psychology is very wide indeed. The subject matter of the science covers all the *overt* or observable behavior that human beings and other organisms exhibit; in the case of human beings it is interested in everything that they do or say. The subject matter also includes the *covert* or hidden processes that go on inside human beings —their thoughts, emotions, motives, and so on.

In studying all these matters, psychology has two aims. Its goals are 1) *to understand behavior* and 2) *to predict behavior.*

Like all sciences, psychology attempts to create satisfactory theories —in this case, statements of general principles that provide a plausible explanation for the phenomena of behavior and mental life observed in the past and that, if sufficiently accurate, will be borne out by future phenomena. In the field of learning in particular, as will be seen in the next two chapters, we already have some fairly powerful theories, derived from the evidence of the past, that enable us to predict when and how learning is most likely to take place.

The methods of psychology

What a science is studying determines in large part the methods it will use. Astronomy, for example, cannot in any way manipulate the stars and planets. It must be content to observe them through telescopes, analyze the kinds of light waves they transmit, and draw conclusions from this indirect information about objects that are billions of miles away. Chemistry can use more direct methods. It can simply put two chemicals together in a test tube and see what happens.

Because human behavior and mental processes take such a wide variety of forms, psychologists have had to improvise. No single method can be applied to all the activities that interest the science. Therefore psychologists have had to adopt a number of different ways of studying their subject matter—and they are constantly seeking new ways. Among the most prominent methods of study now in use are the following.

The experiment

The most powerful tool of psychology, as of all sciences, is the study method known as the *experiment*—in which the psychologist, usually in a laboratory, makes a careful and rigidly controlled examination of cause and effect. Just as chemists can determine that combining hydrogen and oxygen will produce water, psychologists can determine that certain conditions will result in certain measurable changes in the behavior of their subjects, either human or animal.

For example, one psychologist was interested in this question: If people are suffering from anxiety—that is, if they are worried and fearful about what might be about to happen to them—are they more likely than usual to seek the company of other people? This is an important question because it concerns the effects of anxiety, which as will be seen in Chapter 8 is one of the most influential of human emotions, and also the operation of the affiliation motive, which will be discussed in detail in Chapter 9. In everyday terms, the question gets to the core of whether it is true, as is generally believed, that "misery loves company."

To answer the question, the psychologist devised an experiment in which women students at a university, when they arrived at the laboratory to take part in the study, found a frightening looking piece of apparatus and were told that it was designed to deliver severe electric shocks. After being thus made anxious about the nature of the experiment, they were told that they had their choice of waiting their turn alone or in the company of other subjects; and the experimenter carefully noted their decisions. It turned out that only 9 percent preferred to wait alone and fully 63 percent preferred company, while 28 percent said that company or lack of it made no difference to them.

The independent and dependent variables. Every experiment is an attempt to discover relationships among certain conditions or events that can be changed or that result from changes; these are called *variables*. The experimenter sets up some of the conditions and controls and manipulates them. Any condition varied in the experiment, because it is set up independently of anything the subject does or does not do, is called an *independent variable*. The change in the subject's behavior that results from a change in an independent variable is called the *dependent variable*. In the experiment with what the university women believed was a shock machine, the arousal or nonarousal of the subjects' anxiety was the independent variable. Their behavior in response to the independent variable — that is, their decision whether to wait alone or in company — was the *dependent variable*.

In most human situations, in and out of the laboratory, there are many variables. Often, however, the experimenter wants to study the effect of only one independent variable; therefore an attempt is made to hold all other variables constant. In the experiment with the shock machine, for example, the experimenter did not want the results to be confused by any differences between women and men; therefore only female subjects were studied. Since the experimenter was not interested in the effect of any age variable, the study was confined to women of college age rather than a mixed group of adults, teenagers, and elementary school pupils. The experimenter manipulated only one independent variable, degree of anxiety, and studied its effect on one dependent variable, the tendency to prefer company.

The control group. As has been said, measurements of the dependent variable in this experiment showed 9 percent of subjects preferring to wait alone, 63 percent preferring company, and 28 percent in the "don't care" category. As you doubtless have already decided, however, these results are strangely unsatisfactory. It is impossible to figure out, from these figures alone, what if anything the experiment proves. The natural questions to ask are: What would have happened if the subjects had *not* been made anxious? What kind of preferences would they then have displayed toward waiting alone or in company?

To answer these questions, the psychologist used another important experimental tool known as a *control group.* An approximately equal number of women students from the same university were asked to report to the same laboratory, were presented with the same choice of waiting alone or in company — but were *not* made anxious. Instead of seeing and being told about a "shock machine," they were told that the experiment would not be at all unpleasant. Of these nonanxious subjects in the control group, it turned out, 7 percent preferred to wait alone, 33 percent preferred company, and 60 percent were in the "don't care" category. As you can see, this information about the control group enables us to interpret the results for the anxious women. The total design of the experiment included manipulation of an *independent variable* (arousal of anxiety) and measurement of the resulting changes in a *dependent variable* (preference for company, or what is called affiliative behavior), for both an *experimental group* (the subjects made anxious) and a *control group* (the nonanxious subjects). The results, which are presented in several forms in Figure 1-5, "How to read a graph," on the following page, show clearly that at least under these particular experimental circumstances college women suffering from anxiety are much more likely to display affiliative behavior than women who are free from anxiety (1).

Control groups are essential to many psychological experiments, and their selection demands considerable care. In dealing with human subjects, the ideal method would be to find many pairs of identical twins, who, as will be seen in Chapter 7, are as nearly alike as any two people can possibly be, and assign one member of each pair to the experimental group and the other to the control group. Since this is usually impossible, experimenters take many other precautions to ensure that their experimental and control groups are similar in all important respects. In most experiments on learning, for example, psychologists would want to make sure that their experimental and control groups were approximately equal at least in average age and average number of grades or years of college completed — as well as, if at all possible, average scores on intelligence tests and average grades obtained in their classes. They might also try to match the two groups in respect to sex, race, and social background.

Single blind and double blind. In many experiments, another precaution is necessary. For example, one way of studying the effect of marijuana on a person's ability to drive an automobile would be to recruit an experimental group who would receive a known dosage of the drug and a control group who would not receive the drug, then measure their performance on a test simulating driving performance. But obviously their performance might be affected by their knowledge of whether they had taken the drug and their expectations of what it

1-5
How to read a graph

The graphs used to report the results of psychological experiments are simply a convenient way of enabling the reader to grasp the results very quickly, often at a single glance. As is explained in the text, most psychological experiments measure what happens to a dependent variable when an independent variable is changed. The measurements can usually be expressed in figures—such as the percentages of subjects in the "shock machine" experiment who preferred to wait alone, preferred company, or were in the "don't care" category. These figures can be shown in a table, as in illustration A. Or the figures can be converted into a bar graph (B) or a line graph (C).

In this bar graph, as in most, measurements made by the experimenter—the dependent variable—are plotted along the vertical axis at the left, called the *ordinate*. Other conditions of the experiment are plotted along the horizontal axis or *abscissa*. The percentages of subjects who preferred each type of waiting condition are shown by the height of the bars—colored bars for those in the experimental group (made anxious), shaded bars for those in the control group (nonanxious). By laying a ruler across the top of each bar to the figures on the ordinate, as indicated by the dashed lines, you can determine that the height of the bars represents exactly the same figures shown in table A—for example, 9 percent of the experimental group and 7 percent of the control group preferring to be alone, 63 percent of the experimental group and only 33 percent of the control group preferring company. The striking difference in the heights of the colored and shaded bars showing percentages preferring company makes the meaning of the experiment quite evident.

In the line graph, dots are put down in their proper place in relation to the ordinate and abscissa and then connected by lines—a colored line for the experimental group, a black line for the control group. Again, the exact percentages can be determined by running a ruler from the line to the figures on the ordinate, as indicated by the dashed lines.

A

	Subjects' preferences while waiting		
	ALONE	COMPANY	"DON'T CARE"
Anxious subjects (experimental group)	9%	63%	28%
Nonanxious subjects (control group)	7%	33%	60%

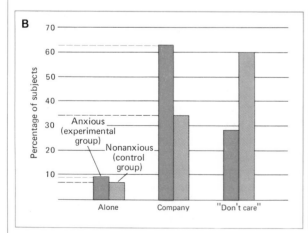

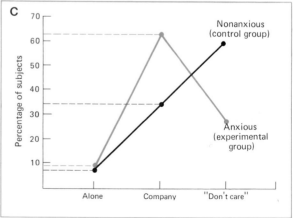

might do to them. To avoid this possibility, it would be important to keep them from knowing whether they had received the drug. This could be done by giving half the subjects an injection of the drug's active ingredient, THC, and the other half an injection of a salt solution that would have no effect, without telling them which was which. This experimental method, in which subjects are prevented from knowing whether they belong to the experimental or the control group, is called the *single blind technique*.

In such an experiment, however, not even the single blind technique would ensure valid results, for the experimenter's judgment of the subjects' driving performance might be affected by knowing which of them had taken the drug and which had not. To make the experiment foolproof, the drug or salt solution would have to be injected by a third party, so that even the experimenter would have no way of knowing which subjects had received which kind of injection. This method, in which neither the subject nor the experimenter knows who is in the experimental group and who is in the control group, is the *double blind technique*. It is particularly valuable in studying the effects of all kinds of drugs—for example, the adrenalin that has been used in studies of emotions (pages 286–88) and the various tranquilizers and antidepressants used in treating emotional disturbances (pages 398–400). It is also used in other experiments where knowledge of the experimental conditions might affect the performance of the subjects or the judgment of the experimenter.

The virtues of the experiment. As developed and refined over the years, and with the checks provided by such methods as use of a control group and the double blind technique, the experiment is indeed psychology's most powerful tool. For one thing, an experiment can be repeated by another experimenter at another time and in another place, ruling out the possibility that the results were accidental or influenced by the first experimenter's personality or preconceived notions of what would happen. (In this connection, a word frequently found in psychological literature is *replicate;* to replicate an experiment is to perform it again in the same manner and obtain the same results.) When facts have been established by the experimental method and verified time and again by other experimenters, we can have great faith in their validity.

Observation

In many cases, unfortunately, experiments are impossible. In particular, it would be highly unethical to perform many experiments that might result in important additions to our store of knowledge. For example, we cannot deliberately rear a group of children under conditions of brutal deprivation and punishment and then compare their behavior with a control group brought up under more humane conditions.

One thing the psychologist can do, however, is what the astronomer does—observe events pertinent to the science with extreme care and precision and with an open and unprejudiced mind. In some cases, psy-

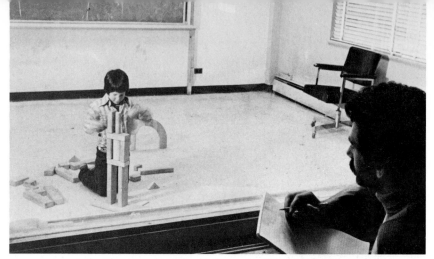

chologists engage in *participant observation,* in which they actually take part in a social situation or a psychological event such as an encounter group. In other cases, they use the method of *naturalistic observation;* they try to remain unseen, as behind a one-way mirror as illustrated in Figure 1-6, or at least to be as inconspicuous as possible, lest their very presence affect the behavior that they are trying to study. Some of our most valuable knowledge of the behavior of infants and how they develop has come from observers who used this method. The famous Masters and Johnson findings on human sexual response were obtained in part in this manner (2).

In a sense all human beings constantly use the technique of observation. Everybody observes the behavior of other people and draws some conclusions from this behavior. If we note that a woman student dislikes speaking up in a classroom and blushes easily in social situations, we conclude that she is shy, and we treat her accordingly. (We may try to put her at her ease, or if we feel so inclined, we may enjoy embarrassing her and making her squirm.) Scientific observations are much more rigorously disciplined than those ordinarily made in everyday life. Scientific observers stick to the facts. They try to describe behavior objectively and exactly, and they are loath to jump to any conclusions about the motives behind it.

Tests

The scientifically designed *test*—itself carefully tested to make sure of its value—is one of the oldest psychological tools. We now have tests that measure intelligence and other abilities, feelings, motives, attitudes, and opinions; and the tests have been tried on enough persons to determine exactly what they measure and how well. As will be seen in Chapter 12 ("Tests of Intelligence and Personality"), the psychological test is a valuable method of exploring human behavior and especially of comparing one human being with another.

Interviews and case histories

One of the best-known studies using the interview method is the work of Alfred Kinsey, who became interested in human sexual behavior when some of his students at Indiana University asked him for sexual advice. When he went to the university library for information, he

Kinsey

found many books of opinion about sexual behavior but almost none that cast any light on the kind and frequency of sexual experiences men and women actually had in real life. So Kinsey determined to find out, and the only possible way seemed to be to interview as many men and women as he could and ask them about their sexual feelings and experiences from childhood until the present time, as he is shown doing at the left. His well-known reports on male and female sexual behavior were the result (3, 4).

A well-known example of the use of psychological interviewing is the *case history*, in which many years of a person's life are reconstructed to show how various kinds of behavior patterns have developed. Case histories are particularly useful in revealing the origins of abnormal behavior. Indeed the whole process of psychotherapy (discussed later in the chapter) may take the form of compiling a long and careful case history as a basis for understanding the problems and correcting them.

Case histories may also be compiled even at times when interviewing is impossible. For example, psychologists may study historical documents, diaries, and the like in an attempt to learn about the behavior and psychological processes of people now dead.

Questionnaires

Closely related to the interview is the *questionnaire*, which is especially useful in gathering information quickly from large numbers of people. A questionnaire is a set of written questions that can be answered easily, usually by putting a checkmark in the appropriate place. In order to obtain accurate results, a questionnaire must be worded with extreme care. Indeed the creation of a questionnaire that will produce accurate results is a fine art, for the slightest change in the way the questions are worded may completely distort the results.

Interviews and questionnaires are sometimes challenged by critics who think that the people who are asked the questions may not tell the truth. Kinsey's work, for example, has been attacked on the ground that people would hardly be likely to be honest about their sexual behavior. But an investigator who is experienced in interviewing or in making up questionnaires and checking them against the facts that can be obtained in other ways knows how to recognize people who are not telling the truth or who are exaggerating. Interviews and questionnaires do not always reveal the complete truth, but when carefully planned and executed, they can be extremely useful.

Applications of psychology

All our modern sciences were founded by people whose chief motive was simply to satisfy their own curiosity about the mysteries of the universe. The first physicists were curious about the nature of light and the behavior of falling objects, the first chemists about the nature of matter.

These pioneers sought knowledge for the sake of knowledge; they were interested in *pure science;* they did not know or especially care whether their discoveries would ever serve any useful purpose.

Yet the discoveries of the pure scientists have of course been put to practical use, and in our modern world we are surrounded on all sides by *applied science.* The physicist's knowledge of electricity has been put to work in lighting and air conditioning the buildings in which we live and work. The automobile is also a product of applied physics, as are radios, television sets, and spaceships. Applied chemistry has produced medicines, plastics, and synthetic fabrics.

Psychology, too, is a pure science that has already had many practical applications, even though it is much younger than physics or chemistry. In today's world, many psychologists are busy studying the pure science; they are interested solely in increasing our knowledge of human behavior. Many other psychologists, however, are engaged in the practice of applied science and are using the knowledge we now have in many practical ways. This work has changed our world more than most people realize. Moreover, it has resulted in a great deal of new psychological knowledge.

Clinical psychology and counseling

Clinical psychology is the diagnosis and treatment of psychological problems. *Counseling* is a closely related field that offers assistance to people who need temporary guidance on problems such as school difficulties, vocational choices, or marriage conflicts. More psychologists today specialize in these two fields than in any other branch of the science; the number has been variously estimated at somewhere between 39 percent (5) and 48 percent (6).

Psychologists have developed many techniques of *psychotherapy,* or the treatment of personality problems. Indeed, as will be seen later in the chapter, these techniques have multiplied to the point where their relative merits have become one of the great current arguments and issues in psychology. The methods themselves will be discussed in Chapter 11.

Psychology in schools and industry

Some clinical psychologists and counselors work in schools, where they not only attempt to diagnose the causes of students' problems but also consult with teachers and families in an attempt to change the conditions that have caused the problems. Others work in industrial firms, where it has been found that many employees fail at the job not because of lack of skill but because of bad personal relations with their fellow workers or bosses. In addition, psychology has found many other applications in the schools and in industry.

In the schools, psychology's best-known contribution has been its standardized tests. Intelligence tests offer a reasonably good prediction of how well a student can be expected to perform—although, as will be

discussed in Chapter 12, they have certain weaknesses and are more successful in rating students from middle-income homes than students from low-income homes. Standardized achievement tests are a generally accurate measure of how well an individual student is progressing year by year in various skills, such as reading and arithmetic, or of how one school compares with others in the nation.

Psychology has also influenced teaching methods, the organization of the curriculum, and the preparation of textbooks and educational films. Indeed most of the principles of learning that will be discussed in Part 2 of this book can be applied to schoolwork. Some colleges have a special course in the applied psychology of learning designed to help students do better in their classes.

In industry, psychologists have discovered many facts about worker fatigue, working hours, rest periods, and employee morale. They have also created many training devices that make it easier to learn particular skills and have contributed to *human engineering,* which is the design of equipment and machinery that will be more efficient and easier to use because they fit the actual size, strength, and capabilities of the human beings who will use them. A new interest of industrial psychologists is the study of pollution created by manufacturing plants, its effect on human beings, and ways to reduce it.

Public opinion surveys

Another field in which a number of psychologists are engaged is the study of public opinion, as typified by the well-known Gallup poll. Such studies have disclosed many previously unknown facts about how people feel about all kinds of important issues, such as military expenditures, welfare programs, racial tensions, sexual behavior, birth control and abortion, marriage and divorce, and many others.

Scientific techniques of sampling have made it possible to show how all the people in the United States are divided on any issue, within a few percentage points of possible error, by polling a mere 1,500 or so. The techniques are extremely complicated and are used not only by psychologists but also by sociologists, economists, and other students of public attitudes. Some of the basic techniques are discussed in an appendix to this book devoted to the subject of *psychological statistics.*

Public opinion surveys have been used to predict election results, by businesses to measure the reaction to various types of products and sales and advertising campaigns, and in many other ways. The Nielsen ratings of the popularity of television shows are another example.

The history of psychology

Humanity's efforts to understand and to predict behavior go back, presumably, to the very origins of the human race. We can assume from what is known about some of the primitive tribes that exist today in isolation from modern civilization that people have always been mys-

tified by their dreams. A man goes to sleep and in his dreams seems to travel. He goes fishing on a distant river; he goes hunting on a distant plain; he meets his friends; he even meets and converses with people who are long since dead. When he wakes up, anyone can tell him that his body has not moved at all from his bed. What could be more natural than to suppose that the human body is also inhabited by a human soul, which can leave and reenter the body at will and survives after death? The ancient Greek philosophers were also fascinated by this apparent division of human existence into body and soul. And they speculated endlessly on the nature of the human mind, which they conceived to be a part of the soul, or perhaps the same thing. This was the age in which the science of mathematics was reaching great heights, and the Greek philosophers marveled that the human mind could create the world of mathematics—a world, though purely imaginary and theoretical, that was much more logical and "pure" than the real world of sleeping and eating and physical illness and death.

As for attempts to predict behavior, the Greeks had their oracles, notably the Delphic oracle, who were supposed to bring them messages from the gods. Presumably all civilizations, and even the generations that preceded civilization, have had soothsayers, witch doctors, and sages to whom they looked for guidance about the future. We still have them today, even in our modern scientific America. Almost every city has its fortunetellers, and the newspapers print columns in which astrologers predict what will happen to us today.

What distinguishes psychology from many previous attempts to understand and predict human behavior is that it refuses to regard the human organism as the possessor or creature of unproved forces. Although a few of its practitioners may perhaps hold to the contrary, psychology does not believe that a person's life is affected by the position of the stars at the moment of birth. It does not seek divine revelations from a Delphic oracle. Nor is it content to describe people as some past philosopher, however brilliant, may have imagined them to be. It does not accept the adages of previous generations, no matter how commonsensical those adages may seem to be. (Many of the adages, as a matter of fact, are mutually contradictory. Is it true that "a bird in the hand is worth two in the bush," or is it better to believe "nothing ventured, nothing gained"?)

Instead, psychology approaches the study of human behavior in much the same manner as chemistry studies the activities of the chemical elements and their compounds, or as physics studies the phenomena of energy and movement. It is based, as has been said, on controlled experiments and on observations made with the greatest possible precision and objectivity. It represents the first application of the methods of science to the study of behavior.

**Wilhelm Wundt,
founding father**

Like other sciences, psychology evolved slowly and was the result of many contributions by many people. The philosophers of the seven-

Wundt

James

teenth and eighteenth centuries helped create the realistically inquiring attitude of mind that made the science possible. The physiologists of the nineteenth century did their part by making numerous discoveries about the human nervous system and the human brain. The year in which all these factors came together and psychology emerged as a science in its own right is usually put at 1879, when Wilhelm Wundt established the first psychology laboratory at Germany's University of Leipzig.

Wilhelm Wundt, shown at left, was a solemn, hard-working, and tireless man who devoted himself to scholarship from the time he was a boy until he died at the age of eighty-eight. A preacher's son, he first became a physician, but instead of practicing medicine he taught physiology. He soon lost interest in the physical aspects of human behavior, for he was much more concerned with consciousness. His laboratory was the first place in the world where a serious and organized attempt was made to analyze and explain human consciousness.

Compared with modern psychological experiments, Wundt's work now seems rather unexciting. For example, he was interested in the human reaction to the sounds of a metronome, and he and his students spent hours in the laboratory listening to the click of a metronome set at low speeds and high speeds, sometimes sounding only a few clicks at a time, sometimes sounding many. As they listened, they tried to analyze their conscious experiences. Wundt decided that listening to some kinds of clicks was more pleasant than listening to others. He noticed that he had a feeling of slight tension before each click and a feeling of relief afterward. He also concluded that a rapid series of beats made him conscious of excitement and that a slow series made him relaxed. Wundt and his students listened to the same kinds of clicks, then carefully reported their conscious experiences and compared notes. They may not have produced powerful laws about behavior, but they did establish a systematic method of study.

Psychology as the study of "mental life"

For many years, following the lead of its founding father, psychology was chiefly interested in the study of the human consciousness. Indeed a textbook written by the most prominent of the early American psychologists, William James, began with the words: "Psychology is the study of mental life."

To make this study of "mental life," the early psychologists used as their tool the practice of *introspection,* or looking inward. They tried to analyze, as carefully and objectively as possible, the processes of their minds. They also asked their subjects to make this same kind of analysis. Thus the technique used by Wundt to examine the conscious experiences resulting from the sounds of a metronome was broadened and applied to a wide range of human experiences. Among the interests of the early psychologists, as James defined them, were people's feelings, desires, thoughts, reasonings, and decisions—as well as their struggles to attain their goals or to become reconciled to failure.

John Watson and the behaviorist revolution

Watson

Is introspection really a scientific method? Or is it merely another name for philosophizing about the human condition? One person who came to the second of these conclusions—and therefore started a revolution in psychology—was John Watson, who about the year 1913 founded the movement known as *behaviorism*. Watson declared that "mental life" was something that cannot be seen or measured and thus cannot be studied scientifically. Instead of trying to examine any such vague thing as "mental life" or consciousness, he concluded, psychologists should concentrate on overt behavior—the kinds of actions that are plainly visible.

Watson did not believe in anything like "free will," or the ability to control one's own destiny. Instead he believed that everything we do is predetermined by our past experiences. He considered all human behavior to be a series of events in which a *stimulus*, that is, an event in the environment, produces a *response*, that is, an observable muscular movement or some physiological reaction, such as increased heart rate or glandular secretion, that can also be observed and measured with the proper instruments. (For example, shining a bright light into the eye of a person or other organism is a stimulus that causes an immediate response in which the pupil of the eye contracts; a loud and unexpected noise is a stimulus that usually causes the response of muscular contraction, or "jumping," and increased heart rate.) Watson believed that through *conditioning*, a type of learning that will be discussed in Chapter 2, almost any kind of stimulus could be made to produce almost any kind of response. Indeed he once said that he could take any dozen babies at birth and, by conditioning them in various ways, turn them into anything he wished—doctor, lawyer, beggar, or thief.

Even the existence of a human mind was doubted by Watson. He conceded that human beings had thoughts, but he believed that these were simply a form of talking to oneself, by making tiny movements of the vocal cords. He also conceded that people have what they call feelings, but he believed that these were only some form of conditioned response to a stimulus in the environment.

Watson's theories burst upon the world at a time when many psychologists were dissatisfied with the progress of their science. The attempts to examine consciousness—or "mental life," to use the James terminology—had not been very fruitful. There was some question whether looking inward into the human mind was really scientific at all. The notion that it is better to examine and measure overt behavior than to try to study the invisible mind was very appealing, and for many years Watson was the most influential of American psychologists.

S-R psychology and B. F. Skinner

One newer school of psychological thought that grew out of Watson's theories is known as *stimulus-response psychology,* or S-R psychology for short. The S-R psychologists emphasize study of the stimuli that produce behavioral responses, the rewards and punishments that help

Skinner

establish and maintain these responses, and the modification of behavior through changes in the patterns of rewards and punishments. One leader of the S-R school has been B. F. Skinner, who ranks as another of the most prominent American psychologists of the past half-century. Skinner has been chiefly interested in the learning process and has revised and expanded Watson's ideas into a theory of learning that continues to influence much psychological thinking. He has made many important contributions to our knowledge of how patterns of rewards and punishments produce and modify connections between a stimulus and a response and thus help control the organism's behavior—often in the most complex ways.

Skinner's best-known book is *Beyond Freedom and Dignity*, published in 1971 (7). Here he argues that people possess neither of the two attributes mentioned in the title. Indeed people are not responsible for their conduct; they are not to blame for their failures or deserving of credit for their achievements. They are simply the creatures of their environments. Their behavior depends on the kinds of S-R learning to which they have been subjected, particularly which of their actions have been rewarded and which have been punished. A "social engineer" aware of all the principles of S-R learning could mold people into any form desired, whether for good or for evil.

Behaviorism and its modern counterpart of S-R psychology, as has been said, have greatly influenced the entire course of the science for many years. Watson and especially Skinner continue to have many followers. But their ideas have always been controversial—and the controversy has been intensified by Skinner's belief that we have no real freedom of choice or responsibility for our own actions. Other schools of psychological thought are now moving in quite different directions.

Gestalt psychology

To understand some of the new trends in psychology one must go back to another school of thought of considerable historical importance. This is *Gestalt psychology*, which originated in Germany at about the same time Watson's ideas were becoming so influential in the United States. Gestalt psychology takes its name from a German word that has no exact English equivalent. *Gestalt* can be roughly translated as "pattern" or "configuration." But it means something more than that. The Gestalt school believed that in studying any psychological subject, from rather simple perceptual processes to the human personality, it was essential to look at the pattern considered *as a whole*. Indeed the Gestalt theories have often been summarized as maintaining that "the whole is greater than the sum of its parts."

A simple demonstration sometimes used in classroom explanations of Gestalt psychology is to draw four lines on the blackboard, as illustrated here in the margin. Students are asked to imagine that these are four sticks of equal length and then to describe what they see. The usual answers are "four sticks," or "four sticks with spaces between them," or

1-7

Seeing a "Gestalt"

What do you see in the left-hand drawing when you look where the arrow points? The Gestalt psychologists would maintain that you do not say to yourself: "I see a head, a body, two arms, two legs; therefore I must be looking at a person." Instead you take in the whole pattern, or Gestalt, and immediately see a person, almost without thinking at all. Because of the uniform, the taxi, and the hotel, you are immediately aware that the person is a doorman. In the right-hand drawing, the same person in a different context seems to be obviously a military officer. This is a good example of how a "whole" dictates the properties of its parts.

"an arrangement of sticks." Then the lines are redrawn to form the geometrical figure shown here at the left—and, lo, the four sticks suddenly become clearly and unmistakably a square.

Another demonstration will be found in Figure 1-7. Note in this figure how your interpretation of what the arrows point to is affected by the surroundings, or what Gestalt psychology refers to as the context. Not only does Gestalt psychology stress the whole rather than the parts but it also emphasizes the importance of the entire situation, or context, in which the "whole" is found.

Gestalt psychology was at direct odds with Wundt's idea, in that it saw no profit in trying to break down human mental experience into individual and fragmented sensations, images, or feelings. It was also at odds with the behaviorists, in that it denied that learning and behavior could be explained as a mere succession of conditioned reflexes. Indeed the Gestalt psychologists argued that learning often takes place in sudden flashes of "insight"—a creative thinking process that will be discussed at length in Chapter 4. Gestalt psychology has largely died out as a movement in its own right, but many of its ideas continue to thrive in two very modern schools of psychology that grew out of its thinking.

Cognitive psychology

One of the new schools related to the old Gestalt movement is *cognitive psychology,* which, as its name implies, stresses the importance of mental processes. Cognitive psychologists reject many aspects of behaviorism and question the importance of the conditioning process that Watson saw as the whole key to human behavior. They maintain that behavior cannot possibly be explained in full by stimulus-response connections and indeed that the human mind is much more than a mere reflection of the stimuli that its possessor has encountered. They tend to think of the mind as operating as a sort of "mental executive" that actively makes comparisons and decisions, thus processing the information it receives into new forms and categories.

A simple example sometimes cited by cognitive psychologists is this: try reading a string of digits to a friend, such as 5, 9, 3, 2, 8, 6. Then repeat the same string with one digit missing, say 5, 9, 3, 8, 6. Your friend will have no trouble stating immediately that the missing number is 2. As the cognitive psychologists interpret it, your friend has not merely made a specific response dictated by a specific stimulus. Instead the listener has engaged in some sort of decision-making process that scanned the two strings of digits, compared them, and noted the difference. What is most important about human mental activity, the cognitive psychologists believe, is that it includes such comparisons and understandings, as well as the discovery of meanings and the use of old knowledge to find new principles that aid in constructive thinking and problem solving.

Like the Gestalt school, the cognitive psychologists tend to think of mental activity and human behavior in general as a pattern and a unity. They regard learning, for example, as a series of very complex but closely related activities that can be described, in the aggregate, as *information processing.* Steps in this processing include seeing and hearing, the organization of what we see and hear into perceptual patterns (for example, perceiving a girl or a boy rather than a collection of arms, legs, and body), and storing what we have seen or heard in memory—then drawing on the information stored in memory to solve problems, make judgments, and decide on appropriate behavior.

Humanistic psychology

The other modern movement that stems in part from the Gestalt school is *humanistic psychology.* Like the Gestalt psychologists, the humanists prefer to view the human personality as a pattern and an entity. To try to study human behavior by breaking it down into fragments, such as individual responses to individual stimuli, is regarded as futile and indeed a matter of "disrespect" for the unique quality of the human spirit (8). For human beings, the humanistic psychologists believe, are totally different from other organisms. They are distinguished by the fact that they have goals and values; they seek to express themselves, to grow, to fulfill themselves, to find peace and happiness. Their thoughts and aspirations, which Watson refused even to acknowledge, are more important than any individual aspects of their behavior.

Rogers

The origins of humanistic psychology also lie in developments in philosophy, literature, and religious writings over past centuries. The humanistic psychologists take a broad and very hopeful view of the true quality of human nature, its accomplishments, and its potentialities. One of their leaders, Abraham Maslow, introduced the theory that human beings are characterized by a motive called *self-actualization* (pages 327–28), which makes them strive to realize fully their possibilities for creativity, dignity, and self-worth. Another, Carl Rogers, invented the optimistic form of treatment of emotional disturbances called *client-centered therapy* (pages 389–90), built around the assumption that people will always grow in a constructive way if their environment permits them to do so.

Sigmund Freud and psychoanalysis

Even a very brief discussion of psychology's history would not be complete without mention of Sigmund Freud, who, though not a psychologist but a physician, has had a profound influence on many aspects of psychological thinking. Freud began his career as a practicing physician and neurologist in the 1880s in Vienna. His attention turned to psychological processes as the result of his experiences with patients who were suffering from hysteria — which sometimes is associated with paralysis of the legs or arms that seems to have no physical cause. The theories he developed — over a lifetime of observing and treating many kinds of neurotic patients and also of attempting to analyze his own personality — are the basis of that well-publicized movement called *psychoanalysis,* first announced to the world around the turn of the century.

Freud himself was rather neurotic in his youth, suffering from feelings of anxiety and deep depression. He retained some neurotic symptoms all his life; he was a compulsive smoker of as many as twenty cigars a day, was nervous about traveling, and was given to what were probably hypochondriacal complaints about poor digestion, constipation, and heart palpitation. However, he managed to overcome his early inclinations toward depression and lived a rich professional, family, and social life — an indication that in his case the physician had managed to heal himself, at least in large part.

One of Freud's great insights into the human personality was the discovery of how it is influenced by *unconscious processes,* especially motives of which we are unaware. At first his ideas were bitterly attacked; many people were repelled by his notion that human beings, far from being completely rational, are largely at the mercy of irrational unconscious thoughts. Many were shocked by his emphasis on the role of sexual motives (which were prominent among those that the society of that period preferred to deny) and particularly by his insistence that even young children have intense sexual desires. Over the years, however, the furor has died out. There is considerable controversy over the value of psychoanalytic methods in treating neurotic patients, but even

Freud

those who criticize psychoanalysis as a form of therapy accept some of Freud's basic notions about personality and its formation. His theories will be discussed in detail on pages 379–82.

Issues in modern psychology

As even a sketchy summary of psychology's history makes clear, the science has moved in many directions. Its practitioners have had many different interests, have conducted their studies in different ways, and have reached different conclusions. In a number of respects the various schools of thought that have arisen over the years — all attracting their share of loyal followers — have been in violent disagreement.

Yet it would seem, as psychology is about to enter its second century, that many of these separate strands of psychological thinking are now in the process of being drawn together. All the pioneers and all the various schools of thought have made important contributions to human knowledge. Today's students of psychology, without agreeing or disagreeing with any of them, can profit greatly from their work. From Wundt we can learn something about the value of trying to make an objective analysis of our conscious experiences. Watson has contributed the warning that psychology should, insofar as possible, stick to the methods of science and be based on what can be seen and measured. The S-R psychologists have cast valuable light on the importance of learning, the cognitive psychologists on the information-processing aspects of mental activity. The humanistic psychologists have reminded us not to lose our concern for humanity's dignity and worth. The psychoanalysts have given us insights into some of the more baffling aspects of human personality.

All these contributions have in one way or another advanced our knowledge of human behavior and mental processes. Perhaps, despite many continuing disagreements, they are now in the process of being synthesized into general theories that will greatly expand our knowledge, will cast new light on human nature, and will suggest new ways to alleviate mental disturbances and improve the quality of human society and human life.

Later chapters of the book will be concerned mostly with specific facts that psychologists have discovered about human behaviors and mental processes in all their great variety from learning to abnormal behavior. Before beginning this kind of detailed discussion, however, it will be useful to examine some of the major overall problems and issues to which modern psychology is addressing itself. Many of these issues go to the very core of the human experience. Since they cut so deep, they are difficult issues to study or to resolve. On most of them, all the facts are not yet in. On many of them, as the discussion of psychology's history has indicated, there is still widespread disagreement. But these are the big issues to which psychology, in the broadest sense, is now dedicated.

Human nature: "good" or "evil"?

The behaviorists and S-R psychologists, as has been said, take a neutral view of human nature. They believe that environment and learning, rather than any inborn qualities, determine human behavior. The humanists, on the other hand, are convinced that human nature is "good." They believe that people are basically destined to live in peace and harmony, to be bound together by ties of affection, to work constructively for the benefit of all. They attribute selfishness, crime, and violence to an environment that thwarts and warps these basic human tendencies. The existence of oppression and cruelty throughout history is believed by the humanists to represent a failure not of the human spirit but of the kinds of societies that have somehow evolved.

The Freudian psychoanalysts are less optimistic. They grant that people are born with great yearnings for life and love—but they also see a darker side of human nature that gravitates relentlessly toward destruction and death. (This conflict between "good" and "evil," in the psychoanalytic view, is often the cause of emotional disturbances.) Least optimistic of all are some scientists who, chiefly from their studies of the behavior of lower animals, have concluded that all organisms including human beings are motivated by hostility and prone to aggression—in other words, are born to fight. Some of these scientists believe that human beings are the most ferocious killers of all (9).

Will we ever be able to determine whether human nature is "good," "evil," or neutral? Perhaps not. This is a philosophical question that defies a purely scientific answer. Scientific observation can determine the conditions under which human beings are aggressive, but the evaluation of aggression as good or evil is an ethical decision made by the members of a society. Our view of "human nature" at any given moment depends on historical developments, social crises, and new knowledge. These are changing and so our notions of "human nature" change with them.

The issue of "nature versus nurture"

This issue revolves around the question: To what extent is human behavior determined by factors present at birth, and to what extent is it molded by experience and learning? Sometimes the question is put another way: To what extent does human nature depend on heredity and to what extent on environment (or the sum total of all the influences exerted by family and society)?

Until a few hundred years ago, majority opinion among history's greatest thinkers seemed to lean toward the side of heredity. It was generally believed that every human being was born with strong predispositions toward certain kinds of behavior. One baby inherited the tendency to be happy, another to be melancholy. One baby was born to be a leader, another a timid follower, another to be a troublemaker or even a criminal. Believers in this theory have been known as *nativists*. Their ideas, it will be noted, constitute a rather fatalistic view of human behavior. If the future of the individual human being is laid down at

Locke

birth, then there is not much point in parents attempting to find better ways of bringing up their children or in the schools attempting to find better ways of educating them.

A groundswell toward the opposite viewpoint was largely the work of John Locke, the seventeenth-century philosopher, who popularized the idea that the mind of the human baby is what has been called a *tabula rasa,* Latin for "blank tablet." On this blank tablet, Locke argued, anything at all can be written through experience and learning. In other words, heredity is unimportant. The child becomes whatever the environment dictates.

Locke's idea greatly influenced other philosophers who helped create the energetic intellectual climate in which psychology was born as a science. It was attractive to many of the early psychologists, who grew up in this atmosphere, and it remains a strong influence to this day. The followers of Locke are known as *empiricists;* their theory, of course, is exactly the opposite of the nativists' beliefs. Some of the empiricists, like Skinner, take a neutral view of what the idea means to humanity. They believe that people can be molded in any direction, vicious as well as benign. But in general the empiricists tend to take an optimistic view of the human condition. If the mind of the human baby is indeed a "blank tablet," then human history would seem to have unlimited possibilities. All the evils that have plagued humanity—jealousy, emotional conflicts, crime, even war—are not inevitable but are the result of the wrong kind of learning. By discovering the principles of learning, we can point the way toward a brighter future for mankind.

On this important issue, psychology has accumulated a great deal of evidence in recent years. Both the nativists and empiricists, it now appears, have been partly right and partly wrong. We human beings, it has been found, are always influenced by both heredity *and* environment.

As will be seen in later chapters, the bodies and nervous systems with which we are born, in accordance with the rules of heredity as described in Chapter 7, do affect our behavior. They help determine many things, such as the way we perceive the world around us and the way we use language. They make some things easy to learn and others more difficult. They influence our emotional makeup and our ability to withstand stress. Even tendencies toward certain severe forms of emotional disturbance (including the crippling mental disorder called *schizophrenia*) seem to be partially inherited. To this extent, the nativists have been right to some degree.

On the other hand, our inborn equipment seems to set only the limits and the broad tendencies of behavior, leaving room for a wide range of possibilities. Even among those who may inherit a tendency toward schizophrenia, only some will actually develop this disorder. Others, thanks to a more favorable environment, will escape. What we learn and how we learn it are still crucial factors in our behavior—so important, indeed, that it is appropriate to begin the main body of this book with the subject of learning (Chapters 2 and 3). Though the new-born baby is not entirely a *tabula rasa,* there is still a great deal of room on the tablet for the writings of experience and environment—and to this extent the empiricists have been right.

Does who you are depend on where you are?

Until fairly recently, psychology was chiefly interested in the individual. The science was content to separate the individual person from others, rather like a zoologist cutting one elephant out of the herd for measurement and tagging, and to study this person's behavior as it appeared in the laboratory or in test results. It was generally assumed that any characteristics that could be observed represented a customary and consistent pattern of behavior. A person found to be helpful and generous would be helpful and generous in general, under any circumstances. An aggressive person would always tend to be aggressive.

It is now well established, however, that the human personality and human behavior are not nearly so consistent as was once believed. Psychology's studies have shown that a child may be a chronic liar in one situation (as to a teacher) but not in another situation (as to a parent). Or the child may cheat in the classroom but never when playing games with friends (10). Adults may be generous in some situations and selfish in other situations, aggressive on some occasions and submissive on other occasions.

Many of the experiments that have most influenced psychological thinking in recent years, indeed, have been studies of how behavior is affected by what the Gestalt school would have called context—that is, the particular situation in which the behavior occurs. The experiments have demonstrated quite clearly that our behavior often depends not so much on who we are as where we are—and particularly on the people around us.

The most dramatic of all studies of how behavior can be affected by the situation—to an extent that is in many ways frightening—was performed by Stanley Milgram at Yale. Like many persons interested in human nature, Milgram found himself haunted by the events in Hitler's Germany, where a great many ordinary sorts of people, presumably with ordinary social backgrounds and moral standards, took part directly or passively in a program that resulted in the mass execution of millions of European Jews. How, Milgram wondered, could such a thing happen? What in the human personality or in the structure of society could account for the willingness of so many people to take part in or at least go along with a slaughter of such magnitude?

Milgram devised an experiment—illustrated in Figure 1-8—in which forty men of various ages and occupations were chosen as subjects and asked to take part in what they were told was an important study of learning. Each subject, working individually with the experimenter, was placed at the controls of a machine that was supposed to

1-8

The Milgram experiment

Some scenes from a film on the Milgram obedience experiment begin with a photograph of the panel supposed to control the level of shock (*A*). In *B*, the "learner" is strapped into a chair and electrodes are attached to his wrists. In *C*, a subject who will be at the controls receives a sample shock of the kind he believes he will administer. In *D*, a subject breaks off the experiment after going to as high a shock level as he is willing to administer. (Copyright 1965 by Stanley Milgram. From the film *Obedience*, distributed by the New York University Film Library.)

deliver electric shocks to a "learner" who was supposedly trying to master an assignment. (Actually the "learner" was a confederate of the experimenter and the machine did not do anything.) The controls appeared to make it possible to regulate the intensity of the shock all the way from "slight" (15 to 60 volts) and "moderate" (75 to 120 volts) to a level clearly marked DANGER: SEVERE SHOCK (as high as 450 volts).

The subject was told that his job was to assist in the learning process by administering a shock each time the "learner" made a mistake—and to raise the intensity of the shock for each new error. The "learner," of course, pretended to make a lot of errors. The shocks began. The controls started moving up. If a subject showed any signs of hesitation about increasing the voltage, the experimenter urged him on with comments such as "It is absolutely essential that you continue" and "You have no other choice; you *must* go on."

The question was: How much of a jolt would the subjects be willing to deliver? As is shown in Figure 1-9, it turned out that all the subjects went as high as what they thought was 300 volts. At that point, the "learner" began pounding on the wall of the room to indicate distress and a few subjects dropped out. But twenty-seven of the forty subjects continued on to what was labeled the danger zone and twenty-six went all the way to 450 volts (11).

How is one to account for the results of this experiment? It can be assumed that the subjects, who were just ordinary people representing a cross-section of the community, were hardly given to cruelty in their

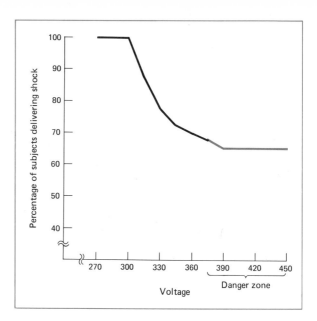

1-9

The strange power of the situation

On command of an experimenter whom they did not really have to obey for any particular reason, all subjects administered shocks as high as what they believed was 300 volts; 65 percent of them went all the way to 450 volts.

daily lives. Yet, in this situation, they proved willing to administer agonizing punishment to their "learners" and even risk killing them. Why?

Presumably they were influenced by the setting—a laboratory designed to advance the cause of science. To an even greater extent, presumably they were impressed by the authority of the scientist who was urging them on. As Milgram has pointed out, the experimenter had no real power to enforce his demands and the subjects had nothing to lose by disobeying him, yet obey him they did. In a different setting, and in response to demands from a figure of less authority, they would surely have behaved much differently.

The manner in which the situation and the people in it can influence behavior is the primary concern of the specialists in social psychology, which is the subject of Chapter 14. But all branches of the science have been greatly influenced by the rise of this new and important issue. More and more, it appears that we cannot fully understand individuals by studying them in isolation. The human personality and human behavior, far from being fixed and unchanging, seem to be in constant flux as the result of interaction between the individual and the environment—the situation of the moment, the number of people found in the situation, and the kinds of people these other participants in the situation happen to be.

Psychology and society

The three modern issues in psychology that have been discussed up to now—the question of whether human nature is "good" or "evil," the question of the relative importance of heredity and environment, and the influence of the social situation on the individual's behavior—all bear strongly on another important concern of many modern psychologists. This is the issue of how psychology's findings can be used, if at all, to help solve some of the problems of our society.

One such problem is the disadvantaged child. It is a well-known and disturbing fact that several million children in the United States do not

seem to be able to profit from the present educational system. These children come from all ethnic and racial groups, but usually from families living at the poverty level. Their chief difficulty in the early grades is an inability to learn to read. This problem cripples their entire educational progress. They fall behind other children their age and eventually drop out of school entirely, often without having acquired any real skills in reading, writing, or arithmetic. In our complex industrial society they are doomed to be unemployable—except perhaps at the most marginal kinds of jobs.

Many psychologists, especially those who specialize in child development and educational psychology, have agonized over this problem. Some feel that the problem is one of motivation; they propose efforts to help parents give these children a greater desire for educational skills. Some believe that the family atmosphere must be made more stimulating, so that the children can enter school with larger vocabularies and more information. Others propose changing the education system itself, to better serve the disadvantaged child. Still others urge some kind of change in our society that would give impoverished families a greater optimism, a greater sense of control over their own lives, and therefore more hope for the success of their children.

Body versus mind

The relationship between body and mind is another of the puzzles that philosophers have pondered over the centuries. Are they two separate and independent parts of the human experience, or do they somehow interact? If they interact, does the body control the mind—or does the mind control the body?

Psychology has now discovered that there are all kinds of relationships between the body and the mind (or, in deference to the followers of Watson who prefer to avoid this word, the mental or cognitive processes of the human organism). As will be seen later in the book, our emotions depend in large part on the activity of various glands inside our bodies. Other kinds of physical changes affect our psychological processes by making us hungry, thirsty, or sleepy; they can make us alert or lethargic, aroused or apathetic. Various physical illnesses have been shown to dull the intelligence and even to cause the severe forms of mental disturbance popularly known as insanity.

Just as the body can influence the mind, so can the mind affect the body. It has been clearly established that psychological stress—worry, anxiety, tension—can cause many physical illnesses such as ulcers, heart disease, high blood pressure, asthma, and many others. (To describe such ailments, medicine uses the term *psychosomatic illnesses,* combining *psycho* for mind and *soma* for body to indicate the cause and effect.)

Though there no longer seems to be any doubt of interaction between body and mind, many aspects of this interaction remain a mystery that psychologists are working hard to resolve. For example, one psychologist recently made a study of people suffering from various kinds of illnesses who went to a faith healer and were miraculously cured. The psychologist discovered some strange facts about the "cures." A physical examination showed no change in the patients' physical conditions. Their actual symptoms remained the same as before. Yet, in their minds, they considered themselves cured and they said they felt better (12). What is one to make of this peculiar example of mind over body?

The brain and behavior

Closely related to the issue of mind versus body is psychology's new knowledge of how the brain operates. In the past decade, this area of research has produced some of the science's most exciting discoveries. As will be seen in Chapter 7, we now know that the human ability to use language seems to depend on one small area in the left side of the brain, larger in human beings than in any other organism. We know that the left side of the brain in general seems to be in charge of processes involving language and thinking in verbal terms, while the right side seems to deal with nonverbal materials such as melodies and pictures.

Above all, we have found that messages get routed through the brain by certain chemicals discharged in tiny amounts at the nerve endings. These *neurotransmitters,* as they are called, are crucial to the brain's activity. Any change in the amounts or kinds of neurotransmitters may have effects on learning and problem solving—as well as on the moods we experience. Any serious disturbance of the neurotransmitter substances may even cause delusions and hallucinations and therefore extremely abnormal behavior. Many of the medicines now used to control mental disturbances—especially depression and schizophrenia—seem to work by affecting the neurotransmitters.

Psychology has also learned a great deal about how the brain operates during sleep and how it is affected by hypnosis, mind-control techniques such as transcendental meditation, and drugs such as marijuana. These matters are generally known among psychologists as *altered states of consciousness* and are discussed in a special section of Chapter 7.

Because of the explosion of knowledge about the brain, some psychologists now believe that eventually all psychological phenomena will be explained in terms of nerve activity and neurotransmitters. That is to say, they propose that all human behavior, including thinking, feelings, motives, and even spiritual aspirations, may depend on chemical processes in the brain and may be capable of change and control through the use of chemicals (or through the kind of electrical stimulation, substituting for chemical stimulation, that so drastically affected the behavior of the bull pictured on page 7). Other psychologists, while recognizing the importance of brain activity, refuse to believe that it can explain everything about human nature or behavior. In a

Lourdes, France. Crutches discarded by pilgrims to the shrine at Lourdes.

sense they are agreeing with the old Gestalt psychologists that the whole of human nature is greater than the sum of its parts — even including such a vital part as brain chemistry has proved to be.

The revolution in therapy

In the early days of the science, psychologists had only a minor interest in therapy. Those who did eventually begin to try to help people suffering from behavior disturbances usually adopted the theories and methods of Freud. It was generally believed that the only effective method of resolving personality problems was a prolonged relationship in which therapist and client met regularly, just the two of them, to try to discover the psychoanalytical roots of the problems.

Today, as has been well publicized, there are dozens of forms of therapy. Almost everyone has heard, at least in passing, of behavior-modification therapy, transactional therapy, and many others. Private discussion between therapist and client, though still practiced, is no longer so common as encounter groups and other forms of interaction in which the therapist meets with many people at once.

The rise of all the new forms of psychotherapy has introduced a number of questions of great importance. Some psychologists continue to believe that one or another form of therapy — ranging all the way from the formal discipline of psychoanalysis to the nude encounter group — is the only helpful approach. Others have come to believe that the type of therapy is relatively unimportant; they feel that what actually matters is some kind of sense of kinship, respect, and trust that the person suffering from problems feels for the person trying to help. The whole question of what kinds of therapies and therapists help most — and indeed whether any of them can help very much at all — is one of today's burning issues in psychology. It will be discussed in detail in Chapter 11.

Summary

1 Psychology is the science that systematically studies and attempts to explain observable behavior and its relationship a) to the unseen mental processes that go on inside the organism and b) to external events in the environment.
2 The subject matter of psychology includes the operation of the senses and the process of perception that bring us our "inputs" — also the way we process this information through learning, thinking, and problem solving.
3 The subject matter also includes emotions, motives, personality, and abnormal behavior — as well as the way we acquire our psychological characteristics (developmental psychology) and the way we interact with other people and society as a whole (social psychology).
4 The goals of psychology are to understand and predict behavior.
5 The methods of psychology include the experiment, naturalistic observation, tests, interviews, and questionnaires.

6 In an experiment, the experimenter controls the *independent variable,* which is set up independently of anything the subject does or does not do, and then studies the *dependent variable,* which is a change in the subject's behavior resulting from a change in the independent variable.

7 Although psychology is a pure science, interested in knowledge for the sake of knowledge, many of its findings have had a practical application in modern life. Examples of *applied psychology* include:

a *Clinical psychology,* which is the diagnosis and treatment of psychological problems, and *counseling,* or assistance to people who need temporary guidance on problems such as school difficulties, vocational choices, or marriage conflicts.

b The use of standardized tests and of the principles of learning.

c The use by industry of studies of the effects of fatigue, working hours, and employee morale; also of human engineering, which is the design of equipment and machinery that fit the actual size, strength, and capabilities of the human beings who will use them.

d Public opinion surveys.

8 Psychology began as a science when Wilhelm Wundt opened the first psychology laboratory in 1879.

9 The early psychologists used *introspection,* or looking inward, to attempt to study their conscious processes. In the words of the American pioneer William James, psychology was considered to be "the study of mental life."

10 The school of *behaviorism,* a rebellion against the introspective method, was founded by John Watson, who declared that "mental life" cannot be seen or measured and therefore cannot be studied scientifically. The behaviorists concentrated on studying *overt* behavior—the kinds of actions that are plainly visible.

11 A more modern version of behaviorism is B. F. Skinner's school of *stimulus-response psychology,* or *S-R psychology.* The S-R psychologists emphasize study of the stimuli that produce behavioral responses, the rewards and punishments that help establish and maintain these responses, and the modification of behavior through changes in the patterns of rewards and punishments.

12 Another school of historical importance is *Gestalt psychology,* named after the German word for "pattern" or "configuration." Gestalt psychologists believed that in studying any psychological process it was essential to look at the pattern considered as a whole—and at the context in which it occurred.

13 A modern school of thought that has grown out of Gestalt psychology is *cognitive psychology,* which stresses the importance of mental processes. Cognitive psychologists think of the mind as operating as a "mental executive" that actively makes comparisons and decisions, thus processing the information it receives into new forms and categories.

14 Another modern school that had its origins in the Gestalt movement is *humanistic psychology,* which holds that human beings are unique because they have goals and values; they seek to express themselves, to grow, to fulfill themselves, to find peace and happiness.

15 Psychological thought has also been greatly influenced by Sigmund Freud's theory of *psychoanalysis,* which holds among other things that personality and behavior are affected by *unconscious processes —* especially motives of which we are unaware.

16 In modern psychology, some of the issues that have aroused the greatest interest and controversy are:

a The question of whether human nature is inherently "good" or "evil."

b The question of whether heredity or environment is more important in influencing behavior (the issue of "nature versus nurture").

c The manner in which personality and behavior are influenced by the social setting — that is, the number of other people who are present at the time and the kinds of people they are.

d The question of whether and how psychological knowledge can be used to help relieve social problems — as for example the problem of disadvantaged children who are presently unable to profit from the kinds of schools we now have.

e The question of the interrelationship between body and mind.

f The role of the brain and its chemical processes in influencing behavior.

g The rise of new forms of psychotherapy and the question of which if any of them is most effective.

Recommended reading

Borger, R., and Cioffi, F., eds. *Explanation in the behavioural sciences.* Cambridge: Cambridge University Press, 1970.

Boring, E. G. *History of experimental psychology,* 2nd ed. New York: Appleton-Century-Crofts, 1950.

Carpenter, F. *The Skinner primer.* New York: Free Press, 1974.

Chaplin, J. P., and Krawiec, T. C. *Systems and theories of psychology,* 3rd ed. New York: Holt, Rinehart & Winston, 1974.

Chein, I. *Science of behavior and the image of man.* New York: Basic Books, 1972.

Coopersmith, S., ed. *Frontiers of psychological research.* San Francisco: W. H. Freeman, 1966.

Marx, M. H., and Hillix, W. A. *Systems and theories in psychology,* 2nd ed. New York: McGraw-Hill, 1973.

Murphy, G., and Kovach, J. K. *Historical introduction to modern psychology,* 3rd ed. New York: Harcourt Brace Jovanovich, 1972.

Scott, W. A., and Wertheimer, M. *Introduction to psychological research.* New York: John Wiley, 1962.

Watson, R. I. *The great psychologists: from Aristotle to Freud,* 2nd ed. Philadelphia: Lippincott, 1968.

TWO

LEARNING, REMEMBERING, AND THINKING

As was explained in Chapter 1, some of the characteristics that each of us displays are obviously the result of heredity. Our physical traits are certainly inherited from our ancestors. Some of us are born to be short, others tall; some light skinned, others dark skinned; some muscular, others fragile. Even many of the traits generally considered to be psychological are at least in part the result of inheritance. As will be explained in detail in later sections of the book, heredity appears to influence (though it does not entirely control) such matters as intelligence, tendencies to be introverted or extroverted, emotionality, and susceptibility to serious forms of emotional disturbance.

Yet, despite these inherited differences, all human beings are far more alike than unlike at the moment of birth. All babies, whether born to an illiterate woman in a South American jungle tribe or to a college-educated mother in Chicago, have much the same kinds of bones and muscles. They also possess very similar forms of the bodily structures that are of special importance in psychological events—the sense organs that bring us our information about the outside world (Chapter 5), the nervous systems that process this information (Chapter 7), and the glands (also discussed in Chapter 7), that help determine emotions and reactions to stress.

We are born very much alike. We turn out very different. Indeed it can be said with some confidence that no human being, not even an identical twin, has ever been exactly like another. Each of us is *unique,* unlike anyone who lived before or will again. Why?

The answer lies to a large extent in the process of learning, which, from the beginning, has been a central concern of psychology. Much of the behavior and mental activity that characterize us as adults has been learned. Indeed virtually everything discussed in the introductory psychology course is at least in part the result of learning—for example, the process of perception with which we view the world (Chapter 6), the events that trigger our emotions (Chapter 8), our motives (Chapter 9), our personalities (Chapter 11), and our relations with the society in which we find ourselves (Chapter 14).

Because learning is so all-pervasive in our lives and in the concerns of psychology, it is the logical place to start studying the science. This second part of the book, therefore, contains two chapters on various aspects of learning and remembering and a third on the closely related topics of language, thinking, and problem solving.

2

The principles of learning and memory

Pavolv (at right)

The most famous experiment in the history of psychology was performed in the early years of this century by the Russian scientist Ivan Pavlov. His subjects were dogs, such as the one shown in the photograph at left. His experimental apparatus was the simple but effective device illustrated in Figure 2-1 on the following page.

Pavlov's concern was a type of behavior known as a *reflex*, exhibited by all organisms that possess a nervous system. Some examples of human reflexes are these: If we touch a hot coffee pot, we automatically pull our hands away. If a bright light strikes our eyes, our pupils automatically grow smaller. These are forms of behavior that are not learned and that take place without any conscious effort. Our nervous systems are just naturally "wired" in such a way that we exhibit these reflexes.

The reflex starts with a *stimulus,* which can be defined as any form of energy capable of exciting the nervous system (the heat of the coffee pot, the bright light.) The stimulus sets off nervous impulses that travel to the central nervous system, that is, the brain and spinal cord. There, in accordance with a built-in pattern, they in turn set off other nervous impulses that travel to the muscles and produce a *response* (the hand pulling away, the pupils growing quickly smaller).

Reflex responses, as has been said, are not learned. They are built in. The question is: Can they be modified by learning?

Learning through conditioning

Pavlov set about answering the question by investigating the salivary reflex—which results in secretions by the salivary glands of the mouth when food is presented. He strapped a dog into the harness shown in

43

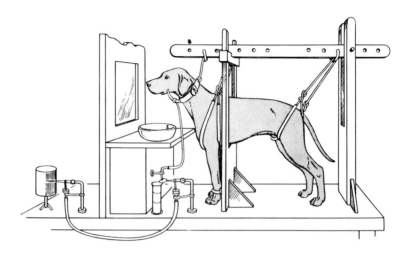

2-1

Pavlov's dog

The dog is strapped into a harness in which it has grown used to standing. A tube attached to the dog's salivary gland collects any saliva secreted by the gland, and the number of drops from the tube is recorded on a revolving drum outside the chamber. The experimenter can watch the dog through a one-way mirror and can deliver food to the dog's feed pan by remote control. Thus there is nothing in the chamber to distract the dog's attention except the food, when it is delivered, and any other stimulus that the experimenter wishes to present, such as the sound of a metronome. For the discoveries Pavlov made with this apparatus, see the text. (1)

Figure 2-1 and then introduced a sound, such as the beat of a metronome. The dog made a few restless movements, but there was no flow of saliva. This was what Pavlov had expected. The stimulus for reflex action of the salivary glands is the presence of food in the mouth —not the sound of a metronome. As far as the salivary reflex is concerned, sound is a neutral stimulus that has no effect one way or the other. When food was delivered and the dog took it into its mouth, saliva of course flowed in quantity.

Now Pavlov set about trying to connect the neutral stimulus of the sound with the reflex action of the salivary glands. While the metronome was clicking he delivered food to the dog, setting off the salivary reflex. After a time he did the same thing again—sounded the metronome and delivered food. After he had done this many times, he tried something new. He sounded the metronome but did not deliver any food. Saliva flowed anyway. The sound alone was a sufficient stimulus to produce the salivary response (2).

An animal's reflex behavior had been modified—so thoroughly that a stimulus having nothing whatever to do with food now produced the reflex response. Pavlov had discovered the form of learning famed among psychologists ever since as *classical conditioning*.

The elements of classical conditioning

In the terminology of classical conditioning, the food in the Pavlov experiment was the *unconditioned stimulus*—the stimulus that naturally and automatically produces the salivary response, without any learning. The sound was the *conditioned stimulus*—neutral at the start but eventually producing a similar response. The reflex action of the salivary glands when food was placed in the dog's mouth was the *unconditioned response*—the one that is naturally built into the dog's "wiring" and takes place automatically, without any kind of learning. The response of the glands to the sound was the *conditioned response*—resulting from some kind of change in the "wiring" caused by pairing the conditioned stimulus with the unconditioned stimulus and therefore with the salivary response.

Extinction, reinforcement, and spontaneous recovery

Once Pavlov had established the conditioned salivary response, he was interested in discovering how long and under what circumstances it would persist. When he merely kept sounding the metronome without ever again presenting food, he found that in a very short time the flow of saliva in response to the sound began to decrease, and soon it stopped altogether, as shown in Figure 2-2. In accordance with Pavlov's terminology, this disappearance of the conditioned response is known as *extinction*.

Pavlov also discovered, however, that if he occasionally followed the sound with food—not every time but sometimes—the conditioned response could be made to continue indefinitely. Since pairing the food with the sound not only established the conditioned response but also strengthened it and kept it alive, Pavlov called this process *reinforcement*—another of the well-known terms he contributed to the study of learning.

He also tried withholding reinforcement and letting the conditioned salivary response undergo extinction, then giving the dog a rest away from the experimental apparatus, and later trying again to see if there

2-2

Extinction

The graph shows what happened to Pavlov's dog when the conditioned stimulus of sound was no longer accompanied by the unconditioned stimulus of food. The conditioned salivary response, very strong at first, gradually grew weaker. By the seventh time the metronome was sounded the conditioned response had disappeared. Extinction of the response was complete.

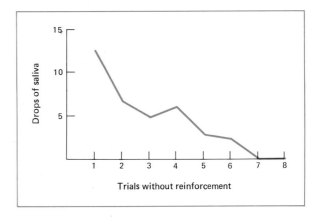

would be any response to the metronome. Under these circumstances, the conditioned response that had undergone extinction and had seemed to disappear took place all over again. He called this phenomenon *spontaneous recovery*.

Stimulus generalization and stimulus discrimination

In Pavlov's experiments, there was nothing magic about the sound produced by the metronome. Indeed he later used many other kinds of stimuli—and found that he could just as easily condition the salivary response to the sound of a bell or to a flash of light as to the metronome. He also discovered that a dog conditioned to the sound of a bell would also salivate to the sound of a different bell or of a buzzer. This phenomenon is called *stimulus generalization*—meaning that once an organism has learned to make a response to a particular stimulus, it tends to display this behavior toward similar stimuli as well.

After Pavlov had established the principle of stimulus generalization in the dog, he went on to demonstrate its counterpart, which is called *stimulus discrimination*. He continued to reinforce salivation to the bell by presenting food. But, when a different bell or a buzzer was sounded, no reinforcement was presented. Soon the dog learned to salivate only to the sound of the original bell, not to the other sounds. The animal had learned to discriminate between the stimulus of the bell and the other stimuli. If the experiment is carried far enough, it can be shown that a dog is capable of quite delicate stimulus discrimination. It can learn to respond to the tone of middle C, yet not to respond to tones that are only a little higher or a little lower.

All these principles of learning discovered by Pavlov—and the terms he applied to them—are still very much a part of psychology's view of the learning process. Moreover, they have had a profound influence on psychology's whole attitude toward not only animal behavior but also human behavior and human nature. They were responsible in large part for the rise of John Watson's behaviorist school of psychology (which was discussed in Chapter 1, page 22) and are today the subject of an important debate between members of the behaviorist school and the cognitive school (which was discussed on page 25). But discussion of this very dramatic role of Pavlov in psychological history and in contemporary controversy must be preceded by the story of another famous series of experiments in learning.

Operant conditioning

The second of the two influential learning experiments was performed by B. F. Skinner, who will be remembered from Chapter 1 (pages 22–23) as a leader of the stimulus-response school of psychology. Like Pavlov, he used a very simple piece of apparatus—the little animal cage illus-

2-3

With this simple but ingenious invention, a box in which pressing the bar automatically releases a pellet of food or a drop of water, B. F. Skinner demonstrated many of the rules of operant behavior. For what happens to a rat in the box, see the text.

trated in Figure 2-3. On one side was a small horizontal bar and a sort of cup built into the wall beneath it. Otherwise the cage was bare. On the outside, a mechanical device operated automatically to deliver a pellet of food into the cup each time the bar was pressed down.

Placed in such a cage—or indeed in any new environment—a rat will typically engage in a number of activities. Some of them seem rather random; the animal may scratch itself or wash itself. Some seem exploratory; the animal may stand up as if to get a better look; it may sniff at and touch various parts of the cage. It should be noted that these are not reflex activities. Instead of having a stimulus in the environment activate some built-in "wiring" of the nervous system to produce a reflex response, we have here just the opposite situation. The organism is "operating" on the world around it, so to speak. Hence this type of activity is known as *operant behavior.*

What happened to the rat in the Skinner box, as the type of cage used in the experiment has become known, demonstrated some important facts about operant behavior and learning. The rat, exhibiting its operant behavior more or less at random, eventually pressed the bar. Automatically, a pellet of food dropped into the cup. Still, no learning took place. In human terms, we might say that the animal did not even "notice" any connection between the bar and the food but continued its random movements as before. Eventually it pressed the bar again, and another pellet dropped. This time the animal "noticed" the connection between pressing the bar and the appearance of food. It began pressing the bar as fast as it could eat one pellet and get back to the bar to produce another (3).

This type of learning, so simply but eloquently demonstrated by the rat in the Skinner box, is known as *operant conditioning.* In the language of conditioning, originated by Pavlov and continued by Skinner, the presentation of the food constituted a *reinforcement* of the bar-pressing behavior, which thus became a learned response. The basic premise of operant conditioning, established by the Skinner experiment, is that operant behavior that is reinforced tends to be repeated, while operant behavior that is not reinforced takes place only at random intervals or is abandoned.

47

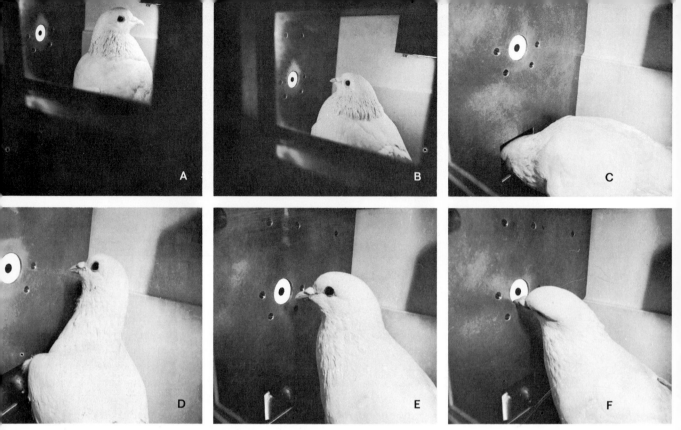

2-4

Shaping a pigeon's behavior

At first the pigeon merely looks about the box at random *(A)*. When it faces the circle *(B)*, it receives the reinforcing stimulus of food in the tray below *(C)*. The next time the pigeon approaches the circle *(D)*, it is again rewarded with food. Later the pigeon is not rewarded until it approaches closer to the circle *(E)*, and still later it is not rewarded until it pecks at the circle *(F)*. The next step, not illustrated here, will be to withhold reward until the pigeon pecks at the small black dot inside the circle.

Some principles of operant conditioning

For many years, experiments in operant conditioning dominated the study of learning. It was found that operant conditioning followed many of the laws laid down by Pavlov for classical conditioning. Conditioned operant behavior, like the conditioned reflex response, was subject to *extinction;* if the rat was no longer rewarded with food for pressing the bar, it eventually would stop pressing. *Spontaneous recovery* also occurred; after a rest away from the Skinner box, the rat would start pressing again.

Experiments with pigeons, which are especially good subjects in their own version of the Skinner box, clearly showed *stimulus generalization.* Once a pigeon had learned to obtain food by pecking at a white button, it would also peck at a red or green button. But *stimulus discrimination* could also be demonstrated if only the operant behavior toward the white button was reinforced. In that case the pigeon could learn to peck only at the white button and ignore the red and green.

Psychologists interested in operant conditioning also developed a method of teaching animals many rather complicated and unusual forms of behavior, a process called *shaping.* Figure 2-4 illustrates how

Skinner

this process can be used to teach a pigeon to peck at a black dot inside a white circle. The bird is led step by step, through reinforcement by food as it approaches closer and closer, to a form of behavior that it might never have hit upon spontaneously. The technique of shaping, with food or affection as the reward, is responsible for the almost unbelievable tricks that animal trainers have been able to produce, some examples of which are shown in Figure 2-5.

2-5

Some results of shaping

Among the accomplishments of animal trainers, using the technique of shaping, are elephants and bears that play musical instruments, a rabbit that hoards its money in a piggy bank, and a dolphin that leaps through a hoop.

2-6

Secondary reinforcement
of a chimpanzee

The chimpanzee has been
operantly conditioned by the secondary reinforcement of a poker
chip, which it now drops into a
vending machine to obtain the
primary reinforcement of food.

The question of reinforcement

One important concern of all the research in operant conditioning has been the matter of reinforcement, which seems to lie at the very core of the process. To a hungry or thirsty animal, food and water constitute an obvious kind of reward; these have been known, to experimenters in operant conditioning, as *primary reinforcers*. But human beings seldom do any learning in order to receive food or water; rather they seem to learn for less tangible rewards such as praise or self-esteem. Indeed even animal trainers, as has been said, often use the reward of affection rather than anything so elementary as food. Such rewards have been called *secondary reinforcers*, and it has been assumed that they have gained their value through some kind of conditioning process that linked them originally with primary reinforcers. One rather simple example of secondary reinforcement is illustrated in Figure 2-6.

Schedules of reinforcement have also been widely studied. In most animal experiments, it has been found, immediate reinforcement produces the most rapid learning; any delay reduces the amount; and too long a delay results in no learning at all, as is shown in Figure 2-7. It has also been found that operant conditioning is affected by the number of

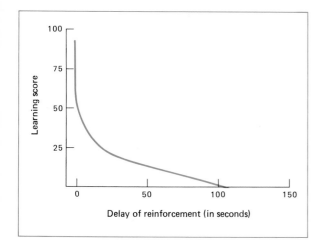

2-7

The effect of delayed reinforcement

The steep drop in the curve shows how rapidly learning fell off when reinforcement—in this case food obtained when rats pressed a bar in a Skinner box—was delayed for intervals varying from a few seconds to about two minutes. Note that no learning at all took place when reinforcement was delayed for slightly more than 100 seconds. (4)

times the reinforcement occurs. Experimenters have made many studies of the effects of *constant reinforcement* (reward for each performance) as compared with *partial reinforcement* (reward on some occasions but not on others), often by measuring the ability of animals to learn to run a maze, such as the one shown in Figure 2-8. The results have indicated

2-8

A maze used in learning experiments

This is one type of maze frequently used in operant conditioning experiments. The animal's progress at learning the maze can be measured by the time it takes to get from start to finish, by the number of errors made by entering the fourteen blind alleys, or by both.

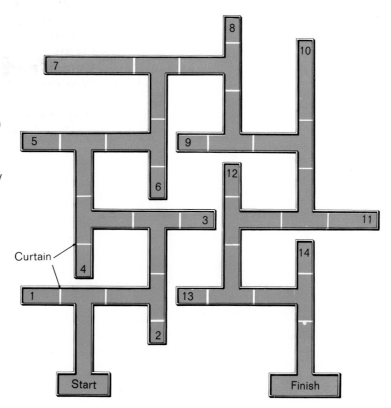

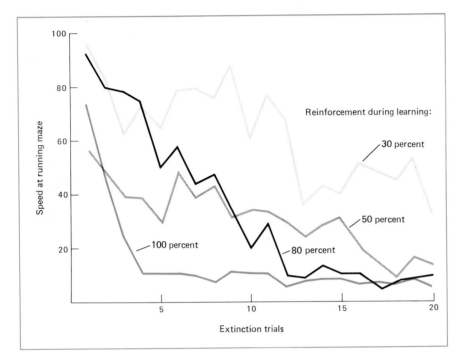

2-9

Partial versus constant reinforcement

In this experiment in maze running by rats, some of the animals were on a schedule of constant reinforcement (100 percent). Others received partial reinforcement—after 30, 50, or 80 percent of their successful trials. Once they had learned to run the maze quickly, they were given twenty trials without any reinforcement at all. Note that the process of extinction during these twenty trials was fastest for the animals that had received constant reinforcement and that the animals on a 30 percent schedule of partial reinforcement resisted extinction the most. (5)

that operant conditioning learned on a schedule of partial reinforcement is the most resistant to extinction. A typical result is shown in Figure 2-9.

Another discovery that greatly influenced the thinking of learning theorists was the fact that animals can be conditioned not only by rewards but also by punishments. In a Skinner box arranged so that the floor is an electric grill and the bar turns off the current, an animal will learn to press the bar to end the shock—a type of learning known as *operant escape*. Or, if the box is arranged so that the shock will occur ten seconds after the flashing of a light, the animal will learn to press the bar when the light appears to keep the shock from taking place—a type of learning called *operant avoidance*.

The implications of conditioning

Between them, the Skinner and Pavlov experiments had a tremendous impact on the world of psychology. The school of behaviorism founded by John Watson, as has been said, was a direct outgrowth of Pavlov's experiments. Watson believed that human behavior, including thinking, was strictly a matter of S-R connections established through conditioning. One of his own influential studies along this line was the famous "Albert experiment"—referring to the name of the eleven-month-old boy who was the subject. The experiment was based on the fact that a loud noise is an unconditioned stimulus that produces the reflex response of fearful behavior in a child. The goal of the experiment was to show that the noise-fear reflex could be conditioned to a previously neutral stimulus.

As is illustrated in Figure 2-10, Watson conditioned the child Albert to display the fear response to the previously neutral stimulus of a furry animal. Moreover, because of stimulus generalization, Albert displayed the same fearful behavior to anything furry, including a man with a beard. To Watson and his fellow behaviorists, the import of the experiment was obvious: human fears are simply the result of classical conditioning. And if fears, why not all other human feelings and activities? In light of the Albert experiment and Pavlov, Watson felt quite confident of his statement that he could take any dozen babies at birth and turn them into any kinds of adult he wished.

In the S-R school of behaviorism founded by Skinner, the emphasis is on reward (encouraging repetition of the behavior that produced the reward) and punishment (encouraging escape or avoidance, in other words abandonment of the behavior that produced the punishment).

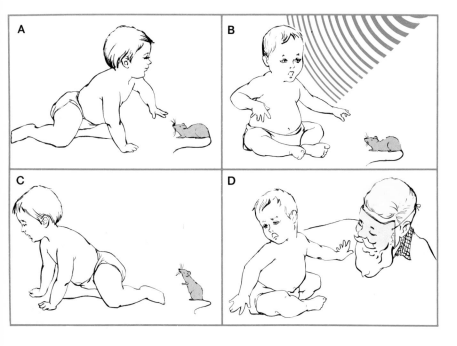

2-10

Conditioning the fear response

The unconditioned baby reaches eagerly toward a rat (*A*). Then a loud noise is presented at the same time as the rat (*B*). After this conditioning, the baby fears the rat (*C*) and even a man whose beard resembles the furry animal (*D*). (6)

But the S-R school also regards human learning and human behavior as determined largely by outside influences. It takes the view that we behave as we do because we are repeating actions that have been rewarded by our environments in the past—and are refraining from actions that have been punished.

In general, the Pavlov and Skinner experiments seem to make the individual's thoughts, feelings, or motives seem rather unimportant. How the individual behaves, at any given moment in life, appears to be simply the total result of prior classical conditioning, operant conditioning, and operant shaping. The idea that individuals can possess a "free will" —or the ability to control their own destinies—is largely ruled out by the behaviorist and S-R schools of thought.

Is conditioning enough?

There is still widespread agreement that the two forms of conditioning take place as Pavlov and Skinner showed, and that their various findings about such matters as stimulus generalization, extinction, and so on are correct in general. But new experiments have raised some doubts about the reason conditioning takes place and about the importance of conditioning in human experience. Four findings in particular have greatly changed the attitude of many psychologists toward learning. These four findings and their implications will be the subject of this section of the chapter. As the title of the section indicates ("Is conditioning enough?"), they raise the question whether classical and operant conditioning can even explain everything that happens in learning—much less everything about human behavior.

Learning without a response

Even in classical conditioning, is the result a simple stimulus-response connection? If so, then how is one to explain what happens in the following experiment?

A dog is strapped into a harness like Pavlov's with one paw resting on a metal plate. A low-pitched tone is sounded. Nothing else happens. Then a high-pitched tone is sounded, an electric current is passed through the metal plate, and the dog by reflex response pulls its paw away. Very quickly the dog learns to stand still when the low tone sounds—but to pull its paw away immediately when the high tone occurs.

Now the experimenter does the same thing with another dog—except that this dog's leg is paralyzed with a drug, so that it cannot pull away. The animal makes no response. Yet, when the experiment is tried again after the drug has worn off, it turns out that the dog has learned. It does nothing when the low tone sounds but pulls its paw away immediately when it hears the high tone (7). During the learning process the dog made no response at all—but nonetheless it learned. To many psychologists, the experiment seems impossible to explain in terms of a stimulus-response connection.

Why you can't teach even a young dog every new trick

Other findings have questioned an assumption that is implicit in the behaviorist and S-R theories—namely, that any response can be conditioned to any stimulus. The organism itself has been found to show some inborn tendencies that seem to challenge this assumption. The individual, it might be said, has been shown to be more important than Pavlov and Skinner believed.

Some of the most interesting findings along this line come from a man-and-wife team of psychologists who became professional animal trainers, using their knowledge of shaping to present performances by such rather far-out entertainers as raccoons, cockatoos, reindeer, pigs, chickens, and whales. They began with the theory that they could teach almost any animal to do almost anything. Some 6,000 animals of thirty-eight different species later, they were forced to admit that they were wrong.

The animals' learning, they found, was limited by what is called *species-specific behavior*. Chickens have an inborn tendency to scratch for their food, pigs to root for it, raccoons to wash it. Thus the two psychologist-animal-trainers never were able to teach raccoons to pick up two coins and drop them into a piggy bank; the animals insisted on going through their natural washing motions by rubbing the coins together, dipping them into the bank, then rubbing them together some more. The pigs insisted on rooting, the chickens on scratching (8).

Other experiments have shown that it is very difficult to teach a rat, whose species-specific behavior inclines it to flee from danger, to press a Skinner-box bar to escape from a shock (9). It is fairly easy, however, to teach the rat to jump or run away to escape the shock (10, 11). On the other hand it is almost impossible to teach certain other animals, whose species-specific behavior is to "freeze" in a dangerous situation, to do the running.

One experiment that is considered a classic on species-specific behavior was performed in this manner: a rat was permitted to drink some sweet-flavored water while a bright light was flashed and noise was sounded. Later the rat was made sick to its stomach through x-ray irradiation. Under these circumstances, what did the rat learn? It turned out that the animal learned to avoid sweet-tasting water. It did not learn to avoid the light or the noise (12). Presumably rats have a species-specific tendency to associate taste with feelings of being sick to the stomach. They "refuse," to use a human concept, to learn a connection between light or noise and sickness.

Thinking in evolutionary terms, one might say that the ability to learn a connection between food and stomach discomfort is a valuable asset to rats. Those possessing this ability would tend to survive and pass on their traits to new generations. Those associating the sickness with anything like a noise or a light, rather than food, would tend to eat the same thing again and die.

If one thinks of the rat in the experiment as acquiring a fear of the sweet-flavored water that preceded the illness, there is an interesting analogy to human behavior. Human beings display many kinds of fears, often to such an irrational degree that they are called phobias (as

will be explained in Chapter 10). To at least a certain extent these phobias are learned, perhaps often in as simple a manner as Albert learned to fear furry animals and beards. Yet, as one psychologist of the cognitive school of learning has pointed out, human phobias tend to take a species-specific form. People are usually afraid of the dark, open spaces, falling, or certain animals or insects—all of which have presented a real danger during human history. People seldom if ever acquire a phobia about electric sockets, lawn mowers, bath tubs, or power tools—even though all these things are potentially much more dangerous than the dark or open spaces in today's world (13).

Learning despite reinforcement delay

The experiment with the nauseated rat was doubly surprising to the world of psychology because it also seemed to offer proof that a delay of reinforcement does not necessarily prevent learning. The reinforcement in this case was the effect created by the x-rays—the punishing reinforcement of illness. But the sickness did not occur until an hour or more after the animal had drunk the sweet-tasting water. Under all the generally accepted rules of delayed reinforcement (page 50), no learning should have taken place at all. Yet the animal unquestionably learned to avoid the water. This fact is very difficult to explain in terms of simple conditioning.

Learning without reinforcement

Perhaps the most startling development of all in the field of learning has been the accumulation of evidence that learning can actually take place without any reinforcement at all. There is now ample proof that this happens at least at certain times and under certain conditions—and some psychologists have concluded that in human experience it happens much more often than does learning as a result of reward or punishment.

Oddly, the fact that learning can take place without reinforcement was discovered in an experiment performed nearly a half century ago. At the time, the results were considered puzzling and their implications were not realized—but the experiment still remains the best and simplest demonstration of nonreinforced learning.

The experimenter used a maze and three groups of rats, all treated differently in regard to reinforcement. Group 1 always found food at the end of the maze—an obvious and immediate reinforcement. Group 2 never found food at the end of the maze; the rats in this group were simply placed in the maze and permitted to move around in any way they chose. Group 3 was treated the same way as Group 2 for the first ten days, receiving no reinforcement. After the tenth day, however, Group 3 always found food at the end of the maze.

How the three groups performed, as measured by the number of errors they made going into blind alleys of the maze, is illustrated in

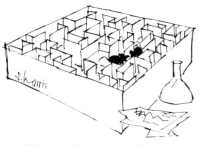

"Act confused. They like to feel superior."

Figure 2-11. The rats in Group 1, it will be noted, improved every day right from the beginning, learning rapidly. The rats in Group 2, never reinforced, displayed little learning. But the important line in the graph shows what happened to Group 3. For the first ten days, this group also showed little learning. But as soon as a reward was provided at the end of the maze, on the eleventh day, they immediately began running the maze like veterans. Even in just wandering about the maze for ten days, without any reinforcement, they apparently had learned a great deal about the correct path. As soon as a reward was provided, they began to demonstrate this knowledge.

Many other experiments have also challenged the importance of reinforcement. In one such experiment, pigeons were taught to peck a lighted key to get food. Then they no longer had to peck the lighted key. All the food they could possibly eat was made available in another feeding cup. Yet they kept on pecking the key anyway (15). Another experiment was arranged so that pecking at the key actually turned off the feeding apparatus. In other words, every peck produced a delay in reinforcement. Yet, again, the pigeons kept pecking away—even though getting quite hungry (16).

2-11

Maze learning with and without reinforcement

The graph shows the progress at learning a maze made by three groups of rats under different conditions of reinforcement. For the meaning of these results, see the text. (14)

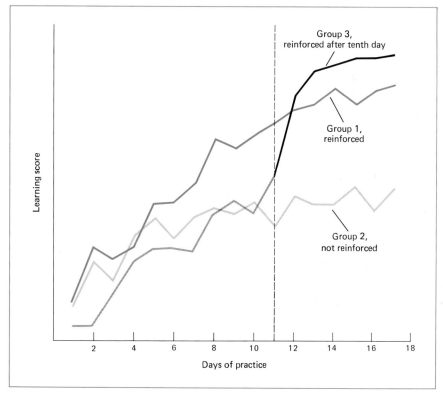

The cognitive theory of learning

In addition to the experimental evidence that has challenged the Pavlov-Skinner idea that all learning is a matter of simple conditioning, there are also some rather imposing facts that we can draw from our own experiences. It seems obvious that we remember things that we have no particular reason to remember. We must somehow have learned these things though we made no response at the time and received no reinforcement. How, in simple S-R terms, can we explain how we know what we had for lunch yesterday, what was in an item read in last week's newspaper, a joke heard last year on television, the name of a movie seen five years ago, something that happened to us in the first grade of school?

For all these reasons, a growing number of psychologists have come to regard learning less as a matter of conditioning and more as a cognitive process. As was stated in Chapter 1 (page 25), the cognitive psychologists think of the mind as being—or possessing—a "mental executive" that actively makes comparisons and decisions. In learning, they believe, this "mental executive" constantly examines the information that our sense organs bring us about the environment. Out of all the information that bombards us, the "executive" selects and pays attention to what seems important; it compares this information with what we already know from previous experience; it weighs and judges the information. By forming meaningful associations between the new information and the old, it often stores the new information in our memories—and in that case we have learned something (17).

As one psychologist has put it, we do not seem to learn just to respond to a specific stimulus. We do not learn just to make a specific response. Rather, what we learn is *knowledge* (18). Thus, to cognitive psychologists, learning is a highly active and complicated process. Indeed it is regarded as only one of a closely related and even more complex series of mental processes (19) discussed later in the book—notably perception (Chapter 6) and language, thinking, and problem solving (Chapter 4), but also any other psychological phenomena that can affect the way we are likely at any given moment to regard and process new information. These would include emotions (Chapter 8), motives (Chapter 9), and the social setting (Chapter 14). The idea that these various elements play a part in how we view our environments and learn from them is called the *information-processing theory*.

The cognitive view of conditioning

Even Pavlov's dog, according to the cognitive theory, did not learn a simple S-R connection (20). Instead it learned some kind of cognitive pattern, the meaning of which was that the sound of the metronome would be followed by food. The nauseated rat acquired a cognitive pattern, put together from two events occurring more than an hour apart, the meaning of which was that drinking the sweet-tasting water would result in sickness.

Some psychologists think of the cognitive pattern as an "expectancy" (21). They would say that Pavlov's dog salivated because it had learned to expect food when the metronome sounded; Skinner's rat pressed the bar because it had learned to expect food when the bar was pressed. Similarly, we human beings tend to behave as we do because we have learned to expect that some event in the environment is likely to be followed by some other resulting event. To cite a very simple example, we head for cover when we hear thunder, because we have learned to expect thunder to be followed by rain. Or we behave as we do because we have learned to expect that a certain kind of action we take will produce certain results. Again to cite a very simple example, we take an aspirin when we have a headache because we expect the aspirin to help.

Other cognitive psychologists emphasize motivation rather than expectancy; they feel that the core of learning is the acquisition of motives to behave in certain ways under certain conditions (22). But regardless of the details, this new school of thought is agreed that learning represents some kind of mental process that cannot be explained as the mere establishment of an S-R connection.

Learning through observation

Cognitive theorists also believe that the most common and important form of learning, especially by human beings, is what has been called *learning through observation,* or, as some psychologists prefer, *learning through modeling* or *learning by imitation.* All three terms are more or less self-explanatory. They refer to the process through which we learn new behavior by observing the behavior of others.

Many experiments have shown quite clearly how animals learn by imitation. For example, one cat was taught in a Skinner box that it could obtain food by pressing the bar when a light went on. Another cat, permitted to watch this process, was then placed in the box. This second cat began very quickly to press the bar when the light went on. Through observation, it learned much faster than the first cat (23).

One well-known and dramatic demonstration of observation learning in human beings was recorded on film by Albert Bandura. In his experiment, children watched a movie showing an adult playing with a large doll in a highly aggressive manner, striking it with a hammer. When they then had an opportunity to play with the doll themselves, they showed remarkably similar behavior. The photographs of this experiment, some of which are shown in Figure 2-12, have greatly

2-12

Imitation of aggression

Why are the boy and girl at the left acting so aggressively toward the toy? And why does their aggressive behavior take such a remarkably similar form? The answer is that they were imitating the behavior of a model—the woman at the right, who had behaved in exactly this fashion in a movie they had watched.

Bandura

"I don't know where he learned that. We don't even have a television set."

influenced psychology's attitude toward observation learning. (They have also raised some serious questions about the effect of all the violence shown in the movies and on TV.)

The cognitive theorists do not, however, think of observation learning as a mere automatic and unthinking imitation of what one has seen. Rather they would say that we begin in early childhood, and continue throughout our lives, to observe what goes on around us and to store up the information that these events provide. We observe what other people seem to value, how they go about getting these things, their behavior in general, and the results of their behavior. At the same time we make judgments. We may or may not decide to value what they value. We may imitate their behavior, adopt some but not all of it, or reject it entirely. As Bandura has written, learning by observation is "actively judgmental and constructive rather than a mechanical copying" (24).

Learning from teachers and books. As every student knows, the human organism can learn a great deal from a teacher or from books. All of us have done this kind of learning ever since we first stepped inside a schoolroom—and in fact even before that, when our parents taught us how to dress ourselves and turn on a TV set. Most psychologists regard this as a form of learning through observation. The observations are not made directly but symbolically, through the use of spoken language or the written word. Except for this added and uniquely human refinement, however, the process appears to be very similar to learning through direct observation. In human experience, of course, it is one of the most important of all the learning processes.

How we remember

Whether one chooses to think of learning from the cognitive viewpoint or in Pavlov-Skinner terms, there can be no doubt that learning represents some kind of *change* inside the organism—frequently a permanent change. Often we speak of this change as residing in memory. If we can remember something, we know we have learned it. If we cannot remember, then we have failed to learn—or have forgotten. Thus psychology's study of memory goes hand-in-hand with its study of learning.

The brain and learning

The change created when learning occurs almost surely takes place in the nervous system. More specifically, it usually takes place in the complicated network of nerve cells and associated fibers in the brain. Just how the change takes place, however, is not fully known.

We do know that chemical activity goes on continuously in the individual cells and fibers that make up the nervous system, especially at the connection points where messages are transmitted from one nerve cell to another. Indeed the usual way for a message to be passed along from one nerve cell to another, as will be explained in detail in Chapter 7, is for the first nerve fiber to secrete a chemical that prods the second nerve cell into action. Some psychologists believe that this chemical activity tends to lay down a more or less permanent pattern or pathway. Once a message has been passed through the nervous system along one particular pathway, the same pathway is likely to be followed again. Learning is regarded as the establishment of such pathways.

Other psychologists believe that learning sets up some kind of chemical code inside the individual nerve cells, rather than between them. Some believe that these changes inside the nerve cells may be of such a nature that they can be facilitated by some as yet undiscovered drug—in other words, that we may someday have a "learning pill" that will help us acquire and remember new knowledge (25). Indeed some psychologists have reported that animals sometimes seem to acquire a new skill more quickly if they are injected with brain tissue from other animals that had learned the skill previously (26), although attempts to repeat their experiments have been generally unsuccessful (27). About all that can be said at the moment is that we must be content to speculate about the changes that learning produces and wait for future investigations to tell us exactly why and how.

What we remember

The behaviorists and S-R psychologists, as has been said, tend to regard the changes produced by learning as the establishment of a rather simple and direct connection between a stimulus in the environment and a behavioral response. The cognitive psychologists tend to regard it as the establishment of an expectancy or a motive—or, in more general terms, as the acquisition of information and of the ability to remember this information and manipulate it in useful and sometimes even creative ways.

These different viewpoints may result in part from the different kinds of experiments that members of the two schools have performed. The S-R psychologists have chiefly studied lower animals, such as rats and pigeons, where the results of learning can be observed only in the form of overt behavior. The cognitive psychologists have chiefly studied human beings, from whom it is possible to obtain reports of the unseen mental processes that go on inside the organism. Indeed the differences in viewpoints may someday be found to have merely reflected the fact that the learning process itself takes a number of different forms. Perhaps the various forms range all the way from the establishment of rather direct associations between a stimulus and a behavioral response to the acquisition of very complex forms of information and rules for using it.

Pending a final resolution of the debate, an increasingly popular and relatively noncontroversial term to describe a change established by learning is *mediational unit*. This is a neutral term because those who prefer S-R psychology can regard it as an intermediary, or go-between, that links stimulus and behavior, while those who prefer cognitive psychology can regard it as a go-between in complex chains of thinking and decision making, with or without resulting in any observable behavior.

Thus *mediational unit* is a useful term that will appear frequently throughout the book. Indeed the mediational units that we acquire through learning—whether one chooses to regard them in S-R or cognitive terms—constitute the great bulk of psychology's subject matter. Nearly everything discussed in the later chapters of this book is a mediational unit or is affected by mediational units.

How we remember: the three kinds of memory

As to the all-important question of how we manage to remember some mediational units while forgetting others, the discussion can best begin with an example that could happen anywhere to anybody. Let us suppose that a college woman is driving across the country to her campus. She expected to arrive at about five o'clock in Indianapolis, where she has been invited by some friends to have dinner and spend the night. As she nears the city, however, her automobile develops engine trouble. A mechanic at a roadside garage tells her the repairs will take an hour or two. So she goes to a phone booth to call her friends and explain that she will be late.

In the phone book, she looks up the number 624-1958. But at that moment there is a loud squeal of brakes out on the highway. Startled, she looks up and sees that there has been a near collision. Turning back to the phone, she finds that she has completely forgotten the number. Indeed it seems that the number never registered at all in her memory. She looks it up again and this time starts silently repeating it to herself —*six, two, four, one, nine, five, eight*—as she turns from the book and drops her coins into the phone. She dials the number correctly but gets a busy signal. By the time she has fished the coins out of the return slot, dropped them back into the phone, and waited for a dial tone, she finds that she has forgotten the number again. She remembered it longer this time—but not long enough.

So she looks up the number again. This time, while repeating it to herself, she notices a peculiarity. The number is exactly the same as her birth date, for she was born on June 24, or 6/24, in 1958. Now she remembers the number no matter how many times she gets a busy signal and has to try again. In fact she may remember it the rest of her life.

This case of the college woman in the phone booth—which is quite

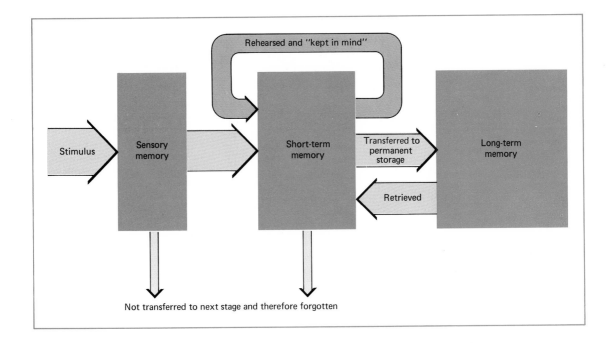

2-13

How we remember

The three systems of human memory appear to operate as shown here. Stimuli from the outside world register briefly in the *sensory memory;* some are promptly lost, but others are transferred to *short-term memory.* There again some are lost, but others are rehearsed and "kept in mind" long enough to be transferred to permanent storage in *long-term memory,* from which they can later be retrieved. The process is described in further detail in the text. (28)

similar to many incidents that occur in all our lives—indicates that there may be several different kinds of memory processes. One theory is that there are three such different processes or systems of memory. To understand them, it will be helpful to refer to Figure 2-13 while reading the following discussion of the three systems.

Sensory memory

Everything that impinges on our sense organs seems to be remembered for at least a brief instant, but sometimes no longer. Thus the woman in the phone booth remembered the numbers 624-1958 after she had stopped looking at them in the directory. But the squeal of brakes on the highway knocked the numbers right out of her head, so to speak. She forgot them completely.

The three-part theory of memory holds that this type of remembering is *sensory memory,* which is just the lingering traces of information

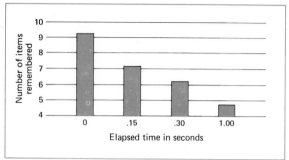

2-14

Sensory memory: how fleeting it is!

Arrangements of twelve letters and numbers, such as those at the left, were shown briefly to subjects. Through a method described in the text, the amount of information they held in sensory memory was then investigated. As the bars show, the amount was quite high at the start but declined very quickly. The base line for the bars is four because that was the average number of items remembered after the sensory memory had faded completely.

sent to the brain by the senses. The nature of sensory memory has been demonstrated by the experiment shown in Figure 2-14. Twelve letters and numbers were shown briefly to subjects. The subjects were asked how many of the letters and numbers they could remember. Without any kind of help, they remembered an average of four. However, if a signal was quickly flashed asking them to try to remember the letters and numbers on one particular line, they could usually recall at least three and often all four of the symbols on this line. This was true no matter which of the three lines was signaled, indicating that the subjects retained a brief impression of almost the entire pattern of the dozen letters and numbers.

As is shown in the bar chart of Figure 2-14, an average of about nine of the twelve letters and numbers was found to persist in sensory memory when the signal was flashed immediately. But the ability to recall the pattern faded very rapidly (29). As the experiment indicates, information that reaches the sensory memory deteriorates rapidly—within a few tenths of a second—and ordinarily has vanished by the end of a full second. That is, unless it is transferred to the next of the three memory systems.

Short-term memory

The second of the three systems is *short-term memory*, into which some but not all of the information about the environment that arrives in the sensory memory is transferred. In the case of the college woman at the telephone, her second look at the phone book resulted in transfer of the number 624-1958 to short-term memory. There it remained long enough for her to dial once—but, when she tried to dial again after getting a busy signal, it had already disappeared.

Unless some further processing takes place within the short-term memory, information held there deteriorates rapidly as is shown in Figure 2-15 and seems to be forgotten completely within about thirty seconds (31). Indeed so much information is lost in this way that one psychologist has aptly described short-term memory as a "leaky bucket" (32). However, this is not entirely a disadvantage. For example, the cashier in a supermarket remembers only briefly that she must give the customer $3.92 change from a twenty-dollar bill. By the time she starts checking out the next customer, the figure $3.92 has already vanished

from her memory. This is just as well—for she would be totally confused by the end of the day if she recalled every transaction starting with the first one of early morning. Similarly, when we add a column of figures such as

37
49
65
<u>22</u>

we say to ourselves (adding the right-hand digits from the top down) 16, 21, 23; then write down the 3 and start over on the left-hand numbers, 5, 9, 15, 17; thus we get the answer 173. All the intermediary numbers that flash through our consciousness—the 16, 21, 23, 5, 9, and 15— disappear almost as rapidly as they are formed. If they did not, we would find it almost impossible to add the columns. The numbers would get hopelessly confused.

Indeed it appears that much of the forgetting we do from short-term memory is intentional (33). We have no need to remember the information. We do not want to remember it—and it would only get in our way, for the capacity of the short-term memory is quite small in terms of amount of information as well as time span. Therefore we throw out the information deliberately. We do so by manipulating the processes that appear to go on in short-term memory, which will now be described.

Processes in short-term memory. Quite a number of different kinds of information-processing activities are associated with short-term memory (34). First, there must be some kind of *scanning* of the information briefly held in sensory memory. From the constant flow of sights,

2-15

Short-term memory: gone in seconds

In a study of short-term memory, the experimenters spoke a group of letters and a number, such as KRG 297. Subjects were asked to begin immediately to count aloud, going backward by threes beginning with the number (for example, 297, 294, 291, etc.). At various intervals, a signal was flashed informing them to stop counting and try to recall the letters. Under these circumstances, which kept them too busy counting to do any further processing of their memory for the letters, their recall dropped rapidly as shown by the graph line (30).

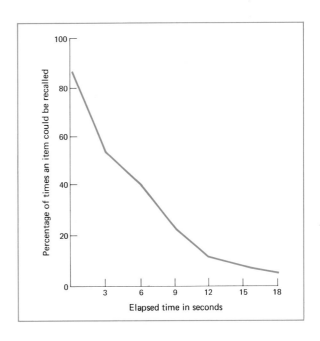

sounds, and other sensory messages some particular items must be selected as worthy of attention. (This scanning and selection process is closely related to the psychological phenomenon of perception and will be discussed more fully in Chapter 6.)

If the information selected for attention is to be held for any length of time, some sort of *rehearsal system* must also be set up. That is, the information must be deliberately kept in mind and prevented from slipping out of the "leaky bucket." Through rehearsal, information can be kept in short-term memory as long as desired—though the amount of information that can be kept alive, as has been stated, is quite small. The seven phone numbers represent just about the top limit of separate items (35).

To help with further processing, the information held in short-term memory is often transformed in some way that makes it as simple and easily handled as possible. This process is called *coding*—for it resembles the manner in which a business machine can take some rather complicated facts (such as a customer's name and address, past-due balance, and new purchases) and code them into a series of holes on a punch card. When the information involves language or numbers, the coding is usually done in acoustical terms—that is, the information is coded into sounds (36). The woman at the telephone coded the visual image of the numbers 624-1958 as seen in the directory into the sounds *six, two, four, one, nine, five, eight.*

Finally, if the information is to be remembered more or less permanently, it must be passed along and stored in the next of the memory systems, which is *long-term memory.* This process, called *transfer,* seems to take place somewhat as follows. The new information, held in short-term memory and kept alive through rehearsal, is associated with any relevant pieces of information already existing in long-term memory. Comparisons are made and relationships sought. When the transfer process is successful, it might be said, new mediational units are associated with mediational units already held in long-term memory and are added to them.

The transfer process may require additional coding and recoding. Its efficiency also depends to a great extent on *organization.* Materials that are themselves well-organized, as for example a self-contained little two-line poem, are more easily transferred to long-term memory than a meaningless string of digits. The transfer process can also be helped by any kind of organization the learner can impose on the materials (37).

Long-term memory

In the case of the woman at the telephone, the transfer of the numbers into lasting memory can be seen to have included all the processes just described. Visual images of the numbers in the directory arrived in sensory memory. These images were scanned, coded into sounds, and kept in mind through rehearsal. They were then lost from short-term memory as the woman did the dialing, listened to the busy signal, and reached to get back her coins. On the next occasion, while she was again rehearsing the sounds of the numbers, she managed to impose an organization on them by noting that they were the same as her birth date. With the help of this pattern of organization, the new information was readily associated with existing mediational units and transfer to long-term memory became easy and effective. The importance of organization — which is the secret of effective learning and a "good memory" — will be further discussed in Chapter 3.

Long-term memory is thought of as a more or less permanent storehouse of information — that is, of all the mediational units that we have placed in it, through learning, in our lifetimes. True, we do forget (for interesting and not completely understood reasons that will be discussed later). But the mediational units laid down in long-term memory are remarkably resistant to extinction. Many of them are likely to persist as long as we live.

Memory and retrieval

If the information in long-term memory is to be of any use to us, however, it must not only be stored but also be available. We must be able to find it and call upon it when needed. This process is called *retrieval*. It is closely related to coding, organization, and transfer — for the manner in which the information was originally stored helps determine how easily it can be retrieved, when, and under what circumstances.

You can observe some elementary principles of coding, organization, and retrieval by trying an experiment of your own. Ask several of your friends to try to remember as many names as they can of cities in the United States. How they respond will probably tell you a great deal about how they have organized these names into their memories and how they go about retrieving the names.

As you listen to them start reciting a list, you will probably find that many of them — and particularly those who are good at quickly naming a considerable number of cities — are making some sort of systematic search of memory. Some may go through the alphabet, starting with cities that begin with A (Atlanta, Albany, Altoona), then, after they can think of no more, moving on to B (Boston, Birmingham, Boise). Others may proceed state by state; for example, they may start with California and call out San Francisco, Los Angeles, San Diego. Others may start with the city in which they were born and the towns around it. Someone who has enjoyed the study of geography may begin by listing all the state capitals. A baseball fan may begin by listing the cities in the major leagues.

As this informal experiment shows, there are many possible ways that information can be organized in memory and retrieved, and different people use different methods. But, in one way or another, the information is somehow organized and stored away in an appropriate manner so that it can — usually — be retrieved.

To use a very rough analogy, we might say that the information stored in long-term memory is something like the definitions in a dictionary. If the words in the dictionary were listed totally at random rather than in alphabetical order — in other words, if *aardvark, metaphysics,* and *zoology* were all on the same page — the book would have little value; we would never be able to find what we were looking for. Similarly, the information stored in memory has to be listed or filed away in some way that makes it easy to find.

The human memory, however, is a good deal more complicated than a dictionary. Suppose, for example, that someone asks us to name the word that is defined "navigational instrument used in measuring angular distances, especially the altitude of sun, moon, and stars at sea." Knowing the definition would not help us find the word (which is *sextant*) in the dictionary, for the dictionary is not organized in a way that makes it possible to work back from definition to word. But if we have the word *sextant* successfully stored in long-term memory, the definition may well provide sufficient cues for us to call it out.

The "tip of the tongue" phenomenon. The definition of *sextant*, indeed, was used in a study that has quickly become famous among psychologists who specialize in learning. The subjects were university students, and they were asked to recall, from hearing the definitions, such words as *sextant, sampan, nepotism,* and *ambergris*—all being fairly unusual words that they probably once had an opportunity to learn but would not have had many occasions to use. As was expected, it turned out that often they could not remember the word but felt that they had it "on the tip of the tongue." The study is important for what it has demonstrated about the nature of the "tip of the tongue" phenomenon and the light this sheds on the process of retrieval.

Often students who had the word "on the tip of the tongue" but could not actually recall it thought of words that had a similar sound. When trying to remember *sampan*, for example, they thought of such words as *Saipan, Siam, Cheyennne,* and *sarong,* and even such made-up words as *sanching* and *sympoon*. Often they thought of words that had not a similar sound but a similar meaning. For example, in the case of *sampan*, which is defined as a small Chinese boat, they thought of *barge, houseboat,* and *junk*.

The students could often—indeed in 57 percent of the cases—guess the first letter of the word they were seeking. They also seemed to have

2-16

"Tip of the tongue" results

In this experiment described in the text, students who had a word "on the tip of the tongue" but could not quite recall it were asked to guess how many syllables it had. As shown by the figures in the colored band, their guesses were more often right than wrong unless the word had more than three syllables.

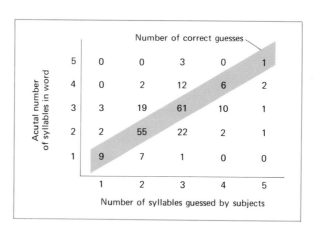

Number of correct guesses

Acutal number of syllables in word	1	2	3	4	5
5	0	0	3	0	1
4	0	2	12	6	2
3	3	19	61	10	1
2	2	55	22	2	1
1	9	7	1	0	0

Number of syllables guessed by subjects

considerable recall for the last letter of the word. Moreover, as is shown in Figure 2-16, they were quite accurate in guessing how many syllables were in the word—at least if the number of syllables, as in the great majority of English words, was no more than three. There was even some indication that they knew which syllable the accent was on (38).

The study indicates that coding, organization, and retrieval are extremely complex processes. Information in the human memory is coded and organized in a way far more complex, sophisticated, and efficient than any dictionary. The storage of a word in long-term memory takes into account the auditory characteristics of the word (that is, how many syllables it has and how it sounds when pronounced), the visual characteristics (the letters with which it begins and ends), and meaning (the word is linked to other words that mean more or less that same thing).

A word about memory theory

Now that the three-part memory system has been explained in full, a word of caution is in order. The theory that there are three different memory systems is not universally accepted. A number of psychologists believe that remembering is probably one single process, even though the process may produce strikingly different results (39). They would say that whether we remember something for just a very brief period or forever depends not on the existence of a short-term memory and a long-term memory but rather on how the information "registers" on the brain and what kinds of changes it produces in the nervous system. When the changes represent a mere processing of a sensory impression (like the glance at the phone book), they tend to have only a very short life. When they represent the formation of some meaningful association (like connecting the phone number with date of birth), they tend to last for a long time (40).

To students who plan to make a career out of psychology, the debate over theories of memory will doubtless be important, for this promises to be a major field of future research. To most students, however, the three-part theory is a useful concept whether it eventually proves to be correct or not. It embraces and explains the various processes that seem to be essential to learning, retaining information, and calling on the information when it is needed. The diagram of the three memory systems on page 63 provides a convenient method of organizing these processes into a logical flow of events. In the context of this chapter, it might be said that the theory and the diagram are helpful guides toward organizing the facts about memory so that they remain in long-term memory.

Why we forget

Memory cannot be discussed without also discussing forgetting. They are opposite sides of the same coin. We learn something; in other words we store some piece of information in our memory. Sometimes this

© 1959 United Features Syndicate

mediational unit that we have learned persists in memory. It continues to exist and to be available to the retrieval process—and we say that we remember. Sometimes it seems to disappear or to become somehow beyond our ability to recapture it—and we say that we have forgotten.

How remembering and forgetting are measured

To the psychologist, the study of the twin processes of remembering and forgetting poses more problems than might be supposed. There is no way that one can examine the nervous system to see what kinds of changes have been laid down in it by learning and how well these changes persist. One can only devise tests that will try to determine how much is remembered and how much is forgotten. Unfortunately, these tests can never make a direct measure of memory. All they really measure is how well people *perform* on the tests—and their performances may not be an entirely accurate reflection of how much they remember.

To explain why this should be true, let us say that two girls in elementary school are taking the same arithmetic course. They listen to the same explanations by their teacher and study the same textbooks. Now one day the teacher gives a written examination. Girl *A* gets 90. Girl *B* gets 70. The logical conclusion is that girl *A* learned her arithmetic very well and remembered it and that girl *B* either learned it rather badly or quickly forgot it.

The truth, however, is that we do not really know. All we are actually justified in saying is that girl *A performed* much better on the examination than did girl *B*. It may very well be that girl *B* had learned addition, subtraction, and the multiplication tables backward and forward and did badly on the examination because these subjects were so old hat to her that she was bored when asked to show how well she could perform and did not do her best.

70

Performance on a test of remembering can be influenced by many factors. Prominent among them is motivation. But subjects may also do badly because of anxiety or distractions or for any of a number of other reasons. Tests of remembering and forgetting are always subject to these kinds of errors—and must always be viewed with reservations.

Psychologists must do the best they can, however, and they have adopted three standard methods of measurement.

Recall. One way to prove you have learned the Gettysburg Address is to recite it—which means to demonstrate that you can *recall* it, that you can retrieve it intact from wherever it is stored in memory. In school, a common use of recall as a measurement of learning is in the essay type of examination. When teachers ask a question such as "What is classical conditioning?" they are asking you to recall and write down what you have learned.

Recognition. There are many situations in which we cannot recall what we have learned, at least not completely, but can prove that we remember something about it by being able to recognize it. For example, you might not be able to recall the Gettysburg Address. But if you were asked what begins with the words "Fourscore and seven years ago," you might immediately recognize the speech, thus demonstrating that you certainly remember something about it.

Multiple-choice examinations are a test of recognition; you are asked to choose the right answer from among several possible answers and thus to prove that you recognize it. Because recognition is easier than recall, many students would rather take a multiple-choice test than an essay examination.

Relearning. The most sensitive method of measuring learning is one that is seldom used. This is the method of *relearning,* which is accurate but cumbersome. All of us once learned the Gettysburg Address, or, if not that, then some other well-known piece of writing, such as the funeral oration in Shakespeare's *Julius Caesar.* We may not be able to recall them now. Our ability to recognize them proves that we learned and remember something but is not a very precise measure of how much. If we set about relearning them, however, the length of time this takes us will serve as a quite accurate measure.

The curve of forgetting

The method of relearning was used in psychology's most famous study of forgetting—an experiment that is as famous in its own way as the work of Pavlov and Skinner. The experimenter was a nineteenth-century German named Hermann Ebbinghaus, who set himself the difficult task of studying remembering and forgetting in their purest possible forms, unaffected by any previous learning, any other previous experiences, emotional factors, or any other aspects of personality. A

2-17

A study of forgetting

In his classic study of forgetting, Ebbinghaus memorized lists of thirteen nonsense syllables similar to those shown here, then measured how much he could remember after various intervals. After twenty minutes, he remembered only 58 percent and after about an hour only 44 percent. After the initial sharp dip, however, the curve flattened out. After one day he remembered about 34 percent and after two days about 28 percent. Although the graph line does not extend that far, he still remembered 21 percent after a month. (41)

BIK	TAF
ROP	GOK
DAF	MIK
PEM	BUL
FUM	HAN
NIF	RIN
GOR	KUF
MEF	JUN
JAL	LEP
KUL	DAL
LUF	FOM
HIR	REL
WOK	TUR

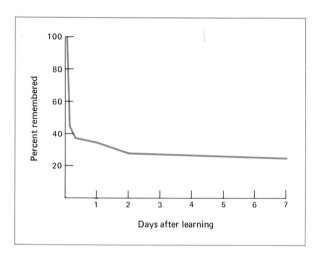

difficult task indeed—for what can a person possibly learn that does not somehow relate to these other factors?

Ebbinghaus solved the problem by using what is called a nonsense syllable—a totally meaningless combination of three letters, such as CIM. He drew up lists composed of thirteen nonsense syllables each—and, using himself as the subject of his experiment, set about memorizing the lists until he could repeat them twice without error, keeping track of the amount of time this took him. Then, after an interval in which forgetting naturally took place, he set about relearning them, again keeping track of how long this took. The difference between the amount of time it took to learn the lists originally and the amount of time it took to relearn them was his measure of how much he remembered.

Using many different lists and varying the time between original learning and relearning, Ebbinghaus came up with the graph shown in Figure 2-17. This is the typical *curve of forgetting* for many kinds of learning. It does not always apply because we learn some things so thoroughly that we never seem to forget anything about them. However, it tells a great deal about the forgetting of such varied kinds of learning as motor skills, poems we have memorized, and college courses we have taken; and its message is this: *When we learn something new, often we quickly forget much of what we have learned, but we remember at least some of it for a long time.*

Theories of forgetting

As to why we forget, the answer is not now known—and indeed may never be known for sure. But there are a number of theories well worth considering. It may be, in fact, that all the theories are correct at least in part, for forgetting may be such a complex process that it takes place in different ways under different circumstances.

Theory 1: forgetting as a failure in retrieval. A considerable number of psychologists have concluded that *retrieval* is the key process in remembering and forgetting. These psychologists feel that the mediational units stored in long-term memory represent a more or less permanent change in the nervous system. The units are always there—but, because of the way they have been stored in memory, we cannot always find them. Thus forgetting is viewed as a failure in the retrieval process—like an unsuccessful search for a box that is stored somewhere in a warehouse but cannot be found at the moment.

An experiment that seems to offer considerable support to the retrieval theory is illustrated in Figure 2-18. A picture was flashed on a screen for a very brief time, a tenth of a second. Then the subjects, who were university students, were asked to describe what they had seen in as much detail as possible and at the same time to make a drawing of the picture, with labels for the various details they included. Typically, their drawings were rather meager, as can be seen from the first drawing (*A*) by one subject, shown in Figure 2-18.

After making the drawing, the subjects were asked to look again at the screen on which the picture had been flashed, to concentrate as hard as possible on what they had seen, and to say out loud any words that happened to come to mind, regardless of whether they had any appar-

2-18

An experiment in retrieval

When the picture at the top was flashed on a screen for a tenth of a second and a student was asked to reproduce what he had seen, he could do no better than drawing *A*. After the experimenter helped his retrieval process through methods described in the text, however, the student produced the much more detailed drawing *B*.

A

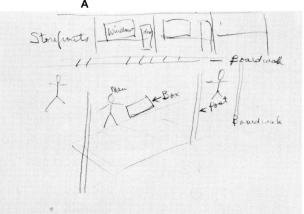

B

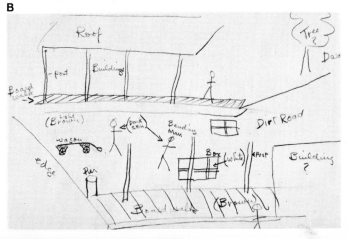

ent connection with the picture. That is to say, they were asked to free-associate to their memory of the picture—to blurt out any associations that occurred to them. The first twelve words they came up with were put on index cards, and these words were used to evoke some further free associations. The subjects were asked to look at each of the twelve words, one at a time, and to say out loud any words that these suggested. They were permitted to look at each of the twelve words until it had suggested ten additional words. Finally, after they had finished going through the twelve words and had come up with a total of 120 associations, they were asked to try to draw the picture again. This time, as can be seen from drawing *B* in Figure 2-18, they came much closer to the original, including many details that they had been unable to remember while making their first drawing. By one kind of scoring, the average improvement by the subjects was about 44 percent (42).

The experiment seems to show that the subjects learned and stored in memory considerably more information about the picture than they were able to retrieve when they made their first drawings. Free association, however, provided new clues that aided the retrieval process—and thus enabled them to remember more about the picture when they made their second drawings.

Similarly, many other experiments have shown how the phenomenon popularly known as "jogging one's memory" aids the retrieval process and thus results in remembering something stored in memory but temporarily forgotten. A simple but convincing example is this: If you are asked to learn a list of words that includes *table* and later find yourself unable to remember *table*, you are likely to recall it immediately if the experimenter helps you by saying, "There was some furniture in the list."

"I joined the Legion two or three weeks ago to try to forget a girl called Elsie or something."
© Punch, London (Rothco).

Theory 2: motivated forgetting. The fact that we seem to deliberately forget some things has already been mentioned in connection with the processes that take place in short-term memory. Many theorists believe that at times we also forget information stored in long-term memory simply because we want to forget it. For example, we forget the name of a person we dislike, or we forget the problems we had at a certain stage of life and look back to that period as a time when we were ideally happy. People who gamble are notoriously prone to remember the times they won and to forget the times they lost, often leading them to a totally false impression of how well they have done over the years.

The theory of motivated forgetting is based in large part on psychoanalytical studies of repression, which seem to show that we push many unpleasant memories into our unconscious minds as a way of getting rid of them. The mediational units that make up these memories are still present, but they are carefully blocked from our thinking. There is also some experimental evidence in support of this theory (43). There seems to be no doubt that motivated forgetting takes place, but it is probably a rather special kind of forgetting that accounts for only a small part of our failure to remember.

Theory 3: fading of the memory trace. One of the oldest theories of remembering and forgetting centers around the phrase *memory trace*. According to this theory, the nerve "trace" (or pattern) set up through learning resembles the marks of a pencil or a path worn into a plot of grass. It can be kept functioning through use, as a pencil mark can be emphasized by tracing and retracing and a pathway can be kept clear by continuing to walk over it. But without use, the memory trace tends to fade away, as a pencil mark fades with time and a pathway becomes overgrown when abandoned.

Some of the most recent speculation about the memory trace is based in part on studies of people who have suffered amnesia, or loss of memory, because of head injuries. This type of amnesia often takes a very strange form. Patients may be completely unable to remember anything that happened in the past five years yet have a normal memory for events that happened earlier. As they begin to recover, they do so according to a definite time pattern. First they recover their memory for events that are five years old, then for four-year-old events, and so on until recovery is complete. It has been suggested that this indicates that memory traces have two separate qualities: 1) resistance to extinction, which increases with the passage of time, and 2) strength, which decreases with time (44). The greater resistance of old memories would account for the ability of the amnesia patients to remember old events. The declining strength of memory traces would account for Ebbinghaus's curve of forgetting.

A

B

C

Theory 4: distortion of the memory trace. Another theory that centers around the notion of a memory trace holds that one type of forgetting occurs when the trace becomes changed or distorted with the passage of time. The theory dates back about a half-century to an experiment performed by a psychologist who presented brief stories to his subjects, then, later on, asked them to reproduce the stories. He found many distortions. His subjects usually remembered the general outline of each story, but often they changed the names of the characters and many other details.

Another psychologist showed his subjects a picture such as *A,* at left. To some of his subjects, he said, "This resembles a bottle." To others he said, "This resembles a stirrup." Later, when he asked his subjects to draw the picture they had seen, they tended to distort the original in the direction of what he had told them. Subjects who had been told the picture resembled a bottle tended to reproduce it as in *B.* Those who had been told it resembled a stirrup tended to draw it as in *C.* Some of the other distortions found in the experiment are shown in Figure 2-19 on the following page.

These experiments indicate that we tend to remember the theme of a story or the general idea of a picture but often forget the details. But whether this means that the memory trace has become distorted is a matter of controversy. Cognitive psychologists have performed many experiments in the learning and recall of sentences and have concluded that the ability to recall depends on how the sentences are stored in

Original picture	Word clue 1	Subject's drawing	Word clue 2	Subject's drawing
(drawing)	eyeglasses	(drawing)	dumbbells	(drawing)
(drawing)	seven	(drawing)	four	(drawing)
(drawing)	crescent moon	(drawing)	letter C	(drawing)
(drawing)	gun	(drawing)	broom	(drawing)
(drawing)	pine tree	(drawing)	trowel	(drawing)
(drawing)	hourglass	(drawing)	table	(drawing)

2-19

Memory distortions

An experimenter showed the drawings in the left-hand column to two groups of subjects. One group was told that the drawings looked like the objects listed under *Word clue 1*, the other that the drawings looked like the objects listed under *Word clue 2*. The use of different word clues sometimes produced distortions as extreme as those shown in the third and fifth columns. (45)

memory in the first place. They believe that it is the *meaning* that is put into memory—not the exact structure of the sentences or the details (46).

Theory 5: interference. The final theory of forgetting centers around the word *interference*. When we learn something new, this theory maintains, our ability to remember it is interfered with by things we have learned previously and also by things we learn in the future. To use a figure of speech, this theory assumes that the mediational units set up by learning are not traces that are prone to fade with the passage of time but instead are more like iron filings clustered in a magnetic field. Like iron filings, they are virtually indestructible—but the patterns in which they cluster can be pulled apart and rearranged when other filings are introduced into the field. The pattern of old filings—the mediational units we have learned in the past—helps determine where new ones will cluster. But new filings may influence and shift the old patterns.

The interference theory of forgetting is based largely on a considerable body of experimental evidence demonstrating two related processes that are called *retroactive inhibition* and *proactive inhibition*.

Retroactive inhibition

Many laboratory experiments in which the task was learning and remembering such things as nonsense syllables or lists of words have demonstrated how new learning can and does interfere with the ability

2-20

Retroactive inhibition

The bars show the results of an experiment in which subjects were asked to learn a list of adjectives, then were tested ten minutes later to find how many of the adjectives they could remember. During the ten minutes some subjects were kept busy at various new learning tasks—such as learning synonyms for the adjectives or their opposites—but some were just permitted to do nothing. The fact that the subjects who worked at new learning tasks recalled fewer of the adjectives than the ''do nothing'' group demonstrates the effect of retroactive inhibition. The more similar the new learning was to the old, the greater was the amount of retroactive inhibition. (47)

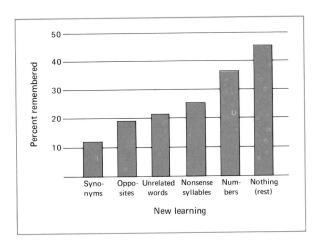

to remember the old. When the learning of task 1 is followed by the learning of task 2, memory for task 1 is less than it would otherwise be—and, the more similar task 2 is to task 1, the greater is the amount of interference. A typical laboratory demonstration of this fact is illustrated in Figure 2-20.

The interference of new learning with old is called *retroactive inhibition*. Retroactive means affecting something that occurred in the past. Inhibition means the act of restraining or stopping. Thus *retroactive inhibition is the partial or complete blacking out of old memories by new learning*.

It has been found that not only new learning but any kind of activity can cause retroactive inhibition, as shown in Figure 2-21. The person who is asleep, and thus as near to a state of suspended animation as possible, forgets less rapidly than the person who is awake and active.

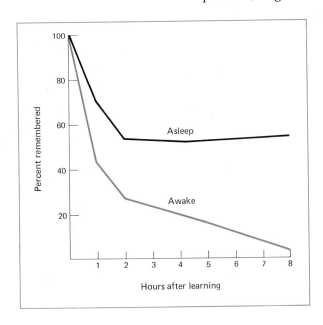

2-21

Forgetting curves when asleep and awake

The black learning curve was obtained from a subject who learned lists of nonsense syllables immediately before going to bed and was wakened for testing at various times of the night. The color curve shows what happened to memory for nonsense syllables when the same subject learned them in the morning, went about the usual daytime activities, and was tested at various times of the day. Question: Why does the curve drop so much more sharply during waking hours than during sleep? For the answer, see the text. (48)

However, some kinds of memory are less subject than others to the effect of retroactive inhibition, as has been demonstrated in a later refinement of the sleeping-waking experiment. In this case, subjects were asked to memorize not just lists of words but some meaningful material — some short stories that had been carefully constructed so that each one contained twelve elements that were essential to the plot of the story and twelve elements that were not essential. The subjects were then tested eight hours later for their recall of the stories, sometimes after sleeping and sometimes after their usual daytime activities.

As far as the nonessential elements of the stories were concerned, the results were much the same as in the earlier experiment with nonsense syllables. The subjects who had slept for the eight hours recalled 47 percent of these nonessential elements. Those who had been awake for the eight hours recalled only 23 percent. But the results for the essential elements of the plots were strikingly different. The sleepers recalled 87 percent, the others 86 percent — scores that are almost identical (49).

Other studies have also shown that retroactive inhibition has a greater effect on the meaningless, the nonessential, and the specific detail than on the more basic elements that underlie meaningful learning. To return to the figure of speech used earlier, the iron filings that cluster together in the firm associations formed around logic and understanding tend to stick together. It is the less tightly bound filings — the mediational units learned by rote, the unimportant, the details — that are likely to be shaken loose by later learning. Again the cognitive psychologists would say that the explanation lies in storing information in memory in terms of meaning.

Proactive inhibition

In retroactive inhibition, as we have seen, the new interferes with memory for the old. When the opposite happens and the old interferes with memory for the new, the process is called *proactive inhibition*.

Proactive inhibition is demonstrated by the experiment illustrated in Figure 2-22, where the learning of previous word lists was found to interfere sharply with the ability to remember new lists. Like retroactive inhibition, proactive inhibition interferes more with the remembering of meaningless materials such as word lists and nonsense syllables than with the remembering of meaningful material and general principles. It also interferes more with the remembering of similar materials than of different kinds of materials. This last point has been demonstrated in an experiment which deserves discussion in detail.

The subjects in this experiment had two seconds to look at a list of three words projected on a screen, like

LAWYER
ENGINEER
BANKER

As soon as the list disappeared from view, a number was flashed — and

2-22

Proactive inhibition

The subjects learned a list of paired adjectives. Two days after learning, they were tested for their recall of list 1 and asked to learn list 2. After a similar interval they were tested on list 2 and learned list 3. Two days later they were tested on list 3 and learned list 4. Finally, after another two-day interval, they were tested on list 4 and the experiment ended. The recall scores, which decline with each list, show the effect of proactive inhibition resulting from the learning of the prior lists. (50)

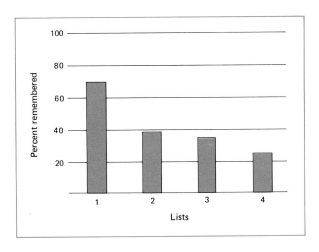

the subjects were asked to begin counting backward by threes. This was to keep them busy and to prevent them from rehearsing the words, as in the experiment described on page 65. Then they were asked to recall the three words before another list was flashed on the screen. This procedure was repeated until they had seen and tried to recall four different word lists.

The experiment was a study of proactive inhibition — but with a difference, as can be seen from a brief glance at Figure 2-23. The subjects were divided into four groups, each of which looked at different categories of words on the first three trials. Group 1 looked at three lists of professions (like the list of LAWYER — ENGINEER — BANKER). Group 2 looked at three lists of meats; Group 3 at three lists of flowers; and Group 4 at three lists of vegetables. Then on the fourth trial, the category was changed. This time all groups studied a list of fruits.

As can be seen in Figure 2-23, the average ability of all the groups to remember their words declined from the first trial to the second and again to the third — just as might be expected from what has been said

2-23

Another experiment on proactive inhibition

As in the experiment that was illustrated in Figure 2-22, subjects were asked to learn four lists of words. As in Figure 2-22, their average memory for the words showed a sharp decline from the first trial through the third. But — in this case — their performance on list 4 went up. Why? And why did Group 1 improve so much more than Group 4? For the answers, see the text. (51)

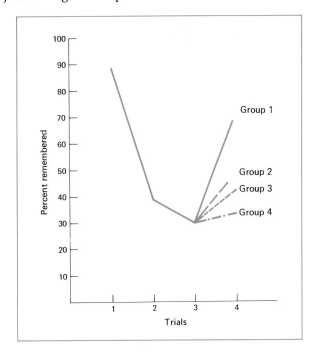

about proactive inhibition. But, on the fourth trial, when a different category of words was presented, the memory scores rose. Note that the improvement on this fourth trial was greatest for Group 1, which switched from professions to fruits—two categories that have nothing at all in common. The next highest improvement was for Group 2, which switched from meats to fruits—categories sharing only the common attribute of being foods. Group 3 showed less improvement and Group 4 showed the least of all—presumably because vegetables and fruits are rather similar in that both come from plants and both can be eaten. In other words, the amount of proactive inhibition was shown to be in direct proportion to the amount of similarity of meaning in the learning materials.

In a whole series of related experiments, it has been found that proactive inhibition is greatly reduced not only when the categories of words are changed (as from professions to fruits) but when a list of words is changed to a list of numbers. Considerable reduction also occurs when lists of words that have pronounced overtones of meaning are changed—as when powerful and destructive words such as *hate, fire,* and *kill* are changed to soft and beneficent words such as *able, mother,* and *wise.* Or when words associated with the male sex (*butler, rooster, tuxedo*) are changed to words associated with females (*queen, nylons, cow*). Or even when words that are frequently used are changed to words that are seldom used. There is little or no effect on proactive inhibition, however, when the change is merely from verbs to adjectives, verbs to nouns, or singular words (such as *child, tooth, mouse*) to plural (such as *oxen, feet, men*).

These experiments are doubly important—for they shed considerable light not only on proactive inhibition but also on the process by which information is stored in memory. They show that coding and organization can often be extremely rapid and efficient. Even in the brief span of two seconds, they indicate, a person can store in memory the meaning of a word, its overtones of meaning, the sex to which it naturally relates, and even something about how frequently it is used. But unimportant grammatical details—such as whether a word is a verb or a noun, singular or plural—tend to be ignored (52).

Summary

1 Pavlov's historic experiment in learning concerned the *reflex,* which is an inborn and built-in *response* to a *stimulus* (any form of energy capable of exciting the nervous system).

2 Through learning, a reflex response can become attached to a stimulus that did not originally cause the response. This process was first demonstrated when Pavlov "taught" a dog to respond to a sound with the salivary reflex response originally caused by the presence of food in the mouth. This type of learning is called *classical conditioning.*

3 In classical conditioning, the stimulus that naturally sets off the reflex (in Pavlov's case, the food) is called the *unconditioned stimulus.* The previously neutral stimulus to which the response becomes attached (the sound) is called the *conditioned stimulus.* The original reflex response is called the *unconditioned response,* and the response to the conditioned stimulus is called the *conditioned response.*

4 The pairing of the unconditioned stimulus and the conditioned stimulus is called *reinforcement.* When reinforcement is withdrawn, the conditioned response tends to disappear—a process called *extinction.* After a rest period, however, it tends to reappear—a process called *spontaneous recovery.*

5 When a response has been conditioned to one stimulus, it is also likely to be aroused by similar stimuli—a process called *stimulus generalization.* Through further training, however, the organism can learn to respond to a particular conditioned stimulus but not to other stimuli even when they are very similar—a process called *stimulus discrimination.*

6 Another influential learning experiment, by Skinner, was concerned with *operant behavior*—the random or exploratory activities in which organisms engage, not in reflex response to a stimulus but as a self-generated way of "operating" on the world around them.

7 Skinner showed that a rat placed in a cage would eventually press a bar through its operant behavior—then would learn to keep pressing the bar if such an action were rewarded with food.

8 The Skinner type of learning is called *operant conditioning.* In this case the reward of food is the *reinforcement.* The basic premise of operant conditioning is that operant behavior that is reinforced tends to be repeated, while operant behavior that is not reinforced takes place only at random intervals or is abandoned.

9 Like classical conditioning, operant conditioning also follows the rules of *extinction, spontaneous recovery, stimulus generalization,* and *stimulus discrimination.*

10 The learning of complicated tasks through operant conditioning is called *shaping,* a process by which complex actions are built up step by step by rewarding simpler actions that lead to the final behavior.

11 In *operant escape,* an organism learns through operant conditioning to get away from an unpleasant form of reinforcement, such as an electric shock. In *operant avoidance,* the organism learns to prevent the unpleasant reinforcement by taking some kind of action before it occurs.

12 A growing number of psychologists, notably those of the cognitive school, have come to regard learning not as the establishment of S-R connections but as the acquisition of *knowledge.* They believe that even classical conditioning sets up not an S-R connection but a cognitive pattern that somehow "tells" the dog that the sound will be followed by food. Some psychologists speak of what is learned as an *expectancy,* others as a *motivation* to behave in a certain way.

13 Cognitive psychologists believe that the most common and important form of learning is *learning through observation* (also called *learning through modeling* or *learning by imitation*), in which the organism learns by studying the behavior of another organism (the model).

14 The physiological explanation of learning seems to be some kind of chemical change that takes place in or between nerve fibers, especially in the brain.

15 What is learned can best be described as a *mediational unit* — a term used throughout the book because it avoids the controversy between S-R and cognitive psychologists. It can be regarded as either a simple and direct go-between linking a stimulus and a response, or as a go-between in the complex chains of thinking and decision making stressed by the cognitive school.

16 One theory of how we remember what we learn is that there are three kinds or systems of memory: a) *sensory*, b) *short-term*, and c) *long-term*.

17 *Sensory memory* is made up of the lingering traces of information sent to the brain by the senses. The information is forgotten within a second at most unless transferred to short-term memory.

18 *Short-term memory* receives coded information arriving from sensory memory, *rehearses* it to "keep it in mind," and *transfers* it to the next stage of memory. The efficiency of the transfer process depends to a great extent on the *organization* inherent in the information or imposed on it by the learner. New materials not transferred to the next stage are forgotten in about thirty seconds.

19 *Long-term memory* is regarded as a more or less permanent storehouse of all the information or mediational units we have acquired. If stored in an accessible code and organization, the information can be called upon when needed through the process of *retrieval*.

20 Remembering and forgetting cannot be measured directly but only by how well people *perform* on tests of memory. The three methods of testing are a) *recall*, b) *recognition*, and c) *relearning*.

21 The *curve of forgetting* shows that when we learn something new often we quickly forget much of what we have learned, but we remember at least some of it for a long time.

22 There are five theories of why we forget, all of which may be true at least in part and at times: a) a *failure in retrieval*, which is the process by which information stored in long-term memory is found and used; b) *motivated forgetting*, which means that we forget because we want to forget; c) *fading of the memory trace*; d) *distortion of the memory trace*; and e) *interference*.

23 When new learning interferes with the memory for old learning, the process is called *retroactive inhibition*. When old learning interferes with the ability to remember new learning, the process is called *proactive inhibition*.

Recommended
reading

Hilgard, E. R., and Bower, G. H. *Theories of learning,* 4th ed. New York: Appleton-Century-Crofts, 1974.

Kintsch, W. *Learning, memory and conceptual processes.* New York: John Wiley, 1970.

Melton, A. W., and Martin, E., eds. *Coding processes in human memory.* New York: Halsted Press, 1972.

Murdock, B. *Human memory: theory and data.* New York: Halsted Press, 1974.

Norman, D. A. *Models of human memory.* New York: Academic Press, 1970.

Seligman, M. E. P., and Hager, J. L., eds. *Biological boundaries of learning.* New York: Appleton-Century-Crofts, 1972.

Solso, R. L., ed. *Contemporary issues in cognitive psychology; the Loyola symposium.* New York: Halsted Press, 1973.

Tulving, E., and Donaldson, W. *Organization of memory.* New York: Academic Press, 1972.

Efficiency in learning

For all of us, in our everyday lives, learning often takes on rather puzzling aspects, some pleasant and others highly frustrating. Sometimes learning seems to occur almost by accident. We learn all sorts of things in this way—for example, how to get to the classroom, the drugstore, the laundromat, our favorite lunchroom. If we are sports fans, we have no trouble learning to recognize our favorite players on the field. If we like music, we have no trouble learning the melodies and words of new songs.

At other times, learning does not take place no matter how hard we try—or think we try. We may attempt to become good bridge players and fail utterly. We may try hard to learn higher mathematics, in hopes of an engineering career, and have no success whatever.

How can we avoid these failures? On the many occasions when we want very much to learn and remember something, how can we best go about it? What are the easiest and best ways to learn?

For example, in using a textbook is it better to keep studying without any breaks—or to study for a number of short periods, with rests in between? Is it better just to read—or to combine reading with reciting? If we want to memorize something, like a speech we must deliver, is it better to try to learn it a paragraph at a time—or to learn the whole thing as a unit?

The answers to questions such as these have been sought in the interests of pure science—but the findings have also been put to immediate practical use and now constitute one of the largest fields of applied psychology. Since the findings are most often used by teachers and in classroom situations, they are called *management of learning,* which means the attempt to arrange the most favorable possible conditions for learning to take place.

Management of learning is closely related to the theory of memory discussed in the previous chapter. It assumes that the key processes in determining whether we remember or forget are the way information is stored in long-term memory and the retrieval of this information. How these processes can be made most efficient is the subject of this chapter.

85

The importance of attention

All of us know from personal experience that attention and learning are closely related. When we pay attention—eagerly and single-mindedly—learning tends to be easy. When we do not pay attention, learning tends to be difficult or even impossible. But, as every student knows, these simple facts are not in themselves very helpful. Try as we may to pay attention, we often fail. While listening to a classroom lecture, we may find ourselves giving our attention not to the words but to the sound of rain on the windowpanes. Reading a textbook, we may find ourselves thinking how pleasant it would be to have a hamburger or go to sleep.

Why is attention so important? And what are the factors that sometimes help us pay attention and sometimes turn our thoughts elsewhere? What, if anything, can we do to control these factors?

The effect of attention

In terms of the three-part theory of memory, attention is important because it serves as a sort of catalyst that helps us transfer information from sensory memory to short-term memory, then helps the short-term memory do the work of rehearsing the information and transferring it to long-term memory. This process takes time. The longer and harder we work at it, the more efficient it is likely to become.

Paying attention seems to have a marked effect on the brain's activity. As is shown by the tracing of brain waves in Figure 3-1, a pattern that has been called an "expectancy wave" occurs when subjects get ready to respond to a stimulus. The same sort of wave appears if they are told that they are about to see something interesting, such as a photograph. In one recent experiment, indeed, it was found that the strength of the expectancy wave was affected by how interesting the subjects expected the photograph to be. Male subjects showed a stronger wave if told that they would view a female nude rather than a male nude, while for women the results were just the opposite (2).

It is known that anything that decreases the brain's general state of

3-1

The "expectancy wave"

The colored line represents a typical tracing of the brain waves of subjects who were told that they would see a flash of light, that the light would be a warning that a tone would soon be sounded, and that they should be prepared to press a key the instant they heard the tone. The tracing was made by an electroencephalograph, a device that will be described in more detail in Chapter 7. (1)

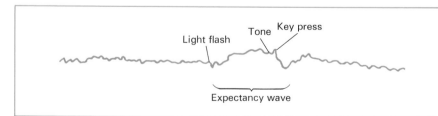

arousal and activity interferes with the learning process. For example, certain drugs have been found to hamper learning when given just before, during, or just after the attempt to learn. These drugs include alcohol (3), tranquilizers (4), and mild doses of anesthetics such as ether or laughing gas (5). On the other hand, anything that increases brain arousal tends to speed up the learning process, unless of course the arousal is so intense as to cause confusion. The reason mild stimulation helps learning seems to be, at least in part, that it sharpens attention. Among the many drugs that have been found to have this effect are caffeine, nicotine, and amphetamines (6). Listening to white noise—which provides stimulation without producing any sounds that might be meaningful and therefore distracting—has also been found to improve efficiency at learning (7).

This does not mean that psychologists recommend that studying should be done with the help of a lot of coffee, cigarettes, and noise—for this kind of stimulation can be effective only for brief periods. It does mean that any kind of self-generated arousal and enthusiasm is helpful.

Motivation and attention

One powerful aid to paying attention is motivation. Some people seem to have an almost insatiable thirst for knowledge—any kind of knowledge. They find it easy to pay attention regardless of the subject matter. Some students who are motivated mostly by the desire for good grades also pay close attention regardless of whether they are studying psychology, philosophy, or ancient history. Most of us, however, are somewhat more selective. We are strongly motivated to learn some things, less strongly motivated to learn others. We are most likely to pay attention when we are learning something that seems to satisfy our own particular and rather specialized motives.

If we can somehow relate the subject matter to our motives, attention can usually be sharpened. Thus the study of Spanish becomes easier if students keep reminding themselves that they may someday be traveling or even working in a Spanish-speaking country.

Feedback and attention

Psychologists have long been aware that feedback—a term borrowed from the field of automation—plays an important role in learning. Feedback means information on how well the learning process is going—that is, on how we are progressing, how much we have learned, how many mistakes we are making, and what kinds of mistakes.

One reason feedback helps is that it enables us to correct our mistakes. This is especially important in the learning of motor skills. For example, if we try to learn typing on a dummy keyboard, we may keep hitting the wrong keys without ever knowing it. On an actual typewriter, feedback from the printed page tells us at once when we make a mistake.

When a man's hand is touched by a hot surface or receives an electric shock, the hand is immediately withdrawn. Since this reflex was not established by previous conditioning, it is a(n) ____ ____ . 2-24	unconditioned reflex 2-24
In this unconditioned hand-withdrawal reflex, heat is the ____ ____ . 2-25	unconditioned stimulus 2-25
In the unconditioned hand-withdrawal reflex, the movement of the arm is the ____ ____ . 2-26	unconditioned response 2-26
If a bell sounds 30 seconds before a hot object touches the hand (and the procedure is repeated several times), ____ will take place. 2-27	conditioning 2-27

3-2

A programed psychology book

Frames from a programed textbook in psychology discuss classical conditioning. The student fills in the blank in each frame at left, then looks at the correct answer (right) before going on to the next frame. (8)

Another reason—even more important—is that feedback helps capture and hold attention. By providing evidence that learning is actually taking place, it maintains our interest. If we are strongly motivated to learn, it shows us that we are beginning to satisfy our motives and thus encourages us to go on.

One of the most interesting applications of feedback has been the development of *programed learning,* in which the contents of a course are broken down into a series of very small steps. At each step a single new term or new idea is introduced or material that has been covered previously is reviewed. When programed learning is offered in printed form, as shown in Figure 3-2, students ordinarily fill in a blank or several blanks at each step. They can then uncover the correct answer—and get immediate feedback as to whether their response was right or wrong—before going on to the next step.

Programed instruction is often presented through a mechanical teaching machine that can be operated manually to show the steps one at a time. Or it may be presented through a computer; the student uses a keyboard or light pen to make responses, as illustrated at the left, and a correct answer produces the next step. Some such systems—called computer-assisted instruction, or CAI for short—have been developed to the point where they can virtually hold dialogues with students and if necessary switch them to remedial steps that will lead to the right

"If this machine isn't out of whack, reading is going to be even harder than I expected."

answers. All programed learning, however simple or complex the apparatus it uses, is essentially an attempt to make maximum use of the value of feedback.

Rewards and attention

As was explained in Chapter 2, many psychologists have come to doubt that reinforcement—or reward—plays the all-important role in learning that has been assumed by the S-R school. Nonetheless, it is generally agreed that rewards can and do have an influence. At least at times, and under certain conditions, they may help sharpen our attention and spur us to do the work required in learning. Psychologists speak of two kinds of rewards, each worthy of separate discussion.

1 External rewards. Some rewards, known as *external rewards* (or *extrinsic rewards*), come from the outside. Babies are rewarded for each new accomplishment with a smile and a pat. Older children are rewarded with gold stars, candy, and trips to the movies. Even college students are rewarded for learning—with good grades and eventually diplomas, and sometimes with increased allowances or presents from their parents. All these tokens of success are in a sense merely bribes provided by another person. Nonetheless, they can be effective and useful.

In one study that demonstrated the value of external rewards, a psychologist worked for a period of years with about 400 boys between the ages of thirteen and eighteen who had done so badly in school that they were considered "uneducable." To give them an incentive to learn, he first paid them small sums of money, then later rewarded them for successes by permitting them to study subjects that they especially liked. On the average these boys managed to cover between two and three years of schoolwork in a single year, and even their scores on intelligence tests improved substantially. The psychologist has concluded that the external rewards of money and permission to study favored subjects served to get the boys going—and finally to reach the point where they really began to enjoy learning (9).

2 Internal rewards. The second group of rewards is *internal rewards,* also sometimes called *intrinsic rewards.* These are inward feelings of personal satisfaction. They might be called the pleasure of learning for the sake of learning.

An example is a boy learning to ride a bicycle. In part his attention

may be drawn by external rewards, such as the respect of his friends. But the rewards are primarily internal—pleasant feelings arising from the satisfaction of his desire to prove his ability and from the sense of power derived from traveling faster on wheels than he can travel on foot. Other examples are adults who try very hard to learn to dance, to play a musical instrument, or to take beautiful photographs. Their attention is absolutely riveted on the learning situation—not because they seek any external reward but because they want the internal reward of learning a new skill, the reward that comes from meeting an internal standard of perfection. Of the two kinds of rewards, the internal seem to be clearly the more effective and lasting aid to attention.

Punishment and attention

As a tool for the management of learning, punishment occupies a unique position. Unlike the other topics that make up this chapter, it is not a tool that we can use to improve our own learning skills. In fact we would not want to use it on ourselves even if we could. But all of us have been subjected to it. And there comes a time in all our lives—as owner of a young pet if not as a parent—when we must wonder whether to use it, and if so when and how.

Animal experiments. A great deal of what psychology knows about the effectiveness of punishment comes from studies of animals, because ethical considerations rule out certain kinds of studies with human beings. Hence the findings have to be regarded with reservations, for what has been found true about animals may or may not be true of human beings.

In general, the animal experiments have shown that punishment often results in rather rapid and long lasting learning (10). As might be expected, the punishment is usually most effective if administered as soon as possible after the behavior that the experimenter wants to eliminate—so that, to use human terminology, the animal can "recognize" a connection between the two events.

Punishment is most effective of all when combined with reward—that is to say, when the "wrong" response is punished and the "correct" response is rewarded. For example, if a rat is placed at the entrance of a T-shaped maze in which the "correct" response is to turn right, it will learn this response very quickly if rewarded with food when it turns right and punished with shock when it turns left. A real-life demonstration of the same principle is provided by the housebreaking of a young puppy, which, as countless dog owners have discovered, is best accomplished by punishing the animal immediately with a slap with a rolled-up newspaper when it wets a rug but giving clear indications to the animal that the same act is praiseworthy outdoors.

Adverse effects of punishment. Even in the case of animals, however, there is experimental evidence that punishment may have drastic and rather horrible results. In one experiment, for example, dogs were strapped into a type of harness similar to the one used by Pavlov (page 44). While thus immobilized, they received a series of sixty-four electrical shocks, each lasting five seconds, delivered at random intervals. There was no way that they could avoid the shocks or escape from them. They were helpless to prevent the shocks or cut them off before the five seconds were up. Next day the dogs were placed in a box with two compartments separated by a shoulder-high hurdle. From time to time the light inside the box was dimmed, and ten seconds later a shock was administered through the floor of the compartment in which the dog had been placed. The animal could avoid the shock altogether by jumping over the hurdle into the other compartment before the ten seconds were up, or it could escape the shock by jumping after the electricity was turned on. If the dog did not jump into the other compartment, the shock continued for a full fifty seconds.

The results of the experiment, shown in Figure 3-3, were quite dramatic. The dogs had ten trials in which they could learn to avoid or escape the shock, but the amount of learning that took place was very small. In most cases the dogs simply accepted the shock for the full fifty seconds, making no attempt to leap over the hurdle. By contrast, a control group of dogs that had not previously received inescapable shocks learned very quickly to jump the hurdle in time to avoid the shock or to escape in a hurry once the shock had begun.

How are we to account for the failure of the experimental dogs to learn—for their passive acceptance of a severe and long lasting shock? The experimenters attribute it to what they have called *learned helplessness*. While in the Pavlov harness, the dogs learned that nothing they could do had any effect on whether they received a shock or for how long. To speak about animals in human terms again, they carried this knowledge over to the situation in the hurdle box. They had no "expectation" that they could do anything about the shock and therefore no "incentive" to try to escape (11).

Punishment in human education. The experiment on "learned helplessness" suggests some of the dangers of the use of punishment in

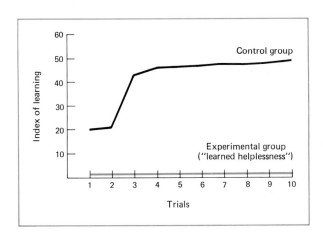

3-3

How punishment can backfire

The graph lines show the results of the experiment, described in the text, in which a group of dogs acquired "learned helplessness" because of receiving unavoidable punishment. When these dogs were later placed in a hurdle box from which they could easily avoid or escape a shock, they showed very little learning. Indeed most of them took no action and endured the shock for its full duration (colored line). Animals that had not previously received unavoidable punishment, on the other hand, were very quick to learn to avoid the shock or escape from it after it began (black line).

human situations. Many parents who believe in the old adage "Spare the rod and spoil the child" are quick to punish almost any kind of activity, often with the same degree of verbal or physical intensity regardless of how major or minor the child's transgressions may be. Some parents seem to operate by whim. Depending on their moods, they may at times severely punish exactly the same kind of behavior that they ignore at other times.

It seems reasonable to assume that children who are continually "bawled out" or spanked—especially if the punishment is often inconsistent—may very well acquire a "learned helplessness" of their own. They may decide that they have no control over when, how, or why they are punished. Like the dogs that never learned to escape the shock in the hurdle box, they may give up trying to learn what their parents are trying to teach them, in which case the parents' attempts to punish them into learning the difference between good behavior and bad become self-defeating. Such children may even become what the experimental dogs would have to be called in human terms—that is, seriously neurotic. The same unfortunate results may occur when elementary school teachers who are "down" on the slow learners in their classes constantly berate them for their stupidity.

Observation of children who received a considerable amount of verbal or physical punishment has shown that they tend to acquire a considerable dislike for the people who punish them (for example, their parents or teachers). Such children also tend to shun any activities that have led to punishment, such as schoolwork (12). Children who are frequently criticized tend to develop an expectation of failure and soon may stop working at their school tasks. It appears, too, that children who are harshly punished tend to be aggressive and punishing toward other children—perhaps as a result of learning through observation, perhaps in an attempt to take out their own sufferings on others. Punishment may attract attention—but often it does so at a price.

Organization as an aid to learning

Attention, as has just been said, is one of the keys to learning. Indeed it is essential—for we cannot learn unless we do pay attention. Yet attention in itself is not enough. What we want to learn must still be stored in long-term memory—and how well we remember depends on the efficiency of that process.

Here the magic word, as was mentioned briefly in Chapter 2, is *organization*. By and large, how well we learn depends on how well we can make sense out of the materials we want to remember, how well we can group and organize them, how well we can fit them together with what we already know.

3-4

Which list is easiest to learn?

These are the kinds of lists used in a well-known learning experiment, which you can repeat for yourself. Study list 1 for two minutes, then test yourself to see how many of the ten items you remember. Now do the same for each of the other three lists. To find how your scores compare with those obtained in the original experiment, see Figure 3-5. (Nonsense syllables, 13)

List 1	List 2	List 3	List 4
SIT	DOZ	SIQ	ZOJ
HAT	RAV	CUK	JYQ
BIN	ROV	BYS	XUY
COW	SOF	NOK	QOV
RIM	HOL	GEV	GIW
RAN	SUR	RYS	VAF
MET	LIF	CYP	CEF
POT	GYM	FYS	XYH
HUG	RUF	JAL	VYQ
FIG	BEV	QAT	ZYT

The search for meaningfulness

Because organization is so important, we are often at the mercy of the materials we are trying to learn. If the materials "make sense," if they are *meaningful,* then they are usually easy to organize. This would be true, say, of many of the rules of mathematics. But if the materials do not make sense, if they do not hang together, then they are usually difficult to organize. This would be true in the case of trying to learn the vocabulary of an entirely unfamiliar language.

One experiment that has clearly demonstrated the advantages of meaningfulness used the word lists shown in Figure 3-4. You can try the experiment for yourself by following the instructions given in the caption. If you do this, your scores on each of the four lists will probably be quite similar to the results found in the original experiment, which are shown in Figure 3-5.

It should come as no surprise that list 1, composed of actual three-letter words, should be the easiest of all the lists to learn. But why is list 2 easier to learn than list 3, and list 3 in turn easier than list 4? The answer is that the lists were deliberately drawn up to contain less and less meaningfulness from number 1 to number 4. Each of the nonsense syllables in list 2 is meaningful in the sense that it tends to remind almost everyone of some actual word. That is to say, all of us already have some word in our vocabulary with which the nonsense syllables of list 2 can easily be associated. In list 3, about half the words have this sort of meaningfulness. In list 4, none of the syllables do; in this list, all the syl-

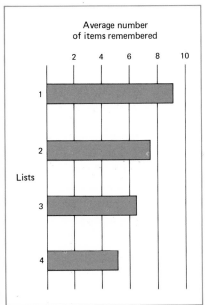

Average number of items remembered

3-5

One group's scores on the lists

These are the scores made by the subjects in the original experiment with the word lists in Figure 3-4. For an explanation of why there was such a large variation in how much was learned from the different lists, see the text. (14)

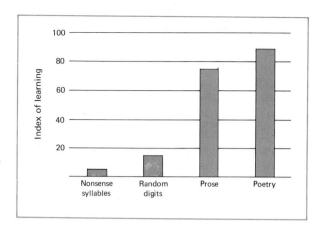

The height of the bars demonstrates how much more easily subjects in one experiment learned
meaningful information than lists
of random digits and nonsense
syllables. (15)

lables are truly "nonsense" in that they do not suggest associations
with actual words. Thus the results shown in Figure 3-5—and probably
your own results if you tried the experiment—demonstrate how meaningfulness helps in learning and how lack of meaningfulness hinders.

Many other experiments have produced similar results. In one of
them, subjects were asked to learn lists of 200 items or words each made
up of either nonsense syllables, digits in random order, a passage of
prose writing, or a passage of poetry. The results are illustrated in Figure 3-6. Note how much easier it was for the subjects to learn the passages of prose or poetry than the nonsense syllables or the nonsense arrangements of digits. Poetry—which has not only meaningfulness but
also a sort of internal logic and organization provided by the cadence
and rhymes—proved easiest of all to learn.

Learning by rule versus learning by rote

Closely related to the role of meaningfulness in helping organize materials is another well established fact about learning: we usually learn
more easily and remember longer if we learn by rule—or, as some might
prefer to say, by logic—than if we learn by rote. An experiment that
neatly demonstrates this is illustrated in Figure 3-7. Most of the students who tried to learn the numbers shown in the right-hand photograph, it should be mentioned, managed to discover the principle that
lay behind the arrangement. You may want to try to discover it also
before reading on to the next paragraph.

As you may have figured out for yourself, the numbers following the
first number 5 are obtained by regularly adding 3-4-3-4-3-4-3-4 to the
preceding number. Thus 5 is followed by 8 (which is 5 plus 3); 8 is
followed by 12 (which is 8 plus 4); 12 is followed by 15 (which is 12 plus
3); and so on. Number 26 at the end of the first line is followed by 29 (26
plus 3) to start the second line, and 29 is then followed by 33 (29 plus 4).

As the experiment was set up, the first class was in effect asked to
learn the numbers by rote—that is to say, by sheer repetition, mechanically, without any regard to meaning. The second class learned by rule
—with an understanding of the meaningfulness and logic of the pattern. When the students were tested three weeks later, not one of those
who had learned by rote remembered the numbers correctly. Of the

students who had learned by a logical rule, 23 percent still knew the numbers perfectly (16).

Indeed the logical rules that we have grasped tend to stay in our memories for a long time—much, much longer than most details that we have learned largely by rote. Five years from now, for example, you may have forgotten words from this course such as *operant* and *reinforcement*. But the general rules of how learning takes place and its importance in human behavior will probably have stuck with you. One study that demonstrates this fact about college students and what they remember from a course is illustrated in Figure 3-8.

3-7

Rote versus rule

In both these classes the students have been asked to memorize the numbers on the blackboard. In the class at left the instructor suggests that the easiest way to remember them is in groups of three, as he has arranged them. In the class at right the instructor points out that the two lines of numbers are not arranged in random order but according to a definite and logical pattern, with the pattern the same for both lines. The students are left to find the pattern for themselves (as you may also want to try to do). The experiment was designed to see which class would learn the numbers more easily. For an explanation of the logical pattern into which the numbers fall and the results that were obtained by the psychologist who devised the experiment, see the text.

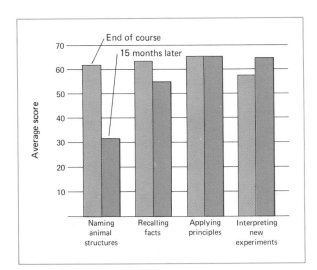

3-8

What college students remember

These scores were obtained by testing college zoology students, first at the end of their course and again more than a year later. They show that the students had forgotten about half the terminology they had learned for animal structures and many specific facts. But they still knew the principles as well as ever and could apply them to new situations. On the matter of interpreting experiments that they had never heard of before, they were actually better than at the end of the course. This improvement was probably due to the greater general knowledge and maturity acquired in an additional year of college. (17)

How categories help

How to remember this list?

SLATE
BRONZE
IRON
EMERALD
GOLD
GRANITE
DIAMOND
LEAD
MARBLE
STEEL
LIMESTONE
PLATINUM
SAPPHIRE
ALUMINUM
SILVER
BRASS
RUBY
COPPER

Another useful method for organizing materials is to lump similar items together in convenient pigeonholes — or, to use more scientific terminology, to try to learn them by categories. This generally efficient method of learning can best be explained by citing an experiment that used word lists such as the one shown at the left. A random list of this sort is not easy to learn, as subjects in the experimenter's control group found out.

The other group of subjects, however, received some help. To these subjects, the words on the list were presented in the manner illustrated in Figure 3-9. That is to say, the subjects were helped to see that all the words fell into the general category of minerals, that this category could be broken down into the subcategories of metals and stones, and that these subcategories could again be divided into three different kinds of metals (rare, common, and alloys) and two different kinds of stones (precious stones and stones used in masonry).

The control group and the experimental group were both asked to try to learn four lists, containing 112 words in all, within four trials. The difference in the amounts learned by the two groups proved quite striking. As is shown in Figure 3-10, the subjects who had been helped to organize the words into categories proved far superior. Indeed they remembered all 112 words perfectly on the third and fourth trials — a level never even approached by the subjects who tried to learn the words at random (18).

3-9

Learning by category

This is how the words shown above in the left margin were presented to the experimental group in the learning study described in the text. Question: Do the categories make learning easier, and if so by how much? For the answer, see the text and Figure 3-10.

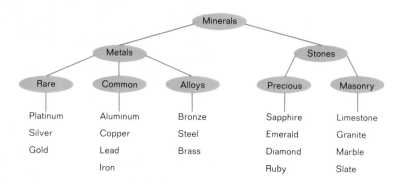

3-10

Results of learning by category

The graph lines show how much more rapidly word lists were learned by subjects who saw them arranged by category, as in Figure 3-9, than by subjects who saw them in random order.

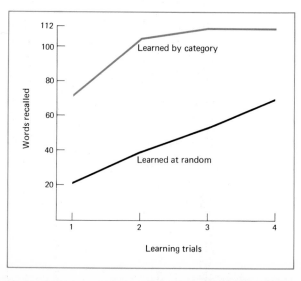

The technique of clustering

Organizing materials into categories is one form of what memory students call *clustering*—that is, the lumping or clustering together of materials that have some sort of affinity. Materials stored in memory in clusters—either by categories, in terms of meaningfulness or logic, or in some other way—tend to hang together in a tightly bound mass that resists the erosion of forgetting.

The clustering process also aids retrieval. Within each tightly bound and cohesive cluster there may be a considerable number of individual items of information. In the search of memory that goes on during retrieval, we have a much better chance of hitting on one of many items than on any single item—just as we have a much better chance of making a hit if we throw a dart at a whole board full of balloons instead of just a single balloon. And when we manage to find this one item, we can pull the whole cluster of information out with it.

An example might be this: in an essay examination, you are asked to define the term *stimulus generalization.* At first the meaning of the term eludes you. You seem to have forgotten it. But then the term suggests the category of learning principles; this suggests the subcategory of classical conditioning—and out pour all the facts you have clustered under that heading, including the meaning of stimulus generalization.

Made-up stories as an aid to retrieval

Even when there is no real logic to the materials that must be learned, and no really meaningful way of grouping them into categories, sometimes we can find a way of organizing them into clusters nonetheless. There are little tricks that can be developed and used effectively.

It has been found, for example, that one good way of learning word lists is to make up stories about the words. In one experiment demonstrating this fact, subjects were asked to memorize in order words such as those on the lists shown in Figure 3-11. One group of subjects simply

3-11

An experiment in memorizing word lists

These are two of the word lists used in the experiment described above, along with examples of the kinds of stories made up by the subjects to help them remember the words.

Word Lists		Stories Built Around Them
1. LUMBERJACK 6. DUCK 2. DART 7. FURNITURE 3. SKATE 8. STOCKING 4. HEDGE 9. PILLOW 5. COLONY 10. MISTRESS		A LUMBERJACK DARTed out of a forest, SKATEd around a HEDGE past a COLONY of DUCKS. He tripped on some FURNITURE, tearing his STOCKING while hastening toward the PILLOW where his MISTRESS lay.
1. VEGETABLE 6. BASIN 2. INSTRUMENT 7. MERCHANT 3. COLLEGE 8. QUEEN 4. NAIL 9. SCALE 5. FENCE 10. GOAT		A VEGETABLE can be a useful INSTRUMENT for a COLLEGE student. A carrot can be a NAIL for your FENCE or BASIN. But a MERCHANT of the QUEEN would SCALE that fence and feed the carrot to a GOAT.

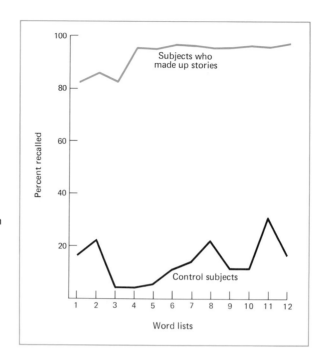

3-12

Results of the word-list experiment

As the graph shows, the subjects who made up stories to help them remember the word lists remembered far more of the words in their correct order than did the control subjects, who tried to memorize the lists by rote. In fact the subjects who made up stories showed almost perfect memory for the fourth through the twelfth lists of words.

received this instruction and no more. Another group was asked to try to do the memorizing by making up stories about the words. They seemed to find this quite easy. Usually they made up their stories, two of which are shown in Figure 3-11, in less than two minutes.

Both groups worked for an equal amount of time at learning twelve such lists. Later their memory was tested by giving them the first word on each list, then asking them to recall the others. As can be seen in Figure 3-12, the difference between the two groups was quite remarkable. The subjects who had made up stories remembered almost all the words. The subjects who had not used this method had forgotten most of them (19).

What happened, of course, was that the subjects told to make up stories found some sort of theme—meaningful to them if not necessarily to anybody else—into which the words on each list could be integrated. This central theme helped them organize the words into clusters, and the clusters persisted in their memories. It is worthy of note that their stories often made a liberal use of *imagery*, or mental pictures. For example, the subject whose story is shown at the left in Figure 3-11 apparently coded into long-term memory a sort of picture of a lumberjack darting out of a forest, skating around a hedge, and so on. Many studies have shown that the formation of such images is of considerable help in retrieval (20, 21).

At left is a mnemonic device used by monks in medieval times to help them remember prayers and religious writings. The device is based on the location of various objects in the monastery in which they lived, in the order in which these would be seen in strolling through the buildings. The middle row, for example, is made up of a chair, shelves, and other objects in the library. The monks made mental images of the items they wanted to remember as placed on or against the various objects. The hand in every fifth frame and cross in every tenth frame helped in remembering the sequence.

98

Mnemonic devices

Closely allied to the trick of making up stories about word lists are the various learning techniques called *mnemonic devices,* after the Greek word for memory. Like the term itself, these devices probably date back to the ancient Greeks (22). Among the well-known ones are the jingle that begins ''Thirty days hath September'' (for remembering how many days there are in each month), the sentence ''Every good boy does fine'' (for remembering the notes in music), and ''I left port'' (for remembering the difference between the port, or left side of a ship, and the starboard, or right side).

A somewhat more complicated mnemonic system, helpful in learning short lists of words or objects, has been used in a number of psychological experiments—and can easily be used by anyone who might want help in remembering such things as shopping lists or chores to be done during the day. To adopt the system, one begins by memorizing this easily remembered jingle:

> One is a bun; two is a shoe;
> Three is a tree; four is a door;
> Five is a hive; six is sticks;
> Seven is heaven; eight is a gate;
> Nine is wine; ten is a hen.

Let us say that the jingle is to be used to help remember, in order, the following list of words: 1) pencil, 2) knife, 3) horse, 4) battleship, 5) briefcase, 6) newspaper, 7) apple, 8) wheelbarrow, 9) table, 10) lightbulb. The trick is to form some kind of mental image, like those shown below, connecting the words to be remembered with the words that rhyme with the numbers.

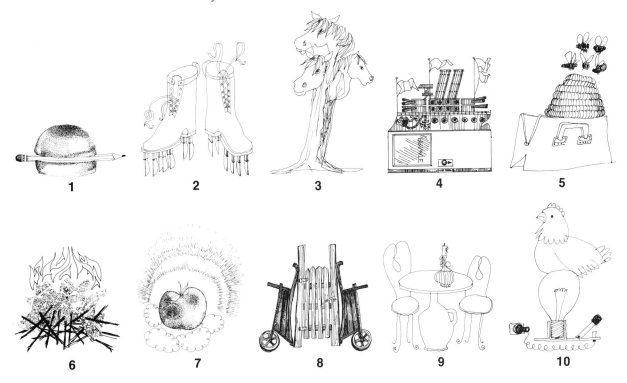

1   2   3   4   5

6   7   8   9   10

3-13

How "one is a bun" can help

In the experiment described in the text, subjects using the "one is a bun" mnemonic device did better than other subjects (the control group) as soon as learning time was increased past two seconds per word. When they had eight seconds, they almost reached the perfect learning score of 20. (23)

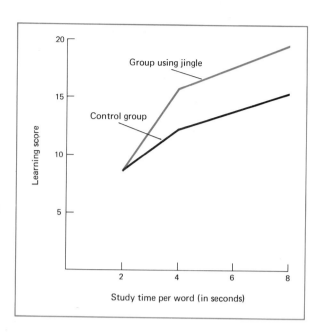

How well the "one is a bun" device works can be seen in Figure 3-13. The graph in Figure 3-13 shows the results of an experiment in which one group of subjects learned lists of ten words with the help of the jingle while a control group learned without it. When subjects had only two seconds to study each word on a list, there was no difference between the two groups. But when more time was allowed—to permit subjects using the jingle to form their mental images—the experimental group did much better.

The experimenters found that the subjects who used the jingle liked the idea and "felt genuinely indebted for being let in on a 'valuable' secret." Similar systems, more elaborate in that they often provide memory hooks for as many as 100 items, are the secret of the "memory experts" in show business who perform such seemingly incredible feats as quickly learning long lists of objects or of people's names. For learning things that do not hang together through any organization or logic of their own, mnemonic devices are unquestionably useful. The reason is that they provide a ready-made framework into which the new information can be integrated and clustered (24).

How learning builds on learning

Though mnemonic devices can serve as a sort of crutch in cases of emergency, nothing is so generally and pervasively helpful in learning as the ability to organize new information into some kind of natural and "sense making" entity—with the new items clustered together and logically related to other information previously held in memory. In the last analysis, indeed, all the factors that have been mentioned in the chapter up to now as aids to learning depend in large part on what kind of information we already possess, and how much.

100

We are most likely to pay attention to something that immediately strikes us as related to something we already know. A physician, for example, may take just one glance at a patient and note that the patient's appearance indicates a disease described in a medical textbook—though the patient's family and friends never noticed anything wrong.

We also are helped to find meaningfulness in new information when it somehow relates to the old. To the art student, a new painting may be meaningful because it uses the same technique Picasso used in one of his early periods. To the nonartist, the painting may have no meaning at all.

We form categories and clusters on the basis of what we already know. To the subjects in the experiment illustrated in Figures 3-9 and 3-10, the categories of *metals* and *stones* would have been of no value had they not already known what these words meant and the kinds of objects they embraced. The subjects in the experiment illustrated in Figures 3-11 and 3-12 could not have made up their stories without all kinds of prior knowledge that enabled them to organize the miscellaneous words into a step-by-step narrative.

The role of component parts

One way in which prior learning helps is demonstrated by this simple example: a young boy has a difficult time learning to ride a bicycle; later on, however, he has no trouble at all learning to ride a motorcycle. The reason is that when he learned to ride the bicycle he had none of the required skills. He had to learn from scratch to balance himself, how to steer, and how to pedal. By the time he got around to the motorcycle, he already knew how to balance and steer. The only thing new to learn was the mechanical operation.

In all kinds of learning, it helps to possess what are called the *component parts*—or units of skill or information that help make up the total pattern that is to be learned and remembered. If you try to teach the word *horizon* to a four-year-old child, you will find the task impossible. But ten-year-olds usually need only one explanation to grasp the meaning and add *horizon* to their vocabularies. The reason is that by the age of ten children have learned the various component parts—concepts of space, earth, and sky—that go to make up the meaning of *horizon*.

Similarly, memorizing the Gettysburg Address would be a difficult task for children in the lower grades. They would first have to learn to recognize and pronounce words such as *conceived, dedicated,* and *consecrated.* Older children, already familiar with these words, find it much easier to link them together.

The importance of component parts in learning explains what would otherwise be a rather baffling fact about schoolwork. Insofar as can be measured, children entering high school have matured to the point where they seem to possess all the neurological equipment that makes learning possible. Their innate ability to learn will not increase very much if at all. They are already just about as smart, to use the popular term, as they will ever be. Yet everybody knows that high-school seniors can learn things that would be beyond a high-school freshman — and college students can go a long step farther. The reason is that each year the students acquire more and more of the component parts of higher learning — a bigger vocabulary, more concepts, more mathematical symbols and rules.

How other information helps

Not only component parts but any other kind of information held in memory can be a significant aid to learning. As an example, let us imagine that a woman who teaches kindergarten has spent her summer in Europe and takes two coins to her class. "This one," she says, passing it around to her pupils, "is an Austrian schilling." Then she passes the other around and says, "This is a French franc."

Now there is nothing very complicated about learning the words *schilling* and *franc*. Thinking in terms of component parts, these parts are only sounds that every kindergarten child has learned.

Let us suppose, however, that there is one girl in the class whose family has frequently gone traveling in Europe. This girl has often heard her parents talk about Austria and France and about exchanging American dollars for foreign money. In addition, she has been entrusted with sums of money that she has been permitted to spend for herself. She knows the difference between a United States nickel and a United States quarter or half dollar. On the other hand, there is a boy in the class who has never heard the words *Austria* and *France* mentioned in his home. He does not know that there is any nation in the world except the United States, and he has never had any money of his own to spend, so that he has only a vague notion of what a coin is.

Which of these two pupils is likely to remember, on the following day, which of the two coins the teacher holds up is the schilling and which is the franc? Naturally the girl is more likely to learn and remember. She has prior information with which the words *schilling* and *franc* can be organized and clustered. In the case of the boy, the new words tend to fall on deaf ears. He simply has no items in memory to which the new words can be attached.

For another example of the importance of prior knowledge and information, consider the case of college students of a generation ago who happened to read a newspaper story about some event in the Middle East. They would probably not have had any previous information about the Middle East and its role in world affairs to which the news story could readily be associated and thus effectively stored in memory. Thus they probably would not have learned very much. More recent students, however, are likely to know a great deal about the Middle East's geography, people, politics, armies, and world importance. They can readily remember the contents of a news article about the Middle East because they have a framework of information into which it can easily be organized.

Clustering
"like grapes to
a stem"

It has been known for a long time that the greatest possible aid to learning is the possession of prior knowledge—mediational units, if you will—to which the new information can "stick." Indeed this principle has never been explained more beautifully than by William James, even though James lived and wrote many years before the discovery of most of what is now known about the processes of memory and retrieval. James put it in these eloquent words:

> *The more other facts a fact is associated with in the mind, the better possession of it our memory retains.* Each of its associates becomes a hook to which it hangs, a means to fish it up by when sunk beneath the surface. Together, they form a network of attachments by which it is woven into the entire tissue of our thought. The "secret of a good memory" is thus the secret of forming diverse and multiple associations with every fact we care to retain. . . . Most men have a good memory for facts connected with their own pursuits. The college athlete who remains a dunce at his books will astonish you by his knowledge of men's records in various feats and games, and will be a walking dictionary of sporting statistics. The reason is that he is constantly going over these things in his mind, and comparing and making series of them. They form for him not so many odd facts but a concept-system—so they stick. So the merchant remembers prices, the politician other politicians' speeches and votes, with a copiousness which amazes outsiders, but which the amount of thinking they bestow on these subjects easily explains. The great memory for facts which a Darwin and a Spencer reveal in their books is not incompatible with the possession on their part of a brain with only a middling degree of physiological retentiveness [by which James means inborn ability for remembering]. Let a man early in life set himself the task of verifying such a theory as that of evolution, and facts will soon cluster and cling to him like grapes to their stem. Their relations to the theory will hold them fast; and the more of these the mind is able to discern, the greater the erudition will become (25).

Unfortunately, the fact that learning builds on learning has some unpleasant implications for our society. It is one reason—perhaps the chief reason—that children from low-income families often have a difficult time in school, thus continuing a vicious circle that leads one generation after another to have trouble getting along. Children whose parents had very little formal education and use a limited vocabulary start school with a severe handicap. There are hundreds and perhaps even thousands of words and concepts that they have never heard of but that are already familiar to other children whose parents are better educated. They simply do not have the mediational units required for the attachments between new and old that come easy to children whose parents speak a richer language.

School would be easier for these children if teachers could develop some technique of building on the mediational units that the children actually do possess—that is, on the kind of previous knowledge that the children take to school from their own backgrounds. Unfortunately, most teachers come from middle-class backgrounds and assume that all children have had the opportunity to acquire the kind of knowledge available in middle-class homes. Therefore many children from low-income families give up and eventually drop out of school, even though they may have a great deal of inborn learning ability. Had they been helped to build a vocabulary, they might quickly have acquired a storehouse of information and caught up by leaps and bounds.

Study methods

Many of the general principles of efficient learning that have been discussed up to this point have a direct bearing on one of the most urgent concerns of the college student—namely, the question of how best to go about the job of studying. As every student knows, there are times when many hours put in at this job result in very little learning. And there are other times when a great deal seems to get accomplished in a hurry. What psychology has learned about the learning process offers a number of clues to avoiding the first of these two possibilities and encouraging the second.

Guidance

Perhaps the greatest help of all in learning is *guidance*. Nothing else is so likely to help us find meaningfulness in new materials, grasp the logical pattern into which the materials fall, and organize them into categories and other forms of clustering.

A textbook is one form of guidance. Enterprising students, if they had enough time, could find every fact and every theory in this book somewhere else in a library. They could find all the experiments reported in some psychological journal. They could read the original books by the pioneers who have been mentioned here, such as Wundt, James, Pavlov, and Watson. But this would be the hard way to learn psychology. Students who tried it would probably have considerable difficulty in relating Pavlov's experiments on classical conditioning to Skinner's experiments on operant conditioning. Many of the words they found in the literature would be completely unfamiliar. The underlying principles of the science would not be apparent for a long time —and the students would therefore have to make a dogged attempt to memorize many things by rote that proper guidance would have enabled them to learn by logical rule.

Even better is the special kind of guidance that can be provided in person, by a good teacher. The art of teaching, indeed, revolves largely around the manipulation of meaningfulness and organization, as well as of attention. If it can be said that there is a first law of efficient learning, it is this: If you want to learn something, get all the guidance you possibly can.

Whole versus part learning

Ebbinghaus

A question that keeps cropping up in all kinds of learning situations is one that was mentioned at the start of the chapter: If you want to learn a speech, is it better to try to learn the whole thing at once, or a paragraph at a time? The same question can be asked about a textbook chapter: Is it better to try to learn the chapter as a whole, or to tackle one part at a time?

To psychologists interested in the management of learning, these questions hinge on the relative merits of what is called *whole learning* versus what is called *part learning*. These two techniques of learning have been studied for a long time, and some of the findings deserve special mention.

Ebbinghaus's discovery. For one of the findings, we are again indebted to Ebbinghaus and his exhaustive studies of nonsense syllables (previously mentioned on pages 71-72). In one of his experiments, he measured how much time it took him to learn a short list of seven syllables, then how much time it took to learn progressively longer lists. The results, in terms of the time required to learn one syllable, are illustrated in Figure 3-14.

As the figure shows, the time required to learn each syllable went up sharply as the number of syllables was increased. Indeed when Ebbinghaus increased the number of nonsense syllables from seven to thirty-six, or to slightly more than five times the original length, the learning time per syllable increased by fifty-five times!

It must be pointed out that nonsense syllables can be learned only by rote. They cannot be compared directly with learning a speech or a textbook chapter. Nonetheless, the Ebbinghaus study does indicate that in general it takes longer, per unit of what is studied, to learn a great deal of material than to learn a small amount of material.

The law of primacy and recency. Another fact that bears on the relative merits of whole versus part learning is something that you may have noticed in your own classroom experience—and indeed in other situations as well. All of us, when we listen to a lecture, have a tendency to remember the first part of it better than the rest. We also have a tendency to remember the last part rather well, though not so well as the first part. The middle is much harder to remember.

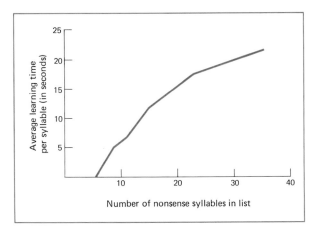

3-14

The more to learn, the harder the task

The results of the Ebbinghaus experiment described in the text are shown by the graph line. Note the steep rise in the curve from the time it took Ebbinghaus to learn each of the nonsense syllables in a list of seven (a mere 0.4 second) to the time it took him for each syllable in a list of thirty-six (22 seconds).

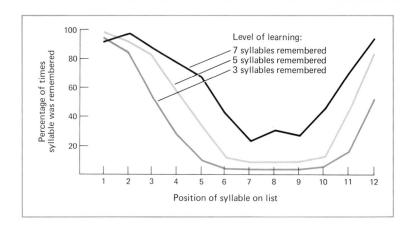

3-15

Out of twelve items, which do we remember?

The graph shows what happened when subjects were asked to study a list of twelve nonsense syllables and were tested at various stages of the learning process to see how many syllables they remembered—especially *which* ones they remembered. To interpret the graph, note first the bottom line, which shows what had happened by the time the subjects had reached the level of learning where they knew three of the twelve syllables. In almost all cases the subjects were successful at remembering the first syllable on the list; well over 80 percent of the time they remembered the second syllable. The third syllable on the list was remembered about half the time, as was the last syllable on the list. Very few of the subjects remembered the fifth through the tenth syllables on the list. By the time the subjects had learned seven of the twelve syllables they still favored the ones at the beginning of the list and to a lesser extent those at the end. The seventh, eighth, and ninth syllables stuck in their memories least of all. The findings demonstrate the *law of primacy and recency,* which is explained further in the text. (26)

Similarly, if we watch a half-hour news broadcast, and someone asks us afterward to tell about it, we tend to remember the first items and the last ones but to forget the ones in the middle. If we make out a shopping list and lose it, we are more likely to remember the first and last items than the middle ones. In any series of items, the ones we are likely to learn and remember seem to be determined by what is called *serial position*—in other words, whether they come first, last, or somewhere in between.

The importance of serial position has been demonstrated in many psychological experiments, such as the one illustrated in Figure 3-15 above. The experiments have led to the formulation of a general principle of learning called *the law of primacy and recency.* The law states that out of any series of items we try to learn, we find it easiest to remember the ones that came first (had primacy) and the ones that came last (had recency).

The answer to whole versus part. The law of primacy and recency would seem to be a strong argument for the part method of learning. If you try to learn a textbook chapter as a whole, it follows from this law that you will learn the beginning and the end of it first. You will know these parts almost by heart before you master the middle. And it seems a waste of time to keep working on the beginning and end long after you know them so well.

106

What Ebbinghaus discovered about the time it takes to learn a great deal of material, rather than small amounts of material, also seems to argue for the part method. This particular chapter of the book you are studying is divided into five parts. And Ebbinghaus seems to prove that learning five parts considered as a single entity takes much longer than learning each of the five parts individually.

However, there are other matters to be considered. Chief among them are meaningfulness and the importance of learning by rule rather than learning by rote. To your own way of thinking, does the chapter as a whole tend to "hang together" and form a meaningful entity? Does it have more meaning as a whole than when broken up into individual parts? If so, this would be an argument for using the whole method.

In cases where you want to learn something word for word—as when memorizing a speech—the problem of transitions must also be considered. If you learn a speech a paragraph at a time, studying each paragraph over and over until you know it, the last words of each paragraph tend to become associated with the first words of the same paragraph. To avoid repeating yourself when you deliver the speech, like a record player with a stuck needle, you must break these associations and establish new associations between the end of each paragraph and the start of the following paragraph. This is not always easy—so score another point for the whole method.

How does the score add up? It all depends. Generally speaking, the whole method seems to be indicated when the material to be learned is relatively brief and has a logical theme that ties it into a meaningful unit. The question of who is doing the learning must also be taken into account. In general, the whole method works best for people who have had considerable practice with it and who are above average in their interest and experience in learning similar materials—factors that help in making new material more meaningful.

Combination methods

Often a combination of the two methods seems most efficient. In studying a chapter in a textbook, for example, one good system is to begin by skimming through it quickly, trying to grasp the general pattern and logic without paying very much attention to the details. Usually the introductory paragraphs and the summary are especially helpful. Sometimes, indeed, it is possible to get a good idea of the sense of a chapter simply by reading the first few paragraphs, glancing at the various headings and the words and ideas emphasized by italics or heavy type, and then reading the summary. Once this feel for the chapter as a whole has been acquired, a slower and more detailed study of the individual parts is in order—with particular attention to the parts that seem difficult to remember.

In learning a speech or any other material that has to be remembered word for word, there often seem to be definite advantages to the *progressive part method*, as it was termed by the psychologist who first

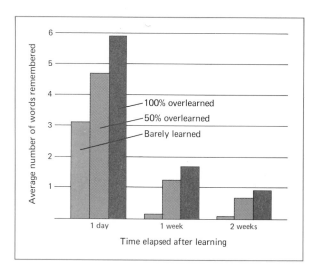

How overlearning aids remembering

These are the results of an experiment in which subjects learned a list of twelve single-syllable nouns. Sometimes they stopped studying the list as soon as they were able to recall it without error—in the words used in the chart, as soon as they had "barely learned" the words. At other times they were asked to continue studying the list for half again as many trials as bare learning required (50 percent overlearned) or to continue studying for the same number of extra trials as the original learning had required (100 percent overlearned). Whether measured after a day or at later intervals, the subjects who had overlearned by 50 percent remembered considerably more than those who had barely learned, and the subjects who had overlearned by 100 percent remembered most of all. (28)

suggested it (27). In this method, you learn the first paragraph (or first stanza or whatever unit seems natural). Then you learn the second. Next you learn to put the first and second together. Once you have these two down pat, you put them aside and learn the third, then combine the first, second, and third into a unit—and so on to the end. This method seems to combine many of the virtues of both whole and part learning and to minimize some of the disadvantages.

One of the troubles, of course, is that you still spend more time than is necessary on the early paragraphs or stanzas, particularly the first one. You *overlearn* these parts. But overlearning, it should now be pointed out, is not necessarily bad.

The advantage of overlearning

Adults are often surprised by how well they remember something they learned as children but have never practiced in the meantime. All of us who once learned to swim can still swim as well as ever even if we have not been in the water for years. We can get on a bicycle after years or decades and still ride away. We never seem to forget such jingles as "twinkle, twinkle, little star" or the stories of Cinderella or Goldilocks and the three bears.

One explanation is the *law of overlearning*, which can be stated as follows: Once we have learned something, additional learning trials increase the length of time we will remember it. A laboratory demonstration of this law is shown in Figure 3-16.

In childhood we usually continue to practice such skills as swimming and bicycle riding long after we have learned them. We continue to listen to and remind ourselves of "twinkle, twinkle, little star" and childhood tales such as Cinderella and Goldilocks. We not only learn but overlearn—and therefore we remember for a long, long time.

The law of overlearning explains why cramming for an examination, though it may result in a passing grade, is not a satisfactory way to learn a college course. By cramming, students may learn the subject well enough to get by on an examination, but they are likely to soon forget almost everything they learned. A little overlearning, on the other hand, is usually a good investment toward the future.

Distribution of practice

Another argument against cramming is that it represents an attempt to learn through what is called *massed practice* — that is, a single long learning session. Studies of a wide range of situations involving both human and animal learning have indicated that massed practice is generally less efficient than *distributed practice* — that is, a series of shorter learning periods. As Figure 3-17 shows, the same total amount of time spent in learning is often strikingly more efficient when invested in short, separated periods than all at once. This is true, as the figure shows, for simple classical conditioning as well as for more complex intellectual tasks.

3-17

Massed versus distributed practice

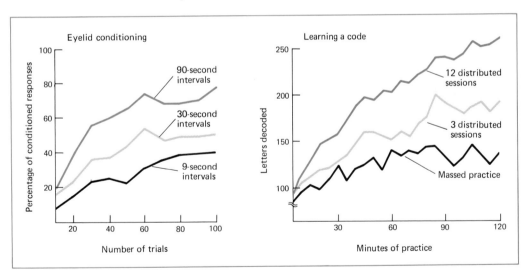

This graph shows the results of an experiment in which the eyelid blinking reflex, produced by a puff of air directed at the eye, was conditioned to a light. More conditioned responses were obtained when there were 90-second intervals between trials than when the intervals were shorter — that is, when the practice was more massed. (29)

This graph shows the results of an experiment in which the subjects learned to substitute numbers for letters. Progress was slowest in a single massed session of 120 minutes of practice, higher when the subjects worked in three 40-minute sessions spread over six days, and highest of all when twelve 10-minute sessions were spread over six days. (30)

Three possible explanations have been suggested for the superiority of distributed practice:

1 Distributed practice reduces the fatigue that often accompanies massed practice in motor learning and the boredom that often occurs in massed practice in verbal learning.
2 In the intervals between distributed practice sessions we may continue to mull over the material we have learned, even without knowing that we are doing so. This process is called *covert rehearsal* and results in what is called *consolidation* of what has been learned.
3 In many kinds of learning it seems likely that we learn not only what we want to learn but a number of useless and irrelevant habits that may actually interfere. When we first learn to type, for example, we might at the same time learn to grit our teeth, squint, and blink our eyes — habits that do not improve our skill but hurt it. During the intervals between distributed practice sessions these extraneous habits may be forgotten more quickly than the basic subject matter of the learning. The process is called *differential forgetting.*

It must be added, however, that distributed practice does not always give such spectacular results as those shown in Figure 3-17. It seems less helpful in learning by logical rule than in learning by rote, possibly because rule learning involves less boredom. In learning situations that require a lot of "cranking up" time — getting out several books and notebooks, finding some reference works on the library shelves, and finding a comfortable and well-lighted place to work — short practice periods may be less efficient than long ones.

In general, however, distributed practice is a useful tool in the management of learning. Not only does it reduce the time required for learning in many cases, but also it has recently been shown to improve one's ability to remember what has been learned (31). Probably all learning tasks can best be accomplished through *some* pattern of distributed practice — in some cases many short periods separated by long intervals, in some cases fewer and longer periods separated by shorter intervals, and in some cases perhaps a combination. The trick is to find the pattern that best suits the particular situation.

Recitation: the best tool of all

We come now to another of the questions posed at the beginning of the chapter: Is it better just to keep reading when you study or to read a while and then attempt to recite? To this question, the answer is clearcut and emphatic. As is illustrated in Figure 3-18, recitation is the most powerful tool of all in learning.

Experimenters have found that it makes no difference whether the subjects are children or adults or whether the material being learned is nonsense syllables, spelling, mathematics, or a foreign vocabulary. In every case it is more efficient to read and recite than to simply read.

Let us say that you have eight hours to devote to learning this

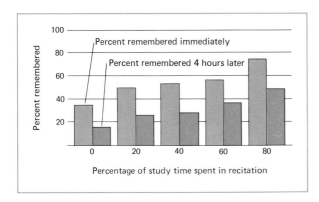

3-18

The value of recitation

The subjects were elementary school pupils and university students who studied a list of sixteen nonsense syllables. The total time spent in study was the same for all the subjects. Some subjects, however, spent the entire time reading the material, while others spent 20 to 80 percent of the time reciting. When the various groups were tested immediately and four hours later, the results were as shown here. (32)

chapter and that reading through the chapter takes you two hours. The least efficient way to spend your study time would be to read through the chapter four times. You would do much better to spend more time in trying to recite what you have learned than in reading—for, as Figure 3-18 shows, devoting as much as 80 percent of study time to recitation may be more efficient by far than mere reading.

Recitation seems to assist learning in a number of ways. It sharpens attention—for just knowing that you are about to try to recite what you are reading stimulates the desire to learn. It provides an immediate form of feedback that tells you clearly what you have grasped and what you have not, or what you understand and what you still find obscure. It helps you find meaningfulness and logical principles in the material—and to organize and cluster it. Of all study techniques, recitation is the one of most clearly proved value.

The SQ3R system of studying

The value of recitation lies at the heart of a method of studying that has produced excellent results for students who have tried it. This is the so-called SQ3R system (33), which holds that the most efficient way to study—for example, to learn a chapter such as this one—is to systematically undertake five steps that can readily be remembered by their first initials (SQRRR):

1 Survey. That is, study the outline at the beginning of the chapter (if there is one, as in this book) and then glance through the chapter to get a general idea of how much attention is devoted to each point in the outline and to the subheadings.

2 Question. Look through the chapter again in a more inquisitive fashion, asking yourself questions that the headings and subheadings suggest. Let the topics you find there whet your curiosity.

3 Read. Now read the chapter straight through, without taking notes.

4 Recite. You have made a survey of the chapter, asked some questions about it, and read it. Now see how much of the chapter you can recite, either to yourself or to a cooperative friend.

111

5 Review. Go through the chapter again, making another survey of its topics and noting how much of it you were able to recite and what points you left out. The reviewing process will show you where you must devote further study.

Transfer of learning

A final word on management of learning concerns a topic to which psychology has made a considerable contribution, not so much by coming up with new knowledge as by proving that a once popular theory was wrong. There was a time, not too many decades ago, when every student preparing for or attending a college was expected to spend many hours studying Latin and ancient Greek. It was believed by educators that learning these two languages would exercise and discipline the mind—and that the beneficial effects would transfer to other kinds of learning. Once students had mastered Latin and Greek, it was thought, their minds would be improved and they would be that much better at learning anything else, from basket weaving to higher mathematics.

This theory that there can be a *general transfer* of learning influenced the education of many generations of students. But in the early 1920s one of the most impressive psychological surveys ever made completely demolished the notion.

The fallacy of general transfer

In the 1920s survey the subjects were no fewer than 13,000 high-school students. They were tested for learning ability—then, after a full year had gone by, tested again. In the meantime, careful records were kept of the subjects they studied. For example, it was noted that some of the subjects spent the year taking algebra, history, English, chemistry, and French. Others took algebra, history, English, chemistry, and Latin. The only difference between these two groups was that one took French and the other Latin. If the second group had shown a substantially higher increase in learning ability than the first group, it would have seemed reasonable to conclude that taking Latin is in fact better than taking French.

By analyzing many kinds of groups taken from the big sample of students, it was possible to study the effects of all kinds of different subjects on changes in learning ability. It was found that the greatest increases in learning ability occurred not among students of Latin but among those who had taken mathematics courses. Close behind were students who had taken social sciences, including psychology. Latin was way down the list. At the very bottom were biology and dramatic art (34).

The most important finding of all, however, was that the entire range of differences was quite small. Though the students who took mathematics improved more than students who took biology or dramatic art, they did so only by an amount that was hardly worth mentioning. For all practical purposes, it made no difference what was studied.

Much more significant in determining how much the students improved was the amount of learning ability they started with. The students who were the best learners to begin with improved the most. The slow learners improved the least. In line with what has been mentioned earlier in the chapter, one might say that the study offered just another proof that learning builds on learning.

As to why the mathematics students came out on top, the authors of the survey concluded that this was because mathematics tended to attract the ablest learners. In the days when the theory of general transfer was popular, it can been assumed, the best students were attracted to Latin and Greek. Or perhaps they were persuaded by their teachers to take these subjects. At any rate it was undoubtedly the quality of the students, not the subject matter, that made Latin and Greek seem so stimulating to the mind.

Although the old theory of general transfer has been disproved, nonetheless it is true that certain specific kinds of transfer do take place, sometimes making new learning easier and sometimes making it more difficult. Helpful and harmful transfer are best discussed separately.

Positive transfer

Everyday examples of helpful transfer of learning are all about us. As children we learn to turn on a water faucet. In later life we have no trouble adjusting to any kind of faucet, regardless of its size, shape, or color. Learning to use the handlebars of a tricycle helps us later to use the handlebars of a bicycle and still later the steering wheel of an automobile.

Indeed the principle of *positive transfer*—as the helpful kind of transfer is called—has been of great practical value in the construction of relatively inexpensive training aids that teach people to operate the most complicated and expensive kinds of machinery. Commercial pilots, for example, learn almost everything they have to know about flying new planes without ever leaving the ground. And astronauts have been similarly trained for space flight and work on the moon.

 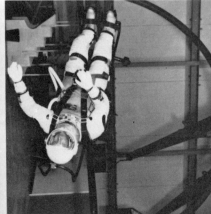 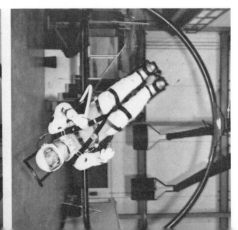

In the psychological laboratory, the circumstances that encourage positive transfer have been demonstrated in the classic experiment illustrated in Figure 3-19. Note that learning list 1 is a clear case of forming simple associations between a stimulus, namely the first of each pair of syllables, and a response, namely the second syllable. In list 2, the responses remain exactly the same, and the stimuli are only slightly different from those in list 1. From what we know about stimulus generalization (page 46), we would expect anyone who had learned list 1 to do very well on list 2. This indeed proved to be the case. It took the subjects only 44 percent as many trials to learn list 2 perfectly as it took subjects who had not learned list 1, which means that the *positive transfer* of learning from list 1 to list 2 was 56 percent—a very substantial amount.

But what about list 3? Here, though the responses remain the same, the stimuli are totally different. Stimulus generalization cannot operate. What can operate, however, is something else that has been discussed at considerable length—that very important role played in learning by previously learned information, or mediational units, to which something new can become attached. All the responses required by list 3, being the same as those in list 1, have already been learned. To learn list 3, the responses need merely become associated with new stimuli. It should come as no surprise, therefore, that the amount of positive transfer from list 1 to list 3, though smaller than to list 2, was also substantial—37 percent.

As a sort of shorthand helpful in discussing learning, the symbol S_1 is often used for the original learning stimulus and R_1 for the original response. Many kinds of learning, especially those easiest to study in the laboratory, consist in forming the association S_1-R_1. When a new learning situation calls for the same response to become associated with a new stimulus, as in the experiment in Figure 3-19, the formula becomes S_2-R_1—in other words, results in positive transfer. The more similar S_2 is to S_1, the greater is the amount of transfer likely to be.

Negative transfer

To continue with the shorthand, S_1-R_1 followed by S_2-R_1 usually results in positive transfer. What happens, however, when S_1-R_1 is followed by

3-19

An experiment in transfer

List 1		List 2		List 3	
REQ	KIY	REF	KIY	FIZ	KIY
TAW	RIF	TAS	RIF	MIP	RIF
QIX	LEP	QIL	LEP	BUL	LEP
WAM	BOS	WAP	BOS	NIC	BOS
ZED	DIB	ZEL	DIB	CAJ	DIB

Subjects first learned the pairings in list 1, so that when presented with the stimulus of REQ they responded with KIY and when presented with TAW they responded with RIF. Some of them then learned list 2, in which the responses are the same and the first syllables in the list are quite similar to those in list 1. Others learned list 3, in which the responses are the same but the first syllables are totally different. Question: Did learning list 1 help in learning lists 2 and 3, and, if so, which did it help more? For the answer, see the text. (35)

"You can't miss it. Go down to the corner and make a left, then another left, then a right . . ."

List 1		List 2	
REQ	KIY	REQ	SEJ
TAW	RIF	TAW	BOC
QIX	LEP	QIX	PUW
WAM	BOS	WAM	GIT
ZED	DIB	ZED	LIM

3-20

A demonstration of negative transfer

Again, as in Figure 3-19, the subjects first learned the pairings in list 1. Then they learned list 2, in which the first syllables remain the same but call for totally new responses. For an explanation of how learning list 1 affected learning list 2 in this case, see the text.

S_1-R_2? In other words, when the learning task calls for the same stimulus to become associated with a new response?

The same investigator responsible for the experiment in positive transfer that was illustrated in Figure 3-19 went on to study the S_1-R_2 situation as shown in Figure 3-20. This time he used two lists of syllables. The first syllables remained the same on both lists — but the second syllables were completely different. And this time, it developed, learning list 1 did not help the new learning but actually hindered it. There was a *negative transfer* amounting to 9 percent.

In another experiment with the S_1-R_2 situation, rats were placed in a simple T-maze. They started at the bottom of the T. At the point where they had to turn to either the right or the left, a light gave them the clue. If the light was on, they found food to the right. If the light was off, they found food to the left. They learned this, on the average, in 286 trials. Once they had thoroughly acquired this S_1-R_1 pattern, the task was reversed. When the light was on, the food was to the left, and, when the light was off, the food was to the right. In the new S_1-R_2 pattern, R_2 was exactly the opposite of R_1. The result was so much negative transfer that the rats required 603 trials to master the new S_1-R_2 situation (36).

Negative transfer causes considerable trouble in everyday situations. Having grown up with faucets that we turned, we may have trouble with some of the new faucets that must be pressed. Being used to faucets that we turn to the left, we run the risk of scalding or freezing ourselves in some of the new showers where the cold water faucet has to be turned in one direction and the hot water faucet in the other. Knowing how to steer a bicycle and an automobile only confuses us when we first try to operate the tiller of a boat.

Learning sets

Closely allied to positive and negative transfer is another fact that has been discovered about learning. When we learn, we do not learn merely specific behaviors or items of information. We often learn something that is equally important: we learn how to learn. We tend to develop what are called *learning sets* — that is, attitudes and strategies that help us in similar learning situations in the future.

115

One well-known demonstration of learning sets was conducted with the monkey shown in Figure 3-21. The monkey, asked to perform a long series of learning tasks that were similar in general but different in detail, got better and better at learning as the series went on. As is shown

3-21

A monkey "learns to learn"

A monkey in a cage learns to discriminate between two objects, one of which has food beneath it. Sometimes, as in this photo, the food was always under the funnel and never under the cylinder. Sometimes it was under a circle but not a rectangle, a cube but not a sphere, or a black object but not a white object. In all, the monkey was asked to learn to discriminate between more than 300 different pairs of objects. Question: Did the animal learn faster toward the end of the series than at the beginning? For the answer, see Figure 3-22.

3-22

The monkey's progress

On each of the learning problems the monkey had a 50-50 chance of finding the food on the first trial, and its score on this trial averaged 50 percent. On the first eight problems the animal made rather slow progress and still was averaging less than 80 percent correct on the sixth trial. Note, however, how much more rapidly it learned on problems 25-32 and especially on 257-312. (37)

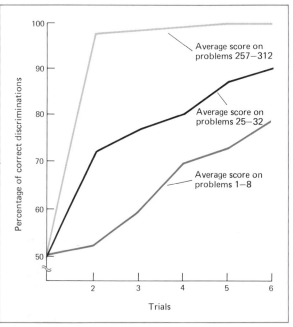

Average score on problems 257—312

Average score on problems 25—32

Average score on problems 1—8

Percentage of correct discriminations

Trials

in Figure 3-22, toward the end the animal was able to master each new problem in a single trial. Whether or not it found the food on the first trial, it went almost unerringly to the correct object on the second and subsequent trials. In most convincing fashion, it had learned to learn.

In an experiment with human beings, using a similar but more difficult series of problems, the results were much the same. It was found in addition, as might be expected, that college students were quicker to develop effective learning sets than fifth-graders. In turn the fifth-graders were considerably quicker than preschool children (38).

In aiding the learning process, the development of various kinds of learning sets goes hand in hand with the acquisition of a larger storehouse of information with which new information can be associated and organized. It is another reason that students who stick to the task become more efficient learners in high school than they were in elementary school — and then go on to become more efficient still in college.

Summary

1 The attempt to arrange the most favorable and efficient conditions for the learning process is called *management of learning.*

2 One tool in management of learning is *attention.* Paying attention helps by a) transferring information from sensory memory to short-term memory and b) enabling the short-term memory to rehearse the information and transfer it to long-term memory.

3 Attention can be attracted by *motivation, feedback, rewards,* and *punishment.*

4 One type of reward is an *external* (or *extrinsic*) *reward.* This is something provided by another person, such as praise, good grades, or a cash reward. Another type is an *internal* (or *intrinsic*) *reward.* This is the learner's own feeling of personal satisfaction.

5 Punishment seems to help produce learning in at least some situations but often has unfortunate side effects. Children who are severely punished seem to acquire a dislike for the people who have punished them and for any activities that have led to punishment, such as schoolwork. The children may "give up," become aggressive, or become neurotic.

6 *Organization* is a key word in management of learning because effective storage in long-term memory depends in large part on "making sense" out of new information and fitting it in with what is already known.

7 Materials are easiest to organize if a) they are *meaningful,* and b) they can be *learned by rule* (or by *logic*) instead of by rote.

8 *Clustering* is a method of organizing materials by lumping together items that have some sort of affinity. Methods of clustering include the use of *categories* and *made-up stories.*

9 *Mnemonic devices,* like the "Thirty days hath September" jingle, are

methods of providing a memory framework for materials that cannot be organized in any logical way.

10 Learning builds on learning. This is because the greatest possible aid to learning is the possession of prior knowledge (or mediational units) to which new information can "stick."

11 Among the important findings about study methods are the following:

a *Guidance* (by a textbook or teacher) is useful because it helps the student find meaningfulness, grasp logical patterns, and organize the new materials in categories and other forms of clustering.

b Studying by the method of *part learning* has certain advantages. One stems from the fact that the difficulty of learning increases disproportionately as the amount to be learned increases. The other stems from the *law of primacy and recency,* which summarizes the fact that in any series of items it is easier to remember the ones that came first or last than the ones in the middle.

c *Whole learning* also has advantages, chiefly in making materials more meaningful and logical.

d Often a *combination method,* utilizing the advantages of both part learning and whole learning, is the most efficient of all.

e The more time we spend continuing to learn, beyond the point where we can barely remember the materials, the longer we tend to remember. This is called *overlearning.*

f *Distributed practice,* in which the learning process is broken up into separated periods, is generally more efficient than *massed practice.*

g *Recitation* has been demonstrated to be the most effective of all study techniques. It is far better to spend as much as 80 percent of study time in an active attempt to recite than to spend the entire time reading the material.

h The very effective *SQ3R system* of studying is named for the five steps it recommends taking in order: *survey, question, read, recite, review.*

12 The old theory of *general transfer* of learning, which held that studying Latin and Greek disciplined the mind and made future learning easier, has been discredited.

13 In many cases, however, learning task 1 makes it easier to learn task 2. This is called *positive transfer.* It occurs most often in situations where task 2 calls for making the same response to a different stimulus (the S_1-R_1/S_2-R_1 situation).

14 In other cases learning task 1 makes it more difficult to learn task 2, and this is called *negative transfer.* It occurs most prominently in situations where a new response must be made to an old stimulus (S_1-R_1/S_1-R_2).

15 When we learn, we also develop *learning sets*—or attitudes and strategies that help us in similar learning situations in the future.

**Recommended
reading**

Bruner, J. S. *Toward a theory of instruction.* Cambridge, Mass.: Harvard University Press, 1966 [reprinted by Norton, New York, 1968].

Hilgard, E. R., ed. *Theories of learning and instruction.* 63rd Yearbook, Part I, National Society for the Study of Education. Chicago: University of Chicago Press, 1964.

Kintsch, W. *Learning, memory and conceptual processes.* New York: John Wiley, 1970.

Kintsch, W. *The representation of meaning in memory.* New York: Halsted Press, 1974.

Lindsay, P. H., and Norman, D. A. *Human information processing.* New York: Academic Press, 1972.

Morgan, C. T., and Deese, J. *How to study,* 2nd ed. New York: McGraw-Hill, 1969.

Riessman, F. *The culturally deprived child.* New York: Harper & Row, 1962.

Tulving, E., and Donaldson, W. *Organization of memory.* New York: Academic Press, 1972.

Language, thinking, and problem solving

If you have ever been in a foreign country, unable to speak a word in the native tongue and unable to find anyone who spoke English, you have had an object lesson in the importance of human language —an importance so vast and all encompassing that it is almost impossible to comprehend.

When you are a stranger in another land, you cannot ask or receive directions. You cannot order food, except by pointing. If you become ill, you cannot ask for a doctor, except perhaps by making gestures of distress. If you do find a doctor, you cannot describe your symptoms. Your situation—as you know if you have experienced it—is one of almost utter helplessness.

Language has been described as humanity's most distinctive and perhaps most complex achievement (1). True, lower animals also communicate with one another—but in limited and rather fixed ways. Bees that have found a new food supply go back to the hive and perform a dance; the nature and speed of this dance "tell" the other bees how to get to the food (2). Birds sing their characteristic songs to attract mates and discourage interlopers. Chimpanzees use sounds and gestures to warn their friends of danger and to threaten their enemies. But these other organisms seem to possess only a small "vocabulary" of sounds and gestures and to use them infrequently. Wild chimpanzees, for example, usually call to one another only when excited, as in case of danger. Under ordinary circumstances, they are generally silent (3).

Human beings, on the other hand, use language constantly and in an almost infinite number of ways. So rich and complex is the English language that it contains more than one-half million words, each with its own meaning. So many sentences can be constructed from these words that nobody could ever begin to speak them within a lifetime. In fact it has been estimated that saying aloud all the possible twenty-word sentences that could be constructed from our language would take at least 1,000 times as long as the earth has been in existence (4).

We use language to communicate everything from our physical needs to our spiritual desires. We use it to tell one another how we think and feel and what we have learned about the world around us. It is a special human technique that permits us to communicate an unlimited number and variety of messages, from the simple request of a child for a drink of water to the theories of an Einstein.

In evolutionary terms, language gives humanity a tremendous advantage over all other organisms. People need not learn everything for themselves; they can share what they have learned. Moreover, written language makes available to us all the learning of the past—the philosophies of the ancient Greeks, the mathematical systems of the ancient Arabs, the scientific discoveries of Galileo. Thanks to language, each of us knows more than any one person, starting from scratch, could discover in a thousand lifetimes. As one psychologist has put it, language "makes life experiences cumulative . . . [and therefore] cultural evolution takes off at a rate that leaves biological evolution far behind (5)."

The structure and rules of language

Why is humanity so proficient in using this invaluable tool called language? Certainly our ability to use language creatively does not depend entirely on the structure of our vocal cords, for other animals have vocal cords and even birds can make many of the sounds of human language. It probably depends instead on the structure and dynamics of the human brain. As far as is known, human beings are the only organisms in which one particular part of the left half of the brain is larger than the corresponding part of the right half—and it has been found that the ability to understand and speak language depends primarily on this particular area of the brain (6).

Somehow or another, probably through the development of this one small but distinctive area in the left half of the brain, nature seems to have designed us for the use of language. To put this another way, the use of a complex and infinitely varied language appears to be a species-specific behavior dictated by our biological inheritance. Just as fish are born to swim and moles to burrow, we seem to be born to speak.

The building blocks

One of the strange facts about the language we speak is that all its variety and richness is based on a rather simple foundation. All spoken language depends on the number of sounds that can be produced by the human vocal cords, and the number is quite limited. This may seem hard to believe, in view of the apparent complexity and variety of all the sentences that can be heard in the halls of the United Nations Building —English, French, Spanish, German, Russian, and all the languages of Asia and Africa—but it is true. No language contains more than eighty-five different basic sounds. English has forty-five, and the simplest language known has fifteen. These basic sounds are called *phonemes* and are the building blocks of language. In English they include such sounds as the vowel *e,* pronounced as in *be,* the consonant *t* at the beginning of *tack,* the *ch* in *chip,* the *th* in *the,* and the *sh* in *shop.*

By themselves, the phonemes usually have no meaning. But two or more of them can be put together to form a combination of sounds that does have meaning. For example: we can start with the phoneme *t,* add the phoneme pronounced as *ee,* then add the phoneme *ch,* and arrive at the combination *teach.* The result is called a *morpheme*—a combination of phonemes that possesses meaning in and of itself. Like *teach,* many morphemes are words. Others are prefixes or suffixes, which can in turn be combined with other morphemes to form words. For example, we can combine the three morphemes *un-* (a prefix), *teach* (a word in itself), and *-able* (a suffix) to form the word *unteachable.*

Thus from the forty-five English phonemes is built a language that makes possible a tremendous variety of expression. The phonemes are combined in various ways to produce more than 100,000 morphemes, or basic units of meaning. The morphemes are in turn combined with one another to produce the approximately 600,000 words found in the largest dictionaries.

The rules and meaning of language

An important feature of language is the manner in which the phonemes and morphemes are put together into meaningful utterances. This is accomplished by virtue of the fact that every language is in essence a set of rules for combining meaningful sounds into an almost infinite number of sentences conveying an almost infinite variety of meaning. These are the rules of *grammar*—or, as it is also called, *syntax.*

Some of the rules of grammar, or syntax, are rather simple. An example is the rule in the English language dictating that a singular noun can be turned into a plural by adding an *s* (one *cat,* two or more *cats*). Other rules are more complex and regulate the manner in which nouns, verbs, adverbs, and adjectives are placed in proper order to form phrases—and phrases are combined in turn into sentences that convey a meaning readily understood by anyone else who speaks the language. For example, every child knows the individual words *cat, to, the, runs, yellow, milk, now,* and *drink*—but the words when presented in that order do not convey any message. When rearranged according to the rules of grammar into *the yellow cat runs to drink milk now,* the words immediately become a meaningful sentence. They now follow the rules of English grammar decreeing that an article such as *the* must precede the noun it modifies; verbs follow their agents of action; adverbs follow verbs.

As will be noted a little later, we acquire the rules of grammar during early childhood. We may not be aware of all of them, either as children or as adults. But we follow them even if we cannot explain what they are — and they are the magic key to human communication (7).

How language is learned

Even if language and its rules are easy to learn because of the nature of the human brain, the rules and meanings of words must still be learned. The American child is not born knowing the meaning of the word *house* and may never discover that the French word meaning the same thing is *maison*. Nor does the child know that *house* can be made plural by adding an *s*. Acquiring a knowledge of all the many words and the rules for stringing them together seems an almost awesome accomplishment — yet children achieve this knowledge quickly. By the age of two, they are already speaking such simple sentences as "Baby drink milk." By the age of five, they understand the meaning of about 2000 words (8). By about the age of six, they have learned virtually all the basic rules of grammar. How do young children accomplish all this so quickly?

It is well established that babies do not have to learn to make the basic sounds of language — the phonemes. They begin very early in life to produce many phoneme sounds spontaneously, presumably because of movements of the mouth, throat, and vocal cords associated with breathing, swallowing, and hiccupping. The fact that all normal babies "babble" and produce many phoneme sounds spontaneously — rather than by imitating anything they hear — has been demonstrated by observations of a deaf baby, both of whose parents were deaf and mute. During the first two months of life this baby who never heard a sound did substantially the same kind of babbling as any other (9).

Indeed it appears that children of all nationalities make the same sounds in their earliest babbling. It has been found, for example, that there are no differences among the babbling sounds of infants born to families that speak English, Russian, or Chinese (10). American infants have been observed to utter phonemes that are not used by English-speaking adults but only by the French or Germans (11). Soon, however, babies begin to concentrate on the sounds appropriate to their own language, which they hear from their parents and others around them. The other phonemes, not useful in speaking English, disappear through disuse. (Rather sadly for those of us who attempt to learn foreign languages after we have grown up, these other sounds are eliminated quite thoroughly. Many of us who try to learn French or German are never able to pronounce some of the phonemes properly, even though we did it quite naturally when we were babies.)

From the simple to the complex

Although uttering the phonemes comes naturally, obviously something more is required to turn these simple building blocks into meaningful language. Babies must learn first what the various sounds of the language mean, also the rules for combining meaningful sounds into sentences. They can do so only through exposure to the sounds of language as used by older people.

What happens to a child who never hears the language of others has been demonstrated by the unfortunate case of a girl named Jeannie who spent most of the first thirteen years of her life shut up in a small room, isolated from human contacts. When she was finally found by the Los Angeles police, she could not speak and in fact made no sounds at all except for a whimper. But perhaps it may never be too late to learn language. Taken first to a children's hospital and then to a foster home, Jeannie soon began to discover the meanings of words and to speak brief sentences such as "Jeannie love Marilyn." By the time she was sixteen, when her case was reported by psychologists who had studied her progress, she was beginning to catch up with children of normal backgrounds (12).

Babies who receive normal exposure to language learn quite rapidly. Their first accomplishment is to speak single morphemes in the form of meaningful words: *baby, mama.* But rather quickly, within a few weeks or months, they begin to string words together: *baby walk, see mama.* The average length of their utterances increases as shown in Figure 4-1 on the following page. Some children learn more quickly than others—but all of them, if normal, show steady and consistent progress.

Acquiring the rules of grammar

At first the child's words may seem to be thrown together haphazardly and their meaning to be unclear. For example, a child of about two may say "Put suitcase for?" when an adult would say "What did you put it in the suitcase for?" Or the child may say "Who dat . . . somebody pencil?" when an adult would say "Whose pencils are they?" (14).

Yet even at rather early ages children organize what they say on definite principles, though not the same kind as they will adopt later, and there is meaningful content to their utterances. Children's speech has been called *telegraphic,* meaning that it is condensed and abbreviated. Young children use only words most important to their meaning and omit the articles, adjectives, and often even verbs. Their speech is also *holophrastic,* meaning that they often use a single word to stand for an entire idea or a complicated sentence. They may, for example, simply say "ball" to convey the thought that they want a ball or want to play ball with their parents.

They soon catch on, however, to the rules of grammar as practiced by the adults around them. When children say something such as "Kitties runned"—as they often do at age two—they reveal that they have learned a rule about forming the plural and the past tense, even though they are incorrect. They have discovered that a word can be made plural by adding an -s and that ordinarily a verb can be turned into the past tense by adding an -ed. (We can hardly blame them for the fact that our language is not always consistent and that the past tense of *run* is *ran* rather than *runned.*)

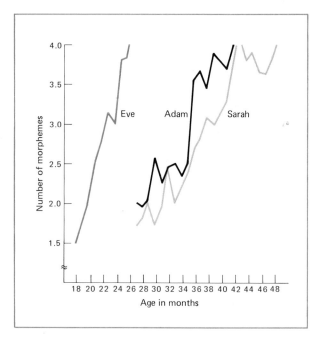

4-1

The rapid progress of children's speech

Charted here is the increasing complexity of the language spoken by three children whose utterances were carefully recorded over a period of months to determine the average number of morphemes they strung together each time they talked. The fastest progress was made by Eve, the daughter of a graduate student,who was observed from the time she was 18 months old. Less quick to use longer strings of words were Adam, the son of a minister, and Sarah, the daughter of a clerk, both of whom were studied beginning at 27 months. Although the three children progressed at different rates, there were some remarkable similarities in their development, as explained in the text. (13)

The way children learn the rules shows a remarkable consistency. Whether they are fast learners or slow, and regardless of the size or nature of their vocabularies, they seem to acquire knowledge of the rules in a predictable order. In the study of the three children illustrated in Figure 4-1, for example, a careful record was kept of the age at which they showed an ability to use morphemes that have grammatical significance. The first such morpheme generally used was *-ing,* added to a verb to denote an action going on at the moment (in the phraseology of grammarians, the present progressive tense). One of the girls, trying to explain that her father was at work, said he was ''making pennies.''

Somewhat later for the three children came the addition of an *-s* to words to make them plural. And still later—again for all three—the use of an *-'s* to indicate possession. They learned to use some of the articles (*the, a, an*) before they added an *-ed* to a verb to show the past tense (15).

Theories of language learning

At one time it was generally believed that the manner in which language is learned could be explained fully in terms of stimulus-response psychology (pp. 22–23 and 43–46) and operant conditioning (pp. 46–54). It was thought that some of the sounds made by babies in their early babbling were reinforced by their parents' smiles or fondling or other behavior. These sounds tended to be repeated. Other sounds, not appropriate to the language, were not reinforced and tended to disappear. The same process of reinforcement or lack of it, it was believed, accounted for the manner in which babies started to string sounds together into meaningful sentences.

Psychologists who became impressed by the importance of observation learning (pp. 59–60) had a different theory. They believed that the stringing together of phonemes into words and words into sentences was more a matter of direct imitation of the parents than of operant conditioning.

Both these theories still persist. Indeed it is generally agreed that both operant conditioning and observation learning play at least some part in the way we acquire our ability to use language (16). But the majority opinion today has been greatly influenced by the new studies on the importance of the grammatical rules, the fact that these rules are so similar in all languages, and the fact that children seem to acquire them in such a similar and orderly progression. Many psychologists today accept the theory that we possess what has been called an "innate mechanism" for acquiring language (17). This "innate mechanism," probably some inborn characteristic of the way in which the human brain operates, enables us as children to do some very rapid information processing on the language we hear from our elders. We quickly develop our own theories of how they are stringing words together to convey their meaning. Later we modify and expand these theories as we get more experience at communicating with others—and soon we are using the rules of grammar in such a sophisticated fashion that we can understand or express almost anything.

It is interesting to note that this sophistication in the rules of language and its endless complexities can be acquired without exposure to any very complicated forms of adult speech. As one investigator has discovered, parents do not ordinarily speak to their young children in the same way they would speak to other adults. Instead they tend to use what has been called "motherese"—a very simplified form of speech that more or less imitates the childish level of language skills. They keep their language as brief and direct as possible—and as closely related to their meaning as they can. If the child does not immediately understand, they try to help by repeating what they have said in different and easier words (18). Yet even from this simple "motherese," often as telegraphic and holophrastic as the child's own utterances, children somehow manage to extract a knowledge of the grammatical rules and the meanings of words. They do so, it should also be noted, without any special training such as is required to learn arithmetic. Children do not have to be formally taught to use language. This is a skill that they simply pick up—as if indeed some "inner mechanism" were at work.

Can animals learn language?

Psychologists who work with lower animals have long been fascinated by the question of whether any of them could be taught to use language. Until recently, their attempts always ended in failure. Experimenters who raised chimpanzees in their homes just like their own children found that the chimps rather readily learned such human habits as eating with a spoon and brushing their teeth—yet never learned to speak more than a few simple words (19). Even dolphins, which seemed promising subjects because they have brains that closely resemble the human brain, proved unable to learn.

A few years ago, however, one group of investigators had a brilliant idea. Perhaps chimpanzees simply find it difficult to learn to use their vocal cords like human beings. Instead of trying to teach them to speak, why not try to teach them a sign language, such as used by the deaf? This experiment proved surprisingly successful. A chimpanzee named Washoe, shown in Figure 4-2, managed to learn an expressive vocabulary of more than 130 signs in a little more than four years of training. (Among the signs were *toothbrush, you, please, cat, enough, time,* and many others.) Moreover, Washoe learned to string the signs together into fairly complex sentences, such as *hurry gimme toothbrush* and *you me go out hurry* (20).

Another ingenious approach has been made with a chimpanzee named Sarah, who has been taught to communicate by using symbols for words in the form of pieces of plastic cut into various shapes. The plastic symbols have a metal backing and can be arranged on a magnetized board as shown in Figure 4-3. In this manner, Sarah too has learned the meaning of more than 130 words and the use of sentences such as *Mary give apple Sarah* (21).

4-2

A chimpanzee "talks"

At the age of two and a half, the chimpanzee named Washoe makes the sign language signal for "drink."

4-3

Another chimpanzee's language symbols

This chimpanzee, trained like Sarah to understand and use magnetized language symbols as described in the text, follows spelled-out instructions to hand over an apple.

These new experiments indicate that animals may be more adept at learning to use language than was formerly believed. Further experimentation, now that these new techniques have been developed, may show an even greater aptitude. It is worthy of note, however, that both Washoe and Sarah had to be taught—very skillfully and very patiently. They did not spontaneously begin to use language as human babies do just from being exposed to the speech of others.

Language and concepts

All words are *symbols*—that is to say, they are learned mediational units that stand for or represent something. Thus *water* is a symbol for the colorless fluid that we drink; *fire* is a symbol for the process of burning. Because we have acquired and know the meaning of such symbols, we can respond as readily to a shout of "*Fire!*" as to the actual sight of flames. Using words as symbols, we can express a need for water (or food or an aspirin tablet) without the actual presence of these objects.

In every language, however, only a few words are symbols for specific, one-of-a-kind objects—in the English language, for example, the names of the planets Mars and Jupiter. All other words are symbols for groups of objects, events, actions, and ideas. Even a word of such apparent simplicity as *water* is a symbol not only for the colorless fluid in the glass we may be holding in our hands but for any somewhat similar fluid anywhere, including the salty contents of the oceans and the drops that fall from the sky as rain. The word *justice* is a symbol for many different abstract ideas held by people around the world at various times in history and embodied in many forms of legal codes and practices. Thus most words constitute a complicated form of symbol called a *concept*, defined as *a symbol that stands for common characteristics or relationships shared by objects or events that are otherwise different.*

The use of concepts lends a tremendous variety and versatility to our mental processes. Think, for example, of how complicated life would be if we had to have a separate word for every object and event in the world—or had to learn anew how to behave every time we encountered a new stimulus. But we do not have to deal as a unique event with every

129

new object or experience that we encounter; usually we can fit it into an already existing concept (22). A tree of a species we have never seen before is instantly recognizable as a tree. A strange new sculpture by a modern artist is immediately recognizable as a piece of art. Studying a book of this sort is greatly helped—indeed made possible—by the concepts represented by such words as *college, course, psychology, theory, experiment*, and many others.

Concepts without words

A concept does not have to be associated with a word, although that is often the case. Babies have a nonverbal concept of a face even though they have no word for face. Even lower animals with no language apparently can acquire and manipulate concepts, though only in a limited way. This has been demonstrated in experiments on stimulus generalization and discrimination (forms of learning that have been discussed on pages 46–48). In one such experiment, shown in Figure 4-4, the duck has learned that food is always found beneath the three-sided stimulus, regardless of its size or exact shape. It must therefore have some kind of concept of triangularity. But for a duck or a rat, learning this is a slow and laborious process.

Verbal concepts

Let us suppose that we now go a step beyond the experiment with the triangles and try to teach a duck or a rat that it will find food behind any of the objects in the left-hand column below but not behind any of the objects similar in appearance listed in the right-hand column:

Cap pistol	Revolver
Building block	Brick
Small rubber ball	Orange
Basketball	Cantaloupe
Tricycle	Motorcycle
Drum	Barrel
Doll	Child
Paintbox	Cigarette case

4-4

An animal's concept of shape

In this learning experiment, the duck has found that food is always found beneath some kind of three-sided figure, never beneath a four-sided figure. Even if the size and exact shape of the figures are changed, the duck will look under the triangle. It must have some kind of concept of triangularity—gained, as explained in the text, without the use of language.

Photo courtesy of Dr. Nicholas Pastore, Queens College

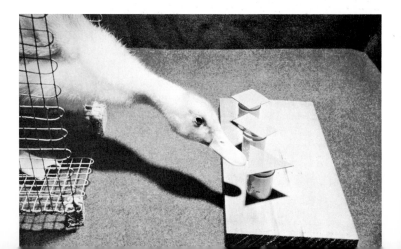

Note that all the objects in the left-hand column are toys. The objects in the right-hand column, though they look much the same, are not toys. But an animal, trying to learn a distinction between the look-alike objects, is really in trouble. Lacking the concept of *toy*, it can learn only by trial and error. Even if it manages to learn, one by one, that food is found behind the objects listed on the left, it will again be baffled if we introduce a miniature xylophone or piano, a rag doll, a stuffed tiger, or a toy train.

The child acquires the meaning of the word *toy*, and the concept it represents, at about the age of three or four. Ever afterward, all toys have something in common. Thus does language—and the concepts that it helps us acquire and use—enable us to react in the same manner to objects as different in physical size, shape, color, and texture as a little black stub of crayon and a giant stuffed tiger. On a more complex and sophisticated level, language helps us deal with the kind of world we live in through concepts represented by such words as *industry, profession, salary, taxation, capitalism, communism*. It enables us to think of our own and others' conduct in terms of concepts represented by such words as *friendliness, hostility, cheerfulness, moodiness, generosity*.

How children build their concepts

As children grow, they acquire the general meaning of many commonly used concepts very quickly. They soon learn to apply the word *clothes* as a concept that includes many different articles of apparel, the word *food* to a wide range of things that are eaten. At first, however, the boundary lines of their concepts are rather hazy. They include some things in the concept that do not really belong—and leave out many things that do belong.

In one study that helps demonstrate this fact, the experimenters showed children pictures of various objects and asked them to pick out those that were called clothes. Even the youngest children (five to six years old) usually were aware that the word *clothes* is applied to such

131

4-5

The older the child, the richer the concept

Does the concept *clothes* include such items as *buttons, belt,* and *shoes?* It takes children quite a while to learn that the answer is yes. The bar chart, which illustrates the result of an experiment described in the text, shows how much richer is the concept *clothes* at age eleven and twelve than it was five years earlier.

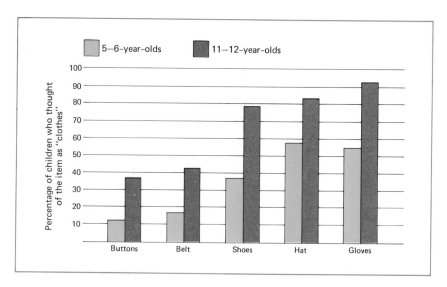

objects as a dress, a shirt, or a sweater. But, as is shown in Figure 4-5, relatively few of them picked out the pictures of such objects as buttons, a belt, shoes, or other articles of clothing that are not made of cloth and worn between the shoulders and knees. Far more older children had learned that the concept *clothes* includes such items.

When asked to pick out the pictures that could be called food, a number of the younger children (about 21 percent) ignored such items as a lollipop, an ice-cream cone, and a cookie. The older children unanimously classified these objects as food. Indeed about half the older children also included pictures of a cow, a pig, and a turkey — indicating that they had broadened and enriched their concept of *food* to include its sources, even when these sources look like nothing ever seen on a dinner table (23).

In another experiment on children's concepts, a different method was used. In this case, the experimenter gave the children a word representing a common concept, such as *clothes, furniture,* or *vegetables,* and asked them to name as many things as they could that are known by these terms. One group of subjects averaged five years old, the other eight years old. The far greater richness of the older children's concepts was demonstrated by the fact that they could name nearly twice as many objects for each term as the younger children — an average of 8 as compared with about 4.5.

The older children had not only enlarged their concepts but also refined them. Under *furniture,* for example, the younger children tended to include almost anything that can be found around the house, such as telephone, clock, wall, or door. Under *vegetables,* the younger children sometimes included such irrelevant items as meat, soup, pizza, or ice cream. The older children were less likely to make such mistakes. They showed considerable progress in weeding out items inappropriate to the concept (24).

The concepts of adults

By the time we have reached adulthood so many factors have gone into our building of concepts that it is impossible to trace or even list them. Indeed most of the words we use as adults involve concepts within concepts. What, for example, do we mean by *human beings*? To a certain extent, we still think of human beings in the way we probably did in childhood: in terms of such characteristics as their physical attributes (two legs and two arms) and what they do. But we also tend to have a concept of human beings as the highest (another concept) of all mammals (still another kind of concept!) — a mammal being a particular kind of organism (another concept!) that produces its young inside the body of the mother (another!) which nurses (another!) the baby (another!) after birth (another!).

As a figure of speech, it might be said that the adult's concepts are like the catalogue file of a library, indexed and cross-indexed so that a search starting with a term such as *human beings* can lead almost anywhere. One card lists the physical attributes of human beings; this card in turn leads to other cards that list the functions of the various organs and the ailments to which they are subject. Another lists all the things that human beings can do; this card leads in turn to other cards that list the details of human history. Another lists the places where human beings are found; this leads in turn to detailed lists of the characteristics of the continents, cities, and types of buildings in which people dwell and work. There are innumerable other cards that list the more abstract and sophisticated aspects of human beings — characterizing them in terms of philosophy, religion, and science and including their aspirations, triumphs, doubts, and failures.

One of the measures of how much a person has learned is how many cards there are under each concept in this mental filing system. A child, for example, makes no connection between the concept *human being* and the concept *whale,* but the educated adult knows that these two very dissimilar organisms are related in that both are mammals. To the young child, the concept *human being* never calls up an association with an ancient Egyptian pharaoh or with the lamas of Tibet; to an adult, it may very well do so. The richness of our adult concepts depends on how many similarities we have found to exist among all the apparently diverse elements in our environment and our history.

The "salient characteristic" of concepts

We can follow the trail of cross-indexed concept cards almost anywhere. In our thinking and problem solving we often rummage through them at length and in depth. Most of the time, however, we tend to ignore the great bulk of the cards and to think of a particular concept in terms of what we consider its one outstanding feature. To a theologian, for example, the term *human being* might ordinarily call up the concept of a creature of God, possessing a soul. To a physician, *human being* might ordinarily mean a functioning collection of physiological apparatus, all subject to various diseases. To the zoologist, it might mean simply another kind of animal.

Thus all of us have our own primary definition of each particular concept we use, based on what to us is the *salient characteristic* of the various objects, events, or ideas that are included in the concept. A group of adults may be well aware that *salt* is a concept that means a certain kind of chemical compound, found in various forms in nature, in the laboratory, and in the human body. But to a cook in the group the salient characteristic of salt is that it is a seasoning used on food. The chemist usually thinks of it as a compound in which the hydrogen of an acid has been replaced by a metal. The physician thinks of it as a component of the human body. This tendency to concentrate on the salient characteristic and ignore other aspects depends in part on a feature of concept formation that is called *concept hierarchies.*

Concept hierarchies

In any list, one item must be at the top and the others must then follow in order to the bottom. So it is with the various lists in our filing system of concepts. This can best be illustrated in the case of a concept such as *vegetable.* Most of us, asked to draw up a list of vegetables, would think first of the very familiar ones such as tomato and potato. Only much later, if at all, would we think of such seldom encountered ones as artichoke or kale. Asked to draw up a list of animals, most of us would not immediately recall that human beings are the most familiar animals of all; we might head our list with dog or cat, or, if we happened to come from ranch country, horse. Way down toward the bottom of the list would come such unfamiliar animals as aardvark and lynx. Asked to list colors, most of us would start with red and take a long time to get to puce and cerise.

The term used to describe this fact is *concept hierarchies*—a hierarchy being a power structure in which the rank of each individual is clearly defined, from bottom to top, and each individual is subordinate to the one immediately above. In concept hierarchies the links between the concept and the associations at the top of the list are very powerful; the links between the concept and the associations toward the bottom of the list are weaker.

Systems of concept hierarchies

One of the interesting facts about concept hierarchies is that they tend to vary depending on the situation and the subject. When we talk about inanimate objects such as buildings, for example, concepts based on physical attributes are usually well up in the hierarchy. When we talk about people, however, our concept is based mostly on what might be called their personality characteristics. We tend to think of them as aggressive or meek, ambitious or easygoing, hostile or friendly.

We build these concepts of people just as we develop our other concepts — by noticing similarities. For example, we notice over a period of time that a man on one occasion argues over who has the right to a parking space, on another occasion pushes his way to a crowded store counter, and on still another occasion dominates the conversation at a party. These are all different kinds of behavior, taking place in different situations, but they all have a common thread that fits into the concept *aggressive*. We note that another man seems a little shy in company, prefers to stay home and read rather than go out to a movie, and spends a good deal of his time alone. In these different forms of behavior we find a similarity, and we call him an introvert.

Our concepts of our own selves form a still different hierarchy. We tend to use evaluative concepts; we think of ourselves as good or bad, smart or stupid, popular or unpopular. Thus do our concept hierarchies vary according to the subject at hand. We use one system of hierarchies for inanimate objects, another for the people we know, and still another for ourselves.

Concepts and connotations

In the system of concept hierarchies that we apply to ourselves, as has just been stated, we make evaluations. But, even in situations where we think we are being objective and using neutral concepts, we are also making evaluations of a sort. This is because most words — and particularly the words used as concepts — not only have the meaning that is apparent on the surface but also carry other implied meanings known as *connotations*. That is to say, they connote (or imply or suggest) certain qualities and values. A good example is the concept word *landlord*. Its dictionary definition is "a person who owns property and rents it to others." That is its plain and simple meaning. But the word also has some highly unpleasant connotations; one may think of a landlord as grasping, unkind, and miserly.

The importance of connotations has been studied by C. E. Osgood, who devised the type of scale shown in Figure 4-6 on the following page. Each line of the scale, you will note, contains seven steps from an adjective such as *weak* at one end to its opposite such as *strong* at the other. To large groups of subjects, Osgood presented a wide variety of words, which they were asked to rate somewhere along each of the lines on his scale, only ten of which are included in Figure 4-6. As it turned out, there were considerable individual differences in the way people rated each word, but the average ratings made by one group were remarkably similar to the average ratings made by another group at a different time and place.

The scale is what Osgood called the *semantic differential*. It measures difference in meaning—not in the dictionary sense of meaning but in terms of the patterns of qualities and values that words connote. To a majority of people, for example, the word *success* proved to have connotations of being strong, large, active, good, hot, healthy, and happy. To a somewhat lesser extent, it suggested young and smooth. Other words turned out to have quite different patterns on the semantic differential, as can be seen for *death* in Figure 4-6.

Osgood found that the most important dimension of all on his scale was good-bad; a very large number of words carry strong connotations of goodness or badness. To enlarge upon the figure of speech used earlier, one might say that our catalogue file of concepts, with its cross-indexed hierarchies, is also organized in another way—as if the "good" concepts were printed in black ink on white paper, the "bad" concepts in white ink on black paper. Our tendency to think in terms of good and bad starts in childhood: among the "good" concepts are mother, father, friend, day, obedience, present, warmth; among the "bad" ones are stranger, night, disobedience, spanking, cold. As adults, we still think of a common thread of goodness running through such different concepts as health, angels, cleanliness, food, bed, work, Sunday, peace, freedom, wealth. We find a common thread of badness running through such varied concepts as sickness, devil, hunger, fatigue, idleness, war, slavery, poverty.

4-6

A scale of connotations

The lines show the ratings given by one subject for three different words on ten lines of the Osgood *semantic differential*. For an explanation of what the ratings indicate, see the text. (25)

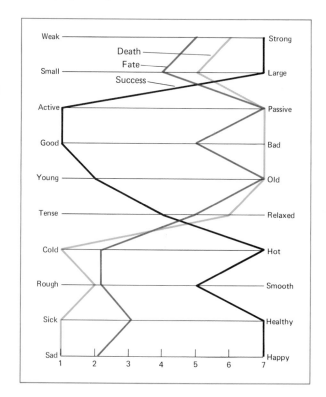

The second most important dimension on the scale, Osgood found, was strong-weak; this line accounted for the second largest number of significant connotations. Success is strong; so are concepts such as father, war, and devil. Mother is weak; so are such varied concepts as poem and illness. The third most important dimension was active-passive: many concepts have connotations of activity (such as success, social, and play), and many others have connotations of passivity (such as fate, death, introvert, and water).

A great majority of all words and concepts have significant connotations on one or more of the top three dimensions. This has proved true not only for Americans but for peoples of other nationalities. Different cultures may disagree as to what particular things are good or bad—for example, a Polynesian would regard work as "bad" and idleness as "good," in contrast to many Americans. In some societies the father is "weak" and the mother is "strong." But all people everywhere seem to use goodness, strength, and activity as important dimensions along which to organize most of their concepts.

Concepts and personality

Although Osgood's work shows some significant similarities in the way all human beings organize their concepts and concept hierarchies, it must also be pointed out that there are many individual differences. As was mentioned earlier, we form our concepts on the basis of our experiences. The similarities to which we are exposed most often are the ones that we notice first. They are also the ones that tend to be bound together by the most powerful associations and to occupy a high place in our concept hierarchies. The mechanic's daughter builds strong and persistent concepts of a mechanical nature; to her an automobile and a boat powered by the same kind of engine may seem more alike than two automobiles with different engines. The philosophy professor's son tends to form highly abstract concepts; his concept of an automobile may involve associations with Phoebus' chariot in Greek mythology.

In one experiment, subjects were asked which word did not belong among the following four:

prayer, skyscraper, temple, cathedral

As you will note, this is an ingenious grouping of words. A person who has a tendency to respond to religious concepts can argue that *skyscraper* is different from the other words. A person who responds to the words as belonging to a hierarchy of architectural concepts can argue that *prayer* is out of place. As it happened, 70 percent of the subjects in the experiment chose *skyscraper* as being the word that did not belong. Then the same words were presented to another group but in different order:

skyscraper, prayer, temple, cathedral

This time the number who chose *skyscraper* dropped to 40 percent (26).

Obviously the decrease was caused by the set created by the first word in the series. When *prayer* was the first word, most subjects were set for religious concepts; when *skyscraper* was the first word, most were set for concepts involving buildings. But even the effect of *skyscraper* in creating a set did not influence all the subjects. Many subjects' own concept hierarchies, with religious concepts occupying a prominent place, still led them to associate *prayer, temple,* and *cathedral* and to consider *skyscraper* the wrong word in the series.

As this fact indicates, each of us has a personal catalogue file — to use that figure of speech again — with its own system of lists and cross-indexing. The same stimulus — the same word, the same action by another person, the same event taking place — may set off in different people entirely different lines of search through the files, leading each of them eventually to take down a different book from the shelves — that is, leading them to engage in very different kinds of behavior.

To put it another way, the concepts we have learned and the way we have built them into hierarchies and have related and interlocked them one with another constitute our own personal system of organizing our environments. They influence what we select to pay attention to in our environments and how we organize what we see and hear. Moreover, most of our concepts carry connotations of goodness and badness, strength and weakness, activity and passivity. We use our system of concepts to label and understand ourselves, our fellow human beings, and the objects and events in our environments. The labels themselves then help determine whether we approve or disapprove, admire or deplore. In our development from infant to adult we have learned not only concepts but ways of responding to these concepts.

Thinking

The most important of all covert behavior is *thinking,* a word that all of us understand but that is difficult to define precisely. Perhaps it can best be described as *the mental manipulation of images, symbols, concepts, rules, and other mediational units.* Sometimes thinking manipulates objects that are physically present in the environment, as does the thinking of carpenters while working with tools and lumber to build a cabinet. But note that carpenters do not just move these objects about; they think about the uses and measurements of the objects in relation to the as yet unfinished products they are building. In other cases, thinking is entirely independent of physical objects. We can think about objects that are not present, about events that occurred in the distant past, or about abstract concepts that have no physical reality at all. Thinking is our most useful tool precisely because it can range so widely and is so free from restrictions imposed by the immediate environment. In the process of thinking we can manipulate any or all of the mediational units acquired in our lifetimes.

Some tools of thinking

One of the kinds of mediational units manipulated in thinking, as has been stated, is the *image*—or the recollection of a sensory experience. Dreaming is this type of thinking. When we dream, we seem to see a series of events happening much as if we were watching a movie. Besides the visual images, our dreams also contain images of sounds; we often seem to speak or be spoken to. Certain kinds of thinking of a high level of complexity and discipline are also possible through the manipulation of images. Mathematicians often think in "pictures" of space and of intersecting planes. Some musicians can compose or orchestrate by manipulating the images of sounds that they "hear" only inside themselves. Beethoven, for example, wrote many of his greatest works after he became deaf and could not actually hear tones at all.

We also manipulate various kinds of nonverbal symbols. The musician may manipulate symbols standing for notes and keys; the scientist may think in terms of mathematical formulas. The most commonly used tools of thinking, however, are verbal concepts. They enable us to label the objects and events in our environment and thus to manipulate them without seeing or touching them. Concepts enable us to treat an event as part of a larger set of relationships.

Facts and premises

Among the mediational units of particular importance in thinking are *facts* and *premises*—or the statements we have learned to know or believe are true about the objects and events of our environment. We have discovered, for example, that holding a finger in a flame causes pain and if continued long enough causes physical damage. We know from experience that if we slip off an edge we will fall. In thinking about fire and about mountain climbing, these facts are among the elements we manipulate.

When we have great faith in a relationship, we call it a *fact*. Thus we consider it a fact that fire burns flesh or that gravity causes falls. Many of what we accept as facts come from our own observations. Others represent the pooled observations of many people in our society—the kind of pieces of information found in various handbooks of fact in our libraries. Our thinking about the desirability of various cities as places to live, for example, might take into account the following: New York City is the largest in the United States; the average annual rainfall in Oregon is high; the sun shines in Miami, Florida, on most days of the year. We may base our thinking about automobiles on various facts about the horsepower and miles per gallon of different models.

Other facts come from the observations of science. When we think about the sky and the solar system, we take for granted the astronomer's observation that the moon revolves around the earth and that the earth and the other planets revolve around the sun. We accept the physiologist's observation that the bloodstream carries oxygen from the lungs to the cells of the body, the finding of medical science that surgery is the

best cure for appendicitis, the chemist's finding that an alkali neutral-
izes an acid.

A *premise* is a basic belief that we accept even though it cannot be
demonstrated so convincingly as the relationships we call facts. The line
between premise and fact is often hazy and difficult to draw, for many
of the beliefs generally accepted as fact cannot actually be proven and
are in truth merely premises. In science, for example, such ideas as the
theory of evolution and many advanced mathematical theories are
really still only premises, though they are in accord with the best observations currently possible and have at least a certain claim to validity.

Many premises are the result of individual experiences and learning.
They are not necessarily based on objective observation, and they may
vary greatly from one person to another. Some of us, from what we have
seen and observed, believe that most people are honest—and much of
our thinking about other people is based on this firmly held premise.
Others of us hold just as firmly to the belief that most people are dishonest. Some of us base much of our thinking (and overt behavior) on
the premise that it is wise to keep one's nose to the grindstone, others
on the premise that all work and no play makes Jack a dull boy.

Thinking by "clustering"

One important type of thinking is based on the manner in which we
have stored into memory our various premises, facts, and concepts. We
carry around with us, as has been said, elaborate systems of concepts
arranged in hierarchies and connected with one another by a sort of
cross-indexing. Moreover, the concepts suggest powerful connotations
of such qualities as goodness, strength, and activity. When we tap any
part of this store of information, we in effect tend to tap all of it. A chain
of thinking begins and adds link after link through a process called
mediational clustering.

A good example of thinking through mediational clustering is this:
let us say that we are asked to think of the word *angel* and to report
every word and idea that it suggests. As we start thinking about *angel,*
all sorts of associated pieces of information occur to us. We may start by
describing the physical attributes of an angel (the white robe, the benign expression), some of the functions of an angel (playing a harp),
and the location (in heaven). We may next think of some of the connotations of the word (notably goodness). Then we may go on to thinking
about the concept of religion and the concepts that this word arouses in
turn—and at last to the opposites that *angel* suggests, such as the word
devil and all its evil associations and connotations.

This kind of thinking is simply based on the way we have stored
various mediational units in memory and the association between clusters such as angel-good and their opposites such as devil-bad. It is the
kind of thinking that is sometimes called free association or stream of
consciousness. Yet the associations are not altogether "free." Each new
link in our chains of thinking depends largely on the way in which we

have organized our concepts into hierarchies and systems of hierarchies, with some associations powerful and others weak. A clergyman, starting with the word *angel,* might forge a chain of thought directly to the philosophical implications of the newest papal encyclical. A musician might make a chain of associations from angel to harp to some special musical interests. An athlete might link angel-fly-fly ball-baseball.

Thinking by logical rules

Another important and much more formal type of thinking is forging a chain of associations by means of *logical rules.* One of the best examples is the application of mathematical rules. One such rule tells us that the circumference of a circle is always $2\pi r$, and π is defined as 3.1416. Therefore we can reason that if r (the radius) is 5 feet, the circumference has to be 31.416 feet. Any other conclusion would be totally illogical.

Outside the field of mathematics, a well-known example of logic is the *syllogism,* a three-step kind of thinking that goes as follows:

1 All mammals nurse their young.
2 A whale is a mammal.
3 Therefore a whale nurses its young.

In the syllogism, statement 1 is known as the major premise, statement 2 is the minor premise, and statement 3 is the conclusion. If the major premise and the minor premise are taken for granted, the conclusion follows inescapably. Note the difference between the inescapable logic of this syllogism and the incorrect logic represented by the following three sentences:

Some mammals live on land.
All whales are mammals.
Therefore some whales live on land.

Logical thinking means to draw conclusions that follow inescapably from facts and premises. One basic form of syllogism following the rules of logic, illustrated by the top drawing at left, is as follows:

1   All A's are B.
2   All B's are C.
3   Therefore all A's are C.   (*True.*)

It is not logical, however, to reason as follows:

1   All A's are B.
2   Some B's are C.
3   Therefore some A's are C.   (*False,* as shown by the possibility illustrated in the middle drawing.)

Nor is it logical to think:

1   Some A's are B.
2   All B's are C.
3   Therefore all A's are C.   (*False,* as shown by the bottom drawing.)

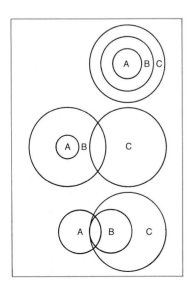

Errors in logic. To draw valid conclusions by applying logical rules, however, is not always easy. People often fall into error. For example, a young woman may decide to become a schoolteacher as a result of this line of thought: "My mother says she was extremely happy when she was teaching school; therefore I will be happy teaching school." The fallacies here are that the young woman may have very different tastes and that school teaching may have changed as a profession in the meantime. A man with a stomachache takes a pill that was once prescribed for a friend on the ground that "the pill helped him; therefore it will help me." But his stomachache may be of an entirely different kind and may only be aggravated by the medicine.

Often when we accuse people of being illogical, however, we are wrong. Their logic is sound, granted their premises, and it is the premises that we disagree with. For example, the navigators of the Middle Ages were quite logical in believing that anybody who kept sailing due west from Europe would eventually fall off the earth. Their reasoning was as follows:

All flat surfaces have edges.
The earth is flat.
Therefore the earth has edges and anyone who sails that far will fall off.

The logic was sound, but the minor premise was wrong. In actual fact, the earth is not flat.

Many arguments and misunderstandings, among statesmen and nations as well as between husbands and wives, are caused not so much by fallacies of logic as by belief in different premises. One government economist, using faultless logic, may reach the conclusion that taxes should be raised this year. An equally brilliant economist, using equally flawless logic, may conclude that taxes should be lowered. One person decides, after much reasonable thought, that capital punishment should be abolished. Another person decides that it is essential. Which economist and which of the two opinions on capital punishment is right, and which is wrong? We cannot really say, because we have no way of establishing the validity of most of the premises that various people hold.

We cannot be sure that a premise is wrong unless it clearly violates proven fact, and this is seldom the case. We know now for a fact, as the navigators of the Middle Ages did not know, that the earth is spherical rather than flat. And, if a man claims to be Napoleon, we know that he

is definitely and unquestionably wrong, and we label him a psychotic. Mostly, however, we hold our premises more or less on faith; we can agree or disagree with another person's premises but cannot usually prove them right or wrong. Thus, even though rules of logic such as the syllogism are formal and well disciplined, people adhering to the rules can reach very different conclusions.

Thinking by inference

Another type of thinking is generally called *inference*. Inference means generating conclusions about possibilities, often through the use of logic, from facts we already know or are experiencing.

An example is this. Someone says to us, "There is a bird in Brazil called a cariama. Does it have wings?" Almost immediately, we answer yes. There is no way that we can know for sure because we have never seen a cariama—but we infer that our answer is correct. In reaching this conclusion, we apply a syllogism—though without realizing it:

A cariama is a bird.   (As we have just learned.)
All birds have wings.   (A fact that we have previously observed and
   stored in memory—a part of our concept of bird.)
Therefore a cariama has wings.   (The inference we make).

The process of inference enables us to think about many questions of this sort without having any direct knowledge of the situation (27). At the end of a long day's drive, we feel confident that we will find a motel room if we push on another fifty miles toward Denver because Denver is a big city and it has been our experience that all big cities have many motels at their outskirts. We may never have read *A Midsummer Night's Dream,* but we are confident it is in blank verse because we know it was written by Shakespeare and everything else we have read by Shakespeare was in blank verse.

We are constantly making inferences. When we hear a sentence such as "John pushed Bill into the water," we think of it in far richer terms than the mere string of words conveys. We automatically assume that John pushed with his hands, that Bill is now in the water, that Bill is wet, that Bill is either swimming or struggling, and so on (28).

Our inferences may sometimes be wrong. Suppose, for example, that the question about the Brazilian bird had been, "Does a cariama fly?" Again the process of inference would doubtless have led us to answer yes, on the premise that all birds fly. But there are a few birds that do not fly—and the cariama just might happen to be one of them.

Many of our conclusions, however, are correct and are therefore useful. Just as the rules of grammar enable us to generate sentences we have never spoken before and to understand sentences we have never heard before, so does the process of inference enable us to think about all kinds of matters we have never actually encountered. We can generalize about the new and unfamiliar from what we have observed about similar objects or events. Indeed it is probably true that most of what we know—or think we know—is based on inference rather than on direct observation.

Problem solving

Many years ago an experimenter put cats into a number of "puzzle boxes"—little cages from which the cats could escape only by lifting a latch or pulling a loop of string. Outside each box he placed food. The cats had a goal—namely, to get out of the box and get the food. But how? This was the problem.

It developed that the cats could solve the problem only through the method of *trial and error*. They made all kinds of movements; they stretched, bit, and scratched. Eventually, by chance, they stumbled on the solution and made their escape (29).

The chimpanzee shown in Figure 4-7 is also faced with a problem. High above its head hangs a bunch of bananas. Its goal is to reach them. But how? The solution to the problem, as the chimp has just discovered, is to pile the boxes one atop another and climb up. In this case the animal caught on; it got the idea; the solution came to it not after long and laborious trial and error but in a flash of what is called *insight*.

The chimpanzee in Figure 4-8 has solved a different kind of problem through insight. In both cases there may have been some trial and error in the sense that the chimps thought of other possible ways to try to solve the problems and had to discard these methods as impracticable. But, if there was trial and error, it took place covertly, through the manipulation of symbols. In a way that is beyond the capacity of lower animals, the chimpanzees solved the problems by thinking. Exactly how they did it—what kind of symbols they used and how these symbols were linked—we of course cannot know.

Techniques of problem solving

Human beings are constantly faced with problems. Students must solve not only the theoretical problems in their mathematics courses but also many real-life problems. You have a certain number of dollars available for tuition, books, clothes, housing, food, and entertainment: How can the dollars best be allotted to these expenses? A motorist driving from California to New York has problems of a different sort: What highways will make the trip fastest? How can the trip best be broken up into how many days on the road? The mechanic looking at an automobile that refuses to run must ask: What is wrong? How can I fix it?

In our attempts to solve problems, we sometimes are lucky enough to have a flash of insight, like the chimpanzees with the boxes or sticks. Sometimes we are reduced to using trial and error, like the cats in the puzzle box. More often, we think and think and think—drawing on all the knowledge we have stored in memory, applying the logical rules we know, relying also on the techniques of mediational clustering and

4-7

A chimp does some thinking

The chimpanzee is in a cage with a bunch of bananas hanging high above its reach and with three boxes, none of which is high enough in itself to enable the chimp to climb up and reach the bananas. After looking the situation over for some time, it starts to pile one box atop another for additional height and thus manages to reach the bananas.

4-8

Another example of insight

This chimpanzee was confronted with some sticks that posed a problem. The very short stick was within reach but was too short to pull in the piece of fruit. The very long stick that would pull in the fruit was well out of reach. At last the animal has caught on and is using the shorter sticks to reach the longer ones; it will have the fruit in a moment.

inference. Sometimes, after much mental work, we succeed. Sometimes we are baffled.

Efficiency at problem solving can be improved through practice, and one can learn to become a better problem solver just as one can learn anything else. Psychologists have found a number of interesting and effective techniques that can be applied to various kinds of problems. But the art of problem solving is a whole field of its own that is too large to be covered adequately in an introductory textbook. Any brief discussion of the subject must be limited to pointing out some of the pitfalls that often lie in wait for the would-be solver.

Pitfall 1: taking too much for granted

One of the common errors in problem solving is beautifully illustrated by the ingenious experiment shown in Figure 4-9, which you should try for yourself before going on to the next paragraph.

The problem presented in Figure 4-9 is really quite simple—yet few people manage to solve it. The answer is that you must turn over cards 1 and 3. If card 1 has a colored circle on the back, or if card 3 has a colored triangle on the back, then the statement you are asked to prove or disprove is false. But if card 1 has a black circle on the back, and card 3 has a black triangle on the back, then the statement is true.

Most people insist that the cards to turn over are 1 and 4. But in fact card 4 has no bearing on the problem. Regardless of whether the triangle on the back is colored or black, this card cannot prove or disprove the statement. The reason people tend to fall into the error of picking this card seems to be that they take too much for granted in reading the problem. From the statement given in the experiment, "*every card that has a colored triangle on one side has a black circle on the other side,*" they assume that it is also true that every card that has a black circle on one side must have a colored triangle on the other side. But this has never been stated and is not part of the problem.

The psychologist who devised this experiment has made many similar studies and has found that in general all of us have a tendency to jump to unwarranted conclusions. We are especially likely to assume that if *all a is b* (red triangle has black circle), then it follows that *all b is a* (black circle must have red triangle).

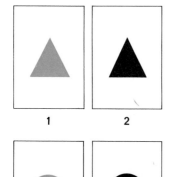

1   2

3   4

4-9

A test in problem solving

Shown here are four cards that have symbols on both sides. Each card has on one side a triangle, which may be either colored or black, and on the other side a circle, which also may be either colored or black. You are asked to prove or disprove the following statement about the cards: *Every card that has a colored triangle on one side has a black circle on the other side.* How many cards—and which ones—would you have to turn over to find out whether the statement is true or false? For the answer, see the text. (30)

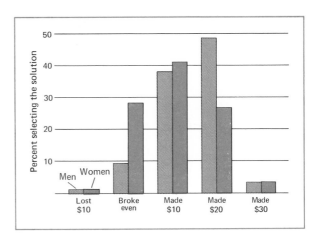

4-10

Male-female differences in problem solving

The bars show the percentages of men and women college students who selected the various possible answers to the horse trading problem described in the text. Note how many more women then men selected "broke even" and how many more men than women selected "made $20."

Pitfall 2: thinking what we would like to think

Closely allied to the error that makes most of us wrong about the cards is another pitfall in problem solving: the fact that we sometimes tend to let our own personal biases get in the way. We try hard—and sometimes against all the weight of evidence and logic—to find the answer we would like to find. The way our personality traits can affect problem solving has been demonstrated by an experiment in which each of the students in a psychology course received a piece of paper on which was written the question: "A man bought a horse for $60 and sold it for $70. Then he bought it back for $80 and sold it for $90. How much money did he make in the horse business?" The students were asked to check one of five possible answers: lost $10, broke even, made $10, made $20, or made $30. (Think about the problem for a moment and decide on your own answer.)

In the original experiment, it turned out that men students and women students reacted quite differently to the problem. As is shown in Figure 4-10, considerably more women than men checked "broke even." Considerably more men than women got the correct answer, which is "made $20." The psychologists who conducted the experiment concluded that the women tended to favor the "broke even" answer because they were more conservative and less aggressive than the men; they preferred to think of people as breaking even in financial transactions rather than as taking risks and winding up with a substantial profit (31).

It should be noted that this experiment was conducted in the 1960s, before much had been heard about the women's liberation movement. You might find it interesting to try the problem on some friends of both sexes to see if the results are different in today's world.

Pitfall 3: persistence of set

Another tendency all of us share is to suffer from what is called *persistence of set*. We develop our own methods of approaching problems—and we tend to use them even in situations where other methods would be more appropriate. In other words, we get into a rut. It is persistence of set that makes it so difficult for most of us to solve brain-teasers that require a fresh approach to familiar situations. For example, there is the old puzzle about the man who lived on the top floor of a nine-story apartment building. Every morning, when he went to work, he got on the elevator at the ninth floor. But in the evening, returning home, he got off at the eighth floor and walked up the remaining flight. Why? A somewhat similar puzzle concerns the man, bitter about life, who planned one last grim joke on humanity. His body was found hanging, with his feet a good 24 inches from the floor, in an otherwise empty closet. How did he manage to hang himself? Only by a determined effort to avoid persistence of set can we come to the answers.*

Pitfall 4: functional fixedness

A special form of set, deserving mention of its own, is called *functional fixedness*. This is a tendency to think of objects as functioning only in one certain way and to ignore their other possible uses. A demonstration of how functional fixedness can interfere with problem solving is illustrated in Figure 4-11. Test your own skills on the problem presented in Figure 4-11 before going on to the next paragraph or turning the page to Figure 4-12, which shows the solution.

As can be seen in Figure 4-12, the key to solving the problem is to forget about the ordinary uses of a pair of pliers and to turn the pliers instead into a support for the flower stand. In an experiment in which subjects were asked to solve the problem by actually manipulating the objects, it was found that their attempts were hampered if they had to begin by using the pliers to loosen the wire. This seemed to serve as a reminder that the usual function of pliers is to loosen or tighten wires,

---

* The man in the elevator was a midget who could reach only as high as the button for the eighth floor. The man who hanged himself stood on a cake of ice that had melted by the time his body was discovered.

4-11

The flower stand problem

Subjects were asked to arrange any or all of these objects so that the board would stand firmly on supports and could serve as a stand for a vase of flowers. The problem is particularly difficult to solve from a photograph, without actually manipulating the objects, but you may be able to visualize the solution before turning to Figure 4-12, which demonstrates how the job can be done. The first step, of course, is to use the pliers to loosen the wire and detach the wooden pin.

turn bolts, or pull nails—not to serve as the legs of a flower stand. Subjects for whom the wooden bar was merely tied to the board and could be removed by simply untying a knot—and who therefore did not have to use the pliers to loosen a wire—were considerably more successful at finding the solution (32).

The flower stand was one of several similar problems devised by the same experimenter; some of the other solutions required using a box as a platform instead of a container or bending a paper clip and using it as a hook. The subjects who had to begin by using the objects in the normal way—the pliers to untwist wire, the box to hold things, the paper clip to fasten papers together—managed to solve 61 percent of the problems. The subjects who did not start this way and thus had less functional fixedness to overcome solved 98 percent.

Does functional fixedness remind you of something that was discussed earlier in the book? It may very well do so—for it is a classic case of negative transfer, S_1-R_1 followed by S_1-R_2 (pages 114–15). Having learned to use the pliers or the paper clips in one way, we find it difficult to cast aside the S_1-R_1 association and use them in an entirely different S_1-R_2 fashion. The old associations keep cropping up and interfering with the establishment of the new.

In many real-life situations functional fixedness reduces our efficiency at solving problems. A nail file is for filing nails; we may overlook entirely the fact that it might help us tighten a screw and thus repair a broken lamp. A goldfish bowl is for fish; the first person who used one as a terrarium for growing house plants had to break some powerful old associations. Similarly, we have a tendency to think that things that perform the same functions should look alike. As old photographs show, the first automobiles strongly resembled buggies.

Why creative people are so rare

Functional fixedness and persistence of set, it must be noted, have certain important advantages in helping us meet the routine problems of daily living. We are set to use many of the articles around us in certain ways—the soap and toothbrush in the bathroom, our clothing, the knives and forks on the table. These sets help us bathe, dress, and eat breakfast almost without thinking about what we are doing. We are set to start an automobile in the routine way, to stop at red lights and start at green lights, to step on the brake when something gets in our path. Sets are particularly valuable when we must react quickly, as when avoiding another automobile or a pedestrian, and do not have time to ponder all the possible answers to the problem.

On the other hand, it is persistence of set and functional fixedness that account for the fact that truly creative thinking is so rare. For example, early attempts to teach language to chimpanzees failed because the experimenters were set to think of language in terms of speech; it was not until this set was broken by the brilliant idea of using sign language that the attempts began to be more successful.

4-12

The solution to the flower stand problem

The problem posed in Figure 4-11 can be solved only by using the pliers in an unusual way, as two "legs" for the flower stand. The metal joints go unused.

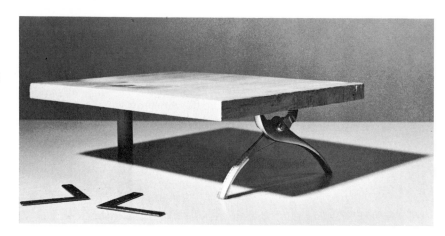

Studies of creative people have disclosed that they tend to have a number of traits in common that are not shared by most other people. Generally speaking, they were lone wolves in childhood; they either were spurned and rejected by other children or sought solitude themselves. If being different from other children caused them anxiety, they eventually overcame it. They grew up with no need to conform to the people and the ways of life around them. In fact creative people tend to *want* to be different and original and to produce new things. They are not afraid of having irrational or bizarre thoughts, are willing to examine even the most foolish-seeming ideas, and are not worried about success or failure. Many of them are aggressive and hostile, not at all the kind of people who win popularity contests or elections (33).

Creativity of any kind—the invention of a new mechanical device such as the airplane, the discovery of a new scientific principle, the writing of a great and original poem or novel—demands superior intelligence. But of the people who have the required intelligence perhaps not even as many as 1 percent are in fact creative. Even more than intelligence, creativity demands the kind of personality that scorns the tried and true, does not get imprisoned by persistence of set, but on the contrary seeks out new and unusual hypotheses even in the face of failure and ridicule.

Attempts have been made to devise tests that would spot creative people early in their school careers so that they might receive special treatment that would encourage their talents. Two such tests are shown in Figure 4-13 and Figure 4-14. Unfortunately, it is easier to test and study sheer originality of response than other qualities that are also necessary for true creativity. Mere novelty is not enough. Besides being new and unusual, a creative hypothesis must also be *appropriate*. A new scientific theory must, like Einstein's theory of relativity, be in accord with the known facts. When we look at a creative painting or hear creative music we must have some kind of perception of aptness, of a disciplined relationship to the world as we know it, if we are to consider the work of art esthetically pleasing. Studies of creativity, therefore, are very difficult to devise.

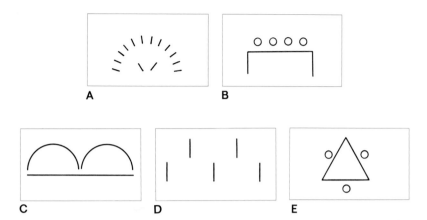

4-13

A test of creativity

These drawings are shown to fifth-grade children, who are asked to try to imagine what they might look like when completed. Most children make routine responses, but a few come up with original and creative ideas. The usual responses are: (A) the sun, (B) table with glasses on it, (C) two igloos, (D) raindrops, and (E) three people sitting at a table. Unusual responses would be: (A) a lollipop bursting into pieces, (B) a foot and toes, (C) two haystacks on a flying carpet, (D) worms hanging, and (E) three mice eating a piece of cheese. (34)

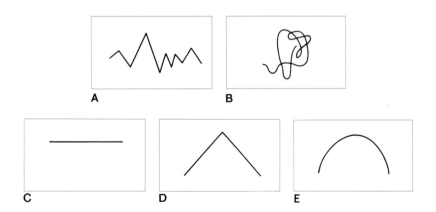

4-14

A variation of the creativity test

In this variation of the creativity test, children are asked what these lines suggest to them—the lines as a whole, not just in part. Ordinary responses would be: (A) mountains, (B) string, (C) stick, (D) arrow, and (E) rising sun. Unusual and original responses would be: (A) squashed piece of paper, (B) squeezing paint out of a tube, (C) stream of ants, (D) alligator's open mouth, and (E) fishing rod bending with a fish. (34a)

Summary

1 Language is humanity's most distinctive and perhaps most complex achievement. It is a special tool that enables us to communicate an unlimited number and variety of messages and to pass knowledge along from one generation to the next.

2 The ability to use language probably depends upon the structure of the human brain and the dynamics of how the brain operates.

3 The building blocks of language are the basic sounds called *phonemes.* English uses forty-five phonemes, and no language uses more than eighty-five. The phonemes are combined into meaningful units known as *morphemes,* which may be words themselves or may be combined with one another to produce words.

4 An important feature of language is that it is a set of rules, notably the rules called *grammar,* or *syntax,* for combining words into an almost infinite number of sentences conveying an almost infinite variety of meaning.

5 Learning to use sounds to express meaning is explained by some theorists in terms of operant conditioning. Others consider observation learning more important. A new and increasingly popular theory holds that we possess some kind of "innate mechanism"—probably an inborn characteristic of the way in which the human brain operates—that enables us to acquire language quickly.

6 All words are *symbols,* but only a relatively few words are used as symbols for specific, one-of-a-kind objects, such as the names of the planets Mars and Jupiter.

7 Most words, however, are *concepts.* A concept is *a symbol that stands for a common characteristic or relationship shared by objects or events that are otherwise different.* Thus the word *water* is a symbol that stands not only for the fluid that comes out of a faucet but for any somewhat similar fluid anywhere, including the salty contents of the oceans and the drops that fall as rain.

8 The concepts used by adults represent many kinds of shared similarities and relationships that have been found to exist among all the apparently diverse elements in the environment and in human history. Ordinarily our primary definition of a concept is based on what is to us the *salient characteristic* of the various objects, events, or ideas that are included in the concept.

9 The associations that make up concepts are arranged in *concept hierarchies,* meaning that some of the associations are very strong and likely to be thought of immediately, whereas others are weaker and less likely to come to mind.

10 Besides their dictionary meanings, most words and concepts also have implied meanings called *connotations.* A great many words carry connotations of goodness or badness, strength or weakness, and activity or passivity.

11 There are many individual differences in the way people learn concepts, build them into hierarchies, and relate and interlock them. Thus we all have personal systems of organizing our environment and responding to it.

12 Thinking is *the mental manipulation of images, symbols, concepts, rules, and other mediational units.*

13 Three important forms of the thinking process are:

  a *Mediational clustering,* based on the way we have stored mediational units (information) in memory.

  b *Logical rules,* such as mathematical rules and formal types of thinking such as the *syllogism.*

  c *Inference,* or drawing conclusions about new objects or situations from what we already know about similar objects or events.

14 Two methods of *problem solving,* displayed by animals as well as by human beings, are *trial and error* and *insight.*

15 Pitfalls in problem solving include a) taking too much for granted, b) thinking what we would like to think rather than what the facts dictate, c) persistence of set, and d) functional fixedness.

Recommended reading

Blumenthal, A. L. *Language and psychology: historical aspects of psycholinguistics.* New York: John Wiley, 1970.

Brown, R. *A first language.* Cambridge, Mass.: Harvard University Press, 1973.

Chomsky, N. *Language and mind,* enl. ed. New York: Harcourt Brace Jovanovich, 1972.

Deese, J. E. *Psycholinguistics.* Boston: Allyn & Bacon, 1970.

Kintsch, W. *Learning, memory and conceptual processes.* New York: John Wiley, 1970.

Mandler, G., and Mandler, J. M., eds. *Thinking: from association to gestalt.* New York: John Wiley, 1964.

Wallach, M. A., and Kogan, N. *Modes of thinking in young children: a study of the creativity-intelligence distinction.* New York: Holt, Rinehart and Winston, 1965.

Wason, P. C., and Johnson-Laird, P. N. *Psychology of reasoning: structure and content.* Cambridge, Mass.: Harvard University Press, 1972.

Wickelgren, W. A. *How to solve problems.* San Francisco: W. H. Freeman, 1974.

THREE

PERCEIVING
THE WORLD

The computer is totally dependent on its inputs—that is, on the kind of information that is fed into it. Rather similarly, the organism is dependent on the kind of information it receives from its environment and the manner in which it is able to organize this information into patterns of meaning.

Hence the importance of the human senses, which will now be discussed in Chapter 5. Note the difference, for example, between the kind of information a human being receives through such sense organs as the eyes and ears and the information on which a paramecium must rely. The paramecium is sensitive in a general way to light and dark and to heat and cold, and it can move toward or away from them. But it is not at all influenced by many of the things that influence human beings. It is unaware of the existence in the environment of colors and the rise of the sun, of sounds and words, of newspapers and books. Its behavior is limited to a few simple functions, such as moving, feeding, and its own primitive kind of reproduction.

As important as the raw information provided by our senses is the manner in which we organize and interpret the information—the processes described in Chapter 6, on perception. For example, your own behavior and thinking at this moment depend not so much on the fact that you can see the book as on the fact that you regard it—or perceive it—as a particular kind of object called a college textbook. A child, though seeing the book exactly as you see it, might interpret it as something to draw on or to build into piles like blocks.

The senses provide the raw information that enables us to behave and think like human beings. The process of perception gives meaning to what we see, hear, feel, taste, and smell. Together, they enable us to understand the objects and events in our environment and to start dealing with them successfully.

The senses

To those of our ancestors who thought about the matter, the human senses were one of life's most puzzling mysteries. Here you stand, and out there, many yards away, totally unconnected in any apparent way with your body or your eyes, is a tree. How are you able to see that tree? Why does its trunk look brown and its leaves green? Why are the roses near it red and the marigolds yellow?

A friend standing near the tree opens his mouth, and you hear words. What has happened—and why does his voice sound different from the voice of anyone else you know? Why does a piano sound different from a violin, and a violin from a trumpet?

Those roses you see out in the yard smell entirely different from the marigolds. Sugar does not taste at all like lemon juice or quinine. Some objects that you touch seem cold; some seem warm and some so hot that you have to draw your hand away in pain. Why?

For centuries nobody knew the answers to these questions. Even the best-informed people could only guess. Some of the guesses, as we now know, came fairly close to the truth. For example, one Greek philosopher who lived around 400 B.C. speculated that all objects gave off some kind of invisible substance that penetrated our eyes or the pores of our skin and then traveled to our brains. Not until recently was there any better explanation.

How the senses operate

As you sit reading this book you are demonstrating the two basic principles now known to be involved in the operation of our senses.

First, there must be a *stimulus*. As the Greek philosopher rightly guessed, something must actually impinge upon our bodies. In this case it is the light waves reflected off your book. Turn out the light and darken the room, thus removing the light waves, and you can no longer see the book, even though it is still there.

Second, there must be *receptors* that are sensitive to the stimulus. The philosopher was wrong in thinking that anything could enter our

159

pores and then travel to the brain. What happens is that the stimulus activates the receptors—in this case the light-sensitive nerve endings in your eyes—which then send nervous impulses to the brain, where they are translated into conscious sensations. Block off the receptors by closing your eyelids, and again you cannot see the book. You cannot see with your skin or your ears because they do not possess any receptors that respond to the stimulus of light.

A *stimulus* has already been defined as any form of energy capable of exciting the nervous system. Among the sensory stimuli are light waves, sound waves, the chemical energy that causes the sensations of taste and smell, and the mechanical energy that we feel through the skin as pressure and pain. A *receptor* can be defined as a specialized nerve ending capable of responding to energy.

If we regard the human organism as a sort of computer, then our senses provide our inputs. They tell us what kind of world we are living in and how the world is changing from moment to moment. Without the evidence provided by our senses, all the rest of our complicated physical and nervous equipment would be useless—just as a modern heating system would be useless without the sensitive element in the thermostat that says the building is now warm and the heat must be turned off, or the building is getting cold and the heat must be turned on. Our sensory receptors relay the fact that the traffic light up ahead has turned red, and by a complicated process of mental and motor activity we step on the brake and stop the automobile. Our sensory receptors inform us that the weather has turned cold, and we put on more clothing lest we freeze to death.

**The range
and limits of the
human senses**

The receptors in the human eye are so sensitive that on a night when the air is clear but the moon and stars are blacked out by an overcast, a person sitting on a mountain can see a match struck fifty miles away. Our noses can detect the odor of artificial musk, a perfume base, in as weak a concentration as one part musk to thirty-two billion parts of air.

Even so, our senses are by no means perfect. Owls can see far better in the near-dark than we can. Hawks soaring high in the air can see mice that we would never be able to distinguish at such a distance. Bees can see ultraviolet light (the rays that produce sunburn), which we cannot see at all. Dogs and porpoises hear tones that go unheard by the human ear. (You can buy whistles that will call your dog without disturbing your neighbors.) The minnow, which has taste receptors all over its body, has a far sharper sense of taste than we do. Bloodhounds are used to track down criminals because they have a far sharper sense of smell.

In some ways the deficiencies of our sense organs are a blessing. Light waves, as the physicists have shown, are one form of electromagnetic radiation. So are many other things, such as cosmic rays, X-rays, radio and television signals, and the electric currents passing through the wires of our houses. The length of the wave determines which of these forms the radiation takes. Light waves, the only wavelengths to which our eyes are sensitive, are a tiny fraction of the entire range. If we could see all the wavelengths—everything from cosmic rays to the flow of electricity and the radio and television signals passing through the air—we would surely be completely confused. Our eyes would give us a hopeless jumble of impressions.

The absolute threshold

With the help of a friend, you can make a simple test of your own hearing that points to one of the important facts about the senses. Have your friend hold a watch somewhere in the vicinity of one of your ears, moving it closer and farther away. The watch is constantly ticking, sending out sound waves. But sound waves decrease in volume as they travel through the air, and if the watch is too far away, you cannot hear it at all. As it is moved closer, eventually there comes a spot at which you can hear it quite clearly. At one distance the sound waves are too weak to make the receptors in your ear respond. A little closer the waves are strong enough; the receptors send signals to your brain and you can hear the watch. The test is a crude measurement of the *absolute threshold* of hearing in that ear—in other words, the minimum amount of stimulus energy to which the receptors will respond. By comparing your threshold with that of other people, you can get a rough idea of whether your sense of hearing is average, sharper than average, or below average.

Measurements establishing the precise absolute thresholds for the various senses under various conditions have been made with procedures known as *psychophysical methods*—techniques of measuring the psychological equivalents of changes in the physical strength of a stimulus. In a typical psychophysical experiment a subject is placed in a dark room and brief flashes of light are presented, with the exact intensity of the light controlled down to the tiniest fraction. Some flashes are so weak in intensity that the subject never sees them. Other, stronger flashes are seen every time. In between, there is a sort of twilight zone of intensities at which the subject sometimes sees the flash and sometimes does not.

There are many reasons for this "sometimes" factor. The human body is constantly at work: the heart is beating, the lungs inhaling or exhaling air. Each cell of the body, including the sensory receptors, is being fed by the bloodstream and is throwing off waste materials. All sorts of spontaneous nervous activity are constantly going on in the brain. Sometimes all these conditions work together in favor of detecting a weak stimulus; sometimes they work against it. So the absolute threshold is not really "absolute." It is arbitrarily considered to be the intensity at which the subject sees the flash half the time.

A synonym for threshold is the word *limen;* a *subliminal* stimulus is below the threshold, a *supraliminal* stimulus above it.

The difference threshold

Let us return for a moment to the psychophysical method of measuring a subject's absolute intensity threshold for a brief flash of light. This time let us change the experiment and present two lights to the subject, side by side. We start with two lights of exactly equal intensity, and the subject, as we would expect, sees them as exactly the same. We show the two lights again, but this time we have increased the intensity of the light on the right by a tiny fraction. If we continue the experiment long enough, keeping the left-hand light at the same intensity and varying the intensity of the right-hand light, eventually we will discover the smallest possible difference that our subject's eyes are capable of recognizing 50 percent of the time. This is the *difference threshold*, or *difference limen*, an important concept in sensory psychology.

The difference threshold—often called the *just noticeable difference*, or j.n.d. for short—is a measurement of our basic capacity to discriminate among different stimuli. Psychophysical measurements have shown that if the left-hand light in our experiment has an intensity of 1, the right-hand light must have have an intensity of 1.016 to be recognized as different. If the left-hand light is 10, the right-hand light must be 10.16. If the left-hand light is 100, the right-hand light must be 101.6. In other words, the difference in intensity between two lights must be 1.6 percent before it can be recognized. For sound, the just noticeable difference is about 10 percent.

This rule that the difference threshold is a fixed percentage of the original stimulus is called *Weber's Law* in honor of the physiologist who discovered it more than a century ago. The law does not apply at very low intensities or at very high intensities, but it holds generally over the greater part of the range of stimulation. In practical terms, it means this: The more sensory stimulation to which the human organism is being subjected, the more additional stimulation must be piled on top of this to produce a recognizable difference. In a room where there is no sound except that of a mosquito buzzing, you can hear a pin drop. On a noisy city street you can hear the honk of an automobile horn but may be completely unaware of the fact that a friend is shouting to you from down the block. At an airport where jet planes are warming up, a small cannon could go off close beside you without making you jump.

Sensory adaptation

At this moment, unless you happen to be sitting in a draft or in an unusually hot room, you almost surely are not conscious of feeling either hot or cold. And you probably feel the same all over. You are not conscious that your feet are cooler or warmer than your hands or that the skin on the calves of your legs is any cooler or warmer than the skin on the small of your back. Yet careful measurements of your skin temperature would probably show small but significant differences for your feet, which are encased in shoes; your uncovered hands; your calves; and the small of your back, covered by several layers of clothing and a belt.

Nor are you conscious of any special pressures against your skin. But wherever your clothing touches your skin, there certainly is pressure; and at some places the pressure is made so intense by a wrist-watch band or by a belt that you may find marks on your skin tonight when you undress.

Why do you not feel these stimuli? The answer lies in the principle of *sensory adaptation,* which means that after a time the sensory receptors adjust to a stimulus—they "get used to it," so to speak—and stop responding.

The classic example of sensory adaptation is this simple experiment. Fill a bowl with water of just about skin temperature—water that feels neither hot nor cold to your hand, water that we may say has a neutral temperature. Fill a second bowl with cold water and a third bowl with water that feels quite warm to the touch. Now put your left hand in the bowl of cold water and your right hand in the bowl of hot water. After a minute or two, put both hands in the bowl that contains water at the neutral temperature. Even though you know perfectly well that both hands are in the same water, your left hand will feel warm, your right hand cool. The receptors in your left hand have become adapted to cold water, and water of neutral temperature now seems warm. The receptors in your right hand have adapted to warm water, and water of neutral temperature now seems cold.

In some ways, the tendency of our senses to adapt to stimuli makes them less accurate than they would otherwise be. The human skin would make a poor thermostat for a heating system; what we want in a heating system is a thermostat that will invariably turn the heat on when the room temperature drops to 69 degrees and turn the heat off as soon as the temperature rises to 71 degrees. But in everyday living, sensory adaptation is generally an advantage. It would be distracting indeed if we were conscious all day of the pressure of every garment we wear and of every slight temperature change from one patch of our skin to another. If our noses did not gradually get used to the odors about us and stop sending signals to our brains, the people who work in fish markets would be a lot less happy than they are.

Because of the principle of sensory adaptation, some scientists like to define a stimulus as a *change in energy* capable of exciting the sense organs. Such a definition is not literally correct, because we never adapt completely to a pressure strong enough to cause severe pain, and we continue to feel uncomfortably warm in a 110-degree room no matter how long we stay there. But the definition is nonetheless useful to keep in mind because it emphasizes the fact that our sensory apparatus is best equipped to inform us of changes in our environment, and it is awareness of change in the environment that is most valuable to us.

With these general principles of the operation of the senses in mind, let us now examine our senses separately and in detail. It is popularly assumed that we are gifted with five senses; the best order in which to explore the five is to start with the simplest and least efficient one, which is *taste,* and proceed to *smell,* the *skin senses, hearing,* and *vision.* Even after we have examined the so-called five senses, however, it will be necessary to add two more—*bodily movement* and *equilibrium*—to explain the full range of human sensory apparatus.

Taste

In view of the variety of foods we recognize and either enjoy or reject, it may seem strange to call the sense of taste our simplest and least efficient. What is generally called the "taste" of food, however, turns out to depend only in small part on our sensory receptors for taste. Much of the sensation depends on other factors—on warmth, cold, the consistency of the food, the mild pain caused by certain spices, and above all on smell. When our noses are stuffed up by a cold, food seems almost tasteless.

If you examine your tongue in a mirror, you will note that it is covered with little bumps, some very tiny, others a bit larger. Inside these bumps, a few of which are also found at the back of the mouth and in the throat, are the *taste buds,* which are the receptors for the sense of taste. Each bump contains about 245 taste buds, and each taste bud in turn contains about twenty receptors sensitive to chemical stimulation by food molecules. Food in solution spreads over the tongue, enters small pores in the surface of the bumps, and sets off chemical changes that depolarize the receptors and thus set off nervous impulses that are sent to the brain.

What psychology has learned about the sense of taste accounts for several well-known but previously unexplained facts. The reason people who quit smoking often find that food tastes better is that tobacco smoke temporarily reduces the sensitivity of the taste receptors (and also of the receptors for smell). The reason people past middle age tend to use large amounts of salt and spices is that the number of sensitive taste buds declines with age, so that older people simply do not have as many receptors capable of responding to the taste of food. People who live to extremely advanced ages sometimes lose the sense of taste entirely.

Animals—at least some of them—apparently have a very different sense of taste from the human kind. Cats do not seem to be sensitive to sweetness; they show no fondness for candy. Dogs usually like candy, and horses seem to prefer a lump of sugar to any other kind of taste.

"I forgot the salt."
(C) *Punch,* London (Rothco).

The taste "map" and pattern theory

Perhaps the most important thing about the sense of taste is that it provides a clear-cut example of how psychology's view of the way the human senses operate has changed over the years as new experimental methods have been developed. The search for the truth has been almost like a long-continuing mystery story. At first a few clues were found and they clearly seemed to point to Suspect A. Later careful research un-

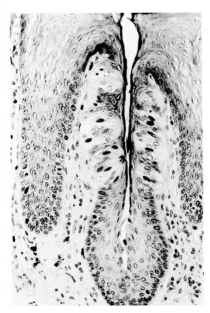

A photograph of a human taste bud, magnified 400 times.

covered new clues, casting grave doubt on Suspect A's responsibility. Still later, additional clues pointed first in one direction, then in another —until now we know that the whole mystery of the senses is complicated beyond any dreams of the original researchers.

At the beginning, the facts seemed ridiculously simple. The taste receptors, it was found, respond to four basic types of stimuli: sweet, sour, salty, and bitter. Moreover, our ability to respond to these four qualities is not uniform over the surface of the tongue but can be mapped as shown in Figure 5-1. What could be more logical, given these facts, than to assume that there were four kinds of taste receptors, each sensitive to one of the four basic taste qualities?

Indeed the same thing found true for taste also seemed to apply to the other senses. It seemed logical to assume further that some of the receptors in the skin were sensitive to pressure, others to warmth, others to cold, still others to pain, while specialized receptors in the eyes were sensitive to certain colors, and so on for the other senses.

Alas, the logic has proved wrong. Evidence disproving the original assumptions has piled up over the years, especially since the development of delicate instruments that can measure the activity inside a single sensory receptor and a single brain cell receiving messages from the sensory receptors. For the sense of taste, it now appears that individual receptors on the tongue are by no means finely tuned to respond to a single taste quality, as a radio might be tuned to receive one wavelength and one only. Instead, they are what one investigator has called "broadly tuned" (1). They may show a maximum sensitivity to one kind of taste quality, but they respond to other qualities as well.

The new explanation of how the senses operate is called the *pattern theory*. This theory holds that there is no simple one-to-one relationship between a sensory receptor and the sensation that we feel. In other words, we do not have a sensation of bitterness because a bitter substance has stimulated a receptor or several receptors that are specifically geared to respond to that kind of substance and that kind only. Instead,

5-1

A "map" of the tongue

Sensory theories were influenced for years by the fact illustrated in this drawing of the tongue's surface—namely that there are certain well-defined areas where we can best distinguish the four basic qualities of taste. For discussion of the theoretical implications and why they have proved wrong, see the text.

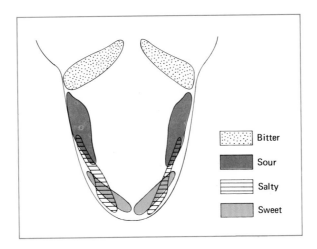

the substance on the tongue affects a great many "broadly tuned" receptors—stimulating some of them to a high rate of activity, others to a lesser rate, perhaps still others to a kind of activity that tends to cancel out what is happening to the other receptors. It is the entire pattern of messages sent to the brain by the various receptors that accounts for the sensation. Similar kinds of patterns are believed to explain the operation of the other senses as well, as will be seen.

Smell

The receptors sensitive to smells are contained in a membrane called the *olfactory epithelium*, which, as can be seen in Figure 5-2, lies at the very top of the nasal passages leading from the nostrils to the throat. As we breathe normally, the flow of air from nostrils to throat takes a direct route, as the drawing indicates, but a certain amount rises gently to touch the olfactory epithelium. The receptors for smell are sensitive only to gases and to substances that become dissolved in the air much as sugar dissolves in water. An actual molecule of the substance must touch the smell receptors; this is the stimulus that causes the receptors to "fire" and send nervous impulses to the brain.

It has been suggested that there are seven basic classes of molecules, different in size and shape, that produce seven basic odors: camphorlike, musky, flowery, pepperminty, etherlike, pungent, and putrid (2). But again the pattern theory maintains that any given smell sensation is produced by the firing of many different types of receptors with maximal firing of one type.

5-2

The receptors for smell

A cross section of the human head shows the position of the *olfactory epithelium*, containing the receptors for the sense of smell. The air we breathe goes to our lungs along the routes shown by the solid arrows, but some of it takes the path shown by the arrows with dashes and thus touches the receptors.

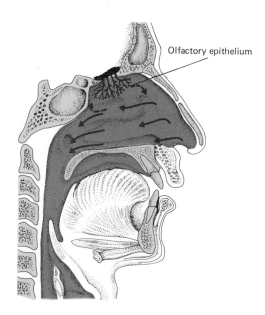

Olfactory epithelium

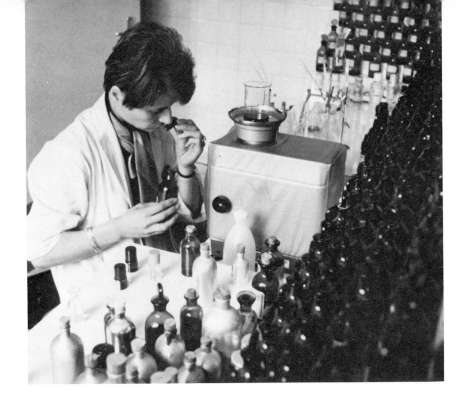

The skin senses

In the search for an explanation of the sensations from the human skin, psychologists ran into a strange coincidence. Just as our tongues are sensitive to four basic taste qualities, our skins seem to produce four different sensations: pressure, pain, cold, and warmth. In the case of the skin, moreover, there was a further and even more misleading coincidence. Microscopic examination of skin taken from the human body clearly shows that it contains four different kinds of nerve endings. Some of the nerve fibers end in little branches, some in globular bulbs, some in egg-shaped swellings, some in the form of tiny baskets surrounding the roots of the hairs.

Four sensations and four types of nerve endings—what could seem more logical than a belief that there had to be a cause-and-effect connection between these two facts? For years investigators made many painstaking studies, mapping the skin for spots that were sensitive to mild pressure or to the warmth of a tiny rod, expecting to find that the sensitive spots were related to the types of nerve endings just under the surface of the skin. Surprisingly, nobody could find good evidence that the four sensations were connected with the four types of receptors (3). Careful research has revealed a new view. There seem to be two types of nerve fibers serving the skin sense. Fibers of the first type are sensitive to pressure and touch and carry their information to the brain rapidly; fibers of the second type are sensitive to pain and temperature and convey information more slowly. Although a sensation of pressure is likely to involve more of one kind of receptor than another, it is the total pattern of discharge in the receptors and in the nerve fibers that carry the information from receptor to brain that determines the final sensation we feel. Again the best explanation for sensation appears to be provided by a pattern theory.

167

The strange phenomenon of paradoxical cold

One of the discoveries made by researchers while mapping the skin deserves special mention. This is the fact that when a spot on the skin is touched by a small rod heated to 110 degrees Fahrenheit or more (which is really quite hot), the stimulus sometimes feels not hot but just the opposite. The name *paradoxical cold* has been given to the sensation produced in this fashion.

It was believed for a long time that paradoxical cold explained how we can distinguish a hot stimulus from a merely warm stimulus. When we touch anything heated to more than 110 degrees, it was thought, the stimulus produced a response both from the nerve endings sensitive to warmth and from the nerve endings sensitive to cold; and the combined responses resulted in the sensation of heat. Indeed an ingenious device was invented that seemed to prove this belief, as illustrated in Figure 5-3. When cool water is passed through both coils, the device naturally feels cool to the touch. When warm water is passed through both coils, it feels warm. But when one coil is warm and the other cool, the device suddenly—and to the amazement of anyone who touches it—feels hot. In terms of the pattern theory, of course, the two coils merely point to one of the many kinds of complex messages that the sensory receptors can produce in response to various kinds of stimuli.

A special word on pain

Receptors that contribute to the sensation of pain are found not only in the skin but also in all our muscles and internal organs. Indeed some of the most excruciating pains come from muscle cramps or from distension of the intestines by gas. Yet most of the receptors in the internal organs do not respond to stimuli that would cause pain if applied to the skin. The intestines, for example, can be cut or even burned without arousing any sensation of pain.

Although pain seems to be one of the crosses that we must bear, it actually serves a purpose. Without the warning given us by pain we might hold our hands in a flame until the tissues were destroyed or cut off a finger while peeling an apple. Even the pain of headache, which cannot be attributed to any specific outside stimulus, is probably a warning that we have subjected ourselves to too much physical or psychological stress. By forcing us to slow down or even take a day off, the headache takes us away from a situation that, if continued, might cause some serious damage to the tissues of our bodies or to our mental stability.

5-3

Warmth plus cold = what?

Warm water can be passed through both coils, or cool water can be passed through both, or warm water can be passed through one coil and cool water through the other. For a description of the unexpected result of passing warm water through one coil and cool water through the other, see the text.

169
HEARING

Hearing

When you hit the key for middle C on a piano, a hammer strikes the string for middle C, the string vibrates, and you hear a sound. Not just any sound, but a very definite sound. You can distinguish it from other notes on the piano; it seems higher than the B just below it and lower than the D just above it. It also sounds different from the middle C on other musical instruments. If someone in the room were playing the same note on a clarinet, you would recognize at once that the sounds were alike yet somehow different.

If you hit the key a little harder, the sound, though remaining the same in every other respect, is louder. Hit the key a little more gently, and the sound is softer.

Striking the piano key is a start toward exploring some of the basic facts about the sense of hearing. Sound is an extremely complicated stimulus, ranging from the lowest notes of a tuba to the highest tones of a shrill whistle, changing in volume from the merest hint of a whisper to the most deafening clap of thunder, taking such diverse and varied forms as the click of two coins in a pocket, the human voice, and the blended richness of a hundred different instruments in a symphony orchestra. The receptors in the human ear have to be very sensitive indeed to respond to such a wide range of stimuli.

The physical nature of sound

The stimulus for sound is sound waves, rippling unseen through the air. Sound waves are roughly analogous to waves on water. If you throw a stone into a quiet pond, waves start to radiate out. It looks as if the surface of the water is moving away from the stone, forming circles of ever increasing size. Actually, as you can tell if there are some twigs or fishing corks floating on the surface, this is not true. The twigs and corks stay in the same spot and merely bob up and down.

What happens when the stone hits the surface of the pond is that it puts pressure on the water. The surface is pushed up, then falls, and in so doing passes the pressure along to the adjoining water. The rising and falling motions continue outward in ever widening circles, with the ripples getting smaller and smaller as the pressure of the stone's impact is absorbed.

When you hit that middle C on the piano, something very similar happens in the air. The piano string starts to vibrate. As it vibrates in one direction, it compresses the air, just as an accordion player compresses the air inside the instrument by pushing the ends together. As the string vibrates in the other direction, it expands the air and creates a partial vacuum, as the accordion player does by pulling the ends of the instrument apart. These alternations of compression and expansion are passed along through the air, growing weaker in volume as they go, until at last the energy from the string's vibration is used up and the waves disappear. The sound waves, then, are ripples of compression and expansion of the air. Regardless of how loud or soft they may be or whether they are high sounds or low sounds, they travel through the air at a standard rate of speed; the speed of sound is around 750 miles an hour, or 1100 feet per second.

Frequency = pitch. Fortunately for our study of sound waves, it is possible to turn these unseen air ripples into pictures that tell us a great deal about them. This is done with a device called a cathode-ray oscilloscope, as shown in Figure 5-4. The wavy lines that flicker across the screen of the oscilloscope are one of our most useful tools for exploring the varied nature of sound waves.

The kind of picture we see on the oscilloscope screen is shown in Figure 5-5. Note how the characteristic called *frequency,* meaning the number of waves per second, determines the *tone* (or *pitch*) that we hear.

Amplitude = loudness. The drawings in Figure 5-6 illustrate the second important characteristic of sound waves, called *amplitude;* that is, the height of the waves, which determines the *loudness* that we hear. It has to be pointed out, however, that amplitude and loudness are not entirely synonymous. If tones of 100 cycles, 1000 cycles, and 10,000 cycles are sounded at exactly the same amplitude and therefore seem exactly the same in volume to the oscilloscope, to our ears the middle tone sounds much louder than the high tone, and the high tone sounds louder than the low tone. The absolute threshold of hearing follows the same pattern. We can hear small amplitudes at 1000 cycles that we could not hear at 10,000 cycles and can hear amplitudes at 10,000 cycles that we could not hear at 100 cycles.

These last facts raise an interesting question. If our sense of hearing

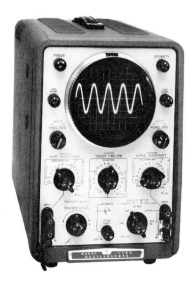

5-4

Turning sound waves into pictures

Sound waves picked up by a microphone are converted into electric currents and fed into an *oscilloscope*, which has a screen similar to a television screen, where "pictures" of the waves can be studied.

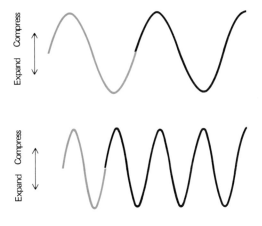

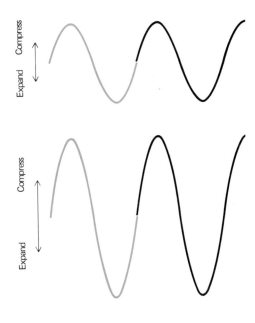

5-5

How sound varies in frequency

The tone of middle C would look as at top on the oscilloscope screen. As the air is compressed the line rises; then the line drops back to the base line and continues downward as the air expands. A single cycle of the curve is shown in color on the graph. For middle C, 256 of these cycles flash across the oscilloscope screen every second; in other words the *frequency* of the sound wave for middle C is 256 cycles per second.

The C above middle C, sounded at the same degree of loudness, would look as at bottom. Here the waves flash across the screen exactly twice as fast, for the frequency of the C above middle C is 512 cycles per second. Thus the oscilloscope screen demonstrates that the higher the frequency of the sound waves, the higher the pitch we hear. The height of the waves, however, remains the same.

5-6

How sound varies in amplitude

At top is the oscilloscope picture of middle C, sounded as before in Figure 5-5. A single cycle is shown in color.

At bottom the same tone is sounded with double the force. The wave frequency remains the same, but the wave is now twice as high as before. The height of the waves is called their *amplitude,* and the oscilloscope screen demonstrates that it is the amplitude of the waves that determines how loud they sound to our ears.

is least sensitive of all to very low tones, why is such a low tone used for foghorns? The answer is that sound waves of low frequency travel much farther than waves of high frequency. High-frequency waves are absorbed much faster by the air through which they travel and by any objects that get in their way, while low-frequency waves travel on and on. The next time you hear a band playing in the distance—as when a parade is approaching or when you are driving toward a football stadium—notice that it is the tubas you hear rather than the flutes.

A familiar measure of amplitude is the *decibel;* the decibel scale is

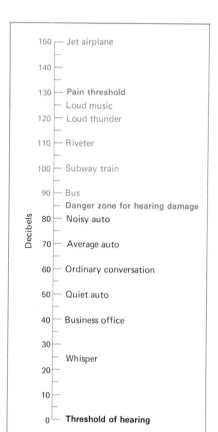

5-7

Decibel scale of loudness

The zero point on the decibel scale is set at the absolute threshold of hearing, and from there the readings go up to the neighborhood of 60 decibels for the sound of ordinary conversation, around 120 for a clap of thunder, and 150 for a jet airplane engine. (4, 5)

shown in Figure 5-7. You will note, of course, that this is not an absolute scale. A clap of thunder at 120 decibels is far more than twice as loud as conversation at 60 decibels. But it is an ingenious scale (of the type mathematicians call logarithmic) that condenses the entire range of possible amplitudes of sound into meaningful numbers. Sound-sensitive devices that give readings expressed in decibels can be used to measure everything from the applause at television shows to the effectiveness of a sound-absorbent ceiling in reducing the noise level in a business office. An absolute scale of amplitude would have to use numbers going all the way up to 500,000, for the smallest amplitude we can hear is just about 1/500,000 as great as the largest amplitude.

Prolonged exposure to sounds above about 85 decibels can cause hearing damage—a fact of considerable importance because the noise level in city streets often goes above that figure. Moreover, many people like to have the sound level very high when listening to modern music; in a small and crowded hall the decibel reading on electric guitars and amplified drums is often around 125. Tests of college freshmen who have listened to a great deal of rock music have shown that many of them can hear no better than the average person aged sixty-five (6). At about 130 decibels or more, sounds actually cause pain.

Complexity = timbre. In the previous diagrams of sound waves as they are seen on the oscilloscope screen, we have been showing pure tones. In fact, however, pure tones do not exist outside sound laboratories. The closest thing to a pure tone in real-life situations is the sound made by that very simple musical instrument, the flute.

The sound waves that actually reach our ears have a third characteristic, in addition to frequency and amplitude, that is called *complexity*. When you strike middle C on the piano, as has been mentioned, the string vibrates at a frequency of 256 cycles a second, creating its characteristic pitch. However, it also vibrates in other and more complicated ways. Each half of the string vibrates separately, at a rate of 512 cycles a second. Each third of the string vibrates, at a rate of 768 cycles a second. And each quarter of the string also vibrates, at a rate of 1024 cycles a second. These additional vibrations are called *overtones*. They have less amplitude than the fundamental tone, but they play an important role in changing the shape of the sound wave that comes from the piano.

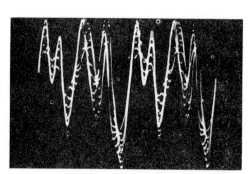

5-8

A complex sound wave

A trumpet note takes a much more complex form than the "pure" tones that were shown in Figures 5-5 and 5-6. This is the oscilloscope pattern of A above middle C as altered by the characteristic overtones of the trumpet.

The complexity of the sound wave (see Figure 5-8) determines what is called its *timbre*. Each musical instrument has its characteristic pattern of overtones, and the note of middle C struck on a piano therefore has a noticeably different timbre from the middle C of a violin or a clarinet. Timbre, as well as pitch, helps account for the ease with which we distinguish one voice from another.

Locating sounds

You are walking across the campus and a man behind you, where you cannot see him, calls to you. You know immediately that he is toward your left or toward your right; you turn in that direction without even thinking. Or you are sitting in a room, not looking out the window. An automobile passes by and you know without thinking that it is moving from left to right. Something about the sound waves gives the receptors in the ears some important clues about the direction from which the sound is coming and the direction in which it is moving. What are the clues?

The answer has been provided by experiments with the pseudophone (see Figure 5-9), a set of earphones that capture the sound waves at the right ear and transfer them to the left ear and send the sound waves that would ordinarily reach the left ear to the right ear. When the young woman wearing the pseudophone keeps her eyes closed, the automobile that goes past from left to right sounds as if it were moving in the opposite direction, from right to left.

Obviously the stimulus that arrives at one ear is not the same as the stimulus that arrives at the other ear. Under ordinary circumstances, a sound wave from the left reaches the left ear a tiny fraction of a second before it reaches the right ear. It is in an earlier phase of the curve from compression to expansion of the air. It is also a tiny bit louder because it has not traveled quite as far. And its overtones are slightly different. The clues to locating sounds thus are *timing, phase, amplitude,* and *complexity*.

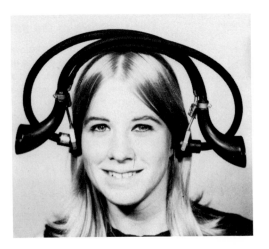

5-9

A device to fool the ear

The young woman wears a pseudophone, a laboratory device that carries the sounds that would ordinarily reach her right ear to her left ear instead, and the sounds that would ordinarily reach her left ear to her right ear. As explained in the text, experiments with the pseudophone have revealed how we locate sounds.

The ear and its receptors

The structure of the ear is shown in Figure 5-10. Sound waves enter the outer ear and set up vibrations in the eardrum. These vibrations then pass through the middle ear, which is an air-filled cavity containing three small bones that conduct and amplify the vibrations, and finally enter the inner ear. Here they reach the *cochlea,* a bony structure shaped like a snail's shell, which contains the receptors for hearing.

The cochlea is filled with fluid, and stretched across it, dividing it more or less in half, is a piece of tissue called the *basilar membrane.* Sound waves are transmitted to the *oval window* of the cochlea, where they set up motions of the fluid that bend the basilar membrane. Lying on the membrane is the *organ of Corti,* a collection of the receptors for hearing.

How the hearing receptors work

When sound waves are transmitted to the cochlea through the oval window, the entire basilar membrane responds with complicated wavelike motions that travel along its length and breadth (8). These motions in turn activate the hearing receptors, which are shaped like very fine hairs resting on the membrane. When the "floor" beneath the receptors moves, the hair-shaped cells jiggle like little dancers—setting off nervous impulses that are sent to the brain and account for our sensations of sound.

The basilar membrane varies in width from one end to the other, rather like the shape of a harp. Moreover, it is quite flexible and easily moved in some places, more rigid and difficult to move in others. Thus different sounds—and especially different pitches of sound—cause its wavelike motions to take many different forms. At times the waves have their greatest effect on the hearing receptors in one spot, at other times on the hearing receptors in other spots. Where the membrane is flexible, the "dancing" of the hair-shaped cells tends to stimulate other nearby cells. Where the membrane is stiffer, this is less likely to happen. Thus there are almost endless patterns of nervous activity that can be

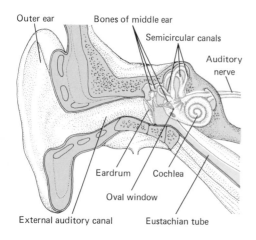

Outer ear
Bones of middle ear
Semicircular canals
Auditory nerve
Eardrum   Cochlea
Oval window
External auditory canal   Eustachian tube

5-10

The structure of the ear

Sound waves reaching the outer ear pass through a short canal across the end of which the eardrum is stretched. Vibrations of the eardrum are then conducted and amplified by the three bones of the middle ear, the last of which connects to the *oval window* of the *cochlea* in the inner ear. The receptors for hearing lie in the cochlea. The *Eustachian tube* connects with the air passages of the mouth and nose and keeps the air pressure in the middle ear the same as the pressure outside. (When this tube is temporarily blocked, as it often is when we have a cold or when we go up or down in an elevator, we feel a sense of pressure against the eardrum.) The *semicircular canals* of the inner ear play no part in hearing but will be discussed later for their role in the sense of equilibrium. (7)

set up in the hearing receptors by different kinds and amplitudes of sounds. It appears that our sensations of pitch and loudness depend on the particular receptors that are stimulated, the number of them, the rate of firing of nervous impulses sent to the brain, and especially the pattern of these impulses (9, 10).

Vision

From all sorts of everyday observations comes evidence that the sound waves that account for hearing are a very different form of energy from the light waves that account for vision. A boat whistles in the distance, and we see the blast of steam well before we hear the sound. We see the lightning flash before we hear the thunder. Quite obviously, light travels much faster than sound.

Sound waves, as has been mentioned, are alternations of compression and expansion of the air; they travel at a speed of around 750 miles an hour. Light waves, on the other hand, are pulsations of electromagnetic energy, closely related to such other wavelike forms of energy as cosmic rays, x-rays, radio waves, and electricity. They do not create any motion of the air and indeed can travel through a total vacuum, as they do when light from a star reaches us across the vast expanses of empty space. If you could arrange to make two coins hit together inside a vacuum tube, you would hear no click, because sound waves cannot be formed in a vacuum. But the light waves from a filament inside a vacuum tube shine brightly. They travel at a speed of 186,000 miles a second, the fastest speed known and presumably the fastest possible. (If a light wave could be reflected around the world, it would get back to the starting point in less than one-seventh of a second.)

In the daytime, light waves intense enough to illuminate our entire landscape reach us from the burning fires and explosions of the sun. At night, they reach us by reflection from the moon and, at much lower intensities, from the more distant suns that we call stars. Light waves can be produced by burning a candle or by using electricity to heat a lightbulb's filament.

The physical nature of light

Although light waves are very different from sound waves, there is a close parallel in the way the two kinds of waves produce sensations. Sound waves, it will be remembered, vary only in frequency, amplitude, and complexity, yet variations in these three characteristics produce a wide range of pitch, loudness, and timbre. Light waves also have three variables. They vary in *wavelength,* which is the distance between the peaks of the waves. (The shortest light waves are about 16/1,000,000 inch long; the longest are about twice that length.) They vary in *intensity,* which is the amount of energy they possess. And they vary in *complexity*—that is to say, the light that reaches our eyes may be composed of waves of only a few different lengths or it may be composed

A seventeenth-century concept of vision.

of many lengths. As in the case of sound, these three differences account for the range of sensations produced by light waves.

Wavelength = hue. Just as the frequency of the sound wave contributes to its pitch, so does the wavelength of the light wave help determine its *hue* — the scientific name for the characteristic usually called color. The hues produced by various wavelengths range from violet, for the shortest, to red, for the longest — a range that includes what are ordinarily called "all the colors of the rainbow."

All the sensations of hue, however, can be produced not only by a single wavelength but also by mixtures of various wavelengths — a fact of importance, as will be seen later, to theories of color vision. Light that appears white to us is actually a mixture of the wavelengths of all the hues. When a white light such as a sunbeam is broken down into its components, as by a prism as shown in Plate I,* the wavelengths are separated and the result is a *spectrum* of all the wavelengths and corresponding hues from shortest to longest.

Intensity = brightness. The harder we strike a piano key, the more amplitude we produce in the sound wave and the louder the sound we hear. In vision, the strength of the light wave is called the intensity, and the sensation that the intensity produces is called *brightness*. A 100-watt electric lightbulb produces light waves of stronger intensity than does a 50-watt bulb and thus looks brighter. Or, much as a band sounds louder when it is close than when it is far away, the light from the sun looks much brighter than the light from other, more distant stars, even though some are much bigger.

Just as was noted for hearing, however, the intensity of light waves does not fully account for all the degrees of brightness we see. Our eyes are most sensitive to the green and yellow at the middle of the spectrum, and under good illumination these hues look brighter than violets or reds of equal intensity.

Complexity = saturation. The third way in which light waves vary is illustrated in Plate II. In the squares of Plate II the hue of red does not change. Nor does the brightness. But as more and more gray is added — thus mixing in wavelengths of all the other hues — the red that we see becomes what might be called "less red," or "duller," or "muddier."

This characteristic of the visual sensation is called *saturation,* which can be defined as the degree to which one particular hue is "pure," or unmixed with other wavelengths. You will note that again there is a parallel of sorts with hearing. In hearing, the complexity of the sound wave determines timbre. In vision, the complexity of the mixture of light waves determines saturation.

*The color plates can be found between pages 178 and 179 of this chapter.

The structure of the eye

The receptors for the sense of vision lie in a small patch of tissue at the back of each eyeball, called the *retina*. Each retina, if flattened out, would appear as an irregular circle with a diameter of a little less than an inch and a total area of only about three-fourths of a square inch—about the size of a quarter. Yet with these two very small items of sensory apparatus we can clearly see the much larger pages of a book such as this and indeed an entire room; from an airplane we can see thousands of square miles of the landscape.

This would be impossible unless the eye, in addition to its receptors, had some sort of equipment for bending light waves and focusing them sharply on the retina, much as a fine camera takes a sharp photograph of a wide sweep of landscape by focusing the light waves on a small piece of film. The structure of the human eye, indeed, greatly resembles a camera. If you have ever taken photographs, particularly with one of the more complicated cameras that must be focused and set before each picture, you will feel right at home with the diagram of the eyeball in Figure 5-11, which should now be studied carefully.

5-11

A cross section of the eye

Light waves first strike the *cornea*, a transparent bulge in the outer layer of the eyeball. The cornea serves as a sort of preliminary lens, gathering light waves from a much wider field of vision than would be possible if the eyeball merely had a perfectly flat window at the front. The waves then pass through the *pupil*, which is an opening in the *iris*, a circular arrangement of muscles that contract and expand to make the opening smaller in bright light and larger in dim light. (When you look at your eyes in a mirror, the pupil is seen as the dark, almost black circle at the center; the iris is the larger circle around it and contains the pigments that determine eye color.) Behind the pupil lies the transparent *lens*, the shape of which is controlled by the *ciliary muscles.* The lens focuses the light rays on the *retina*, which contains the light-sensitive receptors of the eye; the most sensitive part of the retina is the *fovea*. Messages from the receptors are transmitted to the brain by way of the *optic nerve*, which exits from the back of the eyeball, a little off center. Attached to the eyeball are muscles that enable us to look up, down, and sideways. The space inside the eyeball is filled with a transparent substance, as is the space between the cornea and the iris. (11)

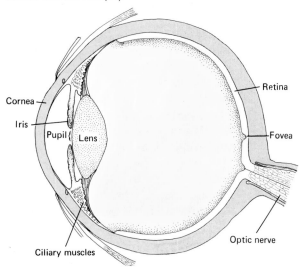

5-12

Hold the book at arm's length, close your right eye, and look at the face on the right. Now move the book slowly closer. When the image of the cat at the left falls on the blind spot of your left eye, it will disappear. To demonstrate the blind spot of the right eye, repeat with the left eye closed and your gaze concentrated on the cat at the left.

The iris and pupil of the eye resemble the diaphragm at the front of a camera. When the pupil is opened to its maximum size, it admits about seventeen times as much light as when it is contracted to its smallest size. The lens of the eye serves the same purpose as the lens of a camera but in a way that would not be possible with even the most carefully designed piece of glass. The lens of a camera has to be moved forward and backward to focus on nearby or faraway objects. The lens of the eye remains stationary but changes shape. The action of the ciliary muscles makes the lens thinner to bring faraway objects into focus and enables it to thicken to focus on nearby objects.

As we grow older, the lens of the eye starts to harden gradually; the process begins almost at birth and continues constantly throughout life. Therefore most people over the age of forty-five have to wear glasses for reading. By the mid-forties the lens has grown so hard that it can no longer thicken sufficiently for sharp focusing on a nearby object such as a book, and the help of an artificial lens is needed.

At the point where the optic nerve exits from the eyeball it creates a small gap in the retina; there are no receptors for vision at this point. The area is almost insensitive to light and is therefore known as the *blind spot*. We are never aware of this blind spot in ordinary life, but you can discover it by examining Figure 5-12.

The receptors of the eye

Any experienced photographer would tell you that the lens of an expensive camera is sharper than the lens of the human eye and that the camera diaphragm has a much wider range than the iris. But a comparison of the very best camera film to the retina is something else again. The retina is sensitive to very low intensities of light that would not register at all on photographic film and at the same time it can function under very high intensities of light that would completely burn out a photographic film. Most important of all, it responds continuously, without any winding from one frame to the next. At this instant you see these words on the page; if you raise your eyes slightly, you immediately see the wall of the room; if you shift your eyes again, you look out the window and see the landscape—all in one continuous and uninterrupted series of visual sensations. In photographic terms, the retina is a highly versatile "film" capable of constantly renewing itself.

Packed into the small area of each retina are about 125,000,000 recep-

178

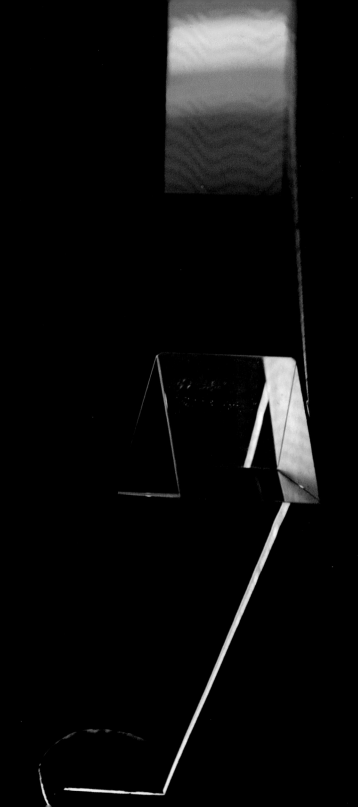

Plate I THE HUES OF THE SPECTRUM

A beam of white light passing through a prism is turned into a *spectrum*. The explanation is th[at] sunlight is a mixture of all the wave lengths to which our eyes are sensitive: the prism, bend[s] each wave length at a slightly different angle, separates the mixture into all the component w[ave] lengths, each of which has its own color or, to use the more scientific term, *hue*. The violets [are] the shortest wave lengths to which our eyes are sensitive, the reds the longest.

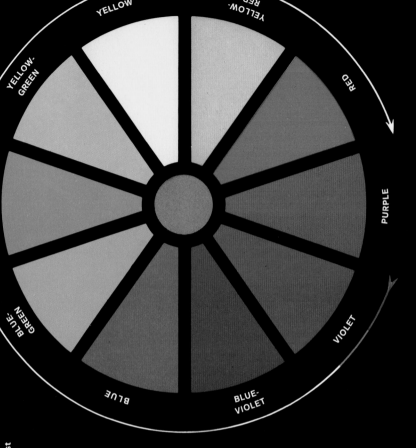

HUES OF THE SPECTRUM

YELLOW-GREEN

YELLOW

YELLOW-RED

GREEN

RED

PURPLE

BLUE-GREEN

VIOLET

BLUE

BLUE-VIOLET

Plate II SATURATED VERSUS UNSATURATED COLOR

This series of colors shows what happens if we start with the purest possible red wave length and then gradually add more and more gray of equal brightness. The square at the extreme left is said to be completely saturated. The square at the extreme right is the least saturated red that can be distinguished from pure gray.

Plate III COLOR MIXTURE

When light waves are combined by projecting filtered light waves onto a screen, some of the results are these. One projector provides the hue at left, the other the hue at right. The mixture of the two hues is in the center. For an explanation, see Plate IV and the text.

Plate IV A CIRCULAR GUIDE TO THE HUES

The laws of color mixture can be summarized by bending the spectrum into an incomplete circle, as shown here, and filling in the gap with the purple that is also seen as a very distinct hue. (Purple is a combination of the wave lengths at the red end of the spectrum and the wave lengths at the violet end.) To find what hue a mixture of any two colors will produce, draw a line between them. If the line passes through the center of the circle, the result will be gray. If not, the result will be the hue midway between the two hues being mixed.

Plate V A TEST OF COLOR BLINDNESS

In the circle at left, people with normal color vision see the number 92; in the circle at right, they see a 23. Totally color-blind people see no number at all in either circle. These are two of the ingenious combinations of hues and brightnesses that make up the Dvorine Pseudo-Isochromatic series of color-blindness tests.

(Reproduced by permission of the author of the Dvorine Pseudo-Isochromatic Plates, published by the Scientific Publishing Co., Baltimore. Md.)

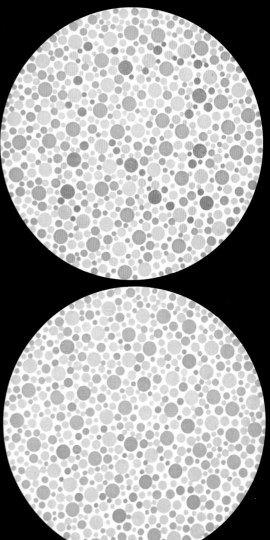

Plate VI   THE VISUAL AFTERIMAGE

The principle of the afterimage produces a startling effect in this modern painting. Look at the top rectangle for about half a minute, fixing your gaze on the
white spot in the center. Then shift your eyes quickly to concentrate on the
dark spot in the lower rectangle. (This painting, ''Flags,'' is by Jasper Johns. Oil
on canvas with raised canvas, 1965. Collection: the artist.)

tors. Most of them are rather long and narrow in shape, a fact that has given them the name *rods.* About 5 percent of the receptors are somewhat thicker and are tapered; these are called *cones.* The rods function chiefly under conditions of low illumination and send information to the brain about movement and about whites, grays, and blacks but not about color. The cones function in bright light and provide information not only about movement and about the black-white dimension but also about color. The cones are most numerous toward the center of the retina; indeed there is one small but important area at the very center, called the *fovea,* that contains only cones, packed together more tightly than anywhere else.

The manner in which light waves stimulate the receptors of the retina was discovered many years ago when physiologists managed to extract a substance known as *visual purple* from the rods. Visual purple is highly sensitive to light, which bleaches it at a rate depending on the intensity and wavelength. Thus light waves striking the retina produce chemical changes in the visual purple, and these chemical changes cause the rods to fire (12).

More recently, it has been found that the cones also contain substances somewhat akin to visual purple. There are three kinds of cones. All three show chemical changes, and therefore fire off their messages, in response to a broad range of wavelengths—but one is most sensitive to the wavelengths at the red end of the color spectrum, another to the middle wavelengths of green, and the third to the wavelengths at the blue-violet end (13, 14).

From receptor to brain

When the receptors fire, they discharge their messages into a highly elaborate network of very short nerve fibers at the back of the retina, as shown in Figure 5-13. This network, which is extremely important in

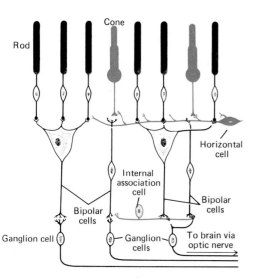

Rod
Cone
Horizontal cell
Internal association cell
Bipolar cells
Bipolar cells
Ganglion cell
Ganglion cells
To brain via optic nerve

5-13

The retina's rich network of nerves

This is a simplified diagram of the elaborate network of nerves through which messages from the rods and cones of the retina are transmitted to the optic nerve and thence to the brain. Messages from a number of individual receptors are picked up by tiny nerves known as *horizontal cells, bipolar cells,* and *internal association cells* and eventually are transmitted to the *ganglion cells.* A single ganglion cell may receive messages from only a few receptors, as do those serving the cones in the fovea, or from several thousand receptors, as do those serving the rods in the outer part of the retina. Moreover, messages from the cones are routed through the network to not just one but several ganglion cells. When you remember that there are about 125,000,000 rods and cones in the retina, constantly being fired by light waves and discharging their messages into this network, you can appreciate the very complicated nature of the patterns of nervous activity that go on at the back of the retina and the wide variety of messages that can then be transmitted to the brain through the fibers of the optic nerve. (15)

vision, acts as a sort of funnel between the retina, with its 125,000,000 rods and cones, and the ganglion cells of the optic nerve, which has only about 1,000,000 fibers over which messages are finally transmitted to the brain.

Ganglion cells serving the outer part of the retina, composed mostly of rods, get messages from as many as several thousand receptors. But ganglion cells serving the densely packed cones in the fovea get messages through the network from only a relatively few receptors. Moreover, each cone in the fovea sends its messages to several different ganglion cells, each of which compares the information coming from this and other cones and thus extracts different kinds of information from the different patterns of messages it receives. Thus our vision is sharpest—in scientific language, has the most *acuity*—at the fovea. When we read or do anything else that requires a very sharp image, we keep the object in the center of our field of vision so that its light waves fall on the fovea. Because fewer receptors feed into each ganglion cell — and because each ganglion cell is capable of distinguishing among many possible patterns of messages—the ganglion cells serving the fovea can send along rather precise information on the exact part of the retina that has been stimulated and by what kind of object.

On the other hand, the outer part of the retina is most sensitive to low intensities of light. This can be noted by finding a very dim star in the skies at night. If you look directly at the star, so that its light waves fall on the fovea, it disappears. But if you glance at it from the side, so that its waves fall on the outer part of the retina, it reappears. One or more ganglion cells, picking up messages from many thousands of receptors, has gathered in enough stimulation through the network to fire off its own message to the brain. The greater sensitivity to light of the outer part of the retina, however, is accompanied by a considerable loss of acuity. The message sent to the brain by the ganglion cell could have originated in the stimulation of any one of the many thousands of receptors it serves. Therefore the exact spot at which the retina was stimulated and the exact nature of the stimulus cannot be specified (16).

How we see color

To understand how the visual sense can produce sensations of color, it is first necessary to know what happens to our sensations when the various hues of the spectrum are mixed—and what happens is not at all what everyday experience would seem to indicate.

For example, every schoolchild who owns a paint set knows that if you have no green, you can produce it by combining blue and yellow — but every schoolchild is wrong. If you combine the wavelength of blue with the wavelength of yellow, you do not get green at all. Until fairly recently, as a matter of fact, nobody had ever combined any of the various hues. You cannot do this with paint, for the following reason.

As was demonstrated in Plate I, the white light from the sun, which illuminates our world by day, is a combination of all the wavelengths of the spectrum. So is the artificial light by which we see at night, though in an imperfect way. (Candlelight and electric light are both yellowish.) The reason that black paint looks black is that it absorbs nearly all the waves, of all lengths, and reflects almost no waves at all back to our eyes. Blue paint looks blue because it absorbs most of the wavelengths except those in and around the blue portion of the spectrum, including, since no paint is a pure blue, some of the green waves. Yellow paint absorbs most of the waves except those in and around the yellow part of the spectrum, including some of the green waves. When you add blue and yellow paint together, you get a mixture that absorbs all the wavelengths of the spectrum except the greenish ones that both the paints happen to reflect. But this is not *adding* light waves; it is more like *subtracting* them.

It was not until the invention of some modern devices that the addition of one light wave to another became possible. One of these devices is the color filter, which permits only waves of a certain length to get through. With two slide projectors equipped with two different kinds of filters, hues of two wavelengths can be thrown on the same white screen and thus mixed, as shown in Plate III.

What happens when two colors are combined in this manner can be summarized by arranging the various hues in a circle as shown in Plate IV. Hues opposite each other on the circle combine into a neutral gray; they are known as *complementary hues* because they cancel each other out. Blue and yellow are complementary hues and therefore a true mixture of the two produces a gray—not the green produced by mixing blue and yellow paint. Two hues that are not opposite each other on the circle combine into a hue that is somewhere in between them on the circle.

As for psychology's attempt to explain how the eye can detect all the various hues, alone or in mixture, one of the most interesting aspects is the fact that a theory proposed more than a century ago, before much was known about the chemistry of the retina or the transmission of nerve impulses from retina to brain, has held up remarkably well. This was the *Young-Helmholtz theory,* which occupies a justly famous place in psychological history. The theory held that the eye contained three types of color receptors, for red, green, and blue, and that a combination of activity by the three receptors could account for all possible sensations of color. The facts about color mixture would appear to support the theory—especially the fact that yellow, though it looks like a basic hue in its own right, can be produced by mixing red and green, as shown in the middle picture of Plate III.

Color vision and color blindness. There are other facts, however, that do not fit so neatly into the Young-Helmholtz theory. One is the matter of color blindness, a phenomenon interesting both in its own right and for its relevance to theories of vision.

For a good test of color blindness, turn to Plate V. Take a quick look at the two circles. Note the numbers you see in them, if any. Then read the caption. . . . If you yourself have passed the test, try showing it to some of your friends—especially male friends. You should soon come to one who fails; and if so, you will have an experience that is worth going to some trouble to obtain. It seems almost unbelievable that you can look at the circle and clearly see one number, while someone else clearly sees another number or is absolutely sure that there is no number at all.

The reason for picking male friends for the test is that far more men than women suffer from color blindness. Only about one woman in a thousand is color blind, but about seven men in a hundred have some form of this visual defect. Total color blindness, in which the world is seen only in shades of gray, like a black-and-white photograph, is extremely rare—probably limited to only about 5000 people in the entire United States. The most common form involves a difficulty in distinguishing between reds and greens. Less common is an inability to distinguish blues and yellows.

The fact that color blindness tends to affect one or the other of these two pairs of colors, red-green and blue-yellow, indicates that there is some kind of connection in the visual process between red and green and between blue and yellow. The same indication, for which the Young-Helmholtz theory provides no ready explanation, comes from another visual phenomenon called the *afterimage*.

Color vision and afterimages. A striking demonstration of the afterimage is provided in Plate VI, and you should experiment with the illustration, according to the instructions, before you go on to the next paragraph.

What happens when you look at Plate VI as suggested is this: by staring fixedly at the pattern of colors, you provide a prolonged stimulus to the retina. When the stimulus is then withdrawn (as you withdrew it by transferring your gaze to another part of the page), you see an afterimage that is in complementary colors to the original stimulus. If you follow the instructions carefully, this afterimage should be so vivid as to startle you—if not on the first try, at least after a little practice.

You can get the same effect anywhere by staring fixedly at a color or a pattern of colors and then quickly transferring your gaze to a blank surface such as a ceiling or a blank wall. The afterimage also occurs with blacks and whites. If you look for a long time at a white square and then at some kind of neutral gray surface, you will see a black square—and vice versa.

Actually, although this is difficult to show except under laboratory conditions, there are two afterimages. Immediately after the stimulus is withdrawn you see a *positive afterimage,* in the same color as before. But this quickly vanishes and is replaced by a longer-lasting *negative afterimage,* in which the complementary colors appear. Only the sense of vision, and no other sense, operates in this fashion.

How can the afterimages be explained? Like the facts of color blindness, they indicate some kind of pairing between red and its afterimage of green, and between blue and its afterimage of yellow. Since the

Color theorist Hering.

Young-Helmholtz theory cannot account for any such pairing, a different kind of theory was proposed, also many years ago. This attempt at explaining color vision, the *Hering theory*, is also famous in psychological history and another example of an early guess that has proved to be remarkably close to the facts, though not entirely correct.

The Hering theory proposed that the eye has three kinds of receptors, each working in two ways: black-white, red-green, or blue-yellow. Thus a red stimulus would produce a change in the chemical substance of a red-green receptor, causing it to fire off signals producing the sensation of red. When the red stimulus was withdrawn, the chemical change in the receptor would continue momentarily, accounting for the positive afterimage. Then the opposite kind of chemical change would occur as the receptor "returned to normal," so to speak. This change would cause the receptor to fire off the opposite kind of signal producing the afterimage of green.

The current theory. Now that scientists have methods of examining nerve impulses in individual receptors and in nerves leading from the eye to the brain, it has been found that a more accurate explanation of color vision seems to be this: the Young-Helmholtz theory was correct in regard to the receptors of the eye; the Hering theory, though wrong about the receptors, was very close to correct about the chain of processes that conveys messages from the receptors to their eventual destination in the brain.

As was said earlier, it has been found that there are three types of cones, one most sensitive to red, another to green, and another to blue — very much as the Young-Helmholtz theory proposed. But it also appears that the nerves between the receptors and the visual area of the brain, starting with the bipolar cells that were shown in Figure 5-13 and continuing with the other links of the chain, operate much as the Hering theory suggested. They pick up messages from the receptors that are then sent along as signals paired either as red-or-green or as blue-or-yellow.

There appear to be four kinds of nerve cells for color vision that make up the chain, all behaving in different ways in response to different kinds of stimuli reaching the eye. One shows a burst of activity when the stimulus is red but is "turned off" by a green stimulus. Another shows a high rate of activity when the stimulus is green, a low rate when the stimulus is red. The third type is activated by blue and slowed down by yellow, the fourth type activated by yellow and slowed down by blue. There are also two other kinds of nerve cells that appear to be responsible for black-and-white vision and sensations of brightness. One is "turned on" by white or bright stimuli and "turned off" by black or dark stimuli; the other works in exactly the opposite fashion and is "turned on" by dark stimuli (17).

Because of these off-and-on pairings of the nerves, the new explanation of vision is known as an *opponent-process theory*. The opponent process explains why color blindness tends to exist in red-green or blue-yellow pairs and helps explain the phenomenon of negative after-images. It also explains why we can see colors such as greenish-yellow but never experience a sensation such as greenish-red. The nerve cells activated by green and yellow can operate at the same time—but the nerves responsible for green and red operate by the opponent system and are "off" for one of the two colors when they are "on" for the other.

The contemporary view of how vision takes place is of course a pattern theory. Because of the especially complicated nature of the visual process it is more complex than explanations of the other senses, but it is a pattern theory nonetheless. A visual stimulus sets up a pattern of response from the rods and the three kinds of cones in the retina. This pattern in turn stimulates the bipolar cells and the ganglion cells (again see Figure 5-13) to their own pattern of nervous activity, with the six kinds of opponent cells for red-green, blue-yellow, and bright-dark all behaving in different ways. It is the total pattern of these nervous impulses, arriving at the brain, that determines what we see.

Visual adaptation and eye movements

One important aspect of vision remains to be discussed: this is the fact that the eyes can function under an extremely wide range of illumination. Many everyday experiences bear this out. For example, you are walking down a street in the glare of the summer sun; then you enter a movie theater where there is hardly any light at all. At first the inside of the theater seems pitch-black, and you have trouble finding your way down the aisle and into an empty seat. But after a while, as your eyes get used to the dark, you find that you can clearly see the aisles, the seats, and the people around you—so well that if you happen to have sat down near some friends, you will easily recognize them.

Full adjustment to dark conditions takes about an hour, and at this point the eyes are about 100,000 times more sensitive to light than they were in the bright sunlight. Note that we do not see colors in a dimly lighted place such as a theater—nothing but shades of gray. This is because our vision then depends on the rods; the color-sensitive cones cannot function at such a low intensity of light.

Under special conditions, the receptors of the eyes can be shown to obey the general rule of sensory adaptation, which, as has been mentioned, is that all receptors tend to adapt to a steady level of stimulation and eventually stop responding. One investigator has invented a sort of miniature "slide projector" that can be attached to the cornea of the eye, where it continues to throw its picture on the same receptors of the retina despite any eyelid blinks or eye movements by the subject. Under these circumstances, the receptors of the eye adapt and stop responding rather quickly (18). Indeed a small stimulus such as a fine line disappears within a few seconds (19).

Under ordinary circumstances, however, we never have this kind of experience; and certainly our field of vision never goes completely blank as the rule of sensory adaptation might predict. The reason is that our eyes are in constant motion, shifting all the various stimuli in our field of vision from one part of the retina to another. For one thing, the eyeballs make spontaneous movements—like tiny but very fast pendulum swings, at the rate of 30 to 100 per second. For another, we are continually making voluntary shifts of our eyes. This is quite obvious in reading. You can observe that when studying this paragraph you gaze first at a word or two at the beginning of a line; then your eyes "jump" to the next word or words, and so on until you have reached the end of the line, when they jump to the start of the next line. In a line of print the width of this one, your eyes make five to fifteen jumps and stops.

Even when we think we are looking steadily at some stimulus such as a photograph, our eyes move constantly, as is shown in Figure 5-14. We do not stare fixedly at an object, even when we think we are doing so, but instead scan it—almost feature by feature and line by line. Our eyes, making these scanning movements, receive an impression of one part of the object, then another, then another, on and on until we have seen the whole as a succession of many different parts. The process can be compared to the creation of a mosaic, put together by the brain from a rapid succession of pieces of information from the eyes.

To prove for yourself the importance of this scanning and "putting together," try a little experiment next time someone is driving you through the countryside. As the automobile approaches the top of a hill, close your eyes. When the car starts down the other side, open your eyes, take a quick look at the new landscape that spreads out in front of you, close them again—and discover how little your eyes have told you about that landscape. Perhaps you know that you saw some horses and cows—but how many? Were they moving or grazing? How many houses did you see? What color were they? Did the road ahead of you curve to the left or to the right?

You will probably be surprised to realize how few such questions you can answer. You *thought* you saw the landscape—but you actually saw very little of it.

5-14

A pattern of eye movements

The pattern of lines was made by bouncing a light beam off the white of a man's eye as he looked at the photograph of the girl, thus recording his eye movements. Note how many movements took place and how they trace all the important elements of the photograph.

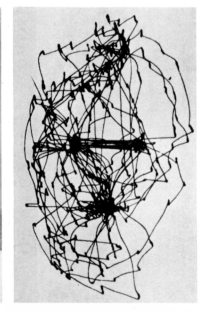

Bodily movement

Exploration of the "five senses" has now been completed, but, as was pointed out earlier, there are two other senses that are less prominent and less obvious but equally important in enabling us to function.

Perhaps the most vital of the senses is our sense of bodily movement —a sense that most people never even realize they possess. One way of demonstrating the existence and importance of this sense is as follows. Close your eyes and then point a finger straight up toward the ceiling, down toward the floor, off to your due left, and then to your due right; stand up; raise your left knee and touch it with your right hand.

What you have just done may not seem very remarkable; it is something that we take for granted. But think about it for a moment. How did you know where your arm was to begin with, and how did you know when you had moved it so that your finger was pointing up, down, or to the sides? How did you know where your left knee was and how to move your right hand to touch it?

None of your "five senses" helped you do this; they had no way of telling you about the position of your arms and legs and could only verify the fact, through the pressure receptors of the skin, that you had actually succeeded in finding and touching your knee. You could never have done what you did without the sense of bodily movement, which keeps us constantly informed of the position and movement of our muscles and bones.

The receptors for the sense of bodily movement are nerve endings found in three parts of the body. The first are in the muscles, and they are stimulated when the muscle stretches. The second are in the tendons that connect our muscles to our bones; they are stimulated when the muscle contracts, putting pressure on the tendon. The third, and apparently most important, are in the linings of the joints between our bones, and they are stimulated by movement of the joint.

Without these receptors we would not be able to walk without great difficulty; we would have to keep constant watch with our eyes to help guide the motions of our legs and feet. Even with the help of our eyes we could never perform the rapid and closely coordinated movements required to dance or to play baseball.

Equilibrium

When we walk, we walk erect, not at an angle to the ground. When we lose our footing and start to fall, we catch our balance through reflex action, without even thinking about it. Standing in a closed elevator and unable to see any motion, we nonetheless know when we start to move and whether we are moving up or down, and we also know when we stop. If we sat blindfolded in a totally silent swivel chair, we would know immediately when someone began to rotate the chair.

All these facts depend on our sense of equilibrium, the receptors for which are in the inner ear. If you look back at Figure 5-10, you will note that the cochlea, containing the receptors for hearing, is only one part of the inner ear. The rest of the inner ear is made up of three *semicircular canals,* extending out from a *vestibule*. The canals are filled with liquid, and the liquid in one or more of the canals is set into motion any time we move in any direction whatever. The movement of the liquid stimulates hairlike receptors with which the canals are equipped. In the vestibule, which is also filled with liquid, the hairlike receptors are matted together and tiny pieces of stonelike crystal are embedded in the mattings. The little crystals put pressure on the receptor cells in the direction of the force of gravity and keep us oriented to an upright position even when we are not moving. Between them, the receptors of the canals and the receptors of the vestibule are constantly aware of the

position of the head and any change in position, thus providing the messages needed to keep us in balance and oriented to the force of gravity. The messages operate by reflex action to produce the muscular movements required to preserve our equilibrium.

Perhaps the most dramatic evidence of how the sense of equilibrium operates is an old experiment involving a lobster—chosen because its equivalent of the human inner ear is readily accessible when the lobster sheds its shell. For the stones that are the lobster's equivalent of the crystals in the human vestibule the experimenters substituted iron filings. These worked just as well as the stones, and the lobster had no problem of equilibrium. But when a magnet was placed above the lobster, exerting a stronger upward force on the iron filings than the downward force of gravity, the lobster turned right over on its back.

Summary

1 The role of the senses in human behavior is to keep us informed about the kind of world we live in and especially about how the world around us is changing from moment to moment.

2 The two essentials of sensation are a *stimulus,* any form of energy capable of exciting the nervous sytem, and a *receptor,* a nerve ending capable of responding to a particular stimulus.

3 To cause a receptor to fire, a stimulus must be of an energy above the *absolute threshold* of the receptor, and a change in stimulus must be above the *difference threshold.* The thresholds are affected by *adaptation,* the tendency of all receptors to stop responding to a continued level of stimulation.

4 The taste receptors respond to four basic types of stimuli: sweet, sour, salty, and bitter. However, the receptors are "broadly tuned" to respond to a fairly wide range of chemical stimulation.

5 The *pattern theory* of the senses holds that our taste sensations result from the total pattern of nervous impulses sent to the brain by the "broadly tuned" taste receptors. Similar kinds of patterns are believed to explain the operation of the other senses as well.

6 The receptors for smell are stimulated by gases or by molecules that have become dissolved in the air we breathe, much as sugar dissolves in water. The sense of smell accounts for most of the "tastes" we associate with foods—as can be noted from the fact that food seems quite tasteless when our noses are stuffed up by a cold.

7 The skin senses account for our sensations of pressure, pain, cold, and warmth.

8 The stimulus for hearing is sound waves, which are alternations of compression and expansion of the air. Sound waves vary in *frequency, amplitude,* and *complexity.* The frequency determines the *pitch* we hear; the amplitude determines the *loudness* (although not entirely), and the complexity determines the *timbre.*

9 Our ability to tell whether a sound is coming from the left or right is

based on the fact that the sound wave arrives at one ear before the other ear. When it arrives at the second ear, the wave is slightly different in *timing, phase, amplitude,* and *complexity.*

10 Sound waves strike the eardrum and are amplified and conducted by the bones of the middle ear to the *cochlea* of the inner ear, where they set up complicated wavelike motions of the *basilar membrane.* The receptors for hearing are the hairlike cells of the *organ of Corti,* lying on the basilar membrane.

11 The stimulus for vision is light waves, a pulsating form of electromagnetic energy closely related to cosmic rays, x-rays, radio waves, and electricity. Light waves vary in *wavelength, intensity,* and *complexity.* Wavelength helps to determine *hue;* intensity determines *brightness* (although not entirely); and the complexity of the mixture of waves determines *saturation.* White light is a mixture of all the wavelengths, as can be demonstrated by passing it through a prism and obtaining a *spectrum* of the hues.

12 Light waves enter the eyeball through the transparent *cornea* and the *pupil,* which is an opening in the *iris,* and then pass through a transparent *lens,* which is changed in shape by the *ciliary muscles* to focus the waves sharply on the *retina* at the back of the eyeball. The receptors for vision are nerve endings in the retina called *rods* and *cones.*

13 The rods function chiefly under conditions of low illumination and send information to the brain about movement and about whites, grays, and blacks but not about color. The rods contain *visual purple,* a substance that is bleached by light; presumably it is the chemical reaction of the visual purple to light that causes the rods to fire.

14 The cones function in bright light and provide information not only about movement and about the black-white dimension but also about color. There are three kinds of cones; one contains a chemical particularly sensitive to the wavelengths at the red end of the color spectrum, another to the middle wavelengths of green, and the third to the wavelengths at the blue-violet end.

15 In the chain of nerve cells extending from the receptors of the eye to the visual center of the brain, there appear to be six different types, operating on what is known as the *opponent-process theory.* These nerve cells are stimulated by the receptors. One type shows a burst of activity when the receptors respond to a red stimulus but is lowered in activity when the receptors respond to a green stimulus. Another type does exactly the opposite; it is "turned on" by a green stimulus but "turned off" by a red stimulus. There is a similar pair of nerves responding in opposite ways to a yellow or blue stimulus, and another pair responding in opposite ways to white (or brightness) and black (or darkness). The total pattern of nervous impulses, set up by a stimulus in the three types of cones and in the rods, then carried along toward the brain by the six types of visual nerves, accounts for our visual sensations.

16 One outstanding quality of the human eye is the wide range of in-

tensities to which it is sensitive. When the eye is completely adjusted to the dark, its absolute threshold declines to the point where it will respond to a stimulus with only 1/100,000 of the intensity required to cause a response under sunlight conditions. At low intensities only the rods function, and color vision is absent. The cones have a much higher absolute threshold.

17 Under ordinary circumstances, our eyes make a rapid and constant series of movements, focusing on one part of the field of vision, then jumping to another. These fragmentary "pictures" or pieces of mosaic are then put together, by the brain and presumably also by the elaborate network of connecting nerves at the back of the retina, into a unified pattern, so that we seem to be seeing the entire field of vision as a single whole.

18 In addition to the "five senses" we ordinarily think of—*taste, smell,* the *skin senses, hearing,* and *vision*—we have two other important senses. The sense of *bodily movement,* the receptors for which are nerve endings in the muscles, tendons, and joints, keeps us informed of the position of our muscles and bones and is essential for the coordination of such complex movements as walking. The sense of *equilibrium,* the receptors for which are hairlike cells in the inner ear, keeps us in balance and oriented to such forces as movement and gravity.

19 The stimuli and receptors of the human senses are as follows:

Sense	Stimulus	Receptor	Sensation
Taste	Molecules of soluble substances	Taste buds of tongue	Flavors (sweet, salty, sour, bitter)
Smell	Molecules of substances in the air	Nerve endings in olfactory epithelium	Odors (camphorlike, musky, flowery, pepperminty, and so on)
Skin senses	Mechanical energy, heat	Nerve endings in skin	Pressure, warmth, cold, pain
Hearing	Sound waves	Hairlike cells of organ of Corti	Sounds, tones
Vision	Light waves	Rods and cones of retina	Colors, movement, patterns
Bodily movement	Mechanical energy	Nerve endings in muscles, tendons, joints	Position and movement of muscles and bones
Equilibrium	Mechanical energy and gravity	Hairlike cells of semicircular canals and vestibule	Movement in space, pull of gravity

Recommended reading

Gregory, R. L. *The intelligent eye.* New York: McGraw-Hill, 1970.
Hochberg, J. E. *Perception.* Englewood Cliffs, N.J.: Prentice-Hall, 1964.
Kenshalo, D. R., ed. *Skin senses.* Springfield, Ill.: Charles C. Thomas, 1968.
Melzack, R. *The puzzle of pain.* New York: Basic Books, 1973.
Uttal, W. R. *The psychobiology of sensory coding.* New York: Harper & Row, 1973.

Outline

Perception

We human beings move around the world confidently, secure in the belief that we understand the nature of our environment. When we look out a window, we know without thinking that it is a rectangular pane of transparent glass and that through it we see a long stretch of grass, a roadway, and other houses down the block. We know that the houses are three-dimensional and that behind their fronts lie rooms. We know which is farthest from us and which is closest. If there is an automobile in sight, it does not matter whether we see a motionless hood and windshield, a motionless rear window and rear bumper, or a silhouette streaking across our field of vision. We know what we are looking at; if it is moving, we know in what direction and approximately how fast. A sound comes to our ears and we know that it is an ambulance siren. Another sound comes to our ears and we know that it is a voice; the sounds form a natural pattern of words and meaning without any effort on our part. We notice a smell and know that an apple pie is baking and that dinnertime is near.

All this we take for granted. Actually, it represents a quite remarkable accomplishment, as can be realized if we think for a moment of how the world must have seemed to us when we were babies.

Babies can see and hear; they can smell and taste food; their skin is sensitive to pressure, pain, warmth, and cold; they receive sensations from their own bodies arising from such states as hunger and thirst. In other words, they have all the equipment of the senses; and their senses operate, if not nearly so efficiently as they will a little later, at least well enough to bring them many sensations from the outer world and from inside their own bodies. The main difference between the world of babies and the world of adults is not so much that babies lack clear sensations as that they have not yet learned to interpret the meaning of what they see, hear, and feel.

193

Evening Falls, by Rene Magritte (1964)

To babies lying in their cribs, the image of an approaching mother's face that reaches their eyes grows larger. But quite possibly they are not aware that this means she is moving; her head may merely seem to be expanding, like a balloon being inflated. When the mother turns away, she may seem to disappear and to be replaced by a totally different image, that of her back, which the baby has not yet discovered to have any connection with her face. When a baby happens to put a hand under a blanket, quite possibly the hand no longer seems to exist.

Babies have no idea, at first, that the palms of their hands also have backs; they do not know that the bars of their cribs have an opposite side or that beyond the walls of their rooms lie other rooms. A window must seem like a sort of painting on the wall, for babies have no idea that beyond the window is a three-dimensional world full of streets and trees and other buildings down the block. To them the world is a strange panorama in which objects appear and disappear, grow smaller and larger, and vanish entirely when they close their eyes. They are unaware of any connection between the movement of a mother's lips and the sounds that simultaneously reach their ears. When they cry, they do not know that they themselves are the source of the sound they hear.

The baby grows up and becomes a mature human being who sees the world and interprets its sights, sounds, and sensations much as all of us do, yet also in a way that is probably individual and unique. These adult impressions of the world are determined by the important psychological process called *perception*.

Perception is a rather difficult term to define. In making the attempt, we can best start with an example that most of us have experienced. We are riding along a highway. Ahead of us, at the side of the road, we see a dead dog. Then, as we draw closer, we find that we do not see a dead dog at all. It is a piece of rumpled cloth. At one moment there is no doubt in our minds that we are looking at a dog. The next instant we know that we are looking at a piece of cloth. The fact is that we did not see a dog. We did, however, *perceive* a dog. In perception, we scan the stimuli in our world much as an electronic computer in a bank might scan the face of a check, looking for the numbers that will identify it (1). We seek to identify and "make sense" out of the objects in the environment. The process is rapid and more or less automatic; we seem to leap to our conclusions. Sometimes our interpretations, when based on insufficient evidence as in the case of the nonexistent dog at the side of the road, are incorrect. Usually, however, they give us an accurate picture of what is going on around us—and thus help us to take appropriate action.

Perception, then, is *the process through which we become aware of our environment by organizing and interpreting the evidence of our senses*. The word is also applied to the impressions of the environment that we obtain as a result of this process. The process of perception—and the perception or interpretation of the environment in which it results—is usually immediate and made without any apparent effort or deliberate thought. We perceive the nonexistent dog, for example, without trying, in fact almost in spite of ourselves, for perception is often a process over which we have little or no conscious control.

Perception influences our entire impression of the world around us, including all the sights and sounds that the world presents to us. As one psychologist has said, "Perception is extracting information from stimulation" (2). Perception also influences our impressions of other people and their behavior. For example, at the end of a day you might think, "My professor sneered at me today." Did the professor really sneer, or did you merely perceive his facial expression that way? Or a young man might say, "My girlfriend was delighted with the present I bought for her birthday." Was she really delighted, or did he merely perceive her behavior that way?

Perception as information processing

As strange as it may seem at first thought, many of the things we seem to see and hear in the world are not really there, or at least not there in exactly the form we believe them to be. The "dog" at the side of the road is by no means unusual in human experience. Some of the illustrations in this chapter will show how easily the perception of an event can be in error. Identical objects seem to be of different size; stationary objects seem to be moving. Many of the ways other people apparently behave toward us—the affection or dislike that they seem to show or the criticism, anger, envy, disapproval, approval, warmth, or praise that they seem to express—are not realities but merely our own biased and incorrect perceptions.

Our senses of vision, hearing, touch, smell, and taste are constantly being bombarded by many kinds of stimuli from the outside world—by light waves, sound waves, the mechanical energy of pressure, and the chemical energy of the things we smell and taste. Out of these stimuli we organize our impressions of an endlessly varied yet stable and consistent world of space and time and three dimensions.

To realize how perception modifies the evidence of the senses, you need only glance at a tree. Look first to the left of the tree, then move your gaze slowly to the right. As you do this, the image of the tree that reaches your eyes definitely moves; the stimuli coming from the tree fall first on one part of your eyes, then cross over to another part. As far as the evidence reaching your sense of vision is concerned, that tree has moved just as surely as if it were an automobile passing across your field of vision as you held your eyes stationary. But the tree does not seem to move. It stays in place. Your perceptual organization of the world says that a tree is a stationary and motionless object, and this is the way you perceive it. This is something that you have learned, as you can tell if you look at the tree again through a pair of binoculars. Since you have never had the opportunity or need to build up a perceptual organization of the world as seen through binoculars, the images seen through the lenses catch you by surprise. As you swing the binoculars from left to right, the tree seems to move.

Perception and learning

Traditionally, perception has been regarded as an independent process, intervening between the operation of the senses and any response to sensory stimuli; and it was thought that this process could be studied and understood without reference to any other psychological activities. But the role that learning seems to play in influencing at least some of our perceptions has inclined many of today's psychologists to view perception in terms of the theory of information processing, which has been previously touched upon on pages 25 and 58–69. These psychologists believe that perception is merely one of a number of interconnected and mutually dependent links in the chain of cognitive activity. In particular, they regard perception as an interaction among the three operations involved in learning, the storage of memories, and the retrieval of these memories (3). In other words, they regard perception as an interaction among the three memory systems that were discussed in Chapter 2 and are again illustrated in Figure 6-1, this time with an emphasis on the perceptual process.

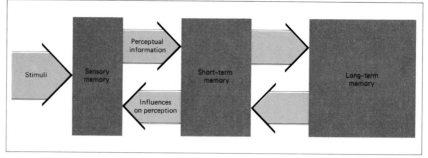

6-1

The perceptual process

The information-processing view of perception holds that it can best be viewed in terms of the three-part memory system that was illustrated on page 63. The brain's store of long-term and short-term memories acts upon information that arrives in the sensory memory from stimulation of the sense organs. Perceptual information is in turn transferred from the sensory memory to the short-term memory, perhaps for further processing and storage in long-term memory.

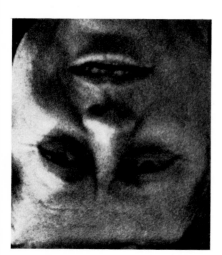

6-2

Whom do you perceive?

Who is this? To find out, you will probably have to turn the page upside down—then the identity will pop right out. For what this demonstrates about perception, see the text. (5)

The information-processing view holds that stimuli in the environment reaching our sense organs result in a sensation held briefly in sensory memory. There the sensation is processed and modified in various ways by the workings of the perceptual process. The resulting perception is then transferred to short-term memory; it may next be stored in long-term memory and later used in thinking and problem solving. But this continuous chain of events also works in the opposite direction: Knowledge held in long-term memory helps determine what is held in short-term memory, and what is held in short-term memory helps determine how our raw sensations are processed into our perceptions (4). Figure 6-1 is only a sketchy attempt to describe the complicated chain of events that the theory assumes. Our perceptions are probably processed and modified not only in sensory memory but elsewhere in the system — and not only by what we have learned but also by some built-in tendencies of the human brain to perceive in certain ways.

Perception versus sensation

Numerous experiments have shown how actively and profoundly the process of perception can alter the raw materials of sensation supplied by the sense organs. One of the simplest demonstrations is provided by an upside-down photograph such as the one in Figure 6-2. The face is very difficult to recognize when presented in this manner but can be identified immediately when turned right side up — even though the elements of the visual stimulus received by the eye have not changed but merely shifted position.

As a variation on the upside-down photograph, note Figure 6-3 and try the suggestion made in the caption before you read on.

Once you have seen that Figure 6-3 is an outline of the map of Africa, try this further experiment. While still holding the book sideways, so that Africa is right side up, tilt your head to the right until your ear is pointing straight down to the floor. Now the drawing occupies exactly the same position in respect to your eyes as it did when you first looked at it without moving the book or your head — yet you see Africa perfectly clearly and right side up.

What Figures 6-2 and 6-3 demonstrate is that a set of stimulus elements is not always perceived in the same fashion. Depending on how we process the information received from our senses, the stimulus may result in very different perceptions. Conversely, stimuli that are very different from one another may result in perceptions that are alike or quite similar. A common example is this: The telephone rings; you pick up the receiver, and a friend says, "How are you?" The friend happens to have a bad cold, so that the voice you hear is completely different from what you are used to. An analysis of the sound waves would show substantial changes in such qualities as pitch and timbre. Yet you recognize the voice immediately; you perceive it clearly as the voice of your friend.

Similarly, you may from time to time encounter many varied forms of the capital letter A. It may be printed large or small, in many different kinds of type face, ranging from simple to very fancy. It may be drawn with a crayon by a young child, with lines that are all crooked and not joined together properly. Yet, no matter how the stimulus varies, you always perceive an A because the pattern of relations among the three lines that compose the letter remains the same.

Presumably the information that is stored in memory and affects perception is not concerned with the absolute value of a stimulus. We do not seem to carry around in our brains a perfect soundtrack of a friend's voice or a perfect picture of the letter A. Instead we apparently store some kind of general pattern of sound and form that is made up

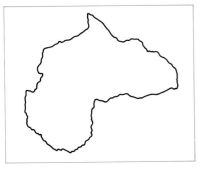

6-3

What is this strange object?

If this drawing looks like anything, it might be a rather poor attempt to depict a horse's head. But turn the book sideways so that the right-hand edge is at the bottom and you will see something very different. (6)

of various relationships among the elements of a sensation. It is this general pattern that influences our perceptions.

Some perceptual illusions

The fact that there is not a perfect relation between a stimulus and a perception has been known for a long time, and many psychologists have been interested in finding ways to demonstrate it. Their efforts have resulted in the invention of some ingenious drawings that bear on the matter. Three of the most famous are shown in Figure 6-4—and it is suggested that you examine this illustration and try to answer the questions in the caption before reading on.

No matter how the drawings in Figure 6-4 may look, the fact is that line A is exactly equal in length to line B in each of them—as you can determine for yourself by measuring them. Here is another case where two stimuli, exactly alike, are perceived in very different fashions.

One of the most common real-life perceptual illusions occurs at the movies. Motion pictures do not really move at all; they are simply a series of still pictures, like snapshots, flashed on the screen at the rate of about twenty per second. When we think we see an automobile crossing a movie screen, we actually see it for about one-twentieth of a second at one spot on the screen, then for one-twentieth of a second a little farther along, and so on. We ourselves "fill in" the gaps and seem to see a continuous movement. Our eyes are the victims—or perhaps one should say the beneficiaries—of the phenomenon called *stroboscopic motion*, meaning apparent motion produced by a rapid succession of images that are actually stationary. The simplest form of stroboscopic motion, called the *phi phenomenon*, is illustrated in Figure 6-5. If the time interval between the flashing of the two lights is arranged properly, the illusion of motion is totally convincing (7).

Going to the movies often produces another kind of perceptual illusion. If you have ever had to sit toward the very side of the theater, down front, close to the screen, you no doubt noticed that the men and women on the screen seemed distorted—very tall and thin, like figures seen in an amusement park mirror. This is indeed the pattern of visual stimuli reaching your eyes at that unusual angle. After a time, however, the distortion probably disappeared; the people on the screen began to

6-4

A test of perception

In the drawing at left, which is longer, line A or line B? In the middle drawing? In the right-hand drawing? After you have decided, see the text to find out if your answers are correct.

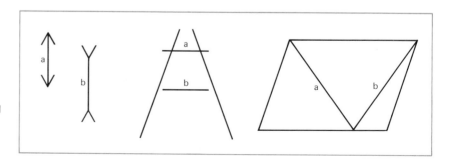

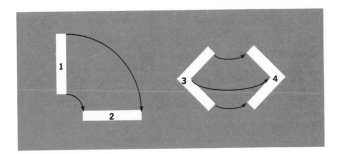

6-5

The phi phenomenon

When a light is flashed behind opening 1 in a screen and an instant later behind opening 2, the bar of light seems to move as shown by the arrows. We perceive light moving across the screen between the two openings even though no light is actually there. When a light at opening 3 is quickly followed by a light at opening 4, the light seems to flip over and move in three dimensions, as if the page of a book were being turned.

look normal again, as if you were viewing them from a better seat. The visual stimuli had not changed: What you saw halfway through the picture was distorted just as at the beginning. But somehow your perception of the stimuli had changed. You had made allowance for the distortion and now saw the people on the screen as having the normal shapes that you know people to have. Much the same thing happens when you watch television. A television picture ordinarily contains considerable distortion; the lines forming the edges of buildings and doors are not quite straight, and the faces are somewhat lopsided. You perceive the picture, however, as perfectly symmetrical.

Attention, selection, and perception

As the previous pages of the chapter indicate, there is by no means a perfect correspondence between the evidence of the world that reaches our senses and our perception of the world. Regardless of whether one chooses to accept the information-processing view or a simpler expla-

nation, it is obvious that perception is some kind of active process with which we greatly modify the evidence of our senses and manipulate it in various ways.

There are two aspects of the perceptual process that deserve special mention. First, perception involves *selection*; that is to say, it represents some kind of decision about which of all the stimuli in the environment to pay attention to. Second, perception also involves *organization*; that is to say, once we have selected the stimuli, we then organize them into our own patterns of meaning. Discussion of these two basic parts of the perceptual process will make up the rest of the chapter.

The problem of selection and attention

During every waking moment our senses are bombarded with a barrage of miscellaneous stimuli. At this instant, for example, your eyes are receiving stimuli not only from this page of the book but also from many other objects that are within your field of vision—the light by which you are reading, the walls of the room, many objects of furniture, perhaps the outdoors as seen through a window. To your ears come many sounds—the crackle of a page as you turn it, someone talking, an automobile going past, perhaps a radio playing softly in the distance. The smell of food cooking may be reaching your nostrils, and on your tongue may linger the taste of a salted peanut. Your skin senses feel many things—the pressure of clothing, the warmth of a sweater, the coolness of a draft blowing across the back of your neck.

You cannot pay attention to all these stimuli at once. You have to select some to which you will give your attention and thrust the rest into a sort of neutral gray background of which you are only dimly aware or perhaps not aware at all. As long as you attend to the words on the page you do not perceive all the other visual stimuli that strike your

eyes. You do not perceive the voice talking, the automobile going by, or the radio playing unless you shift your attention. You are not aware of smells or of the pressure of your clothing unless you deliberately choose to pay attention to them.

Driving an automobile often furnishes striking examples of the selective nature of perception. As you drive along a highway where the traffic is light, you are listening to a football game on the radio. It is an interesting game and you are paying close attention, following every word and every play. Then suddenly an intersection looms ahead. Other cars are moving into the intersection; the lights are changing; you have to slow down, veer into a different lane, watch out for a car that has moved slowly into your path. When the traffic crisis is over, you start listening to the game again and find to your surprise that the score has changed. While your attention was directed elsewhere, a touchdown was scored without your knowing it. The radio was on just as loud as before, but you did not seem to hear it.

Limits and mechanisms of the attention span. Some of the most important laboratory studies of attention have been made with sets of earphones designed to deliver one spoken message to the right ear and a completely different message to the left ear. The results have demonstrated that it is impossible to understand both messages; a subject can pay attention to one or the other, but not to both at the same time. For example, subjects might be asked to listen carefully to the message in the right ear but also to tap with a ruler any time they heard the word *the* in either ear; in one such experiment the subjects caught the word 87 percent of the time in the right ear but only 8 percent of the time in the left ear (8).

If the task is made easier, subjects do somewhat better. For example, they can perceive the sound of a bell or of their own names in the "unattended" ear more often than they can recognize a word such as *the*. If the task is made harder, as by asking them to tap every time any word naming a color is mentioned, they do worse. Experiments of this kind seem to show that some aspect of the messages from both ears is getting through to the brain but that the perceptual process cannot operate efficiently on both if both require mental effort. The more cognitive effort required for processing the messages, the less chance there is of perceiving information with the "unattended" ear (9).

Trying to attend to two different stimuli at once is especially difficult when they involve the same sense organ, as in the case of the earphone messages that both involve the sense of hearing. It is much easier when two different senses are involved — as you may have discovered for yourself by noting that you can continue to read, with fairly good comprehension, while listening on the telephone. Apparently the mental processes required for perception can work better on two different kinds of sensory information than on two messages in the same sensory channel. This fact is probably due to the dynamics of the brain — that is to say, the innate way in which it operates.

The brain and "feature detection"

Indeed, many aspects of perception appear to depend on inborn tendencies. This is not to say that learning is unimportant, but there is no doubt that the perceptual process is determined in many ways by the way the brain just naturally operates, without training or effort.

Using very delicate equipment that makes it possible to measure the activity of individual cells in the brain, experimenters have found that there seem to be specialized cells that respond to specific kinds of sensory stimuli. In one such experiment, measurements were made of the activity of the nerve cells of monkeys or cats in the part of the brain to which the eyes send messages. The animals were placed in front of a screen on which various kinds of visual stimuli were flashed. It was found that some of the brain cells responded sharply to a vertical line on the screen but did not fire at all when the stimulus was a horizontal line (see Figure 6-6). Other cells responded to a horizontal line but not a vertical line. Others responded to angles and still others to movement rather than to any spatial characteristic (11).

Similarly, it has been found that the area of the brain to which the ears send messages contains some specialized cells that are activated only by low-pitched sounds, others by high-pitched sounds, still others only by a change in pitch (12).

These experiments indicate that the brain is so constructed as to be particularly sensitive to certain patterns of sensory stimuli. The specialized brain cells have been called *feature detectors.* As the phrase implies, the cells respond to various specific characteristics of what we see and hear. They detect such features of a visual stimulus as movement and pattern (horizontal and vertical lines and angles), such features of an auditory stimulus as pitch and change of pitch.

Stimulus characteristics and selection

Presumably because of the way the brain and its "feature detector" cells operate, some stimuli in the environment attract us more than others. They seem to compel our attention, dominating the selection process

6-6

How a "feature detector" cell works

The spikes in the graph lines represent the activity of one of the "feature detector" cells in a cat's brain. In response to a horizontal line, the cell displays only its normal amount of spontaneous activity; to an oblique line, there is a small response; to a vertical line—the kind of feature to which this cell is specifically sensitive—there is a sharp burst of activity. (10)

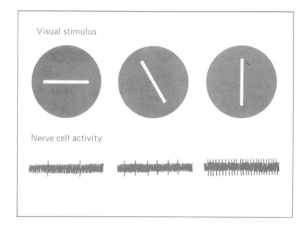

automatically. Among the stimulus characteristics that we are most likely to select to pay attention to are the following.

Change. This is the most compelling stimulus characteristic of all; any change in the environment is likely to be perceived immediately and without effort. When a radio is playing softly in the next room while we are reading, we are likely to ignore it; but we notice at once if the sound stops. We are instantly aware of the change when a light dims because a filament has burned out or when it becomes brighter because of a sudden surge of electricity. This may be partly a matter of sensory adaptation. As was explained in Chapter 5, our sense organs adapt rather rapidly to any steady and continued level of stimulation and quit responding. But this awareness of change also seems to depend on perceptual processes in the brain. Thinking in evolutionary terms, it seems logical that an organism with a nervous system geared to detect change — such as the sudden appearance of a dangerous intruder — would have an advantage over organisms lacking this built-in ability.

Besides being attracted to a change in the intensity of a stimulus, we tend to be attracted to a change in its quality. For example, we are in a restaurant where a number of people are talking at once, all around us. After a while we hear only the conversation at our table; the rest is just background noise to which we have adapted and stopped responding. But now a baby cries in the room. The cry does not make the background noise any louder or softer than before, but we are immediately aware of it.

One attention-compelling form of change is *movement*. Even very young babies try their best to follow with their eyes any kind of moving object. If we adults look at a pasture full of horses, those that are running attract our attention more than those that are quietly grazing. An advertising sign that uses stroboscopic motion is a better attention-getter than a sign whose message remains stationary.

Another important form of change is *contrast*—for example, the sharp difference in intensity between two stimuli. If a black triangle is placed in the field of vision of babies only two days old, they will spend most of their time focusing on one of the triangle's sides or angles—the places where there is the sharpest contrast between the black of the triangle and the light background (13). Babies also show an early interest in the human face, especially the face of the mother, and this too is dictated largely by the strong effect of contrast as an attention-getter. What babies notice particularly is the high degree of contrast between a light face and dark eyes or hairline, or between a dark face and the whites of the eyes and the teeth.

Another kind of contrast can involve size. One mountain among many does not necessarily attract our attention; the same mountain on an otherwise level plain would attract us at once. A six-foot man stands out in a room full of smaller men because he is so tall and at a meeting of seven-foot basketball players because he is so short.

Repetition. Repeated presentation of a stimulus often attracts attention. For example, suppose that you are in a football stadium, which in itself constitutes a sort of sea of change—a football game unfolding play by play on the field, the voice on the loudspeaker following the progress of the game, the crowd moving and shouting in reaction. Now, a friend of yours is paged over the loudspeaker. You may not notice the name the first time or two, but, if it is repeated often enough, you eventually will.

Size. Another factor in attracting attention is absolute *size;* in general, a large object is more likely to be noticed than a small object. A mountain that looms on the horizon is a more compelling stimulus than a hill. When we look at the front page of a newspaper, we are attracted to the biggest headlines first.

Intensity. All other things being equal, it is the brightest or loudest stimulus that is likely to attract our attention. If we are driving at night through a downtown street where all the advertising signs are by some coincidence of equal size, the brightest of them seems the most compelling. The blasting noise of a sound truck passing by is likely to draw our attention away from the softer sounds of conversation or of a radio. Similarly, we are more likely to pay attention to a sharp poke in the shoulder than to a gentle tug at the elbow.

Color. Certain colors command more attention than others; they have been found to be more attractive and more easily recognized in experiments both with young children (14) and with members of a primitive tribe whose language does not possess color names that could influence their selection (15). Even very young babies will look longer at red and blue than at green or yellow. Adults tend to report that red and blue are more pleasant colors than green and yellow.

Organization as an element of perception

The "dog" at the side of the road mentioned earlier in the chapter is eloquent proof of how, in the process of perception, we organize the evidence of our senses into patterns. We do not perceive the world as the chaotic and miscellaneous collection of stimuli that reaches our senses. On the contrary, the perceptual process organizes these stimuli into meaningful objects. We perceive not mere patches of light but houses, people, trees, and roadways. (And sometimes, because an error has been made in organizing the pattern, we perceive a nonexistent dog lying at the side of the road.) We hear not miscellaneous sound waves but voices, musical tunes, and doorbells.

Indeed the very goal of perception is to make sense of what we see, hear, touch, taste, and smell. In a way it is a process of finding meaningful relationships among the events in our environment. The manner in which we find and organize these relations appears to be determined in part by the dynamics of the brain and in part by learning.

Note, for example, the picture in Figure 6-7. The sharp contrast between the roof and the sky—or between the trees and the rock—forces us to perceive these objects as separate; in this case our perceptual process seems to be automatic and unlearned. However, there is no pronounced physical separation between the horse and the rider; it is our knowledge of horses and men that makes us perceive them as separate objects. The building and the water wheel *are* separated physically, yet we perceive them as a unit because we know that water wheels are attached to buildings.

6-7

Perception of hidden figures

The drawing contains a number of hidden objects that you are not likely to see at first glance. After you look long enough, however, you will perceive the objects so clearly that they will almost seem to leap out at you.

6-8

The checkerboard pattern

As you look at this collection of colored squares of uniform size and spacing, what do you see? Look at it closely for a time, letting your eyes shift from one part of it to another if you are so inclined, and compare your perceptions with those described in the text.

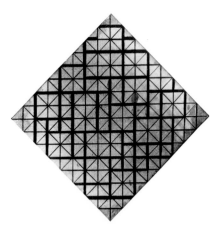

Composition in Black and Gray, by Piet Mondrian (1919)

It should be added that in looking at such a picture we usually select a point of focus or reference, without realizing it, and organize the other information around this focal point. Most people would describe this picture as "A man on a horse passing a house," indicating that they have chosen the rider and horse as their point of reference, probably because a human being is a more compelling stimulus than an inanimate object. It would be very unusual for a viewer to describe it as "A house and some trees with a rider approaching."

Note also that on more careful examination the picture turns out to contain some hidden objects, such as a large cat in the upper left corner. These hidden objects may go unnoticed at first, but once you have become aware that some of the visual stimuli are organized in this manner, it is almost impossible *not* to see them.

For a further demonstration of the part organization plays in perception, you can try an old experiment that requires no more equipment than a few headlines cut from a newspaper. All must be of the same size, and you must not have seen any of them before. Have a friend determine the farthest distance at which you can read the type by testing you with a new headline each time she moves back. Once she has reached a spot just beyond your range of vision, so that you cannot make out the words, have her read the headline out loud and then show it to you again. After you have heard the words, you will find you can read them so easily that you will wonder why you ever had any trouble with them. Here knowledge of the stimulus received through the sense of hearing has helped you to organize the visual stimulus into a pattern, and your perception, at first a blur, is now sharp and meaningful.

One of psychology's first experiments concerned the organization of perceptions. Subjects listened to the sounds of a metronome and it was noted that the clicks were always perceived in some kind of pattern, even though each of them was of exactly the same loudness and presented after exactly the same time interval. One person might perceive them in march time: *click*-click, *click*-click, *click*-click. Another might perceive them in waltz time: *click*-click-click, *click*-click-click, *click*-click-click. Or the sounds might be perceived in more complicated patterns such as CLICK-click-*click*-click, CLICK-click-*click*-click. At any rate, some kind of pattern was always perceived in sounds that of themselves had no pattern.

Another early experimental tool in the study of visual organization was the checkerboard shown in Figure 6-8. Here, much as in the case of the metronome, all the colored squares are of equal size and are equidistant from one another. There is no inherent pattern in the drawing. As we look at it, however, we tend to perceive various patterns, which shift as we continue to stare at it and move our eyes from one point to another. We may perceive horizontal lines, vertical lines, or diagonals. Or we may perceive various patterns in which the individual squares seem to be arranged in pairs or in groups shaped like rectangles or squares.

Factors in organization

Sky and Water II, by M. C. Escher (1938)

6-9

The figure and ground phenomenon

Most people first perceive the drawing at right as a white goblet against a dark background. It can also be perceived, however, as two dark faces in profile against a white sheet. The drawing below is usually perceived as a series of rather strange black figures against a white ground. If you look at it long enough, however, the figure and ground shift into something quite different.

In one way or another, then, we organize our sensory stimuli, often imposing a pattern where in fact none exists. The way we organize seems to be partly a matter of inborn tendencies and partly a matter of learning, though it is difficult to say where one leaves off and the other begins.

Figure and ground. One of the ways we organize our sensory stimuli is demonstrated by what you perceive as you read this paragraph. In terms of light waves, it is composed of many irregularly shaped splotches of white and of black. But you do not perceive a mere jumble of white and black. You perceive letters and words of black, against a background of white. You organize the stimuli into figures that are seen against a ground.

This tendency to organize visual stimuli into *figure and ground* is one of the basic rules in perception. A picture on the wall is perceived as a figure against a ground. So is a chair, or a person, or the moon seen in the sky. The figure hangs together; it has shape; it is an object. The ground is primarily a neutral and formless setting for the figure. What separates the two and sets the figure off from the ground is a dividing line called a *contour*.

One interesting example of how we organize visual stimuli into figure and ground is shown in Figure 6-9, where the contours can be interpreted in two quite different ways. In the upper drawing, you can perceive a white figure against a dark ground, the goblet, or a dark figure against a white ground, the faces. But you cannot perceive both at once.

6-10

Some examples of closure

Though the figures are incomplete in one way or another, we perceive them at once for what they are. (Drawing of cat, 16)

When you perceive the goblet, the faces recede into a formless background. When you perceive the faces, the goblet fades. In the drawing at the bottom of the page the stimuli are meaningless until you organize them into figure and ground; then you clearly see TIE.

Closure. To perceive a figure, we do not need a complete and uninterrupted contour. If part of the contour is missing, our perceptual process fills it in. Indeed we tend to fill in any of the gaps that might interfere with our perceiving an object. This perceptual process, called *closure,* is illustrated in Figure 6-10.

Continuity. Closely related to closure is *continuity,* which is illustrated in Figure 6-11. We tend to perceive continuous lines and patterns, and in any complex visual field we tend to perceive the organization that hangs together with the greatest continuity. The two lines shown at the left of Figure 6-11 have their own kind of continuity, but when they are put together a more compelling kind of continuity makes us perceive them quite differently.

Every beginning photographer has had the embarrassing experience

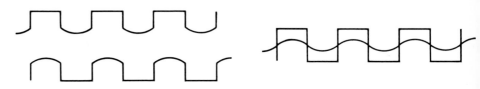

6-11

Continuity in perception

At the left we clearly perceive two continuous lines that are combinations of straight and curved segments. When the two lines are put together as at the right, however, we find it difficult to perceive the original pattern. Instead we perceive a continuous wavy line running through another continuous line of straight horizontal and vertical segments.

of taking an apparently fine snapshot of a friend, only to discover, when the film was developed, that a tree could be seen growing out of the friend's head. At the time the picture was taken the photographer was completely unaware of the tree. This is partly the effect of figure and ground, for the photographer perceiving the friend as figure tends to ignore the rest of the visual field as merely a neutral ground. But it is also partly the result of the continuity factor. When we look at a person's head, we perceive a continuous curved line and are not aware that—seen another way—the curved line merges into the spreading foliage of a tree.

Proximity. When we listen not to a metronome giving out a steady series of clicks but to a device that varies the intervals between the clicks, the patterns we perceive depend on the timing. When we hear click-click . . . click-click . . . click-click (with the dots indicating a pause), we organize the sounds into pairs. When we hear click-click-click . . . click-click-click, we perceive patterns of threes. Indeed, several quite different sounds presented this way, such as click-buzz-ring . . . click-buzz-ring . . . click-buzz-ring, would still be perceived in groups of three.

Such is the effect of *proximity;* we tend to make patterns of stimuli that are close together. This is true not only of sounds presented close together in time but also of visual stimuli that are close together in space, as can be seen in Figure 6-12, square *B.*

Similarity. Much in the same way as we tend to organize stimuli on the basis of proximity, we also make patterns of those that have *similarity.* In Figure 6-12, square *C,* the checkerboard pattern is unchanged except

6-12

The effects of proximity and similarity

Checkerboard *A* is a repetition of Figure 6-8. Note what happens to our perception of the pattern when some of the squares are moved closer together, as in *B,* or when some are changed in color, as in *C.*

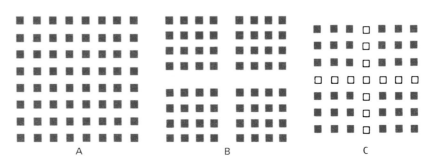

A   B   C

209

6-13

The effect of context

In which of the photographs—un-altered or jumbled—does perception operate more efficiently? For the answer, see the text. (17)

that some of the colored squares have been changed to white—yet the cross fairly leaps from the page at us.

Common movement. Let us try to imagine ourselves in a clearing in an Indian jungle, looking toward a dense growth of trees and foliage. Somewhere in our field of vision is a tiger, poised motionless. Try as we will, we cannot see it. Its stripes blend in so perfectly with the jungle pattern that it is totally camouflaged. Then it moves. Immediately the stimuli become a pattern of their own. The tiger is now an object, and we perceive it clearly. This is the result of the perceptual factor called *common movement*—the fact that when stimuli move together, we tend to organize them into a pattern of their own.

Context. The photographs in Figure 6-13 were used in a recent experiment pointing to another factor in perceptual organization that has been neglected in the past. This is the matter of *context,* or the entire setting in which we view a particular stimulus. In the experiment, some subjects looked at the top photograph, projected briefly on a screen. Then an arrow was projected on the otherwise blank screen, pointing to the spot where the bicycle had been, and the subjects were asked to recall what they had seen at that spot. For other subjects the procedure was the same except that the photograph at the bottom was used. The results showed that subjects who had seen the real-life scene were significantly better at recalling the bicycle than were those who had seen the jumbled photograph. It would appear that meaningful context plays an important part in the organizational qualities of perception.

6-14

What we really see

To the human eye, as to the camera, a close view of the giraffe presents an enormous muzzle, an elongated head, giant eyes and ears, and legs that are tiny by comparison. But we *perceive* the giraffe in proper proportion, without the distortion that the camera records.

Perceptual constancy

Several other factors that play a large part in determining how we organize the evidence of our senses can be grouped together under the term *perceptual constancy*—the fact that we tend to perceive a stable and consistent world even though the stimuli that reach our senses are inconsistent and potentially confusing.

Consider, for example, a stimulus such as the Empire State Building. We may see this building from the sidewalk right in front of it, looking up, or from a very different angle if we are in an airplane. We may see it as a tower in the distance or even as a tiny photographic image on a printed page. All these events constitute very different kinds of visual stimuli—yet we perceive the building as constant and unchanging. When a friend extends a hand to us, the image of the hand on our eyes is far bigger than the image cast by the friend's entire body when at a distance, yet we perceive the friend as of constant size and proportion. The camera, which does not possess the perceptual process, "sees" all kinds of distorted images, as is shown in Figure 6-14. We *see* the same kinds of images, but we *perceive* them without the distortion.

Once we have learned about the objects in our world, we tend to perceive them as constant and unchanging. This perceptual constancy operates with regard to shape, brightness, color, location, and size.

Shape constancy. A door is of course a rectangle—yet we only see it as such when we are directly facing it. While it is swinging open, the visual image of it that reaches our eyes changes constantly and takes many other shapes. But we continue to perceive the door as a rectangle. This is just one common example of the fact that we perceive objects as retaining their shape regardless of the true nature of the image that reaches our eyes—a visual phenomenon called *shape constancy*.

Brightness and color constancy. The light reflected from a black shoe in sunshine may be as bright as the light reflected from a patch of snow in deep shade. A photographic light meter would "see" them as the same and give them the same reading. But to us the shoe looks definitely black and the snow definitely white. Our perceptions of the shoe and the snow are influenced by what is called *brightness constancy*. Similarly, we continue to see a red coat as red and a blue carpet as blue regardless of changes in the light waves that they reflect to our eyes under different lighting conditions—a fact called *color constancy*.

Location constancy. As was explained in Chapter 5, our sense of direction for sounds depends on the fact that sound waves coming from the left strike the left ear a fraction of a second before they strike the right ear, while sound waves from the right strike the right ear first. This has been demonstrated, it was pointed out, by experiments with a laboratory device called the pseudophone, a set of earphones that picks up sound waves that would ordinarily reach the left ear and transfers them to the right ear, while also transferring sounds that would ordinarily reach the right ear to the left ear instead. When a person puts on a pseudophone, sounds get completely turned around; the person may see an automobile traveling from left to right but hear it as moving from right to left. After a few days, it should be pointed out, this changes. The wearer adjusts the perceptual processes and perceives the sounds to be coming from the proper direction.

A similar experiment with vision was performed many years ago by an investigator who built an unusual and elaborate pair of "eyeglasses" that turned the world he saw upside down and reversed right and left. The glasses were a bulky and heavy device, but he persisted in wearing them during his waking hours for eight days. At first he was confused and helpless. Every time he moved his head the world swam about (a fact we might expect from what happens when we look at a tree through binoculars). He had trouble recognizing even the most familiar surroundings and found it almost impossible to feed himself. Gradually, however, the world began to straighten out. Toward the end of the eight days he was able to function quite well; he could avoid bumping into objects and could perform acts such as eating almost without thinking about them. The world no longer moved when he moved his head. Most of it still looked upside down, but he had adjusted his perceptual processes and perceived the location and movement of objects more or less automatically. Indeed he had established new perceptual patterns so thoroughly that when at last he took off the glasses, he again was confused and disoriented for a time (18).

The pseudophone and the upside-down glasses demonstrate that even under the most difficult circumstances we manage to establish *location constancy,* which enables us to perceive objects as being in their rightful and accustomed place and as remaining there even when we move.

Size constancy. The final type of perceptual constancy can be demonstrated by an experiment that requires no more equipment than a full-sized dinner plate and a salad plate of the same pattern, the same in every respect except that it is much smaller. Put the dinner plate on a table, trying not to look at it. Now stand above it, hold the salad plate in front of your face, and look down toward the table. Keeping one eye closed, move the salad plate away from you until it just blots out the dinner plate—in other words, to the point where, if you moved it any farther away from your eye, you would begin to see an outline of the dinner plate.

What you have done, as is shown in Figure 6-15, is set up a situation where the visual images of the two plates are exactly the same size. Now move the salad plate to one side and open both eyes. What you perceive, without question or doubt, is a small plate fairly close to you and a large plate on a table. The dinner plate looks big; the salad plate looks small. You cannot perceive them any other way.

This simple but convincing experiment demonstrates *size constancy*—the fact that we tend to perceive objects in their correct size regardless of the size of the actual images they cast on our eyes. Indeed, we can

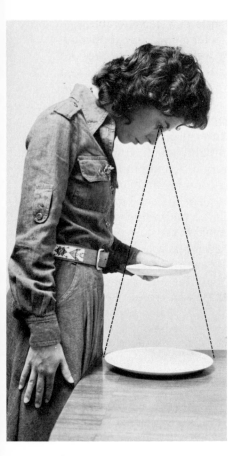

6-15

Which plate looks larger?

Both plates cast images of exactly equal size on the young woman's eye. When she moves the plate she is holding to the side so that she can see both, do they look the same size or does one look larger? You can try the experiment yourself or find the answer in the text.

"Excuse me for shouting—I thought you were farther away."

make excellent estimates of the size of objects at a considerable distance, provided that we have clues as to how far away they are. For example, the Air Force once made tests of how well pilots could judge the height of stakes planted in a field and found that, even when a stake about 6 feet high was nearly a half mile away, the subjects erred by an average of less than 4 inches (19).

Experimenters have devised numerous optical illusions that fool the tendency toward size constancy. The one shown in Figure 6-16 is an interesting manipulation of the relationship between perceived size and perceived distance.

Perception of distance

In our three-dimensional world, the ability to perceive distance is extremely useful. Merely to walk through the world without bumping into doors, furniture, trees, and other people, we must not only perceive these things as objects but also know how far away they are. Our skill at distance perception, which is usually quite accurate, seems to depend on the following clues.

Perceived size. Just as perceived size depends in considerable part on perceived distance, so does perceived distance depend on perceived size. To a large extent, we judge how far away the Empire State Building is—or a basketball being thrown down the court—by how large it seems in relation to other objects in our visual field. Our perception of distance can be thrown off badly if we misjudge size. For example, experiments have been conducted with playing cards much larger or much smaller than the kind people ordinarily use for playing bridge or poker. When seen in a room that affords no other visual clues, the oversized cards always seem closer than they really are, the undersized cards farther away.

Binocular vision. Since our eyes are about 2½ inches apart, they receive different images—a fact that you can demonstrate for yourself by looking at some object in the distance while holding a finger twelve inches

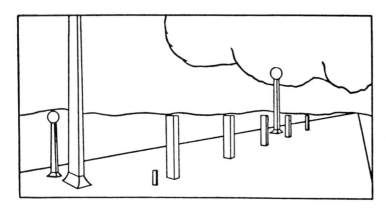

6-16

Perceived size as a function of perceived distance

The lamppost and block of wood at the far right look much bigger than the lamppost at the far left and the block of wood in the foreground. We perceive them as larger because we perceive them as farther away. Actually—as measurement with a ruler will show—the two lampposts and blocks of wood are exactly the same size. (20)

or so in front of your nose. If you close first your left eye and then your right, your finger seems to move, because the image it casts on one eye is in a noticeably different part of the visual field from the image it casts on the other eye.

Ordinarily we focus both eyes on the same object, and the two images are somehow put together in the brain. (Although sometimes, if we are ill or have had too many drinks, this process is disturbed and we "see double.") The slight difference between the two images greatly assists our perception of distance. This fact is the secret of the three-dimensional, or stereoscopic, camera, which simultaneously takes two pictures through two different lenses and on two different pieces of film that are about as far apart as the human eyes. When the two pieces of film are seen through a viewer that presents one to the left eye and one to the right, we perceive a vivid and unmistakable three-dimensional effect.

Focusing our eyes also requires movements of the muscles that control the position of the eyeballs and the shape of the lens of the eye. It is believed that the sensations produced by these movements may also provide clues to perception.

Interposition. This is the term used for the fact that nearer objects interpose themselves between our eyes and more distant objects, blocking off part of the image. The manner in which interposition serves as a clue to distance—such an important clue that when manipulated in the laboratory it can completely fool the eye—is illustrated in Figure 6-17.

6-17

Interposition and distance perception

Two playing cards are arranged as shown in A and are the only objects visible in an otherwise dark room. If we look at them through one eye we see them exactly as shown in A—and the relative size of the two cards tells us clearly that the smaller card is farther away. Now a corner is clipped from the near card, as shown in B, and the stand holding this card is moved to the right, so that the images are seen as in C. When we look at the cards in this arrangement, the cue of interposition now makes us think that we are looking at a small card, close to us, and a larger card farther away. (21)

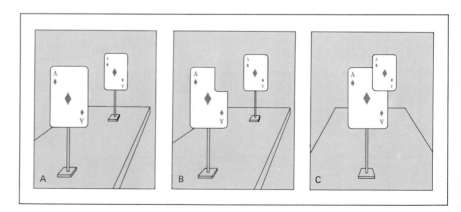

6-18

Perspective and distance

Serving as clues to distance in this single photograph are all three kinds of perspective — linear, aerial, and gradient of texture.

Perspective. Artists learned many centuries ago that they could convey the impression of distance and three dimensions on a flat piece of canvas by following the rules of *perspective,* which all of us use in real life as clues to distance.

Artists speak of two kinds of perspective. One, *linear perspective,* refers to the visual phenomenon that parallel lines seem to draw closer together as they recede into the distance. A good example is railroad tracks or the edges of a highway seen on a level stretch of ground. *Aerial perspective* refers to the fact that distant objects, because they are seen through air that is usually somewhat hazy, appear less distinct and less brilliant in color than nearby objects. If you have lived within sighting distance of mountains or the skyscrapers of a large city, you may have noticed that the mountains or buildings seem much closer on days when the air is unusually clear.

Another factor in perspective is *gradient of texture,* which you can best observe by looking at a large expanse of lawn. The grass nearby can be seen so well that every blade is distinct, and therefore its texture looks quite coarse. Farther away, the individual blades seem to merge, and the texture becomes much finer. This and the other aspects of perspective as a clue to distance are illustrated in Figure 6-18.

Shadowing. The pattern of light and shadow on an object often offers clues that aid in perception of three-dimensional quality. It is shown in

6-19

How shadows create the third dimension

The mere addition of shadowing turns the flat circle into a three-dimensional ball. (22)

Figure 6-19 how the addition of shadows turns what we perceive as a circle on the printed page into a ball. Figure 6-20 demonstrates how an unexpected pattern of shadows can mislead our perception.

Perception of height and depth

One special kind of distance perception concerns the vertical dimension of our world. Imagine yourself standing on a high diving board. At what height are you? Or, to put it another way, how deep is the space beneath you? And how do you know?

Some interesting facts about the perception of height and depth have been disclosed by experiments with the apparatus shown in Figure 6-21. This device, which its inventor has termed a "visual cliff," is a piece of heavy glass suspended above the floor. Across the middle of the glass is a board covered with checkered cloth. On one side of the board the same kind of cloth is attached to the bottom of the glass, making this look like the solid, or shallow, side of the cliff. On the other side

6-20

An illusion formed by shadows

The road seems to be winding down a long hill. But turn the page upside down to see what this really is.

6-21

A baby and the "visual cliff"

At left, a six-month-old baby fearlessly crawls toward his mother on the glass covering the shallow-looking side of the visual cliff. But, at right, he appears afraid to cross over the glass covering the "deep" side. (23)

the cloth is laid on the floor, and to all appearances there is a drop at that side.

As is shown in Figure 6-21, a six-month-old baby crawls without hesitation over the shallow-looking side but hesitates to crawl to the deep side. Animals also show this tendency. A baby chick less than twenty-four hours old avoids the deep side. So do baby lambs and goats tested as soon as they are able to walk.

By manipulating the various clues on which depth perception on the visual cliff might be based, it has been found that the essential one is *motion parallax*. This refers to the fact that when we move our heads, near objects move across our field of vision more rapidly than objects that are farther away. You may have noticed this when on a moving train: the telephone poles along the tracks seem to race past the window, while buildings in the distance do not. When the baby or animal on the visual cliff moves its head, the checks on the cloth at the shallow side move rapidly across its field of vision; the checks on the deep side do not. This clue to depth perception appears to depend on inborn dynamics of the nervous system. It is probably the secret of how even very young animals—particularly those such as goats born into an environment full of mountains and sharp drops—manage to avoid falls.

The perceiver and perception

Many of the rules of perception discussed up to now operate in much the same manner for everyone. Whether because of built-in dynamics of the nervous system or learning experiences common to everyone, or both, all of us seem to base the selection process of perception at least in part on the fact that our attention is attracted to stimuli by change, size, and intensity. We tend to organize the stimuli in general accordance with the rules of figure and ground, closure, continuity, proximity, similarity, common movement, and context. We perceive objects as having constancy of shape, brightness, color, location, and size. We use the same clues and have about the same degree of accuracy in the matter of distance perception.

There are also many factors in perception that depend to a large extent on who is doing the perceiving—and on that person's prior experience, learning, and physical and emotional state at the moment. Since these influences on perception can vary greatly from one person to another, two people exposed to exactly the same stimuli may interpret them in entirely different ways.

Perceptual expectations

One of the most important influences on individual differences in perception is the fact that we tend to perceive what we expect to perceive. At any given moment we are likely to have a sort of "mental set" toward the events in the environment. What we perceive depends to a considerable degree on this set—in other words, on what might be called our *perceptual expectations.*

You can demonstrate for yourself, by trying the simple but convincing experiments suggested in Figures 6-22 and 6-23, how perceptual expectations can influence one's interpretation of a stimulus. It seems al-

6-22

Man or rat?

To demonstrate how perception is affected by expectations, cover both rows of drawings, then ask a friend to watch while you uncover the faces in the top row one at a time, beginning at the left. The friend will almost surely perceive the final drawing as the face of a man. Then try the bottom row in similar fashion on another friend. This friend will almost surely perceive the final drawing as a rat. The psychologists who devised this experiment found that 85 to 95 percent of their subjects perceived the final drawing as a man if they saw the other human heads first, as a rat if they saw the animals first—though of course the final drawings are exactly alike in both rows. (24)

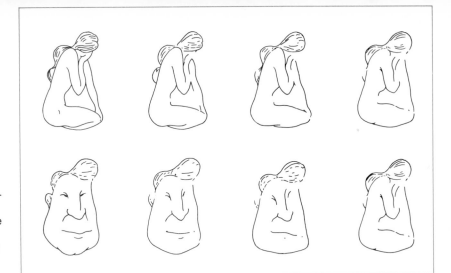

6-23

Face or figure?

Try these drawings on two friends, following the same procedure as in Figure 6-22. Though the final drawings in each row are exactly alike, your friends will almost surely perceive the figure of a woman in the top row, the face of a man in the bottom row. (25)

most impossible that the same drawing could be perceived as a man by one person and as a rat by another—or as a woman's figure and a man's face—yet this is what happens.

Other impressive demonstrations have been made with a laboratory tool called the tachistoscope, a device with which words or pictures can be shown to a subject for very brief exposure times, as small a fraction of a second as the experimenter desires. Many experiments with the tachistoscope have shown that subjects who know in general what to expect can recognize words and objects much faster than subjects who have no idea what is coming. If subjects are told that they will see the names of fruits or vegetables, for example, they perceive the words much more readily than do subjects who have no clues about the nature of the words.

In one of the early experiments with the tachistoscope, one group of subjects was told to expect words dealing with birds or animals and another group to expect words dealing with transportation and travel. Among the words that were then shown, each for a mere tenth of a second, the experimenter slipped in some combinations of letters that were not words at all, though they resembled real words. The first group had a strong tendency to perceive them one way, the second group a very different way. *Pasrort* was often seen as parrot by members of the first group and passport by members of the second group; *dack* as duck and deck; *wharl* as whale and wharf; and *sael* as seal and sail (26). Thus did perceptual expectations influence what the subjects perceived.

Perceptual expectations and context

Many different factors can affect perceptual expectations and therefore what is actually perceived. One of the simplest is the matter of what has happened just before a new stimulus is encountered. This matter of the context in which the stimulus appears is the basis of the different interpretations of the drawings in Figures 6-22 and 6-23. What has just happened creates a mental set; this set affects our perceptions. Experiments have shown, for example, that subjects' estimates of whether various objects are light or heavy depend to a great extent on what they

219

have lifted just before the experiment. If they have lifted a heavy object, they judge other objects to be lighter than the objects really are; if they have lifted a light object, they judge other objects to be heavier (27). Baseball players have made this discovery intuitively; they swing a weighted bat before stepping up to the plate so that their own bat will seem light.

The results of the experiment illustrated in Figure 6-24 show that the same principle applies to the perception of how many objects subjects believe they see. The Group 1 subjects, who consistently overestimated the number of dots shown to them, had looked at a small group of four dots just before the experiment began; the Group 2 subjects, who consistently underestimated the number, had looked at a large group of thirty-two dots. The influence of context has also been found to affect perception of how loud a sound is, the pitch of a sound, the quality of a color, and other sensations.

Perceptual expectations and internal factors

Many different factors that affect the perceiver have also been found to influence perception. For example, the influence of hunger has been demonstrated in an experiment in which three groups of people were asked to describe "pictures" that they were told they would see dimly on a screen. Actually there were no pictures, merely blurs or smudges, but the subjects did their best to perceive some sort of pattern. One group had gone only an hour since eating, another group four hours, and the third group sixteen hours. It turned out that the subjects who had gone four hours without eating thought they saw more objects related to food than did those who had gone merely an hour and that the subjects who had gone sixteen hours without eating "saw" the most food-related objects of all (29).

In another experiment, two groups of subjects were used—one

6-24

Why are these estimates so different?

Subjects in Groups 1 and 2 all looked at patterns of dots shown with a tachistoscope for a half second. The number of dots varied from ten to eighteen. Group 1's estimate of the number shown was consistently too high, while Group 2's estimate was consistently too low. For the reason, see the text. (28)

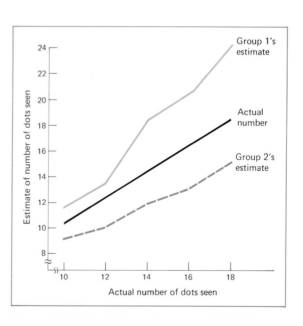

group highly motivated for achievement, the other group with low motivation for achievement. Both groups were tested on words shown with a tachistoscope, some of which, such as *strive* and *perfect,* were related to achievement and others of which were not. It was found that the subjects who had high achievement motivation could recognize the words related to achievement more rapidly than could the other subjects (30).

Another experiment using the tachistoscope was performed with six groups of people who had a high level of interest in religion, politics, economics, society, the arts, or theory. It was found that most of them were quicker to recognize words relating to these special fields than other words. The subjects interested in religion were quick to recognize *sacred,* for example, and those interested in economics were quick to recognize *income* (31).

As has been said, we tend to perceive what we expect to perceive, and the experiments just cited demonstrate that we tend to expect to perceive what we would like to perceive at the moment or what in general we value most highly. In everyday terminology, our perceptual expectations depend on our "state of mind," and our state of mind, in turn, depends on the situation of the moment and on all kinds of prior experience and learning that have resulted in such motives as desire for achievement or acceptance, our various interests and values, and such temporary states as hunger or emotions such as fear or anger.

Some everyday examples

The world is full of everyday examples of how perception depends on the perceiver. The stimuli to which we give our attention, and therefore select for organization and interpretation, frequently are chosen on a highly individualistic basis, so that people who go through the same situation often perceive very different things. For example, a family takes an automobile trip to visit some relatives who live some distance away. The husband, who is thinking about trading in his car, concentrates his attention on the new cars on the highway. The wife, who is a teacher, is hardly aware of the new cars but keenly aware of all the details of the school buildings passed on the way. A son who wants a new bicycle perceives the trip as a succession of children riding various types of bikes.

How we organize and interpret the evidence of our senses is also affected by individual factors. For example, two sisters, living at college, go home for a weekend visit. After an evening of talking with their mother, one sister has noticed that the mother smiled on several occasions, which she takes to mean that the mother is in a happy mood. The other sister has noticed several frowns, which she takes to mean that something is troubling the mother.

Our own individual perceptual expectations have their effect. When we are around an elderly uncle whom we have decided is cranky and critical, we notice his more acid remarks and may not even be aware that a good deal of his conversation is just as pleasant as that of anyone else. Indeed we may interpret as sarcastic many remarks that, said in exactly the same words and tone by someone else, would probably strike us as harmless or perhaps even good-natured. When we are around someone we know likes us and from whom we expect warmth and acceptance, we may be totally unaware of a momentary outburst of anger or hostility.

The role of heredity and learning

For many years, psychologists have been interested in the question of which aspects of perception depend chiefly on inborn factors (such as dynamics of the nervous system) and which depend chiefly on learned factors. Many ingenious experiments have been devised, such as the one illustrated in Figure 6-25, bearing on the influence of early learning experiences on the perceptual abilities of cats. In this experiment, the two kittens had an equal amount of exposure each day to the visual contrast and patterns provided by the striped walls. But one kitten did all the walking, while the other received no experience at coordinating its own movements with its environment. At the end of ten days, the kitten that had done the walking behaved as if it had developed normal perceptions and reactions to its perceptions; it blinked at approaching objects and put up its paws to avoid collisions. The kitten that rode in the gondola showed retarded behavior (32).

The experiment with the two kittens and the gondola is an indication that learning (and especially early learning experience) is important to perception. But other findings, such as the role of "feature detector" cells in the brain as was described on page 202, show the importance of inborn characteristics of the nervous system. The consensus among psychologists today is that both innate factors *and* learning influence the perceptual process—and that it is almost impossible to separate the two of them.

6-25

The kitten that hitched a ride

Two kittens were raised in darkness except for three hours a day in this apparatus. One kitten always did the walking; the other always got a ride. But note that the harness and the gondola are connected in such a way that the kitten that rides faces the striped walls at exactly the same angle as the kitten that walks. For a comparison of the perceptual abilities of the two kittens after using the apparatus, see the text.

The special problem of ESP

Psychological studies of ESP, or *extrasensory perception*, began more than a half century ago but remained a neglected stepchild of the science until very recently. Only a small number of psychologists were interested in the subject. Although these psychologists continued over the years to report experiments indicating that some people seemed to demonstrate an ability to receive messages through channels other than the ordinary senses such as seeing and hearing, their work did not attract much attention.

In recent years there has been a growing interest in ESP. Much of the attention comes from outside scientific circles. ESP has become a popular subject for magazine and book writers and for lecturers, and informal experiments have been attempted by many people—including one of the nation's astronauts, who tried to send and receive mental messages between the earth and his space capsule on its flight to the moon. But the number of psychologists who are seriously concerned with ESP has also increased. There appears to be something about the spirit of the times that encourages a search for phenomena such as ESP.

ESP and parapsychology

ESP, it should be explained, is one of several phenomena that make up the field of *parapsychology*, or the study of psychological events that seem to go beyond normal limits and to defy explanation in any normal scientific way. The increased interest in all these phenomena is reflected in the fact that for some years there has been an official organization called the Parapsychological Association, now affiliated with the American Association for the Advancement of Science.

Three forms of ESP have been studied:

1 *Mental telepathy*, commonly known as "mind reading," in which one person becomes aware of what another person is thinking.
2 *Clairvoyance*, or the ability to perceive an object, such as the next card to be turned up from a shuffled deck, without use of the ordinary sensory channels.
3 *Precognition*, or the ability to perceive something that has not yet happened.

In addition, parapsychologists have also been interested in what is called *psychokinesis*, or the ability to move objects without touching them. An example would be the ability to make a roulette ball drop into a certain number on the wheel through an act of will.

The case for parapsychology

Many experiments in parapsychology have been performed with decks of cards, usually special decks of twenty-five cards made up of five cards each of five different symbols—a star, a cross, a square, a circle, and a set of wavy lines.

In experiments on mental telepathy, the experimenter shuffles the deck and turns the cards over one at a time, concentrating on each symbol that appears. The subject, unable to see the deck, tries to read the experimenter's mind and thus identify each card as it appears. If subjects are merely guessing, the rules of chance would dictate that they would pick the right card one time in five—or five times for each trial of the full deck of twenty-five symbols. Experimenters have reported that many subjects, however, do better than this. One woman tested in England over a period of four years, for example, averaged 6.8 cards correct (33), a result that proponents of ESP say could not possibly be explained by any mere stroke of luck.

In experiments on clairvoyance, subjects are also asked to name the next card that will be turned up, but in this case without any attempt by the experimenter to send a mental message; indeed the experimenter does not know what the card will be. In experiments on procognition, subjects are asked to predict the order of the twenty-five cards before the deck is shuffled. These two types of tests have also produced results, with some subjects, that seem more accurate than mere luck could have accounted for (34).

Another kind of parapsychological experiment was performed with men who were identical twins. The twins were separated and one of them was asked to close his eyes—an action that produces a special pat-

tern of brain waves that can be detected with an instrument called an electroencephalograph (as further discussed in Chapter 7). The other twin was also checked for brain waves at the same instant, to determine what if anything might happen. Out of the fifteen pairs of twins who took part in the experiment, nothing at all happened in thirteen cases. But in the other two cases, the second twin immediately showed the same pattern of waves and did so time after time as the test was repeated (35).

Other researchers have reported apparent success at influencing a sleeper's dreams through mental telepathy. In one such experiment the "sender" of the telepathic message concentrated on a reproduction of a painting; the "receiver," asleep some distance away, reported a dream that had similarities to the painting (36). In one case the "senders" were the entire audience at a rock concert, who concentrated on pictures projected on a screen. The "receiver," asleep 40 miles away, had dreams that seemed to bear a resemblance to the messages (37).

The case against parapsychology

Whether one chooses to view the parapsychological experiments as proof of ESP or as merely some kind of interesting happenstance is another of the perceptual phenomena that seem to depend to a great extent on one's "set." The set of a very large majority of psychologists, it must be reported, continues to be negative.

In the majority view, the whole idea of parapsychological phenomena violates all rules of scientific explanation of events in the universe. As far as mental telepathy goes, the only reasonable explanation would seem to be that brain waves can be transmitted from one person to another—yet brain waves are such a weak form of energy, as will be seen in Chapter 7, that only the most delicate of instruments attached directly to the skull can pick them up. On the matter of clairvoyance, it is impossible to conceive of what kind of signal can pass from a hidden card to the brain of a subject trying to identify it.

Besides having a natural set against any belief in ESP, the skeptics are unimpressed by the evidence. If there is such a thing as ESP, why do only some subjects display it? If only certain people possess it, why can these specially gifted people not name every card in the deck rather than a mere 6.8 out of 25? Why are not all dreams controlled by the thoughts of another person—and, if they can be controlled from 40 miles away, why not by all the hundreds or thousands of people living within that forty-mile radius?

One argument against parapsychology is based on the events that occur every day in Las Vegas. If even a few people possessed the power of precognition, the argument goes, they would bankrupt the gambling casinos because they would know what number was coming up next on the dice or the roulette wheels. If they possessed the power of psycho-kinesis, they could *make* the right number come up. Yet the casinos go on merrily making a profit. Indeed, psychologists have actually made an experimental attempt to use ESP to break the bank in Las Vegas. The experiment failed (38).

Summary

1 Perception is the process through which we become aware of our environments by organizing and interpreting the evidence of our senses. The word is also applied to the impressions of the environment that we receive as a result of this process.

2 Traditionally, perception has been viewed as an independent process, intervening between the operation of the senses and any response to sensory stimuli. The new information-processing view of perception holds that it is merely one of a number of interconnected links in the chain of cognitive activity—closely related in particular to sensory memory, short-term memory, and long-term memory.

3 Perception may profoundly alter the raw materials of sensation supplied by the sense organs; the same stimulus may be perceived in different ways or very different stimuli may be perceived as similar.

4 Examples of how perception alters sensation are supplied by many optical illusions, including *stroboscopic motion,* in which images that are stationary but shown in rapid succession seem to move.

5 One key factor in perception is *selection,* or paying attention to only certain stimuli in the environment rather than all stimuli.

6 Inborn characteristics of the way the brain operates appear to influence selection and other aspects of perception. For example, the brain has been found to have "feature detector" cells that respond only to certain kinds of stimuli. These cells detect such features of a visual stimulus as movement and pattern (horizontal and vertical lines, and angles), such features of an auditory stimulus as pitch and change of pitch.

7 Probably because of the way the brain operates, we appear to have an inborn tendency to select certain kinds of stimuli in preference to others. Among the stimulus characteristics that automatically attract our attention are *change* (including movement, contrast, and sometimes repetition), *size, intensity,* and certain *colors.*

8 Another key factor in perception is *organization.* The tendency to organize stimuli is so compelling that we tend to perceive patterns in stimuli that do not of themselves possess any pattern—such as the steady clicks of a metronome or a uniform mass of checkerboard squares.

9 Factors influencing organization include *figure and ground* (the tendency to perceive an object as a figure set off from a neutral ground by a dividing line called a *contour), closure, continuity, proximity, similarity, common movement,* and *context.*

10 Another important factor in organization is *perceptual constancy,*

which refers to the fact that we tend to perceive objects as constant and unchanging even though the images of them that reach our eyes vary because of changing distance and angle. Perceptual constancy takes the form of *shape constancy, brightness and color constancy, location constancy,* and *size constancy.*

11 In perception of distance, we use the clues of *perceived size, binocular vision, interposition, perspective,* and *shadowing.*

12 *Perceptual expectations* (a form of set) are a strong influence on perception. All other things being equal, we tend to perceive what we expect to perceive. Perceptual expectations are influenced by events that have just happened in the environment and by such factors as motives, interests, values, and emotions.

13 *Parapsychology* is the study of psychological events that seem to go beyond normal limits and to defy normal explanation.

14 One field in parapsychology is ESP, or *extrasensory perception,* which includes *mental telepathy* (mind reading), *clairvoyance* (the ability to perceive an object without use of the ordinary sensory channels), and *precognition* (the ability to perceive something that has not yet happened).

15 Another field in parapsychology is *psychokinesis* (the ability to influence the movement of objects through an act of will).

16 A small but apparently growing number of psychologists believe experiments have established that some people possess parapsychological powers. A majority continue to be unimpressed by the evidence and to regard parapsychology as implausible.

Recommended reading

Carterette, E. C., and Freidman, M. P., eds. *Handbook of perception,* 2 vols. New York: Academic Press, 1974.

Chase, W. G. *Visual information processing.* New York: Academic Press, 1973.

Gibson, E. J. *Principles of perceptual learning and development.* New York: Appleton-Century-Crofts, 1969.

Gregory, R. L. *Eye and brain: the psychology of seeing.* New York: McGraw-Hill, 1966.

Gregory, R. L. *The intelligent eye,* 2nd ed. New York: McGraw-Hill, 1973.

Hochberg, J. E. *Perception.* Englewood Cliffs, N.J.: Prentice-Hall, 1964.

Melzack, R. *The puzzle of pain.* New York: Basic Books, 1973.

Moray, N. *Attention: selective processes in vision and hearing.* New York: Academic Press, 1971.

Reed, S. K. *Psychological processes in pattern recognition.* New York: Academic Press, 1973.

Uttal, W. R. *The psychobiology of sensory coding.* New York: Harper & Row, 1973.

FOUR
THE BODY AND THE BRAIN

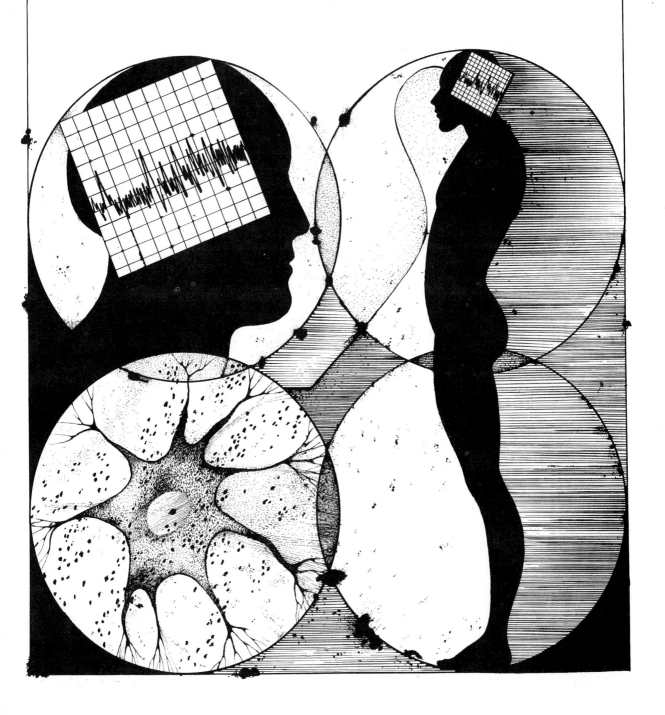

Although psychologists are chiefly interested in human behavior and the mental processes that help influence behavior, they are constantly aware of the fact that all psychological events depend in the last analysis on the human physical structure and the way it operates.

For example, our information about our environments (as was explained in Part 3) depends on the ability of our sense organs to detect stimuli in the world around us and the manner in which our brains select and organize these messages from the sense organs into our perceptions. Our ability to learn, think, and solve problems (discussed in Part 2) depends on the kind of nervous system we possess and especially on the structure and dynamics of the brain. As will be seen later in the book, inborn physical characteristics also help account for our emotions and motives and can be responsible in part for abnormal behavior.

Part 4 therefore describes the various physical characteristics that are most closely related to human behavior—making it possible, sometimes enriching it, sometimes limiting it. Part 4 consists of a single chapter, "Behavior Genetics, Glands, and Nervous System," which begins with a discussion of how we inherit these characteristics.

The second part of the chapter describes the roles played in human behavior by those rather small but extremely important structures called the *endocrine glands*. The third part describes the *nervous system*—particularly that remarkable coordinating, learning, and thinking device called the brain.

One reason these three topics are important is that we cannot rise above our physical limitations; we are born to behave and think in ways dictated by the kinds of muscles, glands, and nervous systems we have inherited from our ancestors. No human being can swim like a fish, fly like a bird, or run as fast as a race horse. Nor can any human being perform arithmetical calculations as fast as a computer—though, as will be seen, the human brain performs marvels of its own.

A final section of the chapter discusses a topic that has aroused much interest in recent years—altered states of consciousness, or how the workings of the brain are affected by such things as sleep, hypnosis, meditation, and drugs. Also discussed in this connection is the controversy over whether science can—or should—control people's minds.

7

Behavior genetics, glands, and nervous system

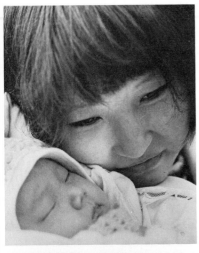

In physical characteristics, all organisms are more or less like the others of their species. Horses may vary in coloring, but certainly we have no trouble recognizing a horse; we would never confuse one with a cow or a sheep. This is true of human beings as well. True, they are more complicated and highly developed than other organisms and therefore show a wider range of differences than do the members of other species. They vary considerably in size, strength, color of skin, facial characteristics, and many other traits. Nonetheless, human beings vary only within limits. As a poet once said, we are all brothers and sisters under the skin. The surgeon and the witch doctor, the dwarf and the giant, the Einstein and the high-school dropout, all have more in common than they have in contrast.

Why are we all alike, yet each one different? The answer is that we inherit our physical makeup from our ancestors—and this makeup is roughly the same for all of us in general, yet infinitely varied in detail. The study of heredity is known as *genetics,* and the aspect of heredity of most interest to psychologists is called *behavior genetics,* which concerns the inheritance of traits that are of prime importance in determining the organism's conduct—such as the glands and most of all the nervous system.

The behavioral traits that we inherit from our ancestors are of course modified by environment. For example, as will be seen later in the chapter, the baby's capacity for intelligence will flourish in a stimulating environment and can be stunted by an unfavorable environment. But for many important traits heredity sets the limits. Environment can only encourage or discourage the development and operation of the traits the organism possesses at birth.

233

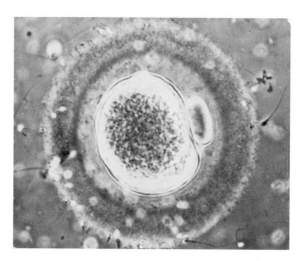

A photomicrograph of the union of sperm and egg.

The genes: key to heredity

Human life starts, of course, when the egg cell of the mother is penetrated and fertilized by the sperm cell of the father. In this process the two join into a single cell—and this single cell eventually grows into a human baby. It does so by a process of division; the single cell splits and becomes two living cells, then each of these in turn splits to make four, and so on.

Thus the original fertilized egg cell must somehow contain the whole key of life. Something inside it must direct the entire development from single cell to the baby at birth (whose body contains about 200 billion cells organized into the various specialized parts of the body) and beyond that from infant to fully matured adult. Something in it must also determine the inherited characteristics of the individual to be born—the color of the eyes, the shape of the facial features, the potential size, the learning capacity.

This "something" is the *chromosomes*—the tiny structures shown in Figure 7-1 as seen under a powerful microscope. The original fertilized

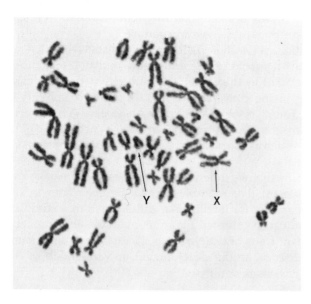

7-1

The human chromosomes

When enlarged 750 times, the human chromosomes look like this. These are from a man's skin cell, broken down and spread out into a single layer under the microscope. The labels point out the X- and Y-chromosomes, the importance of which will be discussed on pages 236–37.

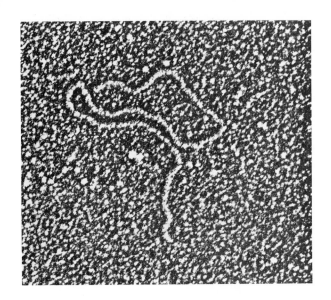

7-2

A single gene

The first gene ever isolated and photographed under high magnification was this twisted strand taken from one of the bacteria frequently found in the human intestinal tract. It is fifty-five millionths of an inch long. (1)

cell contains forty-six chromosomes. When the cell splits, the chromosomes also divide. Thus each cell of the newborn baby as well as of the fully grown human body contains exactly the same forty-six chromosomes that were present in the fertilized egg with which life began. The chromosomes are the key to the development of the human being and are the carriers of heredity.

Each chromosome, though tiny in inself, is composed of hundreds of even smaller structures called *genes,* each of which is a molecule of a complex chemical called *DNA* (deoxyribonucleic acid). Recently scientists managed to extract a single gene from a chromosome of one of the lower organisms and, through a microscope, take the photograph of it shown in Figure 7-2.

Human genes have not yet been isolated, examined, or counted. But it is believed that there are at least 20,000 of them in each human cell and perhaps as many as 125,000. Each gene is believed to be responsible —sometimes by itself but more often in combination with other genes —for some particular phase of development. The genes direct the process by which some cells of the body grow into skin and others grow into nerves or muscles and also the process by which cells become grouped into organs such as the heart, the stomach, and the liver. They control such aspects of development as the color of the eyes and the length of the bones.

Our heredity depends on those many thousands of genes, organized into our forty-six chromosomes. It is the particular kinds of genes present in the original fertilized egg that make us develop into human beings and into the individual kind of human being that each of us is.

Where we get our genes

In the living cell, it must now be emphasized, the chromosomes are not arranged as in Figure 7-1, where they were deliberately separated and spread out to pose for their microscopic portrait. Instead they are arranged in pairs—twenty-three pairs of chromosomes. In each pair the two chromosomes are similar in structure and function and are composed of genes of similar structure and function. For purposes of exposition, we can think of them as pairs A_1-A_2, B_1-B_2, C_1-C_2, D_1-D_2, and so on.

In growth, the twenty-three pairs of chromosomes with their matched genes duplicate themselves exactly, so that each new cell also has pairs A_1-A_2, B_1-B_2, C_1-C_2, D_1-D_2, and so on. But the cells of reproduction—the mother's egg cell and the sperm cell of the father—are formed in very different fashion. Here the pairs split up. Half of each pair goes into one egg or sperm cell, the other half into another cell. Thus each egg or sperm cell has only twenty-three chromosomes, not twenty-three pairs.

When two cells of reproduction are formed by this process, it is a matter of chance whether cell 1 will receive A_1 or A_2, B_1 or B_2, C_1 or C_2, and so on. Cell 1 may receive A_1, B_2, and C_1, in which case cell 2 will receive A_2, B_1, and C_2. Or cell 1 may receive A_2, B_2, and C_1, in which case cell 2 will receive A_1, B_1, and C_2. This random splitting of the twenty-three pairs can itself result in 8,388,608 different possible reproductive cells with different combinations of the two halves of the original pairs. Moreover, the splitting has a further complication. Sometimes A_1, in breaking away from A_2, leaves some of its own genes behind and pulls away some of the A_2 genes. Any of the twenty-three chromosomes can and often does behave in this way, with anywhere from one to several hundred genes from its paired chromosomes. All in all, there are many billions of possible combinations of the original pairs of chromosomes and genes.

An egg cell containing one of these combinations of the chromosomes and genes present in the mother is fertilized by a sperm cell containing one of the combinations of the chromosomes and genes present in the father. The chromosomes and genes pair up, and life begins for another unique human being. Never before, unless by a chance so mathematically remote as to be almost impossible, did the same combination of genes ever exist. Never again is it likely to be repeated.

The one exception to the fact that each human being is unique is in the case of identical twins. Here a single egg cell, fertilized by a single sperm cell, develops into two individuals. They have the same chromosomes and genes in the same combination, and, as all of us have noted, they tend to be very much alike in every basic respect. Their differences are due to events that occurred after conception—possibly starting with different positions in the womb and slight variations in the food supply they received there and certainly including their varied learning experiences, food intake, and chance encounters with disease germs or physical accident after birth.

How sex is determined

One of the twenty-three pairs of chromosomes present in the fertilized egg cell plays a particularly important role in development: it determines whether the fertilized egg will develop into a boy or a girl. In Figure 7-1 you will note that two chromosomes are pointed out by arrows. One of them, as the caption states, is called an X-chromosome, the other a Y-chromosome. Despite their different appearances, they constitute a pair—the only exception to the rule that paired chromosomes are similar in structure. You will also note that the chromosomes in Figure 7-1 are from a cell taken from a male. The X-Y pairing always produces a male. When there is an X-X pair, the result is always a female.

This, then, is how sex is determined. When the mother's X-X pair of chromosomes splits to form an egg cell, the result is always a cell containing an X-chromosome. When the father's X-Y pair splits to form two sperm cells, however, the X-chromosome goes to one of the cells, the Y-chromosome to the other. If the sperm cell with the X-chromosome fertilizes the egg, the result is an X-X pairing and a girl. If the sperm cell with the Y-chromosome fertilizes the egg, the result is an X-Y pairing and a boy.

Dominant and recessive genes

If a man with blue eyes marries a woman with blue eyes, we can predict with absolute certainty that all their children will also have blue eyes. When a man with brown eyes marries a woman with brown eyes, we can never be sure. All we can say is that their children have a greater chance of being brown-eyed than blue-eyed. The fact that we cannot rule out the possibility of a blue-eyed child has some important implications for our study of heredity.

Eye color is determined by one particular pair of genes or perhaps by a particular group of paired genes. For convenience, let us assume that a single pair is involved, and let us call the pair GEC_1–GEC_2— meaning that gene for eye color 1 was inherited from the father and gene for eye color 2 from the mother. If GEC_1 and GEC_2 are both for brown eyes, the eyes will be brown. If GEC_1 and GEC_2 are both for blue eyes, the eyes will be blue. Sometimes, however, GEC_1 is for brown and GEC_2 for blue, or vice versa. What happens when the genes for blue and for brown compete? The answer is that the gene for brown eyes always prevails; it is a *dominant gene*. The gene for blue eyes is a *recessive gene*, and its effects are always suppressed by the dominant gene. Any person with one GEC for brown and one GEC for blue will have brown eyes. But when that person's chromosome and gene pairs split to form reproductive cells, half the reproductive cells will carry the GEC for brown, the other half the GEC for blue. If one of the reproductive cells containing the GEC for blue happens to fertilize or to be fertilized by another reproductive cell containing the GEC for blue, the result will be a blue-eyed child. Thus can people pass along traits that they themselves do not possess. The mechanics of the process are illustrated in Figure 7-3, on the following page.

Among the genes known to be dominant in producing physical characteristics, besides those for brown eyes, are those that cause baldness in men, dwarfism, and cataracts of the eye. Certain recessive

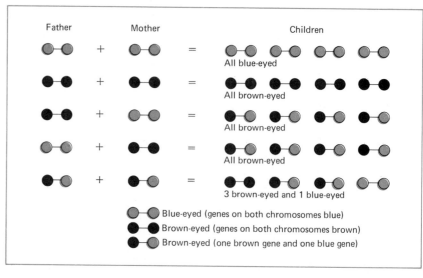

7-3

How eye color is inherited

All blue-eyed people have inherited a gene for blue from each parent; a blue-eyed man and a blue-eyed woman will have only blue-eyed children. Some brown-eyed people have inherited a gene for brown from each parent; all their children will have brown eyes. If one parent has two genes for brown and the other has two genes for blue, their children inherit one brown gene and one blue gene; since the brown gene is dominant, they will have brown eyes. If both parents have one gene for brown and one gene for blue, the probability is that three of their children will have brown eyes and one will have blue eyes.

genes carry color blindness and some rather rare forms of hearing defects and mental retardation.

The implications of heredity

People are born, live their lives, and die. But the chromosomes and the genes are passed on from generation to generation, from parent to child. All of us carry around, in every cell of our bodies, the genes that have influenced human development and behavior since the appearance of humans on earth. They guarantee that we will grow up in the image of our ancestors rather than into apes or fish. Yet the particular combination of genes that each of us carries is unique, coming from a grandfather here, a great-grandmother there, and so on back through countless individuals in countless generations.

So complicated is our inheritance of genes, so vast the possible combinations, that it would have been impossible to predict at the moment of conception what any of us would be like. Two parents who are below average in intelligence can produce a genius. A brilliant husband and brilliant wife may have a mentally retarded child. In a family of twelve children no two may look alike.

From what has been said here about heredity, it should now be clear what was meant by the statement that psychology, although it tends to lean toward the notion that the mind of the human baby is a *tabula rasa,* or "blank tablet," does so with reservations. The particular combination of chromosomes and genes that comes together at the moment of conception constitutes a master key for the development of the new individual's body—potential size, appearance, internal organs, nervous system, glands.

Recent studies indicate that many characteristics that can broadly be characterized as personality traits also are controlled by the genes at least in part, although environment is always a factor. For example, the severe form of mental disturbance called *schizophrenia,* which occurs in only about one person in a hundred, is much more common among people who have a parent or a brother or sister who suffers from the disturbance. This fact cannot be attributed entirely to the environmental effect of living around someone who is schizophrenic. A study of children reared away from their own families in foster homes has shown that of fifty children of normal mothers not one developed schizophrenia, but of forty-seven children born to schizophrenic mothers, five became schizophrenic (2). There is some evidence that heredity also plays a large part in determining whether individuals will be *extroverted,* that is, inclined to be sociable and outgoing, or *introverted,* that is, inclined to be withdrawn and preoccupied with themselves (3).

The glands and their effect on behavior

Among the physical features that we inherit from our ancestors, as a bodily characteristic common to all humanity, are a number of specialized anatomical structures called glands. Some of the glands are of minor interest to psychologists; they simply produce substances that aid the bodily processes in routine ways. For example, the salivary glands deliver saliva to the mouth and thus aid the digestive process; the tear glands keep the surface of the eyeball clean and moist; the sweat glands help keep the temperature of the body constant. There is another group of glands, however, that have a pronounced effect on behavior. All of them have a common characteristic; unlike the salivary, tear, and sweat glands, they possess no ducts for delivery of the substances they produce. Instead they discharge their substances directly into the bloodstream, which then carries them to all parts of the body. For this reason, they are sometimes called the *ductless glands.* They are also known as *endocrine glands,* which means glands of internal secretion. The positions of the important endocrine glands in the body are illustrated in Figure 7-4.

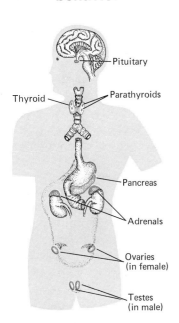

Pituitary

Thyroid — Parathyroids

Pancreas

Adrenals

Ovaries (in female)

Testes (in male)

7-4

The human endocrine glands

These are the endocrine glands most important to human behavior. For their functions, see the text.

Functions of the endocrine glands

The substances produced by the endocrine glands and released into the bloodstream are called *hormones,* meaning activators. The hormones are complicated chemicals that trigger and control many kinds of bodily activities and behavior, as can be seen from the following list of functions performed by the various glands.

Pituitary. This is the master gland, secreting a number of different hormones that have a profound effect on the life process. In the early years the pituitary secretes a growth hormone that regulates the development of the body. As is illustrated in Figure 7-5, if the gland produces too little of this hormone, development is arrested and the child becomes a dwarf, while too much of the hormone causes the child to grow into a giant. At the time of puberty the pituitary secretes another hormone that activates the sex glands, which in turn take over and control the change from child into man or woman. The pituitary also produces hormones that speed up or inhibit the activity of the other endocrine glands.

Thyroid. This gland, a double-lobed mass of tissue lying at the sides of the windpipe, secretes a substance that controls the rate of *metabolism*—the never ending process by which the cells inside the body convert food into energy or into new living protoplasm. When the thyroid manufactures too little of its chemical, the metabolic process is slowed down; a person with an underactive thyroid tends to be sluggish and to tire easily. If the thyroid is overactive, a person is likely to be excitable and "keyed up" and to have trouble sleeping.

Parathyroids. These glands, lying around the larger thyroid gland, help maintain a normal state of excitability of the nervous system by regulating the balance of calcium and phosphorus in the blood.

Pancreas. This large gland, lying below the stomach, secretes hormones that are essential in maintaining the proper level of blood sugar and in the metabolism of blood sugar to provide energy, especially for the brain. One of them is the well-known hormone called *insulin.* An underactive pancreas results in the disease called diabetes, which was invariably fatal before the discovery that injections of insulin from animals could be used as a substitute for the body's own hormone.

Adrenals. There are two of these glands; they lie atop the body's two kidneys. From the psychological point of view, they are of special importance because they secrete two powerful stimulants called *adrenalin* and *noradrenalin,* which play a considerable part in determining our behavior in situations of danger where we must take quick action in the direction of "fight or flight." Although adrenalin is usually associated with fearful behavior and noradrenalin with angry or aggressive behavior, both hormones have rather similar effects. They tend to affect the

7-5

Effects of the pituitary gland

The result of defects of the pituitary is dramatically illustrated in this photograph from Britain of a dwarf (underactivity of the gland) and a giant (overactivity).

rate of heartbeat, raise the blood pressure, and cause the liver to release increased quantities of sugar into the blood to provide additional energy. They also tend to relax the muscles of the digestive system, tense the muscles of movement, shift the flow of blood away from the digestive organs and toward the muscles, and act as a clotting agent that makes the blood coagulate more quickly if exposed to air, as in case of injury. The adrenal glands also produce a number of hormones that perform functions essential to bodily health and activity, such as maintaining a suitable salt balance and providing a readily available supply of energy to be carried around the body by the bloodstream.

Ovaries. In addition to producing the egg cells, the ovaries are also glands of internal secretion. When activated by the pituitary gland, they secrete the hormones estrogen and progesterone that bring about the bodily changes known as secondary sex characteristics—for example, the development of the breasts—as well as being involved in menstruation and pregnancy.

Testes. In addition to producing the sperm cells, the testes are also glands of internal secretion. The hormone they produce, testosterone, brings about such secondary male sex characteristics as the growth of facial hair and change of voice and also plays a part in sexual arousal.

The glands as an integrating system

Taken together, the endocrine glands constitute an elaborate and efficient system that helps integrate many bodily activities. Their hormones, traveling to all parts of the body via the bloodstream, control the metabolic process and thus the rate of bodily activity; they regulate growth and sexual development and activity; they influence the excitability of the nervous system.

In particular, they are closely related to the two powerful emotions of fear and anger, whose effects on behavior will be discussed further in Chapter 8. When we are in the grip of fear or anger, our endocrine systems are working at top speed and we are therefore capable of extraordinary levels of physical activity. We can fight for our lives harder and longer than would otherwise be possible, or we can run away from danger faster and farther.

To a great extent, the endocrine system can operate independently. A hormone from one gland—especially from the pituitary gland—can spur another gland into action. But the operation of many of the glands also depends on the fact that they are connected with the body's nervous system; nerves ending in the glands bring them messages from the brain, directly or indirectly, that make them spring into action. It is the nervous system that is chiefly responsible for the all-important job of integrating bodily activities and behavior.

Basics of the nervous system

To help understand the importance of the human nervous system, it is useful to consider for a moment how some lower organisms manage to function. A one-celled animal such as the paramecium cannot and does not possess any nervous system at all. Its entire single-celled "body" is somehow sensitive to heat and light and capable of initiating its own movements. Larger and more complicated animals, however, have to have some kind of nervous system, composed of specialized nerve cells in the shape of fibers that reach from one part of the body to another and are capable of conveying messages back and forth.

In the lowly little sea creature called the coral there is simply a network of nerves, with no particular central point. The nerves and the various parts of the body work together much like the government of a loose federation of states, each preserving considerable independence. Higher up in the scale of evolution, the network of nerves becomes more complicated and the beginnings of a central nervous system appear. The organism, it might be said, now has the beginnings of a strong central government, exercising control over all its parts. In humans, the central nervous system has reached its peak of development: a large and enormously complex brain serves as a center of power and decision that regulates the behavior of all parts of the body in the most complicated and delicate fashion.

Unlike the paramecium, we would be helpless without a nervous system. We would be unable to react to stimuli from the outside world. We would not even be able to move our muscles. Indeed we could not live at all, for our hearts would not beat and our lungs would not breathe.

The nerve cell

The basic unit of the nervous system is the individual nerve cell, technically called *neuron,* an example of which is shown in Figure 7-6. Some neurons are quite long; for example, the motor neurons that enable us to wiggle our toes extend all the way from the lower part of the spinal column to the muscles of the toes. Others, particularly in the brain, are only the tiniest fraction of an inch in length.

The neuron's *cell body,* which contains the chromosomes and genes that caused it to grow into a nerve cell in the first place, performs the work of metabolism. The *dendrites* are the neuron's "receivers"; when they are stimulated, they start a nervous impulse that travels the length of the fiber to the end of the *axon.* The speed at which the impulse travels depends partly on the size of the neuron; the greater the diameter of the fiber, the greater the speed. It also depends, to a much greater extent, on whether the neuron possesses a *myelin sheath,* as does the one shown in the figure. In neurons that have the sheath, the impulse often travels slightly faster than 300 feet a second, compared with a typical speed of only a little more than 3 feet a second in neurons without the sheath.

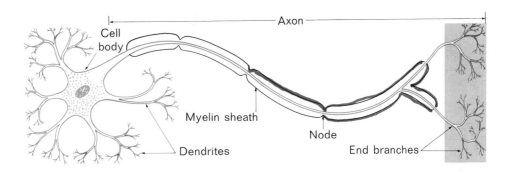

7-6

A nerve cell (neuron)

Like this motor neuron, all neurons are fiber-shaped cells with a *dendrite* or *dendrites* at one end, an *axon* at the other end, and a *cell body* somewhere in between. Stimulation of the dendrites sets up a nervous impulse that travels the length of the neuron to the end of the axon. In the case of this motor neuron, the *end branches* of the axon would be embedded in a muscle fiber, and the nervous impulse would make the muscle contract. The *myelin sheath* is a whitish coating that protects many neurons but not all. The *nodes* are constrictions of the sheath that act as relay stations to improve transmission of the nervous impulse. (4)

The nervous impulse

The nature of the nervous impulse is so foreign to anything else in our ordinary experience that it is somewhat difficult to describe or to comprehend at first. It is a tiny charge of electricity passing from one end of the fiber to the other, but it does not travel like the electricity in the wires of a house—as might be guessed from the fact that electricity travels not at a mere 3 to 300 feet a second but at 186,000 miles a second. The charge can be compared to the glowing band of fire that passes along a lighted fuse, except that no combustion takes place in the neuron. What actually happens is that there is an exchange of chemical particles, carrying different electrical potentials, from inside and outside the membrane that encloses the nerve fiber. Once the nervous impulse created by this exchange of chemical particles has passed down the length of the fiber, the neuron quickly returns to its normal state and is ready to fire off another impulse.

The neuron ordinarily operates on what is called the *all or none principle*. That is to say, if it fires at all it fires as hard as it can considering its physiological state at the moment (which, in complex ways, can be altered by the messages it is receiving from other neurons). All stimuli of sufficient power set off the same kind of impulse—as strong an impulse as the neuron is capable of producing at that moment.

A photomicrograph of a nerve cell in the human spinal cord

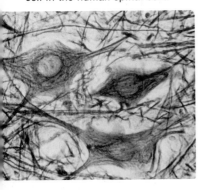

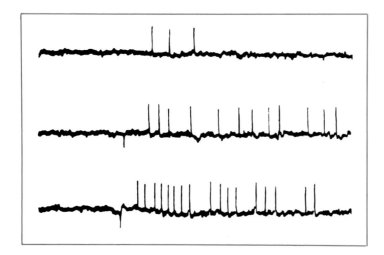

7-7

Records of a neuron's activity

These are tracings from an electrode that was placed on the neuron of a rat. Each upward movement of the lines shows a separate impulse. The neuron was from the rat's tongue, and the stimulus was salt solution in varying strengths. The response of the neuron to the weakest salt solution is shown in the top line. In the center line the stimulus was ten times stronger and in the bottom line a hundred times stronger. (5)

After the neuron has fired, it requires a brief recovery period before it can fire again. This recovery period has two phases. During the first phase the neuron is incapable of responding at all. During the second phase it is still incapable of responding to all the stimuli that would ordinarily make it fire, but it can respond if the stimulus is powerful enough. Some neurons have a fast recovery rate and can fire, when sufficiently stimulated, as often as 1000 times a second. Others recover much more slowly and have a top limit of only a few firings per second.

Figure 7-7 shows the actual sequence of nervous impulses in a neuron over a period of several tenths of a second. Note that each impulse was of approximately equal intensity, as measured by the height of the lines. Stronger stimuli made the neuron fire more often but not with greater intensity.

As remarkable as it may seem, those little movements in the lines in Figure 7-7 are pretty much the whole story of what goes on inside the human nervous system. The neurons fire off their tiny waves of electricity, barely enough to jolt the needle of the most sensitive recording device. For each neuron, each wave is of similar intensity; the major difference is in the number and rapidity of the impulses. Yet somehow these impulses—by the way they are routed through the nervous system and the patterns they form—manage to tell us what our eyes see and our ears hear; they enable us to learn and to think; they direct our glands and our internal organs to function; they direct our muscles to perform such intricate and delicate feats as driving an automobile or playing a violin.

The synapse and neuro-transmitters

The way one neuron connects with another is shown in Figure 7-8. The junction point, or *synapse,* marks the boundary between one neuron and the next and therefore the end of one nervous impulse and the start of a new one. The impulse of the first neuron cannot leap across the synapse; it can go only as far as the end of the axon and no farther. It

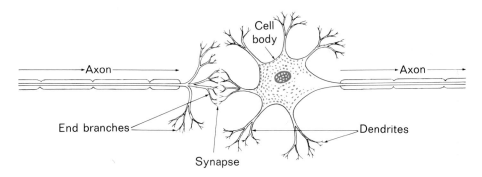

7-8

The synapse

The junction between the axon of one neuron and the axon, dendrites, or cell body of another neuron is called a *synapse*. For an explanation of what happens at the synapse, see the text.

can, however, stimulate the second neuron to fire off its own impulse, thus passing along its "message" to another link in the nervous system.

The major way that stimulation of the second neuron occurs at the synapse is through chemical action. The end of the axon contains very small amounts of a chemical substance known as a *neurotransmitter,* and when the nervous impulse reaches the end of the axon a tiny burst of this substance is released into the synapse (6).

There appear to be a number of chemicals that serve as neurotransmitters responsible for activity at the synapses in various parts of the nervous system (7). One of them, it is interesting to note, is noradrenalin — meaning that some of the neurons, though they are only single cells, are capable of producing one of the same complex chemicals manufactured by the adrenal glands. Another important neurotransmitter is called acetylcholine.

The three kinds of neurons

The neurons of the human body, which number in the billions, come in many different lengths, diameters, and shapes. They can, however, be divided into three classes.

1 *Afferent neurons.* These are the neurons of the senses. The word *afferent* is derived from the Latin words *ad,* which means to or toward, and *ferre,* which means to bear or to carry. The afferent neurons carry messages toward the central nervous system — from our eyes, ears, and other sense organs.
2 *Efferent neurons.* These carry messages *from* the central nervous system. Their axons end in either muscles or glands. Their impulses make the muscles contract or activate the glands.
3 *Connecting neurons.* These are middlemen between other neurons. They are stimulated only by the axon of another neuron. They do not end in muscle or gland tissue but only in other synapses where they

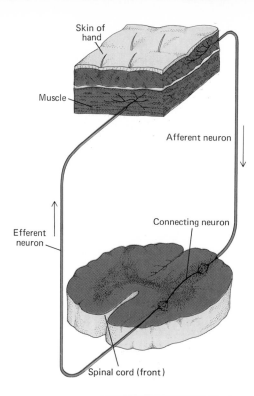

7-9

Connections for the grasping reflex

Stroking the palm of the baby's hand stimulates an afferent neuron whose axon ends inside the spinal cord at a synapse with a connecting neuron. This connecting neuron, in turn, ends at a synapse with an efferent neuron. The impulses from the afferent neuron stimulate the connecting neuron, which in turn stimulates the efferent neuron, which makes the muscle of the hand contract. Note that the afferent neuron enters the spinal cord from the back, and the efferent neuron leaves from the front. This is always the case.

Labels in figure: Skin of hand; Muscle; Afferent neuron; Connecting neuron; Efferent neuron; Spinal cord (front)

stimulate other neurons to fire. Most of them, though not all, are found within the central nervous system.

A simple example of how these three kinds of neurons work together is provided by the infant's grasping reflex, illustrated in Figure 7-9. As will be seen, the nervous messages that produce the reflex begin with the stimulation of an afferent neuron, which in turn stimulates a connecting neuron, which in turn stimulates an efferent neuron—whose impulses cause the muscle to contract.

Multiple nerve connections

Most synaptic connections between neurons, especially the connecting or "middleman" neurons, are far more complicated than the diagrams shown up to this point would suggest. Indeed a synapse can best be thought of as a complex switching point where not just two but many neurons make contact, in the most elaborate kind of way. The axon of each of the many "incoming" neurons that deliver messages at the synapse has many branches, each terminating in a synaptic knob as shown in Figure 7-10. These knobs, which contain the neurotransmitter

7-10

The synaptic knobs

This photograph, shown at a magnification of about 2000 times life size, is the first ever made of the synaptic knobs of a neuron. The photograph is of the neuron connections in a snail. (8)

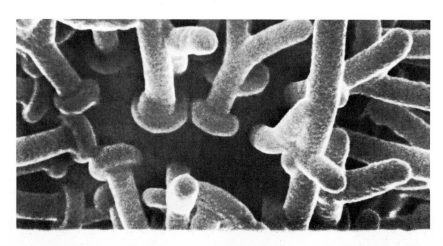

substance, are usually in contact with the dendrites of a large number of "outgoing" neurons. But, to further complicate the picture, some of the synaptic knobs are in contact with the cell bodies of the outgoing neurons, which can be stimulated directly as well as through the dendrites.

Thus each incoming neuron may deliver its message, in the form of its neurotransmitter, to scores or perhaps even hundreds of outgoing neurons. Similarly, each outgoing neuron may receive messages from scores or hundreds of incoming neurons. The outgoing neuron, moreover, does not always respond in the same way to the messages it receives. How it responds depends on where it is stimulated. At some of the many locations, or "receptor sites," where it makes synaptic connections with incoming neurons, stimulation by the neurotransmitter tends to make it fire off its own impulse. At other "receptor sites" the neurotransmitter tends to inhibit it from firing (9).

Ordinarily an outgoing neuron will not fire as the result of a single message arriving at one of its many dendrites or its cell body. Instead the firing process requires multiple stimulation—a whole group of messages arriving at once or in quick succession from several or even a great many of the incoming neurons with which it is in contact at the synapse. Moreover, the messages that it interprets as signals to fire must outweigh any messages that inhibit it from firing.

Thus the multiple connections at the synapses provide an almost astronomical number of possible pathways. The nervous impulses arriving from the incoming neurons may not "get through" at all. They may be too few in number or too far apart in time to fire any of the outgoing neurons, or incoming messages tending to fire the outgoing neurons may be canceled out by messages that inhibit firing. At times the incoming nervous impulses may be of such a number and such a pattern as to fire a single outgoing neuron but no more. At other times several or many outgoing neurons may be fired. The particular ones that are stimulated into activity may vary. So may the number of impulses they fire and the rate at which they fire.

All this means that no new impulses at all may be set up at the synapse, or that new impulses may travel in any one of many directions or in several directions at once. The new impulses that go along to the next switching point or points in the nervous system may be few or many, slow or rapid. Small wonder that the human nervous system is capable of so many accomplishments. By comparison, the nation's telephone network is just a child's toy.

The nerve paths and learning

The multiple connections at the synapses and what is known about transmission across the synapse offer one theory of how learning takes place. When we learn, we obviously route nervous impulses over a particular pathway, going through a number of synapse switching points in a particular pattern. Presumably this pathway can later be reactivated—and we remember.

Studies of lower animals have suggested that at synapses where the axon of one neuron stimulates the dendrite of another neuron to fire by releasing their neurotransmitters, these chemicals produce a change in the efficiency of the synapse (10). That is to say, the second neuron becomes more likely to fire again in the future. The change makes it easier for nervous impulses to follow the same route again. Thus the pathway set up by learning presumably may become, so to speak, a path of least resistance.

Many studies have shown that learning is accompanied by physical changes within the nervous system, notably in the brain. It is known that all the neurons of the brain are present at birth; the number never increases. Yet the brain grows substantially, from about 11 ounces at birth to over 2 pounds in adulthood. Part of the added weight is caused by the fact that the nerve cells grow in size and develop new dendrites (making possible new synaptic connections) much as a young tree develops new branches. The manner in which this growth process is stimulated by learning has been demonstrated in experiments with animals. For example, if one group of rats is raised in ordinary cages and another group in an enriched environment containing numerous visual stimuli and toys, examination after death shows that the animals from the enriched environments have heavier brains (11). Encouraging animals to learn has also been shown to be accompanied by an increase in the number of dendrites in the brain (12) and the amount of neurotransmitter chemical (13).

The peripheral and autonomic nervous systems

How the human nervous system functions is determined in part by the basic elements just discussed — the structure of the neuron, the nature of the nervous impulse, and the manner in which the synapses act as switching points. But the way the system operates is also dependent on its structure — that is to say, how the individual neurons that make up the system are organized and grouped, which is another of the human characteristics determined by heredity.

The most important structure in the nervous system, of course, is the brain, the master control center of all sensations, feelings, mental activity, and behavior. But there are also two other parts of the system — which, since they are simpler, can best be discussed before proceeding to the immense complexities of the brain.

The peripheral nerves

As indicated in Figure 7-11, the neuron fibers of the human nervous system extend to all parts of the body. The outlying neurons comprise what is called the *peripheral nervous system,* a network that extends to the fingertips, the feet, the eyes and ears, the glands, and the various organs of the body — the heart, lungs, stomach, kidneys, and all the rest.

All the neurons of the peripheral system eventually connect either

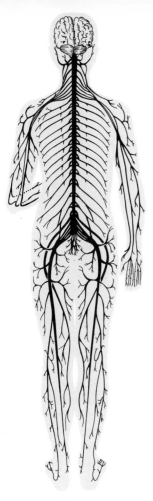

7-11
The human nervous system

Like the tributaries that form a river, individual neuron fibers at all the far reaches of the body join together to form small *nerves*, which is the name for bundles of neuron fibers. The small nerves join with others to form larger nerves, at last becoming the very large ones that join with the central nervous system — the brain and the spinal cord. Twelve *cranial nerves*, in pairs going to the left and right sides of the head, connect directly with the brain. There are also thirty-one pairs of large *spinal nerves*, connected with the spinal cord at the spaces between the bones of the spine.

with the spinal cord, which is a sort of master cable to the brain, or to the brain itself. The afferent neurons of the peripheral system carry sensory messages which, when they reach the brain, account for our vision, hearing, and feelings of touch or of pain. The efferent nerves, originating in the brain or spinal cord, deliver their impulses outward and thus control the glands and organs and muscles as far away as the fingers and toes. The peripheral system is like the wires that radiate out from a central telephone exchange, extending to all the far reaches of the town it serves.

The autonomic nervous system

Another network of neurons that extends into many parts of the body is the *autonomic nervous system,* which exercises its own rather mysterious control over the glands, the so-called smooth muscles, and the heart muscles. (The *smooth muscles* are found in the blood vessels, stomach and intestines, and other internal organs; they are different in appearance and function from the *striped muscles,* which account for motor behavior such as moving the arms and legs. The heart muscles are of a special type found nowhere else in the body.)

The word *autonomic* means independent or self-sufficient, and the autonomic nervous system gets its name from the fact that in many ways it operates like a completely independent integrating system. Although it is connected with the brain and spinal cord, it regulates many bodily activities over which we have very little conscious control. For example, we cannot ordinarily will our adrenal glands to secrete their hormones or our hearts to beat faster. We cannot order our stomach muscles to digest food or to stop the process of digestion so that the flow of blood can be directed away from the stomach and toward other parts of the body. The nervous impulses that give the body such commands are distributed by the autonomic nervous system — a process that goes on constantly, even during periods when we are asleep or in the deep coma caused by an anesthetic or a brain injury.

The autonomic nervous system is composed of centers called *ganglia,* which are masses of nerve cells and synapses forming complex and

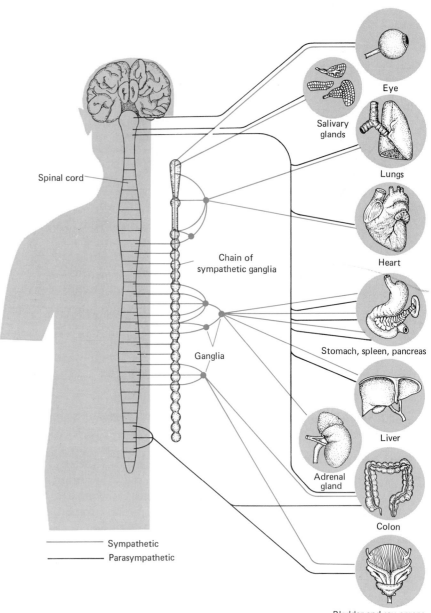

Spinal cord

Chain of
sympathetic ganglia

Ganglia

Eye

Salivary
glands

Lungs

Heart

Stomach, spleen, pancreas

Liver

Adrenal
gland

Colon

Bladder and sex organs

———— Sympathetic

———— Parasympathetic

7-12
The autonomic nervous system

The *parasympathetic division* of the autonomic nervous system connects with the brain and with the lower part of the spinal cord. The *sympathetic division* is composed of long chains of ganglia, one on either side of the spinal column, which connect with the spinal cord in the region of the trunk and the small of the back. Both divisions have fibers extending to the smooth muscles and glands of the body as shown. (14, 15)

multiple connections, just as in the brain itself though on a much smaller scale. Some of the neurons originating in these ganglia have dendrites that receive messages from the central nervous system. Other neurons send messages via their axons to the glands and the smooth muscles, as shown in Figure 7-12.

There are two parts of the autonomic system, and they are quite different in structure. In the *sympathetic division* the ganglia lie in long chains extending down either side of the spinal cord, all connected and interconnected. Many of the axons extending outward from these chains of ganglia meet again in additional ganglia, where they form complicated interconnections with the neurons that at last carry the messages of the sympathetic division to the glands and smooth muscles.

The ganglia of the *parasympathetic division* are more scattered; most of them lie near the glands or muscles to which they deliver their messages. For this reason the parasympathetic division tends to act in piecemeal fashion, delivering its impulses to one or several parts of the body but not necessarily to all. The sympathetic division, with its more central connections and interconnections, tends to act as a unit, delivering its impulses simultaneously to all the glands and smooth muscles.

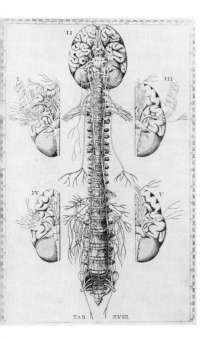

A sixteenth-century drawing of the sympathetic nervous system.

Functions of the sympathetic system. When the sympathetic division of the autonomic nervous system goes into action, as in fight or flight situations, it does many things all at once. It stimulates the adrenal glands and pancreas, resulting in increases in the level of blood sugar and the rate of metabolism. It also stimulates the liver to release sugar into the blood. It causes the spleen, a glandlike organ in which red corpuscles are stored, to release more corpuscles into the bloodstream, thus enabling the blood to carry more oxygen to the body's tissues. It changes the size of the blood vessels, enlarging those of the heart and striped muscles and constricting those of the smooth muscles such as the stomach and intestines. It allows us to breathe harder. It enlarges the pupils of the eyes, which are also smooth muscles, and slows the activity of the salivary glands. ("Wide eyes" and a dry mouth are characteristic of strong emotion.) It also activates the sweat glands and contracts the muscles at the base of the hairs on the body, causing the hair to rise on animals and producing goose flesh in human beings.

Functions of the parasympathetic system. The parasympathetic division is also active at times in situations of emergency, although in ways that are not yet entirely clear. In general, it seems to play its most important role as a regulator of bodily functions during those frequent periods when no danger threatens and the body can relax and go about the ordinary business of living. Impulses from the parasympathetic division constrict the pupil of the eye, stimulate the salivary glands, and lower the blood pressure. They also activate the stomach and intestines, thus setting into motion the normal processes of digestion, and they facilitate the functions of elimination from the intestines and bladder.

Considered as a whole, the autonomic nervous system with its sympathetic and parasympathetic divisions plays a highly important role. More or less independently and automatically, it directs many of the body's functions while we are asleep as well as while we are awake, and it moves quickly to help mobilize the body's resources in case of emergency. It relieves the central nervous system from the necessity of issuing all the continuing demands necessary to keep the body functioning at an optimum level.

The central nervous system

At the center and top of the body's network of neurons lies the *central nervous system* — composed of the *brain,* which is the control center, and the *spinal cord,* which is the brain's trunk line and also the center for some of the body's reflexes, as was shown in Figure 7-12. Inside the central nervous system, it has been estimated, there are about 100,000,000,000 different neurons, capable of making so many synaptic connections and pathways that the number totally defies imagination (16).

The brain's "beautiful interrelationships"

The brain is a truly remarkable organ. Its nerve cells start their pattern of activity long before birth and are constantly at work, humming with their complicated messages even when we are asleep, throughout life. In weight the brain makes up less than 2 percent of the human body, yet it works so hard that it consumes about 20 percent of all the oxygen that the body uses when at rest. It performs a vast array of functions that have been described by one psychologist in these eloquent words:

> The brain is the source of emotions, such as love, fear, and rage. . . . The brain organizes information from our sense organs to provide an orderly basis for our perception of the world about us. It achieves the marvelous coordination of our motor movements. It learns from our experience and stores our memories. It retrieves appropriate memories, plans for the future, thinks, and reasons creatively. Since the brain is the supreme organ of integration; there are many beautiful interrelationships among these apparently diverse functions (17).

One of the characteristics of the brain is its great versatility. Some of its cells function much like sense organs. They are alert to changes in the composition of the blood and other bodily fluids and recognize when the body needs food or water, or they are alert to temperature changes in the bloodstream and send off messages that cause the body to take steps to warm or cool itself. Some of the cells act like glands and secrete hormones. For example, one part of the brain recently has been found to produce a hormone that acts directly on the pituitary and causes the pituitary in turn to release a hormone that controls the activity of the thyroid (18). Other cells of the brain, of course, are primarily concerned with communication. They serve as part of an elaborate network that receives messages from the sense organs, evaluates these

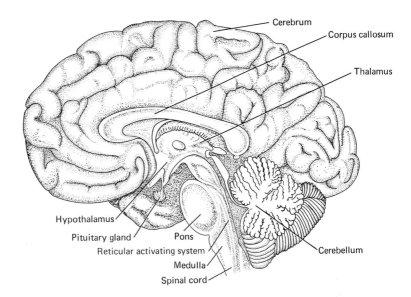

7-13

A sectional view of the brain

The functions of the brain structures shown in the drawing are discussed in the text. (22)

messages, and often translates them into commands to the efferent neurons that activate our muscles of movement or our internal organs.

Another characteristic of the brain is its ability to perform its myriad functions in many different ways, using its multiple connections and pathways to establish new routes of activity when necessary. To use the technical term, the brain exhibits considerable *plasticity,* especially in early life. Thus a woman born without one of the chief communications channels between parts of the brain showed no sign of its absence (19); a man born with several important parts of the brain missing or stunted had a normal personality and intelligence and in fact led his class in school (20). Even adults often manage to function satisfactorily after rather serious damage to parts of the brain (21).

Though the functions of one part of the brain can often be taken over by another, the various parts do ordinarily have their own special roles to play. Hence the importance of Figure 7-13, which shows some of the most prominent structures as they would be seen in a brain divided down the middle. The structures fall into three divisions, starting at the bottom or back part of the brain, which is really an enlarged extension of the spinal cord, and proceeding to the top and front.

The hindbrain

In anatomical terms, the first division is the *hindbrain,* which performs many of the functions essential to life. Making up the hindbrain are three separate structures.

The *medulla* is responsible for coordinating a number of vital bodily processes, including breathing and the beating of the heart. It is also an important relay station, containing neurons that transmit messages between the spinal cord and the upper parts of the brain.

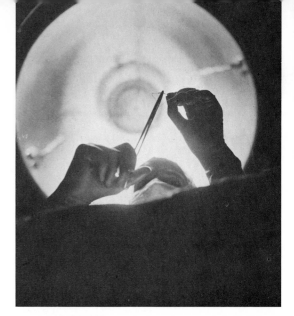

The *cerebellum* controls body balance; it is the part of the brain that keeps us right side up. It has many connections with areas higher in the brain that control conscious movements, and it serves as a coordinator for all the various finely regulated muscular movements of which we are capable, such as typing or playing a musical instrument. The cerebellum is divided into two lobes, or hemispheres, a right and a left—a fact related to the next and last of the hindbrain's three structures.

The *pons* gets its name from the Latin word for bridge, and a bridge it is, for its fibers connect and transmit messages between the two hemispheres of the cerebellum.

It is interesting to note that the hindbrain by itself can perform almost all the functions required to keep an organism alive and capable of the movements necessary for survival. A coldblooded animal such as a fish or snake could get by with a hindbrain and no more. (Warmblooded animals are dependent on a temperature-control center found higher in the brain.)

The midbrain

Just above or in front of the hindbrain lies the *midbrain*. This is a relay and transmission center for messages from our two most important sense organs, the eyes and ears. It is also a major part of what is called the *reticular activating system,* a network that extends downward into the hindbrain and upward into the higher parts of the brain.

The reticular activating system gets its name from the fact that under a microscope it appears as a crisscrossed (or reticulated) pattern of nerve cells and fibers. The nerve pathways bringing messages from the sense organs to the highest parts of the brain have side branches that enter the reticular activating system. These side branches stimulate the system to send impulses of its own in an upward direction, thus arousing the upper part of the brain to a general state of alertness and activity. For lack of such arousal, an animal in which the reticular activating system has been destroyed remains permanently unconscious. Conversely, a sleeping animal can be awakened immediately by electrical stimulation of the activating system (23).

The forebrain

The highest part of the brain, the *forebrain,* contains four structures of special interest.

The *thalamus* has been aptly described as "an information-processing center" (24). Information from the sense organs eventually arrives at the thalamus, where it is organized and sent on to the higher layers of the brain. The thalamus also acts as a relay station for nervous impulses traveling in the opposite direction—messages from the higher layers of the brain, especially for motor activity.

The *hypothalamus* is the brain's most important link with the endocrine glands. (Note in Figure 7-13 that the pituitary gland is attached to it.) Thus it plays a major role in emotional behavior that includes glandular activities. It also helps regulate such bodily processes as hunger, thirst, sexual behavior, and the maintenance of a constant body temperature. It is a terminal for the reticular activating system and as such helps direct sleeping and wakefulness. The hypothalamus and some of the surrounding parts and circuits of the forebrain work together to function in what is known as the *limbic system,* which plays a role in emotions, memory, and escape from danger (25).

The *corpus callosum* is a large nerve bundle, acting as a transmission cable, that is of special importance because of the nature of the next and final structure of the forebrain.

The *cerebrum* is the largest part of the human brain, lying massively atop all the other structures. Like the cerebellum, it is divided into two lobes, or hemispheres. The right and left lobes have a number of interconnections, but the main channel of communication between them is the corpus callosum.

The cerebrum and cerebral cortex

If we could look down through the top of a transparent skull, we would see the human brain as shown in Figure 7-14. We would be looking at only a single one of its many parts—but, as it happens, the very part that most distinguishes human beings from the lower animals. This is

7-14

A top view of the brain

This is the human *cerebral cortex,* the surface of the *cerebrum,* as seen from above. Note how it is divided into two hemispheres of similar size and appearance. Note also the many folds and fissures that add to its area. No other organism except the porpoise has such a large, intricately convoluted, and highly developed cerebral cortex. (26)

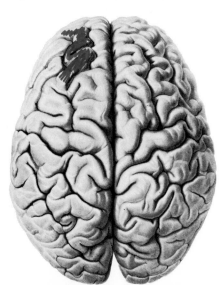

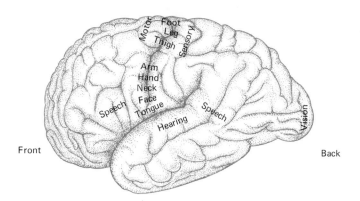

Front   Back

7-15

The cortex and its functions

On this side view of the cerebral cortex the areas that are known
to have special functions have been mapped. (27)

the extremely large, highly developed *cerebral cortex,* the surface of the
cerebrum. The cerebral cortex can best be described as a sort of carpet of
densely packed neurons, with cell bodies, dendrites, and axons forming
a closely knit fabric with innumerable connections and interconnections. This ''carpet'' is elaborately folded and refolded, or convoluted.
We can see only about a third of the cortex; the rest is hidden because of
the convolutions.

A side view of the cerebral cortex is shown in Figure 7-15. Note that
there is a particularly prominent fissure extending downward from almost the very top of the cortex. At the sides of this fissure lies an area
that serves as the control point for our sensory impressions of the body
and the body's motor movements.

This area has been mapped through electrical stimulation in human
patients during brain surgery under local anesthetic. When various
parts of this area are stimulated, the patients report sensations of pressure or movement in various parts of the body, and movement may actually occur. As the figure shows, the body is represented in upside-
down position—with the feet and legs at the top of the area and the
head at the bottom.

The *visual area,* as Figure 7-15 shows, is at the very rear of the cortex.
Stimulation of this area produces various kinds of visual sensations,
and destruction of the area seems to destroy the ability to perceive visual patterns. When the visual area is surgically removed from a
monkey or a rat, the animal cannot distinguish a circle from a triangle.

The *auditory area* lies just below another prominent fissure, which
curves diagonally upward from the bottom left of the cortex toward the
upper right. The two areas marked *Speech* in Figure 7-15, though rather
widely separated, are connected by many neurons traveling from one to
the other. The area at the front seems to be mostly responsible for
speaking words, the area at the back for understanding them.

"I think some of these shows are aimed at the mentality of a rhinoceros."

The cortex and intelligence

The specialized areas of the cortex account for our sensations — for what we see, hear, and feel. They initiate our motor movements and enable us to do what no other animal can do — express ourselves and understand others through a richly meaningful spoken language. The other large areas of the cortex, not labeled in Figure 7-15, play a more general role. Some areas analyze information received from the sense organs, code it, and store it — in other words, they are responsible for learning and memory. Others serve as the "organizer" for all kinds of complex human behavior: they make our decisions; they determine what we are going to do and make plans and programs for accomplishing these aims (28). The cortex, in brief, is the seat of human intelligence. The human cortex is nature's most elaborate and miraculous accomplishment.

The cerebrum's two hemispheres

In general, the left hemisphere of the cerebrum and its cortex receive sensory impressions from and control movement in the right side of the body, while the right hemisphere deals with the left side of the body. In most people, the left hemisphere appears to play the major role in the use of language (29), while the right hemisphere appears to play a more important role in the processing of melodies and other sounds unrelated to language (30), as well as information relating to space and visual patterns.

Although the two hemispheres deal with different sides of the body and perform somewhat different functions, they cooperate closely through the corpus calossum. When this connecting cable is cut, as has sometimes been done for medical reasons, some rather strange results occur. Patients may exhibit little change in intelligence, personality, and general behavior, yet careful testing reveals that in some ways they act as if they possess two separate brains functioning independently.

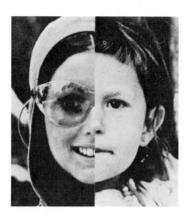

7-16
Whose face is this?

If you saw this composite face, and were asked to compare it with the eight faces shown in Figure 7-17, how would you identify it? Doubtless you would say that the left half was the face of No. 7, the right half the face of No. 2. For the very different reaction of "split-brain" subjects, see the discussion in the text.

One of the most striking demonstrations of this fact has been obtained by using the photographs shown in Figures 7-16 and 7-17. The composite photo in Figure 7-16 is shown to "split-brain" subjects—as those with a severed corpus callosum are known—in such a manner that the right side of the photo is transmitted to the left hemisphere. The left half of the photo is transmitted to the right hemisphere. Asked to say whose photo it is, split-brain subjects have no hesitation in replying that it is "the child" whose full photograph is No. 2 in Figure 7-17. But if subjects are asked to point to whose photo is shown, they point to the young woman with the large glasses, No. 7. When the question requires a verbal response, the left half of the brain prevails. When the question involves a nonlinguistic response—such as pointing—the right half prevails (31).

7-17
The faces for comparison

These are the eight photographs with which split-brain subjects were asked to compare the composite photo in Figure 7-16.

The brain and behavior

Investigations of the brain have included some rather remarkable experiments in controlling the behavior of animals through electrical or chemical stimulation of various parts of the brain or through surgery that destroys some of the brain tissue. For example, when a particular small part of the hypothalamus is destroyed in experimental surgery, animals stay awake until they die of exhaustion. When another small part of the hypothalamus is destroyed, the animals spend most of their time sleeping (32). Injecting different kinds of chemicals into the hypothalamus has been found to make a rat stop eating, even if hungry; or to make it eat, even if already gorged on food (33).

The most valuable thing we know about the brain, however, goes far beyond this knowledge of the functions of its various specific parts. In a normal organism, with an intact and undamaged brain and with no artificial stimulation coming from electrodes, the brain acts as a unit; it works as an entity to integrate behavior and especially as the instrument through which behavior is modified by learning. We know that the pathways of learning laid down in the brain are the real controllers of behavior; they influence how we will interpret and respond to the stimuli that reach our senses; they influence what we find pleasant and what we find unpleasant; they determine what we find psychologically stressful and what we will react to emotionally; they, even more than real physical needs, influence our habits of sleep, hunger, thirst, and sexual behavior.

The controversy over "brain control"

Some of the experiments in controlling the behavior of animals seem to many people to be downright frightening. In the experiment shown in Figure 7-18, for example, it appears that an electrode implanted in one

7-18

Electrical control of behavior

The cat in the photograph at left, under electrical stimulation applied deep in the front part of the cerebrum, ignores its traditional prey the rat. The cat at right, stimulated in the region of the hypothalamus, assumes a hostile posture toward a laboratory assistant with whom it is ordinarily on friendly terms.

part of the brain can make an animal so docile that it will ignore a traditional enemy, while an electrode in another part of the brain will make it hostile and aggressive. Electrical stimulation has even been shown to turn off the charge of a rampaging bull, as was mentioned in Chapter 1 (page 7).

It is also known that many drugs can affect the workings of the brain, chiefly by affecting the amounts and efficiency of the neurotransmitters released at the synapses. Drugs that aid in transmission can relieve the deep depressions suffered by certain kinds of mental patients, while drugs that slow down transmission can combat the anxiety and hallucinations of others. It has been seriously suggested by some writers that what the world needs is a drug that will turn off humanity's aggressive impulses and therefore end crime and war.

Will there come a day when people everywhere are subject to some kind of brain control? When perhaps all of us go around with electrodes in our brains to make us behave as it has been decided—perhaps by government, perhaps by the medical profession, perhaps even by psychologists—that we should behave? Will we perhaps be on a daily dose of drugs to keep us happy, content, productive, and placid?

Science fiction writers have often written about a world of this kind. And many psychologists believe that a considerable amount of brain control, for better or for worse, is indeed possible. Other psychologists believe that we have nothing to worry about. One student of the way the brain functions has suggested that possibly animals such as the cat shown in Figure 7-18 are not really made docile or aggressive; perhaps the electrodes merely set up some kind of motor behavior that gives the appearance of emotion. This investigator has also pointed out that an electrode in any given part of the brain does not always produce the same response; nor does a drug always produce one specific effect. In this psychologist's opinion, the workings of the brain are so complex, the circuits that control any form of behavior so widespread, the alternate pathways so numerous, that it is doubtful whether anybody could exercise brain control over us even if we submitted to the implantation of electrodes or daily medication (34).

Altered states of consciousness

When we think of consciousness, we think of ourselves as going about the usual business of our waking hours, realistically aware of what is going on about us, thinking rationally, sizing up events and responding to them sensibly. Most psychological studies are concerned with this state of "normal" consciousness; they explore the manner in which we learn, solve problems, see, hear, and organize our perceptions when all the complex circuits of the brain are functioning in their usual workaday fashion.

In recent years, however, a growing number of psychologists have become interested in the fact that there are other kinds of brain activity that can best be called *altered states of consciousness*. One of them that we all experience is sleep, which turns out to be a much more complex and interesting phenomenon than the mere state of unconsciousness that most of us assume it to be. Others occur under hypnosis or in the trancelike states sought by the many Americans who have begun in recent years to practice the Eastern arts of yoga and transcendental meditation. Still others are produced by drugs such as marijuana and LSD, which in one way or another affect the transmission of nervous impulses in the brain. (Sometimes they act as neurotransmitters; sometimes they interfere with the brain's own production of neurotransmitter substances or inhibit the activity of the neurotransmitters.)

Sleep and dreaming

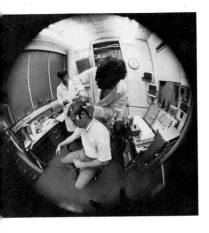

One way scientists have studied sleep is through the use of a device called the electroencephalograph, or EEG for short, which has electrodes that can be placed on the outside of the skull at any given point. The EEG is sensitive enough to produce tracings of the electrical activity produced by patterns of activity in those parts of the brain lying beneath the electrodes.

The EEG studies have shown quite clearly that sleep is by no means a state of suspended animation in which body and brain are shut down for a time. Sleep is not just a slowing down but a kind of activity in its own right. The brain continues to be highly active—though in a different way (35).

Ordinary and paradoxical sleep. One of the peculiar facts about sleep is that it takes two different forms.

1 *Ordinary sleep* is characterized by the fact that the activity of the brain, as can be seen from the EEG tracing in Figure 7-19, is quite dif-

7-19

Brain and muscle activity during sleep

The tracings show typical patterns of brain waves and muscle activity during periods of wakefulness, ordinary sleep, and paradoxical (or REM) sleep. Note that during paradoxical sleep the brain waves resemble the pattern during wakefulness, but the muscles are most relaxed of all. (36)

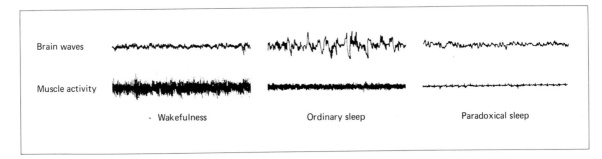

Brain waves

Muscle activity

Wakefulness   Ordinary sleep   Paradoxical sleep

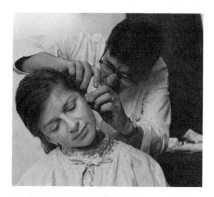

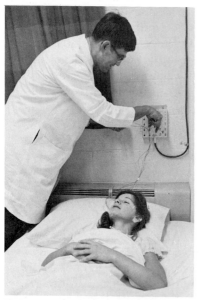

Monitoring brain patterns at the Dartmouth Sleep Laboratory.

ferent from its activity during waking hours and the muscles of the body are quite relaxed. Four stages of ordinary sleep, ranging from light to very deep, can be distinguished in EEG tracings; during the night we move back and forth among these four stages. Most people have three periods of the deepest sleep, the first starting within an hour after dropping off, the last ending after about three or four hours.

2 *Paradoxical sleep* is characterized by the fact that the brain's activity becomes very similar to its waking activity while the muscles become even more relaxed. It is in periods of paradoxical sleep that dreaming occurs. The eyes dart about as if following a series of visual images, and a sleeper who is awakened at this time reports a dream. Thus paradoxical sleep is also known as *REM sleep*—REM standing for the *rapid eye movements* that can be observed during these periods.

Everyone dreams every night, even though the dreams may not be remembered, and the periods of dreaming seem to fall into a pattern common to everyone. The first dream usually occurs about 100 minutes after falling asleep and is the shortest of the night, lasting five or six minutes. The others follow at 100-minute intervals and may last as long as an hour, especially toward morning. On the average, young adult males spend close to two hours of the night dreaming (37). The total is greater for babies and lower for older people.

Why we sleep. Laboratory experiments with subjects who have volunteered to stay awake for long periods show that sleep is definitely essential to our well-being. Such subjects have proved to be able to perform various tasks with their usual accuracy, but their performance was slowed down as if they were having trouble concentrating. They became depressed and irritable (38). In some studies, indeed, the subjects began to talk irrationally and to suffer hallucinations, imagining that they saw or heard something that did not exist (39).

REM sleep appears to be as essential as sleep in general. Experiments have shown that if sleepers are wakened every time they enter an REM period, as shown by their eye movements, and are thus stopped from dreaming, they will make up for it the following night—as if they had a need to put in some definite number of hours of REM sleep (40).

Exactly why we sleep or should need two kinds of sleep is not known. The answer is certainly related to brain activity. As has been said, sleep is known to be controlled by parts of the brain. Moreover, one of the brain structures (the pons) has been found to contain a control center for the rapid eye movements of dreaming. The answer also seems to be related in some way to bodily chemistry. But what kinds of chemicals are involved or where in the body or brain they are produced is not known.

One investigator has suggested a theory that seems a logical deduction from the known facts. The theory is that ordinary sleep performs the function of restoring the body's physical balance, while REM sleep restores our ability to perform psychological functions—perhaps by somehow renewing the chemical substances that transmit messages in the brain (41).

Sleep rhythms. All of us have a physiological rhythm related to our sleeping habits. During sleep, body temperature reaches its low point of the twenty-four hour day, and the release of hormones by the glands is at a minimum. Temperature and glandular activity are at their peak when we are widest awake. For some people, the peak comes right after waking; for others, considerably later in the day. This accounts for the fact that some of us are "day people" who wake up full of energy, do most of our day's work by noon, and are tired early in the evening, while others are "night people" who have a hard time dragging ourselves out of bed, do our best work toward the end of the day, and like to stay up late.

There are some noticeable individual differences in the amount of sleep required. Though most people get along on seven to eight hours a night, some people function perfectly well on much less, while others need much more. One study made a comparison of subjects who slept less than six hours a night with another group of subjects who always slept more than nine hours. Strangely enough, despite the great variations in number of hours spent in bed, both the short and the long sleepers were found to spend equal amounts of time in the deeper stages of ordinary sleep. But there was a striking difference in the amount of REM sleep—nearly twice as much for the long sleepers as for the short sleepers.

Personality tests disclosed some sharp differences between the two groups. The short sleepers tended to be energetic, efficient, hard-working, and self-satisfied; they did not worry or even think very much about their own or the world's problems. The long sleepers tended to do a lot of thinking and worrying about their life styles, their personal problems, and the state of the world. In terms of the theory that REM sleep restores psychological functions, perhaps long sleepers need more REM sleep because they undergo more psychological strain during the day (42). It is also possible, however, that the cause and effect relationship is just the opposite. Perhaps large amounts of REM sleep, whatever the reason may be, produces a tendency to find life's situations stressful.

What do dreams mean? Dreams have always fascinated humanity. In a primitive society, a man goes to sleep and in his dreams seems to travel. He goes fishing on a distant river; he goes hunting on a distant plain; he meets his friends; he even meets and converses with people who are long since dead. When he wakes up, anybody can tell him that his body has not moved at all from his bed. What could be more natural than to believe that the human body is also inhabited by a human soul, which can leave and reenter the body at will and survives after death?

Dreams have also been thought of as portents of the future. With billions of people all over the world dreaming an average of two hours a night, there are bound to be numerous occasions when someone dreams of the death of a friend and the friend actually does die soon afterward, or when a dream seems to "predict" a train wreck, the receipt of an important letter, or the result of a sports event. Such events are

"Oh, to dream once more the untroubled dreams of childhood!"

Drawing by Whitney Darrow, Jr.; ©
1973 The New Yorker Magazine, Inc.

mere coincidences, of course; they tell nothing about the nature or meaning of dreams.

Since the time of Sigmund Freud, a different kind of meaning has been attached to dreams. Freud believed that dreams were an expression of wishes prohibited by the dreamer's conscience. Forbidden sexual desires, in particular, he thought, were likely to crop up—often in a hidden form in which the male sexual organ was symbolized by a snake, a tower, or an airplane, the female organ by a basket or a flower.

Many psychoanalysts and other therapists have followed Freud's lead; they try to analyze their patients' dreams in search of clues to hidden conflicts. Although different therapists use different methods of interpreting dreams, enough successes have been reported to indicate that the content of a dream may indeed reflect the dreamer's personality at times. The recent findings about REM sleep, however, seem to make it clear that dealing with conflicts is not the basic purpose of dreaming. Not only babies but also monkeys, sheep, rats, and chickens have been found to display the rapid eye movements associated with dreaming (43)—and it is hard to imagine that they have any forbidden wishes.

Hypnosis

The most mysterious of all the altered states of consciousness is the one that occurs during hypnosis. To produce this strange phenomenon, the hypnotist may ask the subject to sit as relaxed as possible and stare fixedly at some small object, such as a key, the tip of a pencil, or a point of light. Meanwhile the hypnotist speaks in a quiet and repetitive monotone, suggesting that the subject is growing more and more relaxed, that the subject's eyes are tiring, and that the subject is becoming sleepy. Soon the subject seems to respond to the suggestions: the eyelids flutter and close; the body becomes limp; the head droops; apparently the subject is sound asleep (44).

There is no similarity, however, between the hypnotic state and real sleep. EEG tracings are completely different; so are many measures of bodily activity. Moreover, the subject remains fully conscious of the hypnotist's voice and will respond to the hypnotist's suggestions.

Not everybody can be hypnotized. Perhaps as many as 10 percent show almost no response at all. Only about 25 percent enter the deeper stages of the hypnotic experience and only about 5 to 10 percent enter the very deepest stages (45). Those who are most susceptible tend to be normal, outgoing people of the type who readily become imaginatively involved in events—"carried away" by books or movies, for example. Often they were rather severely punished in childhood, an experience that perhaps inclines them to obey the hypnotist's suggestions (46).

Behavior under hypnosis. A deeply hypnotized subject may behave in ways that seem far removed from any normal experience. At the hypnotist's suggestion, the subject may "see" a chair where none exists; if asked to move about the room, the subject will carefully avoid this hallucinated "chair" as if to prevent a collision. Therapists who use hypnosis have apparently persuaded their subjects to regress in age and act as if they were back in their childhoods, and thus to recall forgotten incidents that created their psychological problems (47).

Some of the most spectacular claims for hypnosis come from physicians and dentists who have practiced it. They report that they have been able to perform the most painful kinds of surgery and dentistry without anesthetics, as if the nerve tracts that carry pain impulses from the body to the brain were somehow blocked off by hypnosis. Indeed it has been claimed that some patients under hypnosis are able to regulate many kinds of bodily activities that are not ordinarily under conscious control (the activities usually carried out by the autonomic nervous system). For example, they are said to be able to regulate their heart beats and to stop bleeding, apparently by clamping down the muscles of the blood vessels.

The controversy over hypnosis. Knowledge of hypnosis is as yet very sketchy. Until recently the entire subject was considered a kind of dubious magic more suitable for being performed on the stage than examined in the laboratory. It was only a relatively short time ago that a few psychologists began making a serious effort to study the phenomenon scientifically, and the number of investigators in the field is still rather small.

Some psychologists continue to believe that hypnosis is highly overrated and not an altered state of consciousness at all. They are convinced that all the various behaviors of a subject under hypnosis are produced by merely manipulating the subject's motivation and suggestibility — and they say they have produced many of the same effects without putting their subjects under hypnosis at all (48).

Meditation

Many Americans are currently seeking another kind of altered state of consciousness through the practice of meditation, which has long been a part of philosophies and religions in the Eastern world. Among the methods followed are yoga, Zen, and transcendental meditation. Though these vary somewhat, they all have as their goal a frame of mind in which ordinary thought processes are suspended and the mind is opened to enhanced perceptions of beauty and truth and perhaps religious insights that defy any attempt to put them into words. This frame of mind is sought through relaxation of the muscles, sometimes through controlled breathing, and in the case of transcendental meditation through the constant repetition in one's thoughts of a word called a mantra, usually taken from the Hindu holy books.

Meditation has been found to change the patterns of brain activity as shown by EEG tracings; in particular, it increases the occurrence of what are called alpha waves (49), which are characteristic of a person

who is relaxed with eyes closed. The rate of breathing and the consumption of oxygen by the body may decline by about 15 percent (50), indicating a very deep kind of relaxation.

Some studies indicate that people who practice meditation may gain long-term physical and psychological effects, carrying over into the ordinary hours of their days. One investigator found that subjects who had been practicing transcendental meditation showed less physical evidence of stress when subjected to unpleasant noises than did other people (51). Students in India taking part in a yoga training program were found to show beneficial changes in glandular functioning and metabolic activity, as well as improved memory, task performance, and resistance to mental fatigue (52).

It is interesting to note that people who report the greatest effects from meditation seem to have some of the same characteristics as people who are most susceptible to hypnotism (53). Moreover, the repetition of a mantra bears resemblance to the repetitious monotone of the hypnotist. It seems quite possible that meditation is a form of self-hypnosis—raising all the mystery and controversy that surround hypnosis itself.

Bio-feedback

Another well-publicized new form of altering consciousness centers around the term *bio-feedback,* used to describe the process of learning to control physiological activities through the feedback of information about changes in these activities. It has been found that it is relatively easy to learn to control the brain's alpha waves in this manner. An electroencephalograph is used to monitor the brain waves—and whenever alpha waves appear, the subject is notified by some signal such as a light or a sound. Eventually, through a form of operant conditioning, the subject is able to produce alpha waves almost at will. Thus the subject can enter into the calm and relaxed mental states associated with these waves (54).

A complex biofeedback experiment.

The typical alcoholic American

young   old   male   female

black   white   rich   poor

employed   unemployed   executive   laborer

student   doctor   immigrant   native born

There's no such thing as typical.
We have all kinds. Nine million alcoholic Americans.
It's our number one drug problem.

NATIONAL INSTITUTE
ON ALCOHOL ABUSE
AND ALCOHOLISM

Drugs

The use of drugs to alter states of consciousness goes far back in human history. It would appear that humanity has always been interested in finding substances that can relieve anxiety, produce feelings of contentment and happiness, and sometimes result in strange experiences that make the user perceive the world in distorted fashion, have hallucinations of imaginary sights and sounds, and perhaps attain a mystical religious sense of oneness with the universe.

Some of the mind-altering substances used today are so routine a part of our social scene that they are seldom even thought of as drugs. *Nicotine*, which constitutes the chief appeal of smoking, is a chemical that acts in several different ways—sometimes as a stimulant, sometimes as a sort of tranquilizer relieving feelings of anxiety. *Caffeine*, found in coffee and tea, is quite a powerful stimulant. *Alcohol* acts as a depressant to the activity of parts of the brain; it relieves inhibitions and encourages the talkativeness and flirtations characteristic of cocktail parties. In large quantities alcohol sometimes releases feelings of hostility and aggressiveness (as in the barroom fight) and often interferes with motor coordination (causing the drunken person to stagger).

All the mind-altering drugs create their effects by temporarily changing the activity of the brain—certainly by assisting or hindering in the transmission of messages at the brain's innumerable switching points, perhaps also by changing the circuits over which messages ordinarily flow. Almost invariably, their effects depend not only on the drug itself and the amount used but also on the frame of mind of the user and the circumstances in which the drug is used. That is to say, what happens depends partly on what the user expects to happen—and partly also on whether the user is alone or in the company of others and how these companions behave. As in the case of hypnosis, suggestibility affects the results (55).

Marijuana. In the case of marijuana, the effects are especially difficult to study because there have been found to be more than 100 different varieties of the marijuana plant, some of which may be 400 times as strong as others (56). Moreover, marijuana users often combine the drug with varying amounts of alcohol, thus further complicating the problem of studying what the drug itself does.

Insofar as can be judged from laboratory experiments, marijuana raises the pulse rate and causes reddening of the eyes and dryness of the mouth and throat; it does not produce any other very marked physical effects. As for the psychological effects, laboratory subjects often report that they get feelings of happiness and elation, become more friendly for a time and then tend to withdraw, become less aggressive, have trouble concentrating, tend to get dizzy and feel as if they were dreaming, and eventually become sleepy. On a simulated test of driving skill they make more speedometer errors, as if they were not watching the speedometer as much as they normally would (57). Tests of ability to think through a series of logical steps have suggested that the drug reduces short-term memory and the ability to make decisions rapidly (58). In one experiment a control group received marijuana from which the active ingredients had been removed, while other groups received various strengths of the drug. The subjects then were asked to start with a number such as 114, subtract 7, then add either 1, 2, or 3, and repeat the process until they reached another number, such as 54. The combined score for speed and accuracy was highest for the control group, which did about 50 percent better than subjects who had received a small dose of marijuana and more than 100 percent better than subjects who had received a large dose (59).

Studies of people who use the drug outside the laboratory have suggested that they probably have different reasons and obtain different kinds of reactions. One investigator, after interviewing a large group of college students and "street people" who were regular users, concluded that they fell into three categories: 1) "insight users," who believed the drug gave them an expanded awareness and made them more creative; 2) "social users," who took the drug mostly for enjoyment and a feeling of warmth and togetherness with their friends; and 3) "release users," who found that it lowered their inhibitions and gave them a feeling of escape from reality (60). This study may explain why there are so many conflicting reports about the kinds of effects that users experience.

Some observers have concluded that the regular use of marijuana produces long-term personality changes, notably loss of motivation, ambition, and judgment (61). Other observers, however, have concluded that it is less likely that the drug causes loss of motivation than that people who have low motivation to begin with are more inclined than others to use it heavily (62).

So far as is known, marijuana does not produce any physical dependence that makes its users crave the drug and suffer withdrawal symptoms in its absence, as do users of a "hard" drug such as heroin. However, it does seem to produce a psychological dependence. In Egypt, where marijuana can be obtained easily despite laws against it, a study of people who use it five to fifty times a month showed that two-thirds wanted to stop—yet continued because of its soothing and mood-elevating effects as well as the fact that they were used to smoking it in social situations (63). Whether the use of marijuana tends to lead to addiction to heroin is not known but seems unlikely. Many heroin addicts began with marijuana (64)—but obviously only a small number of marijuana users go on to hard drugs (65).

LSD (or "acid"). Of all the mind-altering drugs, LSD appears to be the most unpredictable. Even the same person, using it with the same companions and under much the same circumstances, is likely to experience different effects on different occasions.

Often the drug affects the perceptual process; users see brighter colors and new textures and have an increased sense of space. With eyes open, users may stare at a simple object for minutes on end, finding it unbelievably fascinating. With eyes closed, they are likely to have hallucinations, seeing imaginary designs, scenes, and faces, and hearing imaginary music and conversation. On a "bad trip," as an unpleasant experience with LSD is known, users may imagine that their bodies are distorted and rotting, that they are surrounded by darkness and gloom, perhaps that they are dying (66).

LSD is a hallucinogenic drug, so called because of the hallucinations it produces. Other similar drugs are mescaline (which comes from a cactus plant known as the peyote) and psilocybin (found in a Mexican mushroom). It is interesting to note that many people who try these drugs give them up after a time—apparently because of the unpredictable effects and the fact that the perceptual distortions and hallucinations lose their novelty appeal (67).

The amphetamines. The group of drugs chemically labeled *amphetamines* are variously known among their users as uppers, bennies, meth, and speed. All of them are powerful stimulants to the brain, and especially to the centers for arousal and wakefulness. They are often used to combat the effects of fatigue, by people who study or work long hours. They also produce a sense of well-being, a feeling of being alert and on top of the world.

Unfortunately, the amphetamines do not actually relieve fatigue but only mask the feeling; their users are just as tired as before and incapable of performing as well as they think they can. In World War II, for example, pilots who flew long missions over Europe often took amphetamines to keep them awake during the return trip—in many cases only to crash on landing because fatigue had dulled their ability to perform the delicate motor tasks that a landing requires (68).

Amphetamines, indeed, are among the most dangerous of all drugs. Many users tend to become addicted because they build up a tolerance to the drug and must use more and more to achieve the same effect. The

Drawings made under the influence of LSD.

"high" created by amphetamines, especially when injected into the bloodstream, may be accompanied by severe feelings of anxiety and irrational thinking leading to violent behavior, followed by a depression in which the user becomes suicidal. The drug can cause psychological disturbances that make it impossible for the user to keep attending college or work at a job (69), and prolonged abuse of the drug has been found to produce brain damage (70).

Similar in effect to the amphetamines is *cocaine,* a drug extracted from the leaves of the South American coca plant. It, too, may produce dangerous behavior and addiction.

The "downers." The drugs popularly known as *"downers,"* which are in fact sedatives of varying strength and duration of effect, include the barbiturates and other sleep-inducing compounds; among them are Quaaludes, Sopors, Seconals, and Tuinals. They produce a surge of relaxation, well-being, and abandonment—in which, according to their intended use, the user can quickly and blissfully fall off to sleep. When taken for kicks, the user fights off the urge to sleep and tries to maintain the pleasant feelings, which in many ways resemble those produced by alcohol.

Heroin. The most widely publicized drug of all, the subject of countless newspaper stories, movies, and television shows, is *heroin*—a drug considered so dangerous that its use even for medical purposes is prohibited in the United States.

Heroin, like two similar but less potent drugs called *morphine* and *codeine,* is a derivative of the poppy plant. All three drugs are classed as narcotics, meaning that they induce repose or sleep and relieve pain. In illegal use, heroin is usually injected into the flesh or even more commonly into a vein. It produces an immediate rush of pleasure and freedom from anxiety—a "high" in which users forget their problems and feel on top of the world.

Apparently many people can try heroin a few times or use it occasionally over a fairly long period without becoming addicted, but it is impossible to say when casual experimentation with the drug may suddenly turn into total dependence (71). The person who becomes an addict needs the drug desperately to avoid the painful withdrawal symptoms that occur when the effect wears off—the shakes, cold sweats, and stomach convulsions. Moreover, the addict needs more and more of the drug as time goes on.

Some psychologists believe that our society's attitude toward heroin —and the legal prohibitions against its use—cause more trouble than the drug itself. Illegally sold heroin is expensive and the habit may eventually cost as much as $150 a day—a fact that leads many addicts to turn to crime. The uncertain quality of any particular purchase of the drug sometimes leads to fatal overdosing, and the use in secret of contaminated needles can cause the spread of a serious liver ailment called hepatitis. In New York City, one of the centers of the illicit heroin traffic, heroin has been the leading cause of death among young people between the ages of fifteen and thirty-five (72).

Summary

1 *Behavior genetics* is the study of how human beings (and other organisms) inherit characteristics that determine behavior.

2 The mechanisms of human heredity are the twenty-three pairs of *chromosomes,* forty-six in all, found in the fertilized egg cell and repeated through the process of division in every cell of the body that grows from this cell.

3 The chromosomes are made up of a large number of *genes,* which are composed of a chemical called *DNA.* The genes direct the growth of cells into parts of the body and also account for the individual differences we inherit.

4 Egg and sperm cells are created through a splitting process that sends half of each pair of chromosomes and genes to one cell and the other half to another cell in a random manner that makes each egg and sperm cell different, permits billions of variations, and virtually guarantees that every individual will be unique (except for identical twins, who develop from the same fertilized egg cell).

5 A *recessive gene,* such as that for blue eyes, inherited from one parent will be suppressed by a *dominant gene,* such as that for brown eyes, inherited from the other parent. But a recessive gene can be passed along to the next generation.

6 Among the important behavior traits that appear to be influenced by heredity are intelligence, a tendency toward the mental disturbance called *schizophrenia,* and inclinations toward being extroverted or introverted.

7 The *endocrine glands,* or *ductless glands,* influence behavior by secreting chemical substances called *hormones* into the bloodstream. A list of important endocrine glands and their functions follows:

   a The *pituitary* is a master gland that secretes hormones that control growth, cause sexual development at puberty, and regulate other endocrine glands.

   b The *thyroid* regulates the rate of metabolism and affects the body's activity level.

   c The *parathyroids* help maintain a normal state of excitability in the nervous system.

   d The *pancreas* secretes *insulin,* a hormone important in the metabolism of blood sugar to provide energy, especially for the brain.

   e The *adrenals* secrete two powerful stimulants called *adrenalin* and *noradrenalin,* as well as a number of other hormones essential to bodily health and activity.

   f The *ovaries* control the development of secondary female sexual characteristics.

   g The *testes* control the development of secondary male sexual characteristics.

8 The nervous system is made up of fiberlike cells called *neurons,* which are stimulated through their *dendrites* (or through receptor sites on the cell body) and pass along a nervous impulse to the end of their *axons.* The nervous impulse is a tiny wave of electricity traveling at 3 to 300 feet a second.

9 The junction point between one neuron and another is a *synapse.* Here the first neuron stimulates the second neuron to fire, usually by releasing a chemical substance called a *neurotransmitter.*

10 *Afferent* neurons carry impulses from the sense organs to the central nervous system. *Efferent* neurons carry messages from the central nervous system to the glands and muscles. *Connecting* neurons are the middlemen between other neurons.

11 One theory of learning is that the neurotransmitters set up a long lasting change in the efficiency of a synapse, so that a nerve circuit once used becomes a path of least resistance for future activity.

12 The *peripheral nervous system* is made up of the outlying neurons carrying messages to and from the sense organs, muscles, and organs of the body.

13 *The autonomic nervous system* exercises a more or less independent and automatic control over the glands, the heart muscles, and the smooth muscles of the body's organs and blood vessels. It helps regulate breathing, heart rate, blood pressure, and digestion; and in times of emergency it works in conjunction with the endocrine glands to mobilize the body's resources for drastic action.

14 The autonomic nervous system is composed of two parts: the *sympathetic division,* which tends to be active in case of emergency, and the *parasympathetic division,* which is most active under ordinary circumstances. Both divisions are connected with the central nervous system.

15 The *central nervous system* is made up of the *brain* and the *spinal cord.*

16 The spinal cord is the center of some of the body's reflexes and serves as a trunk line for impulses to and from the brain.

17 In structure, the brain is made up of the 1) *hindbrain,* 2) *midbrain,* and 3) *forebrain.*

18 Important parts of the hindbrain and their functions are:

a The *medulla* is responsible for a number of vital bodily processes including breathing and the beating of the heart; it is also a relay station between the spinal cord and higher parts of the brain.

b The *cerebellum* controls bodily balance and the coordination of complicated muscular movements.

c The *pons* serves as a bridge between the two halves (or right and left hemispheres) into which the cerebellum is divided.

19 The midbrain is a relay station for messages from the eyes and ears and a major part of the *reticular activating system,* which keeps the upper part of the brain in a state of arousal and activity.

20 The forebrain contains four structures of special interest:

a The *thalamus* processes information from the sense organs and serves as a relay station for messages to and from the topmost parts of the brain.

    b The *hypothalamus* is the brain's most important link to the glands and helps regulate such bodily processes as hunger, thirst, sexual behavior, maintenance of bodily temperature, sleeping, and wakefulness.

    c The *cerebrum* is the largest and topmost part of the brain. Like the cerebellum, it is divided into right and left hemispheres.

    d The *corpus callosum* is a large nerve bundle connecting the two hemispheres of the cerebrum and enabling them to cooperate.

21 The *cerebral cortex* is the surface of the cerebrum, a densely packed layer of neurons. It accounts for our sensations when the sense organs are stimulated, initiates motor movements and language, and is responsible for learning, memory, and decision-making; thus it is the seat of human intelligence.

22 *Altered states of consciousness,* in which brain functions differ from their normal, workaday, rational operations, include *sleep, hypnosis,* states of *meditation,* alpha wave control through *bio-feedback,* and changes produced by *drugs.*

23 *Sleep* appears to be controlled by the brain's reaction to chemical changes in the body, of an unknown nature.

24 There are two kinds of sleep. *Ordinary sleep* appears to restore physical functions. *Paradoxical sleep* is characterized by dreaming and appears to restore the brain's psychological functions. Because of the rapid eye movements that occur during dreaming, paradoxical sleep is also known as *REM sleep.*

Recommended reading

Brecher, E. M. *Licit and illicit drugs.* Boston: Little, Brown, 1972.

Glass, D. C., ed. *Neurophysiology and emotion.* New York: Rockefeller University Press, 1967.

Lewin, R. *The nervous system.* Garden City, N.Y.: Anchor Books, Doubleday, 1974.

Luria, A. R. *The working brain.* New York: Basic Books, 1973.

Rosenthal, D. *Genetic theory and abnormal behavior.* New York: McGraw-Hill, 1970.

Tart, C. T. *Altered states of consciousness.* New York: John Wiley, 1969.

Thompson, R. F. *Foundations of physiological psychology.* New York: Harper & Row, 1967.

Valenstein, E. S. *Brain control.* New York: John Wiley, 1973.

FIVE
FEELINGS AND MOTIVES

The human brain, described in Part 4, can in some ways be compared to a computer, with network upon network of complicated circuits and switching points. As was discussed in Part 3, it receives the equivalent of the computer's inputs through the sense organs and the process of perception. As was discussed in Part 2, it has its own kind of memory bank, laid down in the pathways of learning, and does its own kind of data processing in the form of thinking and problem solving.

In the remaining chapters of the book, however, we come to a series of topics where any comparison between the human being and the computer breaks down. For example, no human being goes through life as mechanically and dispassionately as the computer. All of us experience swings of mood. Depending on how things are going at the moment, we may feel mildly confident, buoyant, or even elated; on the contrary, we may feel "blue," grief-stricken, or panicky. We experience anger, fear, and anxiety. Moreover, most of us spend a great deal of our energies pursuing some kind of goal. The goal may be a simple one, such as passing a college course or finding time to watch a favorite television show every week. It may be a complicated and long-term goal, such as becoming a surgeon or a successful musician. It may be an abstract goal, such as helping humanity and making the world a better place to live. Indeed we usually have many goals, some simple and immediate and others complex and long-range, some of them selfish and some of them humanitarian.

In the following part of the book, Chapter 8 discusses the origins and consequences of emotions, and Chapter 9 ("Drives and Motives") discusses the search for goals. Between them, emotions and motives go far to account for and clarify the variety and richness of human personality and behavior—and to start demonstrating the contrast between man and machine.

Emotions

At a college football game, an alumnus who is a dignified and usually soft-spoken physician jumps to his feet, boos the referee, moans when the other team scores a touchdown, and sheds tears of joy when his own team comes from behind in the final quarter. In an emergency when a child is seriously ill, a concerned mother who had always considered herself physically fragile finds that she can stay awake and alert for forty-eight hours.

These are some of the more striking examples of how emotions influence behavior. Another is the kind of human drama in which people in the grip of rage commit murders, or people in panic fight to escape from a burning building. In more ordinary situations, emotions involving mild excitement or eagerness often help us to learn faster or get a job done more efficiently. But emotions involving fear and anxiety can make us forget everything we studied when we sit down to take an important examination or strike us dumb when we get up and try to make a speech.

Emotions are among the most powerful of the forces that influence behavior. Generally speaking, we do not seem to have much control over them. They seem to boil up of their own accord. Even in situations where we have determined in advance to remain calm, we often find ourselves unaccountably angry, frightened, or anxious. Our emotions command our attention and we cannot ignore them. When we feel intensely emotional, we cannot concentrate on performing our jobs as we should, or choosing our words carefully, or even listening to music or reading.

Strong emotions—of the kind that made Oedipus gouge out his eyes, Juliet renounce her family for Romeo, and Hamlet kill his uncle the king—have been the chief subject of the world's literature, in all nations throughout history. Philosophers have always tried to understand them, and they have been an important field of psychological investigation ever since the earliest studies of Wilhelm Wundt.

**Bodily changes
in emotion**

Suppose you are riding in a bus, minding your own business. The woman next to you taps you gently on the arm, politely begs your pardon for interrupting you, and says, in a perfectly calm tone of voice and with a facial expression that shows no sign that she is in any way upset or angry, "I don't like you." Then she turns away and quietly resumes reading her newspaper. If you were asked afterward whether she had displayed emotion (not just signs of eccentricity), what would you say?

Now suppose that you carelessly drive through a stop sign, run into another automobile, and badly damage the whole side of it. The other driver gets out and says, "It's all right; don't worry about it; everybody makes mistakes; anyway, I'm insured." You note, however, that his voice is quivering, his facial muscles are twitching, and his hands are trembling. Is he emotional or is he not?

To the first question most people would answer *no,* even though the kind of aggressive behavior involved in a remark such as "I don't like you" ordinarily is highly emotional. To the second question most people would answer *yes,* even though a matter-of-fact remark such as "It's all right" is usually considered to show the absence of emotion. Most scientific investigators of emotion would agree about the driver of the automobile. Before agreeing about the woman on the bus they would want to make sure that she was really as calm inwardly as she appeared on the surface.

Both scientists and laymen reserve the words *emotion* and *emotional* for cases in which physiological changes accompany mental activity. The easiest cases to recognize are those in which the organism is quite obviously "stirred up." We assume that other people are emotional when we note that their voices are unusually high-pitched, when they blush or get pale, when their muscles grow tense or tremble. We know that we are ourselves emotional—even if we manage to conceal all outward signs—when we can feel that we are inwardly shaking, or are "hot under the collar," or that our mouths are dry, our pulses racing, or our stomachs "full of butterflies." But there are also quieter emotions in which the body almost seems to be "toned down." Such are the calm, peaceful, and contented feelings of a person enjoying a sun bath, a beautiful piece of music, or a cup of coffee after a satisfying meal. In these cases too, however, the physiological processes are affected in some manner.

The relationship between mind and body in emotion seems to work both ways. Think about something very pleasant, such as inheriting a million dollars from an unknown relative or anything else that appeals to you. Quite possibly you will soon *feel* pleasant. Think of something that angers you, such as a bad grade, a social snub, being blamed for someone else's mistake. Soon you may *feel* angry. Or try the opposite. Make a smile, hold it, and see if you do not begin to feel happy and have pleasant thoughts. Clench your fist, keep clenching it, and see if you do not begin to feel angry and have aggressive thoughts.

In this connection, an experiment was recently performed in which college students were asked to manipulate their facial muscles without realizing that what they were doing had any relationship to emotions. They were told that the experiment was a study of the effect of muscle movements on perception, and electrodes were attached to the facial muscles to make this explanation seem plausible. With the electrodes in place, the subjects were asked to contract or relax their muscles in a way that at times resembled a smile and at other times resembled a frown. To a very considerable extent, the subjects reported feeling happy when the muscles were in a smiling position and angry when the muscles were in a frowning position—though they were not even aware of their own facial expressions (1).

The nature of the bodily changes

To determine the kinds of physiological changes that take place during emotional states, investigators have used laboratory apparatus of many kinds, such as the device shown in Figure 8-1. Their measurements have shown that the changes are many and varied (2).

Some of the bodily changes in emotion, as is apparent from the experiment on smiling and frowning, represent activity of the striped muscles of movement. One such change is *muscle tension,* as when the teeth are clenched in anger. Another, *tremor,* occurs when two sets of muscles work against each other. Many people, when emotionally excited, have a tendency toward *eye blinking* and other *nervous movements,* such as brushing back their hair or drumming their fingers on a desk. And many emotions result in *vocal expressions,* such as laughter, snarls, moans, and screams, or *facial expressions,* such as frowns, grimaces, and smiles.

The facial expressions of emotion seem to be quite similar for people in all parts of the world and in different kinds of cultures. One inves-

8-1

Measuring the "stirred-up" state of emotion

This instrument produces a continuous record of four physiological processes. The tubes around the young woman's body measure her rate of breathing (thoracic and abdominal), the electrodes attached to her hand her galvanic skin reflex (or change in the electrical conductivity of the skin caused by sweating), and the band around her upper arm her heart rate and blood pressure. These physiological processes and many others that can be measured by more complicated apparatus may be affected in states of emotion. This particular polygraph is often used in the detection of deception and therefore is referred to as a "lie detector."

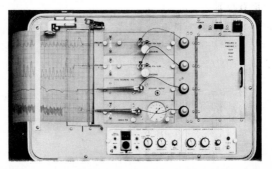

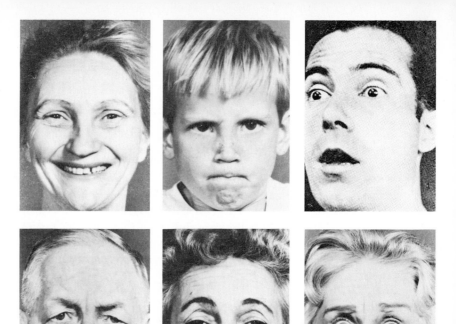

8-2

Facial expressions of emotion

Try to determine the emotions being expressed by these faces before looking at the answers in the footnote. The photographs were among those used in the cross-cultural study described in the text.

tigator presented photographs such as those shown in Figure 8-2 to subjects in a number of different societies. He found that there was a large amount of agreement as to what emotions were being expressed in the photographs—not only among subjects in the United States, Argentina, Brazil, Chile, and Japan but among members of isolated and undeveloped societies in New Guinea. The study indicates that facial expressions of many emotions seem to be universal and unlearned (3).

All the various changes involving the striped muscles of movement are normally under conscious control, but in emotional states they do not appear to be voluntary; they "just happen" as part of the general pattern of change that accompanies emotion. Other changes are controlled by the autonomic nervous system (pages 249–52) and by the endocrine glands (pages 239–41), over which we have little conscious control even under ordinary circumstances. In many emotional states the rate of heartbeat increases, sometimes from the normal of 72 per minute to as high as 180. Blood pressure may also rise sharply, and blood is often diverted from the digestive organs to the striped muscles and to the surface of the body, resulting in flushed cheeks and the sensation of being "hot under the collar." The composition of the blood changes. The number of red corpuscles, which carry oxygen, increases markedly, and the secretion of hormones by the endocrine glands produces changes in the level of blood sugar, acidity of the blood, and the amount of adrenalin and noradrenalin (powerful stimulants secreted by the adrenal glands) in the blood stream.

The emotions being expressed in Figure 8-2, clockwise from upper left, are 1) happiness, 2) anger, 3) surprise, 4) sadness, 5) disgust, and 6) fear.

The normal movements of the stomach and intestines, associated with the digestion and absorption of food, usually stop during anger and rage; in other emotional states they may show changes resulting in nausea or diarrhea (4). The body's metabolic rate tends to go up; food in the blood stream and the body tissues themselves are burned off at a faster rate, creating additional energy. Breathing may change in rate, depth, and ratio between time spent breathing in and time spent breathing out; we may gasp or pant. The salivary glands may stop working, causing the feeling of dryness in the mouth that is often associated with fear and anger. The sweat glands, on the other hand, may become overactive, as shown by the dripping forehead that may accompany embarrassment or the "cold sweat" that sometimes accompanies fear. The muscles at the base of the hairs may contract and raise goose flesh. Finally, the pupils of the eyes may enlarge, causing the wide-eyed look that is characteristic of rage, excitement, and pain.

Development of theories of emotion

As has been noted, the stirred-up bodily states that are a part of emotion are highly diffuse. They include various kinds of tension, tremor, and other movements of the striped muscles controlled by the central nervous system, as well as many changes regulated by the autonomic nervous system that affect the endocrine glands, blood chemistry, and the smooth muscles of the visceral organs, the blood vessels, and the iris of the eye. When we are emotional, we tend to be emotional all over. In the adult human being, who has learned to hide many of the outward signs of emotion, this fact may be apparent only to the delicate measuring apparatus of the laboratory. It is much more obvious in the case of animals, as is shown in Figure 8-3.

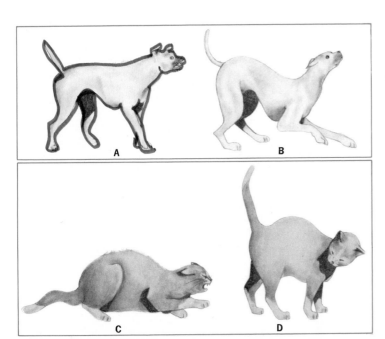

8-3

Emotional postures in the dog and cat

The dog approaching an enemy exhibits many signs of a stirred-up bodily state (A). The bristling hair and the wide and staring eyes are evidence of activity of the autonomic nervous system. The dog's entire posture has been affected: it walks stiffly, holds its tail high, pricks its ears forward, and growls. If it discovers that it is approaching not a hostile stranger but its own friendly master, the pattern immediately changes (B). The hair and pupils return to normal, and the dog may begin salivating. The muscles of its body relax; it lays back its ears and wags its tail. The cat's display of emotion is somewhat different—it crouches toward an enemy (C) and arches its back and purrs for its master (D)—but equally diffuse. (5)

The James-Lange theory

In the long history of scientific investigation of the emotions, these widespread and often dramatic forms of bodily activity have naturally received a great deal of attention. They were the basis of an influential theory of emotion proposed by William James, a theory that has particular interest because it completely reversed all previous thinking about emotions. Common sense says that we cry because we are sad, strike out because we are angry, tremble and run because we are afraid. James made the suggestion—startling to the scientific world of his day and even now to the person who hears it for the first time—that things were exactly the opposite.

James said that emotion occurs in this fashion. Certain stimuli in the environment set off the physiological changes. These changes in turn stimulate the various sensory nerves leading from the visceral organs and other parts of the body to the brain. These sensory messages from our aroused bodies are what we then perceive as emotion. In other words, we do not cry because we are sad; on the contrary, we feel sad because we are crying. Similarly, we do not tremble because we are afraid, but feel afraid because we are trembling (6).

This notion that the physiological changes come first and that the perceived emotion is a feedback from the changes and comes afterward was also proposed at about the same time by the Danish scientist Carl Lange and persisted more or less unchallenged for many years as the *James-Lange theory of emotion.*

The body in anger and fear. If perceived emotion is strictly a matter of feedback from aroused bodily states, then it follows that there should be a different pattern of bodily activity for each emotion, resulting in a distinctive and recognizable pattern of sensory feedback. Many studies have been made, therefore, of the physiological activities that accompany the various emotions.

For anger and fear, the findings have been along lines that the James-Lange theory would predict. In one study, subjects were placed in an apparatus similar to the one shown in Figure 8-1. Laboratory technicians then behaved in ways that angered or frightened the subjects, without disclosing that the actions were deliberate and a part of the experiment. Each subject was made angry on one occasion and fearful on another, and the combined results of the physiological measurements showed some significant differences. In anger there was a tendency for the heart rate to go down, blood pressure to go up, and muscular tension to increase. In fear there was a tendency toward faster breathing and a more spasmodic activity of the muscles. There was also a pronounced difference in the electrical conductivity of the skin (7).

The physiological changes found in this study to be characteristic of anger are the kind known to be produced by the hormone noradrenalin, and the changes found characteristic of fear are known to be produced by the hormone adrenalin. Thus it would appear that the adrenal glands are unusually active in secreting one hormone in anger and a different one in fear—a notion for which additional evidence has been found. In

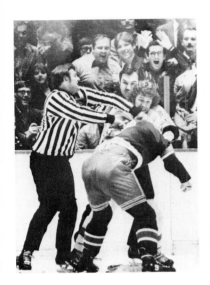

one study, a chemical analysis was made of the urine of players on a professional hockey team to learn how much noradrenalin and adrenalin they were secreting before and after a game. It turned out that the players actively taking part in the game, fighting to win, showed about six times as much noradrenalin after the game as beforehand. But two players who were injured, unable to play, and worried about their future with the team showed increased amounts of adrenalin. The coach sometimes showed more noradrenalin and at other times more adrenalin, depending on how well his team had done in the game (8).

Along the same line, it has been found that animals such as lions, which survive by fighting and killing their prey, have large quantities of noradrenalin in their systems, while rabbits, which survive by running away, have large quantities of adrenalin (9). Thus it appears that anger and "fight" are associated with the physiological effects of noradrenalin, and fear and "flight" with the effects of adrenalin.

The body in other emotional states. Aside from the findings about fear and anger, however, there is not much evidence to support the view that each different emotion depends on a unique pattern of bodily sensations. Certainly no experimenter has ever been able to find a hundred different physiological states to match the hundred different kinds of emotional experience described by our language. In general, the bodily changes in emotion are what recent investigators have called "rather diffuse and global in character" (10). It has proved very difficult to determine, from physiological measurements alone, what kind of emotion a person is experiencing. Indeed the same person, on two separate occasions when he says he feels joyous, may show different bodily changes. And different people may show quite different patterns when experiencing the same emotion. Among students anxious over an examination, one may tend to perspire a great deal, another to show muscle tension, another to have a rapid pulse (11).

In addition, the visceral organs, which James considered to be especially important in emotion, tend to respond rather slowly to impulses from the autonomic nervous system or to stimulation by the hormones. As was noted in Figure 8-3, a dog or cat sometimes changes almost instantly from a posture of rage to a posture of friendliness when it sees that what it thought was a hostile stranger is really its master. The pattern of sensations from the animal's visceral organs could not change that rapidly.

For these reasons and others, the James-Lange theory began to fall into disfavor, and around 1930 a different kind of theory was proposed, based on the rapidly expanding knowledge of how the brain works.

The Cannon-Bard theory

Behavior that appears to be emotional can be triggered by electrical stimulation of the brain: if an electrode is planted in one area of the hypothalamus of a cat, for example, the animal can be made to behave as if enraged by the presence of an enemy. Other studies have also pointed to the importance of the hypothalamus in emotion. Even when the entire cerebral cortex of a dog is removed, the animal still displays most of its typical rage pattern. In fact, the "rage" is produced by mild forms of stimulation that would not disturb a normal dog. The pattern persists in the absence of some other brain structures as well as the cerebral cortex. But the pattern does not occur unless the hypothalamus is intact (12).

It appears that the hypothalamus, with its close relationship to the autonomic nervous system and to the pituitary gland, plays a special role in emotion. This fact led to the formulation of theories of emotion based on brain activity, one of the oldest and best known of which is the *Cannon-Bard theory*. According to this theory, certain stimuli in the environment cause the hypothalamus to fire off patterns of nervous activity that arouse the autonomic nervous system and thus trigger the physiological changes that are associated with emotion. At the same time, the hypothalamus fires off patterns of messages to the cerebral cortex that result in the feelings of emotion. The Cannon-Bard theory, it will be noted, attaches no importance to the feedback of bodily sensations, which is the basic element of the James-Lange theory.

The cognitive theory of emotion

Some newer studies raise the interesting possibility that both the James-Lange and the Cannon-Bard theories of emotion were partially right but that neither offered the full explanation. Modern thinking about emotions has been greatly influenced by experiments performed by Stanley Schachter at Columbia University, which are so important that they deserve discussion here in some detail.

The "happy stooge" and the "angry stooge"

In one experiment Schachter used a volunteer subject, a university student, who agreed to submit to an injection of what he was told was a harmless drug whose effect on vision was being studied. The drug, so the subject was told, would produce certain physical effects—numbness of the feet, itching of the skin, and a slight headache. In truth the subject received an injection of that powerful stimulant adrenalin, in an amount sufficient to produce many of the stirred-up physiological changes that accompany strong emotion.

The subject was asked to sit in a waiting room for a time. In the room was another student, a "stooge" who had specific instructions from Schachter. The stooge began behaving quite strangely. He wadded up paper and used it like a basketball, with a wastebasket as his target. He found a hoop in the room and used it like a hula hoop, dancing around with gay abandon. He folded pieces of paper into toy airplanes and sailed them in all directions. In other words, he acted like a person who was a little out of his head with high spirits. When he invited the sub-

ject to join in the fun, the subject found himself unable to resist. Soon he too was gripped by a feeling of excitement and happiness and was sailing paper airplanes even more boisterously than the stooge.

Another of Schachter's subjects received the same kind of injection and the same story about its effects and also found another student in the waiting room. This time the stooge behaved differently. Instead of acting happy he pretended to be angry; he was bitter and aggressive. Soon the subject, too, found himself feeling angry and behaving in an angry fashion.

The experiment with the two kinds of stooges was performed with a number of subjects. In general, the subjects whose bodies were stirred up with adrenalin felt happy and behaved in a giddy fashion when they were exposed to the happy stooge, and they felt angry and behaved aggressively when exposed to the angry stooge. In each case, presumably, the physiological effects of the adrenalin were more or less the same. The accompanying emotion depended on what was happening around them—the context in which they found themselves.

In another part of the experiment the subjects were treated in exactly the same fashion except that they were told the truth about what kind of physiological reactions to expect from the injections. They were correctly informed that they would experience a fast pulse, hand tremors, and a flushed feeling in the face. These subjects were much less inclined to be influenced by the mood of the stooge; they tended to hold themselves aloof from his high spirits or his anger. A control group of subjects who received a salt water injection also tended to resist the influence of the stooge (13).

Making a funny movie funnier

In another experiment, Schachter had three groups of subjects watch a slapstick movie. Before the movie was shown, group 1 received an injection of adrenalin, and group 2 received an injection of a tranquilizer that suppresses activity of the sympathetic nervous system and therefore has physiological effects that are generally the opposite of those produced by adrenalin. Group 3, the control group, received an injection of salt water. The subjects whose bodies were stirred up by the adrenalin showed the greatest signs of amusement while watching the movie and afterward gave it the highest rating for being funny. The subjects whose physiological activity was suppressed by the tranquilizer showed the least amusement and gave the movie the lowest rating. The control group's reactions were in the middle (14).

Implications of the Schachter experiments

One conclusion toward which the Schachter studies seem to point is that changed bodily states are indeed an essential element in producing feelings of emotion and not just a side effect as the Cannon-Bard theory assumed. It was the group of subjects stirred up by adrenalin who reacted emotionally to the happy stooge and the angry stooge. It was the group of subjects injected with adrenalin who found the movie the most hilarious.

The James-Lange version of *why* feedback from bodily sensations is important, however, appears to be contradicted by the studies. The stirred-up bodily activity produced by the adrenalin injections did not by itself result in a specific emotion or even in any emotion at all. The subjects who had been correctly informed about what kind of bodily sensations to expect did not become giddy when exposed to the happy stooge or angry when exposed to the belligerent stooge. Those who had been misinformed became giddy in one context and angry in another context, even though, presumably, their bodily states were generally alike.

Schachter and his colleagues have concluded that emotions depend on two factors: 1) physiological arousal and 2) a mental process by which subjects interpret or label their physiological sensations. Thus subjects aroused by adrenalin may interpret their sensations as being merely the physical symptoms of rapid heartbeat and tremor that they were told to expect, and they may therefore experience no emotion at all. Subjects aroused by adrenalin and aware of physiological sensations that they do not understand may interpret these sensations as a giddy happiness in one context and as anger in another. Or they may have exaggerated feelings of amusement and joy when they are shown a movie that is funny.

Since the Schachter findings emphasize the mental processes of interpretation and labeling, they are consistent with the position of the cognitive school of psychology (page 25). This new cognitive view of emotions has been colorfully named the "juke box" theory of emotion (15). This is because the stimulus that causes physiological arousal—in normal situations some stimulus in the environment rather than an injection of adrenalin—can be compared to the coin placed in a juke box. It presumably sets off patterns of brain activity, especially in the hypothalamus, that in turn activate the autonomic nervous system and the endocrine glands, causing a general state of physiological arousal. Sensory receptors in the body report these physiological changes to the brain. But the sensations are vague and can be labeled in many different ways, just as the juke box activated by the coin can be made to play any one of a number of different records depending on which button is pushed. We label the sensations on the basis of the environmental context and what we are thinking about at the moment. If they are caused by the sight of a snake, we may feel afraid; if they are caused by a slap in the face, we probably will feel angry.

In the juke box, we start the mechanism by inserting the coin and select the record by pushing a button. In emotion, a stimulus gets physiological changes started, and we ourselves decide what emotion these changes represent.

A tentative definition of emotion

The Schachter findings lead to a definition of emotion that, though it must be advanced with caution, seems to cover many of the known facts: *An emotion is the interpretation of a change in level and quality of internal sensations in a particular context.* The internal sensations result from physiological changes caused by patterns of brain activity, especially in the hypothalamus and limbic system, that act chiefly through the autonomic nervous system. The interpretation is a psychological process that seeks to find the relationship between the sensations and the environmental context and that accounts for our subjective feelings.

There is an interesting parallel between the psychological process involved in emotion and another process discussed earlier in the book. In Chapter 6, you will recall, perception was defined as the process through which we become aware of our environment by organizing and interpreting the evidence of our senses. In emotion, we organize and interpret the sensations from within our bodies. Just as perceptions are the patterns of meaning we find in external stimuli, so our emotional feelings are the patterns of meaning we find in internal stimuli—influenced, however, by our perception of the environmental context.

Note that the definition speaks of a *change* in internal sensations, not an absolute level of sensation. Just as our sense organs are most sensitive to a change in environmental stimuli, so the sensory nerves inside the body are most sensitive to a change in internal conditions. Some emotions are based on a stirred-up condition of the body. Others, such as sadness and loneliness, may involve a level of activity lower than normal, reduced heart rate and blood pressure, and a lack of muscle tone rather than tremor. Hard-driving executives may be more or less stirred up at all times yet unaware of any emotion except when their high rate of physiological activity decreases for some reason.

As for the interpretation we make of the changes in our internal sensations, it is sometimes immediate and automatic. If we find a snake in our path, for example, everything seems to happen at once: our hearts jump, we feel afraid, and we exhibit fearful behavior by leaping back. At other times the interpretation takes longer and is less clear-cut. A student who has a changed pattern of visceral sensations while sitting alone in a room at night may interpret them as loneliness. Another student whose best friend recently died may interpret the same pattern of sensations as grief. A student who has a difficult examination coming up may interpret it as fear or anxiety, and another who has put in an unusually hard day's work may interpret it as fatigue.

Typically, people who become aware of changed internal sensations attempt to explain and understand them. They scan the environment and reach a decision. Sometimes the decision is immediate and often it is reached unconsciously. At other times it involves a longer and more deliberate search that is akin to problem solving; people may select one hypothesis, test it, and discard it in favor of another. At the end of the search they apply an emotionally toned label to their feelings; they decide that they are happy or sad or angry.

The behavior that is undertaken depends largely on how the emotion is labeled. Moreover, the labeling process itself appears in many cases to produce further bodily changes and intensified feelings. Once people have decided that they are afraid, they are likely to experience additional activity of the autonomic nervous system, intensified physiological changes, and greater feedback, all of which add to their feelings of fear.

The behavior that may result from emotion also depends on learning, a fact that has been made quite clear from studies of the differences in expression of emotion in different cultures. When Navajo or Apache Indians are angry, they do not raise but lower their voices; when inhabitants of the Andaman Islands want to show joy at greeting a visiting relative, they sit down in the visitor's lap and weep (16).

Other studies on emotion and interpretation

In one of the many interesting experiments inspired by the work of Schachter and his colleagues, the subjects were men and women who were known to have trouble getting to sleep. They were told that the experiment was a study of how their level of bodily activity, which would be controlled by a pill they were asked to take shortly before going to bed, would affect their dreaming. Actually the pill was what is known in medicine as a placebo—a harmless substance that has no effect on the human body. But half the subjects were told that the pill would arouse them and make them feel as if their minds were racing, the other half that it would relax them and calm down their minds. What the experimenter wanted to discover was what effect, if any, a belief that they were medically aroused or relaxed would have on their ability to get to sleep.

Common sense might predict that the theoretically "aroused" subjects would have more trouble sleeping, while the theoretically "relaxed" would go to sleep more quickly. In actual fact, the results were exactly the opposite—for reasons that you may be able to work out for yourself if you have followed the discussion of emotional interpretations closely. The subjects who thought the placebo had aroused them went to sleep more quickly than usual, presumably because they attributed their keyed-up feelings while lying in bed to the pill rather than to their own emotions. The subjects who thought the placebo had relaxed them stayed awake even longer than they ordinarily did, presumably because they thought they must have been even more emotionally keyed up than usual to remain so tense after taking a pill that was supposed to calm them (17).

In another experiment, subjects were asked to try to solve puzzles while listening to a barrage of loud and unpleasant noises—as part of a study, they were told, of the effect of noise on learning. The experimenters gave them two puzzles and their choice of working on either or both during a three-minute test period. Solving puzzle 1, they were told, would spare them from receiving an electric shock; solving puzzle

2 would bring them a cash reward. Because of the possibility of shock, all subjects showed signs of fear at the beginning of the experiment. But some of them were led to attribute their symptoms of fear—tremors, heart palpitation, and "butterflies in the stomach"—to the noise. The others were told that the noise would merely cause such reactions as ringing of the ears, dizziness, and perhaps dull headache. These subjects presumably knew that their fear symptoms were caused by the prospect of shock.

The real question in the experimenters' minds was how hard the two groups would try either to avoid the shock they thought they would receive if they failed to solve puzzle 1 or to earn some money by solving puzzle 2. (Both puzzles were in fact insoluble.) The answer to the question is shown in Figure 8-4. Of the subjects who recognized that their fears stemmed from the prospect of shock (colored graph line), the majority continued throughout the three minutes to work on the puzzle that would avoid the shock. Of the subjects who attributed their fear to the noise (black line), only a minority continued to work on the shock-avoidance puzzle; when the test period was half over the majority turned their attention to the puzzle that might bring them money (18). Again, interpretation played an important part in emotion and behavior resulting from emotion.

Drugs and emotions. One interesting but not very well understood aspect of emotions is how they are affected by drugs. In one experiment, volunteers in a prison took LSD without knowing what drug had been administered. A number of them reported experiencing very strong emotions of many kinds, ranging from happiness to anger and fear of loss of control. The emotions occurred without any outside stim-

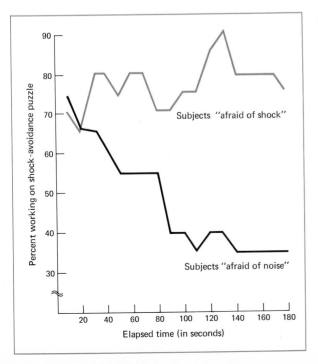

8-4

Is it better to escape a shock or to earn some money?

If you had your choice of trying to solve one puzzle that would spare you from an electrical shock or another puzzle that would bring you the reward of money, which would you choose? The graph lines show what happened when subjects actually faced this situation—and how their choice was influenced by whether they thought their symptoms of fear were caused by the prospect of shock or by noise, as described in the text.

ulus and for reasons that the subjects were unable to interpret. Some of their comments were, "I feel like I'm angry . . . I know that I have no reason to be, yet I'm getting angrier by the minute," and "I feel like something funny has happened—everything seems funny, but I don't know why" (19).

The experimenters have speculated that their findings on LSD may contradict the Schachter theory that emotion depends on a cognitive interpretation. However, people who have knowingly taken LSD on a number of different occasions have reported that whether they had a "good trip" or a "bad trip"—that is, pleasant or unpleasant emotions—depended at least in part on the people they were with and the general situation at the time they used the drug. Thus cognitive interpretations seem to be important to those who use LSD in nonlaboratory situations.

Individual differences in emotions

Evidence of the wide range of individual differences in capacity for emotion lies all around us. We have friends who go into ecstasy over the receipt of a birthday card and others whom we would not expect to be greatly moved by the gift of a diamond. We have bad-tempered acquaintances who seem to be angry most of the time and good-natured acquaintances who never seem to be angry. We know happy people and sad people, brave people and fearful. One person is terrified by a thunderstorm; another is not afraid to fight off and chase a mugger. One student shows signs of tension when asked a question in class; another seems to stay calm while addressing a meeting of several hundred.

The individual differences have two sources. Some of them are the result of learning; all of us have had experiences that have conditioned us to react emotionally to particular kinds of stimuli. Other individual differences, however, may depend on characteristics of the glands, the nervous system, and other physical equipment. These differences may be inborn and determined by heredity. Studies of very young children, who have not yet had the opportunity to do much learning, have shown that some are much more inclined to smile than others, while some have a pronounced tendency to be irritable and to cry at the slightest provocation (20).

Glandular differences

One important difference among animals has already been discussed—namely, the fact that the adrenal glands of lions appear to produce large amounts of noradrenalin, while those of animals such as rabbits produce large amounts of adrenalin. In this connection, it has also been found that the adrenal glands of wild rats are much larger than those of rats that have been bred for generations in the laboratory (21).

In human beings, several individual differences have been found in the endocrine glands. Normal thyroid glands have been found to vary from 8 to 50 grams in weight, testes from 10 to 45 grams, ovaries from 2 to 10 grams. The output of human adrenal glands under similar conditions has been found to vary from 7 to 20 grams, of pituitary glands from 250 to 1100 milligrams (22). Although there is no direct evidence, it seems reasonable to suppose that a person with large and active endocrine glands would experience different physiological changes and therefore different emotions from a person with smaller or less active glands.

Differences in the autonomic nervous system

Laboratory studies have shown that people have their own characteristic patterns of physiological change in emotional situations. For example, one person may consistently show a rapid pulse, while another may show only a small change in pulse rate but a pronounced increase in skin temperature (23). Presumably such findings indicate that there are wide individual differences in the sensitivity and activity of the autonomic nervous system, which controls these types of bodily changes. Indeed studies made with drugs that directly stimulate the autonomic nervous system have shown that there are considerable differences in reaction to these drugs (24). There seems to be little doubt that some people possess autonomic systems that tend to react to weaker stimulation—and to react more rapidly and with more intensity.

Emotions and psychosomatic illnesses

"One businessman's lunch. Will that be ulcer or hypertension?"

© 1972 *Medical Tribune*

These individual differences in the autonomic nervous system and glandular activity (and possibly other individual differences as well) play a large part in determining how susceptible each of us is to psychosomatic illnesses—that is, illnesses in which the physical symptoms seem to have mental and emotional causes. It has been known for a long time that psychological stresses are often closely related to such varied physical disabilities as high blood pressure, heart and circulatory diseases, stomach ulcers, arthritis, kidney trouble, and some kinds of asthma. The psychological stresses can be anything that causes intense and prolonged emotion—for example, the frequently mentioned "stress and strain" of modern life that puts all of us under certain pressures caused by competition (for such things as grades in school, acceptance to colleges, and, in the business world, jobs and promotions) as well as by social demands, worries about economic security and war, the struggle to get through traffic jams and reach our appointments on time, and many other similar situations.

The manner in which stress affects the body has been dramatically demonstrated by Hans Selye, a biologist at the University of Montreal. Selye has subjected various laboratory animals to many kinds of stress, including exposure to cold and the injection of poisons in doses not quite strong enough to kill. What invariably happens in stressful situations, he found, is that the various glands of the body immediately spring into action, just as in the case of emotion, as the body automati-

cally tries to defend itself. The adrenal glands in particular show some striking changes. They become enlarged and produce more adrenalin. They also discharge their stored-up supply of another group of hormones known as steroids that are essential in a number of ways to the body's functions; releasing the steroids causes the adrenal glands to change drastically in color from yellow to brown. Because of this intense activity of the adrenal glands, numerous changes occur in the body. For example, tissue is broken down to become sugar and provide energy, and the amount of salt normally found in the blood stream falls.

In Selye's experiments, animals were subjected to the same high level of stress over a prolonged period. After a few days they seemed to adapt. The adrenal glands returned to normal size, began to renew their supply of stored-up steroids, and changed back to their normal yellow color. The level of salt in the blood rose to normal or even higher. To all intents and purposes, the animals had adjusted to the stress and were perfectly normal; they seemed just like any other animals in the laboratory.

The recovery, however, was only temporary. After several weeks of continued stress the adrenal glands again became enlarged and lost their stores of steroids. The level of salt in the blood fell drastically. The kidneys, as a result of receiving an excess of hormones, underwent some complicated and damaging changes. Eventually the animals died, as if from exhaustion. They had been killed, so to speak, by an excess of the hormones they had produced in their own defense.

Another of Selye's important findings was that even during the period of apparent recovery, the animals were not so normal as they seemed. If a second kind of stress was added in this period, the animals quickly died. One might say that in attempting to adapt to the original stress, they had used their defenses to the maximum and were helpless against a second form of stress (25).

For the sequence of events involved in prolonged stress—the initial shock or alarm, the recovery or resistance period, and at last exhaustion and death—Selye has coined the phrase *general adaptation syndrome*. (To physicians the word *syndrome* means the entire pattern of symptoms and events that characterize the course of a disease.)

The "triggers" for psychosomatic illnesses. There are many indications that the general adaptation syndrome that Selye found in animals also occurs in human beings under prolonged stress—and that to human beings psychological stress resulting in emotion can be as damaging as any of the physical kinds of stress used in the Selye experiments. Investigators have found that damaging kinds of stress are likely to be caused by changes in a social or work situation, by work pressures, and by feelings of responsibility. It has been established, for example, that the pilot responsible for flying and landing a plane shows more physical signs of stress than does the copilot or the radio operator (26). In assessing the chances that a person will suffer a heart attack, some investigators have suggested that there are two types of people. Type *A* people,

Emotional state believed to have triggered the illness	Percentage of cases
Resentment or hostility	17
Frustration or rejection	13
Depression, hopelessness	13
Anxiety	13
Feelings of helplessness	12
Separation from a loved one	9
Stressful changes in life situation or threatening situation	9
Difficulties in relationship with therapist or experimenter	4
Miscellaneous	10

8-5

The emotional background of illness

A survey of case histories of patients suffering from a wide variety of illnesses indicated that the illnesses were always preceded by some kind of psychological stress. The most common "trigger" for the illnesses was an emotion of resentment or hostility. (28)

"I think we can rule out stress."

who are many times more likely to be victims of heart disease, are highly aggressive, competitive, and ambitious, and have a burning sense of urgency about getting their tasks done on time—a description that fits many hard-driving and successful people. Type *B* is quite the opposite: easy-going, rather indifferent to winning and succeeding—and likely to live much longer (27).

It has been suggested that perhaps all diseases, not only those generally considered to be psychosomatic, may be triggered by psychological stress. One group of investigators, examining the backgrounds of patients suffering from many kinds of ailments, including cancer and diabetes, found that all the patients had undergone some kind of stress shortly before the onset of the disease. The types of stress are shown in Figure 8-5. Perhaps emotional stress often reduces the body's ability to resist the effects of germs, viruses, or other causes of disease.

The emotion of anxiety

One emotion that deserves special discussion is *anxiety,* which is among the most powerful of emotions and has far-reaching effects on behavior. Anxiety is *a vague, unpleasant feeling accompanied by a premonition that something undesirable is about to happen.* Anxiety is closely related to the emotion of fear; in fact it is very difficult to draw any sharp dividing line between the two. Generally speaking, fear appears to be a reaction to a specific stimulus and to have a "right now" quality about it. We see a snake and feel afraid; we know what we are afraid of and recognize that we are afraid right here and now. Anxiety is more vague; its cause is not always apparent. Moreover, as the definition states, anxiety is accompanied by a premonition of something that is about to happen—it is not concerned so much with the here and now as with the future.

From the psychological viewpoint, anxiety is an extremely unpleasant experience and particularly difficult to cope with because of its

vagueness. We usually cannot pin down the cause or even the precise nature of what we fear will happen. We can only describe the feeling in the most general terms; we say we are worried, tense, "blue," moody, or "jumpy." The last word, though as vague as the others, is particularly appropriate because people who are in the grip of anxiety have a lower threshold for other kinds of emotional response. They are likely to be irritable and quickly moved to anger; on the other hand they may also overreact to pleasurable stimuli. They tend to have wide swings of mood and their behavior is often unpredictable.

It appears that there are four situations that are likely to produce anxiety:

1 We encounter some kind of unusual event that we cannot immediately understand. (For example, arriving as a freshman at a campus in a strange city.)
2 We are faced with events that are unpredictable. (For example, when we are about to take a difficult test or apply for a job.)
3 We sense a conflict between our thoughts and our behavior. (As when we do something that we have been taught is wrong.)
4 We have two conflicting opinions. (As when we feel strongly about dedicating our lives to helping others, yet at the same time have a strong desire to earn a lot of money.)

One word that can be applied to all four of these common sources of anxiety is *uncertainty*—and therefore the role of uncertainty as a cause of anxiety deserves discussion of its own.

Uncertainty as a source of anxiety

In one of the most significant experiments on the role of uncertainty in producing anxiety, college men were asked to listen to a voice counting to fifteen and were told that at the count of ten they might receive a shock. Whether or not they received the shock, it was explained, depended on the draw of a card from a pack of twenty cards, which was shown to them. For one group of subjects, the deck contained only one "shock" card and nineteen "no-shock" cards — so that they knew their chances of shock were only one in twenty, or 5 percent. For the second group the chances were 50 percent, and for the third group the chances were 95 percent.

In this case, common sense suggests that the group with the 50-percent chance of shock would show the most anxiety, while the 5-percent group would feel relatively secure and the 95-percent group would consider themselves almost certain to receive a shock and would be prepared for it. Indeed even the experimenters expected this result. To the experimenters' surprise, however, the 5-percent group showed the most physiological arousal — as clearly indicated by the graph in Figure 8-6 — and therefore presumably the most anxiety.

The unexpected result of the experiment is probably explained by the comments of some of the subjects in the 50-percent group, who said they had decided that their chances of getting a shock were high enough to lead them to assume that they would get one — thus reducing their suspense — and merely to hope for a pleasant surprise. In other

8-6

Anxiety and uncertainty

Subjects who had only a 5-percent chance of receiving a shock at the count of ten showed more physiological arousal — hence presumably more anxiety — than subjects who had a 50-percent chance or a 95-percent chance. For an explanation of this rather surprising result, see the text. The measure of physiological arousal shown here is electrical conductivity of the skin.

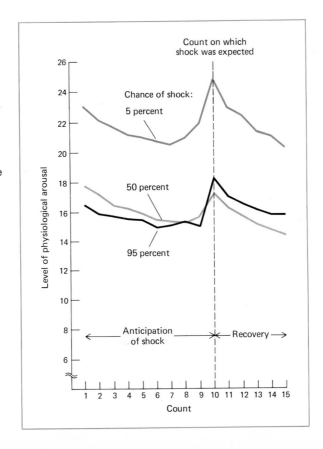

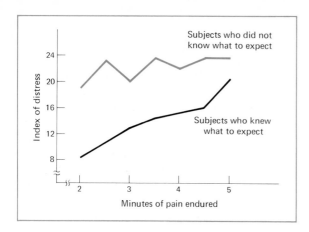

8-7

Uncertainty and pain

Volunteer college students took part in an experiment in which a blood pressure cuff was attached to their upper arms and inflated to a point where it caused the blood to be shut off and pain to occur. Some were told exactly what kinds of sensations and pain to expect. Others did not receive this specific information and did not know quite what to expect. As the graph shows, those who knew what to expect experienced less pain and distress than did the others. (30)

words, they took much the same attitude as the subjects in the 95-percent group, who were almost certain they would get a shock. The subjects in the 5-percent group, on the other hand, seemed to feel the most uncertainty. Their chances of being shocked were so low that they could not resign themselves to the thought, but neither could they dismiss the possibility (29). Because of the uncertainty, they showed the greatest anxiety of all.

Uncertainty may even affect the way we experience pain, as is shown by the experiment described in Figure 8-7. By producing anxiety, it appears, uncertainty makes the unknown much more disagreeable than something that is known and expected, even when the two are in fact equally unpleasant.

Since uncertainty produces anxiety and therefore stress, it is not surprising that uncertainty bears a strong relationship to psychosomatic illnesses. One experiment that offers convincing proof of this relationship is illustrated in Figure 8-8.

8-8

Uncertainty and ulcers

The effect of uncertainty in producing physical damage was demonstrated by an experiment with rats and the stress-producing stimulus of electric shock. One group of rats received no shocks at all. Another group received a series of shocks that came at an expected time, always ten seconds after a tone was sounded. A third group also heard the tone, but there was no relationship between the tone and time at which the shock was administered. As the graph shows, the unshocked rats showed only a small tendency to develop stomach ulcers. Those that received the expected shocks showed only a slightly greater tendency. But the rats that could not know when to expect the shocks suffered considerable ulcer damage. (31)

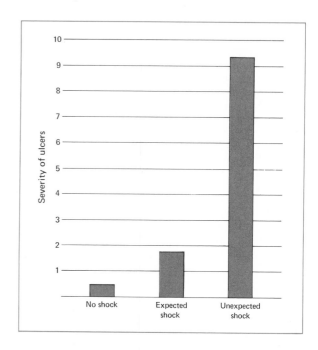

Some effects of anxiety on learning

There is one point about anxiety that deserves special mention because of its particular significance to college students—the effect of anxiety on learning. Does anxiety help learning by increasing the student's desire to learn, or does it interfere with learning?

One thing that is known is that the amount of anxiety a person feels when trying to learn something depends on how difficult the material is. This fact has been proved by experiments such as the one illustrated in Figure 8-9. Note that the students in this experiment showed a sharp rise in feelings of anxiety when their learning task was difficult, then an even sharper drop in anxiety when they switched to an easy task.

It is also known that some people are more likely than others to suffer from anxiety in general or to be especially anxious in learning situations. In general these "high-anxiety" students do better at learning simple tasks but are under a handicap when trying to learn more difficult materials (33, 34, 35). Presumably they have trouble with more complicated learning because their anxiety interferes with the intense concentration that difficult tasks require. People who are high in anxiety seem to do particularly badly at learning when someone is watching them. Their performance at even simple learning tasks has been found to go down rather sharply in the presence of an observer, while subjects low in anxiety do just about as well when watched as when alone (36).

How does anxiety affect actual performance in college? This question was explored by an investigator who selected a group of male students relatively high in anxiety and a group relatively low in anxiety. He then examined their College Board scores, as an indication of their ability, and their actual grades in college. It was found that students

Anxiety and learning

As measured by a test designed to reveal feelings of anxiety, college students displayed considerably more anxiety during a period when they were learning difficult materials than they had displayed before the experiment began. When they were learning easy materials, however, their feelings of anxiety dropped quite sharply. Their blood pressure readings, a physical measure of stress, followed much the same pattern. (32)

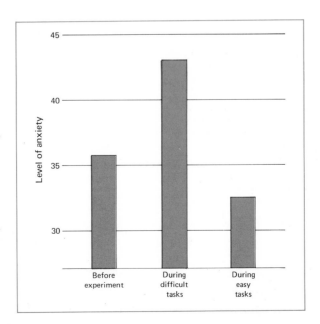

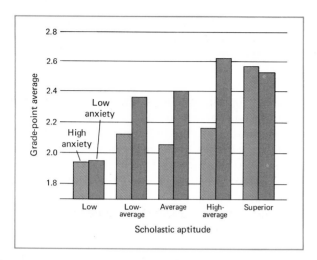

8-10

Anxiety and college grades

The bars show the average grades made by "high-anxiety" and "low-anxiety" students of different levels of scholastic ability as indicated by their College Board scores. Note the pronounced differences in the middle ranges of scholastic ability. (37)

with the lowest levels of scholastic ability made much the same grades regardless of whether they were high or low in anxiety. So did the students with the highest levels of scholastic ability. But at the in-between levels of ability—where, of course, most students fall—the students who were low in anxiety made significantly better grades than did the anxious students. Full results of the study are illustrated in Figure 8-10.

In a follow-up study an attempt was made to select "anxious" freshmen who were making low grades and were in danger of flunking out of college. One group of these freshmen took an active part in a counseling program in which they received advice about their problems in college, methods of study, campus life in general, and their relations with their professors—advice that presumably would reduce their anxiety about the college situation. Another group, matched as closely as possible for College Board scores, type of high school attended, and other factors that influence performance in college, did not receive counseling. From midterm to the end of the first semester the counseled group made an average improvement of more than half a grade point. The group that was not counseled improved by less than a tenth of a grade point (38). Anxiety about the college situation would appear to be a frequent—though perhaps correctable—cause of failure in college.

Since many of us live under crowded and noisy conditions, it is useful to inquire into the effect that noise may have on college work and other forms of learning. The answer seems to be that noise in itself does not usually create any particular problems; we may find it distracting at first but usually adapt to it rather quickly. However, our own emotional reactions to the noise may cause difficulties, especially when we are working on extremely difficult tasks. Experiments have shown that learners are most affected by noise when 1) they believe that others taking part in the same study are not being subjected to as much noise, 2) they have no control over the noise, and 3) the noise occurs at unpredictable intervals (39). The last two factors, of course, are further examples of the anxiety and stress caused by uncertainty.

Anxiety and risk taking

One characteristic that often determines how people will live their lives is the amount of risk they are willing to take. Some people are very conservative; they hate to go out on any kind of limb. Others seem to be born gamblers; they take all kinds of chances with their resources and their lives. Though the idea may seem far-fetched at first, there appears to be a strong relationship between this refusal or readiness to take risks and the emotion of anxiety.

An experiment that demonstrates this fact is illustrated in Figure 8-11. Note that subjects who appeared to be relatively free from anxiety tended to scorn the "sure thing" in the game that was used in the experiment. They made very few throws from the close distances at which they were almost certain to succeed but would receive only a low score. They also tended to avoid the high risk of gambling that they could score from the longest distances, which would have given them the highest scores. Subjects who appeared to be relatively high in test anxiety made many more shots from the short distances but also "went for broke" more often by trying from the longest distances.

One might speculate, on the basis of this experiment, that people who are highly anxious about success and failure tend to adopt either a very conservative or a very risky strategy in life situations. They are inclined to settle for the "sure thing" and thus avoid failure that would add to their anxiety, or else they tend to take the kind of chances at which success is such a remote possibility that failure can readily be excused. All of us, certainly, have observed people who do not take many

8-11

Anxiety, conservatism, and "going for broke"

The curves show the different strategies used by subjects who had been found to be low in anxiety and others high in anxiety in a game where they tossed rings at a peg from any distance they chose. For ringing the peg from close distances they received very low scores, from far distances very high scores, and from middle distances middle scores. Note that the low-anxiety subjects chose a strategy of intermediate risks, while the high-anxiety subjects tended to be very conservative or to "go for broke." The two groups of subjects were matched as closely as possible for desire to succeed at the game—that is, for indications of the achievement motive, which will be discussed in Chapter 9. (40)

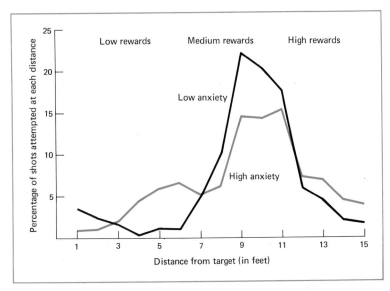

chances in life, settle for jobs that seem beneath their real abilities, and yet occasionally take a flier in a gambling casino or in risky investments. Less anxious people, on the other hand, appear to have sufficient confidence to assume the middle-range risks that are most likely to lead to success in the long run.

Along similar lines, it has been observed that college students who appear to have a high amount of fear of failure tend to leave examination rooms early (41), as if to avoid the further anxiety of continuing to try on the examination. This strategy, of course, only increases the likelihood of the failure that they find such a disturbing prospect.

Summary

1 Emotions involve a wide range of physiological changes — the body may be "stirred up" or "toned down."

2 Some of the changes represent activity by the striped muscles of movement; these changes include a) muscle tension, b) tremor, c) eye blinking and other nervous movements, d) vocal expressions of emotion, and e) facial expressions.

3 Other changes are controlled by the autonomic nervous system and endocrine glands; these include a) heart rate, b) blood pressure, c) blood circulation, d) composition of the blood, e) activity of the digestive organs, f) metabolic rate, g) breathing, h) salivation, i) sweating, j) goose flesh and hair standing on end, and k) pupil size.

4 The physiological changes in emotion were the basis of the *James-Lange theory,* which maintained that the changes were set off by stimuli in the environment, that the changes in turn stimulated sensory nerves inside the organs of the body, and that the messages of these sensory nerves were then perceived as emotion. A striking feature of the theory was its suggestion that we do not tremble and run because we are afraid but instead feel afraid because we are trembling and running.

5 In contrast to the James-Lange theory, the *Cannon-Bard theory* held that stimuli in the environment set off patterns of activity in the brain (notably in the hypothalamus) that were relayed simultaneously to the autonomic nervous system, where they triggered the bodily changes of emotion, and to the cerebral cortex, the higher part of the brain, where they resulted in the feelings of emotion.

6 More recent experiments by Schachter have indicated that physiological changes are essential for emotion but that the same pattern of change can result in different emotions in different environmental contexts. This evidence supports the *cognitive theory of emotion* (sometimes called the "juke box" theory), which holds that emotion depends both on physiological changes and on a mental process that interprets the meaning of the changes.

7 Individual differences in emotion appear to be caused both by a) learning, which conditions the individual to react to particular kinds

of stimuli, and b) constitutional differences in glandular activity and in sensitivity and activity of the autonomic nervous system.

8 Individual differences in emotional tendencies appear to explain the relation between psychological stress and the tendency to suffer from psychosomatic forms of such illnesses as heart disease, high blood pressure, and stomach ulcers.

9 *Anxiety* is an important emotion that can be described as a vague, unpleasant feeling accompanied by a premonition that something undesirable is about to happen. It is usually caused by *uncertainty* (as for example when one is faced with unusual or unpredictable events).

10 People high in anxiety appear to learn faster than people low in anxiety in simple learning situations but more slowly when the learning demands the making of choices. In college, anxiety does not appear to affect the grades of students of lowest or highest learning capacity. Of students of in-between ability, however, those with high anxiety make significantly lower grades than those with low anxiety.

11 Anxiety appears to be related to risk taking. People with high anxiety often seem to adopt a conservative strategy, in which they settle for lower rewards but minimize the chances of failure. Or they may adopt a "go for broke" strategy, in which they take chances with such a remote possibility of success that failure can readily be excused. People with low anxiety appear inclined toward the middle-range risks that usually are the most likely to lead to success in the long run.

Recommended reading

Appley, M. H., and Trumbull, R., eds. *Psychological stress: issues in research.* New York: Appleton-Century-Crofts, 1967.

Darwin, C. *The expression of the emotions in man and animals.* New York: AMS Press, 1972.

Glass, D. C., ed. *Neurophysiology and emotion.* New York: Rockefeller University Press, 1967.

Goethals, G. W., and Klos, D. S. *Experiencing youth: first-person accounts.* Boston: Little, Brown, 1970.

Izard, C. E. *Patterns of emotions.* New York: Academic Press, 1972.

London, H. and Nisbett, R. E., eds. *Thought and feeling: cognitive alteration of feeling states.* Chicago: Aldine, 1974.

Malmo, R. B. *On emotions, needs, and our archaic brain.* New York: Holt, Rinehart, and Winston, 1975.

Schachter, S. *Emotion, obesity, and crime.* New York: Academic Press, 1971.

Stein, D. G., and Rosen, J. J. *Motivation and emotion.* New York: Macmillan, 1974.

Strongman, K. T. *The psychology of emotion.* New York: John Wiley, 1973.

Drives and motives

Sometimes human behavior seems random and without purpose. It is difficult to imagine, for example, what people are seeking to accomplish when they sit idly doodling on a pad of paper or just plain staring into space. Most behavior, however, is a means to an end. In psychological terms, it is goal-directed.

We share some of our goals with other animals. When we are hungry, we take steps to find food. When we are thirsty, we take steps to get a drink of water. When we are tired, we sleep. The forces that make us seek these rather simple, biologically determined goals are called *drives*.

Most of our goals, however, are much more complex than anything found elsewhere in the animal kingdom. Some of us want to have a lot of friends; some of us want to live the solitary life of a forest ranger. We want to be tennis players, reporters, engineers, lawyers, millionaires, Peace Corps workers, police officers, or safecrackers. We may want to be hard-boiled leaders or mild-mannered followers, to be feared or admired. And we may act in many sorts of ways to carry out these desires. The forces that make us seek these complex and in most cases uniquely human goals are called *motives*.

What psychology has learned about motives is especially important for two reasons: 1) it helps answer the age-old question of why people act as they do, which has always fascinated humankind; and 2) it also makes clear that the answer is not nearly so simple as is often assumed. *Motives* has become such a popular word that all of us tend to use it too often and too freely; we like to think that we can rather easily figure out the motives that lie behind another person's behavior. Actually this is very difficult and often impossible.

Take for example the case of a college man who studies constantly and is unhappy with anything less than straight A's. We might suppose that he is highly ambitious, driven by a desire for success, fame, and wealth. In truth, however, he may not be ambitious but merely dependent on the approval of his parents and afraid of losing their support unless he gets good grades.

305

Some very powerful motives, indeed, never show up in behavior at all—for motives cannot operate, as will be seen in the final section of this chapter, unless the circumstances are favorable. To cite a simple example, a young woman might have a burning desire to be a doctor, yet feel that this goal is unattainable for lack of either money or talent and thus never make any attempt to reach it.

Motives and drives are discussed in the same chapter because both are forces that set behavior into motion, organize it, and direct it toward some kind of goal. Whether they have anything more in common is a matter of debate among psychologists. Some psychologists believe that the dynamics of the body and nervous system, which, as will be seen, account for the drives, are also the source of human motives. That is to say, they believe that motives somehow stem from the biological processes that arouse us and make us take action when we are hungry or thirsty. Other psychologists believe that motives are primarily cognitive—in other words, mental processes not clearly related to biological arousal. Whatever the relation between the two, drives and motives have a profound influence on human behavior.

Biological drives

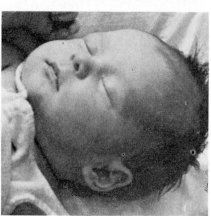

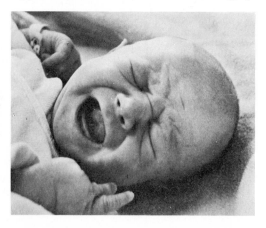

How the drives operate can best be observed among babies whose behavior is still free from any influence of learning. Because of their built-in system of reactions between body and nervous system, newborn babies behave in a number of goal-seeking ways. For example, they seek food, suck vigorously when it is presented, and cry when they lack it. They also cry when unable to achieve the goals of warmth or relief from pain. Each of these forms of behavior is the result of a drive, which can be defined as a *pattern of brain activity that results from certain kinds of physiological conditions*. These physiological conditions usually occur when the organism is in a state of deprivation (that is, in need of food or water) or of imbalance (such as too warm, too cold, or needing to sleep or to eliminate its waste products). The physiological states trigger special patterns of nervous activity in the brain, especially in the hypothalamus and reticular activating system (pages 254–55).

In human beings, the drive pattern usually results in a sensation, such as the feeling of hunger, thirst, or fatigue. It also frequently serves as an energizing force that leads to behavior. When we are hungry, we go to a vending machine for a candy bar or to a restaurant for a meal. When we are thirsty, we go to a water fountain. When we are tired, we go to bed. By so doing, we attain a goal that brings about an end to the physiological condition, changes the pattern of nervous activity, and thus satisfies the drive.

Hunger

As the definition of drive implies, the key to our feelings of hunger lies in the brain, rather than in the stomach as popularly supposed. Although common-sense observation tells us that we have hunger pangs and that these pangs come from the stomach—indeed we can often hear our stomachs growling as if demanding food—these are only secondary factors. There appears to be a sort of feedback process through which the brain affects the activity of the stomach and the stomach in turn has an effect on the brain (1), but this feedback loop seems to play only a minor part in feelings of hunger. One experimenter operated on a rat and severed all sensory nerves leading from the stomach to the brain, yet the rat ate as before (2). In another operation, the entire stomach of a rat was removed, yet the rat continued to show signs of hunger (3). Cases have been reported in which the human stomach had to be removed, without any pronounced effect on the desire for food (4).

Two small areas of the brain, both in the hypothalamus, have been found to control the hunger drive. One of these areas (the lateral hypothalamus) turns on the drive. When an electrode is implanted in this area of an animal's brain and electrical stimulation is applied, the animal will start eating. If the area is surgically destroyed so that it cannot function, the animal loses virtually all interest in eating (5). The other area (the ventromedial nucleus) turns off the drive. When this area is electrically stimulated, the animal immediately stops eating. When the area is destroyed, the animal eats constantly and becomes grossly fat (6).

The two areas of the hypothalamus act as on and off switches for the hunger drive. The question then becomes: What makes the on and off switches operate? One answer is that they respond to changes in the chemical composition of the bloodstream, as has been well established by an experiment with two hungry dogs. One dog was permitted to eat its fill, until it showed no further interest and turned away from the food. Then this well-fed dog received a blood transfusion from the hungry dog. Immediately it started to look for food again, as if it had not eaten at all (7).

The chemical changes that affect the hunger drive appear to center around the level of fatty compounds in the bloodstream, and probably also the level of blood sugar. After a period of not eating, there is a pronounced drop in the amount of these energy-giving substances that the bloodstream carries. To make up for this energy lack, the body begins to draw on its own store of sugar and fat. Fatty compounds leave the tissues and enter the bloodstream to serve as fuel for the body—and also activate the area in the hypothalamus responsible for the hunger drive. Then the food eaten as a result of the hunger drive provides a new source of energy and the body stops drawing on its fat and sugar stores. The level of fatty compounds in the bloodstream drops rapidly. The area responsible for hunger is turned off and the area responsible for ending the drive is turned on (8).

Although the hunger drive can ordinarily be satisfied only by eating, the fact is that eating is merely a means to an end. The drive is actually satisfied by the appropriate change in blood chemistry, however produced. Figure 9-1 illustrates an experiment showing how the hunger drive switches on and off even in the case of an animal never permitted to engage in the behavior of eating.

Hunger and bodily weight. The operation of the hunger drive is closely related to the fact that the body contains a large number of cells, scattered throughout, that are especially designed for the storage of fatty compounds. In evolutionary terms, survival of the species presumably depended on the ability of these cells to store up energy to tide the body over the prolonged periods of starvation that human beings once experienced frequently (and still do in many places). Under ordinary circumstances, the hunger drive keeps these cells filled to an appropriate level with fatty compounds. In an emergency, when the body lacks other sources of food and energy, it can empty out the fat cells, using their contents as fuel.

Since the amount of fat stored in the body largely determines a person's weight, it might be said that the hunger drive operates to keep

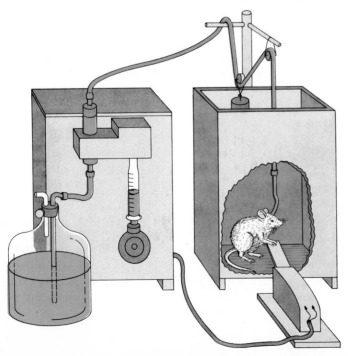

9-1

A well-fed rat that never eats

When the rat presses the bar, a squirt of liquid food is delivered directly to its stomach. The rat never smells, tastes, or swallows the food. Nonetheless, it soon learns to press the bar just often enough to satisfy its hunger and maintain its normal intake of calories. (9)

bodily weight at an individual's ideal level (10). The area in the hypothalamus that switches on the hunger drive keeps the fat deposits and therefore bodily weight from dropping too low (11). The area that turns off the drive keeps the body from acquiring too much fat (12).

Between them, the two areas of the hypothalamus perform an amazingly delicate job of maintaining body weight at a constant level. Even a very slight change in food intake can have a drastic effect on a person's weight. For example, adding as little as ten medium-sized potato chips a day to one's usual diet would result in a gain of about eleven pounds a year. Yet most of us stay at the same weight over long periods of time. The on and off switches for the hunger drive manage to keep our appetites and therefore our weight on a remarkably even keel. One is reminded of the workings of a thermostat that manages, by turning a furnace on and off, to keep a building at never less than 71 degrees and never more than 73 degrees.

Why people get fat. Obviously there are exceptions. Some people are far above the weight ordinarily considered normal for their height. They may be as much as twenty or fifty or in extreme cases even a hundred pounds overweight. The reason has been a mystery that many psychologists have spent years trying to unravel.

The only way one person can get fatter than another, of course, is to eat more, and therefore many studies have explored the eating habits of fat people. These habits, it has been found, are indeed unusual. As the experiment illustrated in Figure 9-2 demonstrated, they tend to eat when they have the opportunity, even if they have already had a meal and would not normally be expected to be hungry. In another experiment, in which clocks were manipulated to make the subjects think that dinner was being served at a later hour than usual, fat people ate more than their ordinary amount, though people of normal weight did not (14). In general, it has been found that fat people eat more food when they sit down to the table and eat faster (15). They are especially likely to eat a lot when the food tastes particularly good and more likely than people of normal weight to be turned off by food that tastes bad (16).

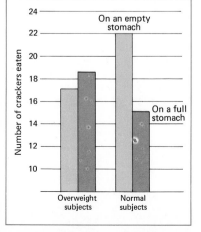

9-2

A clue to why people get fat

An experimenter worked with two groups of subjects, one group of normal weight and the other anywhere from 14 to 75 percent overweight. When the subjects arrived at the laboratory, having skipped the previous meal, half from each group were fed sandwiches, the other half nothing. They then took part in what they thought was an evaluation of the taste of five different kinds of cracker presented to them in separate bowls. They were told that they could eat as few or as many of the crackers as they wished in making their judgments. As the graph shows, the amount eaten by the subjects of normal weight was considerably lower if they had just eaten sandwiches. The overweight subjects, however, actually ate somewhat more on a full stomach than on an empty stomach. For a possible explanation of these results, see the text. (13)

In all these respects, fat people have eating habits that closely resemble those of animals in which there has been surgical destruction of the area in the hypothalamus that turns off the hunger drive. Moreover, they behave in other ways very much like animals with damage to this part of the brain. They tend to be emotional and irritable (17, 18), to be more lethargic and less active than average (19), and to have a weakened interest in sex (20).

Because of these similarities, it was once believed that fat people suffered from some kind of brain abnormality affecting the part of the hypothalamus responsible for turning off the hunger drive. The newest evidence, however, points to a quite different factor. It has been found that people inclined to be overweight have in their bodies an unusually large number of the special cells in which fatty compounds are stored (21); in fact they may have fully three times as many as people of normal weight (22). Similarly, the level of fatty compounds in their bloodstreams tends to be quite high at all times (23). It is possible that the hypothalamus of the overweight person reacts in normal fashion, but the area that turns on the hunger drive is almost constantly active because of the level of fatty compounds in the bloodstream, and the area that turns off the drive is almost never triggered.

Thus fat people, for reasons that cannot be controlled by any act of will power, are constantly hungry. This is particularly true if they try to diet to look more like people of normal weight. Indeed it has been suggested that most fat people, because of social pressure against obesity, are actually underweight rather than overweight—in terms of the requirements of their own bodies (24).

The question remains as to why some people have more fat cells than others. The answer seems to be largely a matter of heredity; they are born that way. Breeding experiments with animals show that some strains are more likely than others to produce fat individuals generation after generation (25)—and anyone who eats a meal in a family restaurant can make the first-hand observation that overweight human parents tend to have overweight children. Besides heredity, another

factor may be early feeding experiences—overeating in the first few months of life.

In one way or another, the number of fat cells in the body seems to be established by the time of very early childhood and to remain relatively constant and unchangeable from then on. People who go on starvation diets show a decrease in the size of these cells, as their contents are drawn on for fuel, but no decrease in the number of cells (26). Similarly, people who deliberately overeat and gain weight show an increase in the size of the cells but no increase in number (27).

It must be pointed out that being overweight may have psychological as well as physical causes. Clinical psychologists have found that many people seem to become fat because of overeating to relieve anxieties over competition, failure, rejection, or sexual performance. But one cause of being overweight seems to be an excess of fat cells, determined at birth or shortly thereafter, urgently demanding to be filled up and constantly triggering the hunger drive.

Thirst

Just as common sense tells us that we get hungry because our stomachs let us know, so does it seem obvious that we get thirsty when our mouths are dry. But again the obvious explanation turns out to be wrong. Sensations from the mouth and throat play only a secondary role; a person can feel thirsty even when these areas are under anesthetic, sending out no messages at all (28).

Again the center for the thirst drive turns out to be the hypothalamus, which has areas that quickly respond when the amount of water in the body drops below the proper level. A lack of water causes the cells of the body to become dehydrated, and there are cells in the hypothalamus that are especially sensitive to this change. Moreover, a lack of water reduces the volume of blood flowing through the body, and this reduced volume of blood causes the kidneys to produce a chemical that also triggers the thirst center of the hypothalamus (29). Thus the thirst drive is set into motion by any sign of imbalance in the body's water level.

Much as in the case of hunger, the goal of the thirst drive is water, not the act of drinking. When the experiment that was shown in Figure 9-1 is changed so that the animal receives water instead of food directly in the stomach, it soon learns to take in the normal amount of water even though it never drinks.

Sex as a drive

Among lower animals sex is almost as direct a drive as hunger or thirst. At most times the female sex drive is quiescent, and the female is not sexually attractive to the male of her species. She has regularly recurring periods of heat, however, in which large amounts of hormones are released from her sex glands and trigger a sex control mechanism in the central nervous system. During these periods, which vary in frequency and length from species to species, the female actively seeks sexual contacts and engages in the kind of courtship and copulatory behavior characteristic of the species. A female in heat is usually apparent to the male of the species through various cues such as odors, the sex "calls" of the cat and other animals, and the reddening of the sexual skin in monkeys and birds.

For some organisms, sexual behavior is largely unlearned; birds, rats, and other lower animals raised in isolation usually demonstrate normal sexual behavior at the first opportunity. But monkeys raised in isolation do not (30). Among human beings sex can hardly be considered only a biological drive. The desire and ability of the human female to perform the sex act are not significantly dependent on her hormone cycles—nor is her sexual attractiveness to the male. Sex is of course a powerful force in human affairs, but much of this influence derives from its motivational rather than its drive qualities. Many forms of human behavior grow out of the learned motives that surround sexual expression—the relations between boys and girls from the time of the first "date," the selection of friends of the opposite sex, marriage, and some of the problems that occur in marriage.

New attitudes toward sex. In recent years there has been a striking change in our society's attitudes toward sexual behavior. In the 1950s public opinion polls showed that a considerable majority of all Americans believed that sex before marriage was wrong. Now a majority no longer consider it wrong. This is especially true of younger people but is also the prevailing opinion, by a smaller margin, among people over fifty (31).

Along with this increased permissiveness there has been an even more startling change in freedom of discussion of sexual matters. In the 1950s, the subject was taboo. Movies and books were strictly censored and the kinds of pornographic film now shown openly in theaters were black market items that the police went to considerable trouble to confiscate and burn. Nowadays even movies that are not x-rated are frequently quite explicit about sexual behavior, and books and magazines often carry reports and advice on how to achieve maximum sexual happiness.

Individual differences in sexual behavior. In the opinion of many sex researchers, the sudden explosion of sexual discussion has had some unfortunate results. Much of the advice in books and magazines is written by people who have never attempted to make any scientific study of the facts, and almost all of it is based on the assumption that for all people at all times sex is the most important activity in human life—an assumption that ignores the finding of serious sex investigators that there seems to be a wider range of human sexual appetite, capacity, and behavior than of almost any other human trait.

As was established by the famous Kinsey reports on male and female sexual behavior, the individual differences are truly amazing. For men in their twenties and early thirties, Kinsey found that the average number of orgasms was two a week. But at the lowest extreme he found individuals who were never having an orgasm, and at the other extreme he found individuals who were having as many as four a day or more, day in and day out (32).

Among women the individual differences were even greater. Kinsey found some women who had never in their lives experienced an orgasm or indeed sexual excitement of any kind. He also found women who had been married for many years but had experienced only one or two orgasms in their lives. At the other extreme, he found women whose sexual desires were so frequent and intense that they could be satisfied only by masturbation—in some cases as many as thirty or more times a week, with numerous orgasms on each occasion (33).

The cause and effect of the differences. To a certain extent, the individual differences in sexual behavior appear to depend on psychological factors. For example, growing up in a family atmosphere that surrounds the sex act with secrecy and shame may tend to inhibit sexual desires and expression. Some sex researchers have concluded, however, that the differences are largely inborn and unchangeable—a matter of glandular activity and perhaps also the dynamics of the nervous system.

Whatever the reasons for the differences in capacity and appetite, it seems obvious that men and women near the bottom of the scale cannot express themselves sexually in the same way as those near the top of the scale. Hence the futility and danger of advice that assumes that all people are alike and that greater sexual activity leads to greater happiness. It has been found, on the contrary, that there is no relation between the frequency of sexual relations and a couple's happiness (34). Moreover, it has been suggested that couples who approach sex rather shyly are just as happy as those who take the uninhibited approach recommended by many marriage manuals (35). The only really useful advice that can be given, one researcher has concluded, is that sexual expression can be satisfactory "only when you engage in it in your own way and at your own choosing—as much or as little as you please, and according to your own tastes and preferences (36)."

Other drives

Five other biological drives deserve brief mention. One of them is the *sleep drive,* which plays an important part in the rhythm of our daily lives but has already been discussed on pages 261–64; it depends, as will be recalled, on some kind of chemical change in the body that activates parts of the brain. Surgical destruction of one area of the brain causes an animal to remain awake until it dies of exhaustion; destruction of another area causes the animal to sleep almost constantly.

The *temperature drive* is common to all warm-blooded animals. In human beings its goal is to maintain the body at about 98.6 degrees

Fahrenheit. The temperature drive is controlled by cells in a lower part of the brain that are sensitive to temperature changes. When stimulated by increased warmth, they send off messages that cause perspiration, which cools the body through evaporation, and that also cause more blood to circulate toward the surface of the body, where it loses heat more quickly. When stimulated by cooling, these brain cells induce shivering, the constriction of blood vessels in the skin, and increased activity of the thyroid gland, which in turn leads to increased bodily activity and the production of more heat (37).

The *breathing drive* goes unnoticed under ordinary circumstances, but people who are drowning or being suffocated will fight as hard for air as they might fight for food when facing starvation. The *elimination drive* acts to rid the body of its waste products. The *pain drive* leads to such reflex behavior as pulling the hand away from fire and such learned behavior as swallowing medicine to relieve a headache.

Drives and incentive objects

Though the drives stem primarily from the brain's reaction to physiological conditions, they also depend in an important way on events in the environment. That is to say, they can be triggered by stimuli—called *incentive objects*—of which the organism becomes aware through the sense organs. Thus a male rat might show no sign of sex drive until it becomes aware, chiefly through its sense of smell, of the presence of a female in heat. Moreover, a rat that has just satisfied the sex drive through copulation may eagerly approach a second female (38).

Rather similarly, an animal that has eaten its fill of one kind of food may begin eating again if a more preferred kind of food is presented. Thus the indications are that many parts of the brain, including the areas that receive messages from the sense organs, cooperate in producing feelings that accompany the drives and drive-satisfying behavior. (Everyone has had the experience, for example, of suddenly becoming quite hungry because of the smell of hamburgers and onions coming from the open doorway of a restaurant.) One theory holds that sensory messages indicating the presence of an incentive object interact with the nerve patterns set up by physiological conditions; in combination the nervous impulses create a *central motive state* that leads the organism to make some kind of *consummatory action*—for example, seeking and eating food (39).

In this connection, one group of experimenters has made a rather strange and interesting discovery. They implanted an electrode in the hypothalamus of a rat—presumably in the center that controls the hunger drive, because the animal would eat when electrically stimulated. But what would happen, the experimenters wondered, if the animal were unable to eat because there was no food in its cage? It turned out that the animal would try to do *something* when the current was applied. If water was present, the animal would drink. If there were some wooden chips in the cage, the animal would start gnawing on them (40).

We do not know, of course, whether electrical stimulation of the hunger center produces the same pattern of brain activity as natural stimulation of the center by changes in blood chemistry. The experiment does raise the possibility, however, that activity in the hypothalamus may serve to arouse the organism rather than make it seek a specific goal. The particular kind of behavior that results may then depend on events in the environment—in the case of the stimulated rat, it depended on the presence of food, water, or wood to gnaw. It may also depend, in human beings, on what other kinds of mental processes are going on at the moment.

This possibility is supported by events that sometimes happen in everyday life. You may suddenly become rather restless and eager—psychologically aroused in some way. If you are near a cafeteria, you may go in and eat. If you are near a water fountain, you may get a drink. If you are sitting on a bench somewhere on the campus, you may get up and go for a brisk walk. Or, if you are in the library, you may throw yourself into an intense effort to study.

Stimulus needs

The biological drives are powerful and dramatic forces. All of them except the sex drive lead to the learning of behavior essential to keeping the organism alive and intact, and the sex drive is essential to the survival of the species. When the drives go unsatisfied, they often result in intense sensations of discomfort and eventually in death. Naturally the biological drives have long been recognized and studied as primary sources for the energizing of behavior.

In recent years, however, more and more evidence has indicated that the basic nature of the organism demands certain other satisfactions. Food, water, sleep, and the other goals that satisfy the biological drives do not seem to be enough. In addition, the organism seems to have inborn tendencies to seek certain kinds of stimulation; it displays what have come to be known as *stimulus needs*. There appear to be at least two kinds of stimulus needs, each of which deserves individual discussion.

The need for sensory stimulation

This need has already been mentioned, although not by name. In Chapter 6, on perception, the importance of early sensory experience for the development of normal perception was discussed. It was also mentioned that human babies, when less than two days old, tend to focus their eyes on the apex of a black triangle that is seen against a light background—the exact spot at which the contrast between black and white is the greatest. Thus the baby seems to exhibit an inborn tendency to seek increased *sensory stimulation*.

What happens to adults who are deprived of sensory stimulation has been demonstrated in the laboratory, with dramatic results. In one experiment, volunteer subjects were kept in bed as shown in Figure 9-3.

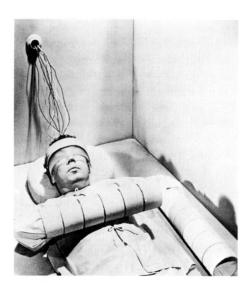

9-3

An experiment in blocking off the senses

This man is taking part in an experiment designed to show what happens when activity of the human senses is reduced as near as possible to zero. The eyeshade permits him to see nothing but a dim haze. The arm casts mask the sense of touch in his hands. The room is soundproofed, and he hears nothing but the constant soft hum of a fan. For what happens to him under these conditions, see the text. (The wires shown at the top of the photo were used to record brain waves.) (41)

In a similar experiment, they were fitted with a sort of diver's helmet and suspended in water held at skin temperature (42). In both cases, the subjects saw nothing but a dim light or no light at all and heard nothing more than a steady low hum. They smelled and tasted nothing, and their sense of touch was masked as much as possible. In other words, activity of their senses was held to almost zero. Rather quickly, it was discovered, many of them found themselves unable to think logically. Their memories became disorganized. Sometimes they felt strangely happy, and at other times they felt anxious or even panicky. Some of them began to develop symptoms that are often associated with severe mental disturbance; for example, they "saw" imaginary sights and "heard" imaginary sounds.

Why a lack of sensory stimulation should have such drastic effects is not completely understood. One possibility is suggested by what has been discovered about the reticular activating system of the brain. Nerve impulses from the sense organs pass through the reticular activating system on their way to the sensory areas of the cortex, or highest part of the brain, where they result in conscious sensations. As they pass through, they seem to set off other impulses, which are sent by the reticular activating system to all parts of the cortex, keeping it in a general state of activity. Without a constant barrage of impulses from the reticular activating system, perhaps the cortex cannot function normally. This may explain the need for sensory stimulation.

The need for stimulus variability

As was also stated in the chapter on perception, there is something inherently attractive about a *change* of stimulus; this is the most important factor of all in attracting perceptual attention. To this statement it should now be added that organisms appear to display a definite need

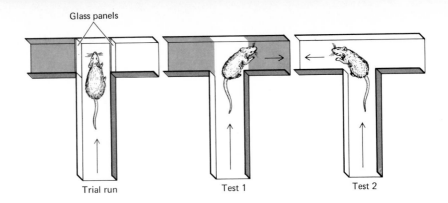
Glass panels

Trial run   Test 1   Test 2

9-4

A response to change

In the trial run a rat enters the T-maze at the bottom and is stopped by the glass panels at a point where it can see that the left arm is dark and the right arm is white. In test 1 the glass panels are removed and both arms are dark. The rat shows a strong tendency to enter the arm that was formerly white. If the trial run is followed by test 2, the rat shows a strong tendency to enter the arm that was formerly dark. As is explained in the text, this behavior is dictated by a preference for a change in stimulus. (43)

for *stimulus variability*. Given the opportunity, they show an innate preference for a change in stimulus and tend to seek it out. This has been demonstrated in the experiment shown in Figure 9-4. Even in this simple T-maze the rat shows a strong tendency to go to the arm that represents a change of stimulus—the dark arm that was originally white or the white arm that was originally dark.

The results of the experiment with the rat and the T-maze fit in with many other observations of animal and human behavior. Monkeys will learn to open a window, as in Figure 9-5, for the reward of seeing what is happening on the other side (44). Presented with the hooks and latches shown in Figure 9-6, a monkey will work hard to open them even though it has discovered that doing so leads nowhere. Human babies seem irresistibly attracted to rattles, toys hanging over the crib, and their own fingers (45). Adults gladly pay for the kind of stimulus change represented by the lights flashing in a pinball game.

9-5

The curious monkey

The monkey, a prisoner in a dimly lit box, learns to push open the window solely for the privilege of watching a toy train in operation for thirty seconds.

9-6

Work for work's sake

Do the latches unlock anything? No. Does the monkey know this? Yes. Then why does it work so hard to open them? For the answer, see the text.

The need for stimulus variability has an obviously useful role for the organism. Every stimulus change represents a new source of information about the environment, and information about the environment is essential to successful adjustment and at times even survival. An organism with an inborn need for stimulus variability has a biological advantage over an organism without it.

One aspect of stimulus variability that deserves special mention is *stimulus complexity*. A very young baby, to whom a toy rattle represents a strange and complicated stimulus, will play with it for a long time. An older infant will put it aside more quickly, and a schoolchild will not play with it at all. To the schoolchild a game of tag is endlessly fascinating; the college student will settle for nothing less than football. To satisfy the organism's needs, the stimulus must have a certain amount of complexity—a factor that is closely related to variability. On the other hand, a stimulus that is too complex is not attractive. A child is more attracted to a nursery rhyme than to a Shakespeare sonnet.

Motives

Behavior undertaken to satisfy stimulus needs can be molded and modified by learning. Similarly, the consummatory behavior set into motion by the biological drives is often affected by learning. For example, the organism has to learn how to find the food that is the goal of the hunger drive. Indeed baby mammals, after being fed their mothers' milk in the early days of life, must learn that solid foods can be a substitute and also how to eat solid foods. But both the stimulus needs and the biological drives are in themselves innate and unlearned. They are inborn characteristics of the organism's nervous system.

Motives, on the other hand, appear to depend more on learning than on any innate factors. Each of us, as a result of life experiences, comes to value certain goals above others. Even in the same family, one brother may exhibit a strong desire to be dependent on other people, another brother to be hostile to authority, a sister to achieve in school and career. Certainly motives vary considerably from culture to culture. For the ancient Greeks, a strong motive was to achieve moderation in all things, especially emotional displays. For the Romans, it was to seem thoughtful and serious. For the Buddhists in classical India and China, it was to be without desire.

Thus the best definition is this: *A motive is a desire for a goal that has acquired value for the individual.* Since the number of goals that we can learn to desire is almost infinite, it is impossible to list all the motives that an individual may possess. It is useful, however, to discuss some of the more common motives on which psychologists have accumulated experimental knowledge.

Affiliation

All of us grow up with strong motives of attachment or affiliation to our parents and other people. The motives differ in strength, of course, among different individuals. Some people are very close to their parents and extremely sociable. They are "joiners," who always like to be in a group, and they prefer to work in situations where they have the help of others. By contrast there are also people, with less affiliation motive, who like to spend much of their time alone and to be on their own in their work.

The affiliation motive affects behavior in many ways. For example, as shown by the study illustrated in Figure 9-7, it can affect performance in college. As the caption explains, students who rated high in affiliation motive were found to make better grades in university classes where their fellow students and instructors provided a warm and friendly atmosphere than in classes where the atmosphere was more impersonal. The psychologists who make the study found that the tendency was considerably stronger among university men than among women, for whom the results were sometimes inconsistent.

Behavior stemming from the affiliation motive has been found to be especially likely to occur in situations that arouse anxiety. You will perhaps recall the experiment described on pages 12–13, where college students made anxious by the prospect of receiving an electric shock showed a much greater tendency to prefer to wait in the company of others rather than alone. Apparently there is considerable truth to the old adage that "misery loves company"; in anxiety-provoking situations people seem to turn to others for both company and comfort.

Dependency

Closely allied to the motive for affiliation is the motive for dependency, which also seems to be universal. As babies, all of us are completely dependent on our parents. They give us food, drink, warmth, comfort, and relief from pain. This tendency to rely on others—at least at times and for certain things—never leaves us. We continue to have strong urges to depend on others to organize our lives, set up our schedules,

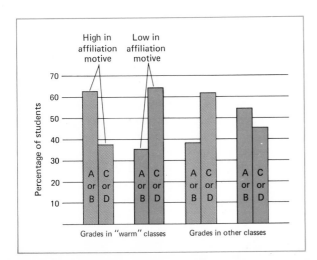

9-7

The affiliation motive, classroom atmosphere, and grades

The bars show the grades made by students who were either high or low in affiliation motive in two kinds of classes: 1) "warm" classes, where students were friendly to one another and the instructor took a personal interest in students and called them by name; and 2) other classes, where these evidences of warmth and acceptance were lacking. Note that the students high in affiliation motive did much better in the "warm" classes, whereas students low in affiliation motive did better in classes where there was less personal warmth. (46)

help us with our work, comfort us in our troubles, and give us support and pleasure.

Behavior that stems from the motive for dependency has been found to be more common among women than among men. But this is because our society, at least until recently, has considered dependency to be appropriate, "feminine," and rather attractive in women. The motive itself is probably equally strong in men — but they are less likely to display it because society has frowned on dependent behavior on the part of males. Often the motive is implemented by men in rather subtle and hidden ways. They may show a tendency to take their problems to the teacher or to the boss (though usually under the guise of being logical rather than emotional). Or it may be noted that they tend to rely on columnists and television commentators for an interpretation of world events — and to give enthusiastic allegiance to political leaders who have strong personalities.

Achievement

The motive for achievement is the desire to perform well and to succeed. Studies of people rated high in achievement motive have shown that their mothers usually demanded that they display considerable independence. These individuals were expected very early in life to go to bed by themselves, to entertain themselves, and later to earn their own spending money and choose their own clothes. Moreover, they were rewarded for these accomplishments with warm displays of physical affection. The mothers of those rated low in achievement motive did not demand the same kind of independence until much later. The striking difference in the kind of training received by people high and low in achievement motive is illustrated in Figure 9-8.

People high in achievement motive tend to try harder and to attain more success in many kinds of situations. In studies where they have been matched with other people of equal ability but weaker in achievement motive, they have been found to do better on tests of speed at mathematical and verbal tasks (48) and on intellectual problems (49). They also make better grades in high school (50) and college (51). As is shown in Figure 9-9, they are more likely to move upward in society and rise above their family origins.

Motivation and risk taking. Individuals who are high in achievement motive tend to be quite realistic about the kinds of chances they are willing to take in life, and this is particularly true if they are not only high in achievement motive but also low in anxiety. (It will be recalled from page 301 that a high level of anxiety inclines people either to be very conservative or to "go for broke.") It has been found that people with a high degree of achievement motive and a low level of anxiety tend to prefer jobs in which they have a reasonable chance of success and can obtain reasonable rewards, while those low in achievement motive and high in anxiety are more inclined either to settle for an eas-

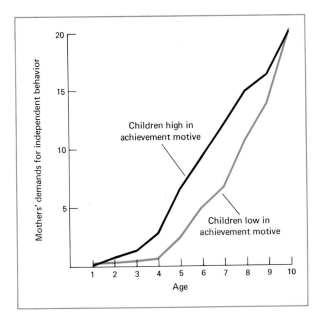

9-8

Early training and the achievement motive

A group of boys was divided into those who tested high and low in achievement motive. Their mothers were then asked at what ages they had demanded that the boys show twenty different kinds of independent behavior, such as staying in the house alone, making their own friends, doing well in school without help, and doing well in competition. All mothers agreed that they had made all twenty demands by the time their sons were ten. But the mothers of sons high in achievement motive made about as many demands at the age of two as the mothers of sons low in achievement motive made at the age of four and about as many at the age of five as the other mothers at seven. (47)

ier but low-paying job or to aim for a high-paying job that is probably beyond their capacities (53). A study made in Germany has shown that achievement motive affects even the kinds of risks taken in driving an automobile. Drivers high in achievement motive tended to commit only minor traffic offenses that represented calculated risks, such as illegal parking. Drivers low in achievement motive tended to get into trouble either for going too slow or for reckless driving (54).

One experiment worthy of special note made an attempt to examine the risk-taking tendencies of people high in achievement motive as

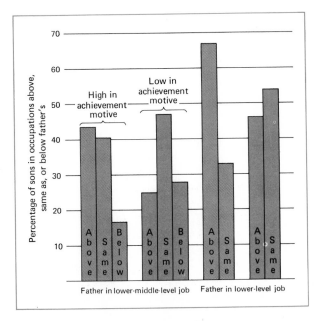

9-9

The achievement motive and upward mobility

The bars reflect the sons' occupation levels as compared with their fathers'. Sons whose fathers had lower-middle-level or lower-level jobs were found more likely to rise above the father's level if they were high in achievement motive, more likely to remain at the same level or drop to a lower level if they were low in achievement motive. (52)

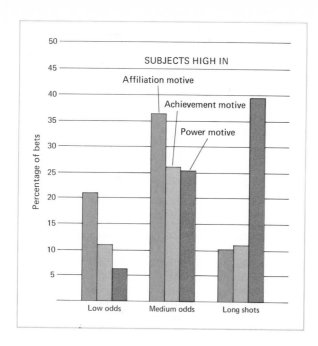

9-10

Motives and gambling strategies

What happens when students who rank high in various kinds of motives have an opportunity to play the gambling game of roulette under laboratory conditions? As the bars show, those high in affiliation motive had a strong tendency to make bets at low odds (even money or less) and medium odds (from 2 to 1 to 5 to 1). Those high in the motive for power preferred to take a chance on long shots (17 to 1 or 35 to 1). Those high in achievement motive fell in between. The experimenters' interpretation of the results is discussed in the text. (55)

compared with those high in affiliation motive and also those high in the motive to acquire power. In playing a gambling game, as Figure 9-10 shows, the three different types of people used noticeably different strategies. The experimenters concluded that the subjects high in achievement motive tended to take medium risks that gave them the best chance of winding up with a sense of personal accomplishment. Those high in affiliation motive tended to shy away from competition by taking low risks. Those high in the power motive took the high risks that they felt would bring them attention and recognition of their daring. In real life situations, the three types probably tend to adopt these same kinds of strategies, for the same reasons.

Motivation and birth order. A sidelight to the achievement and affiliation motives is the fact that both of them tend to be stronger in first-born children (or only children) than among those born later. One study that demonstrates this fact is shown in Figure 9-11. The study is con-

9-11

The affiliation motive and order of birth

The bars show the results of a study of the relationship between being a first-born child (or an only child) and the affiliation motive. Subjects ranging in age from eleven to sixty-two were divided on the basis of tests into those high or low in affiliation motive. A very high percentage of first-born subjects fell into the high group. Of subjects who were born second or later in the family, only a minority proved high in affiliation motive. Note that first-born women were slightly more likely than first-born men to rate high in affiliation motive—but women who were not first-born were considerably less likely than men to do so. (56)

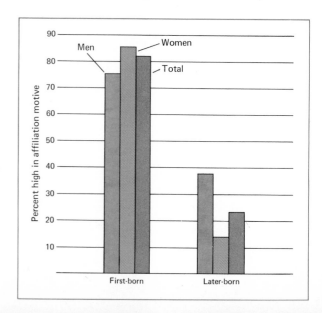

Some first-born high achievers.

Katherine Hepburn

Henry Kissinger

Shirley Chisholm

Billy Jean King

Mick Jagger

Walt Frazier

Winston Churchill

fined to the affiliation motive, but similar findings have been made in regard to the achievement motive. A possible explanation is that mothers appear to treat a first-born child differently from later children. They devote more time to the first-born, are more physically protective, take a greater part in and interfere more with the child's activities, and are more extreme with both praise and criticism (57). The first-born child, it might be said, grows up in an adult world, expected to conform to adult standards (58). Later children receive less attention and guidance from the mother and are more influenced by their relations with other children.

Because first-borns tend to be high in achievement motive, many of them become outstandingly successful. Any list of prominent people—eminent scholars, people in Who's Who, even presidents of the United States—will be found to contain an unusually high proportion of first-borns.

The first-borns' higher level of affiliation motive also tends to be reflected in their life styles. They have been found to be more trusting of authority than later-born children (59). Male first-borns, but not females, have also been found to have strong tendencies to conform to social pressures (60). There seems to be some truth to the cynical observation of the psychoanalyst Alfred Adler, who once described the first-born child as a "power-hungry conservative" (61).

323

The hostility motive

"I love the whole thing. In fact, one day I'm going to take up either animated cartooning or violence."

This is a motive that most of us do not like to admit to but that all of us possess. Evidence of it first appears in children at about the age of two. Up to then, all that they have seemed to want from other people is their presence and the stimulation, help, and approval they provide. But at this stage, children begin to want something else from others. They want—at times—to see other people display signs of worry, fears of discomfort, actual pain. Later they may hope that misfortune will befall others and that they will have the gratification of knowing about it.

Some scientists consider hostility to represent a biological trait that makes aggression as inevitable a part of the human condition as fighting over territories is for baboons and other animals (62). Others, probably a majority, believe that the hostility motive is learned and that it stems from the fact that children cannot have everything they want. Some of their desires are bound to be frustrated by the rules of society and by the conflicting desires of other people. They cannot always eat when they want to. They have to learn to control their drive for elimination except when they are in the bathroom. They cannot have the toy that another child owns and is playing with. Their mothers cannot spend all their time catering to their children's whims. Other children, bigger then they are, push them around.

The aggression that often results from hostility may take such varied forms as argumentativeness, scorn, sarcasm, physical and mental cruelty, and fighting. Yet, while most people are motivated at some time by hostility, not everyone displays aggression. Boys and men are more inclined to do so than are girls and women, for our society has traditionally approved of a certain amount of aggression in the male but has discouraged it in the female.

In recent years there has been considerable debate as to how people's behavior is affected by watching acts of hostility and aggression—particularly the large doses of violence provided by movies and television shows. Some psychologists have believed that watching make-believe scenes of violence may have a cathartic effect; it may help the viewers discharge any aggressive tendencies they may have and therefore discourage any actual aggression (63, 64). But recent studies indicate that the opposite is probably true—that watching violence encourages violent behavior.

In one experiment, subjects thought they were taking part in a learning study in which they were supposed to administer electric shocks every time the learner made a mistake. The severity of the shocks was left to their own judgment. To a marked degree, subjects who had just watched a film showing acts of aggression administered more painful shocks than did subjects who had watched a film that was free of aggression (65). Similarly, it has been found that spectators at a football game, with its violent bodily contact, have greater feelings of hostility when they leave the stadium than when they arrive, but that this is not true of spectators at a less aggressive event such as a gymnastics meet (66).

In another study that bears directly on the question of the possible cathartic effect of watching aggression, subjects were first made angry, then were asked to look at some pictures and to daydream, calling up any fantasies they liked. Some subjects looked at pictures showing aggressive behavior, others at pictures without any suggestion of hostility. Had there been a cathartic effect, the subjects who looked at the pictures of aggressive behavior and had aggressive daydreams in response to them should have shown a greater decline in their own feelings of anger and hostility, but the opposite proved to be true (67).

Many psychologists have concluded that the whole idea of catharsis is wrong, except perhaps under very special circumstances, and that viewing aggression simply breeds more aggression (68). Perhaps the principles of observation learning (pages 59–60) apply. (You may recall the photographs on page 59 of children attacking a doll with a hammer after watching a movie of an adult who had done the same thing.) The suggestion that people learn by observation to commit violent acts is borne out by crime figures, which show that news of a sensational crime is often followed by a sharp rise in similar types of crime, as was the case after the first hijacking of an airplane in 1967 (69).

The certainty motive

Quite early in life children begin to show a desire for the kind of *certainty* represented by their own beds, their own toys, the presence of familiar people and objects in their environments. As they grow a little

older, they like to have rules set for their conduct; they like the certainty of knowing what they are permitted to do and what they are not permitted to do. The prospect of uncertainty—sleeping in a strange house, being taken care of by a strange baby sitter, going to school for the first time—is likely to upset them.

Adults, too, tend to be motivated toward the known and away from the unknown. For some, such as explorers and astronauts, other motives prove stronger; but, in general, the desire for certainty operates strongly in most of us at most times. We like to feel that we know how our relatives and friends will act toward us, what is likely to happen tomorrow in the classroom or on the job, and where and how we will be living next year. Just as children are often upset by new experiences, adults are often upset by such uncertainties as the possibility of unemployment or failure.

The motive for certainty may be said to take three forms.

1 We like to think that we can predict what will happen next—that is, that future events will be orderly and foreseeable.
2 When unusual events surprise us, we like to try to understand them and relate them in some way to previous experiences.
3 We seek some kind of consistency among the various beliefs that we hold and between our beliefs and our behavior. This aspect of the certainty motive is especially important because of its relation to *living up to standards.*

Living up to standards. All of us, as we grow up, begin to set certain standards for our own behavior. Through learning what society values and through identification with our parents and other adults, we acquire inner standards of many kinds. We want very badly—indeed we command ourselves—to be such things as attractive, responsible, friendly, skillful, generous, honest, and fair.

Our standards form what is often called our *ego ideal*—our notion of how, if we were as perfect as we would like to be, we would always think and behave. Many of us acquire such high standards that we cannot possibly live up to all of them at all times. In fact some of our standards demand that we suppress other motives, which may be quite powerful at times; they tell us that we should not take food from another person even if we are hungry, that we should be kind even to people toward whom we feel hostile, that we should play fair no matter how much we want to win. As a result, we often have feelings of shame and guilt, over our thoughts if not actually our conduct. In popular terms, our consciences hurt. The pangs of conscience when we fail to meet our standards can be painful indeed. It has been observed that people who have committed crimes often behave in such a way that they are almost sure to be caught and convicted. Apparently they prefer punishment by imprisonment to the kind of self-punishment that results from a serious failure to live up to one's own standards.

The motive for self-actualization

A discussion of motives would not be complete without including the view of the humanistic psychologists—which is that human beings are distinguished above all by aspirations that go far beyond their desires for such matters as affiliation, achievement, hostility, and certainty. This viewpoint can best be presented in the form of the theory of *self-actualization* developed by Abraham Maslow, who was one of the leading humanists.

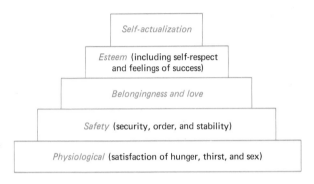

Maslow

9-12

Maslow's pyramid of human motives

According to Maslow's theory, human motives are arranged in this kind of pyramid. Once the *psychological* motives at the bottom have been satisfied, humans are freed to seek the goals of their search for *safety*—and so on up to the top. For the meaning of the self-actualization motive at the apex, see the text.

It was Maslow's belief that human beings are innately inclined to seek beauty, goodness, truth, and the fullest possible development of their own unique potentialities for perfection and creativity. Human motives, he theorized, exist in the form of the pyramid, or hierarchy, shown in Figure 9-12. The physiological motives at the bottom of the pyramid are the most urgent. People must satisfy their hunger and thirst drives in particular before they can undertake the search for safety, which is the next step upward. And only in a safe and stable society can they then begin to seek the higher goals to which human nature aspires.

The goal at the very top of the pyramid, self-actualization, represents a sort of all-encompassing self-fulfillment. Self-actualizing people have satisfied their search for such esthetic pleasures as order, symmetry, and beauty. They are in tune with the meaning and mystery of life. They accept themselves and others and the realities of existence, and they rejoice in the experience of living. Self-actualizers are spontaneous and creative and have a keen sense of humor. They have made the most of their abilities and have become all that they are capable of becoming (70). All this, to Maslow, represented the goal toward which all human beings by their very nature are motivated—though deprivation and unfavorable social pressures may prevent most of them from ever reaching this ideal level of development.

Maslow's view of human nature and human motives must be taken largely on faith. It is not a theory that lends itself to experimental proof or disproof. (Although one study has indicated that high ratings on the qualities Maslow describes as self-actualizing are likely to be accom-

Albert Schweitzer

Eleanor Roosevelt

Helen Keller

Albert Einstein

Some people Maslow considered self-actualizers.

panied by a high degree of freedom from tendencies to be neurotic (71)—in other words, that self-actualization and what is often called "mental health" tend to go hand in hand.) To many psychologists the theory has the intuitive ring of truth; to others it seems too optimistic.

Unconscious motives

Another idea deserving of mention holds that human activities are often a response to *unconscious motives*—that is, to wishes and desires that we are not aware of, that in fact we might vehemently deny, yet that influence our behavior nonetheless, sometimes to a striking and dramatic degree. The idea of unconscious motives was first proposed by Sigmund Freud and is part of his theory of psychoanalysis, which will be discussed in Chapter 11.

Freud's suggestion raises some very thorny psychological problems,

328

among them the question of how a desire that is unconscious can actively operate to produce relevant behavior. But his idea does seem to offer an explanation for some aspects of human behavior that would otherwise be baffling.

One example of what appears to be an unconscious motive is the phenomenon known as posthypnotic suggestion. While subjects are under hypnosis, they may be told that after they awaken from the trance they will go and raise a window the first time the hypnotist coughs— but will not remember that they have received this instruction. Later the hypnotist coughs, and, sure enough, the subjects do open a window. If asked why, they are likely to say that the room was getting stuffy or that they felt faint. They have no suspicion that the real reason was simply to comply with the hypnotist's demand.

Other examples appear to be all around us. A mother may seem to believe in all sincerity that she has the most generous, affectionate, and even self-sacrificing motives toward her daughter, yet an unprejudiced observer might say that the mother's real motives are to dominate the daughter, keep her from marrying, and have her as a sort of maid-servant. A man may earnestly deny that he has any hostile motives, yet we may see that in subtle ways he performs many acts of aggression against his wife, his children, and his business associates. A person may feel genuinely motivated to go to the dentist or to keep a date with a friend, yet conveniently "forget" the appointment.

Although the notion of unconscious motives is puzzling, many psychologists agree that it is valid, including some who reject other aspects of Freud's theories. Accepting the idea leads to a rather startling conclusion: if motives can operate even though they are completely unconscious, then we will often find it as difficult to analyze our own motives as to know the motives that direct the behavior of others.

Motives and behavior

By definition, a motive is a desire for a goal that has acquired value for the individual. We acquire these goals through childhood learning experiences that are more or less common to all people in our society. Thus it appears likely that all of us possess, at least to some degree, all the motives that have been mentioned in this chapter—affiliation, dependency, achievement, hostility, certainty, and (if we accept Maslow's theory) self-actualization—as well as such related desires as power, social approval, and living up to standards. Yet no two of us ever behave exactly alike. Why?

Motive strengths and motive "targets"

One reason we display such vast differences in behavior is that, though we may all have much the same motives, we possess them in widely varying degree. Each of us has built up a highly individual hierarchy of motives in which some of them have a top priority, while others operate with less urgency. And of course the strength of a motive plays a considerable part in determining how hard, if at all, we will try to satisfy it (72). Some of us have such a strong affiliation motive that we will sacrifice our weaker desire for achievement in order not to make any of our friends jealous. On the other hand, some of us are so intent on achievement and power that we will suppress our desire for the friendships dictated by the affiliation motive.

Although it is difficult to measure motive strengths and compare one person to another, the available evidence indicates that there is an extremely wide range of individual differences. The affiliation motive, for example, may be of minimal strength in one person, moderate in another, and of burning intensity in still another.

It is also important to note that motives do not operate in a vacuum. No matter what our hierarchy of motives may be, none of us is always eager for affiliation. We are not always dependent or bent on achievement or hostile. On the contrary, we behave differently toward different people. For example, a man may exhibit a strong motive for affiliation toward his parents, a strong motive for dependency toward his wife, a strong motive for achievement and power toward his business associates, and a strong motive for hostility toward some of the people he knows. This man's behavior will depend in large part on what psychologists call the *targets* of his various motives—that is, the people toward whom they are directed. Similarly, his behavior may or may not reflect these varying motives, depending on the situation in which he finds himself at any given moment.

The importance of opportunity

In many cases, even the strongest of motives do not result in any behavior at all. They cannot operate except under certain conditions—a fact that will make up the remaining pages of the chapter.

The most important of all these conditions centers around the word *opportunity*—for we cannot fulfill any of our motives unless we have a chance to try. The achievement motive is often thwarted in this way. For example, a young woman wants very badly to have a professional career—but for lack of money she cannot get the necessary education. A young man wants very badly to work in advertising—but cannot find any advertising firm that will give him a job.

The affiliation motive may run up against the same kind of insuperable obstacle. Young people eager for the companionship of the opposite sex may live in a community where young men greatly outnumber young women, or vice versa. For older people, the lack of opportunity is caused by the fact that women live much longer than men. Among Americans who are 45 or older, there are nearly six million more women than men (73)—a statistic that tells its own rather grim story of lack of opportunity for single women in that age bracket to satisfy any desire to affiliate with men.

Just as the opportunity must exist in the outside world, so must we have the ability inside ourselves to fulfill our motives. We must have learned how to behave in a way that is likely to result in attaining the goal. Without this knowledge, our motives can never produce results. Thus a child may have strong motives for affiliation and affection yet not know how to go about obtaining them. An adolescent boy may have strong motives for the companionship of girls yet not know how to make himself attractive to girls or ask for a date. An adult may want to earn a lot of money yet lack any skills that have high value in the economic marketplace.

The role of "incentive value"

Even when opportunity is available and we know how to gratify a motive, still nothing may happen. One reason is that motives operate in somewhat the same way as drives. As was explained on pages 314–15, drives interact with the presence of incentive objects to produce consummatory action. Similarly, a motive does not ordinarily result in behavior unless something arouses it and triggers it into action.

For example, a college woman goes home at the end of the day with no particular desires at all concerning the evening's activities. A friend calls and suggests they go to an 8 P.M. tryout for parts in a college drama. Going to the tryout is a potential incentive to implement any one of a number of motives—desires for affiliation and achievement, possibly sexual motives. Whether the student will respond eagerly or turn down the invitation will depend in large part on the *incentive value* that trying out for a drama has for her.

The incentive value of any event or object varies considerably from one person to another. Two students may have equally strong motives for achievement, but one student's motive may center around good grades, the other's around political activity. The offer of a dollar to mow a lawn may have sufficient incentive value for one youngster but not for another.

What are the chances for success?

Another condition that must be met, if a motive is to produce goal-seeking behavior, is that there must be a reasonable expectation of success. That is to say, people are likely to take action only if they believe they have a fair chance to reach the goal and thus obtain satisfaction of the motive. Thus even if the college woman invited to try out for the campus play places a high incentive value on getting an acting part, she is likely to turn down the invitation if she believes that she has absolutely no chance of success. Or let us say that a male student is strongly motivated to call up a girl he has seen in one of his classes and ask her for a date. He places a high incentive value on the date. But if he is shy and awkward around girls and considers himself unattractive and uninteresting, he may not try to satisfy the motive.

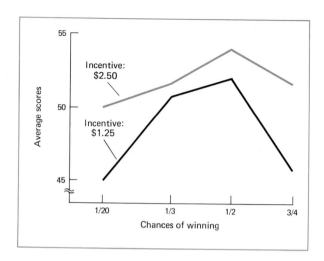

9-13

The effect of incentive and chances of success

The subjects in this experiment were college women who were told they could win a small cash prize in a contest that involved two tasks—one working problems in arithmetic, the other drawing X's inside small circles. Some subjects were offered a $1.25 prize, the others a $2.50 prize. Both groups were divided into four additional groups. One was told that a single prize would be given for the top score among twenty students; in other words, they thought they had one chance in twenty of winning. Others were told that they were in competition with two other students (one chance in three) or with a single other student (one chance in two—or 50–50). A fourth group was told that equal prizes would be given to the top three scorers out of four (three chances in four). Note that the subjects with a chance at a $2.50 prize —in other words, a higher incentive—worked harder than the subjects whose possible prize was only half that amount. In both groups the highest scores were made by those who thought they had a 50–50 chance of winning. (74)

An experiment that explores the role of both chances of success and incentive is illustrated in Figure 9-13. Note how much harder the women in this experiment tried to win their "contests" when the prize —the incentive value of winning—was doubled. Note also that the lowest scores were made by the women who believed that they had very little chance of winning. An interesting sidelight is the fact that the women who believed that winning was almost a sure thing also had low scores, particularly when the incentive value of the prize was low. The highest scores of all were made by those who thought they had a 50–50 chance.

How anxiety thwarts motives

Another thing that often keeps motives from ever taking the form of actual behavior is anxiety—those vague fears and premonitions that plague so many human activities. This fact can be observed even in very young children. When children are separated from their mothers for a long period of time and become anxious over the mother's absence, they may behave very strangely when they have the opportunity to see her again. Although they are strongly motivated to be reunited with her, they may at first actually avoid her rather than approach her.

Because of the different way the two sexes are brought up in our society, girls and women often have particularly strong anxieties about their hostile motives, and boys and men about the desire for help. Therefore anxiety tends to play a particularly important role in inhibiting aggressive behavior on the part of women and dependent behavior on the part of men.

Sexual motives can generate considerable anxiety in both women and men, sometimes to the point of frigidity and impotence that completely block sexual desire or satisfaction. In one experiment on sexual anxiety, young men were asked what stories a series of pictures suggested to them. Although many of the pictures had a strong sexual content, the men tended to ignore this fact in their stories. In fact they were less inclined to read sexual meaning into pictures where it was obviously present — presumably because these pictures aroused anxiety — than into "neutral" pictures. Then they had several alcoholic drinks and were asked to invent stories for another similar series of pictures. This time — presumably because the alcohol had reduced their anxiety — their responses to pictures with a high sexual content were much more sex-oriented than before, and in some cases the researchers found the responses quite blatantly so (75).

Conflicts among motives

For the final word on why motives may never result in behavior, consider this situation: A college man gets ready to eat his evening meal — and a number of motives crowd one after another into his thoughts. The desire to get good grades, representing one aspect of the achievement motive, suggests that he spend the evening studying. Affiliative and sexual motives point toward visiting a girlfriend. His inner standards of proper behavior of a son toward his parents point toward writing a letter home. Obviously he cannot satisfy all these motives. They are in conflict. Only one of them can prevail, and perhaps the conflict will prevent any of them from being translated into behavior. Indeed conflicts among motives are such a complex and important factor in human behavior — and such a strong influence on the human personality — that they deserve a full discussion of their own in the following chapter.

Summary

1 *A biological drive is a pattern of brain activity that results from certain kinds of physiological conditions.* The physiological conditions usually occur when the organism is in a state of deprivation (in need of food or water) or of imbalance (such as too warm, too cold, or needing to sleep).

2 The biological drives are *hunger, thirst, sex, sleep, temperature, breathing, elimination, and pain.*

3 An *incentive object* is a stimulus, such as the presence of food, that helps trigger a biological drive.

4 In addition to biological drives, the organism appears to have tendencies to seek certain kinds of stimulation. These tendencies are called *stimulus needs.*

5 Two important forms of stimulus needs are the need for general *sensory stimulation* and the need for *stimulus variability.*

6 *A motive is a desire for a goal that has acquired value for the individual.*

7 Among important motives are the desires for *affiliation, dependency, achievement, hostility,* and *certainty.*

8 Humanistic psychologists emphasize that human beings are innately motivated to seek beauty, truth, and fullest development of their potentialities. This is called the theory of *self-actualization.*

9 It is widely believed that people may also have *unconscious motives* that influence their behavior even though they are unaware of them.

10 Whether a motive will actually result in behavior depends in part on a) the strength of the motive and b) the "target" of the motive—that is, the person or persons toward whom it is directed. We may have weak or strong urges to display affiliation toward some people, dependency toward others, and hostility toward still others.

11 Often a motive cannot be fulfilled because of lack of opportunity. In particular, we may never have the opportunity to fulfill some of our desires for achievement.

12 A motive does not ordinarily result in behavior unless something with sufficient *incentive value* triggers it into action.

13 If motives are to result in behavior, there must also be a) a reasonable expectation of success, b) freedom from anxiety, and c) an absence of conflicting motives.

Recommended reading

Atkinson, J. W. *An introduction to motivation.* New York: Van Nostrand Reinhold, 1964.

Atkinson, J. W., and Raynor, J. O. *Motivation and achievement.* New York: John Wiley, 1974.

Bandura, A. *Aggression: a social learning analysis.* Englewood Cliffs, N.J.: Prentice-Hall, 1973.

Bolles, R. C. *Theory of motivation,* 2nd ed. New York: Harper & Row, 1975.

Cofer, C. N., and Appley, M. H. *Motivation: theory and research.* New York: John Wiley, 1964.

Epstein, A. N., Kissileff, H. R., and Stellar, E., eds. *The neuropsychology of thirst.* New York: Halsted Press, 1973.

Haber, R. N., ed. *Current research in motivation.* New York: Holt, Rinehart and Winston, 1966.

Kagan, J. *Understanding children: behavior, motives, and thought.* New York: Harcourt Brace Jovanovich, 1971.

Karlen, A. *Sexuality and homosexuality: a new view.* New York: Norton, 1971.

McClelland, D. C., and Winter, D. G. *Motivating economic achievement.* New York: Free Press, 1971.

Maslow, A. H., ed. *Motivation and personality,* 2nd ed. New York: Harper & Row, 1970.

Money, J., and Ehrhardt, A. A. *Man and woman, boy and girl.* Baltimore: The Johns Hopkins University Press, 1972.

Murray, E. J. *Motivation and emotion.* Englewood Cliffs, N.J.: Prentice-Hall, 1964.

Weiner, B., ed. *Cognitive views of human motivation.* New York: Academic Press, 1974.

Zubin, J., and Money, J. *Contemporary sexual behavior; critical issues in the 1970's.* Baltimore: The Johns Hopkins University Press, 1973.

SIX
THE HUMAN PERSONALITY

Discussion of emotions and motives leads naturally to a consideration of the human personality, for, in large part, our personalities depend on the kinds of emotions that life's events tend to arouse in us and on the motives that characteristically influence and guide our behavior. There are people with exuberant personalities who appear to be constantly experiencing the emotion of joy, people with quarrelsome personalities who appear to be constantly experiencing anger, and people with gloomy and frightened personalities who appear to be constantly experiencing anxiety, fear, and guilt. There are "strong personalities" who are highly motivated toward independence and achievement and "weak personalities" who are highly motivated toward dependency and submission.

Personality is made up of many factors—indeed, of all the mediational units that we acquire in our lifetimes, including not only our emotions and motives but also our characteristic ways of perceiving the world, thinking about it, solving its problems, and making all the various kinds of adjustments that it requires. Thus many aspects of personality have already been discussed. This section of the book will point out how the threads already mentioned, and some additional ones, are woven into the richly varied fabric that we know as human personality.

Chapter 10 treats frustration and conflicts, which play a prominent part in determining personality, and also describes the abnormalities of emotion and behavior to which frustration sometimes leads. Chapter 11 concerns the various theories of personality that have been developed by psychologists and psychoanalysts and also discusses the treatment of personality disorders.

Reactions to frustration: normal and abnormal

"The trouble with Ellen is that she's a frustrated actress."

"The trouble with Bill is that he's a frustrated athlete."

How often does one hear such sentences? Time and time again — for the word has spread out from the psychology laboratories and become a part of everyday language. When women and men cannot fulfill a strong motive — such as the desire to be an actress or an athlete — they are said to become frustrated. And frustration, it is generally agreed, often leads to trouble.

Indeed those often-heard observations represent an even greater psychological truth than most people realize. For one of the most important factors of all in determining the whole complex and endlessly varied pattern known as the human personality revolves around two questions at which the observations hint: 1) To what extent are a person's strongest motives gratified, to what extent are they never fulfilled? 2) If the motives are not fulfilled, in what manner and how successfully does the person cope with this fact?

Frustration

Drawing by S. Gross; © 1974
The New Yorker Magazine, Inc.

The word *frustration,* so important in the study of personality, is applied to *the blocking of motive satisfaction by some kind of obstacle.* On a very simple level, our motive to get somewhere on time may be blocked — therefore frustrated — by a flat tire. On a more complex level, any one of a number of obstacles may frustrate our motives to be actresses, athletes, or successful in our relations with people we like.

In popular usage, the term *frustration* is also applied to the unpleasant feelings that result from the blocking of motive satisfaction — that is, the feelings we experience when something interferes with our wishes, hopes, plans, and expectations. But these feelings, or emotional responses to frustration, take on so many forms that they can hardly be described scientifically by a single word. They may range from mild

341

surprise to murderous rage; they may vary from confusion to disappointment to anger to depression to total apathy.

Sources of frustration

Frustration is a universal experience; nobody can possibly go through life without undergoing it innumerable times for innumerable reasons. Our environments are full of events that often seem especially designed to keep us from fulfilling our wishes. And even our own bodies and personalities make frustration inevitable. The possible sources of frustration are usually broken down into a mere four—but note how many possibilities exist in these four categories:

1 *Physical obstacles*—such as a drought that frustrates a farmer's attempts to produce a good crop. Or a broken alarm clock, traffic jam, or flat tire that prevents us from getting to class on time. How many such obstacles there are in the world!
2 *Social circumstances*—such as a refusal by another person to return our affection as we would desire, or social barriers against minority groups, or problems of society that frustrate our motives for certainty by raising the threat of economic dislocation or of war.
3 *Personal shortcomings.* We may want to be musicians but find that we are tone deaf, or aspire to be Olympic champions but lack the physical equipment. None of us is as talented as we would like.
4 *Conflicts.* We may have two motives that cannot both be satisfied and therefore conflict with each other. For example, a woman wants to leave college for a year to try painting—but also wants to please her family by remaining in school. This type of conflict between motives is such a frequent and troublesome cause of frustration that it requires discussion of its own later in the chapter.

The relative nature of frustration

What kinds of physical obstacles, social circumstances, personal shortcomings, and conflicts are likely to be the most frustrating? This is an interesting question to which psychologists have found an interesting answer—which is that frustration is entirely relative. All we can say about what constitutes frustration, and to what degree, is that it all depends.

A classic experiment that demonstrates this fact was performed by observing the conduct of children aged two to five in a playroom that was equipped only with "half toys," such as a telephone without a transmitter and an ironing board without an iron. Despite the missing parts, the children played quite happily—until a dividing screen was removed and they saw much better toys in the other half of the room. Then, when a wire barrier was placed between them and the "whole toys," most of them showed signs of extreme frustration (1).

As the experiment showed, "half toys" are fun to play with if there is nothing better at hand. When better toys lie just beyond reach, the "half toys" are no longer good enough. Adult frustrations are equally relative. A man may be perfectly happy with his old used car until his neighbor buys a new sports model. A woman may be perfectly happy with her job until her friend in the next office gets a promotion. Many people who are quite successful and well liked suffer pangs of frustration because a brother or sister is even more successful and popular.

If modern Americans were by some miracle transported to the America of a century ago, they would undoubtedly suffer all kinds of frustrations—from lack of central heating in winter and air conditioning in summer, from inability to get quick relief from a toothache, from lack of good lighting to read by at night. Yet the Americans who lived a hundred years ago probably suffered no more frustration than exists today. Among blacks in America, indeed, there is probably more frustration today than there was in the past. Although the civil rights movement and increased economic opportunities have greatly improved the *absolute* level of the black's position in society, they have also served to emphasize the *relative* disadvantages under which blacks live and thus have created more intense frustration.

Tolerance of frustration

Though the relative nature of frustration makes it difficult to imagine such a situation, let us suppose that two individuals find a certain set of circumstances equally frustrating. How well will they be able to tolerate these circumstances? To this question the answer is that it depends on the individuals. Some people can tolerate a great deal of frustration; others find it difficult to tolerate even a little.

Differences in the ability to tolerate frustration exist even in children—as has been demonstrated in the experiment illustrated in Figure 10-1. Apparently a child's tolerance can be increased to a certain extent

10-1

Frustration tolerance among children

The bars show the results of an experiment based on the fact that the Stanford-Binet intelligence test ordinarily begins with easy items that the child usually gets all correct and then progresses to more difficult ones that the child cannot answer. The experiment was designed on the hypothesis that for poorly adjusted children this usual progression might constitute frustration and thus produce lower scores than they might otherwise receive. Therefore the children were first divided into two groups, one judged to be well adjusted and the other to be poorly adjusted. Half the members of each group took the test in the usual fashion (deemed "frustrating"). For the other half of each group, the test was given by mixing up the easy and difficult questions and returning to an easy one every time the child experienced a failure (a method deemed "nonfrustrating"). On the average, the well-adjusted children made almost exactly the same scores regardless of how the test was given. But the poorly adjusted children made substantially higher scores when the test was given in the "nonfrustrating" manner—indicating that the performance of poorly adjusted children on this type of test is indeed affected by a lower threshold for frustration. (2)

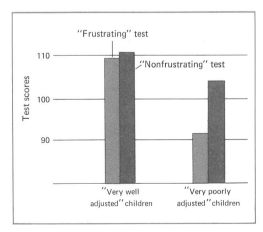

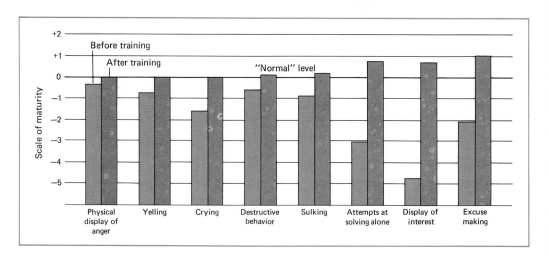

10-2

Results of training in frustration tolerance

The height of the bars shows the amount of improvement in various kinds of behavior made by a group of a dozen children who received special training in an attempt to increase their tolerance of frustration. The shaded bars represent the children's average score on the experimenter's scale of immaturity and maturity before training, the colored bars the average score after training. The children in the experiment were chosen after an initial test in which they demonstrated considerably more frustration when confronted with difficult situations than did other children, whose average scores on the maturity scale are represented by zero. Note that after training the group that originally behaved in an immature fashion actually made better scores on some aspects of behavior than did the more "normal" group. The experimenters trained the children by encouraging them to complete simpler tasks and thus to persist at tasks in expectation of eventual success and by showing them how to attack problems constructively and without the help of adults. (3)

through special training, as has been indicated by the experiment described in Figure 10-2.

Among adults, individual differences in frustration tolerance have been dramatically apparent under wartime conditions. Some soldiers break down under the relatively mild frustrations of training camp and display the various symptoms of abnormal behavior that will be discussed later in the chapter. Others are able to withstand the much more severe frustrations of the battlefield and prisoner of war camps. Under more ordinary circumstances, all of us know men and women who have managed to carry on in normal fashion and even appear relatively cheerful despite serious physical handicaps or tragic disappointments and know others who are reduced to tears or temper tantrums if the breakfast bacon is too crisp.

Conflict

Although the word *conflict* can ordinarily mean many things, ranging from the struggle of two small children over a rubber ball to a world war, for present purposes it has only one meaning. A conflict is the *si-*

multaneous arousal of two or more incompatible motives, resulting in un-pleasant emotions. The emotional factor is an essential part of the definition. The person in conflict experiences uncertainty, hesitation, and the feeling of being "torn" and distressed—elements that are an integral part of conflict and that make conflicts such an unpleasant part of life and a potential threat to normal behavior.

Conflicts fall into two general classes. One class includes conflicts between motives and standards; the other includes conflicts over incompatible goals.

Conflicts with internal standards

Our standards, acquired through learning and identification with our childhood heroes, tell us how we are supposed to behave. When a motive urges us toward behavior that is incompatible with our standards, we have a conflict that often results in intense anxiety. Children, for example, may be motivated by hostility and the desire for independence to strike out in some manner against their parents. But these motives conflict with their desire to live up to standards that tell them they must be obedient children who respect their parents, and the conflict causes them to experience shame or guilt. Adolescents and adults often experience similar conflicts and anxieties over what would happen to their image in society or to their own self-respect if they struck out angrily against a teacher or boss.

Until the last few decades, sexuality was a motive that often conflicted with standards and generated intense anxiety. But society today takes a more permissive attitude toward sexual behavior. We are surrounded by books, movies, and television shows (all of which have an effect on standards) that seem to define sexual expression as desirable rather than shameful. In today's society, a motive that frequently troubles men is the desire to be dependent, which conflicts with the masculine standard calling for independent and even aggressive behavior. A motive that frequently troubles women is the desire to be dominant (for example, to assume leadership in the business or professional world), which conflicts with what has been a traditional standard of our society, calling for dependent and submissive behavior by women. Even the most liberated woman may experience this conflict because of the lingering effect of standards acquired in childhood.

Conflicts over external goals

The other class of conflicts occurs when two motives for different and incompatible goals are aroused at the same time. Most students experience frequent conflicts between the desire to get passing grades and the desire for affiliation and approval (as represented by socializing with one's friends). Many times during a school year these two motives conflict acutely and painfully. For example, it is the night before an examination. The motive to get good grades creates a strong pull toward locking oneself in one's room and studying. But friends call and suggest going to the movies or a party. Various motives for acceptance and affection now pull strongly in the opposite direction. Only one of the two motives can be satisfied. An agonizing decision must be made.

To complicate the situation, the decision will arouse anxieties no matter which way we turn. If we decide to study, we feel anxious about the loss of the goal of being with our friends and also about the possibility that their regard for us may be lowered and that they may be inclined to reject us. If we decide instead to go with our friends, we feel anxious over the possibility of doing poorly on the examination and perhaps also over rejection by our teachers and parents.

In life after college the same kind of conflict often occurs between the motive for success and the motive to be with one's friends or family. Should the young inventor spend the evening in the laboratory (and risk loss of affection from friends or family) or spend the evening with these people (and risk failure as an inventor)?

Life is full of conflicts over pairs of goals that cannot both be attained. Shall I marry now (and lose my chance for other social experiences with the opposite sex) or wait (and risk losing the person I think I love)? Shall I try for a high-paying but difficult job (and risk failure) or settle for a more modest job (and give up the idea of being rich)? Shall I spend everything I earn (and risk my future security) or save some of it (and miss out on things I want to buy now)? Shall I live in a city or in the country? Shall I have a small family or a large one? The list of conflicts could be expanded almost indefinitely.

Achievement versus affiliation

Two motives of special interest in this connection are the desires for achievement and for affiliation, both of which may be quite strong in the same individual. Sometimes the two motives work together toward the same end, as when satisfying the achievement motive by doing well in a class will also gain the approval of a well-liked teacher and thus satisfy the affiliation motive as well. Often, however, the two motives are in conflict. For example, a student may want to make a good grade yet fear losing the friendship of classmates by doing better than they do. Thus in one study of high school boys it was found that those strongly motivated toward both achievement and affiliation tended to do better if told that their performances would be posted on a bulletin board under secret code numbers than if told that the results would be posted by name (4).

Conflict and competition. The conflict between desires for achievement and for affiliation has been found to have some pronounced effects on performance in competitive situations. On many kinds of tasks, it has been shown, most people do better when working alone than when in competition with another person—and this is particularly true of people who are known to be strongly motivated toward both achievement and affiliation (5).

In one study of particular interest, men and women university students worked at the problem of solving a series of anagrams — that is, jumbled-up letters (such as YYPOHLCOSG) that can be rearranged to form a word. Some worked alone, others in competition against a member of the same sex, others against a member of the opposite sex. It turned out that both the men and the women did best when working alone. The men solved an average of 50 out of 100 anagrams when working alone, 43 in competition against a woman, and 40 in competition against a man. The women scored about 47½ alone, a little under 47 in competition against a man, and 44 in competition against a woman.

What is most significant about the study, however, is what the subjects said when asked beforehand how well they expected to do on the anagrams. The men expected to do just as well in competition against another man as if working alone — and to do best of all if competing against a woman. The women, by contrast, expected to do best if working alone, less well if competing against a man, and worst of all if competing against a woman (6).

These expectations, it will be noted, are clearly in line with the standards society has traditionally fostered for the two sexes. Tradition holds that men should welcome competition and feel especially confident when competing against a woman, whereas women should avoid any appearance of being competitive. Yet in actual performance the men in the experiment did not do as well as they expected in competition — an indication, perhaps, that the conflict between a desire to win and a desire not to antagonize the loser bothers even men who believe that they are at their best in competition. The women did relatively better in competition than they had expected — an indication, perhaps, that society's traditions have tended to make women more reluctant to *seem* competitive than to actually shun competition.

The "motive to avoid success." On this matter of attitudes toward competition, it has been suggested that many women acquire a *motive to avoid success* — a desire to keep from seeming prominent or outstanding, especially in any field traditionally considered to belong to men. The motive presumably is based on a belief that a successful woman runs the risk of being considered "pushy" and unfeminine and therefore of being rejected. It has been found to increase from childhood into young adulthood, probably because of increased knowledge of society's expectations and prejudices. Thus one investigator, in a study made a few years ago, found evidence of a pronounced motive to avoid success among 47 percent of girls in the seventh grade, 60 percent of the women in the freshman class at a large Midwestern university, 86 percent of women students in a top-level law school, and, again, 86 percent of the women in a group of highly efficient secretaries (7).

The motive to avoid success (and therefore society's criticism) is of course in direct conflict with the achievement motive. The conflict often produces unfortunate results, as was shown by a study made at a college where women students are chosen for exceptional success in high school and strong ambitions in regard to college studies and future life. The investigator found that most of the incoming freshmen were determined to have distinguished careers. Often they had chosen such difficult and traditionally masculine fields as medicine and law. But by the time they were juniors about 90 percent of those high in the motive to avoid success had changed their plans in a much more modest direction. They had switched to the study of more "feminine" subjects such as the fine arts and many of them had decided to become teachers or housewives. Although they apparently had resolved their conflict by choosing the motive to avoid success over the achievement motive as far as their actual behavior was concerned, the investigator found that this solution "did not occur without a price—a price paid in feelings of frustration, hostility, aggression, bitterness, and confusion." Although men may suffer from the same conflict and resolve it in a similarly unsatisfactory way, they are less likely to do so. Among college men, the investigator found a strong motive to avoid success in only 9 percent of those tested.

A recent study indicates that the situation may be changing, at least to some degree. This study, made at a university in Michigan, found fewer women who displayed the motive to avoid success—perhaps as a result of the influence of the women's liberation movement. But a larger proportion of men at the university were found to display the motive— perhaps as a result of changing attitudes toward lifestyles and material success (8).

Approach and avoidance conflicts

Our conflicts are seldom simple. Indeed they are often so complex that we have trouble understanding them, much less coping with them. To help recognize the complexity, it is useful to note that some of our motives incline us to *approach* a desirable goal (as does the motive for achievement), while others make us seek to *avoid* something that is unpleasant (as does the motive to avoid success). As was noted by psychologists many years ago, these two kinds of motives can result in a truly bewildering array of conflicts (9).

1 An *approach-approach conflict* takes place between two motives that both make us want to approach desirable goals. However, we cannot reach both the goals, for attaining one of them means giving up the other. We cannot simultaneously satisfy the motive to watch the late movie on television and the motive to get a good night's sleep. We cannot simultaneously roam around the world and settle down in a career. Thus we are often torn between alternatives—each of which would be thoroughly pleasant except for our regret over losing the other.

2 An *avoidance-avoidance conflict* occurs between two motives that

make us want to prevent two alternatives that are both *unpleasant.* For example, you are too keyed up over tomorrow's examination to get to sleep. You would like to avoid the unpleasantness of tossing and turning in bed, and you could do so by taking a sleeping pill. But you would also like to avoid the grogginess you will suffer tomorrow if you do take the sleeping pill.

3 An *approach-avoidance conflict* involves mixed feelings about fulfilling a motive that will have some desirable consequences but at the same time some unpleasant consequences. For young people, the thought of getting married often creates an approach-avoidance conflict. Being married has many attractions—but it also means added responsibilities and loss of freedom.

4 A *double approach-avoidance conflict,* the most complex and unfortunately the most common type of all, takes place when we are torn between two goals that both have some good points and some bad points. A college woman from a small community wants to become a certified public accountant. But she knows that the opportunities in this field exist mostly in large cities, and she is worried about the crowded and impersonal aspects of big-city life. Now she falls in love with a classmate who plans to go into his father's business, which is running a small-town automobile agency. She wants very much to marry this man and she likes the idea of living with him in a small community. But she knows that this community will give her very little opportunity for her chosen career as an accountant. Which way shall she turn?

To the double approach-avoidance conflict—so common in life—there is never a fully satisfactory solution. Both goals have their advantages and their disadvantages. Whichever we choose, we are likely to feel at times that we made the wrong decision. Indeed even making the decision can be so difficult that sometimes we are inclined to throw up our hands and give up both the goals.

Effects of frustration and conflict

Conflicts and frustrations are among life's most unpleasant experiences; they result in anxiety and other disagreeable emotions. To escape from the distress, we try in various ways to resolve the conflicts and relieve the frustration. Thus many forms of behavior—some of which, unfortunately, can result in even greater distress—are set into motion. For all of us, the manner in which we more or less typically react in situations of conflict and frustration is an important part of our personalities.

Many of the effects of frustration and conflict appear to be universal; they have been observed in many different kinds of societies. However, there are significant differences in the kinds of reactions that are approved in various societies and are therefore most common. Moreover, even in the same society, there are many dramatic individual differences—and the differences can often be observed even in very young

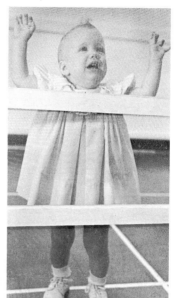

10-3

Different reactions to frustration

Even thirteen-month-olds show pronounced differences in reactions to frustration. When separated by a fence from mother and toys, the child at left first tries to climb the fence, then tries to squeeze around it. The child at right, in the same situation, bursts into tears.

children, as shown in Figure 10-3. Among the most important is the degree of anxiety that the individual suffers. Some people are made extremely anxious and even panicky and will go to great lengths to relieve their distress. Other people are less drastically affected and less likely to react in an extreme manner. Many kinds of feelings and behavior may result from frustration and conflict; among them are the following.

Assertive coping

Any discussion of possible reactions to frustration should begin on a rather hopeful note, with what for lack of a better term might be called *assertive coping*. One of our motives has been blocked; we feel bad about this—yet, if we can keep our wits about us, perhaps we can somehow manage to overcome the obstacle. We can face up to the obstacle and try to find some way to surmount it. We can regard the situation, so to speak, as an exercise in problem solving.

Thus a hungry animal, barred from getting food by a door, will often be observed to try to gnaw through the barrier. The motorist with a flat tire can get busy changing it or try to find a phone and seek help. The student who wants to be an accountant but is weak in some areas of mathematics can tackle these subjects and try to master them. People frustrated by a bad marriage may assert themselves by undertaking counseling for both spouses—or, if necessary, by ending the marriage.

In all these cases, the emotions produced by the frustration may be extremely unpleasant. They may include a high level of anger, even rage. The actions taken to overcome the obstacles may fail. But assertiveness means some kind of meaningful attempt to get rid of the frustration in a constructive way that has a reasonable chance of success. It is a positive kind of reaction and therefore quite different from the others that will now be discussed.

Aggression

Reprinted by permission of Medical Tribune and Joseph Farris

Sometimes the attack on the obstacle causing frustration — whether the obstacle be a physical barrier, a person, or society as a whole — takes the form of *aggression*. Children frustrated by other children who take their toys often get angry and attack with their fists. Adults are more likely to get into verbal battles. But aggression, whatever form it takes, is essentially an attempt to "fight back" — a display of hostility, with destructive intentions and often with destructive results.

Direct aggression. In the experiment with the "half toys" many of the children made a direct though futile assault on the wire barrier that separated them from the better toys they wanted. This is a good example of direct aggression, which is focused sharply on the obstacle that causes the frustration. Adults may display direct aggression by angrily kicking at the tire that has gone flat, by breaking a golf club or hitting a tennis ball into the next county, or by shouting insults to a motorist who has cut in front.

Displaced aggression. In some cases, a direct attack on the obstacle is impossible. But aggression is likely to result anyway and to take some rather strange outlets, as was demonstrated by the following experiment. A group of young boys was organized into two handicraft clubs. One was directed by an adult leader who behaved in a friendly and democratic way, taking the boys into his confidence and letting them help make the group decisions. The leader of the other group deliberately ran it with an iron hand, giving the boys no voice in the proceedings and instead issuing arbitrary orders and presumably arousing considerable frustration. The behavior of the two groups was then observed after the leaders had left the room. The outstanding feature was that the boys who had been frustrated by their iron-handed leader began to release their pent-up aggression by directing it toward the members of the group who were least able to stand up and fight back (10).

This kind of *displaced aggression* — aroused by a source of frustration or conflict that cannot be attacked directly and instead is taken out on an innocent bystander — is very common. The man angry at a demanding and powerful boss goes home and behaves aggressively toward his wife and children. (In everyday language, we would say he uses them as scapegoats.) A little girl angry at her parents takes out her aggression on a smaller child or on a pet. Scapegoating accounts for a great deal of the prejudice displayed against minority groups or the people of other nations. The prime example occurred in Germany when Hitler made the

Jews scapegoats, blaming them for all the frustrations and conflicts that the nation suffered in a time of economic and political tension.

Depression and apathy

Georges Rouault. *It is hard to live* . . . Plate 12 from MISERERE. 1922. Etching over heliogravure. The Museum of Modern Art, New York. Gift of the Artist

Another important reaction to frustration and conflict, found in different degrees among different people, is *depression*. The psychoanalysts, whose theories will be discussed in the next chapter, believe that depression represents a turning inward of anger. That is to say, we may become depressed because we have made ourselves our own scapegoats and accuse ourselves of being stupid, ungrateful, and unlovable—a frame of mind that may lead us eventually to feel totally unable to cope with the problems that the world presents. Other psychologists believe that depression usually results from an inability to live up to an overly rigid set of inner standards of behavior. And of course it may at times result from grief over the loss of a loved one—whether through death or through rejection. Whatever its cause, extreme depression may lead to an *apathy* so severe that its victims live their days in what is commonly called a "blue funk"—so sad and listless that they seem to lose all interest in what happens to them and have a difficult time finding energy for the ordinary chores of life.

Withdrawal

Some individuals, when beset by frustrations and conflicts, exhibit the kind of behavior called *withdrawal*. They try to avoid close contacts with other people and any kind of goal-seeking behavior that may pose the threat of causing further anxiety. We say of such people that they have "retreated into a shell" or that they have "quit trying." Rather than making an attempt to cope with conflicts and frustrations, these people prefer to escape from them by narrowing the horizons of their lives—sometimes in the most drastic and self-limiting kinds of ways.

Vacillation

Often, when faced with a conflict, we engage in the kind of behavior called *vacillation*—the tendency to be drawn first toward one possible resolution of the conflict, then toward another. Torn between studying or working and going out with friends, we may change our minds several times. At one moment we may lean strongly toward studying, at the next moment toward going out. In an extreme case of vacillation, we may take so long making up our minds that we wind up with very little time left for either of the possibilities.

How vacillation operates has been demonstrated in an experiment in which children were placed in front of two attractive toys and a clock that could be set in motion by pressing either of two bars, one under each of the toys. The children were told to select the toy they wanted as a gift by pressing one of the bars. The clock would then run for a full

10-4

Vacillation and anxiety

In a study of anxiety, records were kept of the heart rate of parachute jumpers. As the top graph shows, the heart rate of experienced jumpers increased only until the time of the engine warmup, then gradually decreased—presumably because they felt committed to the jump. The heart rate of the beginners increased all along the way—presumably because of anxiety caused by their continuing to vacillate between jumping and not jumping until the last minute. The effect of anxiety caused by vacillation is shown by the other two graphs. Among both the beginners and the experienced jumpers, the best performers were those who displayed the least anxiety. (12)

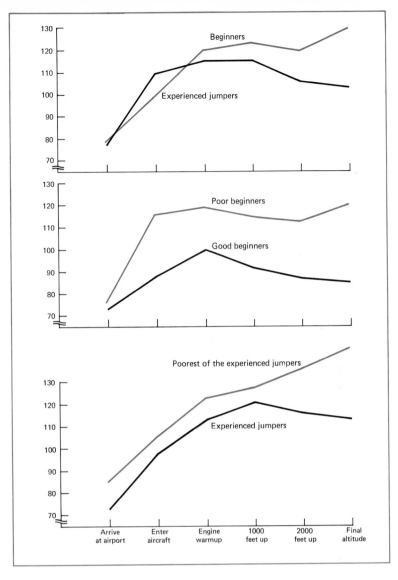

minute, after which the toy above it would be theirs. At any time before the clock had run for a full minute, however, they could change their minds and choose the other toy by pressing the other bar. Many of the children changed their minds at least once and often several times. Frequently they chose one toy, let the clock run for about two-thirds of the minute, then switched to the other toy—as if at that point, when the minute was nearly up, their anxiety over losing the second toy outweighed their desire to obtain the first toy (11).

The close relationship between vacillation and anxiety has been demonstrated by the experiment illustrated in Figure 10-4. The beginning parachutists in this study, who continued to vacillate between jumping and not jumping, showed a steady and pronounced increase in physiological signs of anxiety right up to the moment of making the jump. The experienced jumpers presumably felt committed to the jump much sooner. They stopped vacillating and showed no further increase in anxiety. The experiment also showed how drastically this kind of anxiety can reduce a person's ability to perform.

353

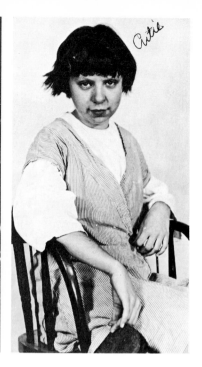

10-5

A case of regression

The girl at left, a seventeen-year-old psychiatric patient, found the old photograph of herself at center, taken when she was five. She then cut her hair and made every other possible attempt to look as she had at five, as shown in the photograph at right. (13)

Regression

The experiment with the "half toys" that was mentioned earlier produced a sort of side effect that demonstrates another possible effect of conflict and frustration. When frustrated by their inability to reach the real toys, the children in the experiment began behaving in a rather strange manner — they suddenly started to act as if they were much less mature than they really were. Indeed they behaved as if they were seventeen months younger, on the average, than their actual ages. This kind of behavior — retreating toward types of activity appropriate to a lower level of maturity — is called *regression*.

Signs of regression are quite common among children. For example, the first-born child often displays them when a baby brother or sister arrives; the child may go back to such forgotten habits as thumb sucking or may want to be fed from a bottle. Frustrated adults may regress to such childish behavior as weeping or temper tantrums. People who are victims of extreme emotional disturbance sometimes display very striking degrees of regression as illustrated in Figure 10-5.

Stereotyped behavior

Another possible reaction to frustration is a tendency to repeat some action over and over again, despite the fact that it appears to serve no useful purpose. This is called *stereotyped behavior*. It is interesting to

354

note that animals as well as people display this tendency, as was shown by an experiment with a rat frustrated in its attempts to reach food.

The rat was placed on a stand from which it could jump toward either of two small doorways, one marked with a white circle on a black card, the other marked with a black circle on a white card. If the rat chose correctly, the door opened, and the rat entered a food compartment. If it chose incorrectly, it bumped into a locked doorway and fell into a net. After the rat had learned to discriminate between the white and the black circles, the problem was made insoluble; half the time food was placed behind the white circle and the door behind the black circle was locked, and the other half of the time this procedure was reversed. The rat's attempts to reach the food and to avoid the bump and fall were now frustrated. After a while it simply remained on the stand and refused to jump at all — a reaction resembling apathy. The experimenter then forced the rat to jump by applying a shock, a blast of air, or a prod with a stick. Under these circumstances the animal's behavior became highly stereotyped; it tended to keep jumping time after time to the same doorway, regardless of the marking or whether it was rewarded or was punished by a fall. This stereotyped tendency to jump in the same direction every time persisted for as many as several hundred trials and sometimes continued even when the other doorway was left open so that the food behind it was clearly visible (14).

As strange as this behavior may seem, it has many counterparts in human activity. People frustrated by a stalled car may keep trying time after time to get it started, even though they know something is wrong, until the battery finally goes dead. Many frustrated people have definite stereotyped patterns of conversation — phrases they keep repeating over and over again, whether they are appropriate to the discussion or not. A pronounced degree of stereotyped behavior is often found among people who have suffered brain damage that interferes with their speech or motor skills. Frustrated by their disabilities, many such patients keep placing their shoes and other belongings in certain definite places and patterns, and they become upset by any variation in the appearance or arrangement of their rooms or lockers.

Defense mechanisms

Among the effects of frustration and conflict, as has just been discussed, are such behavioral symptoms as aggression, depression, withdrawal, vacillation, regression, and stereotyped behavior. In addition, frustration and conflict often result in a group of mental or symbolic processes, first described by Sigmund Freud, that are so important that they deserve discussion in a section of their own. They are called *defense mechanisms*, and they represent an unconscious attempt to reduce anxiety. All defense mechanisms involve some degree of self-deception and distortion of reality. The processes apparently operate in everyone at times, and in psychotic people they are often seen in extreme and exaggerated form.

Rationalization

Perhaps the most common of all defense mechanisms is *rationalization,* familiar even to children—though not by its scientific name—through Aesop's fable about the fox, unable to reach a cluster of grapes, that consoled itself by deciding that they would have been sour anyway. As the fable implies, rationalization is an attempt to reduce anxiety by deciding that you have not really been frustrated—or that a conflict over goals has not really occurred.

Thus a young woman, frustrated because she was turned down by the college of her choice, manages to convince herself that she did not really want to go to that school anyway; it is too far from home or the student body is too snobbish. A young man, frustrated because he was rejected when he asked for a date, convinces himself that the girl is not very attractive and much less interesting than he had supposed.

We also use rationalization at times to conceal from ourselves the fact that we have acted out of motives that conflict with our standards. A mother's real reason for keeping her daughter from dating may be jealousy. She rationalizes by saying that she is acting for the girl's own good. A student may cheat on an examination to avoid the work of studying but rationalize by claiming that everybody cheats. The miser may rationalize a refusal to give money to good causes by claiming that charity weakens the moral fiber of the people who receive it.

"I prefer these imported cigarettes. They don't have a health warning."

Repression

In many cases, people who suffer anxiety over their motives seem simply to banish the motives altogether from their conscious thoughts; they cease to be aware of the motives. This process is called *repression,* and its effects are frequently observed. A woman who at one time suffered severe conflicts and anxiety over sexual urges may now have repressed her motives to the point where she is not aware of any sexual desires or feelings at all. Many people seem to be entirely unaware that they possess such motives as dependency and hostility. Some cases of *amnesia,* or loss of memory, are believed to be exaggerated forms of repression, although amnesia can also be caused by brain damage.

Sublimation

A motive that causes anxiety may also be transformed unconsciously into a different but related motive that is more acceptable to society and to oneself. This defense mechanism is known as *sublimation,* a word chosen because the process enables a "shameful" motive to find expression in a more noble fashion. Freud believed that works of art are often the result of sublimation—that the Shakespeares and Michelangelos of the world may very well have channeled forbidden sexual urges into the pursuit of artistic creativity. Similarly, Freud believed that people with hostile motives may sublimate their urges toward cruelty into a socially approved desire to become surgeons or prosecuting attorneys, or even teachers with the power to discipline the young.

Identification

The term *identification* has already been used in the book to describe one of the processes through which growing children develop their standards. As children we come to think of ourselves as being almost the same person as our parents and other figures of importance and authority in our lives. We feel that we share their power, their virtues, and their triumphs. We adopt their standards and imitate their behavior because we believe that this will help us attain the desirable position that they have reached.

Identification can constitute a defense mechanism when we use it to relieve anxiety over our own conflicts by assuming the virtues of some admired person or of a group that seems free of such anxiety. Thus a man who is anxious about his lack of courage may identify with an astronaut or a group of mountain climbers so that he can believe that he too possesses their courage. A young woman anxious about her own lack of social skill may identify with a more popular roommate.

In a more complex form, an identification can be established with a figure of authority who is resented and feared. Thus a young man may defend himself against the anxiety aroused by hostile feelings toward his boss by identifying with the boss. He may imitate the boss's mannerisms and express the same opinions—thus persuading himself that he possesses the same kind of power. This type of identification may also be made with a group. Thus young people, anxious about their feelings of envy and hostility toward an in-group, may identify with the group and adopt its standards. A study of prisoners in German concentration camps in the Second World War showed that many of them began to imitate the characteristics of the very guards from whose brutality they were suffering (15).

Identification appears in some cases to be a conscious process. People who adopt the tactic seem to be aware of their attempts to make themselves similar to models who possess characteristics that they envy and believe would reduce their own anxiety. In other cases the whole process is unconscious. The people engaging in identification are not aware that they are imitating another individual or a group.

Reaction formation

When people display a trait to excess—that is, in an exaggerated form that hardly seems called for by the circumstances—the possibility always exists that they are using the defense mechanism called *reaction formation*. That is to say, they are pretending to possess motives that are the exact opposite of the real motives that are causing them anxiety. For example, a man appears to be the soul of politeness. He is constantly holding doors open for other people, saying "Yes, sir," and "Yes, ma'am," always smiling, agreeable, and apologetic for his mistakes. This exaggerated politeness and concern for others may simply be a defense mechanism he has adopted to conceal the fact that he has hostile motives and is made anxious by his hostility. A woman who dresses in a sexually provocative manner and is constantly flirting and telling risque stories may only be concealing her basic sexual inhibitions and fear of being unattractive.

Projection

The man who claims that everybody is dishonest and the woman who is convinced of the sexual immorality of the younger generation may have reached these conclusions through honest examination of the evidence. On the other hand, they may be exhibiting another defense mechanism called *projection,* in which people foist off or project onto other people motives or thoughts of their own that cause them anxiety. The man who talks too much about the dishonesty of the human race may very well be concealing his own strong tendencies toward dishonesty. The woman who talks too much about the immorality of young people may be concealing her own strong sexual desires, which cause her considerable anxiety.

In one experimental study of projection, the subjects were college fraternity brothers who lived under the same roof and knew each other well. Each subject was asked to rate his fraternity brothers on a scale that measured four undesirable traits: stinginess, obstinacy, disorderliness, and bashfulness. In the answers the experimenters found general agreement that some members of the fraternity were indeed quite stingy, obstinate, disorderly, or bashful. The subjects were also asked to rate themselves on these traits. These self-ratings showed that some of the men described by their friends as stingy or obstinate freely admitted that they possessed these traits, while others did not. The most significant finding was that the students who were in fact stingy or obstinate, but were unaware of it or unwilling to admit it, were the most inclined to attribute these traits to the others. The student who was generally regarded as stingy but who described himself as generous was likely to rate his friends as possessing a high degree of stinginess (16). Presumably he was relieving his anxiety over possessing this trait by projecting it—by claiming that others, and not he, possessed it.

Projection plays a part in many disagreements in marriage. Many husbands complain that their wives are extravagant, although a disinterested observer can clearly see that it is the husband himself, not the wife, who is wasting money. Wives who are torn by sexual conflicts and urges toward infidelity may falsely accuse their husbands of having affairs. A marriage counselor who hears accusations by husband or wife of bad conduct or improper motives on the part of the other partner always looks for the possibility that the complaints represent projection rather than the truth.

Projection appears to be one of the most powerful but also the most dangerous of the defense mechanisms. It works very effectively to reduce anxiety—but it does so at the risk of a completely distorted view of the truth about oneself and others.

The role of defense mechanisms

In the last analysis, perhaps every person's defense mechanisms are unique. Certainly many investigators would want to add to the list of six that have been mentioned here. Some investigators would use different names for them or perhaps lump some of those mentioned here under the same name. The important thing is that human beings show considerable ingenuity at deluding themselves. In one way or another they persuade themselves that they did not really want the goals from which they have been blocked, that their motives are admirable, that they are living up to their own and society's standards, and that their disappointments are somehow bearable.

Because frustration and conflict are so frequent, all of us use defense mechanisms from time to time. Many of these mechanisms are irrational. Nonetheless, they often serve a useful purpose. They may help us through crises that would otherwise overwhelm and disable us. If nothing else, they may gain time for us—time in which we can gather the strength, maturity, and knowledge needed to cope more realistically and constructively with our anxieties. It is only in the more extreme cases that the use of defense mechanisms—like the other effects of frustration and conflict mentioned earlier in the chapter—slip over into the realm of abnormal psychology.

Normal and abnormal psychology

The dividing line between normal psychological processes and behavior on the one hand and abnormal psychological processes and behavior on the other is difficult to draw. All of us, as has been said, are irrational in our use of defense mechanisms. Moreover, we may be moved to more or less irrational anger and aggression, depression and apathy, withdrawal, vacillation, regression, and stereotyped behavior. At what point does such behavior cease to represent the conduct of a human being who is quite normal (though subject to the usual human frailties) and slip over into the realm of the abnormal? And what is one to say about the fact that sometimes people who behave quite normally most of their lives—and are ordinarily quite successful in their work and their relations with their families, friends, and fellow workers—may go through periods when they seem to be behaving abnormally and may even require treatment?

The normal personality

In attempting to define the normal personality, psychologists for many years stressed the word "adjustment." Normal personality traits, it was generally believed, are those that help people adjust to their environments and to other people—in other words, to accept the realities of the physical world and of society. This general description of the normal personality still persists to some extent. In recent years, however, many psychologists have come to the conclusion that "adjustment" is too passive and negative a word—and that it implies a kind of self-effacing conformity to what others in the society are thinking and doing. Indeed some scholars have decided that "adjustment," if construed as meaning a more or less unquestioning acceptance of some aspects of human society—such as mass killings in warfare and the spending of human resources on military equipment rather than on education and the alleviation of poverty—is itself abnormal (17).

Thus growing numbers of psychologists have come to think less in terms of adjustment than in terms that imply some kind of honest self-awareness, independence, and fulfillment. As was mentioned on pages 327–28, Maslow has suggested the term "self-actualization." Others have suggested that normal people are those who have a continuing and stable sense of identity (18)—or who possess the ability and inner freedom to make their own decisions in accordance with their own desires and the realities of the environment rather than because of real or imagined pressure from others (19).

Some elements of being "normal." Certainly it is very difficult to define the normal personality, especially in times of rapid social change such as the present, and doubtless there will be continued debate and the formulation of new ideas in forthcoming years. But most psychologists probably would agree on the following points.

1 Being normal does not mean being perfect. Even the most normal of us encounter conflicts and frustrations, experience anxiety, and cannot always cope with our anxieties in a completely successful manner. We can only do our best—which probably means continuing to function more or less satisfactorily despite the inevitable problems of the human condition.

2 Being normal means being realistic. Normal people do not expect perfection, either in themselves or in others. They are aware of their own limitations and accept the fact that other people also have limitations. Since they do not have unduly grandiose expectations, they are not surprised or overly ashamed or angry when they themselves fail or when others fail them.

3 Normal people can "roll with the punch." They may be unhappy at times over the state of the world or over personal disappointments, but they can manage to live with these facts. They are flexible and can change their plans. They are confident of their ability to cope with any situations that may arise—not necessarily as well as they would like, but at least after a fashion.

4 Normal people possess a certain amount of enthusiasm and spontaneity. They find things to do in life that give them honest pleasure, whether these be working productively or watching a sunset. They are capable of feeling and showing affection and establishing satisfactory relationships with other people.

The abnormal personality

Just as it is difficult to say what is normal, so is it difficult to say what is abnormal. Indeed it is virtually impossible to make any absolute definition of abnormal behavior. Is it abnormal to believe in witches? It was not so considered by the American colonists. Is it abnormal for a young woman to faint from the excitement of attending a dance or the embarrassment of hearing profanity? It was not so considered in Victorian England. Is suicide abnormal? To most Americans, it may seem like the ultimate in abnormality. Yet in the Far East a Buddhist priest who commits suicide as a form of political protest is regarded as exhibiting strength of character rather than abnormality.

One approach to a description of abnormal behavior can be made in statistical terms—that is to say, it is behavior that is rather uncommon and unusual. But in addition, as the preceding paragraph implies, unusual behavior is not generally considered abnormal unless it is regarded as undesirable by the particular society in which it occurs. For example, working eighteen hours a day is probably even more unusual in our society than being addicted to heroin—but the former is generally considered desirable or at least acceptable and is therefore regarded as normal, while heroin addiction is considered undesirable and therefore regarded as abnormal.

What is considered undesirable or "strange" varies from society to society. In our own society, a man who spent much of his day holding conversations with God would certainly be regarded as abnormal, but in certain parts of rural Brazil such conduct is regarded as perfectly sensible and normal. Our American society has generally regarded drug addiction and homosexuality as abnormal, but this has not been true of all societies and may currently be in the process of becoming less true of our own.

One quality highly valued by the American culture is happiness—and therefore most Americans tend to equate normal personality with happiness. A trait or behavior is considered normal if it leads to personal happiness, at least much of the time, and abnormal if it leads to unhappiness. Though this criterion is widely accepted, there are some rather spectacular exceptions. Many people who commit vicious acts that could hardly be considered normal—such as wartime atrocities and mass murders in peacetime—seem to be perfectly happy.

In general, however, the working definition of abnormal behavior accepted in the United States embraces the three points that have been mentioned. An abnormal personality trait or type of behavior is 1) statistically unusual, 2) considered undesirable by most people, and 3) a source of unhappiness to the person who possesses or displays it. It must be admitted that the definition is not very satisfactory from a scientific point of view and would be rejected by many psychologists—chiefly on the ground that it sets up some rather rigid standards that enable our society to stigmatize as "abnormal" anybody whose behavior is disliked or considered disruptive, whether or not that behavior can be judged abnormal by any scientific measure.

"Do people hate us because we dress this way, or do we dress this way because people hate us?"

Abnormality and stress

Abnormal behavior, however it may be defined, is closely related to all the forces that are lumped together under the concept of stress. It appears that all human beings, and animals as well, can stand a certain amount of frustration, conflict, and the resultant anxiety. But if the burden becomes too great and exceeds the threshold of what they can endure, they may lapse into abnormality, ranging from mild to severe.

It has been known ever since the time of Pavlov that animals can be made to behave abnormally under laboratory conditions that produce frustration and conflict. Pavlov conditioned a dog to discriminate between a circle and an ellipse projected on a screen. The dog learned to salivate to the circle but not to the ellipse. Then the shape of the ellipse was changed gradually so that it became more and more like a circle. Even when the difference in appearance was quite small, the dog still made the discrimination. But when the difference became too small for the dog to perceive and the discrimination became impossible, the dog began to behave strangely. At various times animals placed in this situation became restless, hostile, destructive, and apathetic, and they developed muscle tremors and tics (20).

Many similar experiments have also produced abnormal behavior in laboratory animals. Cats, for example, were taught various means of obtaining food and then, to create a conflict, were given an electric shock or air blast when they performed the act that was rewarded with food. They very quickly—after only one or two repetitions—began to show signs of restlessness, agitation, fear, and panic (21). Among human beings, a common kind of abnormal behavior produced by unusually stressful situations is "battle fatigue," the breakdown sometimes experienced by soldiers—even those who have coped successfully with many difficult problems in civilian life.

Influences on abnormal behavior

Some people have a low threshold for stress, others a much higher one. Three kinds of factors appear to determine which people display abnormal behavior.

Biological factors. As was mentioned in Chapter 7, there appear to be considerable individual differences in glandular activity, sensitivity of the autonomic nervous system, and, possibly, activity of the brain centers concerned with emotion—all of which may incline one person to be more easily aroused and more intensely emotional than another. Among the possible effects of these individual differences may be unusual patterns of physiological change, which produce sensations that cannot be interpreted by any ordinary standards. Any biological deficiency or abnormality in the emotional apparatus may alter the threshold for stress or cause distorted reactions to stress.

There is strong evidence that hereditary factors can be responsible for tendencies toward some of the most severe forms of abnormality, the psychoses, which will be discussed later in this chapter. As was stated on page 239, schizophrenia is more common among the close relatives of schizophrenics than among other people. Indeed a recent survey of all the studies made of children with a family background of schizophrenia — including brothers and sisters and even identical twins who were reared in different environments — offers evidence that a tendency to schizophrenia may be inherited (22). It also appears that hereditary factors may produce tendencies to manic-depressive psychosis (23) and perhaps to some other less extreme forms of abnormal behavior as well (24).

Psychological factors. Regardless of what kind of biological equipment we inherit, our psychological experiences also play a key role in determining how much stress we are likely to experience and how much we can endure without lapsing into behavior that will be considered abnormal. For example, if we acquire motives for achievement or power that we cannot gratify, or if our motives for affiliation and approval are frustrated by a belief that other people dislike us, we become extremely vulnerable. Particularly significant are our standards. An event that produces little or no anxiety in a person with relatively low standards of mastery and competence may produce an almost unbearable anxiety in a person with higher standards. Clinical psychologists sometimes are called on to treat people who appear to have suffered a crippling amount of anxiety over violations of standards of sexual behavior, honesty, hostility, or dependency that would seem trivial to most of us.

Cultural factors. Also important is the kind of culture into which we are born — and thus the kinds of social influences to which we are exposed. For example, statistical studies of schizophrenia appear to show that it is most common among people living in the slum or near-slum areas of large cities (25). Perhaps people who are forced to live in that kind of culture experience more frustration and conflict than people at more affluent levels of society. Or perhaps growing up in a slum environment reduces a person's tolerance for stress.

Cultural factors also determine in large part the symptoms that a person is likely to display. The culture of middle- and upper-class America has maintained that individuals are personally responsible for what happens to them, and people in this culture who fail to live up to their standards of achievement and virtue are likely to suffer intense feelings of guilt and depression. Americans from less affluent homes are more likely to display symptoms that revolve around feelings of anger, bitterness, and suspicion.

One especially significant study of the influence of culture on behavior has been made among isolated tribes in Africa. Some members of these tribes roam the countryside like shepherds, driving small herds of goats and cows in search of forage. Others are farmers, living close together on patches of land on which they grow their food. These two very different kinds of lives were found to have a profound effect on their personalities. The wide-roaming herdsmen proved to be what would generally be called "outgoing"—independent, self-controlled, affectionate, and sexually uninhibited. The farmers, crowded together, competing with, yet dependent on, one another, proved to be what might be called "uptight"—full of suppressed hostility and hatred, secretive, anxious, emotionally inhibited, and oversensitive (26). One might speculate that these farmers have a counterpart in American towns and neighborhoods where people live close together, are forced to be dependent on one another, yet compete for a meager allotment of resources or jobs.

To summarize, the chances that people will display abnormal behavior—and the particular kinds of abnormal behavior to which they are most prone—depend in part on the biological equipment they have inherited, in part on the psychological experiences they have encountered, and in part on the kinds of cultures in which they find themselves in childhood and adulthood. The three factors work together to make some people behave in what is generally considered a normal fashion—and others in ways considered anywhere from just a bit strange to what psychologists call psychotic, or, in popular terminology, insane.

Neuroses

In a sort of twilight zone between normal behavior and the extreme abnormality of psychosis lie the conditions that are known as *neuroses* (or sometimes *psychoneuroses*). In a sense, every neurosis is unique—the product of one person's unique frustrations and conflicts as they affect the tolerance for stress dictated by this person's own unique biological, psychological, and cultural background. Thus any attempt at classification of the symptoms has to be somewhat arbitrary. One popular and useful classification system, based on the work of Freud and used by many psychotherapists, is as follows (27).

Anxiety states

Although anxiety is characteristic of all neuroses, it is a more obvious symptom in some of them than in others. *Anxiety states,* one rather large group of neuroses, include the following.

Anxiety reaction. The outstanding symptom of this anxiety state is a chronic and relatively unfocused feeling of uneasiness and vague fear. People displaying anxiety reaction feel tense and jumpy, are afraid of other people, doubt their ability to study or work, and sometimes suffer from actual panic. They may experience such physical symptoms as palpitation of the heart, cold sweats, and dizziness. One man has described his feelings in these terms:

> I feel anxious and fearful most of the time; I keep expecting something to happen but I don't know what. It's not the same all the time. Sometimes I only feel bad—then suddenly for no reason it happens. My heart begins to pound so fast that I feel it's going to pop out. My hands get icy and I

get a cold sweat all over my body. My forehead feels like it is covered with sharp needles. I feel like I won't be able to breathe and I begin panting and choking. It's terrible—so terrible. I can go along for a while without too much difficulty and then suddenly without any warning it happens (28).

Phobic reaction. When the anxiety becomes attached to a specific object or event, the person displaying it is said to be suffering from a *phobia,* or unreasonable fear. Two common phobias are *claustrophobia* (fear of confinement in small places, which makes some people unable to ride in elevators) and *acrophobia* (fear of high places, which affects some people when they have to climb to a top row of a theater balcony). But phobic reactions may be attached to any object at all. Some people are thrown into panic by a snake, an ambulance, or even a toy balloon.

Obsessive-compulsive reactions

Obsessions are thoughts that keep cropping up in a persistent and disturbing fashion. Some neurotics are obsessed with the idea that they have heart trouble or that they are going to die by a certain age. A common and mild form of obsession is the feeling of people starting out on a trip that they have left the door unlocked or the stove turned on.

Compulsions are irresistible urges to perform some act over and over again, such as washing one's hands dozens of times a day. The hostess who cannot bear to see a knife or fork out of line at the table and keeps emptying her guests' ash trays is exhibiting mild forms of compulsion. So is the businessman who cannot get any work done unless his papers are arranged in neat piles on his desk and he has a half dozen freshly sharpened pencils waiting all in a line. Or the child who steps on every crack in the sidewalk.

Obsessive-compulsive reactions seem to represent an attempt to substitute acceptable thoughts or actions for the unacceptable desires that are causing conflict and anxiety.

Hysteria

As used to describe neuroses, the word *hysteria* has a different meaning from the usual one. It refers specifically to the following two conditions.

Conversion reaction. This form of hysteria results in strange and often dramatic physical symptoms that have no organic basis. People displaying conversion reaction may suffer paralysis of the arms or legs and even blindness or deafness. They may lose all sensitivity in one part of the body. In one type called glove anesthesia they lose all sensitivity in the hand, as if it were covered by a glove; they cannot feel a pinprick or even a severe cut anywhere from fingertips to wrist.

Dissociative reactions. People displaying dissociative reactions set themselves apart in some manner from the conflicts that are troubling them. One type of dissociative reaction is *amnesia,* or loss of memory. Another, quite rare, is *multiple personality;* people with multiple personalities seem to be split into two or more completely different selves that represent sides of their personalities that they cannot integrate into a unity. *Sleepwalking,* in which people move about and perform acts while asleep that they cannot remember after they wake up, is also a dissociative reaction.

Hysteria, obsessive-compulsive reactions, and anxiety states are of course not the only neuroses. There are many others. Indeed it might be said that there are as many different kinds of neuroses, some of which defy classification, as there are neurotics. All of them are characterized by high levels of stress and anxiety, lasting over a considerable period of time; but different individuals display the anxiety in different ways. The neuroses may be mild and cause little trouble, or they may be so severe as to verge on the psychotic.

Psychopathic personality

Before the discussion turns to the psychoses, however, one other form of abnormal behavior must be mentioned. This is *psychopathic personality,* an abnormality that defies any neat classification. It is not a psychoneurosis and it is not a psychosis—but it is a condition that occurs rather frequently and often causes serious trouble.

People exhibiting psychopathic personality seem to lack any normal conscience or sense of social responsibility and to have no feeling for other people. These psychopaths, as they are called, may seem on the surface to be quite charming, candid, and generous—but in truth they are selfish, ruthless, and addicted to lying. They have no love for anyone but themselves and take advantage of others without any feelings of guilt (29). Indeed a total absence of anxiety of any kind is one of the outstanding characteristics of the psychopath—and of course a factor that makes psychopathic personality completely different from the neuroses.

Psychopaths are likely to be in and out of trouble all their lives, for they do not learn from experience and seem to have no desire to change. The word "psychopath" is mentioned frequently in court cases, for criminals who appear to experience no remorse for even the most cruel kinds of deeds are a good example of the psychopathic personality in its most extreme form. Because of the social consequences that often occur, the abnormality is also known as *sociopathic personality* or *antisocial reaction.*

The causes remain a mystery. They seem to entail some kind of failure to grow out of a childish insistence on self-gratification and to acquire more mature and responsible ways of behaving. The psychopath may be a person who just never has "grown up."

Psychoses

Psychosis refers to the extreme forms of mental disturbance that are often known in popular terminology—and also in legal language—as insanity. A psychosis is any form of mental disturbance that is so severe as to make a person incapable of getting along in society. It has been estimated that at any given moment about a million Americans are suffering from mental disorders and that two-thirds of this number are being treated in hospitals, where they occupy about half of all the hospital beds available in the nation (30). It has also been estimated that about ten of every 100 children born today will spend part of their lives in a mental hospital.

Because of these high figures, many people assume that the "stresses and strains" of modern industrial civilization and city life have greatly increased the amount of mental disturbance, but this does not seem to be true. Although more people are admitted to mental hospitals in the United States today than ever before, much of the increase is due to the fact that more people live to an advanced age and therefore become subject to the kind of brain deterioration that accompanies senility and results in psychosis. Among younger people, there appears to have been little if any change. Indeed court records have shown that there were about as many commitments to mental hospitals, in proportion to population, in the relatively rural Massachusetts of the nineteenth century as in the highly industrialized Massachusetts of the present century (31). The same types of mental disturbances found in the United States and other industrialized nations have also been observed in primitive societies throughout the world (32).

A definition of psychosis

In general, people who are psychotic appear to display the following three characteristics.

1 Their thought processes seem to be different from those of the normal person. Their thoughts and conversations are often illogical and unrelated to reality. They may have *hallucinations* (imaginary sensations such as seeing nonexistent animals in the room or feeling bugs crawling under their skins). Or they may have *delusions* (false beliefs, such as imagining that they are Napoleon).

2 They display inconsistent and inappropriate emotions. They may become much more excited than a normal person would be under the same circumstances. Or they may seem happy at times when they should more appropriately be sad.

3 They are unable to control their thoughts and actions. They may be unable to dress themselves, or they may engage in acts of senseless violence.

In some cases the origin of these unusual behaviors is clearly physiological. In *senile psychosis,* for example, there is actual deterioration of the brain caused by aging or by a succession of what are commonly called strokes, or hemorrhages of blood vessels in the brain. Psychoses

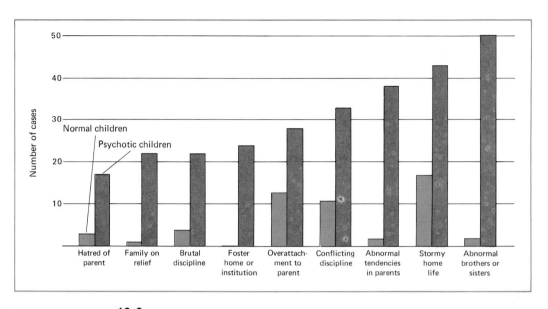

10-6

Backgrounds of normal and psychotic children

The bars show some of the more pronounced differences found in a study of the family backgrounds of a group of psychotic children as compared with a control group of normal children. Note that the bars labeled "abnormal tendencies in parents" and "abnormal brothers or sisters" point to hereditary factors, the others to environment. (34)

can also result from certain diseases, such as untreated syphilis of long standing, from excessive and prolonged use of alcohol and perhaps of other drugs, and, though only rarely, from injuries to the head. Psychoses of these kinds are ordinarily classified as *organic psychoses.*

In other cases, there is no clear-cut physiological explanation. No medical test yet available shows anything physically wrong with the brain, but it simply does not seem to be functioning normally. These cases therefore have been classified as *functional psychoses.* However, the distinction between organic and functional psychoses no longer seems to be as definite and useful as it once did. The evidence that a tendency toward psychosis can be inherited suggests that there may be some kind of physical basis for most or all psychoses, even though the exact nature of the physical defects is not yet known. Some psychiatrists now believe that all psychoses are caused by small and subtle chemical imbalances in the brain and someday should be readily controllable through the use of new medications that will restore the proper chemical balance (33).

Even if all psychoses should indeed turn out to have some kind of physical basis, however, there seems to be no doubt that psychological and cultural factors also are important in determining which individuals will manage to overcome the tendency to psychosis and which will actually display psychotic behavior. As is shown in Figure 10-6, the home and family backgrounds of people suffering from psychosis appear to be less favorable than average in many ways, including many that have no connection with heredity. The manner in which environment operates to encourage or discourage psychosis, however, is some-

368

thing of a mystery. Most people who grow up even in the worst homes do not become psychotic, whereas many people who come from the most privileged homes (at least homes that appear on the surface to be the most privileged) do become psychotic.

For reasons not understood, men appear to be more subject to psychosis than women; the ratio of males to females among first admissions to mental hospitals is about 4 to 3. Married people are less likely to become psychotic than unmarried people, but this is probably because people with psychotic tendencies are less likely to get married in the first place.

The psychoses that have traditionally been classified as functional fall into three categories: 1) *schizophrenia*, 2) *manic-depressive psychosis*, and 3) *paranoia*. The three require separate discussions.

Schizophrenia

This is the most common psychosis of all, accounting for perhaps as much as 25 percent of first admissions to mental hospitals. Its occurence is particularly frequent among young adults in their twenties and is more common among men than among women. As was shown by a survey sponsored by the World Health Organization in nine different countries, therapists generally consider patients to be schizophrenic when they display the following behavior (35):

1 *Poor insight.*
2 *Incoherent speech* (often a spontaneous flow of conversation that cannot be understood).
3 *Delusions* (frequent and often extremely bizarre; schizophrenics may believe that they no longer exist at all or that their heads or arms are missing).
4 *Absence of emotion* (blank and expressionless face; little or no emotion shown in situations where a normal person would be upset or elated).
5 *Remoteness* (making it difficult or impossible for the therapist or others to establish any kind of rapport).
6 *Worry about thoughts* (schizophrenics may seem to hear their own thoughts as if they were spoken aloud and could be heard by others; they may also feel that their thoughts are somehow being broadcast so that everyone knows about them).

In one study of people hospitalized for schizophrenia, an examination of their school records showed that they tended to behave differently from their schoolmates quite early in life. The boys who eventually became schizophrenic were poor achievers in school and tended to be somber, disagreeable, and antisocial, with a generally cheerless and negative attitude toward life. The girls, on the other hand, were unusually quiet, introverted, immature, and overly dependent. As the investigator who made the study has pointed out, the boys destined to become schizophrenic were *actively* maladjusted, as if they were having

Schizophrenia by Boris Art-zybasheff, 1947

trouble establishing control over their hostilities. The girls were *quietly* and passively maladjusted, as if they were having trouble escaping from the dependency of childhood and learning to take part in social experiences without self-doubt and inhibition (36).

Schizophrenia is notably resistant to any kind of treatment yet devised, and recovery is usually very slow at best. Therefore many schizophrenics remain in hospitals for long periods. There also are many schizophrenics who are not in hospitals, either because they manage to function in some sort of minimal way or because their families take care of them. Many of the men and women on city doorsteps and park benches who appear to the casual observer to be alcoholics are in fact schizophrenics. And there are other schizophrenics sitting in front of television sets sixteen hours a day in homes where they are protected from having to cope with life through their own efforts.

Manic-depressive psychosis

This psychosis is characterized, as the name indicates, by extremes of mood, sometimes in the form of wild swings from intense excitement to deep melancholy. In the manic phase, people suffering from manic-depressive psychosis tend to be talkative, restless, aggressive, boastful, uninhibited, and often destructive. In the depressive phase they may become so gloomy and hopeless that they refuse to eat. Some people who have this psychosis, indeed perhaps most, do not exhibit swings from one mood to the other but only one of the two phases, usually the depressive. Manic-depressive psychosis, particularly the depressive kind, is more common among women than among men. It is most likely to occur in middle adulthood.

Even without treatment, manic-depressive psychosis usually disappears—the manic phase ordinarily in about three months, the depressive phase in about nine. Its victims then return to normal, and about a quarter of them never have a second episode. In the other three-quarters the psychosis recurs, often several times.

States of depression that are not severe enough to be called psychotic—but that nevertheless cause a great deal of trouble—appear to be quite common. Indeed one investigator has estimated that perhaps as many as thirty million Americans can expect to suffer from depression at some time in their lives (37). They may not even know what is wrong —for the milder form of depression does not necessarily cause them to feel unhappy or "blue." Nor do they necessarily appear depressed to their friends. But if the activity of their facial muscles is measured with electrodes as shown in Figure 10-7, this sensitive measurement shows a difference in the muscles that create expressions of happiness or sadness. In particular, it has been noted that the muscles show a pattern indicating sadness when a depressed person is asked to think of a "typical day," whereas other people produce a pattern showing happiness (38). These states of depression typically result in feelings of unexplained fatigue and lack of enthusiasm. People experiencing them

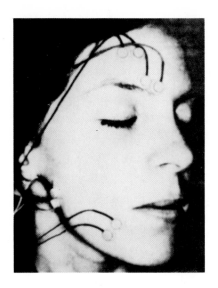

10-7

A test for depression

Electrodes placed on the forehead and cheeks measure the activity of muscles responsible for facial expression even when no change can be seen in the expression. People suffering from depression show characteristic patterns of activity as explained in the text.

have trouble getting any work done. They may lose all interest in activities that once gave them pleasure. Often they feel that they must be suffering from some disease that causes a lack of energy, such as mononucleosis; but a physical examination shows nothing wrong.

Depression often appears to be accompanied by changes in brain chemistry, specifically by a deficiency in the substances called neurotransmitters (see pages 244–45) that are responsible for getting messages through the switching points in the brain. This deficiency appears in particular to slow down the activity of the brain centers concerned with arousal, appetite, sexual desire, and motor activity (39)—all of which tend to be at a low level in people suffering from depression. Moreover, a large majority of people with depression have been found to respond to various types of medication that help encourage activity of the neurotransmitters (40).

Many psychologists believe, however, that the causes of depression are quite complex. It has been suggested that they include not only chemical factors, probably influenced at least in part by hereditary tendencies, but also psychological factors. Often people become depressed after the loss of someone they love, through death or for other reasons, or after an event that causes a loss of social status or self-esteem. Others seem to have become so frustrated that they can no longer cope with their problems, lapse into helplessness, and find consolation in the fact that other people then give them the kind of sympathy and attention that goes along with being "sick" (41). Some therapists believe that this cycle of events can best be broken through medical alteration of the brain chemistry, others that it can best be attacked through psychological therapy, still others that the two approaches should be combined.

Paranoia

This is the least common of the psychoses; it is indeed quite rare. It is characterized by delusions that are spectacular and persistent. Some victims of *paranoia* have delusions of grandeur; they may believe that

371

they are Napoleon or Christ. Others have delusions of persecution; they believe that other people are conspiring to kill them. The delusions of persecution are thought to be an extreme form of projection, in which those suffering from paranoia project to the rest of the world their own hostile motives.

Summary

1 *Frustration* is the blocking of motive satisfaction by some kind of obstacle. (In popular terminology, it is also often used to describe the unpleasant feelings that result from the blocking of motive satisfaction.)

2 Frustration may be caused by a) physical obstacles, b) social circumstances, c) personal shortcomings, or d) conflicts between motives.

3 Some individuals can tolerate relatively large amounts of frustration, whereas others react strongly to relatively small amounts.

4 A *conflict* is the simultaneous arousal of two or more incompatible motives, resulting in unpleasant emotions.

5 Two classes of conflicts are a) conflicts between motives and internal standards (for example, between hostility and standards that prohibit the display of hostility) and b) conflicts over external goals (for example, between the desire to get good grades and the desire to socialize with one's friends).

6 Two motives that often come into conflict are the desire for achievement and the desire for affiliation. This conflict often makes people perform relatively poorly in competition. Particularly among women, because of social pressures against being competitive or "pushy," it has been found to result frequently in what has been called "the motive to avoid success."

7 Conflicts over external goals can be a) *approach-approach* (seeking two desirable goals), b) *avoidance-avoidance* (seeking to prevent two undesirable alternatives), c) *approach-avoidance* (having a motive that has both desirable and undesirable consequences), or d) *double approach-avoidance* (when we are torn between two goals that both have some desirable and some undesirable aspects).

8 Among the possible reactions to frustration are a) assertive coping, b) aggression, c) depression and apathy, d) withdrawal, e) vacillation, f) regression, and g) stereotyped behavior.

9 *Defense mechanisms* are unconscious mental or symbolic processes that act to reduce the anxiety caused by frustration. They include a) rationalization, b) repression, c) sublimation, d) identification, e) reaction formation, and f) projection.

10 *Normal behavior* is defined by many psychologists in terms of honest self-awareness, independence, fulfillment, and a continuing and stable sense of identity.

11 *Abnormal behavior,* though difficult to define, is generally considered to be behavior that is a) statistically unusual, b) considered strange or undesirable by most people, and c) a source of unhappiness.

12 Abnormal behavior is believed to result from stress that exceeds the individual's capacity to withstand stress.

13 The individual's ability to tolerate stress appears to be determined by a) biological factors such as glandular activity and sensitivity of the autonomic nervous system, b) psychological factors such as the individual's internal standards and anxiety over failure to meet them, and c) social and cultural factors.

14 *Neuroses* are forms of abnormal behavior that lie between normal behavior and the extreme abnormality of psychosis. They are frequently classified as a) *anxiety states,* including anxiety reaction and phobic reaction; b) *obsessive-compulsive reactions;* and c) *hysteria,* including conversion reaction (unexplained paralysis) and dissociative reactions (such as amnesia or sleepwalking).

15 Another important form of abnormal behavior, difficult to classify, is *psychopathic personality* (also called *sociopathic personality* or *antisocial reaction*). Psychopaths seem to lack a conscience or sense of social responsibility and to have no feeling for other people. Unlike other disturbed individuals, they are free of anxiety.

16 *Psychosis* is an extreme form of mental disturbance generally characterized by a) disturbed thought processes, b) inconsistent and inappropriate emotions, and c) inability to control one's thoughts and actions.

17 Psychoses have traditionally been classified as either a) *organic* (caused by actual damage to the brain, as in senility), or b) *functional* (having no apparent organic basis).

18 Three types of psychosis traditionally classified as functional are a) *schizophrenia,* b) *manic-depressive psychosis,* and c) *paranoia.*

Recommended reading

Allport, G., ed. *Letters from Jenny.* New York: Harcourt Brace Jovanovich, 1965.

Edgerton, R. B. *The individual in cultural adaptation.* Berkeley: University of California Press, 1971.

Hall, C. S., and Lindzey, G. *Theories of personality,* 2nd ed. New York: John Wiley, 1970.

Kaplan, B., ed. *The inner world of mental illness.* New York: Harper & Row, 1971.

Maddi, S. R. *Personality theories: a comparative analysis,* rev. ed. Homewood, Ill.: Dorsey Press, 1972.

Pervin, L. A., and Levenson, H. *Personality: theory assessment and research,* 2nd ed. New York: John Wiley, 1975.

Rosenthal, D. *Genetic theory and abnormal behavior.* New York. McGraw-Hill, 1970.

Outline

Personality theory and psychotherapy

The preceding chapter has already touched on the study of personality—for two critical characteristics of personality are our sources of frustration and conflict and our behavior and thought processes when we are frustrated or in conflict. The time has come, however, to take a more sharply focused look: What is personality? What are the ways in which individual personalities differ? What is known about the origins, the structure, and the dynamics of personality? In other words, the discussion must now turn to *personality theory* and to the various types of *psychotherapy,* or attempts to treat abnormal personalities, that are associated with personality theory.

What is personality?

Personality is another word that everybody uses but few try to define. It is a concept that has been discussed at least since the time of the ancient Greeks, whose physicians believed there were four types of personalities, each related to different fluids inside the body. *Sanguine* people were believed to have a rich flow of blood, making them happy, warm-hearted, and optimistic. *Choleric* (or bad-tempered) people had an excess of yellow bile. *Melancholy* people had an excess of black bile, making them moody. *Phlegmatic* people were slowed down and made listless by an excess of phlegm.

The human personality takes far more than four forms, and its origins are extremely complicated. But we might still describe the personalities of some of our acquaintances with the adjectives used by the Greeks. Some people are indeed sanguine, choleric, melancholy, or phlegmatic, at least a good deal of the time—and the tendency to display a particular behavior "a good deal of the time" is part of the modern definition of personality.

375

A definition of personality

Personality perhaps can best be defined as the *total pattern of characteristic ways of thinking, feeling, and behaving that constitute the individual's distinctive method of relating to the environment.* There are four key words in the definition, most easily discussed by taking them up in this order: 1) *characteristic,* 2) *distinctive,* 3) *relating,* and 4) *pattern.*

To qualify as a part of personality, a way of thinking, feeling, or behaving must have some continuity over time and circumstance; it must be *characteristic* of the individual. We do not call a man bad-tempered if he "blows up" only once in ten years. We say that a bad temper is part of his personality only if he shows it in many circumstances.

The way of thinking, feeling, or behaving must also be *distinctive*—that is, it must distinguish the individual from other individuals. This eliminates such common American characteristics as eating with a knife and fork, placing adjectives before rather than after nouns, and carrying a driver's license—all of which are more or less the same for every American and do not distinguish one person from others.

Note, however, that a young woman might always wear a ring that is a family heirloom and the only one of its kind in the world; her wearing of the ring would therefore be both characteristic and distinctive. But it would not be considered a part of her personality unless perhaps she attached some deep significance to the ring and acted as if it were an important symbol of personal worth and social acceptance. The word personality is ordinarily attached only to characteristics that play a major part in how people go about *relating* to their environments and especially to the people around them. Moreover, personality characteristics are usually thought of as positive or negative. A positive personality characteristic, such as a friendly manner, helps the individual become related to people and events in a constructive manner. A negative characteristic, such as fear of people, produces anxiety, loneliness, and failure.

There are many kinds of personality characteristics. Indeed psychologists have estimated that the English language has at least 18,000 words to describe them. All of us possess some but not all of them; and our personalities are the *pattern,* or sum total and organization, of the characteristics we possess and display. Some of us have a pattern of relating to our environments that makes us characteristically and distinctively cheerful, outgoing, optimistic, prompt, hard-working, and aggressive. Others may tend to be depressed, introverted, pessimistic, tardy, lazy, and submissive. Still others may be cheerful but introverted, optimistic but tardy, and hard-working but submissive. Or gloomy but extroverted, pessimistic but prompt, and lazy but aggressive. The possible combinations are endless and account for the many varieties of human personality.

The personality hierarchy

One important fact about personality is that, like so many other aspects of human behavior, the various possible thoughts, feelings, and responses within a given personality exist in a hierarchy; some are strong and easily and frequently aroused, while others are weaker and less likely to occur. In a social situation, for example, there are many ways that an individual can try to relate to the others in the group. The individual can be talkative or quiet, friendly or reserved, boastful or modest, bossy or acquiescent, more at ease with men or more at ease with women. One person may characteristically respond by withdrawing into the background, and we say that such a person is shy. Another may characteristically display warmth and try to put the others at their ease; we say that such a person is outgoing. Another may be talkative, boastful, and domineering, and we say that this person is aggressive or "pushy." In each of the three individuals, certain responses are strong in the personality hierarchy and easily aroused.

Each person's hierarchy of actions and thoughts has a certain amount of permanence. The shy person behaves shyly under many circumstances, and the aggressive person has a consistent tendency to be boastful and domineering. However, the hierarchy may change considerably according to circumstances. A young woman who is aggressive around people her own age may behave rather shyly in the presence of older people. A man who is usually shy may have one close friend with whom he is completely at ease. All of us, no matter how friendly or reserved we may be, are likely to have a strong tendency to make friends if we have been isolated for a long time, such as after an illness or a stretch at a lonely job. On the other hand, we are likely to want some solitude after a round of parties. The businessman who is ordinarily interested in his job and eager to talk about it may shun this kind of conversation when he gets home late at night after a hard day's work.

Personality theories

A personality theory is an attempt to organize the great variety of human thinking, feeling, and behavior around some general principles that will help us understand why people are alike in some ways and very different in others. Such a theory attempts to explain which personality characteristics are the most important, the most likely patterns of relationships among characteristics, the way in which these patterns are established, and (at least by implication) the way they can be changed.

The three elements of personality theory

As one student of personality theories has pointed out, all of them are concerned with three aspects of human behavior (1).

1 The theories make certain assumptions about the basic nature of humanity. They assume that there is some kind of *core of personality,* composed of tendencies and characteristics that are common to all of us. Different theories take different views of this common core of personality, as will be seen in a moment, but all of them assume that it exists and is a powerful force in shaping personality.

2 The theories maintain that these common tendencies and charac-

teristics are channeled in various directions by the process of *development*—by all the experiences we have in life, starting with our childhood relationships with our parents. Some of our behaviors are rewarded, others punished (by our parents and other people and society as a whole). We acquire all sorts of knowledge, the nature of which depends in large part on our environments. And thus we are molded into unique individuals.

3 The theories are also concerned with *peripheral characteristics*—that is, all the distinctive ways of thinking, feeling, and behaving that the individual displays under various circumstances. Each of these traits casts some light on the individual's personality; all of them are viewed as the inevitable result of the way the common core of human personality has been channeled in different directions by different developmental experiences.

Three representative theories

So many personality theories have been proposed by psychologists over the years that they can hardly be counted, much less listed. It is of course impossible to do justice to all of them in an introductory course. Fortunately it is possible to select three theories that are of special interest because they demonstrate the wide range of thinking that exists in this field—and also because all three of them have been extremely influential and have had important applications to the practice of psychotherapy, which is the subject of the second half of this chapter. The three are as follows.

1 *Psychoanalysis.* This personality theory, the best-known of all, has had a profound influence on the arts, philosophy, and all the other social sciences as well as on psychological thinking. It assumes that the core of personality is conflict—for example, conflicts between incompatible desires (many of which are unconscious), between desires and fears of punishment for attempts to gratify them, between wishes and defense mechanisms, and between wishes and outside circumstances that frustrate them. In the psychoanalytic view, the personality is decisively shaped by the way an individual learns to cope with such conflicts.

2 *Social learning theory.* This theory, to which many psychologists subscribe, emphasizes the element of development. It tends to regard human nature in *tabula rasa* terms—capable of being molded through learning, reward, and punishment.

3 *Self theory.* This view of personality is generally associated with the name of Carl Rogers, who, it will be remembered from Chapter 1, is a leader of the humanistic school of psychology. The core of personality, according to self theory, is an urge toward integration and self-fulfillment, toward living in harmony with oneself and others. Where the psychoanalysts consider selfishness and hostility to be inherent forces in human nature, Rogers considers them to be abnormalities caused by an unfortunate process of development. All this will be made clearer as the three representative personality theories are discussed one by one.

Psychoanalysis

The most famous of all personality theorists, of course, is Sigmund Freud, the founder of *psychoanalysis*. Rather strangely, the school of personality analysis and therapy started by Freud has never grown very large in actual numbers. In recent years there have been only about 2400 Freudian analysts in the United States and about 6000 in the entire world (2). Nonetheless, his ideas have been widely read and debated and have had a profound influence on the views of human personality held not only by many psychologists but also by many people who have never taken a psychology course.

Anxiety, repression, and the unconscious

Freud's ideas are very difficult to summarize; the student who hopes to understand them fully must be prepared to do extensive reading of both Freud's own writings and the psychoanalytic textbooks and commentaries that have been written by his followers. The discussion that follows here must of necessity omit many aspects of Freudian theory and confine itself to the ones that have had the most lasting influence.

Some of Freud's most influential ideas concerned concepts so central to the study of psychology that they have already been prominently mentioned in previous chapters. One of them was the role of anxiety. Freud was a pioneer in emphasizing the importance of anxiety, which he believed to be the central problem in mental disturbance. Another was the concept of repression and the other defense mechanisms mentioned in Chapter 10. Freud believed that these mechanisms, and especially the process of repression, are frequently used to eliminate from conscious awareness any motive or thought that threatens to cause anxiety. Another influential idea was his concept of the unconscious mind, composed in part of repressed motives and thoughts. Freud was the first to suggest the now widely held theory that the human mind and personality are like an iceberg, with only a small part visible and the great bulk submerged and concealed. All of us, he maintained, have many unconscious motives that we are never aware of but that nonetheless influence our behavior. (An example cited in Chapter 9, where unconscious motives are first discussed, is the case of a man who sincerely believes that he has no hostile motives, yet who in subtle ways performs many acts of aggression against his wife, his children, and his business associates.)

Freud in his Vienna study.

The id

The core of the unconscious, according to Freud, is the *id,* composed of raw, primitive, inborn forces that constantly struggle for gratification. Even a baby, Freud said, is swayed by two powerful drives. One is what he called the *libido,* embracing sexual urges and such related desires as to be kept warm, well fed, and comfortable. The other is aggression—the urge to fight, dominate, and when necessary destroy.

The id operates on what Freud called the *pleasure principle,* which insists on immediate and total gratification of all its demands. Freud felt,

"Good evening, Harry Chadwick. This is your id."

Drawing by W. Miller; © 1969 The New Yorker Magazine, Inc.

for example, that babies in their cribs—though unable as yet to think like human beings, and thus more like little animals—have libidos that demand to possess completely everything they desire and love, and also aggressive urges to destroy everything that gets in their way. As children grow up, they learn to control the demands of the id, at least in part. But the id remains active and powerful throughout life; it is indeed the sole source of all the psychic energy put to use in behaving and thinking. It is unconscious and we are not aware of its workings, but it continues to struggle for the relief of all its tensions.

The ego

The logical part of the mind that develops as the child grows up was called by Freud the *ego*—the "real" us, as we like to think of ourselves. In contrast to the id, the ego operates on the *reality principle;* it tries to mediate between the demands of the id and the realities of the environment. Deriving its energies from the id, the ego perceives what is going on in the environment and develops the operational responses (such as finding food) necessary to satisfy the demands of the id. The ego does our logical thinking; it does the best it can to help us lead sane and satisfactory lives. To the extent that the primitive drives of the id can be satisfied without getting us into danger or harm, the ego permits them satisfaction. But when the drives threaten to get us rejected by society or jailed as a thief, the ego represses them or attempts to satisfy them with substitutes that are socially acceptable.

The superego

In the ego's constant struggle to satisfy the demands of the id without permitting the demands to destroy us, it has a strong but troublesome ally in the third part of the mind as conceived by Freud—the *superego.* In a sense the superego is our conscience, our sense of right and wrong. It is partly acquired by adopting the notions of right and wrong that we are taught by society from our earliest years. However, Freud's concept of the superego represents a much stronger and more dynamic notion than the word *conscience* implies. Much like the id, the superego is mostly unconscious, maintaining a far greater influence over our behavior than we realize. It is largely acquired as a result of that famous process that Freud called the *Oedipus complex,* which can be summarized as follows.

According to Freud, all children between the ages of about two and a half and six are embroiled in a conflict of mingled affection and resentment toward their parents. The male child has learned that the outer world exists and that there are other people in it, and the id's demands for love and affection reach out insatiably toward the person he has been closest to—the mother. Although the child has only the haziest notion of sexual feelings, he wants to possess his mother totally and to take the place of his father with her. But his anger against his father, the

rival with whom he must share her, makes him fearful that his father will somehow retaliate. To further complicate the situation, his demands for total love from his mother are of course denied, a fact that also arouses the aggressive drives of the id and makes him want to retaliate against his mother. Thus he becomes overwhelmed with strong feelings of mingled love, anger, and fear toward both parents at once.

This period of storm and stress was named by Freud after the Greek legend in which Oedipus unwittingly killed his father and married his own mother and then, when he discovered what he had done, blinded himself as penance. Girls, according to Freud, go through very similar torments in the period from two and a half to six, except that their libido centers chiefly on their fathers, their aggression chiefly on their mothers.

The Oedipus conflict must somehow be resolved. The way this is done, according to Freud, is through identification with the parents. That is to say, we resolve our feelings of mingled love and hate for our parents by becoming like them, by convincing ourselves that we share their strength and authority and the affection they have for each other. Our parents' moral judgments, or what we conceive to be their moral judgments, become our superegos. This helps us hold down the drives of the id, which have caused us such intense discomfort during the Oedipal period. But, forever after, the superego tends to oppose the ego. As our parents once did, our superegos punish us or threaten to punish us for our transgressions. And, since the superego's standards were rigidly set in childhood, its notions of crime and guilt are likely to be completely illogical and unduly harsh.

In their own way the demands of the superego are just as insatiable as the id's blind drives. Its standards of right and wrong and its rules for punishment are far more rigid, relentless, and vengeful than anything in our conscious minds. Formed at a time when we were too young to distinguish between a "bad" wish and a "bad" deed, the superego may sternly disapprove of the merest thought of some transgression—the explanation, according to Freud, of the fact that some people who have never actually committed a "bad" deed nonetheless have strong feelings of guilt all their lives.

Superego versus ego versus id

The three parts of the human personality are in frequent conflict. One of the important results of the conflict is anxiety, which is produced in the ego whenever the demands of the id threaten danger or when the superego threatens disapproval or punishment. Anxiety, though unpleasant, is a tool that the ego uses to fight the impulses or thoughts that have aroused it. In one way or another—by using repression and the other defense mechanisms, by turning the mind's attention elsewhere, by gratifying some other impulse of the id—the ego defends itself against the threat from the id or superego and gets rid of the anxiety.

In a sense the conscious ego is engaged in a constant struggle to satisfy the insatiable demands of the unconscious id without incurring the wrath and vengeance of the largely unconscious superego. To the extent that a person's behavior is controlled by the ego, it is sensible and generally satisfying. To the extent that it is governed by the childish passions of the id and the unrelenting demands of the superego, it tends to be foolish, unrewarding, painful, and neurotic.

If the ego is not strong enough to check the id's drives, a person is likely to be a selfish and hotheaded menace to society. But if the id is checked too severely, other problems may arise. Too much repression of the libido can make a person unable to enjoy a normal sex life or to give a normal amount of affection. Too much repression of aggression makes a person helpless in the give and take of competition. Too strong a superego may result in vague and unwarranted feelings of guilt and unworthiness, and even an unconscious need for self-punishment.

The pro and con of Freud

There can be little question that Freud was an important innovator who had a number of extremely useful insights into the human personality. He was the first to recognize the role of the unconscious and the importance of anxiety and defenses as factors in personality. He also dispelled the myth, widely accepted before his time, that children do not have the sexual urges and hostile impulses that characterize adults.

One criticism of Freud is that he may have overemphasized the role of sexual motivation in personality. In Freud's nineteenth and early twentieth century Vienna, with its strict sexual standards, it is perhaps only natural that many of his neurotic patients should have had conflicts and guilt feelings centering around their sexual desires. In today's Western world, with its more permissive attitudes toward sexual behavior, this kind of conflict and guilt seems to be less frequent. Yet people continue to have personality problems, and the incidence of serious mental disturbance seems to remain about the same as ever. This would indicate that conflicts over sexuality cannot be the sole or perhaps even the most important cause of personality disturbances.

Freud (seated left) and Jung (seated right) at a 1909 psychoanalytic conference.

Jung's theory

A number of Freud's disciples broke away from his theories to a greater or lesser degree and established psychoanalytic schools of thought of their own. One of the first of these was Carl Jung, who felt that Freud had overestimated the importance of the sexual drives. To Jung, the instinctive drive called the libido comprised far more than sexual urges; it was an all-encompassing life force that included deep-seated attitudes toward life and death, virtue and sin, and religion. Instead of Freud's id, ego, and superego, Jung emphasized what he called the functions of the personality—modes of viewing the events of the world and making

Jung in his later years.

judgments about them. Ideally, he believed, a person would grasp these events with what he called sensation (the evidence of the senses as to what the objects in the world were like at the moment) and also intuition (an understanding of their past and future potential). In making judgments, a person would ideally employ both thinking (a more or less coldly logical view) and feeling (an emotional judgment of agreeable or disagreeable, right or wrong). But in most people, Jung believed, some of these functions of personality unfortunately tend to develop at the expense of others. The neglected functions are relegated to the unconscious mind and disharmony results.

It was Jung who invented the words *introvert* and *extrovert*. Introverts are people who tend to live with their own thoughts and to avoid socializing. Extroverts are people whose chief interest is in other people and the events of the world. Both introversion and extroversion, he believed, were necessary for fulfillment of the human personality. Unfortunately again, one of these two characteristics tends to develop at the expense of the other, making people either too concerned with themselves or too preoccupied with external events.

Jung's most dramatic suggestion, however, was the idea that human beings possess a *collective unconscious*—a sort of vague, murky repository for all the events that have occurred in human history, and perhaps even in the days before humanity appeared and only lower animals roamed the world. In the collective unconscious lie traces of primitive humanity's fears and superstitions, the belief in magic, the search for gods. There also are memories of the great events in which humanity has participated—its disasters, its conquests and defeats, its happy and unhappy love affairs, its moving experiences with birth and death. Because of the collective unconscious, every person embodies in a sense the entire gamut of human experience. Jung believed that all of us, of whatever sex, have in us elements of both woman and man, mother and father, hero, prophet, sage, and magician.

In Jung's theory, the collective unconscious is an important part of the core of personality, a universal part of the human condition. It influences our behavior in ways that we can understand only dimly or not at all. It finds expression in the work of the artist and accounts for the strong emotions that we sometimes feel, without knowing why, when we look at a great painting or statue. It crops up in our dreams, often giving them a strange and mystical quality that we find beautiful or frightening.

Jung's theory is even more complex than Freud's, and the student who hopes to understand all its varied aspects must be prepared to do some extensive reading of the many books he wrote. Indeed the elements of mysticism it contains cannot be grasped at all in any logical way but can only be felt. It is a theory that emphasizes the intellectual and especially the spiritual qualities of the human personality rather than the primitive drives of sex and aggression that were emphasized by Freud.

Adler's theory

Adler

Another early disciple who rejected Freud's emphasis on sexuality was Alfred Adler, who coined the famous term *inferiority complex.* Adler believed that the core of personality is a universal human desire to be superior and to attain perfection. When this desire is thwarted, as it must often be, the result is feelings of inferiority that may or may not become crippling.

In the development of personality, Adler believed the early years of childhood are crucial. Children brought up by parents who respect them, trust them, and help them are likely to develop courage and independence. Though they cannot be superior and perfect in all respects, and will therefore inevitably suffer from feelings of inferiority, these feelings will merely produce a wholesome ambition to keep improving. But children brought up by parents who neglect, distrust, or belittle them are likely to grow up with all the painful feelings of inadequacy implied by the term inferiority complex. Or they may overcompensate for the feelings of inferiority and become aggressive and ambitious in the destructive sense.

Current trends in psychoanalysis

Fromm

In recent years, new generations of psychoanalysts have also added to and in some ways revised Freud's theories—as indeed he himself was constantly doing throughout his lifetime. These so-called *neo-psychoanalysts,* or new psychoanalysts, have tended to move in two major directions.

One group, headed by Heinz Hartmann, has concluded that Freud overstressed the importance of the unconscious demands of the id and superego and neglected the importance of the conscious and rational ego. They have turned their attention to the role of the ego in dealing with reality through such processes as perception, attention, memory, and thinking. They regard the ego as an important force in itself rather than a mere mediator between the id and the superego (3).

Another group of neo-psychoanalysts have turned their attention to cultural and social influences on personality, which were largely neglected by Freud because of the importance he attached to the primitive, biologically determined drives of the id. One prominent member of this group is Erich Fromm, who has suggested that personality problems are caused by conflicts between the basic human needs and the demands of society. The core of personality, according to Fromm, is the desire to fulfill oneself as a human being—that is, to achieve a kind of unity with nature in the special way that is dictated by the human ability to think. Lower animals have no need to seek such unity; they are simply a part of nature. They are not aware of any separation between themselves and their environment, including their fellow animals. But people must seek the unity through their own efforts; they must fulfill what Fromm lists as the five basic and unique human needs (shown in Figure 11-1).

It would be possible, Fromm believes, to create a society in which these needs could be harmoniously fulfilled. But no such society has

11-1

Fromm's basic human needs

According to the theory developed by Fromm, these are the five basic human needs—frustration of which causes personality problems. (4)

1. *Relatedness* This need stems from the fact that human beings have lost the union with nature that other animals possess; it must be satisfied by human relationships based on productive love (which implies mutual care, responsibility, respect, and understanding).
2. *Transcendence* The need to rise above one's animal nature and to become creative.
3. *Rootedness* The need for a feeling of belonging, best satisfied by feelings of affiliation with all humanity.
4. *Identity* The need to have a sense of personal identity, to be unique. It can be satisfied through creativity or through identification with another person or group.
5. *A Frame of Orientation* The need for a stable and consistent way of perceiving the world and understanding its events.

ever existed, including our own. Therefore all of us tend to have frustrations and personality problems. It is society, Fromm has said, that is "sick"—and it will remain so until it can be transformed so that people can relate to one another "lovingly" and "in bonds of brotherliness and solidarity," can transcend nature "by creating rather than by destroying," and can gain a sense of selfhood through their own individual powers "rather than by conformity" (5).

Social learning theories

Social learning theory represents a different kind of approach entirely from psychoanalysis—at least from Freud's original brand of psychoanalysis. It does not accept the idea that human personality is shaped by the id's powerful demands for sexual gratification and aggression. Indeed it rejects Freud's notion of the id, as well as his ideas of the ego, the superego, and the Oedipus complex. Instead, as its name implies, it holds that personality traits are the result of learning, particularly the kind of learning that takes place in interaction with other people.

There are a number of social learning theories, differing from one another in various respects. All of them, however, regard personality as largely composed of habits—that is to say, of habitual ways of responding to the situations that arise in one's life. These habits have been learned in accordance with the standard principles of learning discussed in Part II of this book; they are *learned responses to stimuli in the environment*. Depending on what kinds of responses have been learned, the individual may be able to cope successfully with life's problems or may be a helpless neurotic.

Learning to be afraid

One experiment often cited in support of social learning theories was a simple but impressive demonstration of some animal behavior that bore a striking resemblance to neurotic human behavior. A rat was placed in a plain white compartment containing a bar that could be pressed, like the bar in a Skinner box. There was nothing unusual about the compartment, nothing that would appear in any way frightening. Yet the moment the rat entered the compartment it behaved in ways suggesting stark terror and immediately pressed the bar—which permitted it to escape into a black compartment alongside.

For some reason, the rat seemed fearful of the white compartment and got right to work at pressing the bar and escaping. Why? If a human being behaved in this manner, a psychoanalyst might suggest that this person had some kind of unconscious conflict, perhaps dating back to the Oedipal period and producing uncontrollable anxiety. But the explanation of the rat's behavior was nothing like this and was in fact almost ludicrously simple.

In a previous stage of the experiment, the rat had received a series of electric shocks in the white compartment, the shocks continuing until the animal learned to press the bar and escape into the black compartment. Its apparently neurotic fear of the white compartment was purely and simply the result of learning (6).

Reward, punishment, and self-evaluation

Just as the rat learned to be afraid, the social learning theorists maintain, so do human beings learn to acquire the whole wide range of characteristics called personality.

Some of the theorists emphasize the role of reward and punishment in the learning process—particularly the kinds of rewards and punishments given by the family and by society. Responses that are reinforced by praise and social reward tend to be repeated and to become habitual; those that are punished by rejection tend to undergo extinction. Two psychologists prominent among social learning theorists, John Dollard and Neal Miller, have suggested that the individual moving through the cultural environment is like a complicated version of a rat moving through a T-maze. Only if we know in which arm of the T the rat will be rewarded by food and in which arm it will be punished by a shock can we predict the rat's behavior. To predict an individual's behavior we would have to know which of this person's responses have been rewarded by society and which have been punished and in what way and to what extent (7).

Other social learning theorists take a more cognitive view. They agree that rewards and punishments influence learning, but they believe that factors inside the person—such as the individual's internal standards—are also important. One of the prominent members of this group, Albert Bandura, has put it this way:

> Humans [have] a capacity for self-direction. They do things that give rise to self-satisfaction and self-worth, and they refrain from behaving in ways that evoke self-punishment. . . . To ignore the influential role of covert self-reinforcement in the regulation of behavior is to disavow a uniquely human capacity. (8)

Rogers' self theory

There is a large group of hypotheses about personality that are known as *self theories,* the best known of which has been formulated by Carl Rogers. Like Freud, Rogers developed his theories out of his treatment of disturbed people. His first professional position after receiving his Ph.D. was in the Rochester (New York) Guidance Clinic, and he has spent much of his life in clinical work with patients seeking therapeutic help. Unlike Freud, however, Rogers was trained in psychology rather than medicine, and the conclusions he has drawn from his observations are very different from those of psychoanalytic theory.

The need for "unconditional positive regard"

Rogers

As has been said, Rogers is an optimist who believes that the core of personality is a human desire to fully realize one's potentialities. His view of human nature is very much like that of Abraham Maslow, whose theory of self-actualization was discussed on page 327. Under ideal conditions of development, Rogers believes, all human beings tend to become trusting, spontaneous, and flexible, leading richly meaningful lives in harmony with themselves and with others.

To attain this full realization of the human potential, however, individuals must grow up in a family and social environment that treats them with what Rogers calls *unconditional positive regard.* That is to say, they must be valued and trusted; their opinions and behavior must be respected; they must be accepted and loved for what they are, even for actions with which others disagree. Unfortunately, few people grow up in such an atmosphere. Most are treated with what Rogers calls *conditional positive regard.* Their families and later the rest of society respond warmly to only some of their thoughts and actions, disapprovingly to others. The "forbidden" thoughts and actions become a source of maladjustment.

Self-image and neurosis

Maladjustments, in Rogers' view, are caused by people's failures to integrate all their experiences, desires, and feelings into their image of self. This idea can best be explained by an example.

A young boy thinks of himself as being good and as being loved by his parents. However, he also feels hostility toward a younger brother, which he expresses one day by breaking his brother's toys. His parents punish him, and he now faces a crisis in integrating the experience into his image of self. He is forced to change the image in some way. He may decide that he is not a good boy but a bad boy and therefore feel shame and guilt. He may decide that his parents do not love him and therefore feel rejected. Or he may decide to deny that he feels any hostility toward his brother, in which case he sets up a conflict between his true nature and his image of himself.

All of us, says Rogers, attempt to perceive our experiences and to behave in a way that is consistent with our images of ourselves. When we are confronted with new experiences or new feelings that seem inconsistent with the image, we can take one of two opposite courses.

1 We can recognize the new experiences or feelings, perceive them clearly, and somehow integrate them into the image of self. This is a healthy reaction. The boy just mentioned, for example, could under ideal circumstances decide that he does feel hostility toward his brother. This is something he must reckon with, but it does not make him "bad" or mean that he will be scorned by his parents and society.

2 We can deny the experiences or feelings or perceive them in distorted fashion. Thus the boy may attempt to deny that he feels any hostility toward his brother and maintain that he broke the toys simply in retaliation for his brother's hostility (thus adopting what has been called the defense mechanism of projection).

Maladjusted people, according to Rogers, are those who perceive any experience that is not consistent with their self-image as a threat, deny it to consciousness, and thereby set up an ever-widening gulf between their self-images and reality. Their images of themselves do not match their true feelings and the actual nature of their experiences. They must set up more and more defenses against the truth, and more and more tension results. Well-adjusted people, on the other hand, are those whose images of themselves are consistent with what they really think, feel, do, and experience. Instead of being rigid, their self-images are flexible and changing constantly as new experiences occur.

Psychotherapy

Psychotherapy—the treatment of personality disorders through psychological methods—is in a sense an ancient technique, dating back to the Greek physicians. For example, the Greeks often attempted to treat their disturbed patients by removing them from their families, thus bringing about a change of environment—a method sometimes recommended today. For women suffering from hysteria the Greek physicians suggested marriage—an interesting form of treatment in light of modern discoveries that hysteria is often associated with sexual maladjustments and anxiety.

During the Middle Ages, however, the Greek approach to personality disorders was cast aside, and people suffering from the more intense and obvious forms of personality and mental disorders were punished for being "possessed by the devil." Even when the first so-called insane asylums were set up in the sixteenth century they were little more than prisons where the inmates were kept in chains and were "treated," if at all, by being whirled around in harnesses or having holes bored into their heads (see Figure 11-2). It has only been in this century that mental hospitals have become more humane institutions (though of course some of them still leave much to be desired). Today the most advanced psychological and medical techniques are being used in an attempt to help psychotics, and considerable numbers of psychologists and physi-

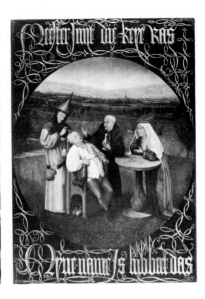

11-2

Old "treatments" for the mentally ill

In the past mental patients were treated by being chained virtually motionless to a wall (left), by being stretched and whirled in harnesses suspended from the ceiling, or by having holes bored in their skulls to release the "evil spirits."

cians have begun to devote themselves to giving treatment and guidance to the less seriously disturbed.

Just as there are many personality theories, there also are many different kinds of psychotherapy. Psychoanalysts now practice a variety of techniques, stemming from Freud's work but often going beyond his emphasis on free association and reconstructing the patient's past. The social learning theories have produced new and quite different techniques, and so has Rogers' self theory. In addition, there are many others; indeed it sometimes seems that there are almost as many forms of psychotherapy as there are psychotherapists. Individual psychotherapists are likely to develop their own methods based on their clinical experiences and the particular problems and needs of the person they are treating. There is also a growing tendency for therapists trained in one method to borrow at times from the methods of other and very different schools of thought.

Client-centered therapy

Since Rogers' personality theory has just been mentioned, the discussion of psychotherapy can perhaps best begin with the kind of treatment that he developed, which is known as *client-centered therapy*. The central idea in client-centered therapy is for the therapist to display unconditional warmth and acceptance toward the people being treated, thus creating a nonthreatening situation in which they are free to explore all their thoughts and feelings, including those that they have been unable to perceive clearly for fear of condemnation by others or by their own consciences.

Originally Rogers refrained from expressing any reactions he might have toward the conduct of the people he treated. More recently he has concluded that he should be more "genuine"—that is, should respond by frankly describing his own feelings. However, the core of client-centered treatment was and is for the therapist to be genuinely empathetic

389

and understanding—in other words, to provide the unconditional positive regard that Rogers believes essential for wholesome development. Indeed client-centered therapists encourage the people they are treating to clarify and expand on even the "worst" aspects of their personalities.

In the safety of this kind of relationship with an understanding and accepting therapist, people who undertake client-centered therapy are expected to gradually acquire the ability to resolve their conflicts. The process, Rogers has said, takes three steps: 1) they begin to experience, understand, and accept feelings and desires (such as sexuality and hostility) that they had previously denied to consciousness; 2) they begin to understand the reasons behind their behavior; and 3) they begin to see ways in which they can undertake more positive forms of behavior. In a word, they learn to be themselves.

Many who hear about client-centered therapy for the first time are struck by the question: If all people were encouraged to be completely themselves, would the world not suddenly be filled with aggressive, brawling, murderous, sexually unrestrained, self-seeking egoists? Rogers, of course, holds that the answer is an unqualified no.

"That's exactly what I mean. When you're late don't bring me a note from your mother."

Psychoanalysis

In the classical psychoanalytic treatment developed by Freud the chief tool is *free association*. If you were to undertake analysis, you would be asked to lie on a couch, as relaxed as possible, and speak out every thought that occurred to you—no matter how foolish it might seem, how obscene, or how insulting to the analyst. In this situation, as when drifting off to sleep, conscious control of mental processes is reduced to a minimum and unconscious forces become more apparent. The analyst would pay particular attention to occasions when your thoughts seemed to encounter what is called *resistance*—that is, when your train of thought seemed to be blocked by anxiety and repressions indicating unconscious conflicts. The analyst would also study your dreams, fantasies, and any slips of the tongue in a search for clues to unconscious desires and conflicts.

Another tool that helps the analyst discover unconscious wishes and fantasies is the phenomenon called *transference*. This means, to the analysts, that all of us tend to transfer to the people we now know the emotional attitudes that we had as children toward such much-loved and much-hated persons as our parents and our brothers and sisters. If you were being analyzed, you probably would find yourself displaying these kinds of emotional reactions toward the analyst; you might at times be overwhelmed by a desire to please the analyst, at other times by resentment and hatred.

"You're just at that stage where you're beginning to identify with me."

Through your transferences, free associations, dreams, and reports of your everyday behavior, a pattern would gradually emerge of the unconscious problems that an analyst would say represented your real difficulties. The analyst would then interpret the problems and help you acquire insights into the unconscious processes and gain control over them. The goal in analysis is to strengthen the ego and provide what one analyst calls "freedom from the tyranny of the unconscious" (9).

In its classical form, psychoanalysis is a long process, requiring three to five visits a week for two to five years or more, and is therefore very expensive. In recent years, however, many analysts have attempted to shorten the treatment period. While still basing their therapy on the underlying principles developed by Freud (or by one of the neo-psychoanalysts), they have adopted various new and faster techniques for helping people achieve, if not full "freedom from the tyranny of the unconscious," at least a working ability to cope with their problems.

Behavior therapy

Psychoanalysis tends to regard personality disturbances as a form of long-term illness that can be cured only by seeking its origin. The psychoanalyst resembles a physician who is not so much interested in treating the symptoms of disease, such as a headache or a fever, as in finding out what is causing the symptoms and then treating the underlying illness. A very different approach is taken by *behavior therapy*, a newer method of treatment that has grown out of social learning theories. Behavior therapy does not regard personality disturbances as deep-seated illnesses but as learned forms of thinking, feeling, and especially behaving that can be modified through relearning.

If you were to undertake behavior therapy, you would find that the therapist would make a direct attack on whatever was bothering you. If you had an unreasonable fear of snakes, or a hot temper that often got you into trouble, or some kind of problem that incapacitated you sexually, the therapist would take the position that you could be helped to learn ways to overcome this difficulty and to substitute more effective forms of behavior.

Behavior therapy has become increasingly popular among clinical psychologists and in recent years has accounted for more studies and research reports than any other kind of psychotherapy (10). As will be seen below, it has produced numerous successes at dealing with various kinds of phobias, sexual problems, speech difficulties, psychosomatic illnesses, and other forms of personality disturbance. When first introduced it was sharply criticized by the psychoanalysts, who maintained that behavior therapy could only get rid of a specific "symptom"—for which the person being treated, since the underlying "illness" was not relieved, might soon substitute another "symptom." (For example, a person relieved of a fear of snakes might soon develop an even more crippling fear of people.) But numerous follow-up studies of people who have had behavior therapy have produced no evidence that symptom substitution actually occurs (11, 12). However, behavior therapy is sometimes combined with other forms of psychotherapy that take a more generalized approach to the personality as a whole. For example, behavior therapy has been used successfully in combination with client-centered therapy to treat a person who had a crippling fear

of going anywhere alone and an inability to admit to deep-seated feelings of anger and hostility (13).

Since behavior therapy is essentially concerned with relearning, it
utilizes many techniques of extinguishing conditioned responses and
substituting new responses. Among its methods are the following.

Extinction. This method attempts to get rid of a conditioned response
that is causing trouble. For example, it was used with spectacular results
to treat a nine-month-old boy who had somehow acquired the habit of
vomiting shortly after every meal and as a result weighed only twelve
pounds and was in danger of starving to death. A nine-month-old
baby, of course, cannot be treated by any method of psychotherapy that
requires the "talking-out" of problems. However, the baby responded
very rapidly to a form of extinction in which an electrode was attached
to his leg and electric shocks were administered whenever he began to
vomit, with the shocks continuing until he stopped. Only a few shocks
were needed. The baby soon learned to stop vomiting when the shock
was applied, then quit vomiting altogether, except for a few relapses
that were quickly ended by further treatment. After a few weeks he
weighed sixteen pounds and was released from the hospital. The baby's
weight increased to twenty-one pounds in his first month back at
home, where he showed no signs of resuming his former behavior (14).

When extinction is achieved by pairing behavior with a disagreeable stimulus, as in this case an electric shock, the technique is called
aversive conditioning. The person being treated learns to abandon the
troublesome behavior to avoid the unpleasant consequences with
which the therapist associates it.

Reinforcement. Another technique used by behavior therapists is
providing reinforcement for more effective and desirable kinds of behavior. For example, one group of behavior therapists, dealing with disturbed adolescents who had never learned to talk very well or to sit
quietly at a school desk, treated them by withholding breakfast and
lunch, then rewarding them with small amounts of food every time they
showed any signs of constructive behavior. Given this kind of push
toward acceptable behavior — which you will recognize as being a form
of operant conditioning and shaping (pages 46–49) with food as the reinforcement — the subjects improved rapidly (15). When learning techniques are used in this manner to encourage changes in behavior, the
process is usually called *behavior modification*.

Behavior modification has been widely used in recent years in mental hospitals — not as an attempt to help the patients get over their personality disturbances but in an effort to improve the general atmosphere in the hospital and the lives of the patients during their period
of treatment by other forms of therapy. The particular method used has
been called a *token economy*. For doing such things as dressing properly,
eating in an acceptable manner, and working at useful jobs, patients
earn tokens that they can exchange like money for movies, rental of

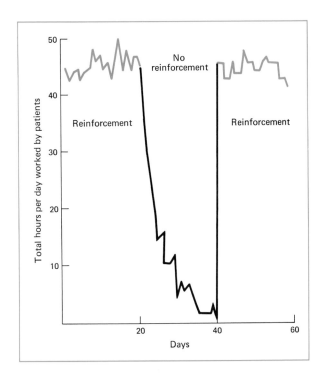

11-3

Effects of a "token economy"

When a group of forty-four patients in a mental hospital operated under a token economy system, in which desirable behaviors were reinforced with tokens that could be used like money, they worked actively at various jobs, helping run the hospital (colored line). When the token economy system was abandoned temporarily and no reinforcement provided, they did very little work (black line). (16)

radios or TV sets, cigarettes, candy, and other privileges. Establishment of these token economies has often produced dramatic improvements in the behavior of the patients. Whether or not it has encouraged their recovery remains to be demonstrated. An example of the effects of a token economy is illustrated in Figure 11-3.

In treating personality problems, behavior therapists often combine the techniques of reinforcement (to encourage positive behavior) and aversive conditioning (to eliminate undesirable behavior). The combination has been effective, for example, in treating men who were sexually incapacitated by sadistic fantasies (17) or by transvestitism (18), which is the desire to dress in the clothing of the other sex.

Desensitization. This is a special technique that has been used successfully to eliminate phobias. When first introduced, the technique attempted to associate the stimulus causing the fear with relaxation rather than with anxiety or fearful behavior. If you sought relief from an unreasonable fear of snakes, for example, the therapist would ask you to relax as much as possible, then to imagine you were looking at a snake in a mildly fear-producing situation, such as from far away. If you were able to do this without losing your feeling of relaxation, you would then be asked to imagine a slightly more threatening sight of a snake—and so on until you could remain relaxed while imagining that you were actually holding a snake.

It has now been found, however, that relaxation is not necessary. The phobia can be eliminated simply by imagining yourself in situations that have caused fear—in the presence of a therapist who encourages the process and praises improvement (19). Apparently just thinking about the fearful stimulus, in an atmosphere that offers support and promises relief from the phobia, is enough to produce results.

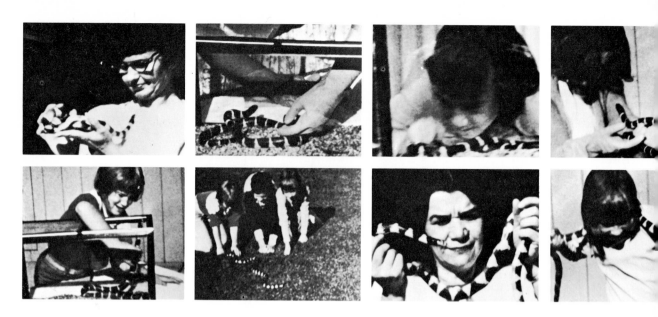

11-4

A cure for snake phobia

These are stills from a movie used successfully by Albert Bandura in the treatment of snake phobia through observation learning, as described in the text.

Many kinds of phobias have been treated successfully through desensitization. In one study, the subjects were college students who suffered extreme anxiety when they had to speak in public. After treatment they reported much less anxiety not only about speaking in public but about other kinds of social situations. Two years after treatment their improvement was still quite pronounced. Moreover, their marks in college had improved somewhat. Ninety percent of them either were still in school or had been graduated, whereas 60 percent of an untreated control group of anxious students had dropped out (20).

Observation and imitation. Another technique used to eliminate phobias is observation learning, which was discussed on pages 59–60. For example, therapists have successfully treated subjects with a fear of snakes by having the subjects watch a movie of other people approaching and eventually playing with a snake (see Figure 11-4)—a movie that the subjects could stop and turn back at any time they began to feel fearful. Snake phobia has also been treated successfully by encouraging subjects to watch live models handle a snake and eventually join the models in playing with the snake. In one experiment, subjects who were fearful of snakes were divided into four groups—a control group that was not treated at all, a group treated through desensitization, another treated by observation of a movie, and the fourth treated through observation and imitation of live models. The results, illustrated in Figure 11-5, showed that observation of live models combined with participation in handling the snake was the best treatment (21).

Interactional therapies

As the previous pages have indicated, behavior therapy concentrates on the individual. Its various techniques are all designed to bring about changes in the individual's own feelings and behavior patterns. By contrast, there is another relatively new group of therapies that concentrate

394

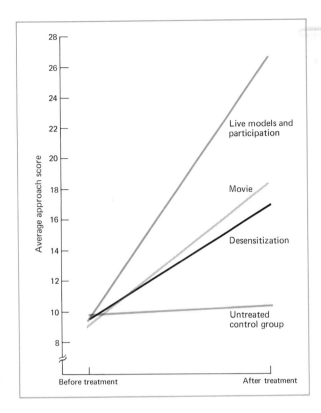

11-5

Eliminating snake phobia

After treatment through behavior therapy, subjects who had been afraid of snakes were able to approach them rather freely. (A score of zero on the approach scale means that the subject was unable even to enter a room in which there was a snake. To achieve a perfect score of 29, subjects had to let a snake crawl over their laps while holding their hands passively at their sides.)

instead on the individual's behavior toward other people. They are collectively known as *interactional therapies,* because they emphasize the individual's interpersonal relations—all the various ways in which the individual reacts to family, friends, schoolmates or fellow workers, and society as a whole.

Although there are a number of different forms of interactional therapy, its practitioners tend in general to take this attitude toward the person they are treating: "In your relations with other people, you are now doing this and it is not working. Give it up for awhile and try something else instead." Thus male homosexuals have been encouraged to stop associating with other homosexuals and force themselves to seek out the company of women, a new kind of interaction that at least sometimes results in a lasting change to heterosexual behavior (22). Other clients with other problems have been invited to play "games" in which they pretend to act like other people or to behave in extremely selfish or extremely generous ways, thus opening up the possibility of new kinds of interaction they have never tried before (23).

One type of interactional therapy is *family therapy,* in which the therapist attempts to help the person under treatment by changing the patterns of behavior that the various members of this person's family display toward one another. In some cases therapists have made television tapes of the interactions between members of a family. Often people who have this kind of opportunity to watch their behavior are helped to see why it is unsuccessful and how it can be improved (24). An even larger-scale approach is represented by *community therapy,* in which the therapist attempts to set up new patterns of interaction to

395

replace existing ones that have caused problems between different groups, between public officials and the citizenry, and so on.

Group therapies

Group therapy is the simultaneous treatment of several patients at a time. It has been used by many therapists of various schools of thought, including some psychoanalysts. The method is in part the child of necessity, for there are not enough trained therapists to treat all prospective patients individually. But it also seems to have genuine advantages with some kinds of patients. The group situation may relieve the individual patient's anxieties by demonstrating that there are other people with the same problems, and it also creates a kind of interactional or social give-and-take that is impossible in a face-to-face session between a therapist and one person. Some studies have indicated that the most effective form of treatment may be a combination of group therapy and individual therapy (25).

In recent years, there has been a great interest in what are called *encounter groups,* in which anywhere from eight to twenty people get together with the goal of throwing off the masks they usually present in public and airing their true feelings. The emphasis in these groups is on activities, games, and conversation that will help their members interact (see Figure 11-6) with open displays of approval, criticism, affection, and hostility rather than with the restraints and tact that usually inhibit the expression of emotions in ordinary social situations. The assumption behind encounter groups is somewhat like the basic premise of client-centered therapy, namely that people will grow in a positive

11-6

Interaction in an encounter group

Group members practice physical togetherness—perhaps as a first step toward greater trust and openness in other social situations.

direction if they can free themselves from artificial restraints on their attempts to perceive their true selves and to interact with others in an honest and open fashion. Indeed Carl Rogers, the founder of client-centered therapy, has led numerous encounter groups.

Encounter groups are usually led by a trained therapist, although sometimes they meet without a leader. The group may meet for several hours a day or evening over a period of time or, as a *marathon group*, for as much as thirty-six hours or more without interruption, except that its individual members drop out occasionally for naps. Whether encounter groups can be considered a form of therapy is a matter of debate. Some psychologists have concluded that they are an effective form of treatment for some kinds of problems. Other psychologists believe that encounter groups merely provide an opportunity for more or less normal people to enjoy the emotional satisfaction of entering into honest interactions of a kind that are difficult to establish in the real world of social restraints. Some psychologists, indeed, consider them a passing fad and potentially dangerous in that they might trigger acute disturbances in some of the more troubled participants.

Somewhat similar to encounter groups are *T-groups* (short for training groups), also called *sensitivity groups*. It should be pointed out that these various kinds of groups are not so new as many people think. As long ago as 1781, Hans Mesmer, whose name is associated with mesmerism (hypnosis), was leading groups of ten to twenty Parisians in activities rather similar to those found in today's encounter groups, such as holding hands and touching one another (26).

Mesmer and one of his groups around a magnetized table.

How effective is psychotherapy?

At this point it is pertinent to ask: How well does psychotherapy work? Which, if any, of the methods is most effective?

These are extremely difficult questions to answer. For one thing, many kinds of people with many different kinds of problems seek therapy. There is no accurate scale on which we can measure what degree of personality disturbance all these people had when they started treatment—or how much, if any, improvement they displayed at the end. For another, even if there were such a scale we could not be sure that the therapy produced the improvement. It is one of life's blessings—though a great handicap to any statistical study of psychotherapy—that many people suffering from personality disturbances get over them even if they receive no treatment at all. The passage of time and perhaps changing life circumstances seem to restore them to normal.

Perhaps because of the difficulty of making adequate studies, the value of therapy is the subject of considerable controversy. Some psychologists have concluded that it is seldom very effective (27). But others take exactly the opposite view; they believe that all the various techniques of psychotherapy have resulted in impressive successes (28). Some take a middle ground. In this connection it is interesting to note that one of the most recent studies of all the available reports on the results of psychotherapy reached the conclusion that everybody who undergoes therapy shows *some* improvement (29) — though the amount may not be entirely satisfactory.

As for which particular type of therapy might be most effective, there is as yet no convincing evidence. For example, studies of Freudian psychoanalysts, Adlerian analysts, and client-centered therapists have shown no important differences in the kinds of results they obtained. The therapist seems to be more important than the type of therapy. The most successful therapists appear to be those who have *empathy* toward those they treat (that is, can put themselves in these people's shoes, so to speak, and understand how they think and feel). It seems to help if the therapist and the person being treated have similar social backgrounds, interests, values, and feelings about interpersonal relationships (30). In addition, it has been suggested that the most successful therapists also have strong feelings of liking and warmth toward the people they are treating and are themselves relatively free of anxieties and other forms of disturbance (31).

The people who are likely to profit most from psychotherapy, it appears, are those who 1) have minor rather than serious disturbances, 2) are highly motivated toward improvement and expect to attain it, 3) are above average in intelligence, and 4) have not suppressed their feelings and lapsed into a state of emotional apathy. In this last connection, it has been found that strong feelings of even such unpleasant kinds as anxiety and depression are favorable indications — possibly because people experiencing them tend to be ready and eager for change. People who have been successful — whether in achieving education, in a job, or in marriage — tend to do well. Men and women appear to have about equal prospects for improvement. Younger people usually do better than older people (32), though elderly people with long-standing problems have also shown marked improvement.

Medical therapy

To complete the discussion of treatment of personality disorders, it must be pointed out that the various forms of psychotherapy are often combined with what is called *chemotherapy* — that is, chemical therapy, or treatment with various kinds of medicines that have been discovered to be helpful to many people. Indeed some psychiatrists rely more on chemotherapy than on psychotherapy. Chemotherapy is also widely practiced in mental hospitals, especially those lacking large enough staffs to offer prolonged psychotherapy to all their patients.

Tranquilizers

One widely used group of medicines are the *tranquilizers,* often prescribed for schizophrenics. The tranquilizers have greatly changed the atmosphere of mental hospitals by calming patients who previously were so noisy, hostile, and destructive as to be unmanageable. They have also enabled some patients, though by no means all, to return to a more or less normal life. Numerous studies have shown that tranquilizers can reduce or eliminate the schizophrenic's hallucinations and delusions.

Because tranquilizers reduce anxiety, they are also widely prescribed for many people with less serious neurotic symptoms—people who find them temporarily helpful in enduring stresses in their lives. The tranquilizers apparently are effective because they reduce the sensitivity of the synapses of the brain (that is, the connection points between nerve cells, as was explained on pages 244–45). They apparently do this by reducing the effectiveness of one of the neurotransmitters (noradrenalin) that is produced at some of the synapses (33). In other words, they slow down the excessive nervous activity in the brain that is characteristic of anxiety, hallucinations, and delusions.

"I see a substantial upswing in the economy by October, but who knows? Maybe it's the Valium talking."
Drawing by Weber; © 1974 The New Yorker Magazine, Inc.

Psychic energizers

Also important in chemotherapy are the *psychic energizers*, used to relieve depression. The energizers have exactly the opposite effect from the tranquilizers; they increase nervous activity in the brain. There are many kinds of energizers, each working in a somewhat different manner and likely to be more helpful for one person than another. In general they seem to increase the effectiveness of noradrenalin as a transmitter of nervous impulses, although they may also affect other transmitter chemicals in the brain (34).

Another method of treating depression is *electroshock therapy*, in which electrodes are fastened to the sides of the head and an electric current roughly as strong as household electricity is passed between them for a fraction of a second. People treated in this manner go into a brief convulsion and then are unconscious for a half-hour to an hour. When they wake up they are drowsy and confused, but advocates of the treatment believe that no permanent harm seems to be done to their memories or learning abilities. The treatment, it has been found, produces a long-term increase in the amount of noradrenalin in the brain (35). Thus it operates in much the same way as the energizing drugs. It produces results more quickly than the chemicals and in many cases has been found more effective (36). But it is a drastic type of treatment and most therapists are loath to recommend it except in case of emergency, as when patients seem close to suicide.

The electrotherapy room in a 1904 mental hospital.

Other medications

There are many other medications that have a pronounced effect on personality and are used in treating various disorders. Several drugs, including Dilantin, have proved outstandingly successful in controlling *epilepsy*, a disorder of the central nervous system characterized by abnormal electrical discharges that produce sudden seizures. With a proper daily dose of Dilantin or the other drugs, most epilepsy sufferers

A hyperkinetic child (right).

can avoid the seizures entirely. Many of them eventually grow out of the condition and can then abandon use of the drugs.

Chemotherapy has also been used successfully in the treatment of an abnormality called *hyperkinesis,* which is estimated to affect perhaps as many as three million American children under the age of fifteen. Hyperkinetic children, for unknown reasons, are "jumping jacks"— overactive, irritable, and unable to concentrate. They are hard to handle, given to temper tantrums, and a source of constant disruptions in their school classes. For reasons as mysterious as the abnormality itself, hyperkinesis can be controlled in a manner that seems utterly illogical— that is, by giving these children steady doses of stimulant drugs such as the amphetamines (pages 269–70). Instead of stimulating hyperkinetic children, these drugs somehow calm them down to the point where they often show marked improvement in behavior and school perform- ance. It must be noted, however, that many psychologists disapprove of the use on children of such powerful drugs, which may have unforeseen results in later life.

The future of chemotherapy

The successes of chemotherapy offer another indication that, as was stated on pages 362–64, most personality disorders seem to have a threefold origin in biological, psychological, and cultural or social fac- tors. Since chemotherapy is a relatively new development, it appears likely that the future will bring many discoveries of new medications that will prove even more effective in attacking the biological roots of the various kinds of personality problems. It may even develop that some disorders are primarily biological, in which case drugs may prove to be a definite cure. The great majority of psychologists, however, believe that most disorders involve functional disturbances as well as biological predispositions and that therefore the individual's thought processes and interpersonal relations have to be explored.

Summary

1 *Personality* is the total pattern of characteristic ways of thinking, feeling, and behaving that constitute the individual's distinctive method of relating to the environment.

2 *Personality theories* are concerned with three aspects of human behavior: they assume a) that there is some kind of *core of personality* common to all human beings, b) that these common tendencies and characteristics of human beings are channeled in various directions by the process of *development*, and c) that the core of personality as modified by development makes each person a unique individual displaying a unique pattern of the *peripheral characteristics* that are generally known as personality.

3 Freud's *psychoanalytic theory* assumes that the core of personality is conflict—for example, conflicts between incompatible desires (many of which are unconscious), between desires and fears of punishment for attempts to gratify them, between wishes and defense mechanisms, and between wishes and outside circumstances that frustrate them.

4 Psychoanalytic theory holds that the human mind has three parts or forces: a) the unconscious *id*, containing the person's instinctive drives toward sexuality (the *libido*) and aggression; b) the largely conscious *ego*, which is the person's contact with reality; and c) the largely unconscious *superego*, which punishes transgressions.

5 The superego is acquired largely as a result of the *Oedipus complex*, a conflict of mingled love and hate toward the parents that all children are assumed to undergo between the ages of two and a half and six. Children resolve the conflict by identifying with their parents and adopting what they consider to be their parents' moral judgments, which form the superego.

6 *Anxiety*, another key concept in psychoanalytic theory, is said to be aroused whenever the demands of the id threaten danger or when the superego threatens disapproval or punishment.

7 Among the successors of Freud who have proposed variations of his theories are Jung, who introduced the concepts of *introvert* and *extrovert* and of a *collective unconscious*; Adler, who introduced the concept of *inferiority complex*; Hartmann, who has emphasized the role of the ego in dealing with reality; and Fromm, who has emphasized the importance of cultural and social influences on personality.

8 *Social learning theory* maintains that personality traits, whether wholesome or neurotic, are *learned responses to the environment*.

9 Rogers' *self theory* holds that the core of personality is a universal

human urge toward integration, self-fulfillment, and living in harmony with oneself and others. To attain this goal, the theory holds, individuals must grow up in a family and social environment that treats them with *unconditional positive regard.*

10 Four influential schools of psychotherapy are a) Rogers' *client-centered therapy,* b) *psychoanalysis,* c) *behavior therapy,* and d) *interactional therapies.*

11 Client-centered therapy holds that maladjustments are caused by people's failures to integrate all their experiences, desires, and feelings into their image of self—caused by the fact that they were not treated with unconditional positive regard and were made to feel anxious or guilty about some aspects of themselves. Client-centered therapists attempt to provide an atmosphere of unconditional positive regard in which these previously unintegrated or repressed characteristics can be explored and acknowledged.

12 Psychoanalysis uses *free association,* dreams and slips of the tongue, and *transference* to provide insights into unconscious conflicts and thus achieve "freedom from the tyranny of the unconscious."

13 Behavior therapy regards personality disturbances as learned forms of thinking, feeling, and behaving that can be modified through relearning. Its techniques include *extinction* (of undesired behavior), *reinforcement* (of more rewarding behavior), *desensitization* (to relieve phobias), and *learning through observation and imitation* (to acquire new and better ways to react to the environment).

14 *Interactional therapies* concentrate on producing changes in the disturbed individual's behavior toward other people.

15 *Group therapy* is the simultaneous treatment of a number of people who meet with the therapist in a group. Currently popular forms of this type of therapy include *T-groups, encounter groups,* and *marathon groups.*

16 Medical therapy is the treatment of personality disturbances through medical methods. These include *chemotherapy,* or the use of medications such as *tranquilizers* (often helpful to schizophrenics) and *psychic energizers* (often helpful to people suffering from depression). They also include *electroshock therapy* (used for depression).

Recommended reading

Bandura, A. *Principles of behavior modification.* New York: Holt, Rinehart and Winston, 1969.

Bergin, A. E., and Garfield, S. L., eds. *Handbook of psychotherapy and behavior change: an empirical analysis.* New York: John Wiley, 1971.

Boszormenyi-Nagy, I., and Framo, J. L. *Intensive family therapy.* New York: Harper & Row, 1965.

Frank, J. D. *Persuasion and healing: a comparative study of psychotherapy,* rev. ed. New York: Schocken, 1974.

Freud, S. *New introductory lectures on psychoanalysis.* Ed. by J. Strachey. New York: Norton, 1965.

Hall, C. S., and Lindzey, G. *Theories of personality,* 2nd ed. New York: John Wiley, 1970.

Jung, C. G. *The basic writings of C. G. Jung.* New York: Random House, 1959.

Levitt, E. E. *The psychology of anxiety.* New York: Bobbs-Merrill, 1967.

Maddi, S. R. *Personality theories: a comparative analysis,* rev. ed. Homewood, Ill.: Dorsey Press, 1972.

Neuringer, C., and Michael, J. L. *Behavior modification in clinical psychology.* New York: Appleton-Century-Crofts, 1970.

Patterson, C. H. *Theories of counseling and psychotherapy,* 2nd ed. New York: Harper & Row, 1974.

Pervin, L. A., and Levenson, H. *Personality: theory assessment and research,* 2nd ed. New York: John Wiley, 1975.

Wiggins, J. S., et al. *The psychology of personality.* Reading, Mass.: Addison-Wesley, 1971.

SEVEN
INDIVIDUAL
DIFFERENCES

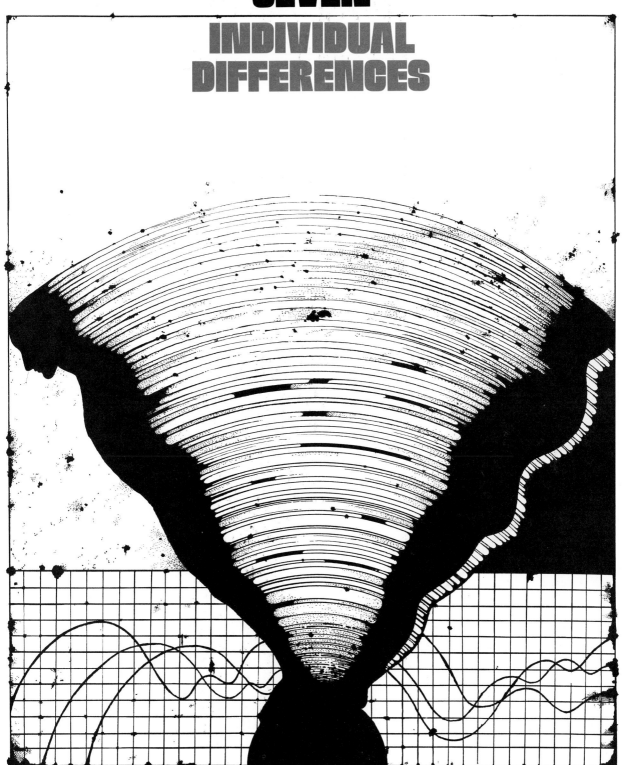

All sciences are interested both in general laws and in predictions about individual events. Thus chemistry is concerned with the general laws that explain what happens when a large number of molecules of an acid meet a large number of molecules of a metal. But it is also concerned with what happens when specific amounts of two specific substances are put together in a test tube under specific conditions of pressure and heat.

Psychology resembles the other sciences in this respect. It is interested in general laws of learning, thinking, perception, emotions, and motivation—all the psychological processes, common to most organisms, that have been discussed up to this point. As will be seen in this section, it is also concerned with individual differences.

It was Sir Francis Galton, an English scientist prominent in the 1880s, who first began collecting proof that no two human beings are ever exactly alike. He studied people's height, weight, hearing, sense of smell, color vision, ability to judge weights, and many other traits and abilities. What he found was that all kinds of human characteristics vary over a wide range from small to large, weak to strong, slow to fast.

Since the time of Sir Francis, psychology has made many advances in the study of individual differences. As Chapter 12 will make clear, much effort has been spent on the development of tests that provide an increasingly accurate measure of human characteristics and abilities, even such vague and complex ones as intelligence and personality. Statistical analysis has provided an interpretation of what the test results mean. Tests and the analysis of their findings have been of particular value in adding to our knowledge about the nature and distribution of intelligence.

Outline

Tests of intelligence and personality

Testing is one area in which everybody, even without ever taking a psychology course, is almost bound to come into contact with psychology. It is virtually impossible to grow up in the United States today without sooner or later taking a test that has been devised by a psychologist or at least in accordance with techniques originally developed by psychologists.

In the early grades many schools give their pupils some kind of intelligence test as an indication of their learning ability. The tests serve as a clue to whether individual students are underachievers who are not living up to their true capacities or overachievers who are working exceptionally hard and doing better than might be expected. In the later grades most pupils take the Iowa or Stanford achievement tests, which measure their progress (and the general level of progress at their particular school) against national averages. As part of the requirement for admission to many colleges, high school seniors take the Scholastic Aptitude Tests, which are a form of intelligence test.

Tests are not the only technique used by psychologists in measuring human beings. Two other scientific methods of investigation mentioned in Chapter 1 as tools of the psychologist—interviews and naturalistic observation—are also important. Thus psychologists interested in children who were having trouble adjusting in school might not only give the children intelligence and personality tests but also talk to the children at length, seeking clues to the problem. They might also try to observe the children's usual behavior in the classroom and at home. This whole battery of ways of evaluating the individual is known as *psychological assessment*. Tests are just a part of the process—but they are of special importance because so much has been learned about how to construct them, use them, and interpret them.

409

Requirements of a test

Informal tests of human characteristics go back to the beginnings of history. Mythology and literature are full of stories of young men who had to slay a dragon to prove that they were brave enough to deserve the hand of a princess. Or sometimes the stories are about people who had to answer riddles posed by wise men to prove that they were intelligent enough to become rulers. The ancient Chinese used tests to select people for governmental posts. The ancient Greeks made selections on the basis of tests they developed for both physical and mental skills (1).

One can safely assume, however, that tests used until recently were not very accurate—for it is extremely difficult to construct a test that will do a good job of measuring what it is supposed to measure. The difficulties can best be explained by discussing the four quite strict requirements that a test should meet to qualify as scientifically sound.

Objectivity

In the first place, a satisfactory test should be *objective*—that is, it should provide results that are uncolored by the personal opinions or prejudices of the person who gives and grades the test. In fact the first intelligence test was an attempt to obtain a more objective measure of a child's ability to profit from classes in school than could be provided by the opinion of the teacher, which might be colored by the child's personality, behavior in class, or family's position in the community.

Insofar as is possible, psychological tests are designed so that any qualified person can present them to the subject in the same manner and under the same kind of testing conditions. A uniform method is provided for scoring the results. Thus the person taking the test should get the same score regardless of who administers the test and who scores it.

Reliability

To describe why a test must also be *reliable,* an analogy can be made between a test and an oven thermometer. If the thermometer is reliable—that is, if it gives the same reading every time for the same amount of heat—the cook can count on roasts and pies to come out of the oven in perfect shape for the table. On the other hand, if the thermometer is damaged and unreliable, it may give a reading of 300 degrees on one occasion and 400 degrees the next, even though the actual temperature is exactly the same. In this case the results of cooking are likely to be somewhat disappointing.

Just as a good thermometer must produce consistent temperature readings, a good test must produce consistent scores. One way of determining the reliability of a test is to compare the same person's score on all the odd-numbered items with the score on all the even-numbered items; these two scores should be similar. Or two versions of the test can be constructed and given to the same person on two different occasions. Again, the scores should be similar.

Validity

The most important requirement of all for a test is that it be *valid*—that is, it must actually measure what it is intended to measure. This is unfortunately the most difficult of the requirements to fulfill and to explain. Perhaps the best approach is to discuss what is meant by the absence of validity.

Suppose that a psychologist wants to develop a test that will predict which college students will make the best teachers in the first three grades of elementary school. On the assumption that the ability to use words is important, the psychologist devises a test that measures how good college students are at such tasks as defining words, completing sentences, and repeating the content of paragraphs read to them. The test is objective. It is also found to be highly reliable. Thus it meets the first two requirements of a good test. But it is not necessarily valid. It may measure not teaching ability but only the ability to understand and manipulate words.

There are a number of ways to determine the validity of a test. Common sense is one of them; the items in the test must bear a meaningful relationship to the characteristics being measured. (For example, the thought of trying to assess musical ability by asking questions on major-league baseball standings does not "make sense" and must be rejected.) Another way is to observe the behavior of people who have taken the test and determine whether they behave as their test scores predicted. Thus, in the case of the test of teaching ability, the scores of a group of college students might be compared with later ratings of the quality of their teaching. Or, to save time, the test might be given to a group of teachers whose ability was already known. If a close relationship was found between their test scores and their ratings as teachers, this would indicate that the test is valid. If there was no relationship or only a small relationship between the scores and teaching ability, the test would have to be rejected as invalid.

Unfortunately, psychology does not yet possess valid tests for many important psychological characteristics. For example, there are no valid tests for anxiety over sexual behavior, tolerance of frustration, or disposition to suicide. The design of such tests is a challenge for psychologists of the future.

Standardization

The final requirement for a test can best be explained in terms of the following imaginary situation. A psychologist has drawn up a 100-question test that can be given and scored objectively and that clearly seems to be a reliable and valid measure of intelligence. The psychologist gives the test to a college student, who answers 60 of the items correctly. What does this score of 60 tell the psychologist? Not very much. The psychologist cannot know, after giving the test to a single person, whether a score of 60 indicates that this person is a genius, a moron, or something in between.

As this imaginary example indicates, the results of a test are generally not very useful unless they can be compared with the scores of other people. Thus most tests, before they are considered ready for use, are themselves tested by administering them to a large and representative sample of the population. Records are kept of how many people score at all the possible levels from highest to lowest. This process, called *standardization,* makes it possible to determine whether the score made by an individual is average, low, or high.

Analyzing test results

A score made on a standardized test can be analyzed in a number of useful ways. It can be compared quite accurately with the scores of the population as a whole—indicating just exactly how much it is above or below average, how many people do better and how many do worse, and other facts that are helpful in interpreting its meaning. Moreover, the score can be used to predict, within limits, how well the individual who made it is likely to do on another kind of test.

The tool used in analyzing the results of tests and other forms of psychological assessment is called *psychological statistics.* As the name indicates, this is the application of mathematical principles to the special problems found in the field of psychology. In today's computer age, the calculations required in psychological statistics are often delegated to computer specialists. They are not especially difficult for anyone with a mathematical turn of mind, however, and the statistical appendix to this book contains all the information needed to use them.

There are two aspects of psychological statistics that are essential for an understanding of intelligence and intelligence testing. The first is discussed in the box titled "The normal curve of distribution" (pages 414–15)—which explains many of the facts about scoring intelligence tests and the differences between an I.Q. (or *intelligence quotient*) of say 85 and an I.Q. of 115. The other is discussed in the box on page 417 titled "The meaning of correlations." This explains a term used frequently in the rest of the chapter in discussing relationships between the I.Q.'s of different groups and of the same people at different times in their lives.

Types of tests

Before discussing some actual tests, their uses, and what has been learned from them, it will be useful to describe some different types of tests. First, a distinction must be made between a *group test* and an *individual test.* The group test is administered to many people at once. It typically takes the form of printed questions, such as those shown in Figure 12-1, which are answered by making penciled notations. The individual test is given to one person at a time by a trained examiner. In this case the test items can call for a verbal answer or for the subject to perform some kind of task, as illustrated in Figure 12-2.

Group tests have made possible the measurement of hundreds of

12-1

A group test

These are sample items for second- and third-graders from the Otis-Lennon Mental Ability Test. At this age level, the person administering the test reads the instructions to the children taking the test. In all intelligence tests the sample items demonstrate how the questions should be answered and are not counted in the scoring. The actual items in this test range from about as difficult as the sample items to much more difficult. (2)

Three of these things are alike in some way. Fill in the answer space beneath the one that is different.

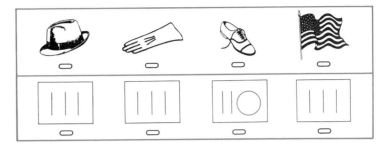

We say: "Boy is to trousers as girl is to what?"

The first two drawings are alike except the second one has a dot inside it. Which drawing goes with the circle in the same way as the first two drawings go together?

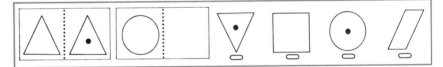

12-2

An individual test

With colored blocks of various patterns, the man is asked to copy a design from the Block Design test, one of the tests that comprise the Wechsler Adult Intelligence Scale. The examiner notes how quickly and accurately he can perform this task.

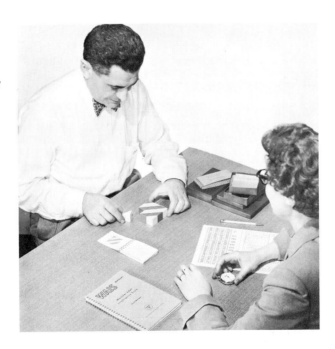

THE NORMAL CURVE OF DISTRIBUTION

When measurements are made of human traits—or indeed of any other phenomena of nature—they are usually found to fall into the same distinct and striking pattern. Let us suppose that we measure a physical trait such as the height of adult American women. We will find that there are a few very tiny women and a few extremely tall women. But most will be found in between these extremes and most of all will cluster around what might be called average. Measurements of intelligence fall into the same pattern, as is shown in Figure A. Nearly half of all people cluster right around the average, with ratings between 90 and 110. Only a very few are found below 60 or over 140.

The kind of curve shown in Figure A is so typical of the results generally found in tests and measurements that it is called the *normal curve of distribution.* The message of the normal curve is that in most measurable traits most people are average or close to it, some are a fair distance below or above, and a few are very far below or above. Those who are about average have a lot of company. Those who are far removed from the average—in intelligence the geniuses and the extremely retarded, in height the seven-footers and the four-footers—are quite rare.

The "Standard Deviation"

Statistical analysis makes it possible to determine how many measurements or scores will be found at any given distance above or below the average—in other words, how many scores will be found under any part of the normal curve of distribution. The statistical tool used for this purpose is called the *standard deviation,* or *SD* for short. The standard deviation is a figure, worked out by a mathematical formula, that in effect divides the normal curve of distribution into equal units above and below the average score as is illustrated in Figure B. The proportion of scores that will be found one, two, or three standard deviation units above or below the average is always the same, as is also shown in Figure B.

For intelligence, the average I.Q. is 100 and the standard deviation is 15. Thus we know, from the rule illustrated in Figure B, that I.Q.'s are distributed according to the following table:

I.Q.	PERCENTAGE OF PEOPLE
130-144	2.14
115-129	13.59
100-114	34.13
85-99	34.13
70-84	13.59
55-69	2.14

In addition a very few people, only .14 percent (or about one in seven hundred), have I.Q.'s over 145; and the same tiny number are under 55.

In interpreting the results of any test, the standard deviation is of great value. Knowing how many standard deviations a person's score lies above or below the average allows us to see quite clearly how this person compares with others.

Percentiles

Another useful device in interpreting test scores is the *percentile,* the meaning of which can best be explained with an example. Take the case of a college man who has applied for admission to graduate school and has been required to take the Graduate Record Examinations, which are nationally administered tests often used to screen applicants. He makes a score of 460 on the verbal part of the test and 540 in mathematics. By themselves, these scores do not mean much to the faculty of the school he wants to attend. But records kept of past results on the test provide a quick means of comparing his scores with those of other college seniors. A score of 460 on the verbal test, the records show, lies on the 40th percentile for men. This means that 40 percent of all senior men who take the test make a lower score and 60 percent make an equal or higher score. The 540 score in math lies on the 66th percentile for men; in other words, 66 percent of senior men make a lower score, and only 34 percent make an equal or higher score. These percentile figures show the student and the school he hopes to attend how his ability compares with that of other prospective graduate students. He is well above average in mathematical ability (only a third of male college seniors make better scores) but below average in verbal aptitude.

Percentile scores can be computed for any kind of measurement, whether or not it falls into a normal distribution. A percentile score of 1—or, to be more exact, .01—means that no one had a lower score. A score of 99—or, to be more exact, 99.99—is the highest. A score of 50 is exactly in the middle.

Figure A   The normal curve and intelligence

The curve shows the distribution of intelligence in the United States, as determined by a test given to a large standardization group in 1937. A total of 46.5 percent of those measured had intelligence quotients between 90 and 109. Fewer than 1 percent scored below 60 and only 1.33 percent scored 140 or over. The meaning of intelligence quotient, or I.Q., is discussed beginning on page 419. (3)

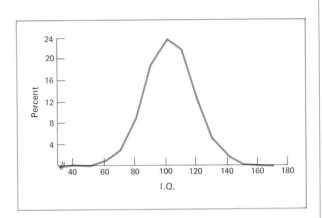

Figure B   The normal curve and the *SD*

In a normal curve of distribution the standard deviation indicates the proportion of measurements or scores that will be found at various distances from the mean. As shown here, 34.13 percent of all measurements lie between the mean and 1 *SD* above the mean. Measurements that are between 1 *SD* and 2 *SD*'s above the mean make up 13.59 percent of the total, and measurements between 2 *SD*'s and 3 *SD*'s above the mean make up 2.14 percent. The same percentages are found below the mean. Note that the figures do not quite add up to 100 percent. This is because 0.14 percent of measurements are found more than 3 *SD*'s above the mean and another 0.14 percent are found more than 3 *SD*'s below the mean. These various percentages hold for any normal distribution, although the size of the *SD* is of course quite different from one curve to another.

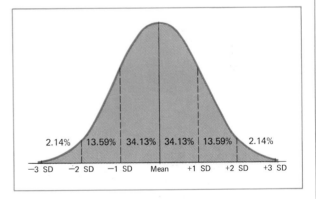

thousands of students each year—a job for which there would never be enough time or testers to use the individual method. They have a limitation, however. A low score on a group test may be caused by such factors as temporary ill health, poor vision, or lack of motivation—which might be apparent to an examiner administering an individual test.

Achievement and aptitude tests. Another distinction separates *achievement tests* from *aptitude tests*. An achievement test attempts to measure how much the subjects have learned or accomplished at the time of taking the test. For example, the Iowa and Stanford achievement tests measure what students have learned about such classroom topics as reading and arithmetic—and how their present skills in these fields compare with those of students around the nation. In general, achievement tests measure how well the subject has mastered some specific topic—usually a topic that has been studied only recently.

An aptitude test, on the other hand, attempts to measure a person's ability to learn a new skill or perform a new task. The Scholastic Aptitude Tests are an example. As the name indicates, they attempt to measure the student's ability to learn the new materials of the college curriculum. However, it is virtually impossible to devise an aptitude test that does not depend at least to some extent on previous learning. Scores on the Scholastic Aptitude Tests, for example, depend to a great extent on the student's past learning achievements, especially in such matters as reading ability and mathematics. This is one weakness of aptitude tests (especially of intelligence tests, as will be explained in more detail later). But aptitude tests are designed to depend as little as possible on previous learning, especially recent learning or knowledge of specific topics. They try to deal in generalities and to measure the ability to solve new kinds of problems.

Norm-oriented and criterion-oriented tests. Until very recently, it should be pointed out, most psychological tests have been constructed and scored in accordance with the statistical principles that were discussed in the box titled "The normal curve of distribution." That is, individuals have been scored in terms of how well they do in comparison with others. They have not been scored in terms of how close they come to making any kind of ideal score—for example, getting all the items right. The tests have been what is called *norm-oriented*. For example, a child takes a reading achievement test in the third grade and scores on the 50th percentile, showing that the child is exactly average in reading ability. In the fifth grade, the same child shows a test score that falls on the 55th percentile. The tests show that the child is now doing a little better than average—but they do not tell us how much the child has actually learned about reading.

In recent years, a number of psychologists have become dissatisfied with norm-oriented tests, particularly as a measure of what is or should be learned in the schools (4). They are seeking to devise what are called *criterion-oriented tests*, which would be geared to some kind of absolute

THE MEANING OF CORRELATIONS

A question that might be of interest to psychologists engaged in intelligence testing is this: Do intelligent parents tend to have intelligent children? One way the question can be answered is through the use of a statistical device called the *correlation coefficient*.

If a high level of intelligence on the part of parents is often accompanied by a high level of intelligence among their children, then these two phenomena must be related to each other in some way. In statistical terms, they are said to be correlated. If the brightest parents in the world have the brightest children, and the second brightest parents have the second brightest children, and so on down the line, then the correlation is perfect. If that one-to-one relationship does not exist (as indeed it does not), then the correlation is something less than perfect.

A sort of rough picture that indicates whether two events are correlated can be obtained by making what is known as a scatter plot, as shown in Figure A. In comparing parents with children, for example, the parents' intelligence score might be plotted along the Y axis, the children's along the X axis. For each family, a dot would be placed as high up as indicated by the parents' intelligence and as far to the right as indicated by the children's intelligence.

After a sufficient number of families had been dotted into the diagram, some kind of pattern would be apparent. If the dots were scattered widely and at random, as in the left-hand panel of Figure A, the pattern would indicate no correlation at all. If the dots were virtually in a straight line, as in the right-hand panel, the pattern would indicate a very high correlation.

Statistical formulas explained in the Appendix provide an accurate method of determining the amount of correlation and expressing it in numbers, ranging from 0.00 for a total lack of correlation to 1.00 for a perfect correlation.

Correlation and prediction

One of the chief practical applications of correlation, as used to interpret test results, is in predicting. For example, guidance counselors know that scores on certain kinds of tests are correlated with success in various kinds of jobs and thus can offer students the prediction that they will probably succeed or fail as computer programers, accountants, auto mechanics, professional musicians, or whatever kind of work they may be considering.

It must be noted, however, that correlations are by no means infallible in making predictions. Only when a correlation is very close to a perfect 1.00, as in the high correlation shown in the right-hand scatter plot in Figure A, does almost every subject tend to show a close relationship between score on scale X and score on scale Y. Even in a correlation of .75, which sounds high, there is a considerable amount of scatter, representing subjects who scored relatively low on scale X but relatively high on scale Y, or vice versa. Since most correlations found in psychological studies are lower than .75, we must be quite tentative in making predictions.

On the question of whether intelligent parents have intelligent children, for example, it has been found that the correlation is .55 (6). This indicates that there is indeed a general tendency for children to resemble their parents, but that there are a great many cases where children score considerably higher or considerably lower. If we predict that intelligent parents will have an intelligent child we will be right more often than we are wrong—but we will certainly not be right every time.

Figure A   A "picture" of correlations
These scatter plots were obtained by making a dot for each subject at a point indicating both score on scale X and score on scale Y. (5)

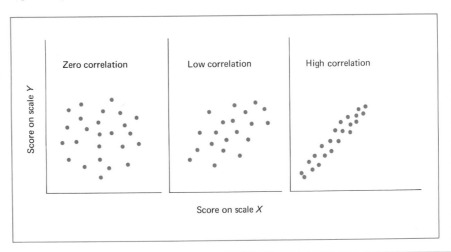

417

standard of performance. On the matter of reading, for example, these psychologists would prefer a criterion-oriented test that would be scored on the basis of how well a child *should* be able to read in the fifth grade if the school has done a good job. This question of the merits of criterion-oriented versus norm-oriented tests promises to be an important psychological issue in coming years.

Intelligence tests

Tests of intelligence are the most widely used of all aptitude tests—and indeed perhaps the best known of all psychological procedures. Everybody has heard about them and about the I.Q., or intelligence quotient, that they produce. Intelligence tests have been widely used for years by schools, industry, and the military services. The results have been analyzed statistically in various ways, resulting in a considerable body of knowledge on how I.Q. is related to success in school and in jobs—as well as to such factors as parents' I.Q., parents' schooling, father's occupation, and the I.Q. of brothers, sisters, and twins. Numerous studies have also been made comparing the I.Q.'s of various nationalities, races, and age groups.

The intelligence test began as a psychologist's answer to a specific and practical problem faced by Paris schools at the beginning of the century. Too many classrooms were crowded, and slow students were holding up the progress of the better ones. One solution, it seemed, would be to identify the children who lacked the mental capacity required by the standard curriculum and put these children in a separate school of their own. But how was the identification to be made?

Binet and daughters

A French psychologist named Alfred Binet who went to work on the problem realized that the identification of the poorer students could not safely be left to the teachers. There was too much danger that a teacher would show favoritism toward children who had pleasant personalities and would be too harsh on those who were bright enough but tended to be troublemakers. There was also the question of whether a teacher could successfully recognize the cases of children who appeared dull but in fact could have done the work had they tried (7). To avoid these pitfalls, Binet developed an objective test that was first published in 1905, has been revised many times since, and is still widely used today.

The Stanford-Binet test

In the United States one of the best-known current versions of Binet's original test is the *Stanford-Binet Intelligence Scale.* This is an individual test that can be given successfully even to very young children; in testing children who are not yet old enough to have developed a wide range of language skills, the examiner uses the kind of physical equipment shown in Figure 12-3. Older children and adults are asked questions that measure such things as vocabulary, memory span for sen-

12-3

Equipment for the Stanford-Binet test

These are the "props" used in administering the Stanford-Binet Intelligence Scale to children.

tences and numbers, and reasoning ability. Some of the test items used at various age levels are shown in Figure 12-4.

Mental age and I.Q.

The scoring method that was originally used by Binet as well as in the initial versions of the Stanford-Binet test was based on the concept of *mental age,* or MA for short. As children mature, they are able to pass

Two years old	On a large paper doll, points out the hair, mouth, feet, ear, nose, hands, and eyes. When shown a tower built of four blocks, builds one like it.
Three years old	When shown a bridge built of three blocks, builds one like it. When shown a drawing of a circle, copies it with a pencil.
Four years old	Fills in the missing word when asked, "Brother is a boy; sister is a _____" and "In daytime it is light; at night it is _____." Answers correctly when asked, "Why do we have houses?" "Why do we have books?"
Five years old	Defines *ball, hat,* and *stove.* When shown a drawing of a square, copies it with a pencil.
Nine years old	Answers correctly when examiner says, "In an old graveyard in Spain they have discovered a small skull which they believe to be that of Christopher Columbus when he was about ten years old. What is foolish about that?" Answers correctly when asked, "Tell me the name of a color that rhymes with head." "Tell me a number that rhymes with tree."
Adult	Can describe the difference between laziness and idleness, poverty and misery, character and reputation. Answers correctly when asked, "Which direction would you have to face so your right hand would be toward the north?"

12-4

Some Stanford-Binet test items

These are some of the test items used at various age levels in the Stanford-Binet scale. (8)

419

more and more of the items on tests of this type; and standardization of the tests reveals exactly how many items the average child is able to pass at the age of six or seven or whatever the child's actual age happens to be. (To testers, actual age in years and months is known as *chronological age,* or CA for short.)

For the average child, mental age and chronological age are equal. But children who have less intelligence than average will not be able to pass all the items suitable to their age level and thus will show an MA that is lower than their CA. Those who have more intelligence than average will pass some of the items designed for older children and thus will show an MA that is higher than their CA.

The relationship between mental age and chronological age was the original basis for that well-known term intelligence quotient, or I.Q. The average I.Q. was arbitrarily set at 100, a convenient figure, and the individual child's I.Q. was determined by the formula

$$\text{I.Q.} = \frac{\text{MA}}{\text{CA}} \times 100$$

As an example of how the formula is applied, we can consider the case of a child whose mental age works out on the test to six years and eight months. To make the arithmetic easier, this mental age is converted into months; six years and eight months equals eighty months. If the child's chronological age is also eighty months, the formula works out as follows

$$\text{I.Q.} = \frac{80}{80} \times 100 = 1 \times 100 = 100$$

If the child is only six years old (seventy-two months) the formula becomes

$$\text{I.Q.} = \frac{80}{72} \times 100 = \frac{10}{9} \times 100 = 111$$

If the child's actual age is eight years (ninety-six months) the formula becomes

$$\text{I.Q.} = \frac{80}{96} \times 100 = \frac{10}{12} \times 100 = 83$$

The intelligence quotient can still be thought of in terms of its original meaning. The average I.Q. is 100; the ability to pass items above one's age level indicates an I.Q. of more than 100; the inability to pass all the items appropriate for one's age level results in an I.Q. of less than 100. In actual practice the I.Q. of an individual taking the Stanford-Binet or other intelligence tests is now determined by consulting a table that lists the I.Q. appropriate to the score of a person of a particular age. These tables are prepared by administering the test in a standard way to people of various ages.

The raw scores of number of items passed are tabulated for each age group to determine the average raw score and the standard deviation for that age group. The average raw score of each age group is then taken to represent an I.Q. of 100; a raw score that is 1 standard deviation above the average represents an I.Q. of 115; and a score that is 2 standard deviations above average represents an I.Q. of 130. Tables make it possible to translate any raw score into an I.Q. without using the MA-CA formula.

The Wechsler tests

Among other widely used individual tests of intelligence are the *Wechsler Adult Intelligence Scale* (called WAIS for short), the *Wechsler Intelligence Scale for Children* (WISC), and the *Wechsler Preschool and Primary Scale of Intelligence* (WPPSI). The distinguishing feature of this group of tests is that the items they contain are divided into two major categories, verbal and performance. The verbal items measure vocabulary, information, general comprehension, memory span, arithmetic reasoning, and ability to detect similarities between concepts. The performance items measure ability at constructing designs with blocks, completing pictures, arranging pictures, working puzzles, and substituting unfamiliar symbols for digits.

The subject's I.Q. can be calculated for the test as a whole or for the verbal items and the performance items considered separately. This feature is often an advantage in testing people who lack skill in the use of the English language. Such people may score much higher on the performance items than on the verbal items.

Group tests

An example of a group intelligence test has already been illustrated. This is the *Otis-Lennon Mental Ability Test,* shown in Figure 12-1, which is actually a series of five tests of varying difficulty designed to cover the school years from kindergarten to college freshman. A well-known test for children in kindergarten and the first grade is the *Pintner-Cunningham Primary Test,* illustrated in Figure 12-5.

12-5

The Pintner test

These are sample items for kindergarten and first-grade pupils from the Pintner-Cunningham Primary Test. (9)

There are *two* things that belong together in this row. Let's see if we can find them. Put a mark on the fork. Now mark something that belongs with the fork.

Look at the picture of the rooster. Find what is gone from the rooster and mark it.

12-6

I.Q. and school achievement

These correlations between I.Q. and achievement in specific school subjects or skills were found in a study that used the Stanford-Binet Scale to measure intelligence. (11)

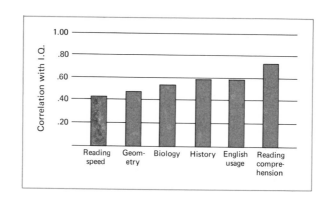

Prospective members of the Army and Navy take the *Armed Forces Qualification Test*. The *Scholastic Aptitude Tests* (SAT) are also group intelligence tests but they have been standardized for high school seniors rather than the population as a whole. The average SAT score is 500, and the standard deviation is 100. Since the seniors who take the test are a rather highly selected group, a score of 500 represents an I.Q. of well over 100.

Virtues of intelligence tests

All modern intelligence tests are objective and standardized and have a high degree of reliability. A person's I.Q. as given by one of the tests will be similar to this person's I.Q. as shown by another test or by the same test given after a reasonable interval. Intelligence tests have also proved valid for predicting success in school. In many studies of the relation between I.Q. and school grades, correlations of .40 to .60 have been found (10). Some forms of school achievement show a higher correlation than others, as is illustrated in Figure 12-6.

Students who have very low I.Q.'s tend to drop out of school before or immediately after the twelfth grade, leaving a rather highly selected group to go on to college. One study made a generation ago showed that the average I.Q. of college freshmen was 118, of graduates 123, and of those who had obtained the Ph.D. degree 141 (12). Because a larger proportion of young people attend college today, the figures for freshmen and graduates now are probably somewhat lower. At universities with the highest entrance standards, however, the figures are very high.

Weaknesses of intelligence tests

One weakness of intelligence tests is the impossibility of devising a test of general or basic mental ability that is purely an aptitude test rather than an achievement test. An intelligence test necessarily relies heavily on the current level of achievement of the people who take it. Their score depends to a considerable extent on the vocabulary they have acquired, their knowledge of the rules of mathematics, and their ability to manipulate numbers and visual symbols. If you study the items from the Stanford-Binet test that were shown in Figure 12-4, you will note that many of the questions are based on what the subject has learned. To answer them correctly, the two-year-old child must have learned the meaning of hair, mouth, and hands; the four-year-old must have acquired some fairly rich concepts of houses and books; the adult must have learned the points of the compass.

The theoretical difference between intelligence and achievement tests is that the intelligence test attempts, insofar as possible, to measure the subjects' ability to use their existing knowledge in a novel way. Thus two-year-olds are asked to apply their knowledge about their own lips and hair to a paper doll. Adults are asked to make a novel spatial orientation based on their knowledge of the compass.

Perhaps the best example of the difference between an intelligence test and an achievement test is the Stanford-Binet item at the nine-year level in which the child is asked to point out the absurdity in the statement: "In an old graveyard in Spain they have discovered a small skull which they believe to be that of Christopher Columbus when he was about ten years old." Finding the absurdity is a novel task, but it also requires the child to know that Columbus lived to be an adult and that people do not cast off their skulls as a snake casts off its skin. A child never exposed to that kind of knowledge might easily miss the question, not for lack of reasoning ability but simply because of confusion over the words (13).

In constructing an intelligence test an attempt is made to base all the items on previously acquired knowledge or skills that everyone has had an equal chance to attain. It is assumed that every two-year-old has had an equal opportunity to learn the meaning of hair, mouth, and hands; every four-year-old knows the words *houses* and *books*; every nine-year-old should know that Columbus discovered America; every adult should have been exposed to information about the points of the compass. No questions are included that can be answered only by a child who has had specialized training in summer camp about nature study or only by an adult who has studied trigonometry or Spanish.

Nonetheless, there is a strong bias in intelligence tests that favors people who have grown up in environments where they have had an opportunity to acquire the kinds of knowledge and language abilities that are typical of the middle and upper classes and are fostered by a school system largely staffed by middle-class teachers. This is one reason that children from middle- and upper-class homes make higher scores than children from lower-class homes (14). City children tend to make higher scores than children from rural areas (15). Whites make higher average scores than blacks and members of ethnic groups that do not share the typical white middle-class culture (16, 17, 18).

Intelligence tests, it must be remembered, were originally designed to measure the ability to learn the tasks typically taught in school, and this is still what they measure today. Indeed it probably would be more accurate to say that intelligence tests provide an A.Q., or academic quo-

"You mean I've been reading to him for the last half hour, and he's not even in bed yet!"

© 1950 by the New York Times Company. Reprinted by permission.

tient, instead of an I.Q., or intelligence quotient. Psychologists are not sure of the degree to which intelligence tests reflect a basic capacity to think intelligently.

Can the tests be improved? Recently there has been much discussion about revising intelligence tests to remove their weaknesses and biases. For example, a panel of scholars appointed to study the Scholastic Aptitude Tests has recommended that these tests be enlarged and diversified. The panel wants the tests to include measurements of such factors as musical and artistic talent, athletic skills, mechanical skills, the ability to express oneself in nonverbal ways, the ability to adapt to new situations, and many others that are not now taken into account (19).

Some critics of intelligence tests would like to prohibit their use entirely in the school system, on the ground that children who make low scores are more or less automatically assigned to a lower-level type of education and never considered as college material, when in fact they might accomplish a great deal if they received sufficient attention, encouragement, and opportunity.

The nature of intelligence

Let us put aside all thoughts of intelligence testing and I.Q.'s for a moment and ask a more abstract question: Just what is intelligence? What does the word mean?

Many investigators would agree with the following definition: *Intelligence is the ability to profit from experience, to learn new information, and to adjust to new situations.* But is it a single ability or a combination of several different kinds of ability?

What is intelligence?

One well-known investigation into the nature of intelligence was made by L. L. Thurstone, who gave dozens of different kinds of tests to schoolchildren and decided that intelligence is composed of seven recognizable factors, which he called *primary mental abilities*:

1 *Verbal comprehension* — indicated by size of vocabulary, ability to read, and skill at understanding mixed-up sentences and the meaning of proverbs.
2 *Word fluency* — the ability to think of words quickly, as when making rhymes or solving word puzzles.
3 *Number* — the ability to solve arithmetic problems and to manipulate numbers.
4 *Space* — the ability to visualize spatial relationships, as in recognizing a design after it has been placed in a new context.
5 *Associative memory* — the ability to memorize quickly, as in learning a list of paired words.
6 *Perceptual speed* — indicated by the ability to grasp visual details quickly and to observe similarities and differences between designs and pictures.

7 *General reasoning*—skill at the kind of logical thinking that was described in Chapter 4.

Thurstone noted, however, that a person who was above average in any one of these abilities also tended to be above average in the others. He concluded, therefore, that intelligence is composed of the seven primary abilities plus some kind of "general factor" common to all (20).

Thurstone's "general factor" is a matter of some controversy among psychologists. Newer investigations have shown that when enough tests of widely different kinds of learning and problem solving are devised and given to children, it turns out that some children do much better on some of the tests, others on very different tests—and that the correlations between an individual's scores on various tests often drop so low as to cast doubt on the existence of any "general factor" (21).

One group of investigators, headed by J. P. Guilford of the University of Southern California, believes that intelligence is probably made up of no less than 120 different factors (or kinds of mental abilities). This 120-factor theory of intelligence, illustrated in Figure 12-7, maintains that an individual may display a very high level of intelligence at some tasks, average ability at others, and rather low ability at still others. Indeed Guilford and his followers have devised finely differen-

12-7
The 120-factor theory of intelligence

The 120 different factors are represented by the small individual blocks contained in this cube. The theory maintains that each factor is the ability to perform one of five different types of mental *operations* on one of four different kinds of material, or *contents*, with the aim of coming up with one of six different kinds of end results, or *products*. Thus the total number of abilities that make up intelligence (or blocks in the cube) is 5 × 4 × 6, or 120. Followers of the theory measure the mental operation called "divergent thinking" by asking a question such as "How many uses can you think of for a brick?"—and noting how many different answers the individual can come up with and how imaginative the answers are. One test of the mental operation called "evaluation" is to present the four words *cat, cow, mule,* and *mare* and ask whether these are best categorized as a) farm animals, b) four-legged animals, or c) domestic animals. The correct answer will be found at the bottom of page 427.

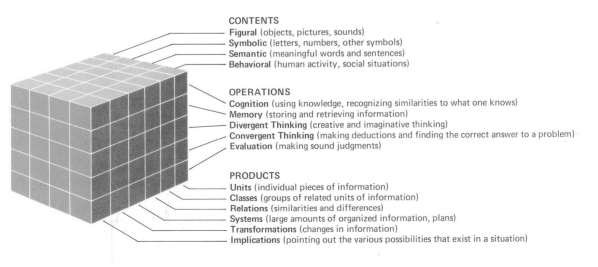

CONTENTS
Figural (objects, pictures, sounds)
Symbolic (letters, numbers, other symbols)
Semantic (meaningful words and sentences)
Behavioral (human activity, social situations)

OPERATIONS
Cognition (using knowledge, recognizing similarities to what one knows)
Memory (storing and retrieving information)
Divergent Thinking (creative and imaginative thinking)
Convergent Thinking (making deductions and finding the correct answer to a problem)
Evaluation (making sound judgments)

PRODUCTS
Units (individual pieces of information)
Classes (groups of related units of information)
Relations (similarities and differences)
Systems (large amounts of organized information, plans)
Transformations (changes in information)
Implications (pointing out the various possibilities that exist in a situation)

tiated tests for many of the 120 factors and have found no correlation at all between an individual's scores on many of the tests (22).

Among other things, Guilford has found that people differ widely in their abilities to deal with different kinds of materials (or *contents* as they are termed in Figure 12-7). Some people excel at dealing with "figural" contents, such as specific objects; these people might be best suited to become master mechanics or painters. Others excel at working with "symbolic" contents, such as numbers; these people might become good mathematicians. Others are best at handling "semantic" contents, such as words and ideas; these might be outstanding as philosophers or writers. A single I.Q. figure, Guilford believes, is incapable of expressing these and the many other differences he has found in mental abilities.

I.Q. and heredity

There are many important questions to be asked about intelligence: Is it inherited or determined by environment? Can it be changed? How is it affected by age? What relation does it have to a person's occupation and success? The answers can be presented only with reservations—for, as has just been said, psychologists are not entirely agreed on exactly what intelligence is and there is considerable question as to whether the standard tests really measure intelligence or only measure such aspects of it as apply to schoolwork. Therefore it will be better to discuss the questions in terms of I.Q. (which is the score based on the most widely used tests) rather than in terms of intelligence (which is more difficult to define and measure).

On the question of whether heredity influences I.Q., there is general agreement among scientists that the answer is probably yes—though the amount of influence is a matter of debate. The reason for believing that heredity has at least some effect is this: the more closely related two people are, the more similar their I.Q. scores are likely to be. Correlations between the I.Q.'s of brothers and sisters, children and their parents, or children and distant relatives all indicate that intelligence as reflected by I.Q. tends to "run in families." The correlation between the I.Q. of one child and of another person chosen at random would be zero, but the correlations between a child's I.Q. and the I.Q.'s of family relatives are always positive. Even for such rather distant relatives as cousins, a correlation of about .30 has been found (23). As is shown in Figure 12-8, there are correlations of close to .60 between the I.Q.'s of brothers and sisters and of children and parents. For identical twins reared together the correlation reaches an almost perfect .97.

I.Q. and environment

It can also be seen from Figure 12-8, however, that environment also plays a part in determining I.Q., because there are positive correlations among people in the same home even when they are not blood rela-

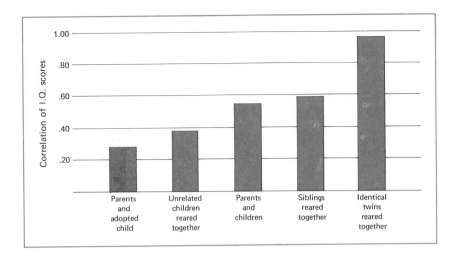

12-8

Family resemblances in I.Q.

Studies of families have shown correlations in I.Q. ranging from .28 between parents and adopted children to .97 for identical twins reared together. (24)

"Why don't you sing, weave, paint, sculpt, compose, or something?"

Drawing by Whitney Darrow, Jr.; © 1974 The New Yorker Magazine, Inc.

tives. The I.Q.'s of foster parents and their adopted children show a correlation; so do the I.Q.'s of children of different parents who happen to be adopted into the same foster home. Conversely, the correlation of .97 shown for identical twins reared in the same home has been found to be lower when for one reason or another twins are separated and reared in different homes (25).

There is also considerable other evidence that the I.Q. is significantly affected by environment. For example, many studies have shown that children's I.Q.'s are correlated with the social class of the parents (26), a finding that is important because of class differences in the kinds of environments provided for children. It has been shown that middle-class mothers tend to spend more time than lower-class mothers in such activities as talking to and playing with their young children and in encouraging them to learn and to solve problems on their own (27)—thus providing exactly the kind of environment that might be expected to result in higher I.Q. ratings. Similarly, the child's I.Q. is correlated with the educational level of the parents; statistically significant correlations, ranging between .32 and .59, have been found for children as young as twenty-seven months to four years (28).

The highest correlations of all between I.Q. and aspects of the environment have been obtained by one investigator who ignored such indirect measures as social class and parents' education and instead made a direct attempt to measure the kind of stimulation provided by the parents. This investigator drew up a scale on which parents were rated on such factors as how much encouragement and help they gave the child in using language and increasing the vocabulary, how much motivation and reward they provided for intellectual accomplishment, and

Although all three of the answers to the question posed in Figure 12-7 are correct, the best answer is c) domestic animals. This makes the finest and neatest distinction between the four animals and other kinds of animals. "Farm animals" is not the best answer because a cat is often found elsewhere. "Four-legged animals" is not the best answer because almost all animals have four legs.

the kinds of opportunities for learning they provided in the home, including personal help, books, and other learning materials. The correlation between the parents' total score on this scale and the child's I.Q. turned out to be .76 (29).

One of the most dramatic examples of the contrasting effects of different kinds of environments was provided by a long-term study of children who began life in the 1930s in an overcrowded, understaffed Iowa orphanage in which they had little opportunity for any kind of intellectual stimulation. Thirteen of the young orphans, with an average I.Q. of only 64 as shown by standard tests, were moved to a less crowded home for retarded teenage girls and women who, despite their own mental handicaps, managed to provide an affectionate and home-like atmosphere for them. Some of the older girls and women served as foster mothers, others as adoring aunts; the attendants in the home provided toys and books; and there was great competition over which of the young children would show the greatest progress in such skills as walking and talking.

Given this kind of personal attention and stimulation, even by "mothers" and "aunts" who were themselves retarded, the children made remarkable advances. After about a year and a half in their new home, their average I.Q. had risen by 28 points to 92 and they were considered suitable for adoption into foster families. A follow-up study thirty years later showed that the children had completed an average of about twelve years of schooling and that all but two, who were women who had married young, had worked successfully at such jobs as office work, school teaching, nursing, vocational counseling, and sales; indeed all of them were living at about the average level of occupation and income for their area of the nation.

The study also followed the careers of twelve other children who, for lack of opportunity to be moved elsewhere, had to remain in the overcrowded and unstimulating environment of the orphanage. These children, as it happened, actually began with a higher average I.Q. than the others, 87. But in the next two years the average declined by 26 points to 61. A follow-up thirty years later showed that they had completed an average of only four years of school, that a third of them were still inmates of an institution, and that only one of them worked at a job above the level of dishwasher or napkin-folder in a cafeteria (30).

Effects
of deprived
environments

All in all, there is considerable evidence that an environment that does not encourage or provide stimulation for the kinds of skills measured by intelligence tests is likely to result in a lower I.Q. score than developing children would be capable of attaining under different circumstances. Moreover, the longer children remain in a deprived environment (in terms of these kinds of skills), the lower their I.Q. score is likely to become. For example, Figure 12-9 shows the results of a study of children brought up by mentally retarded mothers. Note that the

12-9

Effect of poor environment on I.Q.

The bars indicate the average scores on intelligence tests made by the children brought up by mentally retarded mothers. Note that the youngest children proved about normal in intelligence but that the oldest children had an average I.Q. of only about 53. (31)

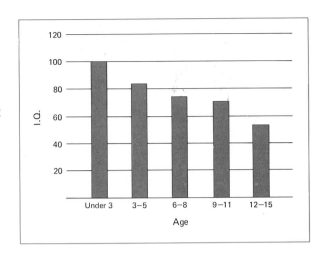

older the child was—in other words, the longer the child had been exposed to the impoverished environment provided by the retarded mother—the lower was the I.Q.

Children who appear to be retarded in early infancy seem to be especially vulnerable to the effects of a deprived atmosphere; a study that points in this direction is illustrated in Figure 12-10. Note that children who appeared to be retarded at eight months had considerably less chance of achieving an I.Q. of at least 80 at the age of four if they grew up in a lower-class home (that is, one less likely to encourage the skills measured by intelligence tests) than if they grew up in a middle-class or upper-class home.

12-10

Environment and the retarded infant

The bars indicate what happened to infants who were retarded at the age of eight months, as shown by tests for motor and mental skills. Their progress by the age of four was found to be related to their home environments. Of those in lower social class homes, only about 88 percent showed an I.Q. of 80 or more at age four, compared with about 93 percent of those in middle-class homes and 98 percent of those in the top-class homes. (32)

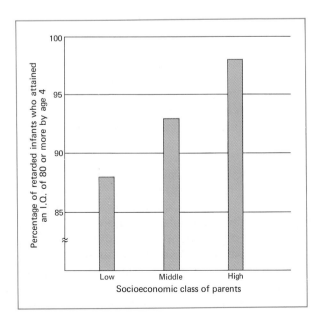

A last word on the heredity-environment issue

The question of whether heredity or environment has the greater effect on I.Q., though it has been the subject of much debate (33, 34), is now regarded by most psychologists as rather meaningless. Mankind's pool of the various genes that may affect performance on an intelligence test is widely varied; no two people except identical twins inherit the same pattern. Moreover, no two people including identical twins are ever subject to exactly the same environmental influences every hour of the day and every day of their lives. The prevailing view among psychologists is that in the constant interaction between heredity and environment, heredity probably sets a top and bottom limit on the individual's I.Q. score and that environment then determines where within this range the score will actually fall (35).

As to the possible range of I.Q. scores set by inheritance, opinions vary. Most though not all psychologists agree that the effect of environment, whatever its range may be, is enough to account for differences that have been found in average I.Q. scores for different groups and to cast serious doubt on the possibility that any social class, race, or nationality might have any significant superiority in the gene pool that might influence the I.Q. (36).

Changes in I.Q.

A change to a more favorable environment, as was shown by the study of the Iowa orpans, often produces a substantial rise in I.Q. Similarly, there is some evidence from studies of identical twins reared in different homes that a change to a less favorable environment may produce a decline in I.Q. These two facts seem perfectly logical. But how is one to account for one other strange finding about I.Q. and environment—which is that even children who remain in the homes in which they were born, and thus grow up in a relatively unchanging environment, often show substantial changes in I.Q. over the years?

This puzzling fact about I.Q. comes from a study in which the progress of 140 girls and boys was carefully followed over a ten-year period, from the time the children were two years old until they were twelve. Intelligence tests given every year indicated that about half the children showed just about the same I.Q. from one year to the next and indeed from the start of the ten-year period to the end. But for the other half there were changes upward or downward that in some cases reached striking proportions. In Figure 12-11, which illustrates some of the individual records from this study, note that one child's I.Q. rose from about 110 to 160, while another's dropped from about 140 to 110.

The children who gained, when compared with those who declined, were found to be more independent, competitive, and aggressive in conversation. They worked harder in school, showed a strong desire to master intellectual problems, and were persistent when faced with difficult tasks. Since these are personality traits that our society encourages in boys—while encouraging girls to be dependent and passive and not to seem smarter than their brothers—it is not surprising that boys were

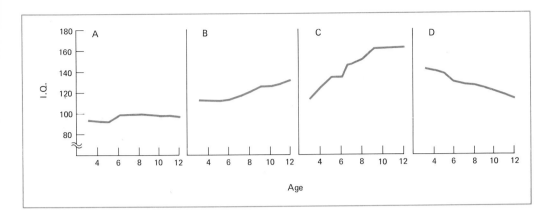

12-11

Changes in children's I.Q.'s

When children were tested annually for I.Q., these were some of the curves obtained. About half the children gave nearly straight-line results as in A, showing little change in I.Q. Some showed pronounced improvement as in B (from about 110 to about 130); some showed striking improvement as in C (from about 110 to about 160); and some showed substantial decreases as in D (from about 140 to 110). (37)

more likely to show increases in I.Q. and that girls were more likely to show decreases.

What conclusions can be drawn from this study? First, it appears obvious that the I.Q. is by no means a constant and unchanging trait like a person's fingerprints. Parents and teachers often take a child's score on an intelligence test too seriously; they give up on the child who has made a low score and expect too much from the child who has made a high score. Second, it appears that intelligence tests as now designed measure achievement motivation as well as ability, for the strength of the child's desire for intellectual achievement seems to be closely related to upward or downward changes in I.Q. Parents who emphasize and reward intellectual accomplishment and independence and who provide a model of intellectual achievement are the most likely to find their children gaining in I.Q. over the years.

The study raises another interesting question: Can people improve their I.Q's. through a deliberate effort toward better achievement? The answer is not known. But certainly some college students who make rather poor grades as freshmen suddenly begin making much better grades later. It may be that retesting of these students would show an increase in I.Q.

Are people getting smarter?

There is no evidence at all that the human species has any greater inborn brain capacity today than it had thousands of years ago—but there is some rather impressive evidence that the average level of intelligence, as measured by standard tests, has been rising, at least in the fairly recent years during which measurements have been kept. It appears quite likely that today the average I.Q. of 100 represents a greater knowledge of the concepts and rules measured by the tests than it did in the past.

The best evidence to this effect comes from a comparison of a large group of presumably representative and therefore "average" soldiers of the Second World War, who were tested in the early 1940s, with a similar group of First World War soldiers, tested a little more than twenty years earlier. On the very similar kinds of group intelligence tests given in the two wars, it turned out that the soldier of the early 1940s who scored exactly average, with an I.Q. of 100, would have been way above

431

average with an I.Q. of 115 if he had been competing with the soldiers of twenty years earlier on the test given at that time (38). There is also some evidence that the average I.Q.'s of children rose during the 1930s and 1940s in Scotland (39) and in England (40).

In view of what was said earlier about the effect of environment on I.Q., it is perhaps only to be expected that the average I.Q. score should have risen. In recent years vast numbers of people have moved from the lower classes into the middle and upper. Millions of people have moved from rural areas into cities. Schools have been improved, and the number of students who complete elementary school, high school, and college has greatly increased. Radio and television have exposed children to verbal stimulation and variety. Thus the average young American today may very well possess more of the kinds of abilities measured by intelligence tests than did the average young American of several generations ago. On the other hand, at least part of the difference in test scores may be due to the fact that people today have had more experience taking tests.

I.Q. and age

As has been said, the ability to pass increasingly difficult items on intelligence tests grows rapidly during the years from birth to about the mid-teens—and particularly in the earliest years of childhood. This fact leads to some interesting questions: At what age does the kind of ability measured by intelligence tests reach its peak? Once the peak is attained, does the ability then decline during the middle and old age?

The answers to these questions are not easy to obtain, because they are complicated by the probability, which has just been mentioned, that the average score on intelligence tests has been rising generation by generation in recent years. If one were to administer the same kind of intelligence test to large numbers of people from teenagers to sixty-year-olds, one would naturally expect the younger people to make higher average scores than the older people—and this is indeed what has been found to happen.

For example, in standardizing a recent version of the Wechsler Adult Intelligence Scale, the test was administered to representative samples of various age groups from sixteen through sixty-four, and the results were as illustrated in Figure 12-12. Note that the average total score rose through the early twenties, remained more or less on a plateau until thirty-four, then began a fairly sharp and steady decline. However, the age-by-age patterns differed for the two parts of the test, the verbal items and the performance items. Ability at verbal skills, after reaching its peak between twenty-five and thirty-four, remained fairly constant through the age of forty-four and afterward showed only a relatively small decline. Ability on performance items began to decline after the early twenties and at a fairly rapid rate.

What would be the results of a study in which the very same people could be tested over the years, beginning in their teens and continuing

12-12

I.Q. by age groups

Various age groups make different scores on the Wechsler Adult Intelligence Scale; the differences are apparent in both the verbal and performance parts of the test and in the total score as well. For a discussion of these results, see the text. (41)

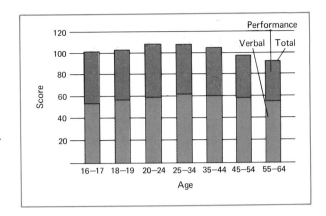

into their sixties? Despite the difficulties of making such a study, fortunately one investigator has managed to compare the scores made on a group intelligence test by nearly a hundred men during the First World War, when they were college freshmen averaging nineteen years old, with their scores on the same kind of test taken when they were fifty years old and again when they were sixty-one. The results are illustrated in Figure 12-13.

As the figure shows, scores on the arithmetic items in the test were highest at the age of nineteen and went down steadily thereafter. Scores on items measuring reasoning ability did just the opposite; they rose steadily and were highest at sixty-one. Scores on items measuring verbal ability were substantially higher at fifty than at nineteen but then declined slightly at sixty-one. The total score rose markedly from nineteen to fifty and afterward showed a slight decline. The results are not entirely satisfactory because they are for men only—and for a group that had an above-average I.Q. at first testing and presumably led lives more

12-13

At what age are we smartest?

The bars show the scores (not I.Q.'s) for three of the skills measured by an intelligence test, as well as the total score, made by men who were first tested when they were nineteen-year-old college freshmen, again when they were fifty, and a third time when they were sixty-one. (42)

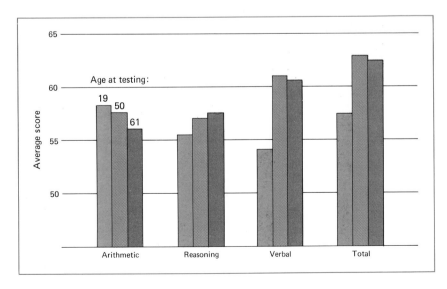

favorable than average to continued intellectual growth. However, they do offer a strong indication that intelligence—at least as measured by present tests—is by no means the monopoly of the young and that there is hardly any cause for despair over what will happen to our mental abilities as we get older.

I.Q. and occupation

The classic study of the relationship between I.Q. and occupation was based on data available from the thousands of men who took the Army's group intelligence test during the Second World War. The results, illustrated in Figure 12-14, show some pronounced differences in the average I.Q. of men in various kinds of jobs, ranging all the way from 93 for miners and 94 for farmhands to around 120 for accountants, lawyers, and engineers.

As Figure 12-14 indicates, there is a fairly large correlation between I.Q. and occupational status, meaning the level of prestige attached to one's job. However, an analysis of this relationship between I.Q. and

12-14

I.Q.'s by occupation

The bars show the range of I.Q.'s found for men in various occupations in the United States and also the average I.Q. for each occupation. Note that the average I.Q. of accountants was 121, of miners only 93, yet some miners had higher I.Q.'s than some accountants. (43)

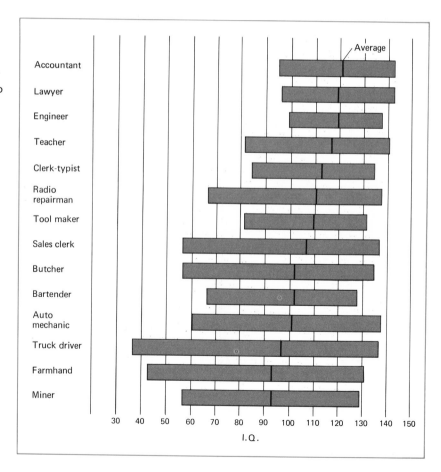

occupation has shown that I.Q. by itself is not very important. The chief factor in determining occupational status is education (44). In general college graduates have better jobs than high school graduates, who in turn have better jobs than those who have not completed high school. I.Q. is related to job status chiefly because it is so closely related to the amount of education a person is likely to receive. (There is a correlation of about .55 between I.Q. and years of school completed.)

Thus two people with equally high I.Q.'s may wind up in very different kinds of jobs. The one able to go to college may become an accountant or lawyer; the one unable for one reason or another to continue past elementary school may have to settle for a job of much lower status. This is undoubtedly the reason for the large range of I.Q.'s found in all the occupations listed in Figure 12-14, from highest to lowest. (Note that some of the miners and farmhands turned out to have I.Q.'s above the average for accountants, lawyers, and engineers.)

It should be noted that a high I.Q. can sometimes be an occupational handicap. This is particularly true for people who, for lack of education or opportunity, wind up in jobs that do not challenge their mental abilities. A study of young women employed in a chocolate factory found that the most intelligent among them were the most easily bored (45). A study of clerks employed at routine jobs showed that the turnover was highest among the most intelligent (46).

The mentally retarded

People whose I.Q.'s are below 70 are called the *mentally retarded,* who make up 2.28 percent of the population. This is a small percentage, but in a nation like the United States, with a population around 215,000,000 it represents a large number of total cases. There are close to 5 million mentally retarded people in the United States, and mental retardation is therefore a widespread and serious problem.

Mental retardation is classified along a scale ranging from mild (I.Q. of 53 to 69) to profound (I.Q. below 20). The mildly retarded, especially if helped with specialized training, can usually learn reading and arithmetic up to about the level of the third to sixth grades in school; and as adults they can usually take care of themselves both socially and in jobs. The profoundly retarded usually need nursing care all their lives; they have trouble speaking and may never even learn to walk.

What causes mental retardation? Some cases stem from specific biological abnormalities. Among these are cases of Down's Syndrome, apparently caused by the presence of an extra chromosome (making a total of forty-seven instead of the normal forty-six). The child with this extra chromosome has many other abnormalities besides mental retardation, including unusual bone structure in the hands, feet, and skull; the condition has been called "Mongolism" because of the round face and slant eyes characteristic of its victims.

Another form of serious retardation is *cretinism,* caused by an abnormally low level of secretion by the thyroid gland. If detected in time, this type of mental retardation can be prevented by giving the child thyroid substance. Other forms of retardation can be caused by biological abnormalities in metabolism, malnutrition, injury to the brain at birth, and brain damage caused by diseases, such as German measles, suffered by the mother during pregnancy.

There are many other cases, however, where no physical cause is apparent. One cannot be sure whether retardation is due to an undetected illness, a poor and unstimulating environment, or heredity.

The mentally gifted

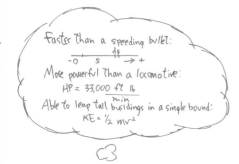

At the opposite extreme from the mentally retarded are the 2.28 percent of the population (again 5 million in all in the United States) who have I.Q.'s over 130. These are the *mentally gifted.* At the very top of the group are the people called *geniuses,* whose I.Q.'s may range up to 190.

A genius is capable of remarkable accomplishments, even early in life. Mozart, who surely would have scored near the very maximum had intelligence tests been invented at the time, began composing music when he was four and wrote a symphony when he was eight. John Stuart Mill, the nineteenth-century economist, read Plato in the original Greek before he was nine. In more recent times Norbert Wiener, the mathematician, graduated from high school at the age of twelve and from college at fifteen.

A classic study of the mentally gifted was begun in 1921 by Lewis M. Terman and continued by him and his associates for many years. He began with 1500 California schoolchildren who had I.Q.'s of 140 or more, and he managed to follow many of them into middle age.

As children, Terman's subjects were superior in many respects besides I.Q. They were above average in height (by about an inch), weight, and appearance. They were better adjusted than average and showed superiority in social activity and leadership.

In later life, not all the gifted children lived up to their early promise. Some of them dropped out of school and wound up in routine occupations; some, even though they went to college, turned out to be vocational misfits and drifters. But these were the exceptions, and their records tended to show problems of emotional and social adjustment and low motivation toward achievement. On the whole the group was outstandingly successful. In large proportion, the gifted went to college, achieved above-average and often brilliant records, and went on to make important contributions in fields ranging from medicine and law to literature and from business administration to government service. Many earned the recognition of a listing in *Who's Who* or *American Men of Science.* The average level of accomplishment was far higher than could be expected of a group chosen at random.

Unfortunately, however, children born with superior mental capacities can meet with serious problems. Presumably many such children are born into homes and social environments that do not encourage their development. They may seem to be know-it-alls and come to be resented by their parents, other children, and teachers. If they stay in

12-15

A special project for gifted children

In a class for the gifted, nine- and ten-year-olds get an early start on the principles of geometry.

the same grade as other children their age, they may be bored by the work and become lazy or difficult to discipline. If they skip grades they may have trouble adjusting socially to other children. In some ways the gifted child can benefit from special training just as much as the retarded child—as some schools have recognized by providing enriched activities as illustrated in Figure 12-15.

Other kinds of tests

Although intelligence tests are the most widely used and generally the most valid, in that they are so useful in predicting academic success, there are scores of other psychological tests, devised for special purposes. Among them, and worthy of special note, are *vocational aptitude tests* and *personality tests.*

Vocational aptitude

Some vocational aptitude tests attempt to measure several different kinds of skills and arrive at a sort of aptitude profile that shows where the test-taker is strongest and weakest. One such test measures skill at spelling and grammar, dealing with numbers, clerical speed and accuracy, mechanical problems, and several types of thinking and reasoning (47). Those taking the test can be advised that they will probably do best in a job requiring the skills for which they score highest.

Other tests are designed to measure the skills required for a particular kind of work. Tests of this sort are often used by industry in select-

ing job applicants and by the military services in assigning people to specific tasks. Tests have been developed for all kinds of special skills, among them musical ability, dealing with details as required in clerical jobs, manual dexterity, and the motor coordination required for operating complicated machinery.

Also used in vocational guidance is another type of psychological assessment known as the *interest test*. As the name implies, this type of test attempts to measure how the subject feels about various kinds of activities. It tries to establish whether the subject is interested in or bored by such things as literature, music, the outdoors, mechanical equipment, art, science, social affairs, and all kinds of specific activities ranging from butterfly collecting to repairing a clock or making a speech. Tests of this type provide an indication of the kind of work in which subjects are likely to be happiest.

In general, the present tests of vocational aptitude are considerably less satisfactory than intelligence tests in that their correlation with actual success on a job is usually much lower than the correlation between I.Q. and success in school. However, they often offer valuable clues about an individual's pattern of skills, and in the hands of trained counselors they serve as a useful adjunct to vocational guidance.

Personality assessment

The search for reliable and valid measures of all the various traits that go to make up personality has been carried on intensively. A test that could accurately measure even a single aspect of personality—for example, degree and type of anxiety—would be an invaluable research tool, opening up almost infinite possibilities for further study. A test that could accurately distinguish between normal and neurotic personalities would enable clinical psychologists to find the people most in need of psychotherapy and perhaps lead to the discovery of new methods. It would make comparisons possible among people who have grown up in different environments and with differents kinds of experiences and thus greatly add to the knowledge of developmental psychology. Conceivably, by spotting certain kinds of disturbed personalities it could prevent tragedies such as assassination attempts.

Thus a great deal of time, energy, and ingenuity has gone into the creation of personality tests. But the goal has been elusive. Although current personality tests are valuable, the ideal kinds of measures have not yet been devised. Personality is a composite of many elements—the product of a tangled and endless web of experiences beginning at birth, continuing throughout life, and unique for each individual—and the difficulties in measuring the elements are staggering.

The personality tests now in use, all of which have some virtues and many limitations, fall into three classes: 1) *objective tests,* 2) *situational tests,* and 3) *projective tests.*

T 1. I have certainly had more than my share of things to worry about.
cs 2. I think that I feel more intensely than other people do.
F 3. I have never done anything dangerous for the thrill of it.
T 4. I think nearly everyone would tell a lie to keep out of trouble.
T 5. I am happy most of the time.
F 6. I tend to be on my guard with people who are somewhat more friendly than I had expected.
T 7. My mother or father often made me obey even when I thought that it was unreasonable.
F 8. I feel uneasy indoors.
T 9. I refuse to play some games because I am not good at them.
cs 10. I find it hard to keep my mind on a task or job.

12-16

MMPI items

The Minnesota Multiphasic Personality Inventory is made up of statements like these, which the subject is asked to score as true, false, or "cannot say." (48)

Objective tests of personality. Not all tests of personality can meet the requirement of objectivity that was discussed at the beginning of the chapter; hence the name *objective tests* is applied to those that do meet the requirement. As the name indicates, these tests are administered and scored according to a standard procedure, and the results are not seriously affected by the opinions or prejudices of the examiner. They are group tests, given with paper and pencil, and usually their results have been standardized for large numbers of subjects.

The most widely used of the objective tests is the *Minnesota Multiphasic Personality Inventory,* called MMPI for short. The test is composed of nearly 600 statements like those shown in Figure 12-16; the subjects are asked to indicate whether the statements are true or untrue of their own behavior or to mark "cannot say." The method of scoring compares the subject's responses with those of other people, on whom the test has been standardized, known to have such personality traits as tendencies to pessimism and depression, anxiety over health, emotional excitability, delinquency, and tendencies toward schizophrenia and paranoia.

Situational tests. In a *situational test,* the examiner observes the behavior of the subject in a situation deliberately created to bring out certain aspects of personality. For example, subjects might be asked to carry out some difficult mechanical task with the assistance of "helpers" who are in fact stooges and who behave in an uncooperative and insulting fashion (49). Or subjects might be put through what is called a stress interview, in which the people asking the questions are deliberately hostile and pretend to disbelieve the answers (50).

12-17

What is happening here?

What kind of story does this picture tell? What led up to the situation? What is happening? How will events turn out? These are the questions asked about the pictures in the Thematic Apperception Test, to which this drawing is similar. You may want to try making up your own story before reading the discussion and the story made up by one subject, described in the text. (51)

One weakness of these tests is that it is difficult to know whether the situation actually seems real to the subjects and whether their motivation and behavior are the same as would occur in real life. Moreover, two different examiners watching a subject's behavior may reach different conclusions about it. Thus situational tests, though they may give valuable clues to personality traits, do not meet the four ideal test requirements of objectivity, standardization, reliability, and validity. They should be used and interpreted with caution.

Projective tests. The *projective test* can best be described in connection with Figure 12-17, which shows a picture similar to those presented to the subject in the *Thematic Apperception Test,* called TAT for short. The subject is asked to make up a story about the picture, telling what has led up to the scene, what is happening, and how events will turn out. The theory is that subjects will project some of their own personality traits into the pictures and that the stories they make up will reveal something about their own attitudes, feelings, motives, and anxieties. For example, there would appear to be a considerable amount of self-revelation in the following story told by one subject about the picture in Figure 12-17.

The older woman represents evil and she is trying to persuade the younger one to leave her husband and run off and lead a life of fun and gaiety. The younger one is afraid to do it—afraid of what others will think, afraid she will regret the action. But the older one knows that she wants to leave and so she insists over and over again. I am not sure how it ends. Perhaps the younger woman turns and walks away and ignores the older woman.

The TAT technique has found its most widespread and successful use in measuring the strength of the achievement motive (52). A tendency to invent stories that contain frequent and intense elements of striving and ambition—or that on the contrary show little concern with achievement—appears to be a better measure of this motive than the judgment of people who know the subjects well (53) or even the subjects' own assessment of their desire to achieve (54). Much of the research that has been done on the origin and operation of the achievement motive has been based on stories told about TAT pictures.

Another well-known example of a projective technique is the *Rorschach Test*, in which subjects are asked to tell what they see in a series of inkblots like the one illustrated in Figure 12-18. There are ten such blots, some in black-and-white and some in color, and ordinarily the subject sees twenty to forty different things in them. Answers are scored for a number of different dimensions. For example, a tendency to respond to the blot as a whole is considered to indicate that the subject thinks in terms of abstractions and generalities; a tendency to pick out many minor details that most people ignore may indicate an overconcern for detail.

Some more informal projective techniques are also frequently used in personality assessment (56). In a *word association test*, the examiner

12-18

What do you see here?

This is an inkblot like those used in the Rorschach Test. Subjects are asked to examine it and report everything they see. (55)

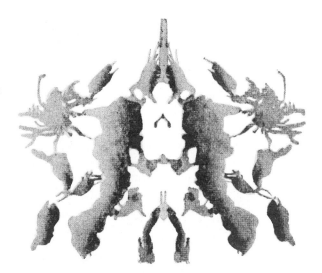

calls out a word, such as "mother" or "bad" or "money," and the subject is asked to respond as quickly as possible with the first word that comes to mind. The examiner notes the nature of the associations that the test words suggest and also the speed with which the subject responds; any unusual delay in responding is taken to indicate that the test word arouses some kind of conflict. In a *draw-a-person test*, the subject is simply asked to draw a picture of a person on a blank paper; the sex of the drawing, its size, the facial expression, and other characteristics may contain personality clues. In a *sentence-completion test*, the examiner gives the subject a series of partially completed sentences such as the following:

I sometimes feel ....
When by myself ....
When I was young ....

The subject is asked to complete the sentences with the first thoughts that come to mind. The responses, like the TAT stories, may suggest motives and conflicts.

Most projective tests require a high degree of skill and experience on the part of the person who gives and interprets them; even trained examiners may reach different conclusions. Aside from the TAT research into the achievement motive, they have been used mostly by clinical psychologists, who often find them a valuable and time-saving supplement to other methods of exploring the problems of patients.

Summary

1 To quality as scientifically sound a test should be:
  a *Objective*—meaning that the test can be given and scored in the same manner by any qualified person and that the results will be unaffected by the tester's personal opinions or prejudices.
  b *Reliable*—yielding similar scores when the same person is tested on different occasions.
  c *Valid*—found to measure the characteristics that it is supposed to measure.
  d *Standardized*—pretested on a large and representative sample so that an individual's score can be interpreted by comparison with the scores of other people.
2 Of particular value in interpreting test results are the following principles of *psychological statistics*:
  a The *normal curve of distribution*, which reflects the fact that intelligence and most other measurable traits are distributed among the population in a definite pattern, with most people at or near the average, some a fair distance below or above, and a few very far below or above.
  b The *standard deviation*, or *SD*, which makes it possible to deter-

mine how many scores will be found at any given distance below or above the average in the normal curve of distribution. About 68 percent of all scores lie between one *SD* below and one *SD* above the average.

    c *Percentiles*, which are a convenient way of expressing how an individual's score ranks in relation to the scores of all other people. A score on the 25th percentile means that the subject has done better than 25 percent of all people taking the test but that 75 percent have done as well or better. A score on the 75th percentile is better than 75 percent of all scores, while 25 percent of all scores are as good or better.

    d *Correlations*, which are a mathematical measure of the relationship between two events or scores, such as the relationship between score on an intelligence test and success in school. Correlations range between 0.00, showing no relationship, and 1.00, indicating a perfect relationship.

3 A *group test* can be given to many people at the same time. An *individual test* is given by a trained examiner to one person at a time.

4 An *aptitude test* measures the subject's capacity to learn a new skill. An *achievement test* measures the subject's present level of skill or knowledge.

5 *Intelligence tests* are aptitude tests that provide a measure of the subject's *intelligence quotient*, or *I.Q.* The intelligence quotient gets its name from the fact that it was originally determined by comparing children's *mental age* (as shown by their ability to pass the kinds of test items that could be passed by the average child of various ages) with their *chronological age* (or actual age).

6 For convenience, the I.Q. is now determined by applying psychological statistics. The individual's raw score on an intelligence test is compared with the scores of a standardization group of people the same age. An average raw score shows an I.Q. of 100; a score one standard deviation below average, 85; a score one standard deviation above average, 115.

7 All modern intelligence tests have a high degree of reliability and a correlation of around .40 to .60 with grades made in school.

8 Since intelligence tests must rely to a certain extent on the subject's present level of knowledge, they tend to favor people who have grown up in environments where they have had an opportunity to acquire the kinds of knowledge and language abilities typical of the middle and upper classes. Children from upper- and middle-class homes make higher average scores than children from lower-class homes; city children tend to make higher average scores than children from rural areas; and whites make higher average scores than blacks.

9 Intelligence can be defined as *the ability to profit from experience, to learn new information, and to adjust to new situations.*

10 According to Thurstone, intelligence is composed of seven *primary mental abilities* (verbal comprehension, word fluency, number, space, associative memory, perceptual speed, and general reasoning) plus a "general factor." Other investigators believe that intelligence is made up of as many as 120 different factors.

11 Studies of blood relatives and foster children have suggested that intelligence is determined partly by heredity and partly by environmental influences. The prevailing view among psychologists is that heredity sets a top and bottom limit on an individual's I.Q. and that environment then determines where within this range the score will actually fall.

12 Even when children remain in the same home environment, their I.Q. may show spontaneous changes over the years—sometimes as much as 50 points, upward or downward. The child's motivation for intellectual achievement seems to be closely related to these changes.

13 The 2.28 percent of the population with an I.Q. below 70 are described as *mentally retarded.* The 2.28 percent with an I.Q. above 130 are described as *mentally gifted.*

14 Tests designed to help people find the most suitable occupations include *vocational aptitude tests,* which measure the individual's ability to perform the various skills required in different kinds of jobs, and *interest tests,* which investigate what kinds of activities the subject likes or dislikes.

15 There are three classes of personality tests:
   a *Objective tests,* such as the Minnesota Multiphasic Personality Inventory.
   b *Situational tests,* in which the examiner observes the behavior of the subject in a situation deliberately created to reveal some aspect of the subject's personality.
   c *Projective tests,* such as the Thematic Apperception Test and the Rorschach Test, in which subjects supposedly insert or project aspects of their own personality into the stories they make up about ambiguous pictures or into the kinds of objects they see in inkblots. Other more informal types of projective techniques include *word association, draw-a-person,* and *sentence completion tests.*

Recommended reading

Anastasi, A. *Psychological testing,* 3rd ed. New York: Macmillan, 1968.

Brim, O. G., et al. *American beliefs and attitudes about intelligence.* New York: Russell Sage Foundation, 1969.

Butcher, H. J. *Human intelligence.* London: Methuen, 1970.

Cronbach, L. J. *Essentials of psychological testing.* 3rd ed. New York: Harper & Row, 1970.

Duncan, O. D., Featherman, D. L., and Duncan, B. *Socioeconomic background and achievement.* New York: Academic Press, 1972.

Garfield, S. L. *Clinical psychology*. Chicago: Aldine, 1974.

Jencks, C., et al. *Inequality*. New York: Basic Books, 1972.

Sattler, J. M. *The assessment of children's intelligence*. Philadelphia: W. B. Saunders, 1974.

Terman, L. M., and Oden, M. H. *The gifted child grows up*. Stanford, Calif.: Stanford University Press, 1947.

Vernon, P. E. *Personality assessment: a critical survey*. London: Tavistock, 1969.

EIGHT

THE CHILD, THE ADULT, AND SOCIETY

Previous chapters have been concerned mostly with the *individual*. Now, in the concluding section of this introduction to psychology, it is necessary to describe some of the ways in which the individual's mental processes and behavior are dependent on other people.

In the poet John Donne's famous words, "No man is an island." We human beings do not live in isolation. Even if we know a great deal about how we as individuals learn, use language, think and solve problems, sense and perceive the world, acquire our emotions and motives, and become unique personalities, our knowledge is still incomplete. We must go on to view ourselves as one person among many—a member of society, constantly interacting with the other members of society.

The final section of the book contains two chapters. Chapter 13, on developmental psychology, describes the manner in which we are influenced from the cradle on by many complex interactions with other people—at first our parents, later our teachers and schoolmates. Chapter 14, on social psychology, explains how our behavior as adults is influenced by other people and by society—to an extent that people who have never taken a psychology course would find it difficult even to imagine.

Developmental psychology

ore than 300 years ago the poet John Milton wrote these
words:

> The childhood shows the man,
> As morning shows the day.

Psychology has shown that Milton was right, at least in part. Studies
of children—especially studies in which the same individuals have
been observed from the time they were babies until they were adults—
have demonstrated that some of the behavior and personality traits of
the adult can indeed be traced to events and influences in childhood,
particularly those occurring during the first ten years. Note, for example, the following reports written by two different trained observers
about the same person, the first when he was a child, the second when
he was a young adult.

Peter X, Age 3½

Babyish in appearance. . . . He showed extreme caution and would back
away from any situation that smacked of danger. When threatened he
would shake his head, clasp his hands, and beg in a frantic tone, "No, no,
no." His role with peers was a sedentary, passive and shrinking one. He
stayed out of the swirl of activities of the other children. . . . With the
staff of the nursery school he was highly conforming and very dependent.
He liked to clean up, liked to wash, liked to take a nap. . . . Whenever he
dirtied something, wet himself, or committed what he regarded as a violation, he became very tense and apprehensive, as if he felt that he had
been a bad boy.

Peter X, Age 21

He was frail of build and spoke in a soft and high-pitched voice. When
interviewed he often meditated for several minutes before answering, and
there was a prevailing air of caution and insecurity in his manner. He
had decided to teach English at a high school. Although he was primarily
interested in teaching at a college, he was afraid to begin there because
he doubted his ability. . . . He admired all his high school and college
teachers and retained a dependent tie to them. . . . He did not want to
marry until he was financially secure, and he had serious doubts about
his ability to support a family. He felt tense and uncomfortable when
with girls and he preferred not to date. Sexual behavior was still a source

Achieving child to achieving adult: Shirley Temple Black as movie star and U.S. Ambassador

Lee Harvey Oswald: a difficult adult who had a difficult childhood.

of fear. . . . He had few friends and most of his leisure was spent alone. Because he felt tense with strange people, he avoided clubs and social groups. If someone irritated him, he walked away; and he rarely insulted or became sarcastic with anyone. With his parents he was close and conforming, and he enjoyed talking over his problems with them. Fearing a feeling of isolation from his family, he had decided to attend a college close to his home (1).

The case of Peter X is extreme, showing an unusually high degree of consistency between the behavior of the child and the behavior of the adult. As will be seen a little later, the human organism is quite resilient and capable of constructive growth. Therefore people may change to a remarkable extent as they grow from infant to child to adolescent to adult. But the case of Peter X suggests that behavior patterns formed in childhood may often help determine whether adults will be dependent or independent, passive or aggressive, shy or friendly. Childhood experiences may also help determine goals, philosophy of life, feelings about marriage, and behavior as parents.

Developmental psychology is the study of the processes by which children gradually acquire patterns of overt behavior, thinking, and problem solving, as well as the emotions, motives, conflicts, and ways of coping with conflicts that will go to make up their adult personalities. For many reasons, developmental psychology is one of the most important and most rapidly growing branches of the science. For one thing, it is virtually impossible to understand adult behavior and the social problems that it often creates without knowing something about developmental psychology. Moreover, developmental psychology points the way to understanding individual children, finding successful methods of rearing them, and handling the difficulties inherent in child rearing.

At this particular period in American history, when there is a strong move toward establishing day-care centers for the children of mothers who are interested in work and careers, developmental psychology can help evaluate such centers and point the way toward operating them most effectively. It also offers what is perhaps the best hope for relieving the psychological problems that now plague so many people in our society—problems such as alcoholism, drug addiction, crime, suicidal depression, and schizophrenia. All these problems when found in established form among adults are difficult to treat and eliminate. But clinical studies of disturbed people and criminals have indicated that their difficulties often began in childhood. Thus developmental psychology may eventually lead to methods of preventing these difficulties or dealing with them more successfully in their early stages.

Individual differences at birth

The human baby, as one group of developmental psychologists has put it, is a "remarkably capable organism" from the moment the very first breath is drawn (2). All normal babies are sensitive from birth to stimuli in their environments and respond to these stimuli with a rather wide

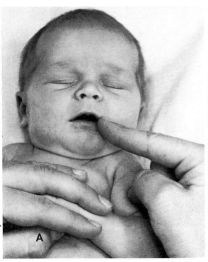
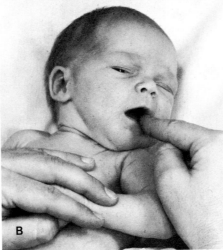
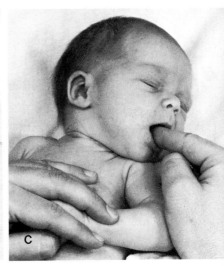

13-1

The newborn's "rooting response"

When the side of an infant's mouth is tickled (A), the reflex response is to turn the head toward the stimulus (B) and then try to suck the finger (C), as if it were a source of food.

range of inborn reflex behavior. Newborn babies can feel, smell, hear, and see. Indeed babies only two hours old will follow a moving light with their eyes. When the sides of their mouths are tickled, they display the reflex illustrated in Figure 13-1—the "rooting response" that enables them to find food at the mother's breast. If the sole of the foot is gently pricked with a pin, they draw the foot away as shown in Figure 13-2—a reflex that results in escape from pain. They display such other protective behavior as closing the eyelids if a bright light is flashed or if the eye is gently touched with a piece of cotton.

Yet, though these "remarkably capable" little creatures are alike in that all normal babies are aware of their environments and can respond to them, it soon becomes apparent that they differ in many ways in their sensitivity and reactions to stimuli. Indeed their interactions with their environments seem to ge governed by what can be called differences in temperament—and these differences, apparently inborn, often tend to persist into later life.

13-2

Reflex escape from pain

When the sole of the infant's foot is touched with a pin, the reflex response is to pull the foot away from the offending stimulus.

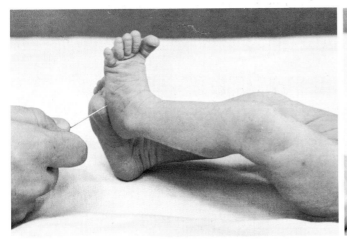
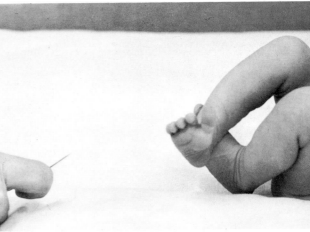

Sensory thresholds and adaptation

Some babies respond with muscular reflexes to a very gentle stroking of the skin; others do not respond unless the stroking is fairly firm. Some display what is called a startle reaction to sounds or light flashes of rather low intensity, others only when the intensity is quite high. The threshold for pain also seems to vary; for example, one study showed that newborn girls responded to mild electrical stimulation of the toe more readily than did boys (3).

When a sound loud enough to produce the startle pattern is repeated over a period of time, some babies quickly adapt and stop responding. Other babies have been found to react with the startle pattern even on the thirtieth presentation of the sound (4).

Similarly, some babies appear to become "bored" with a stimulus more quickly than others. If a series of pictures of the human face is projected on a screen above their cribs, some infants will keep paying close attention for a long time. Others will soon stop looking, as if they have quickly tired of such a repetitive stimulus (5).

Activity and irritability

Even among very young babies, it has been found, some are much more active than others. They move their arms and legs with considerable force, tend to be restless when asleep, suck vigorously when nursing, and appear to have above-average appetites. As they get a little older they tend to make loud noises when they babble, to bang their toys together, and to kick at the sides of their cribs. Other babies are much more placid in all these respects (6).

Another important difference among infants is what for lack of a more precise word might be called irritability. Some babies begin to fret, whine, or cry at the slightest provocation. Once they begin to fret, they often work themselves up into what looks like a temper tantrum and soon are bellowing at the top of their lungs. Other babies do not fret unless their discomfort or pain is quite intense. Even then, they may fret only for a half minute or so, then stop, as if they have some kind of mechanism that inhibits the buildup of extreme upset (7).

Differences in temperament

One group of investigators, on the basis of a study of more than one hundred children observed from birth to past the age of ten, has concluded that the individual differences point to the existence of three distinct patterns of temperament. In the investigators' sample, about 40 percent of the subjects were identified soon after birth as "easy" children—quite regular in their eating and sleeping habits, generally cheerful, and quick to adapt to new schedules, foods, and people. About 15 percent were classed as "slow to warm up"; these children tended to withdraw from their first exposure to a new experience, seemed to be somewhat negative in mood, and displayed a low level of activity. Another 10 percent were classed as "difficult" children; these were

13-3

Three types of childhood temperaments

The three types of children—"easy," "slow to warm up," and "difficult"—have been found to differ most strikingly in the characteristics listed in the table. As discussed in the text, babies have been found to display these characteristics of temperament as early as the age of two or three months and to retain them into later childhood.

		CHARACTERISTICS		
Type of child	Regularity (of hunger, sleep, excretion)	Approach or withdrawal (in presence of a new object or person)	Intensity of responses	Mood (pleasant and joyful as contrasted with unpleasant and unfriendly)
"Easy"	Very regular	Active approach	Low or moderate	Positive
"Slow to warm up"	Varies	Partial withdrawal	Low	Slightly negative
"Difficult"	Irregular	Withdrawal	Intense	Negative

13-4

A contrast between three-month-olds

The top strip of photos shows the eager and positive responses of a three-month-old girl being fed a new kind of cereal for the first time. The bottom strip shows the very different reactions of the girl's younger brother when he was introduced to the same new cereal at the same age. Even at this early age, these babies from the same family displayed far different temperaments.

quite irregular in sleeping and eating habits, very slow in adjusting to new experiences, quite negative in mood, and given to unusually intense reactions, such as loud laughter, frequent loud crying, and temper tantrums. The remaining 35 percent of subjects showed mixtures of these various traits and did not fall into any general classification (8).

The most pronounced differences found among "easy," "slow to warm up," and "difficult" children are listed in Figure 13-3. A photographic record of the positive response of an "easy" child to an experience with a new kind of food—as contrasted with the negative response of a child with a "difficult" temperament—is shown in Figure 13-4. Note that the two children shown responding in such different fashion in Figure 13-4 are sister and brother—a fact that is in keeping with the investigators' finding that differences in temperament among infants do not reflect their parents' personalities or child-rearing methods. The differences appear to be inborn rather than acquired.

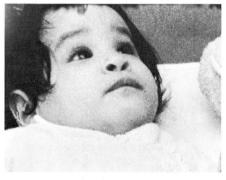 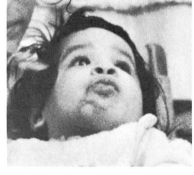 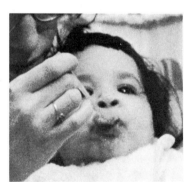

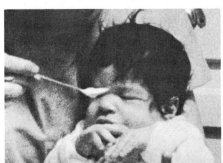  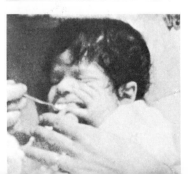

Inborn differences and later life

Follow-up observations of the children who displayed one of the three different types of temperaments showed that the differences tended to persist over the years; most of the subjects identified as "easy" children at two or three months were still cheerful and adaptable at the age of ten, while most of the "difficult" children were still irregular in their habits, negative in mood, and intense in their reactions. How they got along in general in later childhood, however, proved to depend as much on their environments as on their inborn traits.

One of the conclusions reached by the investigators was that the three types of children require very different treatment at home and at school. "Easy" children thrive under almost any kind of treatment in early childhood—but, having adapted so well to the home environment, they may have trouble when their school and schoolmates make different demands. "Slow to warm up" children require considerable patience. They do their best when encouraged to try new experiences but to adapt at their own pace. Too much pressure heightens their natural inclination to withdraw.

"Difficult" children present a special kind of problem. Because of their irregular habits, their resistance to adjustment, their negative attitude, and their boisterousness, they are likely to be found hard to live with by both their parents and later their teachers. But any attempt to force them to behave like other children is only likely to make them more negative and difficult than ever. It requires exceptional understanding and tolerance on the part of their parents to bring them around —slowly and gradually—to obeying the rules and getting along with other individuals.

What developmental psychology has learned about individual differences present at birth can be of inestimable value to parents, the staffs of day-care centers, and schoolteachers, especially in the early grades. In the past, it was generally assumed that all children were more or less alike—or at least that their behavior *should* be alike. The new findings show that, on the contrary, even infants in their cribs are individuals who require individual treatment if they are to attain their maximum potential.

Maturation and environment

In the early development of newborn children, one important factor is *maturation*—the physical changes, taking place after birth, that continue the biological development of the organism from fertilized egg cell to complete adult. Babies mature physically. Their nervous systems become more efficient. Almost day by day, simply as the result of growing older, they become capable of new accomplishments. Yet environmental factors also play a part. In many ways, the environment can speed the maturation process or slow it down. The progress of babies as they grow toward adulthood represents an interaction between their inborn characteristics, gradually blossoming through maturation, and the effect of their experiences.

Physical development

Of all the ways in which children develop after birth, the easiest of all to measure is growth in size and in skill at motor performance. Many studies have been made of physical development, and there is considerable literature from which parents can learn the normal standards for height and weight at all ages from birth on and for the occurrence of such events as crawling, the first step, and other motor skills.

The bodies of newborn babies grow, as shown in Figure 13-5, from all head and tiny legs into quite different adult proportions. The skeleton, which at birth is largely composed of rather soft and pliable cartilage, hardens into bone. The muscle fibers, though they do not increase in number, grow until they eventually weigh about forty times as much as they weighed at birth. Nerve fibers grow and form additional connections to other fibers, and some of them develop protective sheaths that make them faster and more efficient conductors of nervous impulses. The brain, in particular, grows in size and weight—very rapidly during the first two years, then more slowly until adulthood.

13-5
Development of body proportions

Newborn babies have a disproportionately large head and short legs; the head makes up a fourth of the total height, the legs only about a third. From birth to maturity the legs grow the most, to half the total height; and the head grows the least, becoming only a tenth of the total height. (9)

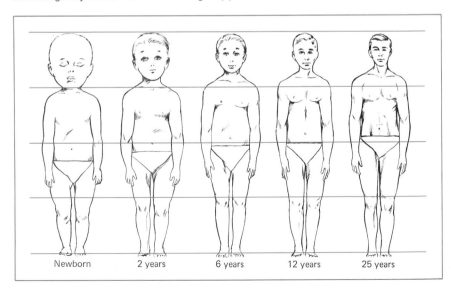

| Newborn | 2 years | 6 years | 12 years | 25 years |

Fetal posture **(Newborn)**

Chin up **(1 month)**

Chest up **(2 months)**

Reach **(3 months)**

Sit with help **(4 months)**

Sit on lap, grasp object
(5 months)

Sit in high chair, grasp
dangling object **(6 months)**

Sit alone **(7 months)**

Stand with help **(8 months)**

Stand holding furniture
(9 months)

Creep **(10 months)**

Walk with help
(11 months)

Pull up **(12 months)**

Climb **(13 months)**

Stand alone **(14 months)**

Walk alone **(15 months)**

13-6

From birth to first step

From birth to first step the
child goes through a number of
stages of gradually increasing
motor ability. The ages indicate
the average age at which each
stage of development occurs. (10)

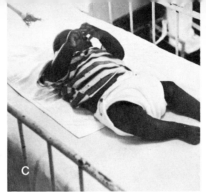
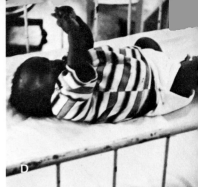

13-7

First attempts at reaching

How soon do babies develop the desire and ability to grasp a bright toy held over the crib? Very young babies, typically lying with neck muscles holding the head to one side (A), pay only slight attention. Later they occasionally watch the hand that is extended to the side toward which the head is turned (B). At this stage they will glance at the toy when it is held on that side but focus on it for only five to ten seconds at a time. Older babies (about three and a half months, as at the right) no longer hold the head to the side and may move their hands in unison. When the toy is held directly above, they clasp their hands together beneath it (C). A little later they begin to raise their clasped hands toward the object (D). This is the final preliminary stage before they actually reach toward the object with an open hand and attempt to grasp it. (11)

Even in the womb unborn babies begin to use their muscles; their movements can usually be felt in about the twentieth week of pregnancy. After birth their muscles of posture, creeping, and standing develop as shown in Figure 13-6, to the point where they are able to walk alone by about the age of fifteen months. Their skill at using their hands and fingers also increases rapidly. At first they cannot reach out and grab objects held in their visual fields, but they gradually begin to reach for them as shown in Figure 13-7. Their ability to grasp objects develops as shown in Figure 13-8. The ability to vocalize, which is also partly a motor skill, appears very early. As was explained on pages 124–25, babies

13-8

Development of grasping ability

Studies made with a motion picture camera showed this sequence of development in the baby's ability at *prehension* — or grasping. The ages in weeks indicate the average age at which each stage is reached. (12)

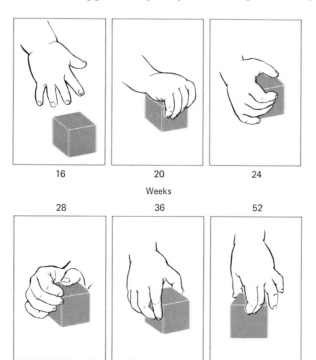

16   20   24

Weeks

28   36   52

begin to utter some of the basic sounds of language in their very first few days of life.

The role of maturation

In performing such physical feats as sitting alone or walking, maturation is the crucial factor. These feats also require some learning, of course, but the learning is impossible until maturation has provided the necessary muscular and nervous structures. Attempts to push children into performing far beyond their level of maturation are futile and may have harmful effects (13).

Maturation also controls many other aspects of development. It has been found, for example, that children all over the world tend to display various skills at about the same average age. They smile when they see a human face at about four months, show vocal excitement to a new voice at nine months, search for a hidden object that they saw being covered by a piece of cloth at about twelve months. Children six months old cannot speak because their brains have not matured sufficiently. By the time they have reached the age of eighteen months they have attained sufficient maturity and speech becomes possible.

The role of environment

In all forms of development, however, environment also plays a part. An environment that encourages infants to perform skills—though without forcing them—is likely to produce the appearance of these skills at an earlier age. An environment that restrains the infant is likely to delay their appearance. Thus infants whose parents talk to them a great deal may themselves begin speaking when they are only twelve to eighteen months old. Infants with less encouragement may not start talking until the age of two or even later. Skill at such cognitive tasks as remembering long lists of objects develops much earlier in societies that consider such activities important for young children than in societies that consider them unimportant.

On the matter of motor skills, the early environment does not seem to have any lasting effect. Certainly there seems to be no lasting impairment of motor development among babies brought up by Indian mothers who carry them about strapped to a board or by Russian mothers who keep them tightly bound in swaddling clothes (see Figure 13-9). In this connection, a study made in an isolated Indian village in Guatemala is pertinent. In this primitive community, babies are kept inside the family's windowless hut for most of the first year of life, in the belief that sunlight, air, and the stares of certain people will cause sickness. The babies seldom have an opportunity to crawl on the floor of the hut or practice creeping or walking, and their parents seldom play with them. When they emerge from the hut, they are behind American children in physical skills. But they soon catch up, once they have the

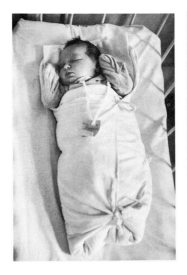 

13-9

Does swaddling inhibit motor development?

Russian babies are still bound tightly in swaddling clothes (left), a custom that was also popular at one time in the United States but has long since been abandoned in favor of greater freedom of movement. Yet Russian children appear to walk as soon and as well as any others and may grow up with the motor skills and physical grace of the girls in the Leningrad ballet class shown at right.

opportunity to practice, and become as well coordinated physically as any other children (14).

How resilient is the "neglected child"?

As to whether other types of development can be permanently retarded by an unfavorable early environment, this is one of the key unresolved questions in psychology. Put another way, the question becomes: What chance does the "neglected child" of our society have to develop into a normal adult? If children grow up in an environment that retards rather than encourages their progress, are they doomed to be ineffective and unhappy throughout life? Or do they have a chance to throw off their early handicaps?

Many of the first studies bearing on this problem produced pessimistic results. In the animal world, it was found that monkeys raised in isolation grew up with many symptoms of maladjustment. They were unfriendly, aggressive, and sexually incompetent (15). Among human babies who had severely deprived childhoods, many lasting effects of deprivation were observed (16). One investigator made a study of children who had spent the first three years of their lives in the impersonal atmosphere of an orphanage, then had gone on to foster homes. Later these children were compared with a control group of children of the same age and sex who had been brought up from the very start in foster homes, where presumably they received considerably more care and encouragement than was possible in an institution. Even after some years had passed, the orphanage children were found to be notably more aggressive, with strong tendencies to have temper tantrums, to kick and hit other children, and to lie, steal, and destroy property. They tended to be emotionally cold, isolated, and incapable of forming affectionate personal relationships (17).

The resilient monkeys. A number of recent studies, however, have produced quite different findings. A new experiment was performed in which monkeys were placed, shortly after birth, in black boxes in which they remained in total isolation until they were six months old. When they emerged from the boxes, their behavior was decidedly abnormal. They were then permitted to associate with other younger monkeys, just half their age, who had developed normal social behaviors. Within a few weeks the "black box" monkeys began to improve and after six months they seemed almost completely normal (18).

Some resilient children. Human subjects have also been found to display some remarkable ability to bounce back from the numbing effects of an unstimulating early environment. In the study of Guatemalan Indians, for example, it was found that the babies restricted to the dark huts for most of the first year were in many ways severely retarded, by the standards of other societies, at the age of two. But by adolescence they appeared to have recovered. They were lively and alert—and on certain tests of perception and memory as intelligent as most children that age.

A Czechoslovakian psychologist has reported the case of twin boys who spent most of the six years of their lives under the most cruelly inhuman circumstances imaginable. They lived with a mentally subnormal father and an apparently psychopathic stepmother who totally excluded them from the family circle. They were never permitted outside the house but were kept in the cellar or in a small closet. None of the other children in the family was permitted to talk to them. Thus they grew up in almost total isolation except for their own company.

When the case was discovered, the twins looked more like three-year-olds than six-year-olds. They were barely able to walk or speak. They were so retarded, in fact, that it was impossible to test their intelligence. Yet, after they were moved to a favorable environment, they soon began to make progress. By the time they were eleven, their I.Q.s were about average and their social and emotional development also appeared to be normal (19).

A final word on resilience. Though the evidence seems on the surface to be conflicting, perhaps one can draw the following conclusion. Human infants are extremely impressionable and their environment has a profound effect on their development from the moment they are born. A highly unfavorable environment can produce drastic damage. But infants are also resilient and malleable, that is, capable of changing under changed circumstances. Under the proper conditions for growth, early handicaps can sometimes be overcome.

Intellectual development

As infants grow into children they display marked advances in their intellectual development—that is, their increased ability to remember past experiences, to make inferences, and to solve problems. Even very

The design to be scanned

Three-year-old

Six-year-old

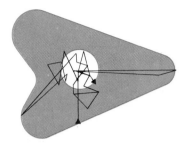

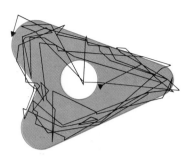

13-10

Age differences in perceptual scanning

When children were asked to try to remember the design at the left, a typical three-year-old scanned the design with the rather simple eye movements shown at center, a typical six-year-old with the much more complex and efficient eye movements at the right. (22)

young children have remarkably good memories. In one experiment, for example, three-year-olds were asked to learn an association between pairs of pictures that were presented together (a variation on the paired word list often used in experiments with adults). It took them longer to learn the pairs initially than older children—but when their memory for the pairs was tested a week later, they did just as well as six-year-olds or nine-year-olds (20). In another experiment three-year-olds watched while five different toys were placed under five boxes of different shapes and colors. The boxes were then hidden by a screen for a few seconds, after which the children were asked to find one of the toys—a doll, for example. Most of the three-year olds were able to remember which box covered the toy they were asked to find, indicating that they could keep track of five different objects without difficulty (21).

Progress in perception and language

The growth of intellectual ability involves many factors. One is improvement in the process of perception. Children begin to know what to search for in the environment and how to go about it. They develop strategies for seeking important information and ignoring the irrelevant. Their attention becomes more selective and they are able to maintain it over a longer time span. Their scanning of the environment becomes more systematic and orderly.

Some of these differences in perception can be observed by making records of children's eye movements, as shown in Figure 13-10. Asked to look at and remember an unfamiliar design, three-year-olds do not yet know how to extract a maximum of information. They tend to keep their eyes fixed on a single spot for a rather long time and may never get around to all the details. Six-year-olds, however, scan the entire design with rapid and quite extensive eye movements, paying particular attention to the contour line that determines its shape. Children also become more adept at perceiving details (23) and in organizing them into meaningful patterns. Looking at the drawing shown at the left, a three-year-old child is unlikely to perceive the dashes as a rabbit. The child of seven or eight recognizes the rabbit at once.

463

Another important factor in intellectual development is a growing adeptness at the understanding and use of language, as was discussed on pages 124–28. In turn, the increasing skill at language facilitates the formation of concepts, which are so important in intellectual development that they deserve discussion of their own.

Acquiring concepts

Children begin to acquire concepts, such as the concept of animal for four-legged living creatures, at a rather early age, perhaps as young as a year and a half. Then, as they grow older, their concepts become broader and move inclusive. For example, the concept of animal may at first include only dogs and cats—but later it is expanded to include other creatures as well. At the same time, the concepts of growing children also become more precise and differentiated. The general concept of animal is broken down into more specific concepts such as pets and nonpets, tame animals and wild.

Children increasingly use concepts as a strategy for organizing new information and storing it in memory. In one study demonstrating this fact, the experimenters used a set of twenty-four pictures that fell into four categories of six pictures each. One category was means of transportation, in which the pictures showed an automobile, bicycle, boat, bus, train, and truck; the other categories were animals, furniture, and clothing. The pictures were spread out on a table in a random arrangement, and the subjects, who were children from the first through the sixth grades, were told that they would have three minutes to study them, during which time they could move them around or do anything else that might help them remember what they had seen. They were not told about the categories. The question was whether the children would of their own accord use the strategy of rearranging the pictures into categories as an aid to learning—and also whether they would tend to recall them in clusters determined by the concepts of means of transportation, animals, furniture, and clothing.

The results of the experiment are shown in Figure 13-11. None of the

13-11

Development of use of concepts

The graph lines show the results of an experiment, described in the text, in which children tried to remember objects they had seen in pictures that could be organized in categories determined by the concepts of means of transportation, animals, furniture, and clothing. The black line demonstrates the tendency to rearrange the pictures into categories, from zero among first-graders to a rather high level among sixth-graders. The colored line demonstrates a similar increase in the tendency to recall the objects in clusters dictated by the concepts.

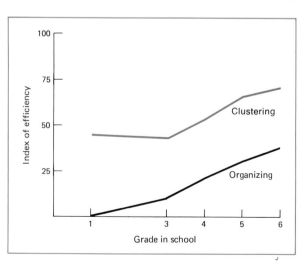

first-graders and only a few of the third-graders rearranged the pictures into categories. Starting with the fourth-graders, however, there was a rapidly increasing tendency to use concepts as a strategy for organizing the pictures into groups and to recall the objects in clusters (24). Other studies have shown that the increasing ability to use concepts in memorizing is correlated with improvement in solving various kinds of problems (25, 26).

Piaget's theory of intellectual development

Piaget

The most influential student of intellectual development is the Swiss psychologist Jean Piaget, who has spent a half-century observing the behavior of his own and other children as they grew from infancy through adolescence. Piaget has concluded that mental growth is basically an increased ability to adapt to new situations and that this growth takes place because of two key processes that he calls *assimilation* and *accommodation*. Assimilation is the process of incorporating a new stimulus into one's existing cognitive view of the world; accommodation is changing one's cognitive view and behavior when new information dictates such a change.

As a simple example, consider a young boy who has a number of toys. To these familiar old toys we add a new one, a magnet. The boy's initial impulse will be to assimilate the new toy into his existing knowledge of other toys; he may try to bang it like a hammer, throw it like a ball, or blow it like a horn. But once he learns that the magnet has a new and unprecedented quality—the power to attract metal—he accommodates his view of toys to include this previously unfamiliar fact. He now behaves on the revised assumption that some toys are not designed to bang, throw, or make noise with but to attract metal.

There is always tension, Piaget has concluded, between assimilation (which in essence represents the use of old ideas to meet new situations) and accommodation (which in essence is a change of old ideas to meet new situations). And it is the resolution of this tension that results in intellectual growth. Piaget believes that the growth takes place in a series of stages, in each of which the child thinks and behaves in quite different fashion than earlier. He maintains that the child grows intellectually not like a leaf, which simply gets larger every day, but like a caterpillar that is eventually transformed into a butterfly. The various stages and approximate ages at which they occur have been charted by Piaget as follows (27).

Sensorimotor stage (birth to age two). During this stage most children have not yet learned to use symbols and language to represent the objects and events in their environments. According to Piaget, they know the world only in terms of their sensorimotor interactions with it—that is, their own sensations, their movements, and the results of their movements. By the age of four to six months, children have started to operate on their environments. They will repeatedly kick at toys hang-

ing over their cribs, apparently to make them swing and thus produce a change of stimulus that they find "interesting." By the age of twelve months they act as if they know that objects are permanent and do not mysteriously disappear. If a toy is shown to them and then is hidden behind two pillows side by side in the crib, they know how to find it. They look first behind one of the pillows; if the toy is not there, they will then look behind the other.

Preoperational stage (two to seven). In this stage the ability to use symbols begins to dominate the development of intellectual ability. As the use of language increases, children begin to attach new meanings to the stimuli in their environments and to use one stimulus to stand as a symbol for another. They may behave toward a doll as if it were a real child and toward a stick as if it were a gun.

By the age of four concepts have become more elaborate, but they are still based largely on the evidence of the senses. Children can learn, for example, to select the middle-sized of three rubber balls. They have attained what Piaget has called an *intuitive understanding* that the middle-sized ball is bigger than the small one but smaller than the big one. But if three balls of very different size from the original three are then shown, they must learn to make the selection all over again (28). Until about the age of seven they are fooled by the puzzle illustrated in Figure 13-12. Apparently the height of the jar is such an outstanding characteristic that they cannot help equating height with the number of beans the jar contains.

13-12

A preschool puzzle

The four-year-old child points to both of the squat jars to acknowledge that they contain an equal number of beans. But when the beans are poured from one of these jars into a tall, thin jar, he says that the tall jar then contains more beans. Not until he is around seven years old will he state that the number of beans remains the same.

Stage of concrete operations (seven to eleven). For the typical American child, this stage begins some time between the ages of six and eight. For children who grow up in isolated and less modern societies, it may begin somewhat later. It is characterized by the fact that children now possess a set of rules, not previously available to them, that help them adapt to their environments. They now know, for example, that if A is as heavy as B, and B is as heavy as C, then A and C must be equal in weight. They also have acquired considerable sophistication in the use of concepts and categories. They realize, for example, that "all the pets that are dogs" plus "all the pets that are not dogs" go to make up a category called "all pets." They also realize that objects or attributes can

belong to more than one concept; they know that animals can be tame or wild, and can also be furry or feathered.

Piaget has conducted many experiments demonstrating the intellectual conquests that children achieve in the stage of concrete operations. One of them is becoming aware that the number of beans does not change in the experiment that was shown in Figure 13-12. They have discovered the important principle of *conservation* — that is, the fact that such qualities as mass, number, weight, and volume remain constant regardless of changes in appearance. If asked why the tall jar and the short jar contain an equal amount, they may say, "Well, this one is taller, but this one is fatter." A little later their explanation may become more sophisticated: "If you poured the beans from the tall jar into the other jar, then it would still be the same."

Thus children in the stage of concrete operations show an ability to reason logically about objects and to apply rules. But as Piaget's name for the stage implies, they seem to reason more effectively about objects that they can see or feel than about verbal statements. Suppose, for example, that children of this age are asked: "A is the same size as B, but B is smaller than C; which is bigger, A or C?" They may not be able to answer — for this question requires the manipulation of pure language rather than concrete objects.

Stage of formal operations (beginning at about ten or eleven). In this stage children can reason not only about actual objects and events but about things that "might be." They can assume hypothetical conditions and make correct inferences about them. They are no longer merely preoccupied with all the ramifications of what is real and concrete. Instead they are able to deal with the possible and the abstract — and they enjoy it. In Piaget's words, "Thought takes wings."

Adolescents can determine the logical validity of a statement such as this, "If X or Y leads to Z then it is false to assume that if Y does not occur Z will not occur." They can deal with hypothetical questions such as: "If all unicorns have yellow feet and I have yellow feet, am I a unicorn?" (They can examine the logic and quickly answer, "No.")

Children in the stage of formal operations are less likely to waste their time with trial and error techniques. Instead, they use abstract strategies. They examine their premises and beliefs systematically, searching for consistencies or inconsistencies. They approach problems with some definite plan, try to think of all the possible solutions, and reexamine their thinking to make sure that they have indeed exhausted all the possibilities. Moreover, their thinking is what might be called "self-conscious." They think about their thoughts and are curious to learn how these thoughts are organized and where they will lead.

There are of course individual differences in the ages at which children attain the various stages described by Piaget. There is evidence, however, that the progression of stages holds true for all children — even children of different nationalities and regardless of what kinds of education they have had (29). There is also evidence that it is impossible to hurry children from one stage to another by trying to teach them the reasoning skills appropriate to a more advanced period (30). It appears that children can only understand experiences and pieces of information that match what they already know about vocabulary, facts, and rules—or that are just a bit in advance of their existing information and cognitive skills. If a new experience or idea has no readily apparent connection with what they already know, they are not likely to learn much if anything about it. Indeed they may not even pay attention to it.

Personality development— birth to eighteen months

As with intellectual development, the development of relations to people and of motives and emotions—processes that we call personality—also seems to progress in an orderly way. As babies grow from the crib to the age where they can move about, then to the preschool age, and finally into schoolchildren interacting closely with their classmates and teachers, they enter into new and widening circles of influence. Their changing social experiences, going hand in hand with their increasing intellectual development, mold their personalities in many different ways, for better or for worse. By the age of ten, many personality traits have become established in a way that is likely to persist into adult life—though the traits are still subject to change if the environment changes because of the continuing resilience and malleability of the human organism.

During the first eighteen months of life, personality development is based largely on the variety of experiences encountered and on the establishment of attachment to the person or persons who are the main sources of interaction, comfort, and care. Usually this person is the mother. It can, however, be someone else—the father, a grandparent, a babysitter, or a day care teacher who takes care of the baby's first needs.

The importance of attachment

Much psychological thinking about the very earliest development of attachment stems from a famous series of experiments by Harry F. Harlow, who took baby monkeys from their own mothers and placed them with doll-like objects that he called "surrogate mothers." As is shown in Figure 13-13, Harlow gave his baby monkeys two such surrogate mothers. One was made of wire, with a bottle and nipple from which the monkey received milk. The other was made of sponge rubber and terrycloth; it was an object to which the baby monkey could cling.

As the photographs show, the baby monkeys had a strong tendency to prefer the terrycloth doll to the wire doll; indeed they clung to the terrycloth mother even when feeding from the other. Note particularly that when a new object was placed in the cage, they clung to the terrycloth mother while making their first hesitant and tentative attempts to discover what this strange and at first frightening object might be (31). Ob-

13-13

Baby monkey and "surrogate mothers"

The baby monkey has been taken from its own mother and placed with two "surrogate mothers." Note how it clings to the terrycloth mother, even when feeding from the wire mother and especially when exploring a new and unfamiliar object that has been placed in the cage.

viously there was something about the terrycloth surrogate that provided the baby monkey with what in human terms would be called comfort, protection, and a kind of secure base from which new aspects of the environment could be explored.

The tendency to stay close to the terrycloth mother and to be more secure in its presence defines what is meant by "attachment." The term *attachment* refers to the human infant's tendency, during the first two years of life, to approach particular people, to be maximally receptive to care from those people, and to be least afraid when in the presence of those people. Human babies, like monkeys, also seem to be born with a kind of innate tendency to become attached to the adults who care for them. They show a strong preference to approach those people who have served as continuous caretakers. This preference is particularly noticeable when they are bored, frightened, or in some kind of distress.

Babies can display attachment toward more than one person—as toward both a mother and father who have frequently ministered to their needs. But usually there is a preference for one caretaker above any others. This has been shown in a study of infants who spent much of their time—twenty to forty hours a week—in a day care center. Each of the infants was placed in a room with the mother, a stranger, and the day care teacher with whom the baby had had many very pleasant experiences at the center. Then an event was arranged that caused the infant to become slightly uncertain and insecure. Invariably, the baby sought comfort from the mother—not from the day care teacher, despite all the close interactions of the past (32).

Attachment versus love

The attachment of the very young baby, however flattering it may be to the adult to whom it is directed, is not to be confused with the love an older child has for a parent. The attachment is the expression of some kind of inherited pattern of behavior and does not necessarily predict the kind of love children may display later. For example, a baby girl may grow to the age of five without ever having seen her father. Then he joins her and she realizes that he values and cares for her. She may

469

quickly attain a very close relationship with him — indeed a love relationship — without any prior attachment to him during her infancy.

Attachment and exploration

The importance of attachment is unquestioned. For one thing, it helps children seek nurturance and protection from distress and dangers, real or imagined. But if the infant's tendency to remain closely attached to the parents prevailed completely, children would never outgrow their dependency on their caretakers. They would never learn to adapt to their environments. For, to become self-sufficient, they must also begin to satisfy their needs for stimulus change (pages 316–18) by venturing away from the caretakers' protection. They must begin to explore the environment, encounter new objects and new experiences, and learn how to cope with them.

The photograph on page 469 of the baby monkey cautiously examining a new object while clinging to its surrogate mother provides one indication of how attachment and exploration work hand in hand. Among wild monkeys, it has been observed, the baby and its real mother seem almost to work as a team in this respect. At first the baby clings constantly to the mother. Later it ventures off a short distance to explore its environment and play with other young monkeys — but always with one eye on the mother, so to speak, as a haven to which it can scurry back at the first sign of danger. At the same time, the mother keeps an anxious watch on the baby, ready to haul it back if it starts getting in trouble. With increasing age the baby becomes more and more daring and the mother more and more permissive (33).

Human babies also seem to gather courage for exploration from their attachment to their mothers. In one experiment, babies just under a year old were placed in a strange room that contained a chair piled high with and surrounded by toys. When baby and mother were in the room together, the baby actively looked at the toys, approached them, and touched them. All this exploratory behavior dropped off, however, if a stranger was present or if the mother left the room (34).

The beginnings of anxiety

The experiment just described also produced results that point to another phase of development in the first eighteen months — namely, the first appearance of behavioral signs of anxiety. When the babies were left alone in the room, many of them very quickly began to cry, to make what appeared to be a rather frantic search for the mother, or to do both. They were exhibiting *separation anxiety,* which first appears among American babies around the age of nine or ten months.

A possible explanation for separation anxiety is the fact that the disappearance of the mother creates a strange and inexplicable situation that conflicts with the motive for certainty — which, as was discussed in Chapter 9, is one of the strongest of all human motives. Babies cannot

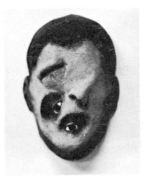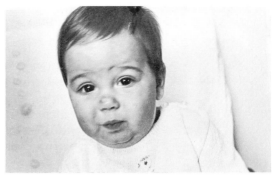

13-14

Perceptual distortion and anxiety

Violation of perceptual expectations makes the baby of about eight months express anxiety upon seeing the distorted mask at left. At an earlier period, before learning what the human face is supposed to look like, the baby might have smiled at the mask.

understand or explain the disappearance of their mothers; therefore this makes them anxious. In an experiment that supports this conclusion, it was found that babies rarely cried if their mothers left them by way of a familiar exit, such as the door from the child's bedroom to the other parts of the home. Presumably this was an everyday event that the babies had assimilated into their experience. But they did cry if their mothers disappeared in an unfamiliar way—for example, behind the door of a closet (35).

It might seem simpler to regard separation anxiety as reflecting the child's attachment to the caretaker, but this does seem to be the case. Babies brought up at home, with their mothers almost always around and opportunities for attachment at a maximum, are no more likely to show separation anxiety than children who spend much of their time at day care centers (36). Indeed American children reared by their mothers display no more separation anxiety than children brought up in Israeli kibbutzim, where the mothers are absent for most of the day (37). Among both groups, separation anxiety begins at the age of nine or ten months and is usually over by the time the children are three years old.

Stranger anxiety. Babies also exhibit *stranger anxiety* during the first year. In fact this type of anxiety appears somewhat earlier than separation anxiety. If the mother shows her face above the crib, the child of seven or eight months will usually smile. But if the face is that of a stranger, the baby may show anxiety by turning away and perhaps crying. Again, the explanation may be that the appearance of the stranger's face is an event that generates uncertainty. The baby has acquired some sort of mental representation or perceptual expectation of the familiar face, which is violated by the unfamiliar face. Indeed the behavioral evidences of stranger anxiety can sometimes be produced by showing the baby a distorted mask of the human face, as is shown in Figure 13-14.

The first social demands: eighteen months through three years

The second important period in personality development, roughly from eighteen months through three years, is dominated by children's first important experiences with the demands of society. When they leave the crib and begin walking about the house, they find innumerable objects that look like toys provided for their own special benefit but which in fact are expensive and fragile pieces of household equipment—or, like knives and electric light cords, are dangerous. For the first time, therefore, they encounter discipline. They discover that they can no longer do whatever they please. The rules of the home say that they must not destroy valuable property and must not get into dangerous situations. At the same time they encounter a rule of society holding that the elimination drive must be relieved only in the bathroom. They undergo that much-discussed process called toilet training.

The horizons of these children widen. They leave the self-centered environment of the crib and begin to take their places in the world of people, property, and property rights. Sometimes smoothly, sometimes with stormy difficulties, they begin to learn to become disciplined members of society.

Punishment and anxiety

In toilet training children must learn *not* to do something—in this case, not to respond immediately to the sensations that call for relief of the elimination drive. They must also learn *not* to respond to such external stimuli as the cupboard full of dishes that they would like to explore or the lamp that they would like to smash to the floor. In other words, they learn in this period to *inhibit* forms of behavior that would ordinarily be the natural response to internal or external stimuli.

They learn partly through reward. When they are successful at using the toilet, they are usually rewarded with praise and fondling. When they refrain from playing with a lamp after being told "No," they usually receive the same kind of reward. But since they are learning inhibition, they also learn through punishment and anxiety.

Children are customarily punished, verbally if not physically, when they soil their pants, break something, or get into places where they do not belong. As a result of the punishment they acquire a twofold anxiety over committing the acts. They become anxious over the prospect of future punishment. They also become anxious over the possibility of losing the affection and regard of their parents.

The anxiety helps them become social beings. The same stimuli that urge them toward an act of elimination or to explore or destroy begin to arouse sufficient anxiety to inhibit what had previously been a natural kind of behavior. The closer their ties with their parents, the more readily does this kind of learning take place. Children also learn appropriate social behaviors through observing the actions of their parents, siblings, and peers.

Exploring and destroying

It is by exploring the world that children come into contact with new experiences and learn about their environments. It is by handling objects—and sometimes, unfortunately, destroying them—that children learn how to operate on the environment. They discover that they can roam around the world and in many cases rearrange it. They can reach for ob-

jects they want; they can move these objects. They learn that they themselves can satisfy many of their desires. By reaching into the cookie jar they can satisfy their hunger. By crawling under the coat that a visitor has thrown on the sofa they can find warmth. By knocking down a tower of blocks (or pulling down a tablecloth) they can satisfy the need for stimulus change.

Parents who want to help their children develop along the most favorable lines face a problem at this period. Children must definitely learn to avoid danger. They must also learn to curb their inclinations to let exploration turn into destruction. But there is a point at which attempts to preserve children's safety and stop them from destroying can begin to thwart normal development.

Some mothers are overprotective. They try to keep their children "tied to their apron strings" and object to any activities the children attempt to undertake on their own. Other parents are too concerned with neatness and order. They scold or punish their children for making the slightest mess, getting the least bit dirty, or merely touching a newly polished table. When disciplined by overprotective or overly neat parents, children can acquire too much anxiety. Their fear of punishment or disapproval may generalize to any new object or new activity. They may therefore grow up with strong inhibitions against trying anything at all that is novel or challenging, including attempts to make adjustments to other people.

Parents who are somewhat more permissive during this difficult period, on the other hand, can set the stage for spontaneous, self-reliant, and effective behavior. Though they must stop their children at times, they do so only when absolutely necessary. They encourage and reward attempts at anything new and constructive, such as drawing pictures or riding a tricycle. Thus their children learn that only some kinds of exploratory behavior are forbidden, not all, and that in fact many kinds are considered "good." These children discover that curiosity and new attempts to operate on the environment are generally approved, and they may very well begin to develop independence and self-confidence.

The preschool years: four and five

Preschool children use language and concepts. They are beginning to roam outside the home and play with other children. They may go to nursery school or kindergarten. These years of four and five witness some important changes. Children develop their first feelings of guilt, representing the workings of that rather strange mechanism called conscience. They learn that the world is divided into males and females, for whom society decrees quite different roles. Boys begin to take on characteristics that society considers appropriate to males, and girls to take on characteristics considered appropriate to females.

One important reinforcement for learning continues to be provided by parents in the form of praise and other rewards. Children in the preschool period also mold their behavior in a continued effort to avoid disapproval or punishment and anxiety over the possibility of these two unpleasant events. However, a new factor now enters. This is the period in which children begin to identify with their parents and to try to imitate them.

Identification

Drawing by Chas. Addams, © 1954
The New Yorker Magazine, Inc.

The process of *identification* is a matter of debate. To the psychoanalysts it is a complex process involving the Oedipus complex and the superego, as was explained on pages 380–81. To many psychologists it has a somewhat different meaning—namely, that children come to feel that they and their parents share a vital bond of similarity. Children bear the same family name. They are often told that they look like their parents. Thus they consider themselves in many deep and important ways to be similar to their parents. This usually makes them feel more secure because they view their parents as stronger and more competent than they themselves are. They begin to imitate the parents' behavior to increase this similarity—and to share vicariously in the parents' strengths, virtues, skills, and triumphs.

Children with intelligent parents often come to think of themselves as intelligent. A boy whose father holds a job requiring physical strength usually begins to think of himself as being strong, and a girl with an attractive mother thinks of herself as being attractive. Unfortunately, children identify with their parents' faults as well as with their virtues, and it is not unusual for children to become aware of the defects of their parents. They may be able to see for themselves that their father is unable to hold a job and is the object of ridicule in the community or that their mother drinks too much and is unwelcome in the houses of her neighbors. They may hear criticism of their parents from relatives. Or divorced parents may bitterly criticize each other's conduct. Under these circumstances many children develop the belief that they too are unworthy, unlovable, hateful, stupid, lazy, or mean. Many children treated in guidance clinics for psychological problems have a background of identification with a "bad" parent.

13-15

The effects of loss of a parent

A study of the home backgrounds of delinquent boys, as compared with a matched control group of nondelinquent boys, found that considerably more of the delinquents had lost a parent through death, divorce, or other causes—particularly when they were very young. (38)

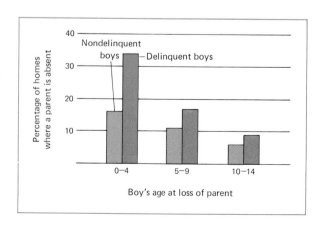

Children can also be affected adversely by the loss of a parent. This is true when the loss occurs at any time in childhood, but especially when it occurs before the end of the preschool years. As is shown in Figure 13-15, it has been found that a substantial number of delinquent boys come from homes in which a parent had died or was absent for other reasons, with the percentage of delinquency greatest among the boys who were youngest when the absence began. Obviously there are many ways in which the death of a parent or divorce can hamper a child's development—but certainly one possibility is interference with the normal process of identification.

Sex typing

Another important phase of development that takes place in the preschool years concerns the matter of *sex typing*. This is a process that occurs universally. Every society assigns different roles to men and women; it expects them to have different duties, attitudes, and standing in the community (39). The assigned roles may vary considerably from one society to another. But whatever the particular customs, men are expected to act like men and women like women. And children are made aware of this fact at an early age.

In the United States, at least in the past, children have been brought up to believe that women should be pretty and preferably slim, while men should be tall and strong. Women should be passive, nonaggressive, and submissive toward men, while men should be active, aggressive, and dominant. Even children's television shows reflect this kind of bias. In a recent attempt by psychologists to analyze the male-female differences depicted in children's programs, it was found that many shows could not be studied at all because no women characters appeared in them. Even in the other shows, most of the characters were men—and the men, as is illustrated in Figure 13-16, were depicted as

13-16

Sex differences in children's TV shows

Are men and women depicted differently in children's television programs? No doubt about it. An analysis of the time spent by the TV characters at various forms of behavior has demonstrated that the men are shown as being much more of everything than women—except deferential.

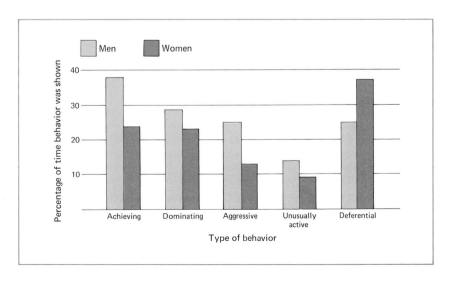

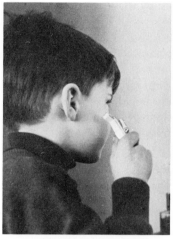

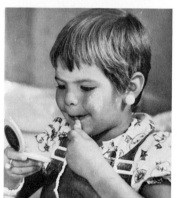

considerably more active, aggressive, dominating, and successful than the relatively rare women characters among them. The women were often shown as being deferential—and when they got "out of line" by being active and attempting to make their mark on the world, they were likely to fail or even be chastised (40).

Teachers in nursery schools attended by many children aged four and five have been found to treat boys and girls quite differently. They pay considerably more attention to the boys. This is true not only when the boys engage in disruptive behavior (as they do to a far greater extent than the girls in these schools) but also when they are on their good behavior. The teachers are likely to talk to the boys at greater length, give them more detailed instructions, praise them more frequently, and even hug them more often as a token of approval (41).

In one way or another, children quickly learn about sex typing. When children of four and five are presented with pictures of various objects associated with play—such as dolls, guns, kitchen utensils, cowboys, and Indians—and asked which they prefer, there are pronounced differences in the responses of boys and girls (42). A recent study of such preferences indicates that girls may now be growing less concerned about choosing items that have traditionally been considered appropriate for them—and that this change is more pronounced in the United States than in England (43). But in general the preschool boy seems to be asking, "How masculine am I?" and the preschool girl to be asking, if to a somewhat lesser extent, "How feminine am I?" Their feelings of how well they measure up to the standards set by society for the two sexes—or perhaps of how well they can resist sex typing—begin to play an increasing part in their evaluation of themselves and of their roles in society.

Children and their peers: six to ten

When children enter elementary school, their lives take on a new dimension. Up to this point their chief social contacts have been their parents, their brothers and sisters, and perhaps a few young playmates. Now they come into close contact with a large number of their peers— boys and girls of the same age with whom they share their experiences of work and play. They also come under the influence of their teachers. They encounter new sources of uncertainty, notably over their competence at school tasks and at skills admired by their peers. Although the home continues to be important in development, these other factors begin to play an increasing role.

The child in school

In the new world that children enter there is a new adult—the teacher— whose discipline they must conform to and whose acceptance they must court. Ordinarily the teacher is a woman, like the mother, and children's behavior toward their mothers can be generalized toward her. But boys who are identifying with their fathers and rebelling against their mothers often have trouble in the early grades. They may be less fearful of rejection by the teacher and therefore more reluctant to accept her influence. They typically get lower marks and cause more disciplinary problems than do girls.

The teacher usually plays a dual role in pupils' development. In the first place, she teaches the intellectual skills appropriate to our society. In the second place, and perhaps even more important to personality development, she tries to encourage a motive for intellectual mastery. It is in the early years of school that children crystallize their inner standards of intellectual mastery and begin to feel anxiety if they do not live up to the standards. By the age of ten, largely because of the school experience, some children have developed a pronounced fear of failure, others an expectancy of success. The desire to avoid the anxiety attached to possible failure can be one of the strongest of motives.

The influence of peers

In addition to making all the new adjustments to their teachers, children must also learn to live with their schoolmates. And when children are six to ten these peers take on a particular importance for three special reasons.

Evaluation. It is by comparing themselves with their classmates that children judge their own value. As they grow to the age of ten, they begin to lose their original faith in the wisdom of adults. They seem to sense that their parents are either too full of praise for their virtues or too critical of their faults. They conclude that they can get a more realistic reading of their value from their relations with other children. For one thing, they can make direct comparisons. They can determine their rank among their classmates on such attributes as intelligence, strength, and skills of various kinds. For another thing, the opinions of their classmates seem more objective, honest, and easily interpreted than their parents' opinions. They have no trouble determining whether they are regarded by other children as competent and likable or foolish and unpleasant.

Assignment of role. It appears to be a characteristic of human society, at least in our own kind of civilization, that every group has a leader, a "closest adviser" to the leader, and a scapegoat on whom the group takes out its aggressions. Often there are also an individual looked up to as a source of wisdom and a court jester, or clown. There may be a rebel and a psychotic. These roles, into which individuals naturally gravitate or are pushed by others, are found in groups of children as well as of adults. Once children have achieved or been assigned a role, they usually take it seriously, receive some kind of satisfaction from it, and assume more and more of the appropriate traits. The child who is a leader in the first grade, for example, is likely to develop many of the traits of skilled leadership. The class clown develops an increasingly buffoonlike personality.

Rebellion. Most schoolchildren, especially boys in our society, are to some degree rebellious against the adult world. In particular, they resent adult restrictions on the display of hostility and demands for cleanliness, order, and quiet. In the company of their peers, these young rebels can express their hostilities, make a mess, be noisy, and do all the other things that the adult world forbids. When they do so, they often receive the admiration of their classmates rather than disapproval.

Peers as psychotherapists

In a sense, children often function for one another as psychotherapists. They help one another toward an objective evaluation of their own talents and position in society. The peer group assigns roles to play and provides models to identify with and imitate. It provides an outlet for feelings, such as hostility, on which the adult world frowns. Thus it is not at all surprising that children between the ages of six and ten begin to learn more from their peer groups than from anyone else.

It is interesting to note, however, that the rebelliousness against adult standards that is fostered by the peer group in the United States is not characteristic of all societies. This fact has been demonstrated in an ingenious experiment in which American and Russian children were asked to respond to a questionnaire about how they would behave if some of their friends urged them to perform such acts as going to a movie disapproved by their parents, running away after accidentally breaking a window, stealing fruit from an orchard, or taking advantage of finding the questions and answers for a school examination. Some of the children were told that no one would see their answers to the questionnaire except the experimenters, others that their parents would see the answers, and still others that their classmates would have an opportunity to see the answers.

In every case, the American children proved far more inclined than the Russian children to perform the forbidden acts. But an even more striking finding was this: when the Russian children believed that their peers would see their answers, they were less willing to admit to an inclination toward forbidden acts than when they thought that no one would see their answers. In other words, the influence of their peers acted as a restraint. For American children, the finding was the opposite; when they believed that their peers would see their answers, they were *more* inclined toward forbidden or rebellious behavior (44). In the Soviet Union, it would appear, the peer group serves to help enforce compliance with adult standards; in the United States, it serves to foster rebelliousness.

Dominance and submission

One personality trait that becomes partially set by the end of the early school years is the tendency to be dominant or submissive in relations with other people. Children of ten who actively make suggestions to the group, try to influence and persuade others, and resist pressure from others are likely to remain dominant in their social relations for the rest of their lives. Children who are quiet and readily follow the lead of others are likely to remain passive and submissive.

The tendency to be dominant or submissive is in part a function of group acceptance. Children who believe that they are admired by the group are likely to develop enhanced self-confidence and dominance with others. Children who do not consider themselves admired by the group are likely to develop feelings of inferiority and to be submissive. In this connection, physical attributes play an important part. The large, strong boy and the attractive girl are more likely to be dominant. The small boy and the unattractive girl are likely to be submissive. Other factors are identification with a dominant or submissive parent and also the kind of control exercised by the parents. Permissive parents tend to influence their children in the direction of dominance, while parents who restrict their children's activities tend to influence them in the direction of submissiveness.

Motives and standards

Another change that occurs in the early school years concerns the relative importance of motives and standards. The desire to live up to standards gradually begins to take top position in the hierarchy. For example, a four-year-old girl values her mother's kiss for its own sake; she has a motive to obtain signs of affection. By the time she is eight she is likely to have developed a standard that in effect says, "I should be valued by my parents." Her desire to live up to this standard of being valued is more general than her earlier motives for physical affection and more difficult to satisfy.

Four important standards that begin to take form in the early school years are these:

1 Being valued by parents, teachers, and peers.
2 Mastery of physical and mental skills.
3 Behavior appropriate to sex typing—particularly strength, independence, and athletic skills among boys; social skills and inhibition of aggression among girls.
4 Cognitive consonance between thoughts and behavior. (Children want to behave rationally and sensibly and in a way that confirms their self-concepts and identification with their parents and other heroes they may have.)

The ten-year-old as a future adult

All in all, a vast array of changes occur during the first ten years of life. Children of ten have matured physically, have grown, and have become capable of performing a vast array of motor skills. Intellectually, they are well along in Piaget's stage of concrete operations and about to embark on the final stage of formal operations. Their personalities have developed in a host of directions; and individual differences in personality are readily apparent to anyone who watches their behavior, as can be seen in Figure 13-17.

To a rather considerable extent, the ten-year-old child offers a reasonably accurate preview of the adult to come. The trend of physical development and the pattern of mental processes have been established. And in many cases the personality traits acquired by that age will be carried through adolescence and into adult life, as indicated by the correlations shown in Figure 13-18. But development, though it proceeds so rapidly and dramatically through the first ten years, does not end there. Many psychologists, indeed, consider it a lifelong process continuing from cradle to grave. Adolescence and adulthood, as will now be seen, may produce changes so drastic as to defy prediction.

13-17

Same stimulus, different response

The two young daughters of an astronaut exhibit very different reactions while watching their father on a space-walk broadcast over television. The girl at right stifles a yawn—while her older sister casts a reproachful glance.

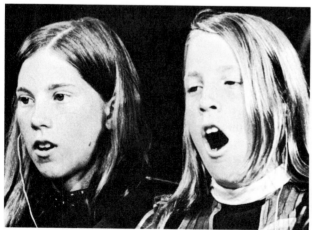

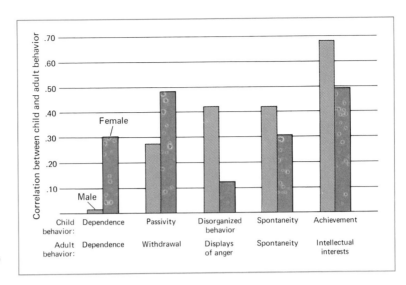

13-18

How child foreshadows adult

The bars show the correlations between the behavior of boys and girls and their behavior later, as young adults. The children rated for dependence, passivity, and disorganized behavior were aged six to ten; those rated for spontaneity and achievement were ten to fourteen. (45)

Adolescence and adulthood

Though our society makes frequent use of the words *adolescent* and *adult*, it is difficult to define them. They are words that some other societies never use at all, and that even our own society did not think about in its early history. In simple, nonindustrial societies there is an easy and almost imperceptible transition from early childhood to full membership in the community. Children begin performing the work of the community as soon as they can—and one day, almost without anyone's taking note of the fact, they become self-sufficient and independent of their parents. They start rearing their own families and the whole smooth cycle starts over again.

In our own society, the situation is more complex. To perform most of the work of our society, a prolonged education is required. Most young people remain in school until they are at least sixteen or eighteen. Many continue on to college until they are twenty or twenty-two. The person who becomes a lawyer may not be able to earn a living before the age of twenty-five, the physician before nearly the age of thirty. At what point, in this extended preparation for full participation in the society, does the child become an adolescent and the adolescent become an adult?

Adolescence and the growth spurt

One way to define the beginning of adolescence is in physical terms. It is considered to begin with the onset of puberty—marked by menstruation in the female, the ability to produce sperm in the male. This can occur at any time between the ages of eleven and eighteen—usually a year or two earlier in girls than in boys.

The age at which adolescence begins for the individual can have important effects. One reason is that puberty is almost invariably accompanied by a spurt in physical growth. Beginning at any time after the tenth year, a girl may suddenly grow three to five inches taller in a single year, a boy four to six inches taller. Along with the growth spurt

481

comes a change in physical dimensions and strength. The girl begins to look like a woman, the boy like a man.

For a girl, the early onset of adolescence may at first be embarrassing. It is somewhat awkward to look like an adult in a classroom full of children—and especially to tower over the boys in the class. Later, however, the girls who matured early seem to have a distinct advantage. By the time of junior high school these girls seem to have a better opinion of themselves and better relations with both their classmates and their parents than girls who entered into puberty much later (46).

For boys, an early adolescence seems to be an unmixed blessing. These boys quickly become physically stronger and thus better athletes than classmates who are slower to mature. It has been found that they are more highly regarded by their peers and by adults; they tend to develop a great deal of self-confidence, social poise, and leadership abilities. Boys who are slow to show the growth spurt, on the other hand, continue to be treated as "little boys" while their bigger and more mature classmates are gaining all this new respect. Sometimes they try to make up for their physical and social disadvantages by working too hard to attract attention. Sometimes they are inclined to draw into a shell. Though they catch up later in physical development, they may continue as adults to be less confident, sociable, and enterprising, and more "touchy" and rebellious (47).

Adolescence and sexual problems

One adolescent activity of overriding importance, of course, revolves around the first serious attempts to establish relationships with the opposite sex. These social contacts between boys and girls—whether formal or informal, called "dating" or something else—occupy much of adolescents' time and preoccupy their thoughts.

Dating is not always, however, a total delight. Both girls and boys often view the first date with a certain amount of fear. One study found that two-thirds of both sexes described themselves as "pretty scared" over the prospect of doing something wrong (48). Experience lessens this fear but does not eliminate it. A study of high school students showed that about 25 percent of the boys and 33 percent of the girls felt that they were failures at dating. About 33 percent of the students admitted they did not know how to act on dates; the same number said they experienced more fear than pleasure (49).

The relations between adolescent boys and girls are further complicated by the question of sexual behavior. And this question in turn is complicated by the attitudes of parents and society in general and by the individual adolescent's own standards of sexual morality. It is also made more difficult because of the fact that most adolescent boys have a much stronger and more insistent sex drive than do most girls who are the same age (50, 51).

Sexual attitudes and the extent to which they create problems vary so widely as to defy analysis. Studies have been made, however, of actual behavior. One of the most recent, based on a statistically valid

sample of American teenagers from all types of backgrounds, showed that 37 percent of those thirteen through fifteen had experienced sexual intercourse. For those sixteen through nineteen, the figure was 64 percent. More males than females had had sexual experience—for the entire group, 59 percent of the males as compared with 45 percent of the females in the sample (52).

Moral development

Moral standards in general—not only on sexual but on other types of behavior as well—tend to change and to become rather firmly established during the adolescent years. They first appear much earlier, for even very young children make judgments of what is right and what is wrong; they develop moral and ethical principles by which they guide (or try to guide) their conduct. But the moral judgments of young children are based on the anticipation of punishment, not on abstract principles. These judgments become abstract and logically coherent as children begin to grow toward adulthood.

The manner in which moral judgments develop has been studied extensively by Lawrence Kohlberg, by the questioning of boys seven years old through adolescence. Kohlberg presented his subjects with a number of hypothetical situations involving moral questions like these: If a man's wife is dying for lack of an expensive drug that he cannot afford, should he steal the drug? If a patient who is fatally ill and in great pain begs for a mercy killing, should the physician agree? By analyzing the answers and particularly the reasoning by which his subjects reached their answers, Kohlberg determined that moral judgments develop through a series of six stages, as shown in Figure 13-19 on the following page. Children in the two stages of what he calls the preconventional level base their ideas of right and wrong largely on their own self-interest; they are concerned chiefly with avoiding punishment and gaining rewards. Later, in the two stages of what he calls the conventional level, they become concerned about the approval of other people. And finally, in the two stages of the postconventional level, they become concerned with abstract moral values and the dictates of their own consciences.

In other words, children's reasons for being "good" progress from sheer self-interest to a concern for the approval of others and finally to a concern for the approval of their own consciences. How this pattern of moral judgments develops with age is shown in Figure 13-20. Apparently such a stage-by-stage development takes place in other societies as well as our own. Kohlberg has found a similar progression among children in Mexico and Taiwan (55).

Is adolescence fun or furor?

The question of whether adolescence is in general a joy or a burden has been pondered by many psychologists (as well, no doubt, as by many adolescents). The first American psychologist to become deeply concerned with the problems of growing up concluded that adolescence

13-19

A stage theory of moral development

Summarized in the table are the six stages in the development of moral judgments found by Kohlberg. For the ages at which American children appear to progress from one stage to the next, see Figure 13-20. (53)

PRECONVENTIONAL LEVEL

Children are oriented to the consequences of their behavior.

Stage 1. Defer to the power of adults and obey rules to avoid trouble and punishment.

Stage 2. Seek to satisfy their own needs by behaving in a manner that will gain rewards and the return of favors.

CONVENTIONAL LEVEL

Children are oriented to the expectations of others and to behaving in a conventional fashion.

Stage 3. Want to be "good" in order to please and help others and thus receive approval.

Stage 4. Want to "do their duty" by respecting authority (parents, teachers, God) and maintaining the social order for its own sake.

POSTCONVENTIONAL LEVEL

Children become oriented to more abstract moral values and their own consciences.

Stage 5. Think in terms of the rights of others; the general welfare of the community, and a duty to conform to the laws and standards established by the will of the majority. Behave in ways they believe would be respected by an impartial observer.

Stage 6. Consider not only the actual laws and rules of society but also their own self-chosen standards of justice and respect for human dignity. Behave in a way that will avoid condemnation by their own consciences.

13-20

Stages of moral development by age

Among seven-year-olds, almost all moral judgments are made at the preconventional level (Kohlberg's stages 1 and 2). By the age of ten, more than half of moral judgments are still made at this level but judgments at the conventional level (stages 3 and 4) are increasing rapidly. By thirteen, judgments at the preconventional level have dropped to a rather small minority, judgments at the conventional level predominate, and judgments at the postconventional level (stages 5 and 6) are beginning to become important. (54)

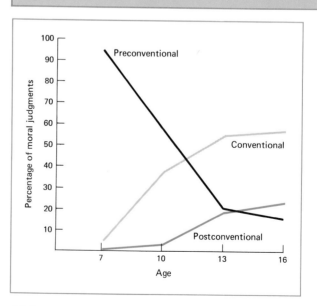

was all in all a very difficult time of life—indeed a period of "storm and stress" (56). Many other psychologists would agree. In one study it was found that substantial numbers of people, looking back on their lives when they had reached the age of thirty, characterized their adolescent years as the time when they were most confused and their morale at its lowest ebb. They mentioned such difficulties as striving for recognition from peers of their own and the opposite sex, being under anxiety-producing pressures from their parents for scholastic and social achievement, and trying to establish their independence while still remaining financially dependent on their parents (57).

Other psychologists, however, have reached quite different conclusions. Some studies have found that most adolescents, far from being in bitter rebellion, have a warm and mutually respectful relationship with their parents (58). And some investigators have concluded that most adolescents, far from being hopelessly confused and demoralized, are actually quite well adjusted (59). The conflicting evidence may reflect the vast range of individual differences—in both experiences and reactions to these experiences—that occur among human beings as they go through a period in which psychological growth may be as breathtaking as those sudden spurts in height.

Psychological development after adolescence

Even a very unhappy adolescence, however, is not necessarily fatal to future development. Life goes on. New experiences occur. The most troubled adolescent—a failure in school, unsuccessful in social contacts, unpopular and despondent—may develop into a happy, successful, well liked, and highly respected adult.

This fact has been strikingly demonstrated in a long-term study in which 166 boys and girls were observed carefully from shortly after birth until they were eighteen years old, then observed again when they were adults at the age of thirty. As an example of the kind of change that some of them displayed between adolescence and adulthood note this finding:

> [One subject]—a large, awkward, early-maturing girl who labored under the weight of her size and shyness, feeling that she was a great disappointment to her mother—worked hard for her B average to win approval and was a pedestrian, uninteresting child and adolescent. She had periods of depression, when she could see no point to living. Then, as a junior in college, she got excited over what she was learning (not just in grades to please her mother) and went on to get an advanced degree and to teach in college. Now she has taken time out to have and raise her children. . . . [She is] full of zest for living, married to an interesting, merry, and intelligent man she met in graduate school.

Similarly, a girl who was expelled from school at sixteen and a boy expelled at fifteen—for failing grades and misbehavior—were found to have developed into "wise, steady, understanding parents who perceptively appreciate the complexities of life and have both humor and compassion for the human race." An adolescent boy who could only be described as a "listless oddball" had turned into a successful architect and excellent husband and parent who called his adult life "exciting and satisfying." All told, just about half the subjects were living richer and more productive lives as adults than could have been predicted from their adolescent personalities (60).

How adulthood brings its changes. What causes such marked changes in many adults? One conclusion reached by the study is that some people are just naturally "slow bloomers." It takes them a long time—and often a change of environment that takes them away from their parents or even to a new community—to find themselves. Taking on a meaningful job may help. So may marriage and especially parenthood, with all its responsibilities and opportunities.

The authors of the study have also concluded that even the problems of a troubled adolescence may sometimes prove a blessing in disguise as the years go on. If adolescents go through a period of "painful, strain-producing, and confusing experiences" but manage to survive them, these experiences may in the long run serve to produce greater insight and stability (61).

In this connection it is interesting to note that subjects in the study who seemed perfectly well adjusted in adolescence did not always turn out well as adults. About 20 percent of the subjects were found to have less fulfilling lives at thirty than would have been expected from the promise they showed at eighteen—and included in this group were a number of men and women whose early lives had been smooth, free from any severe strains, and marked by success in both school and social relations. At eighteen these subjects seemed well poised and self-confident. The boys tended to be much-admired leaders in athletics, the girls to be good-looking and socially skillful. Yet at thirty they were found to be "brittle, discontented, and puzzled." Perhaps too easy a childhood and adolescence, creating no need to face and overcome problems, can at times hinder future development.

Erikson's eight stages of lifelong development

Many students of development, as has been said, view it as a continuous process, extending from birth through adulthood to old age, and ending only with death. Among the most prominent proponents of this idea is Erik Erikson, a psychoanalyst who bases his conclusions on observations of people he has treated at all ages, some in childhood and others in adulthood.

Erikson speaks in terms of *psychosocial development*. That is to say, he holds that development is a twofold process in which the psychological development of individuals (their personalities and views of themselves) proceeds hand-in-hand with the social relations they establish as they go through life. He has suggested that this development can be divided into eight stages, in each of which individuals face new social

Erikson

13-21

Erikson's eight stages of life

This is the life cycle of development, from cradle to grave, as viewed by Erikson. Each stage brings new social horizons and new crises—which, if surmounted successfully, lead to constant growth and a steadily enriched personality. (62)

Stage	Crisis	Favorable outcome	Unfavorable outcome
First year of life	Trust versus mistrust	Faith in the environment and future events	Suspicion, fear of future events
Second year	Autonomy versus doubt	A sense of self-control and adequacy	Feelings of shame and self-doubt
Third through fifth years	Initiative versus guilt	Ability to be a "self-starter," to initiate one's own activities	A sense of guilt and inadequacy to be on one's own
Sixth year to puberty	Industry versus inferiority	Ability to learn how things work, to understand and organize	A sense of inferiority at understanding and organizing
Adolescence	Identity versus confusion	Seeing oneself as a unique and integrated person	Confusion over who and what one really is
Early adulthood	Intimacy versus isolation	Ability to make commitments to others, to love	Inability to form affectionate relationships
Middle age	Generativity versus self-absorption	Concern for family and society in general	Concern only for self—one's own well-being and prosperity
Aging years	Integrity versus despair	A sense of integrity and fulfillment; willingness to face death	Dissatisfaction with life; despair over prospect of death

situations and encounter new problems (or "psychosocial crises"). They may emerge from the new experiences with greater maturity and richer personalities—or they may fail to cope successfully with the problems and their development may be warped or arrested.

Erikson's eight stages are shown in Figure 13-21. They begin, as will be seen, with the child in the first year of life. At this stage the child's social relations are confined to the caretaker; out of this relationship, Erikson believes, the child learns either to trust the social environment and what it will bring in the future or to be suspicious and fearful of others. In later stages the social environment widens and new psychosocial crises occur, again with outcomes that may be favorable or unfavorable. If all goes well, the final stage of old age finds people thinking of their social environment as comprising all of humanity; they feel a kinship with the stream of life and with history; they have a sense of wisdom, integrity, and fulfillment; they face the inevitability of death without fear or regret. The process of development, from its seeds in the newborn child, has come full flower.

Summary

1 *Developmental psychology* studies the processes by which children gradually acquire patterns of overt behavior, thinking, and problem solving, as well as the emotions, motives, conflicts, and ways of coping with conflicts that will go to make up their adult personalities.

2 Babies differ at birth in a) sensory thresholds and adaptation, b) activity and irritability, and c) temperament. On the matter of temperament, most appear to be "easy" children, some "slow to warm up," and some "difficult."

3 The baby's physical development, including the acquisition of such skills as walking and talking, depends largely on the process of *maturation*—the physical changes, taking place after birth, that continue the biological development of the organism from fertilized egg cell to complete adult.

4 In all forms of development, environment also plays a part. An environment that encourages infants to perform skills—though without forcing them—is likely to produce the appearance of these skills at an earlier age.

5 Human infants are extremely *impressionable*. In particular, a highly unfavorable environment can produce drastic and sometimes long-lasting abnormalities. But infants are also *resilient* and *malleable,* that is, capable of changing with changed circumstances. Under proper conditions, even severe early handicaps can sometimes be overcome in later years.

6 The intellectual development of children depends in part on increasing skill at perception, language, and the use of concepts.

7 According to Piaget, intellectual development is basically an increased ability to adapt to new situations. The key processes in development are *assimilation* (the process of incorporating a new stimulus into one's existing cognitive view of the world) and *accommodation* (the process of changing one's cognitive view and behavior when new information dictates such a change).

8 Piaget has charted intellectual development through the following stages: a) the *sensorimotor stage* (birth to age two), b) the *preoperational stage* (two to seven), c) the *stage of concrete operations* (seven to eleven), and d) the *stage of formal operations* (beginning at about eleven or twelve).

9 Personality development during the first eighteen months is characterized by attachment to and a close relationship with the mother or other caretaker. This period is marked by the appearance of *separation anxiety* and *stranger anxiety.*

10 The period from eighteen months through three years is characterized by the *first social demands* on children, asking them to conform

to discipline and to undergo toilet training. Too much discipline or protection during this period may instill a crippling amount of anxiety and create lifelong inhibitions against trying anything novel or challenging.

11 The *preschool years,* four and five, are characterized by identification with the parents; the development of standards, feelings of guilt, and the first notions of sex typing and conduct appropriate to males and females.

12 From six to ten, children come under the strong influence of their *peers* — that is, other children. Peers provide a) evaluation, b) a role, and c) an opportunity for rebellion against the restraints of the outside world. During this period children acquire strong tendencies toward dominance or submission, and their inner standards (toward being valued by parents and peers, mastery of physical and mental skills, etc.) take on overriding importance.

13 Adolescence is characterized physically by the sudden growth spurt that accompanies puberty. Some adolescents find this period a time of "storm and stress" — with much confusion over such problems as striving for recognition from peers of their own and the opposite sex, being under anxiety-producing pressures from their parents for scholastic and social achievement, and trying to establish independence while remaining financially dependent on the parents.

14 Continuing development in the years after adolescence can produce many changes. Some of the most troubled and despondent adolescents turn out to lead happy and fulfilling lives as adults, while some of the most untroubled and self-confident adolescents do not live up to their early promise.

15 One of the prominent proponents of the idea that development is a lifelong process is Erikson, who holds that *psychosocial development* (psychological changes occurring with changes in one's social environment) proceeds in eight stages extending over the life span from infancy to old age.

Recommended reading

Bowlby, J. *Attachment and loss.* Vol. I "Attachment." New York: Basic Books, 1969.

Conger, J. J. *Adolescence and youth: psychological development in a changing world.* New York: Harper & Row, 1973.

Erikson, E. H. *Childhood and society,* rev. ed. New York: Norton, 1964.

Gibson, E. J. *Principles of perceptual learning and development.* New York: Appleton-Century-Crofts, 1969.

Kagan, J. *Understanding children.* New York: Harcourt Brace Jovanovich, 1971.

Mussen, P. H., Conger, J. J., and Kagan, J. *Child development and personality,* 4th ed. New York: Harper & Row, 1974.

Piaget, J. *Six psychological studies.* New York: Random House, 1967.

Stone, J. L., Smith, H. T., and Murphy, L. B. *The competent infant.* New York: Basic Books, 1974.

Social psychology

Imagine for a moment that you are sitting at an upstairs window on a big-city street corner, watching the pedestrians on the sidewalks beneath you. Lights at the corner, instructing the pedestrians, flash bright neon signals: first WAIT, then WALK. You keep a tally and it turns out that the pedestrians pay close attention to the lights. Almost all of them stop and wait until the signal changes. Over a period of time, you discover, only 1 percent violate the command to WAIT.

Now a confederate of yours comes on the scene—a young man who is going to act like a sort of Pied Piper trying to lure the pedestrians across the street against the light. He is a rather unimpressive and untidy young man, in an old shirt, patched trousers, and scuffed shoes. As he marches boldly across the street in defiance of the WAIT signal, how many pedestrians will follow him? How many would have followed him if he had been been dressed neatly in a well-pressed suit?

This series of events actually took place in a well-known experiment on the effect of social influence. As tallied from the observation post in the window, it turned out that 4 percent of the pedestrians followed the untidy young man through the light—four times as many as had previously crossed on their own. When he returned later in more impressive dress, the number who followed him jumped all the way to 14 percent (1).

This is only one of many experiments that have clearly and dramatically demonstrated how human behavior is affected by the behavior of other people. No matter how the experiments are devised, the results are always the same. People, it turns out, have a strong tendency to do what they see other people doing. On a building doorway, a psychologist once hung the urgent sign:

ABSOLUTELY NO ADMITTANCE
USE ANOTHER ENTRANCE

One person after another, even those who had been using the doorway every day, looked at the sign and turned back. But given the example of a confederate of the psychologist who ignored the sign and marched right on in, others followed (2).

In another experiment, movie cameras were set up in a sixth-floor window of a New York City building to record the behavior of the people on the crowded street below. At a signal from the window, some confederates mingling with the crowd stopped and stared up at the cameras. As was captured on the film, other passersby found their example almost impossible to resist. As Figure 14-1 shows, most of them looked up and many actually stopped to stare—especially when there was a large number of confederates who pretended that they saw something interesting.

14-1

If others are doing it, why not me?

When even just one person on a New York City sidewalk stopped to stare up at something that seemed to be going on in a building across the street, 4 percent of passersby also stopped to look up. When fifteen people stopped to stare at the building, fully 40 percent of passersby followed their example. An even larger number of pedestrians looked up even though they did not stop. (3)

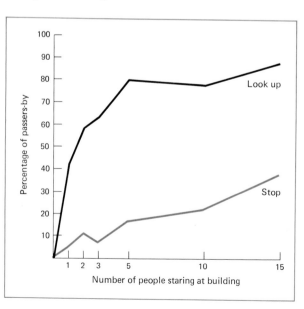

Number of people staring at building

To a very considerable extent, all of us behave as we see the people around us behave—or as we believe they expect us to behave. Our thinking is also molded in large part by the people around us. To a greater degree than most of us ever realize, we are the products of our social environments. Hence the importance of *social psychology,* which *studies the manner in which the human being "thinks, feels, and behaves in social situations"* (4). To put this more broadly, social psychology is the study of how people influence and are influenced by other people, for our behavior is at the same time a response and a stimulus to the behavior of others. What we do is determined at least in part—and sometimes to a very great extent—by what other people are doing or what they seem to expect us to do. At the same time, what we do helps determine what they do (5).

To draw a rough analogy, the individual is something like a football quarterback facing the other team's defensive unit. What the quarterback decides to do depends in large part on the strengths and weaknesses of the defensive team, how the defense is lining up, or how he expects it to line up. In turn, what the defensive team does depends in large part on what it expects the quarterback to do—and, once the play is under way, on how he does it. The influence works both ways.

Society and attitudes

Unlike some animals, human beings do not prowl the world alone or with no company save that of a mate. Human beings are social animals. Ever since they appeared on the face of the earth they appear to have lived in some kind of community, probably starting with the ancient cave communities. The most primitive people still left in the undeveloped parts of today's world are banded together in some kind of mutual living arrangement.

It appears, indeed, that human beings cannot exist in isolation; they need the company and cooperation of other human beings to acquire even such basic necessities as food, clothing, shelter, and protection against enemies. They can survive only by establishing some kind of *society*—which is the name applied to any organized group of people, large or small. The people living in a group of thatched huts in the jungles of South America make up a society. So do the people living in a small rural town or in New York City. The United States itself is a society. Big or little, simple or complex, the society is a universal way of human life.

Socialization: the process of learning society's ways

The society into which we are born begins to influence us almost from the moment of birth. As was explained in the previous chapter, we develop from child to adult not in a vacuum but in close interaction with our parents, families, teachers, and schoolmates. From all these people, we learn the ways of our own society. We learn the English language.

We learn how Americans speak, behave toward one another, and express or conceal their emotions. Later we learn what the people in our society believe and what they value. We learn the customs and laws that dictate a whole host of activities, from courting a mate to conducting a business transaction.

This process is called *socialization;* it is the process through which children are integrated into the society through exposure to the actions and opinions of other members of the society. In many ways, children become creatures of their society, molded by its customs and rules (6).

Since each society has its own customs and rules to instill in its children, the socialization process takes many different forms around the world. The customs in England call for driving on the left side of the road; in the Orient, for eating with chopsticks; in many Latin countries, for disregarding clocks and appointment times. There are societies where the women do all the work and the men do nothing except devote themselves to ceremony and self-adornment (7). There are places where two friends would never dream of competing against each other, as in games or athletic contests (8). There are even places where cannibalism is an approved way of life.

Whatever the customs and rules may be, every society molds its children in accordance with them. Socialization is a universal process. It is a form of learning that everyone undergoes—and that probably has a more pervasive and lasting effect than anything one can learn in school (although school also serves in many ways to socialize its pupils).

Socialization and subcultures

In a society as complex as ours, it must be pointed out, not every child is socialized to follow the same customs and rules. Within our society there exist many *subcultures,* or ways of life that differ from one another in many important respects. Some of these subcultures exist partly because the nation has been settled over the years by people from many different parts of the world, bringing with them their own particular customs and values. Other subcultures have a religious basis. Still others depend on geographical and occupational considerations.

Children are socialized into far different patterns of behavior if they are born in a rural area than if they are born in a small city—and into still other patterns if they are born in a large city. They may grow up into membership in subcultures as varied as a Zen commune, the world of music, the academic community, the business community, or the scientific community. The United States is a nation of many subcultures holding very different views on religion, politics, militarism, sexual behavior, the use of drugs, and life styles in general.

The importance of attitudes

The views that we acquire as a result of the socialization process—if they are strong and deep-seated, as is often the case—are known to social psychologists as *attitudes.* This term represents one of the most important of social psychology's concepts, for all of us grow up with many very definite attitudes toward the people and situations we face in life. We have favorable or unfavorable attitudes — wielding a powerful influence on the ways in which we lead our lives — toward foreigners, ethnic groups, rich people, poor people, men, women, homosexuals, children. We have strong attitudes toward the political parties, militarism, taxation, welfare, crime, labor unions, religion, and almost every other institution or issue in our society.

Attitudes are so ingrained, pervasive, and complex that they defy any brief definition. However, a definition is the best start toward explaining them, and the best possible definition is this: *an attitude is an organized and enduring set of beliefs and feelings toward some kind of object or situation and a predisposition to behave toward it in a particular way.* Note that the definition includes three elements that combine to form an attitude: 1) a cognitive element (beliefs), 2) an emotional element (feelings), and 3) a behavioral element.

Thus a favorable attitude toward religion might include a number of beliefs about the existence of a higher power, emotional feelings of awe and humility connected with these beliefs, and a behavioral tendency to go to church, to respond favorably to the clergy, and to respond unfavorably toward immoral or atheistic actions. A negative attitude toward women's liberation would include a belief that a woman's place is in the home, feelings of attraction to passive women and distaste for militant women, and a tendency to seek out a dependent woman rather than a career woman as a wife.

It is chiefly the emotional component of an attitude that distinguishes it from a mere belief. A belief that the world is round has no emotional flavor. It is merely the cognitive acceptance of what is presumed to be a matter of fact. People who hold this belief are neither for nor against roundness — and in the unlikely event that science should suddenly discover that the world is shaped like a football, they would not hesitate to change their opinion. An attitude, because of its emotional overtones — because we are "for" or "against" whatever it is that the attitude concerns — is much more resistant to change. Since attitudes are so enduring, and since they influence so much of our behavior toward other people, social psychologists have been particularly interested in the study of how attitudes are formed and changed.

Stereotypes and prejudices

Our attitudes are not necessarily based on any real evidence. In many cases we have simply taken them over lock, stock, and barrel from the people around us — without ever looking at the evidence at all. Nor are they necessarily logical or consistent. Some psychologists have concluded, indeed, that the most remarkable thing of all about our attitudes is the amount of inconsistency we somehow manage to tolerate (9).

An example that is not at all unusual would be this: In a mayoralty election, Candidate Smith is running for reelection. Mr. and Mrs. Jones have a strongly favorable attitude toward Mayor Smith and the mayor's political party. But one day something rather upsetting occurs. The local newspaper comes out with a strong and extremely persuasive editorial that describes in detail how Mayor Smith has failed to solve a number of urgent city problems; in fact the mayor has accepted graft as an inducement to permit gambling and to tolerate inferior performance on city construction contracts.

Will Mr. and Mrs. Jones change their attitude toward Mayor Smith? Not necessarily. Instead, they may do any one of several things. They may convince themselves that the newspaper is simply biased against the mayor. They may engage in a sort of mental debate with the editorial, in which they disprove its allegations, at least to their own satisfaction. Or they may put the whole editorial right out of their minds—that is, simply refuse to think about it. Our ingenuity at finding ways of maintaining our attitudes despite strong opposing arguments seems almost boundless.

Two kinds of attitudes that often fly in the face of fact are so common that they have acquired special names in social psychology. An attitude that disregards individual differences and holds that all people of a certain group behave in the same manner is called a *stereotype*. People make judgments on the basis of stereotypes when they assume that all women are emotionally flighty or that all men are male chauvinists. A *prejudice* is an attitude that an individual maintains so stubbornly as to be virtually uninfluenced by any information or experiences that would disprove it. In our society today, one of the more common prejudices is held by some whites against blacks and by some blacks against whites.

How attitudes become changed

Although attitudes are stubbornly resistant to change, they are by no means totally permanent and unyielding. Sometimes the dyed-in-the-wool Republican switches to the Democratic party. Or a confirmed atheist joins the church—and a devout churchgoer drops out. Even the most deep-seated prejudices sometimes give way. Public opinion polls taken at intervals over recent decades have shown sharp changes in prevailing attitudes toward many kinds of issues and institutions.

New experiences and change

One reason attitudes change is that the socialization process continues throughout life. As children, of course, we tend to adopt the attitudes of our parents. Studies have shown, for example, that negative attitudes toward minority groups often start when passed along from parent to child (10). And a very large majority of children in elementary school have been found to favor the same political party as their parents (11). But as we grow older the early influence of our parents begins to weaken. On the matter of politics, for example, the number of children

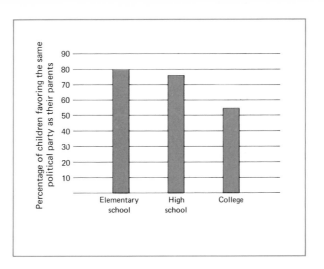

14-2

The waning influence of parents

Among elementary school pupils, 80 percent have been found to share the political attitudes of their parents. But the number begins to drop in high school and sinks to only somewhere around 55 percent by the college years.

who favor their parents' party has been found to drop as shown in Figure 14-2 among high school (12) and college students (13).

In many respects early socialization in the home continues to influence us as adults more than we might like to believe. For example, a study was once made of campus radicals and their parents. Though they held many clashing views and seemed on the surface to represent an extreme case of "generation gap," it turned out that the students and parents were more alike than different in numerous basic ways (14). But growing up does provide new forms of socialization, the influence of new and different kinds of people, and often changes in attitudes.

For college students, the freshman year is often especially influential (15). Up to that time many students have lived in an environment where most people are quite alike in their attitudes. Then as freshmen they suddenly find themselves in the company of many different kinds of teachers and fellow students who hold attitudes they had not previously encountered. Students from a religious and politically conservative background may find themselves exposed to new attitudes of religious skepticism and political liberalism. Students whose family and friends have scoffed at literature and art may find themselves around people who greatly admire Shakespeare and Rembrandt.

Some of the attitudes held by college students of the 1970s are shown in Figure 14-3. Another survey has indicated that college students appear to be growing less trusting of their fellow human beings and social institutions and less hopeful about the future. This study, begun in 1964, has shown a consistent and significant increase in the number of students who agree with such statements as "Hypocrisy is on the increase in our society," "This country has a dark future unless we can attract better people into politics," "The United Nations will never be an effective force for world peace," and "Most people would be horrified if they knew how much of the news the public hears and sees is distorted" (17).

These attitudes of today's student may play an important part in social developments in years to come, for attitudes developed as a result of the college experience tend to last a long time, often throughout life. One well-known study of this phenomenon began in the late 1930s in a women's college attended largely by students from wealthy and con-

BERRY'S WORLD

"You got that haircut to bug me, didn't you, son?"

497

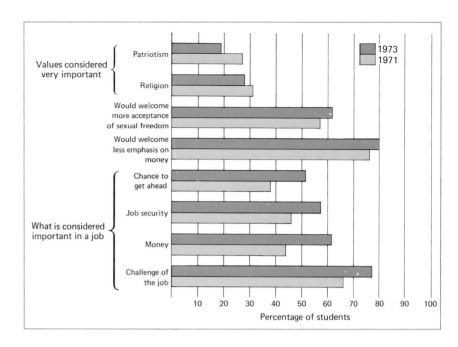

14-3

Some attitudes of college
students in the 70s

A public opinion poll that accurately reflects national trends found that in 1973 only
a minority of American college students considered patriotism and religion to be
"very important values." A majority said they would welcome more acceptance of
sexual freedom and less emphasis on money. Asked what they would value highly in
choosing a job, they prominently mentioned the challenge of the work, money, job
security, and a chance to get ahead. Note the rather sharp changes in some of
these attitudes from those expressed in a similar poll just two years earlier. Note
also that there seems to be a contradiction between students' desires for less emphasis on money and the importance they attach to the amount of money they can
earn at a job. (16)

servative backgrounds but staffed by a faculty that some people would
call extremely "liberal" and others would call "radical." By the time
students at this college reached their senior year, it was found, some
remained quite conservative but most showed pronounced changes
toward a liberal attitude. A follow-up twenty years later showed that
they continued to hold the same attitudes they had held as seniors (18).

But experiences that come after the college years can also have an
important effect. When we take a job we undergo a new kind of
socialization. Each time we change jobs or get a promotion, each time
we move to a new neighborhood or a new community, we come under
new influences. We are also influenced by what we read and by what
we see on television. And the world changes and we must change with
it. Our attitudes can be compared to a house that undergoes frequent
remodeling, expansion, and repainting over the years. In some ways the
house never changes, yet it is never really the same.

498

Cognitive dissonance and attitude change

One possible explanation of how attitudes undergo change is the *theory of cognitive dissonance*. This theory maintains that we have a strong urge to be consistent and rational in our thinking and to preserve agreement and harmony among our beliefs, feelings, and behavior—and therefore our attitudes. When there is a lack of consistency and harmony, we experience cognitive dissonance. We may manage to tolerate the inconsistency, as the Joneses did in the case of Candidate Smith. But cognitive dissonance tends to be highly uncomfortable and we are strongly motivated to restore harmony by making some kind of adjustment in our beliefs, feelings, behavior, or all three.

In the case of attitudes, new factual information is sometimes enough to create cognitive dissonance and bring about a change. For example, it appears that many people who were once strongly opposed to birth control have been greatly influenced by all the factual information that has appeared in recent years about the population explosion and the danger of worldwide starvation. They once had the cognitive belief that a growing population is a good thing; this cognitive belief has now changed, and their entire attitude toward birth control has changed with it.

Events that alter the emotional component of an attitude may also create an inconsistency that calls for a change. For an example, one need only imagine what would happen if a man who had always regarded women as second-class citizens found himself in love with a woman who was an ardent advocate of women's liberation. Or consider an actual laboratory experiment in which college women underwent a deeply emotional experience related to cigarette smoking. The women, all heavy smokers, were asked to act out a scene in which the experimenter pretended to be a physician and they his patients. Each subject, visiting the "doctor," got bad news about a persistent cough from which she had been suffering; her X-rays had shown lung cancer; immediate surgery was required; before the operation she and the doctor would have to discuss the difficulty, pain, and risk. The experimenter attempted to keep the scene as realistic as possible and to involve each subject emotionally to the greatest possible degree. As a result of the experience, almost all the women quit or drastically cut down on smoking —and a follow-up eighteen months later found that they continued to show a significant change in their smoking habits (19).

Behavior change
as the key to
attitude change

It seems only logical that a change in a belief or in an emotional response should act to change an attitude and thus produce a change in behavior. Yet, strangely enough, utterly contrary to common sense, it has been found that attitudes often change because of a change in behavior, not vice versa.

This fact was demonstrated in one of the very first experiments on cognitive dissonance. In this study, college students were asked to work for a long time at some extremely dull and boring tasks. They were then asked to tell other students waiting to take part in the experiment that the tasks had in fact been very interesting and enjoyable. In other words, they were asked to say something that they could hardly have believed—an action neatly calculated to produce cognitive dissonance.

To deceive the waiting students, some subjects were paid twenty dollars, while others were paid only the nominal sum of one dollar. The question was whether the amount of payment would influence the amount of cognitive dissonance experienced by the subjects and their efforts to relieve it. To answer this question, the subjects were asked afterward to express their feelings about the tasks they had performed and had spoken about. They were requested to rate the tasks on a scale ranging from extremely dull and boring (as indeed they were) to extremely interesting and enjoyable (as they had told other students).

The results of the experiment are shown in Figure 14-4. A control group, which did not engage in any deception of other students, expressed the candid and correct opinion that the tasks were far from enjoyable. The subjects paid $20 took a somewhat more favorable view—but still rated the tasks on the unenjoyable side of the scale. Presumably they considered the twenty-dollar payment a sufficient justification for lying to the waiting students, experienced only a low degree of

14-4

The strange effect of
cognitive dissonance

All the subjects in this experiment worked for an hour at some laboratory tasks. The control group, asked immediately afterward to describe the tasks, had no hesitation about calling them anything but enjoyable. The other two groups—and especially the group paid $1 as described in the text, gave the tasks a more favorable rating.

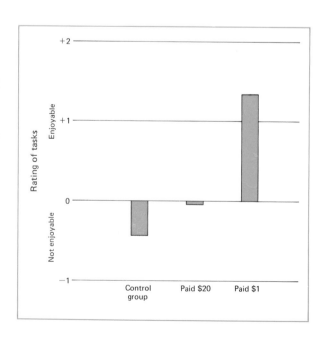

cognitive dissonance, and were not strongly motivated to change their own beliefs. But the one-dollar subjects did something very revealing. They gave the tasks a favorable rating; indeed they claimed that the tasks had actually been almost as "interesting, enjoyable, and lots of fun" as they had told the waiting students. The one-dollar payment had not relieved their cognitive dissonance; instead they relieved it by changing their beliefs (20).

Decision making as a behavior change

As will be noted later in the chapter, some aspects of the theory of cognitive dissonance are controversial. Many social psychologists believe that there are other explanations for attitude changes in situations such as the one just described. However, the fact that changes in behavior tend to produce changes in attitudes is well established and generally accepted. Moreover, there appears to be little doubt that one type of behavior of special importance in creating attitude change is the mere act of making a decision. This fact can best be explained by citing one of the classic experiments on attitude change.

In this study, a psychologist posing as a market researcher asked a woman to examine eight different electrical appliances (such as a toaster or coffee maker) and rate them in terms of how attractive she found them. Once the rating had been made, the psychologist then picked out two of the appliances and asked the woman to take her choice of one of the two as a gift for helping in the study. She made her choice and the appliance she selected was wrapped up and presented to her. Then she was asked to rate the eight appliances once more. This procedure was repeated with a number of different subjects—always with the same results. On the second rating, the women gave a higher mark to the appliance they had selected and received as a gift. But they gave a lower mark to the other appliance that had been offered to them—the one they had rejected (21). Once they had made their decision between the two appliances, they emphasized the good points of the one they had chosen—and looked unfavorably on the one they had turned down.

Similarly, a study of people who had just bought new automobiles showed that they continued to read advertisements for that particular brand—but avoided ads for other cars (22). They seemed to be looking for praise of their car that would confirm the wisdom of their decision to buy it. They shunned any ads that might have raised doubts.

Behavior and moral attitudes

A final word on the importance of decision making and other changes in behavior in bringing about attitude changes comes from an experiment performed with a group of sixth-graders. First the attitudes of the pupils toward cheating were measured. Then they were asked to compete for cash prizes by taking an examination. The exam was made so difficult that it was almost impossible to win without cheating, and the situation was arranged so that it seemed very easy to cheat without being caught—though in fact the experimenters could keep an accurate record of who did and who did not cheat. Afterward the children's attitudes toward cheating were again measured. Among the pupils who had cheated there was a strong tendency to take a more lenient attitude toward cheating. But the children who had not cheated developed a harsher attitude (23).

Summing up all the meaning of this and other studies, one social psychologist has suggested that the following advice might be useful to a ruler cynically interested in controlling the minds of humanity:

1 If you want someone to form more positive attitudes toward an object, get him to commit himself to own that object.
2 If you want someone to soften his moral attitude toward some misdeed, tempt him so that he performs that deed; conversely, if you want someone to harden his moral attitudes toward a misdeed, tempt him—but not enough to induce him to commit the deed (24).

The intervention of a cynical ruler is not required, however, for attitude changes to take place. Just as a matter of course in our changing society, new social situations push us in the direction of changes in behavior, which often lead in turn to changes in attitudes. This has been particularly noticeable in recent years in the attitudes of whites toward blacks and blacks toward whites. Among both blacks and whites, integration is most favored by those who have attended school or worked with members of the other race, and it is least favored by those who have had no interracial contacts (25). Undoubtedly this is a case where new forms of behavior—that is, dealing with members of the other race, studying or working with them, treating them as friendly equals—has produced attitude change.

In this same connection, a study was made of the attitudes of white housewives toward blacks in two different kinds of public housing projects—one in which whites and blacks lived side by side in fully integrated buildings, and the other in which they lived in separate buildings or different parts of the project. As is shown in Figure 14-5, the type of project had a pronounced effect. In the fully integrated projects,

14-5

A change in racial attitudes

In segregated housing projects where white and black families had few contacts, there were rather small changes in the attitudes of the white housewives toward blacks. In fully integrated projects that produced many interracial dealings, there were pronounced changes in a favorable direction. (26)

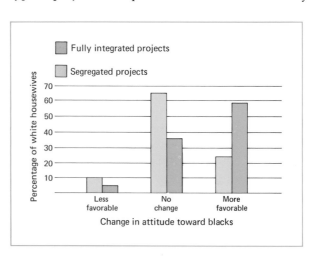

the attitudes of the white housewives toward blacks became more favorable in nearly 60 percent of cases, more unfavorable in only 5 percent. In the more segregated projects, changes of attitude were much less frequent. Again behavior appears to have been the key to the attitude change. The housewives in the integrated projects often found themselves in situations that called for friendly behavior toward their black neighbors. Those in the segregated projects did not.

Some other forces for attitude change

As was stated earlier, there are other theories of how attitudes may be changed. Since attitudes and attitude changes are so central to the study of social psychology, and the theories themselves so interesting, they are well worth our attention. The best place to start is with *attribution theory*. This may at first seem somewhat remote from attitude change. But it is an important aspect of social psychology, deserving discussion in its own right; and its relevance soon will become clear.

Attribution theory

As you stand in a group of people waiting for an elevator, the man next to you steps on your foot, causing you considerable pain. What will your reaction be? The answer depends on the man's behavior in the moments immediately following the incident. If he acts distressed and apologetic you will probably assume that the incident was an accident and will laugh it off. If he seems hostile you will probably assume that he stepped on your foot on purpose, and you will doubtless be angry. In other words, you make a judgment. You attribute his stepping on your foot either 1) to an unfortunate accident, which the man greatly regrets, or 2) to a hostile desire to hurt you.

Attribution theory holds that we are constantly looking for the causes of behavior. We want to know *why* people behave as they do. Only by attributing behavior to some kind of motive or other cause can we acquire the comfortable feeling that we understand the people who constitute such an important part of our environment — and that we can to some extent control their behavior in a way that will enable us to receive a maximum of social rewards and a minimum of punishments.

Attribution theory, it might be said, is devoted to the study of the amateur psychology that people use in trying to interpret behavior. In some ways, the amateur psychology that all of us apply is quite effective. Studies have shown that we look, as we should, for consistency of behavior. We do not decide that a woman is witty simply because she makes one rather funny remark; instead we wait for further evidence. We try to determine, as we should, whether a man tells us he likes his job because he really means it or because his boss is listening. We also seek and listen to the opinions of other people (which are often useful) as to whether the woman is witty, the man sincere or just acting because of external pressures (27).

Errors in attribution

All of us, however, tend to fall into a trap in regard to attribution. In seeking the cause for another person's behavior, we ignore the great message of social psychology, which is that behavior depends mostly on the situation. Instead, we tend to attribute behavior to some kind of lasting and consistent personality traits—or what social psychologists call *dispositional factors* (as opposed to *situational factors*). A woman bank teller smiles at us and wishes us a good morning and we conclude that she is warm and friendly—when her behavior may only reflect the fact that the boss has just warned her against being her natural surly self with customers. We see that a man who lives down the block drives through a red light at a high rate of speed and conclude that he is a reckless driver—though in fact he is merely rushing an injured daughter to a hospital emergency room.

This tendency to attribute behavior to dispositional factors—in other words, deep-seated personality traits—is one of the most powerful of all psychological forces. It operates even under the most unlikely circumstances, as has been shown by an experiment that produced almost unbelievable results. In this study, the subjects were asked to listen to a speech on racial segregation. In some cases the speaker argued vehemently for segregation, in other cases against it. Either way, the subjects were informed that the speaker had no choice about which side to take; the speaker had been ordered to argue pro or con and even told what arguments to use. Thus there was absolutely no reason to believe that the speaker was sincere. Yet so powerful was the effect of observing the speaker's behavior—that is, listening to the speech—that the subjects could not help concluding that the speaker really meant what was said, at least to some extent (28).

Attribution and one's own behavior

Attribution theory states further that we often try to analyze our own behavior just as we try to analyze the behavior of others. We find ourselves doing something that we do not quite understand. We drop a five-dollar bill that we cannot really spare into a Salvation Army kettle. We lose our tempers in the course of what seemed to be a friendly discussion of political differences. We are puzzled—and we ask ourselves, "Why did I do that?"

The manner in which we try to reach conclusions from our own behavior is the subject of what is called *self-perception theory*. The theory holds that when we have done something that cannot readily be explained, we then tend to take the role of an outside observer trying to find the cause. We study our behavior and the situation in which it occurred in order to try to decide what beliefs, feelings, and attitudes produced the behavior (29).

Rather strangely, when we look for the causes of our own behavior we tend to look for situational rather than dispositional factors—just the opposite of what we do when we try to find reasons for the behavior of others. If we do badly in school, for example, our faculty adviser is likely to attribute our failure to lack of ability or laziness. We ourselves are likely to attribute it to too heavy a course load, emotional stress over personal problems, or some other situational factor (30). Even if we do something rather praiseworthy, such as stopping on a highway to help an elderly couple change a tire, the same thing is likely to happen. An outsider watching our behavior would probably attribute it to a consistent disposition to be friendly and helpful. We ourselves would be inclined to emphasize the situational factors. We would point out that the people seemed very nice, unable to cope with their situation, and badly in need of somebody's help.

Self-perception theory and attitude change

We have now come full circle back to the matter of attitude change. Followers of attribution and self-perception theory maintain that these two processes, rather than cognitive dissonance, are often the best explanation of attitude change. What happens, they hold, is that in our search for causes of our own behavior we cannot always find situational explanations, as hard as we may be inclined to try. If we do manage to find such causes, then there is no reason to change our attitudes. But, if we cannot find them, we are forced to attribute our behavior to our attitudes—and in that case a change of attitude may well result (31).

In the case of the study mentioned earlier, in which subjects were paid to lie about how interesting an experiment was, self-perception theory would explain the results in these terms: The subjects who were paid $20 could conclude that it was only natural to be willing to lie for such a sum. Thus they attributed their lying to situational factors and no change of attitude occurred. The subjects paid only $1, on the other hand, were inclined to think, "Nobody would deliberately lie for such a small fee. Anybody who said the experiment was interesting must surely have believed it to at least some extent. Therefore *I* must have believed it." And, lo and behold, an attitude was changed.

Students who take advanced courses in social psychology will doubtless hear more about attribution and self-perception theories and the theory of cognitive dissonance. The important thing for present purposes is not the controversy but the fact that all three theories have shed valuable light on human social behavior in general and on attitude change in particular.

Attitude change and "persuasive communications"

Deliberate attempts to change attitudes are a commonplace feature of our society. Politicians want people to develop favorable attitudes toward them and their party. Advertisers spend many millions of dollars every year to try to create favorable attitudes toward their products. Many organizations work hard to find support for such causes as conservation, kindness to animals, and pollution control. Even religious leaders and educators are in a sense engaged in a constant attempt to in-

fluence attitudes and opinions—in the direction of the particular theology, philosophy, values, and moral code to which they adhere. On the world scene, democracy and Communism are often said to be in "a battle for people's minds."

To social psychologists, all these attempts to change attitudes by transmitting information and making emotional appeals are known under the collective term of *persuasive communications*. Because they have such a potentially great effect on our society and the behavior of individuals in that society, they have of course been studied in considerable depth.

The difficulty of reaching the right person

Every attempt to influence the attitudes of large numbers of people, it has been found, operates under many handicaps. For one thing, persuasive communications do not necessarily reach very many people. A presidential candidate who makes a speech on television may come to the notice of perhaps ten million people directly and several million more through newspaper accounts of the speech—yet even these figures, though they may seem high at first glance, represent only a fraction of the seventy million or more people who vote in a presidential election. A religious leader who makes a speech or writes a book reaches a much smaller audience.

Moreover, the kind of audience that is likely to hear or read any appeal for attitude change is determined largely by a factor called *selective exposure*. This means that, by and large, persuasive communications reach only people who are already persuaded. The audience that turns out for a Democratic political rally is overwhelmingly composed of Democrats. The people who read magazines favoring the conservation of natural resources are people already interested in conservation.

This is not to say that people always deliberately seek out support for their own attitudes and avoid anything that might shake their attitudes. Sometimes they do this, as has been shown in the experiment on reading automobile advertisements and in other studies (32, 33). Often, however, people actually seem to prefer information disagreeing with their attitudes, as if seeking to check their beliefs (34). Selective exposure is chiefly the result of the fact that people naturally tend to associate with people they like and to read or listen to communications they find interesting. Thus they are exposed mostly to people and communications they already agree with.

Perhaps the most concerted effort to change attitudes in our society is represented by a presidential campaign, which is a concentrated attempt to reach the public through all kinds of persuasive communications ranging from door-to-door canvassing to television speeches and commercials and from billboards to giant party rallies. The campaigns produce less attitude change than might be supposed. Many surveys have shown that most voters have their minds made up on the day the candidates are nominated and stick to their selections.

The number who change their preferences has been found to be no more than one in ten (35). This amount of change is of course extremely important to the political parties that wage the campaigns, for most elections are decided by margins of far less than 10 percent—but it is quite small considering all the effort and money that are expended.

The communication and its source

Let us now disregard the matter of selective exposure and assume that a persuasive communication has managed to reach us. It argues a viewpoint to which we are at the moment opposed. To adopt it, we will have to change an attitude. Will the persuasive communication actually persuade us?

Several factors help determine the answer. One of the most important, it has been found, is the matter of who is trying to persuade us—in other words, *the source of the communication.* Some sources are likely to have considerable influence. Others are much less likely to convince us and may in fact only make us more opposed to what they are proposing.

The importance of the source was convincingly demonstrated in one of the very first experiments in effectiveness of persuasive communications. Subjects in this study were asked to read a rather controversial argument on the development of an atomic energy project. Half the subjects were told that the argument had been written by a well-known atomic scientist. The other half were told that it came from the Soviet newspaper *Pravda.* It should come as no surprise that there was a great deal more attitude change among subjects who believed that the source was the scientist (36).

Many subsequent experiments have also demonstrated the importance of the *credibility of the source.* If the communication comes from people who can be assumed to know what they are talking about—in other words from a source of high credibility—it is likely to have considerable influence. If it comes from a source of low credibility, we tend to disregard it.

If the source of the communication is someone we like, we are also more likely to be influenced. In one experiment, for example, subjects listened to an argument presented by a woman who had no special qualifications to speak on the subject—but who, as the experimenters had carefully made sure, was extremely beautiful. Her argument proved very effective. In fact she was most effective of all when she frankly told her audience that she hoped to change their opinions (37).

While people may change their opinions when someone they like deliberately tries to influence them, as this experiment shows, they tend to do so only on matters of rather trivial importance. On important issues, the effectiveness of a persuasive communication is greater when it comes from a source that seems more objective and less interested in wielding influence. The effectiveness is greatest of all when the source is people who seem to be arguing for something that would be contrary to their own self-interest. In an experiment that demonstrates this point, subjects read a bogus newspaper interview with a mythical gangster convicted of smuggling and selling heroin. Half the subjects read clippings in which the "gangster" urged the courts to be more lenient in sentencing criminals. These subjects were not influenced at all; if anything, they became more opposed than ever to leniency. The other subjects read clippings in which the "gangster" seemed to go against his own self-interest by urging the courts to be stricter. These subjects were influenced to a marked extent. They tended to agree whole-heartedly with the "gangster" (38).

The nature of the communication

Just as the source can help determine effectiveness, so can the nature of the communication—that is, what kind of arguments are presented and how and when. In general, appeals to the emotions tend to be quite effective (39). Indeed one experimenter, dealing with actual voters in an actual election campaign, found that an appeal to vote for a candidate was considerably more successful when it was primarily emotional than when it was primarily logical (40). Appeals to fear are often particularly effective, as was shown by the experiment cited earlier in which women acted out the role of patients suffering from lung cancer. But sometimes the arousal of fear may backfire (41)—presumably because the listener becomes so upset as to try to forget the whole matter.

If the communication is addressed to an intelligent audience, its effectiveness appears to be increased if it presents a "fair" rather than a one-sided argument, admitting that the other side also has its points (42). But a one-sided argument may be more effective with a less intelligent audience, perhaps because such an audience is confused by listening to both sides (43). The one-sided argument also has a greater influence on an audience already leaning toward that side, while a "fair" argument is more likely to influence people leaning in the opposite direction (44).

The communication and the listener

A final factor that helps determine the effectiveness of a persuasive communication is the audience it reaches. Who is listening may be just as important as what is said and the source of the communication. For example, there appears to be no doubt that some people are much more easily persuaded than others. Indeed experiments have shown that people who tend to change their attitudes under one set of circumstances and in response to one kind of communication are also likely to change under different circumstances and in response to different kinds of communications (45). The crucial factor seems to be one's own opinion of oneself. People who are low in self-esteem tend to be much more easily persuaded than people who are high in self-esteem (46). Similarly, people who are anxious about social acceptance are more easily persuaded than those who are not anxious (47).

One very important research finding indicates that people are more likely to change an attitude if they think they have learned it than if they think it is something intrinsic—that is, if they think the attitude is a basic part of human nature or at least of their own inborn dispositions. In one experiment, university students were asked whether they thought it was likely that the next five years might change their attitudes about some of their personality characteristics (such as whether they regarded themselves as trusting, curious, and so on) and toward various social issues (such as capital punishment and legalization of marijuana). If they considered the attitude to be largely the result of their learning experiences (as a majority did for being trusting or favoring legalization of marijuana), they were significantly more likely to expect change than if they regarded the attitude as something innate (as a majority did for the trait of curiosity) (48).

The results of the experiment have some important implications for our society. They suggest that the popular but incorrect belief that most aspects of human nature are inherited discourages attitude change. For example, a young man convinced that he was "born" to be a delinquent might consider it hopeless to try to be anything else. He might be totally unresponsive to any appeals to change his attitudes and behavior. On the other hand, the discoveries of social psychology about the importance of situational factors should encourage change. If the young man could be convinced that his delinquency is the result of environmental influences, as indeed it is, then he would be much more receptive to the possibility of change.

Conformity

Up to this point the chapter has been chiefly concerned with the attitudes we acquire as a result of our experiences with other people and how these attitudes sometimes are changed—again chiefly as a result of the influence of other people, their behavior toward us, and most of all our behavior toward them. From what has been said, it should come as no surprise that the word *conformity* is prominent among the concerns of social psychology. Conformity is defined as the *yielding by individuals to pressures from the group in which they find themselves.* It is a prominent aspect of social behavior, closely related to attitude formation and change, and has been the subject of considerable research.

"You're a disgrace to all lemmings!"
Drawing by Chas. Addams; © 1974 The New Yorker Magazine, Inc.

The Asch experiment

One of the classic experiments on conformity was performed in the 1950s at Swarthmore College by Solomon Asch. It utilized the method illustrated in Figure 14-6, in which one actual subject, who thought that he was taking part in a study of perceptual discrimination, sat at a table with a group of confederates of the experimenter. The experimenter showed pairs of white cards with black lines of varying length, such as the lines shown in their relative sizes in Figures 14-7 and 14-8, and asked the group which of the lines in Figure 14-8 matched the test line.

For what the experimenter claimed were reasons of convenience, the people sitting around the table were asked to call out their judgments in order, beginning with the student at the experimenter's left. The real subject was always placed near the other end so that he would hear the judgments of several confederates before making his own. Sometimes the confederates gave the right answer, but on some trials they deliberately called out the wrong answer. On these trials 37 percent of the answers given by the real subjects were also incorrect. In other words, the subjects conformed with the group's wrong judgment much of the time.

Some of the subjects conformed on all trials; others on some but not all; and some remained independent and did not conform at any time. Even the subjects who showed independence, however, experienced various kinds of conflict and anxiety, as is readily apparent from the photographs of the subject in Figure 14-9. Some of their comments later were: "Despite everything, there was a lurking fear that in some way I did not understand I might be wrong." "At times I had the feeling, to heck with it, I'll go along with the rest." "I felt disturbed, puzzled, separated, like an outcast from the rest." Thus the urge to conform—to go along with the group—was strong even among the most independent subjects (49).

14-7

A test line

This was the relative size of one of the lines shown to subjects in the Asch experiment. They were asked which of the lines in Figure 14-8 matched it.

14-8

Which line matches?

Which of these three lines, the subjects in the Asch experiment were asked, matches the line shown in Figure 14-7? In one of the trials the experimenter's confederates insisted unanimously that it was line 1—the one that is in fact least like the test line.

14-9
An "independent"
subject—shaken but
unyielding

In the top photo, number 6 is
making his first independent judgment at variance with the group's
otherwise unanimous but incorrect verdict. In the other photos
his puzzlement and concern seem
to increase, until, preserving his
independence despite the pressure, he announces (bottom), "I
have to call them as I see them."

The Milgram experiment

Another experiment that produced even more dramatic results was performed by Stanley Milgram at Yale. This study was a different version of the Milgram experiment described in Chapter 1 (pages 30-32), in which it was found that subjects were surprisingly willing to follow the orders of the experimenter to administer what they thought were very severe and painful shocks to other people. Having shown that subjects were willing to obey a figure of authority even when the commands seemed outrageous and inhumane, Milgram then asked the logical next question: Would they be equally willing to conform to pressure from a group of their peers?

To answer the question, Milgram selected eighty men of various ages and occupational backgrounds and asked them to take part in what he said was an important experiment in learning. Each subject was assigned to a group of four people—the other three of whom, unknown to the subject, were Milgram's assistants. One of the assistants was the "learner" in the make-believe experiment. The other two assistants and the subject were the "teachers," with the job of instructing the "learner" by punishing him with an electric shock when he made an error. The subject was put at the controls that regulated the amount of shock. Actually, of course, as in the other Milgram experiment, no electricity was hooked up to the controls and no learning took place. The "learner" deliberately made errors and only pretended to feel a shock when punished.

Of the eighty subjects, half were placed in a control group. These subjects were not subjected to any pressure to raise the shock levels and did not raise them very high. Thirty-four of these forty control subjects stopped at shock levels listed as "slight" or "moderate." Only six went above 120 volts. But it was a far different story with the other forty subjects. These forty were strongly urged by their fellow "teachers" to raise the amount of electricity higher and higher—and they did. Only six of them refused to go above 120 volts. The other thirty-four went right on, even though the "learner" at first shouted that the shocks were becoming painful and later began to groan and finally scream in pain. Seven of the subjects went up to what they thought was the maximum they could deliver—a "highly dangerous" shock of 450 volts. Many of the experimental subjects showed signs of doubt and distress, yet they conformed anyway to the pressures of their group (50).

Why do we conform?

Milgram's subjects were just ordinary people who presumably would never be guilty of cruelty under ordinary circumstances. The fact that they were willing to go to such outrageous lengths under group pressure is eloquent and even frightening proof of how strong is the human tendency to conform. The question, of course, is why do we have these tendencies? Why are these tendencies so powerful that they can sometimes make us behave in unexpected and almost unbelievable ways?

The experiment in which the experimenter himself ordered the shocks is perhaps easiest to understand. In this case the subjects displayed obedience to a figure of authority — and obedience probably comes naturally to us because of the ways in which we are socialized from early childhood on. We are taught to believe that there are experts in the world who know much more than we do — and that it is both proper and wise to defer to their judgment.

The experimenter who demanded obedience had a lot of authority going for him. In the first place, he was working on the campus of a highly respected university. In the second place, he bore the imposing title of scientist. Take away either of these factors, and his subjects might have been far less willing to obey. Indeed Milgram proved this in some later studies. One study was conducted not on the Yale campus but in a rundown building in the shopping area of a nearby industrial city. Here the amount of obedience by the subjects was lower (51). In another study, the commands to increase the shock levels were given not by a scientist but by an ordinary layman. Again the subjects proved considerably less willing to obey (52).

Our dependence on our peers

As to why we should conform to the pressure of people who are not authorities — just ordinary people who happen to be in the same group in which we find ourselves — one reason seems to be that we depend on the group for many of our psychological satisfactions. It is pleasant to be a fully accepted, well-liked member of the group. It is highly unpleasant to be rejected by the group and perhaps even subjected to ridicule (53). Thus it is generally easier and more rewarding to conform. It can be very difficult to stand alone as a single dissenting voice.

Studies have shown, indeed, that unanimity within the group is the most powerful factor of all in producing conformity. If we are in a group where everybody agrees, we are under much stronger pressure to conform than if even one person expresses disagreement. This was demonstrated in an ingenious variation of the Asch experiment in which one of the confederates sitting around the table was a black and some of the actual subjects were known to be prejudiced against blacks. When the confederates were unanimous in the incorrect answers they gave, all the subjects showed the usual tendency to conform. But when the black confederate broke the unanimity of the group by giving the correct answer, the subjects were much less likely to conform — including the subjects known to be prejudiced (54).

"The main thing is not to take it personal."
Courtesy of *Saturday Review* and Joseph Farris

Conformity and
the theory of
social comparison

Another reason we tend to conform is that the behavior of the other members of the group is often the only guide we have to how we ourselves should behave. Suppose, for example, that you go as an exchange student to live with a family in Italy. How, in this strange household, do you know what kind of table manners are expected, how you are expected to address the father and mother, what gestures are considered polite, what kinds of conduct are frowned on? The only way you can answer these questions is to see how the members of the family behave — and to model your own behavior on what they do.

Going to Italy is an extreme example, but the same sort of situation arises frequently in the ordinary course of events. On a new campus, how are you expected to dress, behave in the classroom, get along with your fellow students? If you go to a party where you are the only stranger, how do you manage to fit in? Obviously, you have to look to the people around you for information. What they do is your only guide to what you are expected to do.

The human tendency to look to others for information has led to what is called the *theory of social comparison*. The theory maintains that all of us feel the need to evaluate our own opinions and abilities. Usually there is no objective, scientific way that we can do this. Therefore we can only judge ourselves by comparing ourselves with other people — usually our friends or other people we believe to be similar to ourselves (55). The more uncertain we are as to where we stand, the more likely we are to make comparisons and rely on what other people tell us (56, 57).

The theory of social comparison sheds considerable light on why the subjects in the Milgram conformity experiment may have behaved as they did. They were in a highly uncertain situation. After all, they were taking part in a scientific experiment. And, if they were supposed to stop at a low level of electric shock, why did the controls go all the way up to 450 volts? They had no real way of knowing what to think or how to behave — so they looked to the other "teachers," people who seemed to be just like themselves, for information. They compared their own opinions with the opinions of the others in the group. And, when the others proved to be so positive about raising the shock levels, who were they to argue otherwise?

"I'm awfully sorry, Dick, but we've all just had a little meeting, and we've agreed that perhaps it's best you leave the commune."
Drawing by Weber; © 1973
The New Yorker Magazine, Inc.

True and expedient conformity

Before leaving the subject of conformity, it should be added that there are two kinds. *Expedient conformity* is mere lip service to the ideas and opinions expressed by the group, without any real change in attitude. For example, a woman who strongly favors the Democratic candidate in a forthcoming election finds herself at a party where everybody else favors the Republican candidate. She might very well pretend to go along with the group simply to avoid argument.

True conformity represents a change of both outward behavior and private attitude in response to group pressure. For example, a man who has always believed that pollution control laws were bad for business and employment moves to a new job in a new community. His business associates and neighbors are very much in favor of pollution control. Eventually he may come to agree wholeheartedly. One might say that he has internalized the group attitude and made it his own.

To put this another way, sometimes we conform to the group even when we feel that the group is wrong, just because we want to be accepted. This is expedient conformity. But sometimes we conform because we have made our social comparisons and decided the group is right. This is true conformity (58).

Social comparisons and self-esteem

The theory of social comparison, besides explaining some of the facts about conformity, also bears in an important way on how our self-esteem—one might almost say our entire self-image—is affected by the people around us. We judge our abilities as well as our opinions, the theory holds, mostly by comparing ourselves with other people. We cannot state for sure, as a proven fact, that we are good students, good teachers, good athletes, or anything else. We have to try to decide how we rank in comparison with other people—notably our friends and other close associates. And we must also ask, "What do other people think of us?"

The opinions of other people play a far greater part in self-esteem than could ever be imagined by a person who has never been exposed to social psychology and its emphasis on social influences. For dramatic proof of this fact, one need only think for a moment about another experiment that produced surprising results.

In this study, the subjects were women attending high school or college. They were asked to try their hands at a problem-solving task containing twenty-five items. After they had finished, the experimenters pretended to grade their attempts and then told them how they had scored. Actually, no grading was ever done. The experimenters simply decided arbitrarily to tell half the subjects that they had done quite badly, the other half that they had done quite well.

This false information about performance was allowed to "sink in" for a time. Then the experimenters flatly admitted their deception. It was explained to the women that their scores had never actually been compiled—and that there was no truth at all in the information that

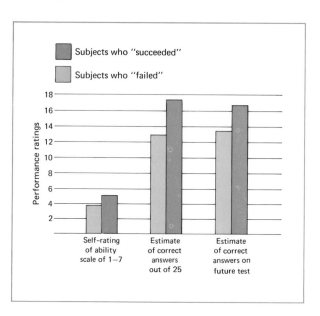

14-10

It's not true — but I believe it!

The graph illustrates the results of the experiment with high-school and college women discussed in the text. Subjects who were told they "failed" at a problem-solving task had a significantly lower opinion of their ability than subjects who were told they "succeeded" — even though they knew that the information about their performance had absolutely no relation to the facts.

they had done badly or well. Once the truth was out, the women were then asked to rate their own ability at that kind of problem-solving, to estimate how many problems they had in fact solved correctly, and also to estimate how many they would solve correctly on a future trial.

As is shown in Figure 14-10, the results were quite startling. Apparently the women who had been told they did badly were never quite able to get over the loss of self-esteem they suffered — even though they knew that the unfavorable rating had no relation to the facts and meant absolutely nothing. The women who had been told they did well, on the other hand, were much more confident — even though they, too, knew that the information was meaningless (59).

There could hardly be more convincing proof of the importance of the social comparison process. If our self-esteem and expectations of future performance depend so thoroughly on ratings by others that these ratings continue to affect us even after we are told they are false, then how can anyone doubt the importance of social influences on our lives?

Attraction to others

As has been discussed in the preceding pages, the people around us play a vital part in molding our self-images, pressuring us toward conformity, forming our attitudes, and sometimes changing our attitudes. Therefore it becomes important to ask: Who *are* these other people? How do we come to be associated with them? Why are we subject to the influences of one particular group rather than of some other very different group?

Sometimes our associations are a matter of sheer accident. In Milgram's experiment, for example, the subjects just happened to find themselves in a group with two other "teachers" who just happened to be confederates of the experimenter. In real life situations as well, accident can play a part. Going to a college because it is close to your home or offers you a scholarship can place you in very different groups of students and teachers than you might find at a different college. Taking a job puts you into close contact with co-workers who are already there, without your having any choice in the matter. The people next door move in or out of the neighborhood without your permission.

All of us, however, choose many or most of the people with whom we associate. We deliberately pick our friends and our less intimate acquaintances. We belong to groups of our choosing. Hence the importance of what social psychologists call *interpersonal attraction* — or the manner in which we are attracted to other people or repelled by them.

What social psychologists have learned about interpersonal attraction can be summed up quite simply: "We like those who reward us, and the more they reward us the better we like them" (60). As to what we find rewarding about others — and why — a number of factors have been found important.

Physical attractiveness

Most of us like to deny that physical appearance has anything to do with our judgments of other people. Beauty, we have been told, is only skin deep. And some of the greatest men and women in the world's history have been physically unprepossessing or downright ugly. It seems totally unfair to like or dislike someone just because an accident of heredity has resulted in beauty or its opposite. For more than a half century psychologists have been asking college students what they value most in a person of the opposite sex, and physical attractiveness has always wound up near the bottom of the list. In one of the most recent studies, college men were asked to rank four characteristics in order of the importance they would attach to these qualities in a woman who was a possible date. The men put "personality" at the top, followed by "character." The factor of "looks" was rated third, ahead only of "intelligence" (61).

But studies have revealed ample evidence that physical attractiveness is more important than most people care to admit. Even in nursery school, it has been found, the attractive boys are the most popular, the unattractive boys the least popular (62). And what adults think about children has also been shown to depend to a considerable extent on physical appearance. In one experiment, women subjects were asked to evaluate the behavior of children who had supposedly been guilty of a serious disturbance in the classroom or on the playground. A written report of the incident was given to the subjects along with what was purported to be a photograph of the child. When the photograph showed an unattractive child, the women tended to be rather harsh in their judgments. When the child was attractive, their judgments were more lenient. Thus an unattractive girl was described by one subject as "quite bratty . . . a problem to teachers. . . . She would probably pick a fight. . . ." An attractive girl who had supposedly committed exactly the same disturbance was described as "charming, well-mannered, basically unselfish . . . but like anyone else, a bad day can occur" (63).

What adults think of other adults is similarly affected by physical appearance. In one experiment, for example, college men were asked to judge the quality of an essay written by a college woman. When the subjects believed that the writer was very attractive, they gave the essay the highest marks. When they did not know about her appearance, the marks were in the middle range. When they believed she was unattractive, they gave the lowest marks (64).

Even just being in the company of someone attractive can produce a favorable impression. This was demonstrated in an experiment in which subjects were asked to express their opinion of a man they had met in the company of a woman introduced as his girl friend. When the "girl friend" was attractive, the subjects gave the man a favorable rating. When she was unattractive, the subjects' rating was negative (65).

As for what constitutes physical attractiveness, there is considerable difference of opinion around the world and in our own society from person to person. In one study in which subjects were asked to judge the attractiveness of photographs of children, teenagers, and adults, every one of the photographs was ranked first by some of the judges (66). On the other hand, most judges in our society usually tend to agree. Rather high correlations have been found between ratings of attractiveness made by different observers (67).

For men, tall is beautiful. One factor that seems to play an extremely important part, as far as men are concerned, is height. One analysis has shown that college graduates applying for a job are more likely to get it if they are tall than if they are short. Moreover, the taller graduates are likely to be started at a higher salary. In presidential elections, the taller of the candidates has consistently been the winner (68). The manner in which height is associated with attractiveness and importance has also been demonstrated in an experiment in which a stranger was introduced to a number of college classes—sometimes as a student, sometimes as a lecturer, and sometimes as a full professor. After he departed,

14-11

How tall is this man?

Estimates of his height, as was discovered in an experiment described in the text, depend on how important he is believed to be by the people making the estimate. The more important he is, the taller he seems to be in the eyes of his beholders.

6'	
5'11''	
5'10''	
5'9''	

Student   Lecturer   Senior lecturer   Professor

the students in the classes were asked to estimate his height. As is shown in Figure 14-11, when he was introduced as a student the average estimate was 5 feet 10 inches. But when he was introduced as a professor the average estimate jumped to over six feet (69).

Why attractiveness counts. As to why physical attractiveness should be such an important factor in interpersonal attraction, one reason seems to be that it is so immediately and obviously apparent. When we meet someone for the first time, we can only guess at this person's I.Q., educational background, interests, tastes, and attitudes. We can see at a glance, however, what the person looks like.

Moreover, all of us tend to hold to a stereotype maintaining that psyically attractive people are also attractive in other ways. In a study in which subjects were asked to judge the personality characteristics of people shown in photographs, the subjects read all kinds of virtues into photos of attractive people. The attractive people were judged to be more interesting, strong, sensitive, sociable, poised, modest, outgoing, and sexually warm and responsive. This was true regardless of whether the photographs showed men or women—and of whether the subjects judging the photographs were men or women (70).

Similarity

All other things being equal, we also tend to be most attracted to people who are very much like us—or at least whom we perceive to be similar. This fact can readily be observed in real-life situations and has also been demonstrated experimentally. At one large university, a psychologist arranged to operate a sort of men's dormitory in which roommates were assigned on the basis of questionnaires and interviews revealing their attitudes, interests, and tastes. Some roommates were put together because they were very similar, others because they were quite different. As time went on, it developed that roommates who were very much alike usually liked each other and became good friends, while those who were dissimilar did not like each other and did not become friends (71).

As might be expected from the earlier discussion of the importance of attitudes, these play a particularly prominent role in helping us decide whether another person is like us or different. In one experiment, a psychologist measured the attitudes of college students on a variety of issues, such as the strength of their attachment to the Republican or Democratic party. The students were then asked to read what were said to be answers to attitude questionnaires by other students they had never met. The supposed answers of these "strangers" were carefully designed so that the stranger sometimes seemed to have no attitudes at all in common with the subject, in some cases seemed to be in total agreement on all attitudes, and in other cases fell somewhere in between, agreeing with some of the subject's attitudes and disagreeing with others. The subjects were asked to rate these various strangers on a scale ranging from "not at all attractive" to "very attractive." As is shown in Figure 14-12, the attractiveness ratings turned out to bear an almost perfect straight-line relationship to the percentage of attitudes the subjects believed were held in common (72).

In a strange way, similarity and physical attractiveness seem to interact. In one experiment, students were placed in discussion groups whose members had a wide range of political attitudes from quite conservative to quite radical. Later the students were asked to rate members of the group for physical attractiveness. They showed a pronounced tendency to think that those with similar attitudes were more physically attractive than those with different attitudes (73). This same phenomenon also seems to work in the opposite direction; if we consider a person physically attractive, we tend to think that this person is similar to us in attitudes (74).

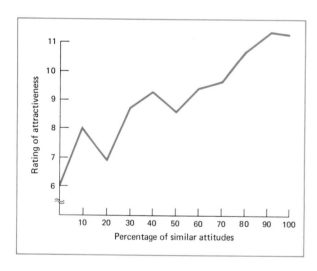

14-12

The more shared attitudes, the greater the attraction

The dependent variable was how subjects would rate a "stranger" on a scale ranging from 2 (not at all attractive) to 14 (very attractive). The independent variable was the percentage of attitudes that the subjects believed they and the "stranger" held in common. Note that the curve is almost a straight line, indicating an almost perfect correlation.

14-13

Familiarity and attraction

The amount of attraction felt toward a person seen in a photograph rises sharply with the number of times the photograph has been seen.

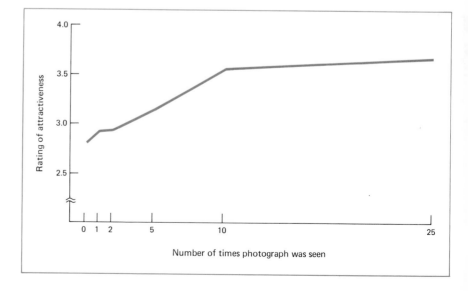

Competence

In general, we have a tendency to be attracted to people who are competent — who are good at what they do, whether this be singing, playing basketball, solving mathematical equations, or repairing automobiles. It is interesting to note, however, that most of us seem to be turned off by people who are *too* competent (75). Apparently we are uncomfortable around people who remind us of our own all-too-human failings; we prefer them to have a few little weaknesses and failings of their own.

This fact was demonstrated in an ingenious experiment in which an actor made four tape recordings of what were purported to be tryouts for a television quiz show. In one recording, the actor pretended to be a near-genius who got almost all the questions right and was well-nigh perfect in every respect. In another recording, the actor was again the near-genius but made an embarrassing blunder near the end of the tape — admitting, in an agonized voice, that he had spilled a cup of coffee all over his new suit. In the other tapes, the actor pretended to be just a mediocre sort of person who got most of the questions wrong. In one of the tapes he made no blunder; in the other he too spilled the coffee.

When the tapes were heard by the subjects in the experiment, and the subjects were asked to say how attracted they felt toward the four supposedly different people trying out for the TV show, the results were these: the competent person who made a blunder turned out to be the most attractive; the mediocre person who made a blunder turned out to be the least liked (76). A blunder by an extremely competent person seems to make that person more human and therefore more lovable. A blunder by a mediocre person reinforces our already low opinion.

The effect of familiarity

One well-established fact in the field of interpersonal attraction is that, contrary to the old adage, familiarity does *not* breed contempt. All other things being equal, the more familiar we are with other people — the more chance we have to get used to them — the more likely we are to be attracted to them. In one experiment, for example, two subjects who did not know each other sat across from each other without talking. Some of them met in this manner on three occasions, others six times, others twelve times. Afterward they were asked how much they liked each other. The more often they had seen the other, the greater was the mutual attraction (77). Indeed the same thing is true even of photographs of people. In another study, photographs of faces were shown to the subjects — some just once, others as many as twenty-five times. Then the photographs were shown again, along with some never seen before, and the subjects were asked if they thought they would like the person. As is illustrated in Figure 14-13, the amount of attraction they felt toward the person in the photograph was closely related to how often they had seen that person's picture (78).

Indeed it appears that just the mere prospect of becoming familiar with other people can make them more attractive. When strangers are

introduced in the laboratory, it has been found that they are more attracted to each other if told that they will work together in the future than if they believe they may never meet again (79). Similarly, we tend to like those who live nearest to us. A number of studies have shown that people are likely to be most friendly with those who live right next door to them in a college dormitory, an apartment building, or a suburban group of houses (80).

Liking those who like us

It seems only logical to assume that we tend to be attracted to people who seem to be attracted to us, and this assumption has been borne out by a number of experimental studies (81). We also tend to like people in whose company we have achieved satisfactions, as can be observed by the general air of camaraderie on a winning athletic team. Similarly, we tend to like people who hold a high opinion of us (82).

Apparently we are especially attracted to other people who at first do not seem to like us or hold a high opinion of us — but later come around to liking us. This fact was demonstrated in an experiment in which subjects held a series of brief interviews with a person they believed was another subject but was in fact an accomplice of the experimenter. After each interview, the subjects overheard a conversation in which the accomplice talked about them to the experimenter. As would be expected, the subjects were attracted to the accomplice when the reports about them were consistently favorable after each interview. But they were even more attracted if the accomplice was critical after the early interviews and gradually came around to a favorable opinion (83). Apparently there is a special satisfaction — and thus a strong tendency toward attraction — in winning over a person who was at first critical.

The importance of first impressions

When we meet new people, our first impressions often have a lasting effect on how attractive they seem. If we like them, we usually continue to like them — even if some of their future conduct is rather objectionable. If we dislike them, we are likely to continue to feel negatively about them — even if their future conduct is above reproach.

In an experiment demonstrating this fact, subjects first saw a stranger — actually a man who was an accomplice of the experimenter — in a laboratory waiting room. In his dealings with a secretary who was in charge of the waiting room, the stranger was at times extremely impolite, belligerent, and demanding. At other times, in the presence of other subjects, he was polite and pleasant. Later the subjects again met the accomplice-stranger on three to twelve other occasions. As would be expected from what is known about the effect of familiarity, they liked the "pleasant" stranger better when they saw him twelve times than when they only saw him three times. But increased contact did not change their ratings of the "unpleasant" stranger (84). The effect of the bad first impression outweighed the effect of familiarity.

The importance of first impressions was also demonstrated in an experiment in which subjects watched and listened to a student answering the items on an intelligence test. The test-taker, again an accomplice of the experimenter, followed three different patterns in giving the answers. In front of some subjects, the student answered the first questions accurately and then began making mistakes. In front of other subjects, the student performed evenly and moderately well throughout. Still other subjects watched the student do badly on the early questions, then improve toward the end. In every case, the net result was fifteen correct answers out of thirty questions. Yet, when the subjects were asked to rate the student's intelligence, the highest marks were given by subjects who had seen the student do well on the early questions—in other words, by those whose first impression had been favorable (85).

The "warm" or "cold" instructor. In another experiment, students reporting for a class were informed that they would have a substitute instructor that day. To prepare them for the substitute (so they were told), slips of paper bearing a written description of him were passed around. Half the slips described the substitute as "a rather cold person, industrious, critical, practical, and determined." The other half said he was "a rather warm person, industrious, critical, practical, and determined." The changing of only one word—*cold* to *warm*—had some interesting effects. The students who had received slips calling the substitute *warm* took more part in the classroom discussion that day than did the others. Afterward, asked their impressions, they described the substitute in much more favorable terms than did the students who had been told he was *cold*. Figure 14-14 shows some of the differences in the students' ratings of the substitute (86).

A note on implicit personality theory. To explain the importance of first impressions, social psychologists have suggested that all of us tend to carry around a sort of working theory of people and their personalities. As was said earlier, we tend to think that people who are physically attractive are also blessed with many other virtues. As the experiment with the substitute instructor shows, we tend to think that a "cold" per-

14-14

What a difference a word makes

These are some of the ratings of a substitute instructor made by a class of students—half of whom had been told he was a "warm" person and half of whom had been told he was "cold." Note how the single word "cold" led students to judge him as also irritable, humorless, and so on—characteristics that the students who expected him to be "warm" were much less likely to find.

Characteristics on which substitute was rated	Substitute instructor believed to be	
	"Warm"	"Cold"
Irritable	9.4	12.0
Humorless	8.3	11.7
Ruthless	8.6	11.0
Unsociable	5.6	10.4
Self-centered	6.3	9.6
Formal	6.3	9.6
Unpopular	4.0	7.4

son is also likely to possess other undesirable traits, such as irritability and lack of a sense of humor.

Social psychologists have termed this phenomenon *implicit personality theory*. Without ever realizing it, all of us have developed such a theory and make many of our judgments in accordance with it. If we notice or are told that a stranger has an important personality trait that we have come to believe is accompanied by other good or bad traits, we immediately draw some conclusions. Thus if we are told that a stranger is "cold" we make many assumptions about the stranger's irritability and lack of humor. If the stranger is "warm," we make entirely different assumptions. Our implicit personality theory leads us into error at times. For one thing, it is likely to make us think of other people as more consistent than they really are. But it does serve a purpose in helping us categorize and deal with other people. Our theory has been acquired through experience and is probably right more often than it is wrong. Right or wrong, it is one of the tools we use in that important form of behavior called responding to others.

Bystander apathy, aggression, and altruism

As a final word on social psychology, mention should be made of some other important questions that its investigators have been asking in recent years. Why do people sometimes go to great lengths to help others—like the brave men and women who, as the newspapers report from time to time, risk their own lives to save someone who is drowning? Why, at other times, do they seem to ignore other people who are in serious trouble? Are human beings basically aggressive and cruel, as crime statistics and warfare might indicate? Or are they basically kind and helpful, as countless stories of self-sacrifice might seem to say?

14-15

Helpfulness to strangers: big city versus small town

The "strangers" were investigators who rang doorbells, pretended to be lost, and asked to use the phone. The people they asked for help were inclined to admit women investigators to their homes, more inclined to turn men investigators away. But to both sexes, people in small towns were much more helpful than big-city residents.

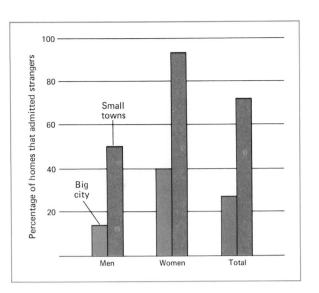

Studies in
bystander apathy

One term frequently used in this connection is *bystander apathy*—the outgrowth of a well-publicized incident in New York City in which a young woman named Kitty Genovese was murdered on the street one night in sight of thirty-eight neighbors who heard her cries and ran to their apartment windows. Although the assault went on for a half hour and many of the spectators watched for the entire time, no one called the police or took any other action. Why?

The Genovese case has inspired many studies designed to shed light on why people sometimes help and sometimes display a remarkable degree of bystander apathy. In one such study investigators rang doorbells, explained that they had mislaid the address of a friend in the neighborhood, and asked to use the phone. Half the investigators were men and half were women, and they went to homes in both a large city (middle-income housing developments in New York) and small towns. The results are shown in Figure 14-15. In both the big city and the small towns the women investigators were admitted to more homes than the men—but both women and men investigators received much more help in small towns than in the city. The psychologists who conducted the experiment believe that one explanation of the results is that big-city residents have a greater suspicion and fear of strangers (87).

Apathy and the big-city rush. Another possible explanation for bystander apathy, especially in large cities, comes from an experiment in which subjects were men attending a theological seminary—and therefore men who might be expected to lend a helping hand to anyone in trouble. The subjects had volunteered to record a brief talk. When they arrived at the experimenter's office they received some printed material that was to be the basis of the talk, studied it, and then were directed to proceed to a recording studio in a nearby building. The route, as shown on a map each received, took them through an alley in which they passed a confederate of the experimenter who was lying in a doorway, coughing and groaning as if in pain. The question, of course, was how

525

14-16

A "Good Samaritan" offers help

One of the subjects in an experiment on bystander apathy stops to offer help to a man lying in an alley doorway. Was he really a "Good Samaritan"—or did he just stop because he was in no special hurry to get anywhere? For the answer, see the text.

many of them would stop to assist the man in trouble—as did the subject shown in Figure 14-16.

The printed material that half the subjects studied was the story of the Good Samaritan, which, it seemed, might help remind them of their duty to help others. The other half studied a discussion of job opportunities for seminary graduates, which, it was presumed, would have no effect one way or the other. In addition, an attempt was made to determine whether the men might be influenced by how much of a hurry they were in to reach the recording studio. Some of the men were told that they were early and should take their time, others that they were just about on schedule, and still others that they were late and should rush to the studio as fast as possible. In other words, a third of the subjects were put in what the experimenter deemed a "low hurry" situation, a third in an "intermediate hurry," and another third in a "high hurry" situation.

Which subjects offered help to the man in pain and which did not? It turned out that it made no difference whether the subjects had just read the Good Samaritan parable or the material on job opportunities. What did make a difference was whether or not they were in a hurry. Of the "low hurry" subjects, 63 percent offered help; of the "intermediate hurry" subjects, 45 percent; and of the "high hurry" subjects only 10 percent (88). The study would indicate that the rush of big-city life—as contrasted with the more leisurely pace of smaller towns—may also contribute to bystander apathy.

The anonymity of big-city life also appears to play a part. In the city, people can walk for blocks without meeting anyone they know. They themselves are mere faces in the crowd. They do not have the intimate contacts with known friends and neighbors that might induce them to offer help.

Studies have shown that any increase in the degree of intimacy—even in the matter of physical closeness—serves to reduce the tendency toward bystander apathy. In one experiment, for example, investigators pretended to collapse on the floor of a New York subway car. In some cases they smelled of alcohol and carried a whisky bottle in a paper bag, as if they were drunk. In other cases they showed no signs of drinking but carried a cane, as if they were sick. Over a large number of trials,

526

someone in the car went to the assistance of the "drunks" half the time, to the assistance of the "sick" investigators 95 percent of the time (89). This is a far higher number of people than have ever been found willing to help a similar sort of "victim" on a big-city street. Doubtless the results were due to the fact that the bystanders—actually "by-sitters"—were in a face-to-face situation with the victims and in a confined space where they could not just ignore these victims and walk past.

There's no safety in numbers. Further light on bystander apathy comes from experiments that have explored the relationship between the number of people who witness an incident—such as a fire, a theft, or a call for help—and the likelihood that anyone will try to help. In a typical experiment of this kind, men students at a university who arrived at a psychology laboratory were asked to sit in a small waiting room until they could be interviewed. Some of the subjects waited alone, others in groups of three, and still others in groups of three that contained only one actual subject and two confederates of the experimenter. Soon smoke began to seep into the room through a ventilator in the wall. The smoke continued until someone took steps to report a fire, or, if no one did, for six minutes.

As is shown in Figure 14-17, most of the subjects who were alone took action to report the smoke—and they usually did so rather quickly. But when three subjects were waiting together, only 13 percent ever reported the smoke. Of the subjects who were sitting with the two confederates—who of course were instructed to pay no attention to the smoke—only 10 percent took action (90).

The moral would seem to be that anyone who needs help is not

14-17

Bystander apathy and number of spectators

How many students, sitting in the waiting room of a psychology laboratory, would report the presence of smoke that seemed to indicate a fire? The answer seems to depend on how many people are present. In group 1, there were three people in the room—one actual subject and two confederates of the experimenter who were instructed to ignore the smoke. In group 2, three actual subjects were waiting in company. In group 3—the only one in which a majority took action—the subject was alone in the room and presumably felt a greater sense of personal responsibility.

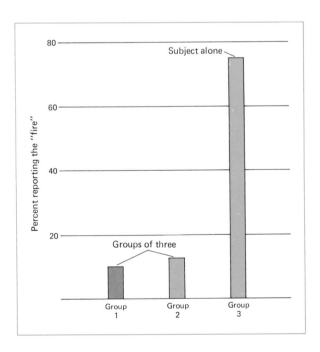

likely to find safety in numbers but is better off when only one other person is around. Several reasons have been suggested. First, the presence of others may produce bystander apathy by relieving any single individual of feelings of personal responsibility. Second, apparent indifference on the part of others may cause the individual bystander to downgrade the seriousness of the situation. The facts can also be explained in terms of what was said earlier about conformity. In any situation where a group appears to be ignoring the plight of a person in need, there is a strong tendency to conform to their behavior.

Aggression

The question of whether human beings are innately aggressive—in a manner that makes oppression, cruelty, and warfare inevitable—was mentioned in Chapter 1 as one of the great issues that concern today's psychologists. Some of the findings about aggression have also been discussed. You may recall, for example, the photographs on page 59 showing how children tend to imitate an adult who aggressively attacks a life-size doll—an indication that aggressive behavior can be acquired through observation learning. In Chapter 9, in the discussion of the hostility motive, mention was made of studies showing that people appear to become more aggressive after watching violent behavior in films or even in sports such as football.

As a result of such studies, many psychologists have concluded that human aggression, though it may have some innate elements, is largely

learned: it is a form of behavior that the individual has acquired through observation learning or has discovered to be effective in some way in obtaining social rewards. These psychologists point out that aggressive children tend to come from aggressive families — and to have been punished rather severely for childhood transgressions. Moreover, it has been found that aggression tends to become a way of life for some individuals. Occasionally the newspapers report what seems to be an inexplicable act of violence by someone who apparently had never been known to show such tendencies earlier. Yet careful study of some such cases has shown that these people actually had a long though secret history of aggressive behavior (91).

In this connection, it is interesting to note that even a monkey's display of aggression is modified by learning and the social situation. When a part of the brain that tends to produce aggressive behavior is stimulated by an electrode, a monkey will indeed attack other monkeys who rank lower in the social hierarchy. But, if the monkey is in the presence of others who rank higher, it will not attack. Instead it will flee. If even a monkey experiencing "brain control" modifies its aggressive behavior so drastically in accordance with the social situation, why should social influences not affect human aggression?

Aggression as a "basic trait." Other psychologists, as well as scientists in other fields such as biology, maintain that aggression is a basic trait of human nature. Indeed one scientist has described it as "an essential part of the life-preserving organization of instincts" (92). Some scientists follow the lead of Freud, who theorized that people have a death instinct that pushes them toward violence or self-destruction. Others base their opinions on observations of animals — the "law of the jungle" dictating that the organism must kill to survive.

It has been found, for example, that certain male fish ordinarily attack only the males of their own species — presumably to protect their territories and their mates. But, if there are no other males of the species around, these fish will start to attack the males of other species. If there are no males of any kind available, the fish will attack females — and sometimes even kill their own mates. This behavior has been cited as proof that the fish has an instinct or drive for aggression so powerful that it has to find some kind of outlet, even if this means violent destruction of the family (92a).

It has also been shown that a rat raised in isolation — that is, without any chance to observe and learn aggressive behavior from others of its species — will immediately attack any other rat that enters its cage. Moreover, in making its threats and carrying out its attack, it will use the same tactics used by rats raised with normal social contacts (93).

At this stage of psychology's history, it is impossible to say for sure whether human beings are "programed" for violence like fish and rats — or whether they merely learn to be violent. Whatever the origin of aggressive behavior, it has been pointed out, doubtless it once had a great value in helping the human race survive — but the development of civilization may have made it obsolete and counterproductive. As one biologist has put it: "The need now is for a gentler, a more tolerant people than those who won . . . against the ice, the tiger, and the bear" (94).

Altruism

The opposite of aggression is what social psychologists call *altruism* — or being kind, generous, and helpful to others. Cases of altruism are not reported in the newspapers so often as incidents of violence, but they occur in great numbers. The Boy Scout helping an elderly person across the street is no exception in our society. And the amounts donated each year to various charities are quite staggering.

Just as a case can be made that animal behavior indicates that aggression is innate or possibly even instinctive, so can a similar case be made from studies of lower organisms that altruism is an inborn trait. Chimpanzees have been found to share their food with another hungry chimpanzee in an adjoining cage — though, it must be conceded, they did so rather grudgingly (95). Other animal studies have also produced evidence of an altruistic concern for others (96).

It has been argued, indeed, that tendencies toward altruism may be an innate trait that has been passed along to today's human beings as a result of the evolutionary process. Human beings have always been more likely to survive, the argument goes, when living with other people rather than when living alone. Therefore it seems likely that over the centuries those who were willing to cooperate with others had a better chance of surviving and passing along their characteristics to future generations (97). Again, as in the case of aggression, it is impossible to make a final judgment of such a theory.

Some people, of course, are more inclined toward altruism than others. Studies have shown that people who are "wrapped up" in themselves — self-centered and concerned about their own welfare — are less likely to be altruistic (98). People who feel a personal responsibility for others are more likely to be altruistic (99). People who have learned to empathize with others — that is, to feel the joys and pains of others as if these were their own — also seem to have strong tendencies toward altruism (100). Having altruistic parents to imitate and identify with also plays a part. One investigator found that boys who were regarded as generous had fathers whom they perceived as being warm and helpful (101). And a study of a group that had devoted itself to advancing the cause of civil rights showed that its members had a close relationship with an altruistic parent — at least one, and sometimes both (102). Whether altruism is or is not a basic and innate human trait, there seems to be no doubt that it can be encouraged or discouraged by learning — and especially by the social influences that have been the whole theme of this chapter.

Some things are worth saving. Join the Peace Corps.

PEACE CORPS -one part of ACTION

Summary

1 *Social psychology* is the study of how human beings "think, feel, and behave in social situations" — or, in broader terms, of how people influence and are influenced by other people.

2 *Socialization* is the process through which children are integrated into society through exposure to the actions and opinions of other members of the society.

3 An *attitude* is an organized and enduring set of beliefs and feelings toward some object or situation and a predisposition to behave toward it in a particular way. Thus an attitude contains a) a cognitive element (beliefs), b) an emotional element (feelings), and c) a behavioral element.

4 One explanation for changes in attitudes is the *theory of cognitive dissonance*. The theory holds that we seek to preserve agreement and harmony among our beliefs, feelings, and behavior. When there is a lack of consistency — and cognitive dissonance occurs — we are strongly motivated to restore harmony by making an adjustment in our beliefs, feelings, behavior, or all three.

5 *Attribution theory,* which also relates to attitude change, holds that we are constantly looking for the causes of behavior; we want to know *why* people behave as they do.

6 Closely associated with attribution theory is *self-perception theory,* which holds that we also look for the causes of our own behavior; we want to know why we ourselves behave as we do.

7 Attribution and self-perception theory hold that the best explanation for attitude change is as follows. When we are unable to find *situational* causes for our own behavior (that is, something about the situation and the people in it that could explain why we act as we do), we are forced to look for *dispositional* causes (that is, we must seek the reason for our behavior in our own attitudes). Therefore our behavior may lead us to change our attitudes.

8 Attempts by other people to change our attitudes — by transmitting information or making emotional appeals — are known as *persuasive communications*.

9 The effectiveness of persuasive communications depends on a) the *source of the communication,* b) the *nature of the communication,* and c) the *listener.*

10 The most effective sources of persuasive communication are persons of high credibility and people we like.

11 On the matter of the nature of a communication, the effectiveness seems to be enhanced if the appeal is emotional (but not so fear-arousing as to backfire). A "fair" argument, presenting both sides of the question, is more effective with intelligent audiences and with people who are leaning in the opposite direction.

12 Listeners who are most likely to be influenced by a persuasive communication are those who are low in self-esteem and anxious about social acceptance.

13 *Conformity* is the *yielding by individuals to pressures from the group in which they find themselves.* Closely related to conformity is *obedience,* or the tendency to behave as directed by a figure or authority. Studies have shown that most people have a strong tendency to conform and to obey.

14 The reason for obedience appears to be the fact that we are socialized to believe that there are experts who know much more than we do — and that it is both proper and wise to defer to their judgment.

15 One reason for conformity appears to be that we depend on the group for many of our psychological satisfactions. It is pleasant to be accepted by the group and highly unpleasant to be rejected.

16 Another explanation for conformity is provided by the *theory of social comparisons,* which holds that all of us feel the need to evaluate our own opinions, abilities, and behavior — and often can do so only by comparing ourselves with other people, who thus serve as our guides.

17 *Expedient conformity* is mere lip service to the ideas and opinions expressed by the group, without any change in attitude. *True conformity* represents a change of both behavior and attitude in response to group pressure.

18 Another major topic in social psychology is *interpersonal attraction,* or the manner in which we are attracted to other people or repelled by them. The study of interpersonal attraction is important because it helps account for the kinds of people we choose to be around — and who therefore influence our attitudes and tendencies to conform.

19 In general, it has been found that we tend to be attracted to people who a) are physically attractive, b) are similar to us, c) display competence (but not so much competence as to make us feel inferior), d) are familiar to us through close association, and e) like us.

20 *Bystander apathy* is the term used to describe the failure to assist others who appear to be in need of help. One factor that seems to induce people to display bystander apathy is the impersonality and rush of big-city life. Also, bystander apathy tends to be greatest when there are large numbers of other people around. Their presence relieves any single individual of feelings of responsibility, and their indifference may influence the individual to downgrade the seriousness of the situation and to conform to their apathetic behavior.

21 The question of whether human beings have an innate tendency to display *aggression* — or whether aggression is the product of learning — is one of the unresolved issues in psychology.

22 The opposite of aggression, known as *altruism* (or the tendency to be kind, generous, and helpful to others), is another concern of social psychology. Studies have indicated that people are most likely to be altruistic if they feel a personal responsibility for others (rather than being self-centered), have learned to empathize with others, and have altruistic parents whom they can imitate and identify with.

Recommended reading

Aronson, E. *The social animal.* San Francisco: W. H. Freeman & Co., 1970.

Bem, D. J. *Beliefs, attitudes, and human affairs.* Belmont, Calif.: Brooks-Cole, 1970.

Berkowitz, L., ed. *Advances in experimental social psychology.* New York: Academic Press, 1974 (Vol. 7).

Berscheid, E., and Walster, E. C. *Interpersonal attraction.* Reading, Mass.: Addison-Wesley, 1969.

Buckhout, R., ed. *Toward social change: a handbook for those who will.* New York: Harper & Row, 1971.

Freedman, J. L., Carlsmith, J. M., and Sears, D. O. *Social psychology.* Englewood Cliffs, N.J.: Prentice-Hall, 1970.

Jones, E. E., et al. *Attribution: perceiving the causes of behavior.* Morristown, N.J.: General Learning Press, 1972.

Milgram, S. *Obedience to authority.* New York: Harper & Row, 1974.

Zimbardo, P. G., and Ebbesen, E. B. *Influencing attitudes and changing behavior.* Reading, Mass.: Addison-Wesley, 1969.

Appendix: statistical methods

The use of statistics as an important tool in psychology began with Sir Francis Galton, an Englishman whose most important work was done in the 1880s, shortly after Wilhelm Wundt's laboratory first opened its doors. Sir Francis was interested in individual differences — how people vary in height, weight, and such characteristics as color vision, sense of smell, hearing, and ability to judge weights. He was also interested in the workings of heredity. One of the questions that fascinated him was whether tall people tend to have taller than average children. Another was whether successful people tend to have successful children.

Since Galton's time, many investigators have pursued similar questions, such as: Do intelligent parents tend to have children of above-average intelligence? Do strict parents tend to produce children who are more or less aggressive than the children of parents whose discipline is more lenient? Do intelligent people tend to be more or less neurotic than people of less intelligence?

To answer these questions, as Galton discovered, one must first make some accurate measurements. Galton himself devised a number of tests for such abilities as vision and hearing. And psychologists have been busy ever since, as is explained in Chapter 12, trying to perfect tests for intelligence and personality traits. But the results of the tests are meaningless unless they can be analyzed and compared in accordance with sound statistical practices.

Psychological statistics is the application of mathematical principles to the interpretation of the results obtained in psychological studies. It has been aptly called a "way of thinking" (1) — a problem-solving tool that enables us to summarize our knowledge of psychological events and make legitimate inferences.

Probability and the normal curve of distribution

As an example of how we can profit from thinking in terms of statistical methods, let us say that someone shows us two possible bridge hands. One is the bridge player's dream — thirteen spades. The other is a run-of-the-mill hand containing one ace, a few face cards, and many cards of no special value. The person who has put together these cards for us asks: "If you play bridge tonight, which of these hands are you less likely to have dealt to you?"

Common sense says that the answer is the hand with thirteen spades. When a bridge player gets such a hand, the newspapers are likely to report it as a great rarity. The player is likely to talk about it the rest of his life. And, in all truth, a hand of thirteen spades is extremely rare. It occurs, as a statistician can quickly calculate, on an average of only once in about 159 billion deals.

But the other hand, whatever it is, is equally rare. The rules of probability say that the chance of getting *any* particular combination of thirteen cards is only one in about 159 billion deals. The reason a hand of thirteen spades seems rarer than any other is that bridge players pay attention to it, while lumping all their mediocre hands together as if they were one and the same.

Let us think about the hand of thirteen spades in another way. Since it occurs only once in 159 billion deals, is it not a miracle that it should ever occur at all? No, it is not. It has been estimated that there are about 25 million bridge players in the United States. If each of them deals twenty times a week, that makes 26 billion deals a year. The statistical method tells us that we should expect a hand of thirteen spades to be dealt on the average of about once every six years.

Coincidences

This last fact—that we can expect a hand of thirteen spades to occur with some regularity—explains some events in life that often seem baffling to people who do not understand statistics. For example, every once in a while the newspapers report that someone shooting dice in Las Vegas has made twenty-eight passes (or winning throws) in a row. This seems almost impossible, and in fact the actual mathematical odds are more than 268,000,000 to 1 that it will not happen to anyone who begins throwing the dice. These are very high odds indeed. Yet, considering the large number of people who step up to all the dice tables in Las Vegas, it is very likely indeed that sooner or later someone will throw the twenty-eight passes.

The laws of probability explain many of the coincidences that seem—to people who do not understand these laws—to represent the working of supernatural powers. A woman in Illinois dreams that her brother in California has died and the next morning gets a telephone call reporting that he was killed in an accident. This may sound like an incredible case of some kind of mental telepathy, but the laws of probability offer a much simpler and more reasonable explanation. Most people dream frequently. Dreams of death are by no means rare. In the course of a year millions of people dream of the death of someone in the family. Sooner or later, one of the dreams is almost sure to coincide with an actual death.

Astrologers and other seers who claim to predict the future also profit from the rules of probability. If an astrologer keeps predicting that a "catastrophe" will occur, the forecast is bound to be right sooner or later, because the world is almost sure to have some kind of tragedy, from airplane accident to tornado, in any given period. And a prophet who makes a reputation by predicting the death of a "world leader" takes advantage of the fact that there are many world leaders and that many of them are in an advanced age bracket where death would not be unusual.

In a world as big as ours, all kinds of coincidences are likely to occur. The rules of statistics say that we should expect and not be surprised by them. Statistical analysis enables us to view these coincidences for what they are—and helps us avoid the error of assuming that they have any real significance.

The normal curve

One of the principles of probability, as Galton was the first to notice, has particular importance for the study of human behavior. This principle has to do with the manner in which many things, including psychological matters, are distributed in the normal course of natural events. The principle can best be approached through a simple experiment that you can try for yourself. Put ten coins into a cup, shake them, throw them on a table, and count the number of heads. Do this a number of times, say 100. Your tally will probably be roughly the same as the one shown in Figure 1.

What you have come up with is a simple illustration of normal distribution. When you toss ten coins 100 times—a total of 1000 tosses—you can expect 500 heads to come up, an average of five heads per toss. As the tally shows, this number of five heads came up most frequently. The two numbers on either side, four and six, were close seconds. The numbers farther away from five were increasingly infrequent. Ten came up only once, and zero did not come up at all. (Over a long period, both ten and zero would be expected to come up on an average of once in every 1024 tosses.)

The tally shown in Figure 1 can be converted into the bar graph shown in Figure 2, which provides a more easily interpreted picture of what happened in the coin

Number of heads						
0						
1	/					
2	ᏞᏞᎢ	/				
3	ᏞᏞᎢ	ᏞᏞᎢ				
4	ᏞᏞᎢ	ᏞᏞᎢ	ᏞᏞᎢ	///		
5	ᏞᏞᎢ	ᏞᏞᎢ	ᏞᏞᎢ	ᏞᏞᎢ	ᏞᏞᎢ	//
6	ᏞᏞᎢ	ᏞᏞᎢ	ᏞᏞᎢ	ᏞᏞᎢ	/	
7	ᏞᏞᎢ	ᏞᏞᎢ	/			
8	////					
9	/					
10	/					

1

A tally of coin tosses

Ten coins were shaken in a cup and tossed on a table 100 times. A tally of the number of heads that appeared on each toss is shown here.

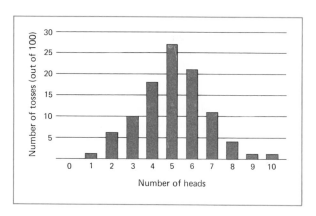

2

The tally in bar form

Here the results of the coin-tossing experiment, which were shown in tally form in Figure 1, have been converted into a bar graph. Note the peak at the center and the rapid falling off toward each extreme.

tossing. Note its shape—highest in the middle, then tapering off toward the extreme left and extreme right. If a curve is drawn, connecting the tops of the bars, we have a good example of the *normal curve of distribution,* sometimes called the *normal probability curve.* Such a curve, obtained by measuring how many digits college women could remember, is shown in Figure 3.

The curve's meaning

The important thing about the normal curve of distribution is that it provides a picture of the way many events —from the results of tossing coins to the ability to remember strings of digits—are distributed in the world. If we measured the length of all the leaves on all the trees of the world, we would get such a curve—high in the middle, tapering off to both sides. Curves of this pattern have been found for human height and weight, and all kinds of other characteristics and skills. The message of the normal curve is that in many measurable traits most people are average or close to it. (Most of the women in the test for memory of digits illustrated in Figure 3 could remember eight to ten.) Some are quite a little distance away from average. (Some of the women could only remember six digits; about an equal number could remember twelve.) And a few people are very far below or above average. (A few of the women could remember only three digits; a few could remember as many as fifteen.)

In a great many human traits, those who are about average have a lot of company. But some people are as rare in the number of digits they can remember—or in height, or in the scores they make on intelligence tests— as are the twenty-eight passes in a dice game. More will be said later about the normal curve of probability and its many important applications to the analysis of psychological findings.

3

Distribution of memory span for digits

The curve shows the distribution of the memory span for digits found in a group of 123 women students. The number of digits is the maximum that the students were able to repeat accurately after hearing them one time only. (2)

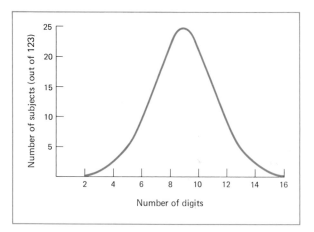

Descriptive statistics

One of the simplest but most useful applications of mathematics to psychological data takes the form of what is called *descriptive statistics,* which provides a quick and convenient method of summarizing the characteristics of any group under study. Let us say that we draw up a new kind of intelligence test and administer it to 10,000 college students. We wind up with 10,000 raw scores on the test. To pass along what we have learned about the test, however, we need not quote every one of the 10,000 scores. Through the use of descriptive statistics we can summarize and condense. With just a few well-chosen numbers, we can tell other people much of what they need to know in order to understand our results. Among the most commonly used such numbers are the following.

Number in group

This number is simply the total number of subjects in the group we have studied. It is an important number because the chances of obtaining accurate results are greater if we study a large group than if we study only a small group. If we test only three people on our new intelligence test, we may happen to select three geniuses or three morons. A larger sample is likely to be more representative of the population as a whole.

The statistical average

Another useful piece of information is what in everyday language is called the *average.* For example, six students take an examination containing a hundred true-false questions and get test scores of 70, 74, 74, 76, 80, and 82. The "average" score—or in technical language, the *mean*—is the sum of the scores divided by the number of subjects who took the test. In other words, it is 456 divided by 6—or 76. Knowing that the mean is 76 tells us a great deal about the kind of curve of distribution that could be drawn up from the scores. We know that the curve would center around a figure of about 76—and that the majority of scores would be somewhere in this neighborhood.

Another measure of the central point around which the scores tend to cluster is the *median,* the halfway point that separates the lower 50 percent of scores from the higher 50 percent. In the example just given, the median would be 75 because half the scores fall below 75 and the other half fall above. The median is an es-

pecially useful figure when the data include a small number of exceptionally low or exceptionally high measurements. Let us say, for example, that the six scores on the true-false examination were 70, 74, 74, 76, 80, and 100. The one student who scored 100 brings up the mean score quite sharply, to 79. But note that 79 is hardly an "average" score because only two of the six students scored that high. The median score, which remains at 75, is a better description of the data.

A third measure of central tendency is the *mode*—the measurement or score that applies to the greatest number of subjects. In the case of the true-false examination it would be 74, the only score made by as many as two of the students. The mode tells us where the highest point of the curve of distribution will be found. In a perfectly symmetrical normal curve the mode, the median, and the mean are the same. If the distribution is not symmetrical, but on the contrary tails off more sharply on the below-average side than on the above-average side, or vice versa (as often happens), it is useful to know all three of these figures.

Variability and standard deviation

Even when the normal curve is perfectly symmetrical, it may take different forms. Sometimes it is high and narrow. At other times it is shorter and wider. This depends on the *variability* of the measurements, which means the extent to which they differ from one another.

A crude way to describe the variability of scores made on a psychological test is simply to give the *range* of the scores—the highest minus the lowest. Another and much more sensitive description is provided by what is called the *standard deviation,* often abbreviated to the initials *SD.* The standard deviation, which is computed from the data by a formula that will be explained later in the chapter, is an especially useful tool because it indicates the proportion of scores or measurements that will be found under any part of the curve. As is shown in Figure 4, the rule is that 34.13 percent of all the scores lie between the mean and a point 1 *SD* above the mean; 13.59 percent lie between 1 *SD* and 2 *SD*'s above the mean; and 2.14 percent lie between 2 *SD*'s and 3 *SD*'s above the mean. Thus the *SD* provides an eloquent description of the variability of the measurements.

On the matter of the intelligence quotient, for example, the mean is 100 and the *SD* is approximately 15. That is to say, an I.Q. one *SD* above the mean is 115. Armed with this knowledge alone, plus the general statistical rule illustrated in Figure 4, we know that human

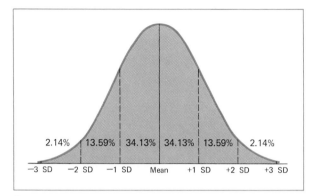

2.14% | 13.59% | 34.13% | 34.13% | 13.59% | 2.14%

−3 SD   −2 SD   −1 SD   Mean   +1 SD   +2 SD   +3 SD

4

Using the *SD* to analyze data

In a normal curve of distribution, the standard deviation indicates how many measurements or scores will be found at various distances from the mean. As shown here, 34.13 percent of all measurements lie between the mean and 1 *SD* above the mean. Measurements that are between 1 *SD* and 2 *SD*'s above the mean make up 13.59 percent of the total, and measurements between 2 *SD*'s and 3 *SD*'s above the mean make up 2.14 percent. The same percentages are found below the mean. Note that the figures do not quite add up to 100 percent. This is because 0.14 percent of measurements are found more than 3 *SD*'s above the mean and another 0.14 percent are found more than 3 *SD*'s below the mean. These various percentages hold for any normal distribution, although the size of the *SD* is of course quite different from one curve to another.

intelligence tends to be distributed according to the figures in the following table:

I.Q.	Percentage of people
145 and over	0.14
130–144	2.14
115–129	13.59
100–114	34.13
85–99	34.13
70–84	13.59
55–69	2.14
under 55	0.14

The *SD* is also used to compute what are called *standard scores*, or *z-scores*, which are often more meaningful than the actual raw scores made on a test. The *z*-score tells how many *SD*'s a score is above or below the mean; it is obtained very simply by noting how many points a score is above or below the mean and then dividing by the *SD*. A *z*-score of 1 is one *SD* above the mean. A *z*-score of −1.5 is one and a half *SD*'s below the mean.

Percentiles

There is one other term in descriptive statistics that deserves special discussion. This is *percentile*, which is used not so much to describe the nature of the distribution as to add further meaning to any individual score.

The meaning of percentile can best be explained with an example. Take the case of a college man, a senior who wants to go on to graduate school and is asked to take the Graduate Record Examinations, which are nationally administered aptitude tests often used to screen applicants. He makes a score of 460 on the verbal test and 540 in mathematics. By themselves, these scores do not mean much either to him or to the faculty of the school he wants to attend. But records kept of other people's results on the test provide a means of comparing his scores with those of other college seniors. A score of 460 on the verbal test, the records show, lies on the 40th percentile for men. This means that 40 percent of all senior men who take the test make a lower score and 60 percent make higher scores. The 540 score in math lies on the 66th percentile for men; in other words, 66 percent of senior men make a lower score, and only 34 percent make higher scores. These percentile figures show the student and the school he hopes to attend how his ability compares with that of other prospective graduate students: he is well above average in mathematical ability (only a third of male college seniors make better scores) but below average in verbal aptitude.

Percentile ratings can be made for any kind of measurement, whether or not it falls into a normal pattern of distribution. A percentile rating of 99 — or, to be more exact, 99.99 — means that no one had a higher score. A percentile rating of 1 — or, to be more exact, 0.01 — is the lowest in the group.

Inferential statistics

When psychologists run a rat through a maze, they are not really interested in how that particular rat will learn the maze. Their primary interest is in discovering some general principle of behavior that says something about the learning process of all rats — and, by implication, perhaps about learning processes in general. Investigators who study the performance of a group of human subjects who memorize nonsense syllables — or their behavior when they receive an injection of adrenalin and watch a funny movie — are not interested in those particular people. The investigators' ultimate interest is in discovering something about the behavior of people in general. This is why *inferential statistics* — which permit us to make generalizations from our measurements —are so important.

Population and sample

Science is interested in what is called the *population,* or sometimes the *universe*—that is to say, all people or all events in a particular category. But we cannot study or measure the entire population. We cannot give an intelligence test, for example, to every human being now on the face of the earth; even if we could, we still would not have reached the entire population, because many people would have died and many new people would have been born in the meantime. We must settle for a *sample,* a group of convenient size taken from the population as a whole.

A sample must be *representative* of the population we wish to study. If we wish to make generalizations about the intelligence of the American population, we cannot use a sample made up entirely of college students or a sample made up of high-school dropouts. If we want to learn about political attitudes, we cannot poll merely Republicans or people who live in big cities or people who belong to one kind of church or one kind of social class. Our sample must be representative of all kinds of Americans.

One way to ensure a representative sample is to choose it entirely at *random.* If each member of the total population has an absolutely equal chance of being studied—and if our sample is large enough—then there is a good likelihood that the sample will represent all segments of the population. For example, the experimenter who wants to study the emotional behavior of rats in a laboratory cannot just reach into a cage and pull out the first dozen animals that are closest at hand. The very fact that they are close at hand may mean that they are tamer than the others and have a different kind of emotional temperament. To achieve a more valid sampling, the experimenter might take the first rat, reject the second, take the third, reject the fourth, and so on. An investigator interested in student attitudes toward marijuana on a particular campus might draw up an alphabetical list of all students, then interview every tenth person on the list.

In the Gallup election polls, the random sampling starts with a list of the approximately 200,000 election districts and precincts in the nation. From this master list, about 300 districts are chosen at random. Then a map of each of the 300 districts is drawn up. On the map, one house is chosen as a starting point—again at random. Beginning at that point, and proceeding along a path drawn through the district, the pollsters collect interviews at each third residence or sometimes each fifth or twelfth residence, depending on the desired size of the sample (3).

Control groups

In selecting experimental and control groups, the random technique of obtaining a representative sample is also standard procedure. Ideally, every individual in the control group should be identical with a member of the experimental group. But this is of course impossible because not even identical twins (who are too scarce anyway) are alike in every respect. To ensure as much similarity as possible between the experimental and control groups, subjects are usually assigned to one group or the other at random. Each individual, arriving at the laboratory, has a 50-50 chance of being assigned to the experimental group—and of course also a 50-50 chance of being assigned to the control group.

Comparing two groups

For an example of how inferential statistics is used to compare two groups, such as an experimental group and a control group, let us imagine an experiment in which we try to determine whether physical health affects the learning ability of high-school students. We select an experimental group of sixteen representative, randomly chosen students, who agree to take part in a rigorous health program. We arrange a supervised diet and exercise, give them regular physical examinations, and promptly treat any illnesses or defects such as impaired vision or hearing. We also select a control group of sixteen similar students, who do not receive any special treatment. At the end of a year, we find that the experimental group has a grade-point mean of 89, with a standard deviation of 3. The control group has a grade-point mean of 85, with a standard deviation of 4. Question: Is this difference of four points between the mean of the experimental group and the mean of the control group just a statistical accident? Or does it really mean that good health produces better grades?

Although four points may sound like a lot, the question is not so easy to answer as it may seem. The reason is that *any* two samples of sixteen people each, taken from the high-school population or any other population, are likely to have somewhat different means. Sup-

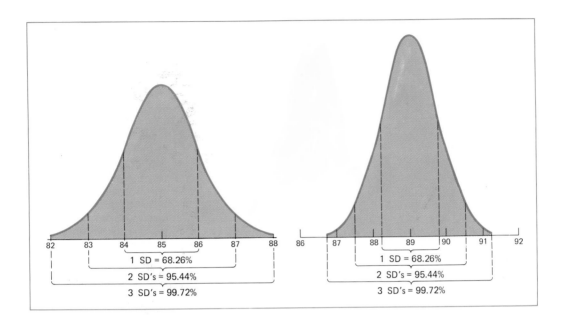

5

How means are distributed

These graphs show how the standard error of the mean of a sample is used to infer the true mean that would be found if the entire population could be measured. In the control group of high school students, at left, the mean is 85 and the standard error of the mean is 1.0. Thus we know that the chances are 68.26 percent that the true mean for the population lies between 84 and 86 (1 standard error above or below the mean of our sample), 95.44 percent that the true mean lies between 83 and 87 (2 standard errors above or below), and 99.72 percent that the true mean lies between 82 and 88 (3 standard errors above or below). In the experimental group, at right, the mean is 89 and the standard error of the mean is 0.75. Therefore the chances are 68.26 percent that the true mean of the experimental population would fall between 88.25 and 89.75; the chances are 95.44 percent that the mean would fall between 87.50 and 90.50; and they are 99.72 percent that the mean would fall between 86.75 and 91.25. Note how the two graphs utilize the same principle that was illustrated in Figure 4.

pose we write the names of all the students in the high school (or in the city) on slips of paper and draw the slips from a hat. The grade-point mean for the first sixteen names we draw may be 85, for the next sixteen names 88, for the next sixteen names 87. If we pull twenty different samples of sixteen students each from the hat, we will find that the means vary from sample to sample, perhaps by as much as several points. So the question now becomes: Is the difference between the mean score of 89 for the experimental group and the mean score of 85 for the control group just an accidental result such as we might get by pulling samples from a hat? Or is it *statistically significant*, meaning that it probably indicates a real difference between our two groups?

Standard error of the mean

Helping answer the question is the fact that the means of randomly chosen samples, like raw measurements or scores themselves, tend to fall into a pattern of normal distribution. From our control group of sixteen with a grade-point mean of 85 and a standard deviation of 4, we can figure out the distribution of all the means we would be likely to get if we continued to pick samples of sixteen students at random, and we find that the curve looks like the one shown on the left in Figure 5. We get the curve by using the formula (shown on page 000) for the *standard error of the mean*. For the control group, the standard error of the mean turns out to be 1.0. For the

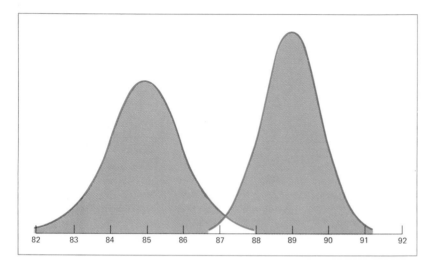

6

Is the difference significant?

When the curves that were shown in Figure 5 are superimposed, they have only the small white area in common. The probability that the difference between the two means is due to chance is represented by this area; the probability that the difference is a real one is represented by the colored areas.

experimental group, we get the curve shown at the right in Figure 5; for this group the standard error of the mean turns out to be .75.

Having found the two curves, we can put them together as is shown in Figure 6—which shows us that the probability is very high that there is a true difference between the grades of students who receive special medical care and the grades of students who do not. The possibility that the difference we found is merely a matter of chance is represented by the small area that lies beneath the extreme right-hand end of the control curve and the extreme left-hand end of the curve for the experimental group.

Probability and ''significance''

The curves in Figures 5 and 6 demonstrate the principle that underlies the comparison of two groups through the standard error of the mean. In actual statistical calculation these curves need not be constructed. We can use the two means and the standard error of each mean to work out what is called *the standard error of the difference between two means* (see page 545). This figure can in turn be used to work out the probability that the difference we found was due merely to chance. In the case of the hypothetical experiment we have been describing, the probability comes to less than .01.

It is an arbitrary rule of thumb in experimental work that a difference is considered *statistically significant* only when the probability that it might have been obtained by chance is .05 (5 chances in 100, or 1 chance in 20) or less than .05.

In reports on experiments that can be analyzed with this kind of inferential statistics, the probability figure is always given; you will frequently find the note

$$p \leq .05$$

meaning that the difference would be found by chance only 5 times or less out of 100 and is therefore statistically significant. In virtually all the experiments cited in this book, p was .05 or less.

Correlation

Galton's question—do successful parents have more successful children than other parents?—is a problem for which statistics provides another useful tool, called *correlation*. If success on the part of a parent is often accompanied by success on the part of a child, then these two events are related to one another in some sort of way. In statistical terms, they are *correlated*. Galton showed that there was indeed a correlation between the two events; other investigators have shown that there are correlations between I.Q. and grades in school, between grades in school and economic success, between a parent's strictness and aggressive behavior in the child, and between many other psychological traits and forms of behavior.

Some correlations are *positive*, meaning that the higher a person measures on scale X (for example, I.Q.), the higher he or she is likely to measure on scale Y (for example, grades). *Negative correlations*, in which a high score on scale X is likely to be accompanied by a low score on scale Y, have also been found. For example, the frequency of premature births has been found to be negatively correlated with social class—meaning that there tends to be less prematurity among upper-income families than lower-income families. Negative correlations also exist between aggressive behavior in children and social class and between test anxiety and grades made in schools.

Scatter plots

A rough idea of the degree of correlation between two traits can be obtained by plotting each subject's score on scale X against the subject's score on scale Y. For each person, a dot is entered at a point corresponding to the scores on both scales, as shown in Figure 7. The result is what is called a *scatter plot*. If the dots are scattered completely at random, we can see that the correlation is 0. If we should happen on one of those extremely rare cases where the dots form a perfectly straight line, running diagonally up or diagonally down, we know that we are dealing with a correlation of +1 or −1. Most scatter diagrams take a form that falls somewhere in between. If a fairly narrow diagonal oval would enclose most of the dots, the correlation is rather high. If the oval must be fatter to enclose the dots, the correlation is lower.

Correlation coefficients

A more precise measure of the relationship between scores on the X-scale and scores on the Y-scale can be obtained—without the need for constructing a scatter plot—by using various statistical formulas for calculating a *correlation coefficient*. (The formulas are presented on page 545.) A correlation coefficient can range from 0 (no correlation at all) to +1 (a perfect positive correlation) or −1 (a perfect negative correlation). But correlations of +1 or −1 are very rare. Even such physical traits as height and weight, which would seem to go together in almost perfect proportion, do not reach a correlation of +1. Some typical correlations that have been found in various studies are the following:

Between I.Q. and college grades	.50
Between parents' I.Q.'s and child's I.Q.	.49
Between I.Q. and ability at pitch discrimination	.00
Between boys' height at age two and height at age eighteen	.60
Between boys' height at age ten and height at age eighteen	.88

Correlation and prediction

The correlation coefficients in the above table show that there is a considerable relationship between boys' height at age two and at age eighteen—and an even greater relationship between height at age ten and at age eighteen. Knowing that these relationships exist, we can make some predictions. We can say that a boy who is taller than average at two—or especially at ten—has a pretty good chance of also being taller than average at eighteen. Because of the .50 correlation coefficient between I.Q. and college grades, we can suggest that high-school seniors who make high scores on in-

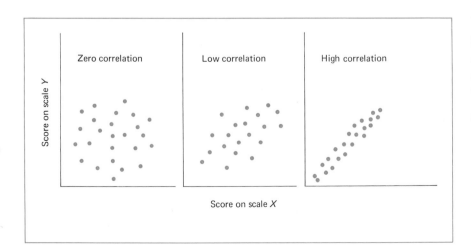

Score on scale Y

Zero correlation   Low correlation   High correlation

Score on scale X

7

Scatter plots of correlations

These scatter plots were obtained by making a dot for each subject at a point indicating both score on scale X and score on scale Y. (4)

N	Number of subjects from whom a measurement or score has been obtained		ample, the difference between the mean (M) of scale X and the mean of scale Y
X	The numerical value of an individual score	SE_{D_M}	The standard error of the difference between two means, used as a measure of whether the difference is significant
Y	If each subject is measured on two scales, the numerical value of an individual score on the second scale	p	Probability, expressed in decimals ranging from .00 (no chance) through .50 (50-50 chance) to 1.00 (100 percent chance). A result is considered statistically significant when $p \leq .05$, meaning that there are only 5 chances in 100 (or fewer) that it was obtained by chance
Σ	The Greek capital letter sigma, standing for "sum of"		
ΣX	The sum of all the individual scores on scale X		
M	The mean, which is the sum of the scores divided by the number of subjects		
x	A deviation score; that is, the difference between an individual score and the mean for the group of which the individual is a member	r	Correlation coefficient obtained by the product-moment method
		ρ	Correlation coefficient obtained by the rank-difference method
y	A deviation score on the second scale, or Y-scale	z	A standard score, expressed in number of SD's above or below the mean
SD	The standard deviation of the scores	C	Coefficient of contingency; type of correlation used to find relationships between events on a nominal scale
SE_M	The standard error of the mean; also called the standard deviation of the mean		
D_M	The difference between two means; for ex-		

8

Some useful symbols

These are the mathematical symbols used in the formulas presented in this chapter.

telligence tests have a good chance of getting high grades in college, and that students with very low scores run the risk of failure in college.

It must always be kept in mind, however, that a coefficient of correlation is less accurate in making predictions than it sounds. Only when the correlation is very close to 1, as in the scatter plot that was shown at the right in Figure 7, does every subject tend to show a close relationship between score on scale X and score on scale Y. Even in a correlation of .75, which sounds high, there is a considerable amount of scatter, representing subjects who scored relatively low on scale X but relatively high on scale Y, or vice versa. Since most correlations found in psychological studies are lower than .75, we must be quite tentative in making predictions.

Correlation, cause, and effect

Just knowing the degree of relationship implied by a correlation coefficient is often of value to psychologists.

For example, it has been found that there is a positive correlation between strict discipline on the part of parents and the amount of aggressive behavior displayed by children. This fact has a number of implications for child-rearing practices and for developmental psychology in general.

Again, however, it is important not to exaggerate the degree of relationship expressed by a correlation coefficient. We cannot say that strict discipline always—or even usually—is accompanied by aggressive behavior. Moreover, we must avoid jumping to conclusions about cause and effect. Did the children become aggressive because the parents were strict, or were the parents strict because the children were aggressive? Is it possible that some third factor caused both the parents' strictness and the children's aggression? (For example, it may be that parents who are generally cold and rejecting of their children tend to be strict and that it is the coldness and rejection, rather than the strictness, that make the children aggressive.)

As a reminder of the danger of jumping to false

conclusions on the basis of correlations, it is a good idea to keep in mind that there is a very high correlation between the number of permanent teeth that have erupted through the schoolchild's gums and the child's raw scores for questions answered correctly on any kind of intelligence or aptitude test. But it would be foolish to conclude that more teeth make the child smarter or that better scores make more teeth appear. Increased maturity produces both the teeth and the higher scores.

The mathematical computations

The use of correlations and other descriptive and inferential statistics is not nearly so difficult as might be assumed. The mathematical knowledge required for these kinds of analysis is really not complicated at all. One need only be able to manipulate mathematical symbols, the most frequently used of which are explained in Figure 8, and to apply the few basic formulas that are presented in Figure 9.

The symbols and formulas are given at the start of this section on computations so that they can be found all in one place for future reference. They may seem rather difficult when shown all together in this fashion, but their application should be apparent from the examples that will be presented as we go along.

The kind of measurement that an investigator often wants to analyze is illustrated in Figure 10. Here seventeen students have taken a psychological test and have made scores ranging from 60 to 97. The raw scores are a jumble of figures, from which we now want to determine the mean, the standard deviation, and the standard error of the mean.

The mean

The formula for computing the mean, as can be seen from Figure 9, is

$$M = \frac{\Sigma X}{N}$$

These symbols denote, as can be found in Figure 8, that the mean equals the sum of the individual scores divided by the number of subjects.

The way the formula is applied is illustrated in Figure 11. The sum of the individual scores, which are shown in column one, is 1326. The number of subjects is 17. Thus the mean is 1326 divided by 17, or 78.

1. For determining the mean:
$$M = \frac{\Sigma X}{N}$$

2. For determining a deviation score:
$$x = X - M$$

3. For determining the standard deviation:
$$SD = \sqrt{\frac{\Sigma x^2}{N - 1}}$$

4. For determining a z-score:
$$z = \frac{x}{SD}$$

5. For determining the standard error of the mean:
$$SE_M = \frac{SD}{\sqrt{N}}$$

6. For determining the difference between two means:
$$D_M = M_1 - M_2$$

7. For determining the standard error of the difference between two means:
$$SE_{D_M} = \sqrt{(SE_{M1})^2 + (SE_{M2})^2}$$

8. For determining the critical ratio:
$$\text{Critical ratio} = \frac{D_M}{SE_{D_M}}$$

9. For determining the coefficient of correlation by the product-moment method:
$$r = \frac{\Sigma xy}{(N - 1)SD_x SD_y}$$

10. For determining the coefficient of correlation by the rank-difference method:
$$\rho = 1 - \frac{6(\Sigma D^2)}{N(N^2 - 1)}$$

9

Some statistical formulas

These are some of the formulas most frequently used in statistical analysis. Their use is explained and illustrated in the text and in the following figures.

1. 78	4. 74	7. 92	10. 74	13. 70	16. 82
2. 97	5. 80	8. 72	11. 85	14. 84	17. 78
3. 60	6. 77	9. 79	12. 68	15. 76	

10

The test scores of seventeen students

These raw scores, obtained by seventeen students on a psychological test, will be analyzed statistically in the text.

TEST SCORES (X)	DEVIATION SCORES (x)	DEVIATION SCORES SQUARED (x^2)
78	0	0
97	+19	361
60	−18	324
74	− 4	16
80	+ 2	4
77	− 1	1
92	+14	196
72	− 6	36
79	+ 1	1
74	− 4	16
85	+ 7	49
68	−10	100
70	− 8	64
84	+ 6	36
76	− 2	4
82	+ 4	16
78	0	0
$\Sigma X = 1326$		$\Sigma x^2 = 1224$

$$M = \frac{\Sigma X}{N} = \frac{1326}{17} = 78$$

$$SD = \sqrt{\frac{\Sigma x^2}{N-1}} = \sqrt{\frac{1224}{16}} = \sqrt{76.5} = 8.75$$

11

Computing the mean and the SD

Using the formulas in Figure 9, we first compute the mean score (M) for the seventeen students, which comes out to 78. Once we have the mean, we can compute the standard deviation (SD)—starting by obtaining the deviation scores ($x = X - M$), then squaring these scores to get x^2.

The standard deviation

The method of finding the standard deviation is also illustrated in Figure 11. The formula for the standard deviation is

$$SD = \sqrt{\frac{\Sigma x^2}{N-1}}$$

This means that we square each of the deviation scores, add up the total, and divide the total by the number of subjects minus 1. The square root of the figure thus obtained is the standard deviation.

The deviation scores shown in column two have been obtained by the formula $x = X - M$—that is, by subtracting the mean, which is 78, from each individual score. These figures in column two have then been squared to give the figures in column three. The sum of the x^2 figures is 1224, and this figure divided by 16 (our $N - 1$) comes to 76.5. The standard deviation is the square root of 76.5, or 8.75.

The standard error of the mean

Finding the standard error of the mean for our group is extremely simple. The formula is

$$SE_M = \frac{SD}{\sqrt{N}}$$

We have found that the SD of our sample is 8.75 and our N is 17. The formula yields

$$SE_M = \frac{8.75}{\sqrt{17}} = \frac{8.75}{4.12} = 2.12$$

Differences between groups

For an example of how the formulas for analyzing differences between groups are applied, let us return to the hypothetical experiment mentioned earlier in the Appendix. We had the school grades, you will recall, of an experimental group of sixteen students who took part in a health program; the mean was 89 and the standard deviation was 3. We also had the grades of a control group of sixteen students; the mean for this group was 85 and the standard deviation was 4.

The difference between the two means is easily computed from the formula

$$D_M = M_1 - M_2$$

which means that the difference between the means is the mean of the first group minus the mean of the second group—in this case, 89 minus 85, or 4. To know whether this difference is statistically significant, however, we must calculate the standard error of the difference between the two means. To do so, as Figure 9 shows, we must use the fairly complex formula

$$SE_{D_M} = \sqrt{(SE_{M1})^2 + (SE_{M2})^2}$$

Our first step is to compute SE_{M1}, the standard error of the mean of our first or experimental group. We do so as shown earlier, this time with 3 as our standard deviation and 16 as our number of subjects.

$$SE_{M1} = \frac{SD}{\sqrt{N}} = \frac{3}{\sqrt{16}} = \frac{3}{4} = 0.75$$

We also compute SE_{M2}, the standard error of the mean of our second or control group, where the standard deviation is 4 and the number of subjects is 16.

$$SE_{M2} = \frac{SD}{\sqrt{N}} = \frac{4}{\sqrt{16}} = \frac{4}{4} = 1.00$$

Thus SE_{M1} is 0.75 and SE_{M2} is 1.00, and the standard error of the difference between the two means is computed as follows:

$$SE_{D_M} = \sqrt{(SE_{M1})^2 + (SE_{M2})^2}$$
$$= \sqrt{(0.75)^2 + (1)^2}$$
$$= \sqrt{.5625 + 1}$$
$$= \sqrt{1.5625}$$
$$= 1.25$$

To complete our analysis of the difference between the two groups, we need one more statistical tool—the *critical ratio*. This is given by the formula

$$\text{Critical ratio} = \frac{D_M}{SE_{D_M}}$$

In the case of our hypothetical experiment we have found that D_M is 4 and that SE_{D_M} is 1.25. Thus

$$\text{Critical ratio} = \frac{4}{1.25} = 3.2$$

This critical ratio gives us a measure of the probability that our difference was due merely to chance. For reasons that mathematically minded students may be able to work out for themselves but that need not concern the rest of us, the magic numbers for the critical ratio are 1.96 and 2.57. If the critical ratio is as high as 1.96, then $p \le .05$, and the difference is considered statistically significant. If the critical ratio is as high as 2.57, then $p \le .01$, and the difference is considered highly significant. The critical ratio we found for our two groups, 3.2, is well over 2.57; thus we can have some confidence that the difference was not the result of chance.

Correlation coefficients

There are a number of ways of computing correlation coefficients, depending on the type of data that are being studied. The most frequently used is the *product-moment method,* which obtains a coefficient of correlation designated by the letter r for the relationship between two different measurements. The formula is

$$r = \frac{\Sigma xy}{(N-1)SD_x SD_y}$$

To use the formula we have to determine the amount by which each subject's score on scale X differs from the mean for all scores on scale X—in other words the value for x, the deviation score, which may be plus or minus. We must also determine the amount by which the subject's score on the second test, or scale Y, differs from the mean for all scores on scale Y—in other words, the value for y, which also may be plus or minus. We then multiply x by y for each subject and add the xy products for all the subjects in the sample. This gives us the top line, or numerator, of the formula. The bottom line, or denominator, is found by multiplying the number of subjects minus 1 $(N-1)$ by the standard deviation of the scores on the X-scale (SD_x) and then multiplying the product by the standard deviation of the scores on the Y-scale (SD_y). An example is shown in Figure 12.

In some cases it is convenient to use the *rank-difference method,* which produces a different coefficient of correlation called ρ (the Greek letter *rho*), which is similar to but not exactly the same as r. The formula is

$$\rho = 1 - \frac{6(\Sigma D^2)}{N(N^2 - 1)}$$

The method of applying the formula is demonstrated in

SUBJECT	TEST SCORES		DEVIATION SCORES		PRODUCT OF DEVIATION SCORES (xy)
	X	Y	x	y	
1.	60	81	−12	+ 1	− 12
2.	80	92	+ 8	+12	+ 96
3.	70	76	− 2	− 4	+ 8
4.	65	69	− 7	−11	+ 77
5.	75	88	+ 3	+ 8	+ 24
6.	85	96	+13	+16	+208
7.	60	64	−12	−16	+192
8.	75	75	+ 3	− 5	− 15
9.	70	77	− 2	− 3	+ 6
10.	80	82	+ 8	+ 2	+ 16
					$\Sigma xy = 600$

$N = 10$
For scale X, $M = 72$, and $SD_x = 8.56$
For scale Y, $M = 80$, and $SD_y = 9.98$

Thus

$$r = \frac{\Sigma xy}{(N-1)SD_x SD_y} = \frac{600}{(10-1) \times 8.56 \times 9.98}$$
$$= \frac{600}{768.9} = .78$$

12
Computing product-moment correlation

Note that in the sample of ten, four subjects who scored above the mean on scale X also scored above the mean on scale Y (subjects 2, 5, 6, and 10). Four subjects who scored below the mean on scale X also scored below the mean on scale Y (subjects 3, 4, 7, and 9). Only two subjects (1 and 8) scored above the mean on one test and below the mean on another. Thus multiplying the x-deviations times the y-deviations gives us eight positive products and only two negative products. Σxy, which is the total of the positive products minus the total of the negative products, comes to 600. The correlation coefficient comes to the rather large figure of .78.

The manner in which SD_x and SD_y were computed is not shown, but you can check the figures of 8.56 for SD_x and SD_y by applying the formula for computing a standard deviation as shown in Figure 11.

Figure 13. Note that the D in the formula refers to the difference between a subject's rank on scale X—that is, whether first, second, third, or so on among all the subjects—and the subjects' rank on scale Y. ΣD^2 is found by squaring each subjects' difference in rank and adding to get the total for all subjects.

Contingency

One other frequently used type of correlation is known as the *coefficient of contingency,* symbolized by the letter C. This is used to find relationships between events that can be measured only on what is called a *nominal scale*— where all we can say about them is that they belong to certain groups. For example, we can set up a nominal

SUBJECT	TEST SCORES		RANK		DIFFERENCE IN RANK (D)	DIFFERENCE SQUARED (D^2)
	X	Y	X	Y		
1.	60	81	9.5	5	−4.5	20.25
2.	80	92	2.5	2	−0.5	0.25
3.	70	76	6.5	7	+0.5	0.25
4.	65	69	8.0	9	+1.0	1.00
5.	75	88	4.5	3	−1.5	2.25
6.	85	96	1.0	1	0.0	0.00
7.	60	64	9.5	10	−0.5	0.25
8.	75	75	4.5	8	−3.5	12.25
9.	70	77	6.5	6	−0.5	0.25
10.	80	82	2.5	4	+1.5	2.25
						$\Sigma D^2 = 39.00$

$N = 10$
Thus

$$\rho = 1 - \frac{6(\Sigma D^2)}{N(N^2-1)} = 1 - \frac{6(39)}{10(10^2-1)} = 1 - \frac{234}{990} = 1 - .24 = .76$$

13
Computing rank-difference correlation

Here the same scores that were shown in Figure 12 have been used to find the rank-difference correlation, ρ, which comes out to .76—very close to the .78 that we found in Figure 12 for r. In computing ρ, we disregard the individual scores on scale X and scale Y and use merely the rank of each score as compared to the others on the scale. Note that subjects 2 and 10 are tied for second place on the X-scale. Their rank is therefore considered to be 2.5, halfway between second and third place.

scale on which all college students taking a humanities course are grouped in class 1, all taking engineering are grouped in class 2, and all taking a preparatory course for one of the professional schools such as law or medicine are grouped in class 3. We might set up another nominal scale on which we designate the students as males or females. If we then want to determine whether there is any relationship between a student's sex and the kind of college course the student is likely to take, we use the coefficient of contingency. Its meaning is roughly the same as that of any other coefficient of correlation.

Summary

1 *Psychological statistics* is the application of mathematical principles to the interpretation of the results obtained in psychological studies.
2 The statistical method is of special importance as a *way of thinking* — reminding us that many events take place in accordance with the laws of probability and that "remarkable coincidences" can often be explained as occurring by mere chance.
3 Many events in nature, including many human traits, fall into the pattern of the *normal curve of distribution*. In this curve, most such events or traits cluster around the average, and the number declines approaching either the lower or the upper extreme.
4 *Descriptive statistics* provide a convenient method of summarizing scores and other psychological measurements. Important descriptive statistics are:

 a The *number of subjects,* or *N.*
 b Measures of central tendency, including the arithmetic average, or *mean* (total of all scores divided by *N*), *median* (point separating the lower half of scores from the upper half), and *mode* (most frequent score in the group).
 c Index of *variability,* including *range* (obtained by subtracting the lowest score from the highest) and *standard deviation,* symbolized by *SD*. In a normal distribution, 34.13 percent of the scores lie between the mean and 1 *SD* above the mean, 13.59 percent between 1 *SD* and 2 *SD*'s above the mean, and 2.14 percent between 2 *SD*'s and 3 *SD*'s above the mean, while 0.14 percent lie more than 3 *SD*'s above the mean. The same pattern of distribution exists below the mean.

5 *Percentiles* are used to describe the position of an individual score in the total group. A measurement on the 75th percentile is larger than 75 percent of the measurements, or, to put it another way, 25 percent of measurements lie on or above the 75th percentile.
6 *Inferential statistics* are procedures that allow us to make generalizations from measurements. They enable us to infer conclusions about a *population* or *universe,* which is the total of all possible cases in a particular category, by measuring a relatively small *sample*. To permit valid generalization, however, the sample must be *representative*. One way to ensure that the sample is representative is to choose it entirely at *random,* with each member of the population having an equal chance of being selected.
7 A set of findings is considered *statistically significant* when the probability that the findings might have been obtained by chance is only 5 in 100 or less; the figure is expressed mathematically as $p \leq .05$.
8 *Correlations* between two measurements — such as scores on two different tests — range from 0 (no relationship) to +1 (perfect positive relationship) or −1 (perfect negative relationship).
9 The symbols and formulas used in the statistical analysis described in the chapter are shown in Figures 8 and 9.

Recommended readings

Arkin, H., and Colton, R. R. *Tables for statisticians,* 2nd ed. New York: Barnes & Noble, 1963.

Freund, J. E. *Modern elementary statistics,* 4th ed. Englewood, N.J.: Prentice-Hall, 1973.

Guilford, J. P. *Fundamental statistics in psychology and education,* 5th ed. New York: McGraw-Hill, 1973.

Hammond, K. R., Householder, J. E., and Castellan, N. J., Jr. *Introduction to the statistical method: foundations and use in the behavioral sciences,* 2nd ed. New York: Knopf, 1970.

Hays, W. L. *Statistics for social scientists,* 2nd ed. New York: Holt, Rinehart and Winston, 1973.

McCall, R. B. *Fundamental statistics for psychology,* 2nd ed. New York: Harcourt Brace Jovanovich, 1975.

McCollough, C., and Van Atta, L. *Statistical concepts: a program for self-instruction.* New York: McGraw-Hill, 1963.

Reichman, W. J. *Use and abuse of statistics.* Baltimore: Penguin Books, 1971.

Siegel, S. *Nonparametric statistics for the behavioral sciences.* New York: McGraw-Hill, 1956.

Glossary

abnormal behavior. Behavior that is statistically unusual, considered strange or undesirable by most people, and a source of unhappiness to the person who displays it.

abnormal psychology. The branch of psychology that studies mental and emotional disturbances and their treatment.

abscissa. The horizontal axis of a graph, along which the independent variable is usually plotted.

Absolute threshold. The minimum amount of stimulus energy to which a receptor will respond 50 percent of the time.

accommodation. The process of changing one's cognitive view when new information dictates such a change; one of the processes emphasized in Piaget's theory of intellectual development.

acetylcholine. One of the neurotransmitters.

achievement test. A test that measures the individual's present level of skill or knowledge. (*Compare* **aptitude test.**)

acuity. A scientific term for sharpness of vision.

adaptation. The tendency of the sensory apparatus to adjust to any steady and continued level of stimulation and to stop responding.

addiction. Physiological or psychological dependence on regular use of a drug.

adrenal cortex. The outer part of an *adrenal gland.*

adrenal glands. A pair of endocrine glands, lying atop the kidneys. Each consists of two parts: an *adrenal medulla,* which produces the stimulants adrenalin and noradrenalin, and an *addrenal cortex,* which produces steroids essential to life.

adrenal medulla. The inner part of an *adrenal gland.*

adrenalin (*also called* **epinephrine**). A hormone, secreted by the adrenal medulla, that affects the rate of heartbeat, raises the blood pressure, and causes the liver to release increased quantities of sugar into the blood to provide additional energy. Adrenalin is associated with the bodily states in fear or "flight" situations.

aerial perspective. A clue to distance perception; refers to the fact that distant objects appear less distinct and less brilliant in color than nearby objects, because they are seen through air that is usually somewhat hazy.

affect. A term used to describe the feelings that accompany emotional states of the organism; it refers specifically to feelings rather than to patterns of nervous discharge, physiological changes, or the behavior that may result from emotion.

afferent neuron. A neuron that carries impulses from the sense organs toward the central nervous system.

afterimage. The visual phenomenon produced by withdrawal of a stimulus. Withdrawal is followed briefly by a positive afterimage, then by a negative afterimage.

aggression. A type of behavior arising from hostile motives; it takes such forms as argumentativeness, scorn, sarcasm, physical and mental cruelty, and fighting.

agoraphobia. Abnormal fear of being in open spaces.

algorithm. A formal rule for solving mathematical problems, thus an important tool in logical thinking. (*Compare* **heuristic.**)

alpha waves. A pattern of regular waves of 7-10 cycles per second characteristically found when the brain is "at rest."

altered states of consciousness. States of consciousness different from normal waking experience, such as those produced by sleep, hypnosis, or drugs.

altruism. Behavior that is kind, generous, and helpful to others.

ambivalence. Mingled feelings of like and dislike toward a person or situation.

amnesia. Loss of memory. It may be caused by physical injury, or it may be a defense mechanism—an exaggerated form of repression.

amphetamine. Any of a group of drugs that excite the central nervous system; of value in the treatment of hyperkinesis but often abused by users who seek to combat fatigue or get "kicks." Also known as "meth," "bennies," "speed," or pep pills.

amplitude. The characteristic of a sound wave that determines the loudness we hear.

anal stage. One of the stages of psychological development according to Freud; the stage at which the child is preoccupied with sensations from the anal area.

anthropology. A behavioral science that is chiefly concerned with the study of societies or large cultural groups.

antisocial reaction. *See* **psychopathic personality.**

anxiety. An emotion characterized by a vague fear or premonition that something undesirable is going to happen; a frequent result of conflicts among motives and a prominent factor in abnormal behavior.

anxiety reaction. A psychoneurosis in which the individual often describes himself as "chronically uneasy" for reasons he cannot explain; the anxiety is the outstanding symptom.

anxiety state. One rather large group of psychoneuroses, in all of which anxiety is a prominent symptom. The group includes *anxiety reaction* and *phobic reaction.*

apathy. A feeling of indifference in which the individual may seem to lose all interest in what happens to him; a result of frustration.

aphasia. The loss of ability to speak or to understand speech.

apparent motion. The perception of motion in stimuli that, though they change, do not actually move, as in *stroboscopic motion* or the *phi phenomenon.* (*Compare* **illusory motion.**)

applied psychology. The application of psychological knowledge and principles to practical situations in school, industry, social situations, and treatment of abnormal behavior.

approach-approach conflict. A conflict in which the aroused motives have two incompatible goals, both of which are desirable.

approach-avoidance conflict. A conflict in which the individual has a single goal with both desirable and undesirable aspects, causing mixed feelings.

aptitude. A capacity to learn or to perform, such as mechanical or musical aptitude; an inborn ability that exists and can be measured even though the individual has had no special training to develop his skills (such as at mechanical or musical tasks).

aptitude test. A test that measures the individual's *capacity* to perform, not his present level of skill or knowledge. (*Compare* **achievement test.**)

aroused motive. A motive the individual is actually thinking about at the moment; an active influence on behavior. (*Compare* **motivational disposition.**)

assertive coping. A constructive attempt to get rid of frustration in a meaningful way that has some chance of success.

assimilation. The process of incorporating a new stimulus into one's existing cognitive view; one of the processes emphasized in Piaget's theory of intellectual development.

asthenic reaction. An anxiety state in which the individual is chronically tired, listless, and unable to concentrate or work efficiently. At one time the condition was called neurasthenia.

astigmatism. A defect of vision caused by irregularities in the shape of the cornea or lens.

attachment. *See* **theory of attachment.**

attachment unit. A unit of innate or previously learned behavior, overt or covert, to which a new stimulus can become attached.

attention. The process of focusing perception on a single stimulus or limited range of stimuli.

attitude. An organized and enduring set of beliefs and feelings toward some kind of object or situation and a predisposition to behave toward it in a particular way.

attribution theory. The theory that social behavior is often influenced by our constant attempts to attribute behavior to a motive or other cause.

authoritarian personality. The combination of traits that has been found common among people who prefer an authoritarian as opposed to a democratic society; the traits include rigidly conventional standards of behavior and obedience and prejudice against minority groups.

autistic. A term used to describe disturbed individuals whose thoughts are extremely self-centered and unrelated to reality.

autokinetic illusion. The illusion of self-generated movement that a stationary object, such as a point of light seen in an otherwise dark room, sometimes creates.

autonomic nervous system. A complicated nerve network that connects the central nervous system with the glands and the smooth muscles of the body organs.

aversive conditioning. A type of behavior therapy that attempts to associate a behavioral symptom with pain and punishment rather than with pleasure and reward.

avoidance-avoidance conflict. A conflict in which there is simultaneous arousal of motives to avoid alternatives, both of which are undesirable.

axon. The fiber of the neuron that has end branches that transmit messages to other neurons or to muscles and glands; the "sending" portion of the neuron.

balance theory. A theory maintaining that, when a person holds two conflicting attitudes, he (1) stops thinking about the problem, (2) changes one of the attitudes, or (3) redefines the meaning of one of the attitudes.

basilar membrane. A piece of tissue dividing the cochlea more or less in half for its entire length; the organ of Corti, containing the hearing receptors, lies on this membrane.

behavior. The activities of an organism, both overt, or observable (such as motor behavior), and covert, or hidden (such as thinking).

behavior genetics. The study of how human beings and other organisms inherit characteristics that affect behavior.

behavior modification therapy. A type of psychotherapy that concentrates on eliminating abnormal behavior, which is regarded as learned, through new forms of learning.

behaviorism. A school of thought maintaining that psychologists should concentrate on the study of overt behavior rather than of "mental life" or consciousness.

benzedrine ("bennies"). One of the amphetamines.

binocular vision. A clue to distance perception; refers to the fact that the two eyes, being about 2½ inches apart, receive slightly different images of any seen object.

bio-feedback. A method of achieving control of bodily and brain functions through the feedback of information about these functions. In popular usage, refers to control of the brain's alpha waves.

biological drive. A pattern of brain activity that results from certain kinds of physiological conditions—usually when the organism is in a state of deprivation or imbalance.

blind spot. The point at which the optic nerve exits from the eyeball, creating a small and mostly insensitive gap in the retina.

brain control. A term for control of behavior through drugs or electrical stimulation of the brain.

brain stem. A group of brain structures, including the cerebellum, pons, reticular formation, and medulla, on which the forebrain rests.

breathing drive. A biological drive aroused by physiological requirements for oxygen.

brightness. One dimension of the visual stimulus; dependent on intensity.

brightness constancy. The tendency to perceive objects to be of consistent brightness regardless of the amount of light they actually reflect under different conditions of illumination.

bystander apathy. The tendency of people, especially under crowded conditions, to ignore others who need help or situations that call for action.

CAI. *See* **computer-assisted instruction.**

Cannon-Bard theory of emotion. A neurological theory holding that stimuli in the environment set off patterns of activity in the hypothalamus and thalamus; these patterns are then relayed both to the autonomic nervous system, where they trigger the bodily changes of emotion, and to the cerebral cortex, where they result in the feelings of emotion.

caretaker period. The period between birth and eighteen months, during which the child's personality development depends mostly on his close relationship with his mother or caretaker.

cell body (of a neuron). The portion of a neuron containing its genes, as opposed to the fiber portion of the neuron.

central motive state. A state of the organism produced by an interaction between a biological drive and an incentive object.

central nervous system. The spinal cord and the brain. (*Compare* **peripheral nervous system.**)

central trait. A personality trait that is generally believed to have an important correlation with other traits—as "warmth" of personality is believed to be accompanied by sociability and a good sense of humor.

cerebellum. The portion of the brain stem that controls body balance and helps coordinate bodily movements.

cerebral cortex. The highest part of the brain, the surface of the cerebrum; a dense and highly interconnected mass of neurons and their cell bodies.

cerebrotonic temperament. A type of temperament ascribed by William Sheldon to the ectomorphic body type; characterized by mental overintensity, secretiveness, emotional restraint, fear of society, and love of privacy.

cerebrum. The large brain mass of which the cerebral cortex is the surface. It is divided into two separate halves called the left hemisphere and the right hemisphere.

character disorder (*also called* **personality disorder**). A type of emotional disorder characterized by failure to acquire mature and efficient ways of coping with the problems of adult life.

chemotherapy. The treatment of emotional disorders with drugs (or chemicals).

chromosome. The mechanism of human heredity. There are twenty-three pairs of the tiny structures, forty-six in all, found in the fertilized egg cell and repeated through the process of division in every cell of the body.

ciliary muscles. The muscles that control the shape of the lens of the eye.

clairvoyance. The supposed ability to perceive something that is not apparent to the sense organs; a form of extrasensory perception.

classical conditioning. A type of learning process through which a response becomes attached to a conditioned (or previously neutral) stimulus. (*Compare* **operant conditioning.**)

claustrophobia. Abnormal fear of being in enclosed places, such as elevators.

client. A term used, in preference to "patient," by clinical psychologists to refer to the people they treat.

client-centered therapy. A type of psychotherapy, developed by Rogers, in which the therapist displays warmth and acceptance toward the patient, or client, thus providing a nonthreatening situation in which the patient is freed to explore all his thoughts and feelings.

clinical psychologist. A psychologist who practices psychotherapy or diagnoses abnormal symptoms.

clinical psychology. The branch of applied psychology concerned with the application of psychological knowledge to the treatment of personality problems and mental disorders.

cochlea. A bony structure of the inner ear shaped like a snail's shell; contains the receptors for hearing.

codeine. A narcotic drug derived from the poppy plant.

cognitive consonance. Consistency and agreement among one's beliefs, feelings, and behavior.

cognitive dissonance. Lack of consistency among beliefs, feelings, and behavior. The theory of cognitive dissonance maintains that people are strongly motivated to relieve such dissonance, often by changing attitudes.

cognitive psychology. A school of thought maintaining that the mind does not merely react to stimuli but actively processes the information it receives into new forms and categories.

cognitive theory of emotion. The theory that an emotion is the cognitive interpretation of a change in level and quality of internal sensations in a particular context.

collective unconscious. In Jung's theory, a repository for the events of human history, superstitions, fears, etc., which influence all people.

color blindness. A visual defect involving deficiency in color discrimination.

color constancy. The tendency to perceive a familiar object as of constant color, regardless of changes in illumination that alter its actual stimulus properties.

communication. A general term for exchanges of information and feelings between two (or more) people. For its special meaning in social psychology, *see* **persuasive communications.**

community therapy. A type of interactional therapy in which the therapist attempts to change conflicts and patterns of behavior through alteration of behavior in the community.

comparative psychology. The study of processes common to several animal species, including man.

complementary hues. Two hues that, when added one to the other, yield gray.

complexity. The characteristic of a sound wave that determines the timbre we hear; caused by the number and strength of the overtones.

compulsion. An irresistible urge to perform some act over and over again.

computer-assisted instruction (CAI). A method of programed instruction in which a computer is used as a teaching machine.

concept. A symbol that stands for a common characteristic or relationship shared by objects or events that are otherwise different.

concept hierarchy. An arrangement of the associations that make up concepts; the very strong ones at the top are likely to be thought of immediately, and the weakest ones at the bottom are less likely to come to mind.

conceptual intelligence. The term used by Piaget to describe the developmental process after the age of two, in which the child increasingly uses concepts to organize the evidence of his senses and to engage in ever more complex thinking and problem solving.

concrete operations. The term applied by Piaget to the stage of intellectual development (ages seven to eleven) when the child can reason logically about concrete objects that he sees but has yet to learn to deal with rules in the abstract.

conditioned operant. Behavior learned through operant conditioning; a type of behavior with which the organism "operates" on its environment to obtain a desired result.

conditioned response. A response that has become attached through learning to a conditioned (or previously neutral) stimulus; an example is the salivation by Pavlov's dog to the sound of the metronome.

conditioned stimulus. In classical conditioning, a previously neutral stimulus (such as a sound) that through pairing with an unconditioned stimulus (such as food) acquires the ability to set off a response (such as salivation).

conditioning. A learning process in which behavior becomes attached to new stimuli. (*See* **classical conditioning, operant conditioning.**)

cones. One of two types of receptors for vision located in the retina. The cones are receptors for color and are also sensitive to differences in light intensity resulting in sensations of black, white, and gray.

conflict. The simultaneous arousal of two or more incompatible motives, resulting in unpleasant emotions.

conformity. The yielding by an individual to pressures from another person or, more usually, from a group. Expedient conformity is mere lip service. True conformity represents an actual change of attitude.

connecting neuron. A neuron that is stimulated by another neuron and passes its message along to a third neuron.

connotation. The implied meaning of a word. Although *landlord* means only a person who rents property, to most people the word connotes stinginess.

conservation. The principle that such qualities as mass, weight, and volume remain constant regardless of changes in appearance; learned by the child during Piaget's stage of concrete operations.

consummatory action. Behavior undertaken by an organism to satisfy a drive or motive.

control group. A group used for comparison with an experimental group. The two groups must be alike in composition and must be observed under the same circumstances except for the one variable that is manipulated in the case of the experimental group. (*Compare* **experimental group.**)

conversion reaction. A form of hysteria characterized by physical symptoms that have no organic basis.

core of personality. To personality theorists, the tendencies and characteristics common to all people.

cornea. The transparent bulge in the outer layer of the eyeball through which light waves enter.

corpus callosum. A large nerve tract that connects the left and right hemispheres of the cerebrum and enables the two hemispheres to cooperate and share in duties.

correlation. The degree of relationship between two different factors; measured statistically by the correlation coefficient.

correlation coefficient. A statistic that describes in numbers ranging from -1 to $+1$ the degree of relationship between two different factors.

cortisol. One of the steroids produced by the adrenal cortex.

counseling psychologist. One who practices counseling psychology.

counseling psychology. The branch of psychology that concentrates on vocational guidance, assistance with marital problems, and advice in other situations regarded as less serious or deepseated than the behavioral problems usually treated by clinical psychologists.

counterconformity. The tendency to be opposed to anything suggested by group pressure, regardless of its merits.

covert behavior. Hidden processes (such as thoughts) that take place inside the organism and cannot be seen by an observer.

creative thinking. A highly imaginative and rather rare form of directed thinking in which the individual discovers new relationships and solutions to problems and may produce an invention or an artistic creation.

cretinism. A biological form of mental retardation caused by an abnormally low level of secretion by the thyroid gland.

criterion-oriented. A term for tests that measure the subject's performance in absolute terms—as for example, a sixth-grader's skill at performing all the arithmetic calculations of which a well-instructed sixth-grader might be capable.

critical ratio. A measure of the degree of difference between two groups.

culture. The ways of a given society, including its norms, customs, beliefs, values, and ideals.

curve of forgetting. A graph plotting the course of forgetting.

---

decibel. A measure of the amplitude of sound.

defense mechanism. A process, generally believed to be unconscious, in which the individual tries to convince himself that a frustration or conflict and the resulting anxiety do not exist or have no importance.

delusion. A false belief, such as imagining that one is already dead.

dendrite. The part of the neuron, usually branched, that has the special function of being sensitive to stimuli and firing off a nervous impulse; the "receiving" portion of the neuron.

denial. A defense mechanism, closely related to repression, in which the individual simply denies the existence of the events that have aroused his anxiety.

dependent variable. A change in behavior that results from changes in the conditions that affect the organism—that is, from changes in an *independent variable.*

depression. The feeling of sadness and sometimes total apathy, often due to guilt or the inability to cope with one's problems; a result of frustration or conflict or possibly influenced by chemical imbalances in the brain.

descriptive statistics. A quick and convenient method of summarizing measurements. Important figures in descriptive statistics are the number of subjects (or *N*); measures of central tendency, including the mean, median, and mode; and measurements of variability, including range and standard deviation.

desensitization. An attempt to eliminate phobias by associating the stimulus that has caused the fear with relaxation rather than with fearful behavior; a technique used in behavior therapy.

developmental psychology. The study of the processes by which the newborn baby acquires his patterns of overt behavior, thinking, and problem solving and the motives, emotions, conflicts, and ways of coping with conflicts that will go to make up his adult personality.

dexedrine. One of the amphetamines.

didactic learning (*also called* **learning through exposition**). A method of instruction in which the teacher explains a concept and then cites examples.(*Compare* **discovery learning.**)

difference threshold (*also called* **just noticeable difference** *or* **j.n.d.**). The smallest difference in intensity or quality of stimulation to which a sensory receptor will respond 50 percent of the time.

Dilantin. A drug that has been used successfully in controlling epilepsy.

direct aggression. Aggressive behavior focused directly on the obstacle that has caused frustration.

directed thinking. A process in which we try to forge a chain of associations that will reach a definite goal. The most important form of directed thinking is *problem solving.*

discovery learning. A method of instruction in which the teacher presents examples of a concept and lets the student discover the concept for himself. (*Compare* **didactic learning.**)

displaced aggression. Aggressive behavior directed against an "innocent bystander" because the cause of frustration or conflict cannot itself be attacked.

dispositional factors. Behavior producing factors that represent lasting and consistent personality traits. Opposite of *situational factors.*

dissociative reaction. A form of hysteria in which the individual undergoes some form of loss of contact with reality; he dissociates himself in some manner from the conflicts that are troubling him. Three forms are amnesia, multiple personality, and sleep walking.

dissonance theory. A theory maintaining that inconsistencies among one's beliefs, feelings, and behavior create a state of cognitive dissonance that the individual then tries to relieve, often by changing his attitude.

distributed practice. A series of relatively short learning periods. (*Compare* **massed practice.**)

dizygotic twins. *See* **fraternal twins.**

DNA (deoxyribonucleic acid). The complex chemical of which genes are composed.

dominant gene. A gene, such as the one for brown eyes, that always prevails over a *recessive gene,* such as the one for blue eyes.

double approach-avoidance conflict. A conflict aroused by motives toward two goals that both have their good points and their bad.

double blind. An experimental technique in which neither the subjects nor the experimenter knows which subjects are in the control group and which are in the experimental group.

"downers". In the parlance of drug users, any drug that has a calming or sedative effect.

Down's Syndrome (*sometimes called* **Mongolism**). A type of mental retardation caused by the presence of an extra chromosome.

drive. *See* **biological drive.**

drug abuse. The use of drugs, especially herion but also psychedelic drugs and others, without medical indication and to excess.

ductless gland. *See* **endocrine gland.**

eardrum. A membrane between the outer part of the auditory canal and the middle ear.

ectomorph. One of three basic types of body build described by Sheldon; the ectomorph is characterized by a skin area and nervous system that are large in proportion to his size.

edumetric test. Another name for a criterion-oriented test (which see).

EEG. *See* **electroencephalograph.**

efferent neuron. A neuron that carries impulses from the central nervous system toward the muscles or glands.

ego. According to Freud's psychoanalytic theory of personality, the conscious, logical part of the mind that develops as a person grows up and that is his operational contact with reality.

ego ideal. The sum total of a person's standards; his notion of how, if he were as perfect as he would like to be, he would always think and behave.

ego theory. One of the neo-psychoanalytic theories, stressing the importance of the ego rather than of the id.

eidetic imagery. The ability, possessed by a minority of people, to "see" an image that is an exact copy of the original sensory experience.

electroencephalograph (EEG). A delicate instrument that measures the electrical activity of the brain.

electroshock. A medical method of treating behavior disorders, especially depression, by passing an electric current through the patient's brain.

elimination drive. A biological drive aroused by physiological requirements to get rid of the body's waste products.

emotion. A word used in four different ways: (1) by physiologists to describe various changes inside the body; (2) by neurologists to describe patterns of nervous activity; (3) by those interested in behavior to describe such actions as weeping or laughing, and (4) to describe the subjective feelings (also called *affects*) that bear such names as fear, anger, and so on.

emotional state. The condition of the organism during emotion, characterized by patterns of activity in the central nervous system and autonomic nervous system and by changes in glandular activity, heart rate, blood pressure, breathing, and activity of the visceral organs.

empathy. Understanding another person by putting oneself in that person's shoes and sharing his thoughts and feelings.

empiricists. Those who accept the theory that behavior is determined more by learning and experience than by inborn factors.

encounter group. A group of people who meet, usually under the leadership of a psychotherapist, with the goal of throwing off the masks they usually present in public and airing their true feelings.

endocrine gland (*also called* **ductless gland**). A gland that discharges chemical substances known as *hormones* directly into the blood stream, which then carries them to all parts of the body, resulting in many kinds of physiological changes.

endomorph. One of the three basic types of body build described by Sheldon; the endomorph is characterized by a strong digestive system and tends to be round in build, with relatively weak bones and muscles.

engram. Some kind of lasting trace or impression formed in living protoplasm by a stimulus; a deliberately vague term often used to describe the learning connection or memory trace.

epilepsy. A form of brain malfunction that produces sudden mental blackouts and sometimes seizures or "fits."

epinephrine. *See* **adrenalin.**

ESP. *See* **extrasensory perception.**

estrogen. One of the hormones secreted by the female ovaries.

Eustachian tube. A passage between the middle ear and the air chambers of the mouth and nose; it keeps the pressure on both sides of the eardrum constant.

existential psychology. A school of thought that emphasizes man's freedom and responsibility for his own existence and experiences.

expectancy wave. A type of brain wave that occurs when a person is in a state of expectancy, as when awaiting a stimulus he knows is coming.

experiment. A scientific method in which the experimenter makes a careful and rigidly controlled study of cause and effect, by manipulating an independent variable (or condition affecting the subject) and observing its effect on a dependent variable (or the subject's behavior in response to changes in the independent variable).

experimental group. A group of subjects whose behavior is observed while the experimenter manipulates an independent variable. (*Compare* **control group.**)

extinction. The disappearance of a conditioned response (or other learned behavior) when reinforcement is withdrawn.

extrasensory perception (ESP). Any of several various forms of supposed ability to perceive stimuli through some means other than the sense organs.

extrinsic motivation. Motivation that comes from the outside, established artifically and created by rewards that have no real connection with the learning situation. (*Compare* **intrinsic motivation.**)

extrovert. An individual who dislikes solitude and prefers the company of other people.

---

factor analysis. A statistical method used to discover the major factor or factors that are measured by a large number of tests or observations; for example, a battery of mental tests usually reveal a verbal ability factor.

family therapy. A type of interactional therapy in which the therapist attempts to change the patterns of behavior that various members of a family display toward one another.

fantasy. Images; daydreams.

fat cells. Cells scattered throughout the body that are designed for the storage of fatty compounds. An excess of such cells is believed to be a common cause of obesity.

feature detector. A brain cell that responds to special features of a stimulus reaching the sense organs—as to a horizontal line but not to a vertical line.

feedback. In learning, knowledge obtained by the learner of how well he is progressing.

figure-ground. In perception, the tendency to see an object as a figure set off from a neutral ground.

forebrain. The top part of the brain mass, including the cerebrum, corpus callosum, thalamus, and hypothalamus.

formal operations. The term applied by Piaget to the stage of intellectual development (beginning at about age eleven or twelve) at which the child becomes capable of thinking in the abstract.

fovea. The most sensitive part of the retina; contains only cones, which are packed together more tightly than anywhere else in the retina.

fraternal twins (*also called* **dizygotic twins**). Twins who develop from separate eggs and do not inherit the same genes. (*Compare* **identical twins.**)

free association. A tool of psychoanalysis in which the patient, lying as relaxed as possible on a couch, is encouraged to let his mind wander where it will and to speak out every thought that occurs to him.

free operant. Random, purposeless action, such as the movements of a baby in his crib.

frequency. The characteristic of a sound wave determining the tone or pitch that we hear; measured in number of cycles per second.

frustration. The blocking of motive satisfaction by some kind of obstacle. (In popular usage, also the unpleasant feelings caused by the blocking of motive satisfaction.)

functional psychology. A school of psychology, associated with James, that emphasized the functions rather than the structure of mental processes.

functional autonomy. A principle holding that an activity that is originally a means to an end frequently acquires an independent function of its own and becomes an end in itself.

functional fixedness. The tendency to think of an object in terms of its usual functions, not other possible functions; a common barrier to problem solving.

functional psychosis. A psychosis having no apparent connection with any organic disturbance. (*Compare* **organic psychosis.**)

---

galvanic skin reflex (GSR). A change in the electrical conductivity of the skin caused by activity of the sweat glands.

gamma phenomenon. The apparent motion of a light when it gets brighter (and seems to draw closer) or dimmer (and seems to move away).

ganglion (*plural:* **ganglia**). A mass of nerve cells and synapses forming complex and multiple connections.

gene. A tiny substance that is a molecule of *DNA*. The genes, grouped together into chromosomes, direct the growth of cells into specific parts of the body and account for inherited individual differences.

general adaptation syndrome. A phrase coined by Selye for the sequence of events involved in prolonged stress; the initial shock or alarm, the recovery or resistance period, and at last exhaustion and death.

generation gap. Differences in attitudes

and behavior between young people and older people.

genital stage. One of Freud's stages of psychological development; the final stage, at which the person is able to enter into a heterosexual relationship.

genotype. The characteristics of an organism that depend on its genetic inheritance and will be passed along to its offspring. (*Compare* **phenotype.**)

Gestalt psychology. A school of thought holding that all psychological phenomena must be studied as a whole (rather than broken down into parts) and in the context in which they occur.

goal. An object or event toward which a biological drive, stimulus need, or motive is directed.

gradient of approach. The changing strength of the desire to approach a goal, dependent on such factors as distance from the goal.

gradient of avoidance. The changing strength of the desire to avoid an unpleasant goal, dependent on such factors as distance from the goal.

gradient of texture. A clue to distance perception; refers to the fact that nearby objects are seen more sharply and therefore appear "grainier" in texture than more distant objects.

"grass". Slang for marijuana.

group dynamics. The forces that operate in a group to produce leaders and to bring about other alignments, activities, and decisions.

group test. A psychological test that can be given to many individuals at the same time.

group therapy. A type of psychotherapy in which several patients are treated simultaneously.

GSR. *See* **galvanic skin reflex.**

hallucination. An imaginary sensation, such as seeing nonexistent animals in the room or feeling bugs crawling under the skin.

halo effect. The fact that our general impressions of another person are strongly colored by any one thing, good or bad, that we initially learn about him.

hashish ("hash"). A concentrated extract of the active substances of the marijuana plant.

Hering theory (of vision). A theory holding that color vision is attributable to two types of cones with double

action, one responsible for red and green, the other for blue and yellow. The Hering theory is now considered incorrect as to the nature of the cones but correct as to the type of nervous impulses sent from the eye.

heroin. A narcotic drug derived from the poppy plant.

heterosexuality. Sexual attraction to members of the opposite sex.

heuristic. A type of thinking that attempts to solve problems less through the application of formal rules than by the use of analogies, rules of thumb, and educated guesses. (*Compare* **algorithm.**)

hippocampus. A part of the brain that appears essential to the transfer of information from short-term memory to long-term memory.

homeostasis. An internal environment in which such bodily states as blood circulation, blood chemistry, breathing, digestion, temperature, and so on are kept at optimal levels for survival of the living organism.

homosexuality. Sexual attraction to members of the same sex.

hormones. Substances produced by the endocrine glands and secreted into the blood stream; complicated chemicals that trigger and control many kinds of bodily activities and behavior.

hue. The proper scientific term for what is commonly called color; determined by the length of the light wave.

human engineering. A branch of applied psychology concerned with the design of equipment and machinery to fit the size, strength, and capabilities of the people who will use it.

humanistic psychology. A school of thought especially interested in the qualities that distinguish human beings from other animals—such as desires for dignity, self-worth, and *self-actualization.*

hunger drive. A biological drive caused by deprivation of food.

hyperkinesis. A mental abnormality that makes children overactive, irritable, unable to concentrate, and "hard to handle."

hypnosis. The act of inducing the hypnotic state, in which the subject is in a sort of dreamlike trance and highly susceptible to suggestions from the hypnotist; sometimes used in psychotherapy.

hypochondriacal reaction. An anxiety state in which the individual tends to

excuse his failures on the grounds of an imaginary physical illness.

hypothalamus. The portion of the forebrain that serves as a sort of mediator between the brain and the body, helping control metabolism, sleep, hunger, thirst, body temperature, and sexual behavior, and that is also concerned with emotions.

hypothesis. A theory, especially as to how a problem might be solved.

hysteria. A form of psychoneurosis; includes *conversion reaction* and *dissociative reactions.*

id. According to Freud's psychoanalytic theory of personality, the unconscious part of the human personality comprising the individual's primitive instinctive forces toward sexuality (the *libido*) and aggression.

identical twins (*also called* **monozygotic twins**). Twins who develop from the same egg and thus inherit the same genes. (*Compare* **fraternal twins.**)

identification. (1) A process in which the child tries to imitate the behavior of his parents or "heroes" so that he can share vicariously in their strengths and triumphs. (2) In psychoanalytic theory, the process through which the child resolves the Oedipus complex by absorbing his parents into himself. (3) As a defense mechanism, the process through which the individual identifies with another person, or more often with a group, in order to reduce his own conflicts and anxieties.

illusion. A perception that is a false interpretation of the actual stimuli.

illusory motion. The perception of motion in a unchanging stimulus, such as in the *autokinetic illusion.* (*Compare* **apparent motion.**)

image. The recollection of a sensory experience.

imitation. *See* **learning through observation.**

implicit personality theory. The assumption, held by most people, that certain personality traits are correlated with others—e.g., that "warmth" of personality is accompanied by sociability and a good sense of humor.

imprinting. A rapid form of learning occurring during a critical period early in the organism's life—as when young ducks learn to follow a moving object, usually the mother.

incentive object (*also called* **incentive stimulus**). A stimulus that arouses a drive or motive.

incidental learning (*also called* **latent learning**). Learning that takes place casually, almost as if by accident, then lies latent until reinforcement is provided.

incremental learning. Learning that takes place in a series of steps, in which the amount of learning increases, sometimes quickly and sometimes slowly, until the learning is complete. (*Compare* **one-trial learning.**)

independence. As used in social psychology, the tendency to make up one's own mind and decide on one's own behavior and thinking regardless of society's norms and pressures.

independent variable. A condition, affecting an experimental subject, that is controlled and varied by the experimenter, thus producing changes in the subject's behavior, called the *dependent variable.*

individual difference. Any difference — as in physical size or strength, intelligence, sensory threshold, perceptions, emotions, personality, and so on — between the individual organism and other members of his species.

individual test. A psychological test that is given by a trained examiner to one person at a time.

industrial psychology. A branch of applied psychology, embracing the use of psychological knowledge in setting working hours and rest periods, improving relations between employer and employees, and so on.

inferential statistics. Statistics that are used to make generalizations from measurements.

inferiority complex. A concept introduced by Adler to describe the condition of a person who for some reason has been unable to develop feelings of adequacy, independence, courage, and wholesome ambition.

inhibit. To suppress behavior; for example, the child in toilet training must learn to inhibit his tendency to eliminate wherever and whenever the elimination drive occurs.

inhibition. The suppression of behavior; also frequently used to describe emotional and psychoneurotic barriers to action — such as an inhibition against competitive or sexual activity.

inner ear. The portion of the ear inward from the oval window; contains the cochlea, vestibule, and semicircular canals.

insight. (1) In problem solving, the sudden "flash of inspiration" that results in a successful solution (*compare* **trial and error learning**). (2) In psychotherapy, and discovery by the patient of psychological processes that have caused his difficulties.

instinct. An elaborate and inborn pattern of activity, occurring automatically and without prior learning in response to certain stimuli in the environment.

insulin. A hormone, secreted by the pancreas, that burns up blood sugar to provide energy.

intellectualization. A defense mechanism in which the individual tries to explain away anxiety by intellectually analyzing the situations that produce the unpleasant feelings and making them a matter of theory rather than of action.

intelligence. The ability to profit from experience, to learn new pieces of information, and to adjust to new situations.

intelligence quotient (I.Q.). A numerical value assigned to an individual as a result of intelligence testing. The average intelligence quotient is set at 100.

intelligence test. A test measuring the various factors that make up the capacity called intelligence. It measures chiefly the individual's ability to use his acquired knowledge in a novel way.

interactional therapies. Types of psychotherapy that concentrate on changing the individual's behavior toward other people.

interest test. A test measuring the individual's interest or lack of interest in various kinds of amusements, literature, music, art, science, school subjects, social activities, kinds of people, and so on.

interference. Failures of memory caused by the effect of old learning on new or new learning on old.

intermittent reinforcement. *See* **partial reinforcement.**

interpersonal attraction. A person's tendencies to like other people, largely determined by such factors as similarities in attitudes, interests, and personality.

interposition. A clue to distance perception; refers to the fact that nearby objects interpose themselves between our eyes and more distant objects.

interval scale. A scale (for example, a thermometer) on which the intervals are equal but no ratio between the intervals is implied.

interview. A scientific method in which the investigator obtains information through careful and objective questioning of the subject.

intrinsic motivation. Motivation that comes from inside the individual. It is an integral part of the learning situation; the individual seeks to learn not for any external reward, but for the joy of knowing. (*Compare* **extrinsic motivation.**)

introspection. Inward examination of a "mental life" or mental process that nobody but its possessor can see in operation.

introvert. A person who tends to be preoccupied with his own thoughts and activities and to avoid social contact.

intuitive thought. The term applied by Piaget to the stage of intellectual development (ages four to six) when the child is developing concepts that become more and more elaborate but are still based largely on the evidence of his senses.

I.Q. *See* **intelligence quotient.**

iris. A circular arrangement of muscles that contract and expand to make the pupil of the eye smaller in bright light and larger in dim light.

James-Lange theory of emotion. A physiological theory holding that stimuli in the environment set off physiological changes in the individual, that the changes in turn stimulate sensory nerves inside the body, and that the messages of these sensory nerves are then perceived as emotion.

"joint". A marijuana cigarette.

just noticeable difference (j.n.d.). *See* **difference threshold.**

---

latent learning. *See* **incidental learning.**

lateral hypothalamus. A part of the brain containing the area responsible for turning on the hunger drive.

learned helplessness. A condition in which the organism has been subjected to punishment over which it has no control, leading to an impairment of the ability to learn or use old habits.

learning. The process by which overt behavior and covert behavior become altered or attached to new stimuli.

learning by imitation. *See* **learning through observation.**

learning curve. A graph plotting the course of learning. In a learning curve of decreasing returns, progress is quite rapid at first; then the curve starts to level off. In a learning curve of equal returns, progress takes place at a steady rate, with each new trial producing an equal amount of improvement. In a learning curve of increasing returns, very slow progress in early trials is followed by rapid progress in later trials.

learning plateau. A period in which early progress in learning appears to have stopped and improvement is at a standstill; the plateau is followed by a new period of progress.

learning sets. Attitudes and strategies acquired in one learning situation and carried over to similar situations; "learning how to learn."

learning through exposition. *See* **didactic learning.**

learning through modeling. *See* **learning through observation.**

learning through observation (*also called* **learning through modeling, learning by imitation**). A type of learning in which the behavior of another organism is observed and imitated.

lens. A transparent structure of the eye that changes shape to focus images sharply on the retina.

libido. According to Freud's psychoanalytic theory of personality, a basic instinctual force in the individual, embracing sexual urges and such related desires as to be kept warm, well-fed, and happy.

lie detector. A device designed to reveal whether a subject is telling the truth by measuring physiological changes, usually in heart rate, blood pressure, breathing, and galvanic skin reflex.

limbic system. A set of interconnected pathways in the brain, including the hypothalamus, some primitive parts of the cerebrum that have to do with the sense of smell, eating, and emotion, and other structures.

limen. *See* **threshold.**

linear perspective. A clue to distance perception; refers to the fact that parallel lines seem to draw closer together as they recede into the distance.

location constancy. The tendency to perceive objects as being in their rightful and accustomed place and remaining there even when we move and their images therefore move across our eyes.

logical thinking. An objective and disciplined form of thinking in which facts are carefully examined and conclusions consistent with the facts are reached.

long-term memory. The permanent storehouse from which information can be retrieved under the proper circumstances.

loudness. The hearing sensation determined by the amplitude of the sound wave.

LSD (lysergic acid diethylamide). A psychedelic drug.

management of learning. An attempt—often made by educators and by people desirous of learning—to arrange the most favorable possible conditions for learning to take place.

manic-depressive psychosis. A functional psychosis characterized by extremes of mood, often by wild swings from intense excitement to deep melancholy.

marathon group. A type of encounter group that meets for a single continuous session, often lasting thirty-six hours or more.

marijuana. The dried leaves and flowers of the hemp plant; a drug that affects different users in different ways, often interfering with short-term memory and concentration and producing feelings of elation.

masochism. Obtaining sexual pleasure from suffering pain or other maltreatment. (*Compare* **sadism.**)

massed practice. A single, long learning session. (*Compare* **distributed practice.**)

maturation. The physical changes, taking place after birth, that continue the biological development of the organism from fertilized egg cell to complete adult.

mean. A measure of central tendency obtained by dividing the sum of all the measurements by the number of subjects measured.

measurement. The assignment of numbers to traits, events, or subjects according to some kind of orderly system.

median. A measure of central tendency; the point separating the lower half of measurements from the upper half.

mediated generalization. A process in which two stimuli are generalized through the use of language, although they do not possess any physical similarities. An example is the generalization of a small rubber ball and a giant stuffed animal because both are called toys.

mediated transfer. A special kind of transfer of learning in which language is the mediating factor.

mediational clustering. The association of words and concepts, not through formal rules of logic but through an informal clustering of ideas that are in some way related.

mediational unit. One term (the preferred term in this book) for the engram, association, bond, or memory trace formed in learning; a connection between a new stimulus and an innate or previously learned unit of overt or covert behavior.

medulla. The connection between the spinal cord and the brain; an important connecting link that is vital to life because it helps regulate heartbeat, blood pressure, and breathing.

memory trace. The basis of a theory of remembering, no longer popular, holding that learning left some kind of trace in the nervous system that could be kept active through use but tended to fade away or become distorted through lack of practice.

mental age. A person's age as measured by his performance on an intelligence test; a person who scores as well as the average ten-year-old has a mental age of ten regardless of his chronological age.

mentally gifted. Having an I.Q. over 130.

mentally retarded. Having an I.Q. below 70.

mental telepathy. The supposed ability of one person to know what is going on in another person's mind; a form of extrasensory perception.

mesomorph. One of three basic types of body build described by Sheldon; the mesomorph is the athletic type, with strong bones and muscles.

metabolism. The chemical process in which the body converts food into protoplasm and energy.

methedrine ("meth"). One of the amphetamines.

middle ear. The portion of the ear between the eardrum and the oval window of the inner ear; contains three bones that aid transmission of sound waves.

mnemonic device. A form of memory aid in which memorized symbols give relation to otherwise unrelated material.

mode. A measure of central tendency; the measurement at which the greatest number of subjects fall.

modeling. *See* **learning through observation.**

Mongolism. *See* **Down's Syndrome.**

monozygotic twins. *See* **identical twins.**

morphemes. The smallest meaningful units of language, made by combining *phonemes* into prefixes, words, or suffixes.

motion parallax. A term describing the fact that, when we move our heads, near objects move across our field of vision more rapidly than objects that are farther away.

motivation. A general term referring to the forces regulating behavior that is undertaken because of drives, needs, or desires and is directed toward goals.

motivational disposition. The possession of a motive; a potential influence on behavior that can at any time be aroused to become an active motive. (*Compare* **aroused motive.**)

morphine. A narcotic drug derived from the poppy plant.

motive. A desire for a goal or incentive object that has acquired value for the individual.

motive targets. The people to whom motives are directed. People may exhibit strong motives of affiliation toward a "target" such as their parents and of hostility toward other "targets."

motor skill. A coordinated series of movements, such as those required in walking or riding a bicycle.

multiple personality. A type of dissociative reaction in which the individual seems to be split into two or more different selves that represent sides of his personality he cannot integrate into a unity.

muscle. Fibers capable of producing motion by contraction and expansion. Human muscles include *striped muscles* and *smooth muscles.*

muscle tension. Contractions of a muscle; one of the bodily changes often observed in emotion.

myelin sheath. A fatty sheath, white in appearance, that covers many neuron fibers and speeds the transmission of nervous impulses.

---

nAch. Short for need for achievement, often used by authors of studies of motivation.

nAff. Short for need for affiliation, often used by authors of studies of motivation.

narcissism. Excessive self-love.

narcotic. A term applied to a group of drugs that produce repose or sleep.

nativists. Those who accept the theory that many of the important factors determining behavior are present at birth.

naturalistic observation. A scientific method in which the investigator does not manipulate the situation and cannot control all the variables; he tries to remain unseen or as inconspicuous as possible.

negative transfer. A process in which learning is made more difficult by interference from previous learning. (*Compare* **positive transfer.**)

neo-psychoanalysts. The recent psychoanalytical theorists who have changed Freud's original ideas in various ways; "neo" means new.

nerve. A group of neurons, small or very large in number, traveling together to or from the central nervous system; in appearance, a single large fiber that is in fact made up of many fibers.

nervous impulse. A tiny charge of electricity passing from the dendrite end of the neuron to the end of the axon.

neuron. The individual nerve cell, basic unit of the nervous system.

neurosis (*also called* **psychoneurosis**). A form of emotional disturbance characterized by high levels of stress and anxiety over a period of time.

neurotic depression. A form of psychoneurosis in which the individual appears to be particularly sensitive to unhappy events; his normal discouragement and grief are complicated and exaggerated by feelings of dejection, hopelessness, and guilt.

neurotransmitter. A chemical released by one neuron that stimulates another neuron to fire; also sometimes inhibits the second neuron from firing.

nomadism. A form of withdrawal in which the frustrated individual wanders through life without ever putting down roots.

nominal scale. A scale in which num-

---

bers are simply assigned to different categories (as when men are called group 1 and women are called group 2).

nonsense syllable. A meaningless syllable, such as XYL or PLAM, used in the study of learning.

nonsocial behavior. Actions that take place when a person is alone.

noradrenalin (*also called* **norepinephrine**). One of the neurotransmitters. Also a hormone, secreted by the medulla of the adrenal gland, that produces bodily changes associated with anger or "fight" situations.

norepinephrine. *See* **noradrenalin.**

normal curve of distribution (*also called* **normal probability curve**). A bell-shaped curve that describes many events in nature; most events cluster around the average, and the number declines approaching either the lower or the upper extreme.

norm-oriented. A term for tests that measure the subject's ability in comparison with other people.

norms. The shared standards and expectations of a social group.

---

obedience. In social psychology, conformity to a figure of authority.

object constancy. The tendency to perceive objects as constant and unchanging, even under varying conditions of illumination, distance, and position.

objective personality test. A paper-and-pencil test administered and scored according to a standard procedure, giving results that are not affected by the opinions or prejudices of the examiner.

obsession. A thought that keeps cropping up in a persistent and disturbing fashion.

obsessive-compulsive reactions. A group of neuroses characterized by obsessions or compulsions.

Oedipus complex. According to Freud, the conflict of mingled love and hate toward the parents that every child undergoes between the ages of two and a half and six.

olfactory epithelium. The membrane, at the top of the nasal passages leading from the nostrils to the throat, that contains the receptors sensitive to smell.

one-trial learning. Learning that takes place in a single step. (*Compare* **incremental learning.**)

operant avoidance. Behavior, learned

through operant conditioning, by which the organism attempts to avoid something unpleasant.

operant behavior. Behavior that is not initially associated with or normally elicited by a specific stimulus. (*Compare* **respondent behavior.**)

operant conditioning. The process by which, through learning, free operant behavior becomes attached to a specific stimulus. (*Compare* **classical conditioning.**)

operant escape. Behavior, learned through operant conditioning, by which the organism seeks to escape something unpleasant.

opium. A drug derived from the poppy plant, most commonly used in the United States in the form of heroin.

opponent-process theory (of color vision). A type of pattern theory maintaining that our visual sensation of color results from three types of cones plus nerve cells, picking up messages from the eye that are sent along as signals paired as red-or-green, blue-or-yellow, and black-or-white.

oral stage. One of the stages of psychological development according to Freud; the first stage, in which the infant receives pleasure in the area of the mouth from acts such as sucking.

ordinal scale. A scale based on rank order.

ordinary sleep. A state of the organism in which brain activity is different from that in the waking state and the muscles of the body are quite relaxed. (*Compare* **paradoxical sleep.**)

ordinate. The verticle axis of a graph, along which the dependent variable is usually plotted.

organ of Corti. The collection of hair cells, lying on the basilar membrane, that are the receptors for hearing.

organic psychosis. A psychosis caused by actual damage to the brain by disease or injury. (*Compare* **functional psychosis.**)

organism. An individual animal, either human or subhuman.

osmotic pressure. The relative concentration of chemicals, such as salt and sugar, in the body fluids; cells in the brain sensitive to osmotic pressure set off the thirst drive.

oval window. The membrane through which sound waves are transmitted from the bones of the middle ear to the cochlea.

ovaries. Glands that, in addition to producing the female egg cells, secrete

hormones that bring about bodily changes known as secondary female sex characteristics.

overlearning. The process of continuing to practice at learning after bare mastery has been attained.

overlearning, law of. The principle that overlearning increases the length of time the material will be remembered.

overt behavior. Observable behavior, such as motor movements, speech, and signs of emotion such as laughing or weeping.

overtones. The additional vibrations of a source of sound, at frequencies higher than the fundamental tone it produces; the overtones account for the complexity and timbre of the sound.

---

pacer stimuli. A term, used in the theory of choice, that refers to stimuli of somewhat greater complexity than stimuli at the individual's ideal level of complexity.

pain drive. A biological drive aroused by unpleasant or noxious stimulation, usually resulting in behavior designed to escape the stimulus.

pancreas. The endocrine gland that secretes insulin.

Papez-MacLean theory of emotion. A neurological theory of emotion that emphasizes the role of the *limbic system.*

paradoxical sleep. A state of the organism in which the brain's activity is similar to that in the waking state but the muscles are extremely relaxed; also known as REM sleep because it is accompanied by the rapid eye movements that characterize dreaming. (*Compare* **ordinary sleep.**)

paranoia. A functional psychosis characterized by delusions, sometimes of grandeur, sometimes of persecution.

parasympathetic nervous system. A division of the autonomic nervous system, composed of scattered ganglia that lie near the glands and muscles they affect. The parasympathetic system is most active in helping maintain heartbeat and digestion under normal circumstances. (*Compare* **sympathetic nervous system.**)

parathyroids. A pair of endocrine glands, lying atop the larger thyroid gland, that regulate the balance of calcium and phosphorus in the body, an important factor in maintaining a

normal state of excitability of the nervous system.

part method (of learning). A method in which one part of the material is learned at a time, as in memorizing a speech. (*Compare* **whole method.**)

partial reinforcement (*also called* **intermittent reinforcement**). Reinforcement provided on some but not all occasions.

participant observation. A scientific method in which the investigator takes part in a social situation, encounter group, or the like in order to study the behavior of others.

pattern theory. A theory of the operation of the sense organs; it holds that our sensations are the result of the entire pattern of nervous impulses sent to the brain by many "broadly tuned" sensory receptors that respond in different ways to different stimuli.

peer group. The group of psychological equals to which the individual belongs; among children, based largely on age.

peers. For any individual, other people of about the same age and standing in the community; equals.

percentile. A statistical term used to describe the position of an individual score in the total group.

perception. The process through which we become aware of our environment by organizing and interpreting the evidence of our senses.

perceptual constancy. The tendency to perceive a stable and consistent world even though the stimuli that reach the senses are inconsistent and potentially confusing.

perceptual expectation. The tendency to perceive what we expect to perceive; a special form of *set.*

performance. Overt behavior; used as a measure of learning.

performance test. An intelligence test or part of an intelligence test that measures the individual's ability to perform such tasks as completing pictures, making designs, and assembling objects. (*Compare* **verbal test.**)

peripheral characteristics. To personality theorists, the observable traits that spring from the core of personality as channeled by individual development.

peripheral nervous system. The outlying nerves of the body and the individual neurons that make up these nerves. (*Compare* **central nervous system.**)

persistence of set. In problem solving, the tendency to continue to apply a certain hypothesis because it has worked in other situations, often at the expense of trying different and much more efficient hypotheses.

personality. The total pattern of characteristic ways of thinking, feeling, and behaving that constitute the individual's distinctive method of relating to his environment.

personality disorder. *See* **character disorder.**

personality test. A test designed to measure the various characteristics that make up the individual's personality.

perspective. A clue to distance perception; refers to the fact that three-dimensional objects can be delineated on a flat surface, such as the retina of the eye. (*See* **aerial perspective, linear perspective.**)

persuasive communications. The transmission of information and appeals to emotion in an attempt to change another person's attitudes.

phallic stage. One of the stages of psychological development according to Freud; the stage at which the child invests interest in the pleasure derived from his sex organs.

phenomenal self. A concept proposed by Rogers in his theory of personality; one's uniquely perceived self-image, based on the evidence of one's senses but not necessarily corresponding to reality.

phenotype. Characteristics displayed by an individual organism that are not necessarily passed along to its offspring—for example, its appearance. (*Compare* **genotype.**)

phi phenomenon. Motion produced by a rapid succession of images that are actually stationary; the simplest form of *stroboscopic motion.*

phobic reaction. An anxiety state characterized by unreasonable fears.

phonemes. The building blocks of language; basic sounds that are combined into *morphemes* and words.

pitch. The property of being high or low in tone, determined by the frequency (number of cycles per second) of the sound wave.

pituitary gland. The master endocrine gland that secretes hormones controlling growth, causing sexual development at puberty, and also regulating other endocrine glands.

PK. *See* **psychokinesis.**

place theory (of hearing). The theory that special parts of the basilar membrane are "tuned" to various pitches and that the response of receptors in each particular place accounts for the sensations of pitch.

play therapy. A type of psychotherapy, usually used with children, in which patients express their feelings by drawing pictures, modeling, or handling puppets or other toys.

pleasure principle. According to Freud's psychoanalytic theory of personality, the demand of the unconscious id for immediate and total satisfaction of all its demands. (*Compare* **reality principle.**)

pons. A structure of neurons connecting the opposite sides of the cerebellum; it helps control breathing and is apparently the origin of the nervous impulses that cause rapid eye movements during dreaming.

population. In statistics, the term for all people or all events in a particular category—such as all male college students in the United States.

position. The particular place or niche that an individual occupies in society.

positive transfer. A process in which learning is made easier by something learned previously. (*Compare* **negative transfer.**)

posthypnotic suggestion. A suggestion made during hypnosis, urging the subject to undertake some kind of activity after the hypnotic trance ends.

"pot". Slang for marijuana.

precognition. The supposed ability to forecast events; a form of extrasensory perception.

preconceptual thought. The term applied by Piaget to the stage of intellectual development (ages two and three) at which the child begins to use language to attach new meanings to the stimuli in his environment and to use one stimulus as a symbol for another.

prehension. Grasping ability.

prejudice. A deep-seated attitude that an individual maintains so stubbornly as to be uninfluenced by any information or experiences that might disprove it.

premise. Something that we believe to be true about the objects and events in the environment; an important tool in thinking.

preoperational stage. The term applied by Piaget to the period (ages two to seven) when the child's ability to use language begins to dominate intellectual development.

primacy. In learning, the fact of being near the beginning of a series of items to be learned. (*See* **primacy and recency, law of.**)

primacy and recency, law of. The principle that the learner tends to remember best the items that were first in a series (had primacy) or last (had recency).

primary mental abilities. According to Thurstone, the seven abilities that make up intelligence. They are verbal comprehension, word fluency, number, space, associative memory, perceptual speed, and general reasoning, plus some kind of "general factor" that is common to all individuals.

primary reinforcement. Reinforcement provided by a stimulus that the organism finds inherently rewarding—usually stimuli that satisfy biological drives such as hunger or thirst.

proactive inhibition. Interference by something learned in the past with the ability to remember new learning. (*Compare* **retroactive inhibition.**)

problem solving. Thinking that is directed toward the solution of a problem; the most common and important kind of *directed thinking.*

progesterone. One of the hormones secreted by the female ovaries.

programed learning. A system of instruction in which the subject matter is broken down into very short steps, mastered one at a time before going on to the next.

progressive part method (of learning). A method of learning, frequently quite efficient, in which the first unit of the whole (such as the first stanza of a poem) is learned, then the second, then these two are combined; then the third unit is learned and combined with the first two; and so on.

projection. A defense mechanism in which the individual foists off or projects onto other people motives of his own that cause him anxiety.

projective personality test. A test in which the subject is expected to project aspects of his own personality into the stories he makes up about pictures or the objects he sees in inkblots.

protoplasm. The basic substance of living tissue, the "stuff of life."

psychedelic drugs. Drugs, such as LSD, that often produce hallucinations and a sense of detachment from one's body.

psychiatrist. A physician who has had special training in treating behavior disturbances.

psychic energizer. Any of a number of drugs used to relieve depression by increasing brain activity.

psychoanalysis. A type of psychotherapy developed by Freud, in which the chief tools are free association, study of dreams and slips of the tongue, and transference. Psychoanalysis attempts to give the patient insight into his unconscious conflicts, which he can then control as they come into his awareness.

psychoanalyst. A person, usually a physician, who practices psychoanalysis.

psychoanalytic theory of personality. A theory originally formulated by Freud that emphasizes three parts of the personality: (1) the unconscious *id*, (2) the conscious *ego*, and (3) the largely unconscious *superego*.

psychodrama. A type of psychotherapy in which the patient is encouraged to act out his problems and fantasies in the company of other patients or therapeutic assistants who have been trained in the techniques of psychodrama.

psychokinesis (PK). The supposed ability of some people to influence physical events through exercise of the mind—for example, to make dice turn up as they wish.

psycholinguistics. The study of the relationship between psychological processes and the structure and use of language. Among its important concerns are the rules of language and the manner in which they are learned.

psychology. The science that systematically studies and attempts to explain observable behavior and its relationship to the unseen mental processes that go on inside the organism and to external events in the environment.

psychometric test. Another name for a norm-oriented test (which see).

psychoneurosis. *See* neurosis.

psychopathic personality (*also called* **sociopathic personality** *or* **antisocial reaction).** A behavior disorder characterized by lack of conscience, sense of social responsibility, and feeling for other people; also selfishness, ruthlessness, and addiction to lying.

psychophysical methods. Techniques of measuring how changes in the intensity or quality of a stimulus affect sensation.

psychosexual development. The Freudian theory that psychological development goes through oral, anal, phallic, and genital stages.

psychosis. The scientific name for the extreme form of mental disturbances often known as insanity. The mental disturbance is so severe as to make the individual incapable of getting along in society.

psychosomatic illness. An illness in which the physical symptoms seem to have mental and emotional causes.

psychotherapy. A technique used by clinical psychologists, psychiatrists, and psychoanalysts in which a patient suffering from personality disorder or mental disturbance is treated by the application of psychological knowledge.

pupil. The opening in the iris that admits light waves into the eyeball.

---

questionnaire. A scientific method similar to the interview but in which information is obtained through written questions.

---

random sample. A statistical sample that has been obtained by chance methods that avoid any bias.

range. A measurement of variability obtained by subtracting the lowest measurement from the highest.

rapid eye movement (REM). Small movements of a sleeper's eyes that occur during paradoxical sleep and dreaming.

ratio scale. A scale of measurement (such as height or weight) in which there is a true zero point and all the numbers on the scale fall into perfect ratios.

rationalization. A defense mechanism in which the individual maintains that a goal he was unable to attain was not desirable or that he acted out of "good" motives rather than "bad."

reaction formation. A defense mechanism in which the person behaves as if his motives were the opposite of his real motives; often characterized by excessive display of a "good" trait such as politeness.

reality principle. According to Freud's psychoanalytic theory of personality, the principle on which the conscious ego operates as it tries to mediate between the demands of the unconscious id and the realities of the environment. (*Compare* **pleasure principle.**)

recall. A way of measuring learning; the subject is asked to repeat as much of what he has learned as he can. (*Compare* **recognition, relearning.**)

recency. In learning, the fact of being near the end of a series of items to be learned. (*See* **primacy and recency, law of.**)

receptor. A specialized nerve ending of the senses.

recessive gene. A gene, such as the one for blue eyes, whose effects are always inhibited if the other member of the pair is a *dominant gene,* such as the one for brown eyes.

reciprocal inhibition. A technique of reducing anxiety by associating the stimulus that causes it with some new and more benign response; one of the techniques used in behavior therapy.

recognition. A way of measuring learning; the subject is asked to show that he recognizes what he has learned—for example, by picking out the right answer in a multiple-choice test. (*Compare* **recall, relearning.**)

redintegration. A special kind of remembering in which the individual appears to reconstruct an entire incident from his past; for example, he remembers not only a poem but also events in the classroom and the appearance of his teacher on the day he learned the poem.

reflex. An automatic and unthinking reaction to a stimulus by the organism. A reflex is inborn, not learned, and depends on inherited characteristics of the nervous system.

regression. A retreat toward types of activity appropriate to a lower level of maturity; a result of frustration.

reinforcement. In classical conditioning, the pairing of an unconditioned stimulus (such as food) with a conditioned stimulus (such as sound). (Here, the food is the reinforcement.) In general, the process of assisting learning by pairing desired behavior with something the organism finds rewarding.

reinforcing stimulus. The stimulus used in reinforcement; anything that strengthens and induces repetition of behavior in learning.

relearning. A method of measuring learning; the subject is asked to relearn to perfection something he had previously learned and partially forgotten, and the amount of time required for the original learning and for relearning are compared. (*Compare* **recall, recognition.**)

releaser. A stimulus that sets off instinctive or species-specific behavior.

reliable test. A test that gives consistent scores when the same individual is tested on different occasions.

REM. *See* **rapid eye movement, paradoxical sleep.**

reminiscence. In psychology, the phenomenon responsible for the fact that performance of a learned task is sometimes better after a lapse of time than at the conclusion of learning.

replicate. To repeat an experiment at a different time with a different experimenter and different subjects but with the same results.

representative sample. A statistical sample in which all parts of the population are represented.

repression. A defense mechanism in which an individual suffering anxiety over his motives seems to banish the motives from his conscious thoughts, pushing them into the unconscious.

resistance. In psychoanalysis, a blocking of the patient's thoughts by anxiety and repressions.

respondent behavior. Behavior that is a response to a definite stimulus. (*Compare* **operant behavior.**)

response. A general term used to describe any kind of behavior produced by a stimulus.

reticular activating system. A network of nerves in the brain stem and hypothalamus, serving as a way station for messages from the sense organs.

retina. A small patch of tissue at the back of the eyeball; contains the nerve endings called rods and cones that are the receptors for vision.

retrieval. The process of extracting information from long-term memory.

retroactive inhibition. Partial or complete blacking out of old memories by new learning. (*Compare* **proactive inhibition.**)

risky shift. The tendency of people to be more willing to undertake risks in decisions made in groups than in decisions made individually.

rods. One of the two types of receptors for vision located in the retina. The rods are receptors for light intensity, resulting in sensations of black, white, and gray.

role. The kind of behavior that society expects from a person in a given position.

role strain. A problem caused by the fact that a person cannot always know what role his fellow men expect him to play, especially when he occupies several different positions in society at the same time or moves from one to another.

---

sadism. Obtaining sexual pleasure from inflicting pain or other maltreatment. (*Compare* **masochism.**)

sample. A relatively small group whose measurements are used to infer facts about the population or universe. To permit valid generalization the sample must be representative and random.

saturation. The amount of pure hue present in a color as compared to the amount of other light wave lengths mixed in; thus the complexity of the mixture of waves determines saturation.

scanning. A process that takes place in short-term memory; the study of information that has arrived in sensory memory from the sense organs. Also the controlled movement of the eyes when the person is studying a stimulus.

scapegoating. Blaming other people, often members of minority groups, for feelings of frustration or conflict of which they are not the cause.

schizophrenia. A functional psychosis in which the patient appears to lose contact with reality and lives in a shell-like world of his own.

search for consistency. A person's tendency to seek consistency among his beliefs, feelings, and behavior.

secondary reinforcement. Reinforcement provided by a stimulus that has acquired reward value through association with a primary reinforcing stimulus.

selection. In perception, the tendency to pay attention to only some of the stimuli that reach our senses.

selective exposure. A term used by social psychologists to describe the fact that persuasive communications usually reach mostly people who already agree with them.

self-actualization. A term used by Maslow in his personality theory holding that men are innately virtuous and that normal and healthy development would enable each person to actualize his own true nature and fulfill his potentialities.

self-perception theory. The theory that we often take the role of an outside observer trying to find the reasons for our own behavior.

self theories. Personality theories based on the importance of the individual's self-image and its relation to reality.

semantic differential. A term coined by Osgood for differences in the qualities and values that words connote, especially along dimensions of good-bad, strong-weak, and active-passive.

semicircular canals. Three liquid-filled canals in the inner ear, containing receptors for the sense of equilibrium.

senile psychosis. A organic psychosis caused by deterioration of the brain cells and other physiological changes due to aging.

sensitivity group (*also called* **training group, T-group**). A kind of encounter group.

sensorimotor stage. The term applied by Piaget to the period of intellectual development during the first two years of life, when the child knows the world only in terms of his sensory impressions and his motor activities.

sensory adaptation. The tendency of sensory receptors to adjust to a stimulus and stop responding after a time.

sensory memory (*also called* **sensory register**). A memory system of very brief duration, composed of lingering traces of information sent to the brain by the senses.

sensory-motor area. A part of the brain's cortex serving as a control point for sensory impressions and motor movements of the body.

sensory register. *See* **sensory memory.**

separation anxiety. Fear of being separated from the caretaker; a form of anxiety that develops in the infant of about ten to eighteen months.

serial position. The position that an individual item occupies in a series of items to be learned. (*See* **primacy, recency.**)

set. A tendency to respond in a certain

way; to be prepared or "set" so to respond.

sex drive. A biological drive aroused by physiological requirements for sexual satisfaction.

shadowing. The pattern of light and shadow on an object; often a clue to perception of three-dimensional quality.

shape constancy. The tendency to perceive objects as retaining their shape regardless of the true nature of the image that reaches the eyes because of the viewing angle.

shaping. The learning of complicated tasks through operant conditioning, in which complex actions are built up from simpler ones.

short-term memory. A memory system in which information is held briefly, then either transferred to long-term memory or forgotten.

sibling. A brother or sister.

sibling rivalry. Jealousy between two chidren in the same family.

single blind. An experimental technique that keeps subjects in the dark as to whether they are in the control group or the experimental group.

situational factors. Behavior producing factors that depend on the situation of the moment, particularly the other people who are in the situation. Opposite of *dispositional factors.*

situational personality test. A test in which the examiner observes the behavior of the subject in a situation deliberately created to reveal some aspects of his personality.

size constancy. The tendency to perceive objects in their correct size regardless of the size of the actual image they cast on the eyes when near or far away.

skewed curve. A type of distribution curve that is irregular in that more scores fall on one side of the mode than on the other side.

sleep drive. A biological drive aroused by the physiological requirements for sleep.

sleeper effect. The term used to describe the fact that persuasive communications that initially have little effect on attitudes because they come from a source of low credibility may have a greater effect once the source is forgotten.

smooth muscle. A muscle of the internal organs, such as the stomach and intestines, or of the pupil of the eye, over which the individual ordinarily

has no conscious control.

social behavior. Actions taken in relation to another person or persons.

social class. A subdivision of society characterized by the access it has or believes it has to power, determined largely by income and education in western society.

social comparison theory. The theory that often we can only evaluate our own abilities, opinions, and behavior by comparing ourselves with other people.

social learning theories of personality (*also called* **stimulus-response, or S-R, theories**). Theories maintaining that personality is composed of habitual ways of responding to the environment that are learned responses to stimuli in the environment.

social psychology. The study of the behavior of the individual in his society and the influence that the actions and attitudes of the other members of his society have on his overt behavior and his thinking.

socialization. The training of the young in the ways of the society.

society. Any organized group of people, large or small.

sociopathic personality. *See* **psychopathic personality.**

somatotherapy. Treatment of behavior disturbances by treating the body, as with drugs or electroshock.

somatotonic temperament. A type of temperament ascribed by Sheldon to the mesomorphic body type; characterized by boldness of manner, physical courage, aggressiveness, and the love of physical adventure, risk, and chance.

spectrum. The range of hues created by breaking up a beam of sunlight with a prism, thus separating all the wave lengths of light from red to violet.

"speed". Slang for amphetamine.

spontaneous recovery. The tendency of a conditioned response that has undergone extinction to occur again after a rest period.

SQ3R system. An efficient five-step study method (survey, question, read, recite, review).

S-R psychology. *See* **stimulus-response psychology.**

S-shaped learning curve. A curve that shows very slow progress at the start, then faster progress for a time, and at last slower progress (or decreasing returns) as the ultimate limit of learning is approached.

standard. A rule that the individual sets for his own behavior. The desire to live up to standards is an important human motive.

standard deviation (SD). A statistical device for describing the variability of measurements.

standardized test. A test that has been pretested on a large and representative sample so that one person's score can be compared with the scores of the population as a whole.

startle pattern. A complex human reflex that occurs in response to sudden and unexpected events, such as a loud noise. The muscles of the neck, arms, and legs tense; the head moves forward; and the mouth may open.

statistical method. The application of mathematical principles to a description and analysis of measurements.

status. As used in social psychology, same as *position.*

stereotype. An attitude that disregards individual differences and holds that all people of a certain group behave in the same manner.

stereotyped behavior. A tendency to repeat some action over and over again, almost as a ritual; a result of frustration.

steroids. Chemical substances produced by the adrenal cortex and essential for life.

stimulus. Any form of energy capable of exciting the nervous system.

stimulus complexity. The relative level of simplicity or complexity possessed by a sensory stimulus. The organism apparently has stimulus needs for stimuli of a particular level of complexity found the most "comfortable."

stimulus discrimination. The ability, acquired through learning, to make distinctions between stimuli that are similar but not exactly alike.

stimulus generalization. The tendency of an organism that has learned to associate a stimulus with a certain kind of behavior to display this behavior toward stimuli that are similar though not exactly identical to the original stimulus.

stimulus need. The tendency of an organism to seek certain kinds of stimulation. The tendency does not have the life-and-death urgency of a drive, nor is its goal as specific and clearcut. Examples are the needs for stimulation, stimulus variability, and physical contact (or tactual comfort).

stimulus-response (S-R) psychology. A school of thought that emphasizes study of the stimuli that produce behavioral responses, the rewards and punishments that help establish and maintain these responses, and the modification of behavior through changes in the pattern of rewards and punishments.

stimulus-response (S-R) theories. *See* **social learning theories of personality.**

stimulus variability. Change and variety in stimulation; believed to be one of the organism's inborn stimulus needs.

stranger anxiety. Fear of unfamiliar faces, one of the first forms of anxiety that develops in the child at about eight months.

stress. In psychological terms, a stimulus that threatens to damage the organism.

stress interview. A form of situational personality test in which the subject is asked deliberately hostile questions and the interviewers pretend to disbelieve his answers.

striped muscle. A muscle of motor behavior, over which the individual ordinarily has conscious control.

stroboscopic motion. Motion produced by a rapid succession of images that are actually stationary, as in motion pictures.

structural psychology. A school of psychology, associated with Wundt, that concentrated on the structure or contents of conscious experience, such as sensations, images, and feelings.

subculture. A culture within a culture—that is, the ways of life followed by a group in a society that does not adhere to all the practices of the society as a whole.

sublimation. One form of the defense mechanism of *substitution*; substituting an acceptable goal for a forbidden one.

subliminal. A word used to describe a stimulus of an intensity below the threshold (or limen) of the senses.

substitution. A defense mechanism in which an unobtainable or forbidden goal is replaced by a different goal.

superego. According to Freud's psychoanalytic theory of personality, a largely unconscious part of the individual's personality that threatens punishment for transgressions.

supraliminal. A word used to describe a stimulus of an intensity at or above the threshold, or limen.

syllogism. A three-step process of logical thinking, consisting of a major premise, a minor premise, and a conclusion that follows inescapably from the first two.

symbol. Anything that stands for something else. The word *water* is a symbol for the colorless fluid we drink; the skull and crossbones is a symbol for poison; mathematics is a collection of symbols.

sympathetic nervous system. A division of the autonomic nervous system, composed of long chains of ganglia lying along both sides of the spinal column. It activates the glands and smooth muscles of the body and helps prepare the organism for "fight or flight." (*Compare* **parasympathetic nervous system.**)

synapse. The junction point between the axon of one neuron and the dendrite of another neuron.

synaptic knob. A swelling at the end of a dendrite; an important structure in the transmission of messages across the synapse.

syndrome. A medical term meaning the entire pattern of symptoms and events that characterize the course of a disease.

---

tabula rasa. A "blank tablet"; a phrase used to describe the theory that the mind of a human baby is a "blank tablet" on which anything can be written through learning and experience.

tactual comfort. Physical contact; one of the stimulus needs.

taste buds. The receptors for the sense of taste; found on the tongue, at the back of the mouth, and in the throat.

teaching machine. A device used in programed learning; the machine presents the program one step at a time and asks a question that the learner answers before going on to the next step.

telepathy. *See* **mental telepathy.**

temperature drive. A biological drive aroused by physiological requirements that the body temperature be kept at a constant level (in human beings, around 98.6° Fahrenheit).

test. A measurement of a sample of individual behavior. Ideally, a scientific test should be (1) objective, (2) standardized, (3) reliable, and (4) valid.

testes. Glands that, in addition to producing the male sperm cells, secrete hormones that bring about secondary male sex characteristics, such as the growth of facial hair and change of voice.

testosterone. A hormone secreted by the male testes.

T-group. *See* **training group.**

thalamus. The brain's major relay station, connecting the cerebrum with the lower structures of the brain and the spinal cord.

theory. A statement of general principles that explains events observed in the past and predicts what will happen under a given set of circumstances in the future.

theory of attachment. The theory that the human baby inherits a strong tendency to orient toward and consort with a caretaker, usually the mother, because inborn behaviors such as rooting, sucking, babbling, and crying are directed toward another person.

thinking. The covert manipulation of images, symbols, and other mediational units, especially language, concepts, premises, and rules.

thirst drive. A biological drive aroused by deprivation of water.

threshold (*also called* **limen**). The minimum amount of stimulation or difference in stimulation to which a sensory receptor will respond 50 percent of the time. (*See* **absolute threshold, difference threshold.**)

thyroid gland. An endocrine gland that regulates the rate of metabolism and affects the body's activity level.

tic. The involuntary twitching of a muscle.

timbre. The quality of a sound, determined by the number and strength of the overtones that contribute to the complexity of the sound wave.

tip of the tongue phenomenon. A partially successful attempt at retrieval in which we cannot quite remember a word (for example) but seem to have it almost available or "on the tip of the tongue."

token economy. An arbitrary economic system, often used in mental hospitals, in which patients are rewarded for good behavior with tokens that they can exchange like money for various privileges.

training group (*also called* **T-group, sensitivity group**). A kind of encounter group.

tranquilizer. A drug that reduces anxiety and often eliminates the hallucinations and delusions of schizophrenics, apparently by slowing down the activity of the brain.

transcendental meditation. A method of inducing an altered state of consciousness.

transfer of learning. The effect of prior learning on new learning. (*See* **positive transfer, negative transfer.**)

transference. A psychoanalytic term for the tendency of the patient to transfer to other people (including the psychoanalyst) the emotional attitudes he felt as a child toward such much loved and hated persons as parents and siblings.

traveling wave theory (of hearing). The theory that the basilar membrane responds as a whole to sound waves and that the sensation of pitch results from the fact that some parts of the membrane are activated more than others.

tremor. A shaking produced when two sets of muscles work against each other; one of the bodily changes observed in emotion.

trial and error learning. A form of learning in which one response after another is tried and rejected as unsuitable, until at last a successful response is made. (*Compare* **insight.**)

truth serum (sodium amytal). A narcotic used in medical therapy to induce a period of drowsiness in which the patient is able to recall and discuss experiences that he ordinarily represses.

---

unconditioned response. An automatic, unlearned reaction to a stimulus—such as the salivation of Pavlov's dog to food.

unconditioned stimulus. A stimulus that is innately capable of causing a reflex action—such as the food that originally caused Pavlov's dog to respond with salivation.

unconscious motive. A motive that the individual is unaware of but that may influence his behavior nonetheless.

undirected thinking. A thinking process that takes place spontaneously and with no goal in view.

"uppers". In the parlance of drug users, any drug that produces a lift in mood, such as the amphetamines.

upward mobility. The tendency of an individual to surmount the barriers between social classes and advance his station in life.

---

vacillation. The tendency to be drawn first toward one resolution of a conflict, then toward the other; a type of behavior typical in conflict situations.

valid test. A test found to measure the characteristic that it attempts to measure.

variability. In statistics, the amount of variation found in a group of measurements; described by the range and standard deviation.

variable. A condition that is subject to change, especially in an experiment. (*See* **dependent variable, independent variable.**)

ventromedial nucleus. A part of the hypothalamus containing the area responsible for turning off the hunger drive.

verbal test. An intelligence test or part of an intelligence test that measures the individual's ability to deal with verbal symbols; it may include items measuring vocabulary, general comprehension, mathematical reasoning, ability to find similarities, and so on. (*Compare* **performance test.**)

vestibule. A chamber in the inner ear containing receptors for the sense of equilibrium.

visceral organs. The internal organs, such as the stomach, intestines, liver, kidneys, and so on.

viscerotonic temperament. A type of temperament ascribed by Sheldon to the endomorphic body type; characterized by relaxed posture, even emotions, love of physical comfort, tolerance, and complacency.

visual purple. A light-sensitive substance associated with the rods of the retina; chemical changes in the visual purple, caused by light, make the rods fire.

vocational aptitude test. A test that measures the ability to perform specialized skills required in various kinds of jobs.

vocational guidance. The technique of helping a person select the right lifetime occupation, often through tests of aptitudes and interests.

Weber's Law. The rule that the difference threshold, or just noticeable difference, is a fixed percentage of the original stimulus.

whole method (of learning). A method in which the material is learned or memorized as an entire unit rather than part by part. (*Compare* **part method.**)

withdrawal. A reaction in which the individual tries to relieve feelings of frustration by withdrawing from the attempt to attain his goals.

X-chromosome. One of the two chromosomes that determine sex; an X-X pairing produces a female, an X-Y pairing a male.

Y-chromosome. One of the two chromosomes that determine sex. (*See* **X-chromosome.**)

Young-Helmholtz theory (of vision). A theory stating that, since the entire range of hues can be produced by combining red, green, and blue, there must be three kinds of cones differentially sensitive to these wave lengths.

References and acknowledgments

Chapter 1
What is psychology?

1. Schachter, S. *Psychology of affiliation.* Stanford, Calif.: Stanford University Press, 1959.
2. Masters, W. H., and Johnson, V. E. *Human sexual response.* Boston: Little, Brown and Co., 1966.
3. Kinsey, A. C., Pomeroy, W. B., and Martin, C. E. *Sexual behavior in the human male.* Philadelphia: Saunders, 1948.
4. Kinsey, A. C., et al. *Sexual behavior in the human female.* Philadelphia: Saunders, 1953.
5. Cates, J. Psychology's manpower: report on the 1968 national register of scientific and technical personnel. *American Psychologist,* 1970, **25,** 254–63.
6. Jones, D. R. *Psychologists in mental health: 1966.* Washington, D.C.: National Institute of Mental Health, Public Health Service Publication, No. 1984, 1969.
7. Skinner, B. F. *Beyond freedom and dignity.* New York: Knopf, 1971.
8. Matson, F. W. Humanistic theory: the third revolution in psychology. *The Humanist,* March/April, 1971, 7–11.
9. Lorenz, K. *On aggression.* New York: Harcourt Brace Jovanovich, 1966.
10. Hartshorne, H., and May, M. A. *Studies in the nature of character,* Vols. I and II. New York: Macmillan, 1928 and 1929.
11. Milgram, S. Behavioral study of obedience. *Journal of Abnormal and Social Psychology,* 1963, **67,** 371–78. Copyright 1963 by the American Psychological Association. Reprinted by permission.
12. Pattison, E. M., Lapins, N. A., and Doerr, H. A. Faith healing: a study of personality and function. *Journal of Nervous and Mental Disease,* 1973, **157,** 397–409.

Chapter 2
The principles of learning and memory

1. Yerkes, R. M., and Morgulis, S. The methods of Pavlov in animal psychology. *Psychological Bulletin,* 1909, **6,** 257–73.
2. Pavlov, I. P. *Conditioned reflexes: an investigation of the physiological activity of the cerebral cortex.* London: Oxford University Press, 1927 [reprinted by Dover, New York, 1960].
3. Skinner, B. F. *The behavior of organisms.* New York: Appleton-Century-Crofts, 1938.
4. Perin, C. T. A quantitative investigation of the delay of reinforcement gradient. *Journal of Experimental Psychology,* 1943, **32,** 37–51. Copyright 1943 by the American Psychological Association. Reprinted by permission.
5. Weinstock, S. Resistance to extinction following partial reinforcement under widely spaced trials. *Journal of Experimental Psychology,* 1954, **47,** 318–23. Copyright 1954 by the American Psychological Association. Reprinted by permission.
6. Watson, J. B., and Rayner, R. Conditioned emotional reactions. *Journal of Experimental Psychology,* 1920, **3,** 1–14.
7. Solomon, R. L., and Turner, C. H. Discriminative classical conditioning in dogs paralyzed by curare can later control discriminative avoidance response in the normal state. *Psychological Review,* 1962, **69,** 202–19.
8. Breland, K., and Breland, M. The misbehavior of organisms. *American Psychologist,* 1961, **61,** 681–84.
9. D'Amato, M. R., and Fazzaro, J. Discriminated lever-press avoidance learning as a function of type and intensity of shock. *Journal of Comparative and Physiological Psychology,* 1966, **61,** 313–15.
10. Baum, M. Dissociation of respondent and operant processes in avoidance learning. *Journal of Comparative and Physiological Psychology,* 1969, **67,** 83–88.
11. Miller, N. E. Learnable drives and rewards. In Stevens, S. S., ed. *Handbook of experimental psychology.* New York: John Wiley, 1951.
12. Garcia J., and Koelling, R. Relation of cue to consequence in avoidance learning. *Psychonomic Science,* 1966, **4,** 123–24.
13. Seligman, M. E. P. Phobias and preparedness. *Behavior Therapy,* 1971, **2,** 307–20.
14. Tolman, E. C., and Honzik, C. H. Introduction and removal of reward and maze performance in rats. *University of California Publications in Psychology,* 1930, **4,** 257–75. Originally published by the University of California Press; reprinted by permission of The Regents of the University of California.

15. Neuringer, A. J. Animals respond for food in presence of free food. *Science*, 1969, **166**, 399–401.

16. Williams, D. R., and Williams, H. Auto-maintenance in the pigeon: sustained pecking despite contingent non-reinforcement. *Journal of the Experimental Analysis of Behavior*, 1969, **12**, 511–20.

17. See, for example, Bower, G. H. A selective review of organizational factors in memory. In Tulving, E., and Donaldson, W. *Organization of memory*. New York: Academic Press, 1972, pp. 93–137.

18. Kintsch, W. Personal communication.

19. See, for example, Jenkins, J. J. Remember that old theory of memory? Well, forget it! *American Psychologist*, 1974, **29**, 785–95.

20. Bandura, A. Behavior theory and the models of man. Presidential address presented at the meeting of the American Psychological Association. New Orleans, August, 1974.

21. Bolles, R. C. Reinforcement, expectancy, and learning. *Psychological Review*, 1972, **79**, 394–409.

22. Bindra, D. A motivational view of learning, performance, and behavior modification. *Psychological Review*, 1974, **81**, 199–213.

23. John, E. R., et al. Observation learning in cats. *Science*, 1968, **159**, 1489–91.

24. Bandura, A. Behavior theory and the models of man. Presidential address presented at the meeting of the American Psychological Association. New Orleans, August, 1974.

25. McGeer, P. L. The chemistry of mind. *American Scientist*, 1971, **59**, 221–29.

26. Babich, F. R., et al. Transfer of a response to naive rats by injection of ribonucleic acid extracted from trained rats. *Science*, 1965, **149**, 656–57. Also, McConnell, J. V. Comparative physiology: learning in invertebrates. *Annual Review of Physiology*, 1966, **28**, 107–36.

27. Byrne, W. L., et al. Memory transfer. *Science*, 1966, **153**, 658.

28. Adapted, as is Figure 6-1, from Shiffrin, R. M., and Atkinson, R. C. Storage and retrieval processes in long-term memory. *Psychological Review*, 1969, **76**, 179–93. Copyright 1969 by the American Psychological Association. Reprinted by permission.

29. Sperling, G. The information available in brief visual presentations. *Psy- chological Monographs*, 1960, **74** (No. 11, Whole no. 498). Copyright 1960 by the American Psychological Association. Reprinted with permission.

30. Peterson, L. R., and Peterson, M. J. Short-term retention of individual verbal items. *Journal of Experimental Psychology*, 1959, **58**, 193–98. Copyright 1959 by the American Psychological Association. Reprinted with permission.

31. Shiffrin, R. M., and Atkinson, R. C. Storage and retrieval processes in long-term memory. *Psychological Review*, 1969, **76**, 179–93.

32. Miller, G. A. Language and psychology. In Lenneberg, E. H., ed. *New directions in the study of language*. Cambridge, Mass.: M.I.T. Press, 1964, pp. 89–107.

33. Bjork, R. A. Theoretical implications of directed forgetting. In Melton, A. W., and Martin, E., eds. *Coding processes in human memory*. Washington, D.C.: V. H. Winston, 1972, pp. 217–35.

34. Sperling, G. Successive approximations to a model for short term memory. *Acta Psychologica* (Amsterdam), 1967, **27**, 285–92.

35. Miller, G. A. The magical number seven, plus or minus two: some limits on our capacity for processing information. *Psychological Review*, 1956, **63**, 81–97.

36. Kintsch, W. *Learning, memory and conceptual processes*. New York: John Wiley, 1970.

37. Mandler, G. Organization and recognition. In Tulving, E., and Donaldson, W., eds. *Organization of memory*. New York: Academic Press, 1974.

38. Brown, R., and McNeill, D. The "tip of the tongue" phenomenon. *Journal of Verbal Learning and Verbal Behavior*, 1966, **5**, 325–37.

39. See, for example, Wickelgren, W. A. The long and the short of memory. *Psychological Bulletin*, 1973, **80**, 425–38.

40. Wickelgren, W. A. Personal communication.

41. Ebbinghaus, H. *Memory*. New York: Columbia University, Teachers College, 1913 [reprinted by Dover, New York, 1964].

42. Haber, R. N., and Erdelyi, M. H. Emergence and recovery of initially unavailable perceptual material. *Journal of Verbal Learning and Verbal Behavior*, 1967, **6**, 618–28.

43. Clemes, S. R. Repression and hypnotic amnesia. *Journal of Abnormal and Social Psychology*, 1964, **69**, 62–69.

44. Wickelgren, W. A. Trace resistance and the decay of long-term memory. *Journal of Mathematical Psychology*, 1972, **9**, 418–55.

45. Carmichael, L., Hogan, H. P., and Walter, A. A. An experimental study of the effect of language on the reproduction of visually perceived form. *Journal of Experimental Psychology*, 1932, **15**, 73–86. Copyright 1932 by the American Psychological Association. Reprinted with permission.

46. See, for example, Bransford, J. D., Barclay, J. R., and Franks, J. J. Sentence memory: a constructive versus interpretive approach. *Cognitive Psychology*, 1972, **3**, 193–209. Also Jenkins, J. J. Remember that old theory of memory? Well, forget it! *American Psychologist*, 1974, **29**, 785–95.

47. McGeoch, J. A., and McDonald, W. T. Meaningful relation and retroactive inhibition. *American Journal of Psychology*, 1931, **43**, 579–88. Reprinted by permission of the University of Illinois Press.

48. Jenkins, J. G., and Dallenbach, K. M. Oblivescence during sleep and waking. *American Journal of Psychology*, 1924, **35**, 605–12. Reprinted by permission of the University of Illinois Press.

49. Newman, E. B. Forgetting of meaningful material during sleep and waking. *American Journal of Psychology*, 1939, **52**, 65–71.

50. Adapted from Underwood, B. J. Interference and forgetting. *Psychological Review*, 1957, **64**, Fig. 1, p. 51. Copyright 1957 by the American Psychological Association. Reprinted with permission.

51. Wickens, D. D. Some characteristics of word encoding. *Memory and Cognition*, 1973, **1**, 485–90.

52. Wickens, D. D. See immediately above.

Chapter 3
Efficiency in learning

1. Tecce, J. J. Contingent negative variation and individual dif-

ferences. *Archives of General Psychiatry*, 1971, **24**, 1–16.
2. Costell, R. M., et al. Contingent negative variation as an indicator of sexual object preference. *Science*, 1972, **177**, 718–20.
3. Goodwin, D. W., et al. Loss of short-term memory as a predictor of the alcoholic "blackout." *Nature*, 1970, **227**, 201–02.
4. Johnson, F. N. The effects of chlorpromazine on the decay and consolidation of short-term memory traces in mice. *Psychopharmacologia*, 1969, **16**, 105–14.
5. Leukel, F. A comparison of the effects of ECS and anesthesia on acquisition of the maze habit. *Journal of Comparative and Physiological Psychology*, 1957, **50**, 300–06.
6. McGaugh, J. L., and Dawson, R. G. Modification of memory storage processes. *Behavioral Science*, 1971, **16**, 45–63.
7. Berlyne, D. W., et al. Effects of stimulus complexity and induced arousal on paired associate learning. *Journal of Verbal Learning and Verbal Behavior*, 1965, **4**, 291–99.
8. From *The analysis of behavior* by James G. Holland and B. F. Skinner. Copyright © 1961 by McGraw-Hill, Inc. Used with permission of McGraw-Hill Book Company.
9. Cohen, H. Unpublished study reported in *Behavior Today*, 1970, **1**, 2.
10. Solomon, R. L. Punishment. *American Psychologist*, 1964, **19**, 239–53.
11. Maier, S. F., Seligman, M. E. P., and Solomon, R. L. Pavlovian fear conditioning and learned helplessness: effects on escape and avoidance behavior of (a) the CS-US contingency and (b) the independence of the US and voluntary responding. In Campbell, B. A., and Church, R. M., eds. *Punishment and aversive behavior.* New York: Appleton-Century-Crofts, 1969, pp. 299–342. By permission of Prentice-Hall, Inc., Englewood Cliffs, N.J.
12. Munn, N. L., Fernald, L. D., Jr., and Fernald, P. S. *Introduction to psychology*, 2nd ed. Boston: Houghton Mifflin, 1969.
13. Glaze, J. A. The association value of nonsense syllables. *Journal of Genetic Psychology*, 1928, **35**(2), 255–69.
14. McGeoch, J. A. The influence of associative value upon the difficulty of nonsense-syllable lists. *Journal of Genetic Psychology*, 1930, **37**, 421–26.

15. After Lyon, D. O. The relation of length of material to time taken for learning and the optimum distribution of time. *Journal of Educational Psychology*, 1914, **5**, 1–9, 85–91, and 155–63.
16. Katona, G. *Organizing and memorizing.* New York: Columbia University Press, 1940.
17. Tyler, R. W. Permanence of learning. *Journal of Higher Education*, **IV** (April, 1933), Table I, p. 204.
18. Bower, G. H., et al. Hierarchical retrieval schemes in recall of categorized word lists. *Journal of Verbal Learning and Verbal Behavior*, 1969, **8**, 323–43.
19. Bower, G. H., and Clark, M. C. Narrative stories as mediators for serial learning. *Psychonomic Science*, 1969, **14**, 181–82.
20. Paivio, A. Mental imagery in associative learning and memory. *Psychological Review*, 1969, **76**, 241–63.
21. Bower, G. H. Mental imagery and associative learning. In Gregg, L. W. *Cognition in learning and memory.* New York: John Wiley, 1972, pp. 51–88.
22. Yates, F. A. *The art of memory.* Chicago: University of Chicago Press, 1966.
23. Bugelski, B. R., Kidd, E., and Segmen, J. Image as a mediator in one-trial paired-associate learning. *Journal of Experimental Psychology*, 1968, **76**, 69–73. Copyright 1968 by the American Psychological Association. Reprinted with permission.
24. Bower, G. H. Mental imagery and associative learning. In Gregg, L. W. *Cognition in learning and memory.* New York: John Wiley, 1972, pp. 51–88.
25. James, W. *Principles of psychology,* Vol. I. New York: Dover, 1950, p. 662.
26. Ward, L. B. Reminiscence and rote learning. *Psychological Monographs*, 1937, **49**(No. 220). Copyright 1937 by the American Psychological Association. Reprinted with permission.
27. Pechstein, L. A. Whole vs. part methods in learning nonsensical syllables. *Journal of Educational Psychology*, 1918, **9**, 379–87.
28. Krueger, W. C. F. The effect of overlearning on retention. *Journal of Experimental Psychology*, 1929, **12**, 71–78. Copyright 1929 by the American

Psychological Association. Reprinted with permission.
29. Spence, K. W., and Norris, E. B. Eyelid conditioning as a function of the inter-trial interval. *Journal of Experimental Psychology*, 1950, **40**, 716–20. Copyright 1950 by the American Psychological Association. Reprinted with permission.
30. Starch, D. Periods of work in learning. *Journal of Educational Psychology*, 1912, **3**, 209–13.
31. Wickelgren, W. A. Trace resistance and decay of long-term memory. *Journal of Mathematical Psychology*, 1972, **9**, 418–55.
32. Gates, A. L. Recitation as a factor in memorizing. *Archives of Psychology*, New York, 1917, No. 40. By permission of the Trustees of Columbia University in the City of New York.
33. Robinson, F. P. *Effective study*, rev. ed. New York: Harper & Row, 1961.
34. Thorndike, E. L. Mental discipline in high school studies. *Journal of Educational Psychology*, 1924, **15**, 83–98.
35. Bruce, R. W. Conditions of transfer of training. *Journal of Experimental Psychology*, 1933, **16**, 343–61. Published by the American Psychological Association. Copyright 1933 by the American Psychological Association. Reprinted with permission.
36. Hunter, W. S. Habit interference in the white rat and in human subjects. *Journal of Comparative Psychology*, 1922, **2**, 29–59.
37. Harlow, H. F. The formation of learning sets. *Psychological Review*, 1949, **56**, 51–65. Copyright 1949 by the American Psychological Association. Reprinted with permission.
38. Levinson, B., and Reese, H. W. Patterns of discrimination learning set in preschool children, fifth-graders, college freshmen, and the aged. *Monographs of the Society for Research in Child Development*, 1967, **32**(No. 7), 1–92.

Chapter 4
Language, thinking, and problem solving

1. Mussen, P. H., Conger, J. J., and Kagan, J. *Child development and personality*, 4th ed. New York: Harper & Row, 1974.
2. Von Frisch, W. *Bees: their vision,*

chemical senses, and language. Ithaca, N.Y.: Cornell University Press, 1950.

3. Gardner, B. T., and Gardner, R. A. Two-way communication with an infant chimpanzee. In Schrier, A. M., and Stollnitz, F., eds. *Behavior of non-human primates.* Vol. IV. New York: Academic Press, 1971, pp. 117–84. Also Gardner, R. A., and Gardner, B. T. Teaching sign language to a chimpanzee. *Science,* 1969, **165,** 664–72.

4. Miller, G. A. Some preliminaries to psycholinguistics. *American Psychologist,* 1965, **20,** 15–20.

5. Brown, R. The first sentences of child and chimpanzee. In Brown, R., ed. *Psycholinguistics.* New York: Free Press, 1970, pp. 208–31.

6. Geschwind, N., and Levitsky, W. Human brain: left-right asymmetries in temporal speech region. *Science,* 1968, **161,** 186–87.

7. Chomsky, N. *Aspects of the theory of syntax.* Cambridge, Mass.: M.I.T. Press, 1965.

8. Smith, M. E. An investigation of the development of the sentence and the extent of vocabulary in young children. *University of Iowa Studies in Child Welfare,* 1926, **3**(5).

9. Lenneberg, E. H. *Biological foundations of language.* New York: John Wiley, 1967.

10. Atkinson, K., MacWhinny, B., and Stoel, C. An experiment on recognition of babbling. In *Papers and reports on child language development.* Stanford, Calif.: Stanford University Press, 1970.

11. Miller, G. A. *Language and communication.* New York: McGraw-Hill, 1951.

12. Fromkin, V., et al. The development of language in Jeannie: a case of language acquisition beyond the "critical period." *Brain and Language,* 1974, **1,** 81–107.

13. After Brown, R., Cazden, C., and Bellugi-Klima, U. The child's grammar from I to III. In Hill, J. P., ed. *Minnesota symposia on child psychology,* Vol. 2. Minneapolis: University of Minnesota Press, 1969, p. 244.

14. Brown, R., and Bellugi, U. Three processes in the child's acquisition of syntax. *Harvard Educational Review,* 1964, **34,** 133–51.

15. Brown, R. *A first language: the early stages.* Cambridge, Mass.: Harvard University Press, 1973.

16. See, for example, Chomsky, N. A review of verbal behavior by B. F. Skinner. *Language,* 1959, **35,** 26–58.

17. Chomsky, N. *Language and mind.* New York: Harcourt Brace Jovanovich, 1969.

18. Newport, E. Unpublished Ph.D. dissertation, University of Pennsylvania, 1974.

19. Kellogg, W. N., and Kellogg, L. A. *The ape and the child.* New York: McGraw-Hill, 1933. Also Hayes, K. *The ape in our house.* New York: Harper & Row, 1951.

20. Gardner, R. A., and Gardner, B. T. Communication with a young chimpanzee: Washoe's vocabulary. In Chauvin, R., ed. *Edition du Centre National de la Recherche Scientific.* Paris: 1972.

21. Premack, A. J., and Premack, D. Teaching language to an ape. *Scientific American,* 1972, **227,** 92–99.

22. Bruner, J. S., Goodnow, J. J., and Austin, G. A. *A study of thinking.* New York: John Wiley, 1956.

23. Saltz, E., Soller, E., and Sigel, I. E. The development of natural language concepts. *Child Development,* 1972, **43,** 1191–1202.

24. Nelson, K. Variations in children's concepts by age and category. *Child Development,* 1974, **45,** 577–84.

25. Osgood, C. E., and Suci, G. J. Factor analysis of meaning. *Journal of Experimental Psychology,* 1955, **50,** 325–38. Copyright 1955 by the American Psychological Association. Reprinted with permission.

26. Judson, A. J., and Cofer, C. N. Reasoning as an associative process. I. Direction in a simple verbal problem. *Psychological Reports,* 1956, **2,** 469–76.

27. Collins, A. M., and Quillian, M. R. How to make a language user. In Tulving, E., and Donaldson, W., eds. *Organization of memory.* New York: Academic Press, 1972.

28. Schank, R. C. Identifications of conceptualizations underlying natural language. In Schank, R. C., and Colby, K. M., eds. *Computer models of thought and language.* San Francisco: Freeman, 1973, pp. 187–247.

29. Thorndike, E. L. *Animal intelligence.* New York: Macmillan, 1911.

30. Wason, P. C. Problem solving and reasoning. *Cognitive Psychology, British Medical Bulletin,* 1971, **27.**

31. Maier, N. R. F., and Burke, R. J. Response availability as a factor in the problem-solving performance of males and females. *Journal of Personality and Social Psychology,* 1967, **5,** 304–10. Copyright 1967 by the American Psychological Association. Reprinted with permission.

32. Duncker, K. (trans. by Lees, L. S.). On problem-solving. *Psychological Monographs,* 1945, **58**(No. 270).

33. Mackinnon, D. W. The personality correlates of creativity: a study of American architects. In Nielsen, G. S., ed. *Proceedings of the XIV International Congress of Applied Psychology, Copenhagen, 1961.* Copenhagen: Munksgaard, 1962, pp. 11–39.

34 and 34a. From *Modes of thinking in young children* by Michael A. Wallach and Nathan Kogan. Copyright © 1965 by Holt, Rinehart and Winston, Inc. Reprinted by permission of Holt, Rinehart and Winston, Inc.

Chapter 5
The senses

1. Uttal, W. R. *The psychobiology of sensory coding.* New York: Harper & Row, 1973.

2. Amoore, J. E., Johnston, J. W., Jr., and Rubin, M. The stereochemical theory of odor. *Scientific American,* 1964, **210,** 42–49.

3. Kenshalo, D. R., and Nafe, J. P. Receptive capacities of the skin. In Hawkes, G. R., ed. *Symposium on cutaneous sensitivity.* U.S. Army Medical Research, Fort Knox, Ky., February, 1960.

4. Champanis, A., Garner, W. R., and Morgan, C. T. *Applied experimental psychology—human factors in engineering design.* New York: John Wiley, 1949.

5. Champanis, A. *Man-machine engineering.* Belmont, Calif.: Wadsworth, 1965.

6. Lipscomb, D. M. High intensity sounds in the recreational environment: hazard to young ears. *Clinical Pediatrics,* 1969, **8,** 63–68.

7. From *Hearing and deafness,* revised edition, edited by Hallowell Davis and S. Richard Silverman. Copyright 1947 by Holt, Rinehart and Winston, Inc. Copyright © 1960 by Holt, Rinehart and Winston, Inc. Adapted and reproduced by permission of Holt, Rinehart and Winston, Inc.

8. Békésy, G. v. *Experiments in hearing.* New York: McGraw-Hill, 1960.

9. Wever, E. G. *Theory of hearing.* New York: John Wiley, 1949.

10. Uttal, W. R. *The psychobiology of sensory coding.* New York: Harper & Row, 1973.

11. Bloom, W., and Fawcett, D. W. *A textbook of histology,* 9th ed. Philadelphia: Saunders, 1968.

12. Wald, G. The photochemical basis of rod vision. *Journal of the Optical Society of America,* 1951, **41,** 949–56.

13. Liebman, P. Detection of color-vision pigments by single cell microphotometry—the method and its efficiency. Summarized in Riggs, L. A. Vertebrate color receptors. *Science,* 1965, **147,** 913.

14. De Valois, R. L. Neural processing of visual information. In Russell, R. W., ed. *Frontiers in physiological psychology.* New York: Academic Press, 1966, pp. 51–91.

15. Polyak, S. I. *The retina.* Chicago: University of Chicago Press, 1941.

16. De Valois, R. L. Neural processing of visual information. In Russell, R. W., ed. *Frontiers in physiological psychology.* New York: Academic Press, 1966, pp. 51–91.

17. De Valois, R. L., and Jacobs, G. H. Primate color vision. *Science,* 1968, **162,** 533–40.

18. Pritchard, R. M. Stabilized images on the retina. *Scientific American,* 1961, **204,** 72–78.

19. Riggs, L. A., et al. The disappearance of steadily fixated visual test objects. *Journal of the Optical Society of America,* 1953, **43,** 495–501.

Chapter 6
Perception

1. Noton, D., and Stark, L. Eye movements and visual perception. *Scientific American,* 1971, **224,** 34–43.

2. Gibson, E. J. *Principles of perceptual learning and development.* New York: Appleton-Century-Crofts, 1969.

3. Reed, S. K. *Psychological processes in pattern recognition.* New York: Academic Press, 1973.

4. Haber, R. N. Introduction. In Haber, R. N., ed. *Information processing approaches to visual reception.* New York: Holt, Rinehart and Winston, 1969.

5. Based on an idea by Rock, I. The perception of disoriented figures. *Scientific American,* 1974, **230,** 78–85.

6. Rock, I. The perception of disoriented figures. *Scientific American,* 1974, **230,** 78–85.

7. Kahneman, D., and Wolman, R. E. Stroboscopic motion: effects of duration and interval. *Perception & Psychophysics,* 1970, **8,** 161–64.

8. Treisman, A. M. Strategies and models of selective attention. *Psychological Review,* 1969, **76,** 282–99.

9. Wilding, J. M., and Underwood, G. Selective attention: the site of the filter in the identification of language. *Psychonometric Science,* 1968, **13,** 305–06.

10. Hubel, D. H. The visual cortex of the brain. *Scientific American,* 1963, **209,** 54–62. Copyright © 1963 by Scientific American, Inc. All rights reserved.

11. Hubel, D. H., and Wiesel, T. N. Receptive fields and functional architecture in two non-striate visual areas (18 and 19) of the cat. *Journal of Neurophysiology,* 1965, **28,** 229–89.

12. Whitfield, I. C., and Evans, E. F. Responses of auditory cortical neurons to stimuli of changing frequency. *Journal of Neurophysiology,* 1965, **28,** 655–72.

13. Salapatek, P., and Kessen, W. Visual scanning of triangles by the human newborn. *Journal of Experimental Child Psychology,* 1966, **3,** 155–67.

14. Heider, E. R. "Focal" color areas and the development of color names. *Developmental Psychology,* 1971, **4,** 447–55.

15. Heider, E. R. Universals in color naming and memory. *Journal of Experimental Psychology,* 1972, **93,** 10–20.

16. Street, R. F. *A gestalt completion test.* New York: Columbia University, Teachers College, 1931. Reprinted by permission of the publisher.

17. Biederman, I. Perceiving real-world scenes. *Science,* 1972, **177,** 77–79.

18. Stratton, G. M. Vision without inversion of the retinal image. *Psychological Review,* 1897, **4,** 341–481.

19. Gibson, J. J. *The perception of the visual world.* Boston: Houghton Mifflin, 1950.

20. *Experiments in optical illusion,* by Nelson F. Beeler and Franklin M. Branley. (Artist: Fred H. Lyon.) Copyright 1951 by Thomas Y. Crowell Company, New York, publishers.

21. From *Elements of psychology,* 2nd ed., by David Krech and Richard S. Crutchfield. Copyright © 1958 by David Krech and Richard S. Crutchfield. Copyright © 1969 by Alfred A. Knopf, Inc. Reprinted by permission of Alfred A. Knopf, Inc.

22. Gibson, J. J. *The perception of the visual world.* Boston: Houghton Mifflin, 1950. Used by permission of the publisher.

23. Gibson, E. J., and Walk, R. D. The "visual cliff." *Scientific American,* 1960, **202,** 64–71. (Photos by William Vandivert)

24. Bugelski, B. R., and Alampay, D. A. The role of frequency in developing perceptual sets. *Canadian Journal of Psychology,* 1961, **15,** 205–11. Copyright 1961, Canadian Psychological Association. Reprinted by permission.

25. Fisher, G. Ambiguity of form: old and new. *Perception and Psychophysics,* 1968, **4,** 189–92. Attneave, F. Multistability in perception. *Scientific American,* Dec. 1971, **225,** 6, 62–70. Drawings originated by Gerald Fisher.

26. Siipola, E. M. A study of some effects of preparatory set. *Psychological Monographs,* 1935, **46**(No. 210).

27. Helson, H. Adaptation-level as a basis for a quantitative theory of frames of reference. *Psychological Review,* 1948, **55,** 297–313.

28. Helson, H., and Kozaki, A. Anchor effects using numerical estimates of simple dot patterns. *Perception & Psychophysics,* 1968, **4,** 163–64. Reprinted by permission of the Psychonomic Society, Austin, Texas.

29. McClelland, D. C., and Atkinson, J. W. The projective expression of needs. I. The effect of different intensities of the hunger drive on perception. *Journal of Psychology,* 1948, **25,** 205–22.

30. McClelland, D. C., and Liberman, A. M. The effect of need for achievement on recognition of need-related words. *Journal of Personality,* 1949, **18,** 236–51.

31. Postman, L., Bruner, B., and McGinnies, E. Personal values as selective factors in perception. *Journal of Abnormal and Social Psychology,* 1948, **43,** 142–54.

32. Held, R., and Hein, A. Movement-produced stimulation in the development of visually guided behavior. *Journal of Comparative and Phys-*

iological Psychology, 1963, **56,** 872–76.

33. Soal, S. G., and Bateman, F. *Modern experiments in telepathy.* New Haven, Conn.: Yale University Press, 1954.

34. Rhine, J. B., and Pratt, J. G. *Parapsychology: frontier science of the mind.* Springfield, Ill.: Charles C Thomas, 1957.

35. Duane, T. D., and Behrendt, T. Electroencephalographic induction between identical twins. *Science,* 1965, **150,** 367.

36. Ullmann, M., and Krippner, S. An experimental approach to dreams and telepathy. *American Journal of Psychiatry,* 1970, **126,** 1282–89.

37. Krippner, S. Experimentally-induced effects in dreams and other altered conscious states. 20th International Congress of Psychology, Tokyo, August, 1972.

38. Brier, R., and Tyminski, W. V. Psi application. In Rhine, J. B., ed. *Progress in parapsychology.* Durham, N.C.: Parapsychology Press, 1971.

Chapter 7
Behavior genetics, glands, and nervous system

1. Shapiro, J., et al. Isolation of pure *lac* operon DNA. *Nature* (London), 1969, **224,** 768–74.

2. Heston, L. L. The genetics of schizophrenic and schizoid disease. *Science,* 1970, **167,** 249–55.

3. Scarr, S. Social introversion-extraversion as a heritable response. *Child Development,* 1969, **40,** 823–32.

4. Evans, C. L. *Starling's principles of human physiology,* 14th ed. Philadelphia: Lea & Febiger, 1945.

5. Pfaffmann, C. Gustatory nerve impulses in rat, cat, and rabbit. *Journal of Neurophysiology,* 1955, **18,** 429–40.

6. Eccles, J. C. *The physiology of synapses.* New York: Academic Press, 1964.

7. Axelrod, J. Neurotransmitters. *Scientific American,* 1974, **230,** 59–71.

8. Lewis, E. R., Zeevi, Y. Y., and Everhart, T. E. Studying neural organization in *Aplysia* with the scanning electron microscope. *Science,* 1969, **165,** 1140–42.

9. Lewin, R. *The nervous system.* Garden City, N.Y.: Anchor Books, 1974.

10. Kandel, E. R. Nerve cells and behavior. *Scientific American,* 1970, **223,** 57–68.

11. Bennett, E. L., et al. Chemical and anatomical plasticity in the brain. *Science,* 1964, **146,** 610–19.

12. Schapiro, S., and Vukovich, K. R. Early experience effects upon cortical dendrites: a proposed model for development. *Science,* 1970, **167,** 292–94.

13. Bennett, E. L., et al. Chemical and anatomical plasticity in the brain. *Science,* 1964, **146,** 610–19.

14. Copenhaver, W. M., ed. *Bailey's textbook of histology,* 15th ed. Baltimore: Williams & Wilkins, 1964.

15. Crosby, E., Humphrey, T., and Lauer, E. W. *Comparative anatomy of the nervous system.* New York: Macmillan, 1962. Based on data in Figs. 337 and 339.

16. Lewin, R. *The nervous system.* Garden City, N.Y.: Anchor Books, 1974.

17. Miller, N. E. From the brain to behavior. Invited lecture at XII Interamerican Congress of Psychology, Montevideo, Uruguay, March 30 to April 6, 1969.

18. Guillemin, R. Characterization of the hypothalamic hypophysiotropic TSH-releasing factor (TRF) of ovine origin. *Nature* (London), 1970, **226,** 321–25.

19. Sperry, R. W. Cerebral dominance in perception. In Young, F. A., and Lindsley, D. B., eds. *Early experience and visual information processing in perceptual and reading disorders.* Washington, D.C.: National Academy of Sciences, 1970, pp. 167–78.

20. Nathan, P. W., and Smith, M. C. Normal mentality associated with a maldeveloped rhinencephalon. *Journal of Neurology, Neurosurgery, and Psychiatry,* 1950, **13,** 191–97.

21. Weiskrantz, L. Problems and progress in physiological psychology. *British Journal of Psychology,* 1973, **64,** 511–20.

22. Wolf-Heidegger, G. *Atlas of systematic human anatomy.* Basel, Switzerland: S. Karger, 1962.

23. Moruzzi, G., and Magoun, H. W. Brain stem reticular formation and activation of the EEG. *Electroencephalography and Clinical Neurophysiology,* 1949, **1,** 455–73.

24. Lewin, R. *The nervous system.* Garden City, N.Y.: Anchor Books, 1974.

25. Pribram, K. H. The neurophysiology of remembering. *Scientific American,* 1969, **220,** 73–86.

26. Wolf-Heidegger, G. *Atlas of systematic human anatomy.* Basel, Switzerland: S. Karger, 1962.

27. Wolf-Heidegger, G. See immediately above.

28. Luria, A. R. The functional organization of the brain. *Scientific American,* 1970, **222,** 66–79.

29. Geschwind, N. Language and the brain. *Scientific American,* 1972, **226,** 76–83.

30. Kimura, D. The asymmetry of the human brain. *Scientific American,* 1973, **228,** 70–78.

31. Levy, J., Trevarthen, C., and Sperry, R. W. Perception of bilateral chimeric figures following hemisphere deconnection. *Brain,* 1972, **95,** 61–78.

32. Nauta, W. J. H. Hypothalamic regulation of sleep in rats: an experimental study. *Journal of Neurophysiology,* 1946, **9,** 285–316.

33. Leibowitz, S. F. Hypothalamic β-adrenergic "satiety" system antagonizes an α-adrenergic "hunger" system in the rat. *Nature,* 1970, **226,** 963–64. Also Leibowitz, S. F. Reciprocal hunger-relating circuits, involving alpha- and beta-adrenergic receptors located, respectively, in the ventromedial and lateral hypothalamus. *Publication of the Proceedings of the National Academy of Science,* 1970, **67,** 1063–70.

34. Valenstein, E. *Brain control.* New York: John Wiley, 1973.

35. Williams, H. L. The new biology of sleep. *Journal of Psychiatric Research,* 1971, **8,** 445–78.

36. Courtesy of Dr. William C. Dement. Prepared by Stanford University Medical Center, Sleep Disorder Clinic.

37. Williams, H. L. The new biology of sleep. *Journal of Psychiatric Research,* 1971, **8,** 445–78.

38. Webb, W. B. *Sleep: an experimental approach.* New York: Macmillan, 1968.

39. Gove, W. R. Sleep deprivation: a cause of psychotic disorganization. *American Journal of Sociology,* 1970, **75,** 782–99.

40. Dement, W. C. The effect of dream deprivation. *Science,* 1960, **131,** 1705–07.

41. Hartmann, E. L. *The functions of sleep.* New Haven, Conn.: Yale University Press, 1973.

42. Hartmann, E. L. See immediately above.

43. Webb, W. B. *Sleep: an experimental approach.* New York: Macmillan, 1968.

44. Moss, C. S. *Hypnosis in perspective.* New York: Macmillan, 1965.

45. Hilgard, E. R. *Hypnotic susceptibility.* New York: Harcourt Brace Jovanovich, 1965.

46. Hilgard, J. R. *Personality and hypnosis: a study of imaginative involvement.* Chicago: University of Chicago Press, 1970.

47. Kline, M. V. Personal communication.

48. Barber, T. X. *Hypnosis: a scientific approach.* New York: Van Nostrand Reinhold, 1969.

49. Banquet, J. P. Spectral analysis of the EEG in meditation. *Electroencephalography and Clinical Neurophysiology,* 1973, **35**, 143–51.

50. Wallace, R. K., and Benson, H. The physiology of meditation. *Scientific American,* 1972, **226**, 84–90.

51. Orme-Johnson, D. W. Autonomic stability and transcendental meditation. *Psychosomatic Medicine,* 1973, **35**, 341–49.

52. Udupa, K. N., and Singh, R. H. The scientific basis of yoga. Letter to the editor, *Journal of the American Medical Association,* 1972, **220**, 1365.

53. Maupin, E. W. Individual differences in response to a Zen meditation exercise. In Tart, C. T., ed. *Altered states of consciousness.* New York: John Wiley, 1969, pp. 187–97.

54. Nowlis, D. P., and Kamiya, J. The control of EEG alpha rhythms through auditory feedback and the associated mental activity. *Psychophysiology,* 1970, **6**, 476–84.

55. Sjoberg, B. M., Jr., and Hollister, L. E. The effects of psychotomimetic drugs on primary suggestibility. *Psychopharmacologia,* 1965, **8**, 251–62.

56. Doorenbos, N. J., et al. Cultivation, extraction and analysis of *Cannabis Sativa L.* Paper presented May 20, 1971, at the Conference on Marihuana sponsored by the New York Academy of Sciences. *Annals of the New York Academy of Sciences,* 1971, **191**, 3–14.

57. Hollister, L. E. Marihuana in man: three years later. *Science,* 1971, **172**, 21–29.

58. Clark, L. D., and Nakashima, E. N. Experimental studies of marihuana. *American Journal of Psychiatry,* 1968, **125**, 379–84.

59. Melges, F. T., et al. Marihuana and temporal disintegration. *Science,* 1970, **168**, 1118–20.

60. Bennett, D. E. Marijuana use among college students and street people: "It just brings out what's there." Unpublished undergraduate honors thesis, Radcliffe College, May, 1971.

61. Tylden, E. A case for Cannabis? *British Medical Journal,* 1967, **2**, 556.

62. U.S. Department of Health, Education, and Welfare. *Marihuana and health.* Washington, D.C.: U.S. Government Printing Office, 1971.

63. Souelt, M. I. Hashish consumption in Egypt, with special reference to psychosocial aspects. *Bulletin on Narcotics,* 1967, **19**(2), 1–12.

64. Ball, J. C., Chambers, C. D., and Ball, M. J. The association of marihuana smoking with opiate addiction in the United States. *Journal of Criminal Law, Crinimology, and Police Science,* 1968, **59**, 171–82.

65. Hollister, L. E. Marihuana in man: three years later. *Science,* 1971, **172**, 21–29.

66. Barron, F., Jarvik, M., and Bunnell, S., Jr. The hallucinogenic drugs. In *Altered States of Awareness: Readings from "Scientific American."* San Francisco: Freeman, 1972.

67. Brecher, E. M. *Licit and illicit drugs.* Boston: Little, Brown, 1972.

68. Second report of the National Commission on Marihuana and Drug Abuse. *Drug use in America: problem in perspective.* Washington, D.C.: U.S. Government Printing Office, March, 1973.

69. Steinhilber, R. M., and Hagedorn, A. B. Drug induced behavioral disorders. *GP,* 1967, **35**, 115–16.

70. Kales, A., moderator. Drug dependency. University of California at Los Angeles Interdepartmental Conference. *Annals of Internal Medicine,* 1969, **70**, 591.

71. Brecher, E. M. *Licit and illicit drugs.* Boston: Little, Brown and Co., 1972.

72. Kogan, B. A. *Health.* New York: Harcourt Brace Jovanovich, 1970.

Chapter 8
Emotions

1. Laird, J. D. Self-attribution of emotion: the effects of expressive behavior on the quality of emotional experience. *Journal of Personality and Social Psychology,* 1974, **29**, 475–86.

2. Lindsley, D. B. Emotion. In Stevens, S. S., ed. *Handbook of experimental psychology.* New York: John Wiley, 1951, pp. 473–516.

3. Ekman, P. Universals and cultural differences in facial expressions of emotion. In Cole, J. K., ed. *Nebraska symposium on motivation, 1971,* Vol. 19. Lincoln: University of Nebraska Press, 1971, pp. 207–83.

4. Shaffer, L. F. Fear and courage in aerial combat. *Journal of Consulting Psychology,* 1947, **11**, 137–43.

5. Young, P. T. *Motivation and emotion.* New York: John Wiley, 1961.

6. James, W. *Principles of psychology.* Vol. II. New York: Dover, 1950.

7. Ax, A. F. The physiological differentiation between fear and anger in humans. *Psychosomatic medicine,* 1953, **15**, 433–42.

8. Elmadjian, F. Excretion and metabolism of epinephrin. *Pharmacological Reviews,* 1959, **11**, 409–15.

9. Funkenstein, D. H. The physiology of fear and anger. *Scientific American,* 1955, **192**, 74–80.

10. Mandler, G. Emotion. In Brown, R., et al. *New directions in psychology.* New York: Holt, Rinehart and Winston, 1962, pp. 267–343.

11. Lacey, J. L., and Van Lehn, R. Differential emphasis in somatic response to stress. *Psychosomatic Medicine,* 1952, **12**, 73–81. Also Lacey, J. L., Bateman, D. E., and Van Lehn, R. Autonomic reponse specificity: an experimental study. *Psychosomatic Medicine,* 1953, **15**, 8–21.

12. Bard, P. A. A diencephalic mechanism for the expression of rage with special reference to the sympathetic nervous system. *American Journal of Physiology,* 1928, **84**, 490–515. Also, Cannon, W. B. The James-Lange theory of emotions: a critical examination and an alternative theory. *American Journal of Psychology,* 1927, **39**, 106–24.

13. Schachter, S., and Singer, J. E. Cognitive, social and physiological determinants of emotional state. *Psychological Review,* 1962, **69**, 379–99.

14. Schachter, S., and Wheeler, L. Epinephrine, chlorpromazine, and amusement. *Journal of Abnormal and Social Psychology,* 1962, **65**, 121–28.

15. Mandler, G. Emotion. In Brown, R., et al. *New directions in psychology.* New York: Holt, Rinehart and Winston, 1962, pp. 267–343.

16. Opler, M. K. Cultural induction of

stress. In Appley, M. H., and Trumbull, R., eds. *Psychological stress.* New York: Appleton-Century-Crofts, 1967, pp. 69–75.

17. Storms, M. D., and Nisbett, R. E. Insomnia and the attribution process. *Journal of Personality and Social Psychology,* 1970, **16,** 319–28.

18. Ross, L., Rodin, J., and Zimbardo, P. G. Toward an attribution therapy: the reduction of fear through induced cognitive emotional misattribution. *Journal of Personality and Social Psychology,* 1969, **12,** 279–88.

19. Katz, M. M., Waskow, I. E., and Olsson, J. Characterizing the psychological state produced by LSD. *Journal of Abnormal Psychology,* 1968, **73,** 1–14.

20. Kagan, J. Discrepancy, temperament, and infant distress. In Lewis, M., and Rosenblum, L. A., eds. *The origins of fear.* New York: John Wiley, 1974, pp. 229–48.

21. Richter, C. P. Rats, man, and the welfare state. *American Psychologist,* 1959, **14,** 18–28.

22. Williams, R. J. *Biochemical individuality.* New York: John Wiley, 1956.

23. Lacey, J. I., and Lacey, B. C. Verification and extension of the principle of autonomic response-stereotypy, *American Journal of Psychology,* 1958, **71,** 50–73.

24. Gellhorn, E., and Miller, A. D. Methacholine and noradrenaline tests. *Archives of General Psychiatry,* 1961, **4,** 371–80.

25. Selye, H. *The stress of life.* New York: McGraw-Hill, 1956.

26. Kiritz, S., and Moos, R. H. Physiological effects of social environments. *Psychosomatic Medicine,* 1974, **36,** 96–114.

27. Rosenman, R., et al. Coronary heart disease in the western collaborative group study: a follow-up experience of two years. *Journal of the American Medical Association,* 1966, **195,** 86–92.

28. Luborsky, L., Docherty, J. P., and Penick, S. Onset conditions for psychosomatic symptoms: a comparative review of immediate observation with retrospective research. *Psychosomatic Medicine,* 1973, **35,** 187–201.

29. Epstein, S., and Roupenian, A. Heart rate and skin conductance during experimentally induced anxiety: the effect of uncertainty about receiving a noxious stimulus. *Journal of Personality and Social Psy-*

chology, 1970, **16,** 20–28. Copyright 1970 by the American Psychological Association. Reprinted with permission.

30. Johnson, J. E. Effects of accurate expectations about sensations on the sensory and distress components of pain. *Journal of Personality and Social Psychology,* 1973, **27,** 261–75. Copyright 1973 by the American Psychological Association. Reprinted with permission.

31. Weiss, J. M. Psychological factors in stress and disease. *Scientific American,* 1972, **226,** 104–12.

32. O'Neil, H. F., Jr., Spielberger, C. D., and Hansen, D. N. Effects of state anxiety and task difficulty on computer-assisted learning. *Journal of Educational Psychology,* 1969, **60,** 343–50. Copyright 1969 by the American Psychological Association. Reprinted with permission.

33. Taylor, J. A. The relationship of anxiety to the conditioned eyelid response. *Journal of Experimental Psychology,* 1951, **41,** 81–92.

34. Farber, I. E., and Spence, W. K. Complex learning and conditioning as a function of anxiety. *Journal of Experimental Psychology,* 1953, **45,** 120–25.

35. O'Neil, H. F., Jr., Spielberger, C. D., and Hansen, D. N. Effects of state anxiety and task difficulty on computer-assisted learning. *Journal of Educational Psychology,* 1969, **60,** 343–50.

36. Ganzer, V. J. Effects of audience presence and test anxiety on learning and retention in a serial learning situation. *Journal of Personality and Social Psychology,* 1968, **8,** 194–99.

37. Spielberger, C. D. The effects of manifest anxiety on the academic achievement of college students. *Mental Hygiene,* 1962, **46,** 420–26.

38. Spielberger, C. D., Denny, J. P., and Weitz, H. The effects of group counseling on the academic performance of anxious college freshmen. *Journal of Counseling Psychology,* 1962, **9,** 195–204.

39. Glass, D. C., and Singer, J. E. *Urban stress.* New York: Academic Press, 1972.

40. Atkinson, J. W., et al. The achievement motive, goal setting, and probability preferences. *Journal of Abnormal and Social Psychology,* 1960, **60,** 27–37. Copyright 1960 by the American Psychological Associ-

ation. Reprinted with permission.

41. Atkinson, J. W., and Litwin, G. H. Achievement motive and test anxiety conceived as motive to approach success and motive to avoid failure. *Journal of Abnormal and Social Psychology,* 1960, **60,** 53–62.

Chapter 9
Drives and motives

1. Ball, G. G. Vagotomy: effect on electrically elicited eating and self-stimulation in the lateral hypothalamus. *Science,* 1974, **184,** 484–85.

2. Morgan, C. T., and Morgan, J. D. Studies in hunger. II. The relation of gastric denervation and dietary sugar to the effect of insulin upon food-intake in the rat. *Journal of Genetic Psychology,* 1940, **57,** 153–63.

3. Tsang, Y. C. Hunger motivation in gastrectomized rats. *Journal of Comparative Psychology,* 1938, **26,** 1–17.

4. Wangensteen, O. H., and Carlson, A. J. Hunger sensations in a patient after total gastrectomy. *Proceedings of the Society for Experimental Biology and Medicine,* 1931, **28,** 545–47.

5. Anand, B. K., and Brobeck, J. R. Hypothalamic control of food intake in rat and cat. *Yale Journal of Biology and Medicine,* 1951, **24,** 123–40.

6. Hetherington, A. W., and Ranson, W. W. Hypothalamic lesions and adiposity in the rat. *Anatomical Record,* 1940, **78,** 149–72.

7. Tschukitscheff, I. P. Über den Mechanismus der Hungerbewegungen des Magens. I. Einfluss des "satten" und "Hunger"-Blutes auf die periodische Tätigkeit des Magens. *Archiv Für die Gesamte Psychologie,* 1930, **223,** 251–64.

8. Nisbett, R. E. Hunger, obesity, and the ventromedial hypothalamus. *Psychological Review,* 1972, **79,** 433–53.

9. Epstein, A. N., and Teitelbaum, P. Regulation of food intake in the absence of taste, smell, and other oropharyngeal sensations. *Journal of Comparative and Physiological Psychology,* 1962, **55,** 155. Copyright 1962 by the American Psychological Association. Reprinted with permission.

10. Stellar, E., and Corbit, J. B., eds. Neural control of motivated behavior. *Neuroscience Research Program Bulletin,* **11**(No. 4), Sept., 1973.

11. Nisbett, R. E. Hunger, obesity, and

the ventromedial hypothalamus. *Psychological Review,* 1972, **79,** 433–53.

12. Hervey, G. R. Regulation of energy balance. *Nature,* 1969, **222,** 629–31.

13. Schachter, S. Some extraordinary facts about obese humans and rats. *American Psychologist,* 1971, **26,** 129–44. Copyright 1971 by the American Psychological Association. Reprinted with permission.

14. Schachter, S., and Gross, L. P. Manipulated time and eating behavior. *Journal of Personality and Social Psychology,* 1968, **10,** 98–106.

15. Schachter, S. Some extraordinary facts about obese humans and rats. *American Psychologist,* 1971, **26,** 129–44.

16. Nisbett, R. E. Taste, deprivation, and weight determinants of eating behavior. *Journal of Personality and Social Psychology,* 1968, **10,** 107–16.

17. Rodin, J. Shock avoidance behavior in obese and normal subjects. Unpublished manuscript, Yale University, 1972.

18. Rodin, J., Elman, D., and Schachter, S. Emotionality and obesity. Unpublished manuscript, Yale University, 1972.

19. Bullen, B. A., Reed, R. B., and Mayer, J. Physical activity of obese and nonobese adolescent girls appraised by motion picture sampling. *American Journal of Clinical Nutrition,* 1964, **14,** 211–23.

20. Nisbett, R. E., and Platt, J. Unpublished data referred to in Nisbett, R. E. Hunger, obesity, and the ventromedial hypothalamus. *Psychological Review,* 1972, **79,** 433–53.

21. Björntorp, P. Disturbances in the regulation of food intake. *Advances in Psychosomatic Medicine,* 1972, **7,** 116–47.

22. Knittle, J. L., and Hirsch, J. Effect of early nutrition on the development of rat epididymal fat pads: cellularity and metabolism. *Journal of Clinical Investigation,* 1968, **47,** 2091.

23. Björntorp, P., Bergman, H., and Varnauskas, E. Plasma free fatty acid turnover rate in obesity. *Acta Medica Scandanavia,* 1969, **185,** 351–56.

24. Nisbett, R. E. Hunger, obesity, and the ventromedial hypothalamus. *Psychological Review,* 1972, **79,** 433–53.

25. Schemmel, R., Michelsen, O., and Gill, J. L. Dietary obesity in rats: Influence of diet, weight, fat accretion in seven strains of rats. *Journal of Nutrition,* 1970, **100,** 1041–48.

26. Hirsch, J., and Knittle, J. L. Cellularity of obese and nonobese human adipose tissue. *Federation Proceedings,* 1970, **29,** 1516–21.

27. Sims, E. A., et al. Experimental obesity in man. *Excerpta Medica Monograph,* 1968.

28. Cofer, C. N. *Motivation and emotion.* Glenview, Ill.: Scott, Foresman, 1972.

29. Epstein, A. M., Fitzsimons, J. T., and Simons, B. Drinking caused by the intercranial injection of angiotensin into the rat. *Journal of Physiology* (London), 1969, **200,** 98–100.

30. Harlow, H. F., and Harlow, M. K. Social deprivation in monkeys. *Scientific American,* 1962, **207,** 136–46.

31. Hunt, M. *Sexual behavior in the 1970s.* Chicago: Playboy Press, 1974.

32. Kinsey, A. C., Pomeroy, W. B., and Martin, C. E. *Sexual behavior in the human male.* Philadelphia: Saunders, 1948.

33. Kinsey, A. C., et al. *Sexual behavior in the human female.* Philadelphia: Saunders, 1953.

34. Gebhard, P. H. Personal communication, 1974.

35. Vincent, C. E. Social and interpersonal sources of symptomatic frigidity. *Marriage and Family Living,* 1956, **18,** 355–60.

36. Messenger, J. Personal communication, 1974.

37. Miller, N. E. From the brain to behavior. Invited lecture at XII Interamerican Congress of Psychology, Montevideo, Uruguay, March 30 to April 6, 1969.

38. Beach, F. A., and Ransom, T. W. Effects of environmental variation on ejaculatory frequency in male rats. *Journal of Comparative and Physiological Psychology,* 1967, **64,** 384–87.

39. Bindra, D. The interrelated mechanisms of reinforcement and motivation, and the nature of their influence on response. In Arnold, W. J., and Levine, D., eds. *Nebraska symposium on motivation,* 1969, Vol. 17, Lincoln: University of Nebraska Press, 1970, pp. 1–37.

40. Valenstein, E. S., Cox, V. C., and Kakolewski, J. W. Reexamination of the role of the hypothalamus in motivation. *Psychological Review,* 1970, **77,** 16–31.

41. Bexton, W. H., Heron, W., and Scott, T. H. Effects of decreased variation in the sensory environ-ment. *Canadian Journal of Psychology,* 1954, **8,** 70–76.

42. Lilly, J. C. Mental effects of reduction of ordinary levels of physical stimuli on intact healthy persons. *Psychiatric Research Reports,* 1956, **5,** 1–9. Reprinted in Teevan, R. C., and Birney, R. C., eds. *Readings for introductory psychology.* New York: Harcourt Brace Jovanovich, 1965, pp. 57–62.

43. Dember, W. N. The new look in motivation. *American Scientist,* 1965, **53,** 409–27.

44. Butler, R. A. Discrimination learning by Rhesus monkeys to visual-exploration motivation. *Journal of Comparative and Physiological Psychology,* 1953, **46,** 95–98.

45. Mussen, P. H., Conger, J. J., and Kagan, J. *Child development and personality,* 4th ed. New York: Harper & Row, 1974.

46. McKeachie, W. J., et al. Student affiliation motives, teacher warmth, and academic achievement. *Journal of Personality and Social Psychology,* 1966, **4,** 457–61. Copyright 1966 by the American Psychological Association. Reprinted with permission.

47. Winterbottom, M. R. The relation of childhood training in independence to achievement motivation. Unpublished doctoral dissertation, University of Michigan, 1953. Summarized in McClelland, D. C., et al. *The achievement motive.* New York: Irvington Publishers, Inc. 1953. Adapted by permission.

48. Lowell, E. L. The effect of need for achievement on learning and speed of performance. *Journal of Psychology,* 1952, **33,** 31–40.

49. French, E. G., and Thomas, F. H. The relation of achievement to problem-solving effectiveness. *Journal of Abnormal and Social Psychology,* 1958, **56,** 45–48.

50. Sadacca, R., Ricciuti, H. N., and Swanson, E. O. *Content analysis of achievement motivation protocols: a study of scorer agreement.* Princeton, N.J.: Educational Testing Service, 1956.

51. Morgan, H. H. An analysis of certain structured and unstructured test results of achieving and nonachieving high ability college students. Unpublished doctoral dissertation, University of Michigan, 1951.

52. Crockett, H. J. The achievement motive and differential occupa-

tional mobility in the United States. *American Sociological Review*, 1962, **27**, 191–204. By permission of the American Sociological Association.

53. Morris, J. L. Propensity for risk taking as a determinant of vocational choice: an extension of the theory of achievement motivation. *Journal of Personality and Social Psychology*, 1966, **3**, 328–35.

54. Hoyos, C. G. Motivationpsychologische Untersuchungen von Kraftfahrern mit dem TAT nach McClelland. *Archiv Für die Gesamte Psychologie*, 1965. Supp. No. 7.

55. McClelland, D. C., and Watson, R. I., Jr. Power motivation and risk-taking behavior. *Journal of Personality*, 1973, **41**, 121–39.

56. Dember, W. N. Birth order and need affiliation. *Journal of Abnormal and Social Psychology*, 1964, **68**, 555–57. Copyright 1964 by the American Psychological Association. Reprinted with permission.

57. Hilton, I. Differences in the behavior of mothers toward first- and later-born children. *Journal of Personality and Social Psychology*, 1967, **7**, 282–90.

58. Feshbach, S. The dynamics and morality of violence and aggression: some psychological considerations. *American Psychologist*, 1971, **26**, 281–92.

59. Suedfeld, P. Sensory deprivation stress: birth order and instructional set as interacting variables. *Journal of Personality and Social Psychology*, 1969, **11**, 70–74.

60. Sampson, E. A., and Hancock, F. T. An examination of the relationship between ordinal position, personality, and conformity. *Journal of Personality and Social Psychology*, 1967, **5**, 398–407.

61. Adler, A. Characteristics of the first, second, and third child. *Children*, 1928, **3**, 14–52.

62. Lorenz, K. *On aggression*. New York: Harcourt Brace Jovanovich, 1966.

63. Foulkes, D., et al. Dreams of the male child: an EEG study. *Journal of Abnormal Psychology*, 1967, **72**, 457–67.

64. Dollard, J., et al. *Frustration and aggression*. New Haven, Conn.: Yale University Press, 1939.

65. Hartmann, D. P. Influence of symbolically modeled instrumental aggression and pain cues on aggressive behavior. *Journal of Personality and Social Psychology*, 1969, **11**, 280–88.

66. Goldstein, J. H., and Arms, R. L. Effects of observing athletic contests on hostility. *Sociometry*, 1971, **34**, 83–90.

67. Paton, R. Fantasy content, daydreaming frequency, and the reduction of hostility. Unpublished doctoral dissertation, 1972, City University of New York.

68. Doob, N. Unpublished study, University of Toronto.

69. Bandura, A. *Aggression: a social learning analysis*. Englewood Cliffs, N.J.: Prentice-Hall, 1973.

70. Maslow, A. H. *Motivation and personality*, 2nd ed. New York: Harper & Row, 1970.

71. Knapp, R. R. Relationship of a measure of self-actualization to neuroticism and extraversion. *Journal of Consulting Psychology*, 1965, **29**, 168–72.

72. Atkinson, J. W. The mainsprings of achievement oriented activity. In Atkinson, J. W., and Raynor, J. O., eds. *Motivation and achievement*. Washington, D.C.: V. H. Winston, 1974, pp. 13–42.

73. U.S. Bureau of the Census. Current Population Reports, Series P-25, No. 519, 1974. Washington, D.C.: U.S. Government Printing Office, 1974.

74. From *Motives in fantasy, action, and society* by J. W. Atkinson. Copyright © 1958 by Litton Educational Publishing, Inc. Reprinted by permission of Van Nostrand Reinhold Company.

75. Clark, R. A. The projective measurement of experimentally induced levels of sexual motivation. *Journal of Experimental Psychology*, 1952, **44**, 391–99.

Chapter 10
Reactions to frustration: normal and abnormal

1. Barker, R. G., Dembo, T., and Lewin, K. Frustration and regression: an experiment with young children. *University of Iowa Studies in Child Welfare*, 1941, **18**(No. 386).

2. Hutt, M. L. "Consecutive" and "adaptive" testing with the revised Stanford-Binet. *Journal of Consulting Psychology*, 1947, **11**, 93–103, Table IV, p. 100. Copyright 1947 by the American Psychological Association. Reprinted with permission.

3. Keister, M. E., and Updegraff, R. A. A study of children's reactions to failure and an experimental attempt to modify them. *Child Development*, 1937, **8**, 241–48. By permission of the Society for Research in Child Development, Inc.

4. Entin, E. The relationship between strength of motivation and performance on simple and complex tasks. Unpublished doctoral dissertation, University of Michigan, 1968.

5. See, for example, Horner, M. S. The psychological significance of success: a threat as well as a promise. In Day, H. I., and Berlyne, D., eds. *Intrinsic motivation in education*. New York: Holt, Rinehart and Winston, 1971.

6. House, W. C. Actual and perceived differences in male and female expectancies and minimal goal levels as a function of competition. *Journal of Personality*, 1974, **42**, 495–509.

7. Horner, M. S. Follow up studies on the motive to avoid success in women. Symposium Presentation, American Psychological Association, Miami, Florida, September, 1970.

8. Feather, N. T., and Raphelson, A. C. Fear of success in Australian and American student groups: motive or sex-role stereotype? *Journal of Personality*, 1974, **42**, 191–201.

9. Lewin, K. *A dynamic theory of personality*. New York: McGraw-Hill, 1935.

10. Lewin, K., Lippitt, R., and White, R. K. Patterns of aggressive behavior in experimentally created social climates. *Journal of Social Psychology*, 1939, **10**, 271–99.

11. Maher, B., Weinstein, N., and Sylva, K. The determinants of oscillation points in a temporal decision conflict. *Psychonomic Science*, 1964, **1**, 13–14.

12. Fenz, W. D., and Jones, G. B. Individual differences in physiologic arousal and performance in sport parachutists. *Psychosomatic Medicine*, 1972, **34**, 1–8.

13. Masserman, J. H. *Principles of dynamic psychiatry*, 2nd ed. Philadelphia: Saunders, 1961.

14. Maier, N. R. F. *Frustration*. New York: McGraw-Hill, 1949.

15. Bettelheim, B. Individual and mass behavior in extreme situations. *Journal of Abnormal and Social Psychology*, 1943, **38**, 417–52.

16. Sears, R. R. Experimental study of projection. I. Attribution of traits. *Journal of Social Psychology*, 1936, **7**, 151–63.

17. See, for example, Laing, R. D. *The divided self.* Baltimore: Penguin, 1960.

18. Erikson, E. H. *Identity, youth, and crisis.* New York: Norton, 1968.

19. Bühler, C. Psychotherapy and the image of man. *Psychotherapy*, 1968, **5**, 89–94.

20. Pavlov, I. P. *Conditioned reflexes: an investigation of the physiological activity of the cerebral cortex.* London: Oxford University Press, 1927 [reprinted by Dover, New York, 1960].

21. Masserman, J. H. *Behavior and neurosis.* Chicago: University of Chicago Press, 1943.

22. Rosenthal, D. Hereditary nature of schizophrenia. In Kety, S. S., and Matthysse, S., eds. Prospects for research in schizophrenia. *Neurosciences Research Program Bulletin*, 1972, **10**(4), pp. 397–403.

23. Reich, T., Clayton, P. J., and Winokur, G. Family history studies: V. The genetics of mania. *American Journal of Psychiatry*, 1969, **125**, 64–75.

24. Gottesman, I. I. Beyond the fringe — personality and psychopathology. In Glass, D. C., ed. *Genetics.* New York: Rockefeller University Press and Russell Sage Foundation, 1968, pp. 59–68. Also Gottesman, I. I. Double talk for twins' mothers. (Review of A. Scheinfeld's *Twins and Supertwins.*) *Contemporary Psychology*, 1968, **13**, 518–20.

25. Hollingshead, A. B., and Redlich, F. C. *Social class and mental illness, a community study.* New York: John Wiley, 1958.

26. Edgerton, R. B. *The individual in cultural adaptation.* Berkeley: University of California Press, 1971.

27. Coleman, J. C. *Abnormal psychology and modern life*, 3rd ed. Chicago: Scott, Foresman, 1964.

28. Denike, L. D., and Tiber, H. Neurotic behavior. In London, P., and Rosenhan, D., eds. *Foundations of abnormal psychology.* New York: Holt, Rinehart and Winston, 1968, pp. 345–90.

29. McCord, W., and McCord, I. *The psychopath: an essay on the criminal mind.* Princeton, N.J.: Van Nostrand, 1964.

30. Coleman, J. C. *Abnormal psychology and modern life*, 3rd ed. Chicago: Scott, Foresman, 1964.

31. Goldhamer, H., and Marshall, A. W. *Psychosis and civilization.* New York: Free Press, 1953.

32. Benedict, P. K., and Jacks, I. Mental illness in primitive societies. *Psychiatry*, 1954, **17**, 389.

33. Kline, N. S. Personal communication, 1970.

34. Yerbury, E. C., and Newell, N. Genetic and environmental factors in psychoses of children. *The American Journal of Psychiatry*, 1944, **100**, 599–605. Reprinted by permission of the University of Illinois Press.

35. Carpenter, W. T., Jr., Strauss, J. S., and Bartko, J. J. Flexible system for the diagnosis of schizophrenia: report from the WHO international pilot study of schizophrenia. *Science*, 1973, **182**, 1275–78.

36. Watt, N. F. Childhood roots in schizophrenia. Unpublished study, University of Massachusetts.

37. Kline, N. S. *From sad to glad: Kline on depression.* New York: Putnam's, 1974.

38. Schwartz, G. E., et al. Facial expression and depression: an electromyographic study. Paper read at annual meeting of the American Psychosomatic Society, Philadelphia, March 29, 1974.

39. McGeer, P. L. The chemistry of mind. *American Scientist*, 1971, **59**, 221–29.

40. Kline N. S. *From sad to glad: Kline on depression.* New York: Putnam's, 1974.

41. Akiskal, H. S., and McKinney, W. T., Jr. Depressive disorders: toward a unified hypothesis. *Science*, 1973, **182**, 20–29.

Chapter 11
Personality theory and psychotherapy

1. Maddi, S. R. *Personality theories: a comparative analysis*, rev. ed. Homewood, Ill.: Dorsey Press, 1972.

2. Whitman, A. Freudian analysts gather for the first time in Vienna. *The New York Times*, July 26, 1971, **120**, 1–3.

3. See, for example, Hartmann, H. Ego psychology and the problem of adaptation. In Rapaport, D., ed. *Organization and pathology of thought.* New York: Columbia University Press, 1951, pp. 362–93.

4. Based on Chapter 3, The human situation — the key to humanistic psychoanalysis, from *The sane society* by Erich Fromm. Copyright © 1955 by Erich Fromm. Reprinted by permission of Holt, Rinehart and Winston, Inc.

5. Fromm, E. *The sane society.* New York: Holt, Rinehart and Winston, 1955.

6. Miller, N. E. Studies of fear as an acquirable drive. I. Fear as motivation and fear-reduction as reinforcement in the learning of new responses. *Journal of Experimental Psychology*, 1948, **38**, 89–101.

7. Miller, N. E., and Dollard, J. *Social learning and imitation*, New Haven, Conn.: Yale University Press, 1941.

8. Bandura, A. Behavior theory and the models of man. Presidential address delivered before the American Psychological Association, New Orleans, August, 1974.

9. Kubie, L. S. *Practical and theoretical aspects of psychoanalysis.* New York: International Universities Press, 1950.

10. Gendlin, E. T., and Rychlak, J. F. Psychotherapeutic processes. *Annual Review of Psychology*, 1970, **21**, 155–90.

11. See, for example, Gelder, M. G. Desensitization and psychotherapy research. *British Journal of Medical Psychology*, 1968, **41**, 39–46.

12. See, for example, Paul, G. L. Two-year follow-up of systematic desensitization in therapy groups. *Journal of Abnormal Psychology*, 1968, **73**, 119–30.

13. Naar, R. Client-centered and behavior therapies: their peaceful coexistence: a case study. *Journal of Abnormal Psychology*, 1970, **76**, 155–60.

14. Lang, P. J., and Melamed, B. G. Avoidance conditioning therapy of an infant with chronic ruminative vomiting. *Journal of Abnormal Psychology*, 1969, **74**, 1–8.

15. Martin, M., et al. Programing behavior change and reintegration into school milieux of extreme adolescent deviates. *Behavior Research and Therapy*, 1968, **6**, 371–83.

16. Ayllon, T., and Azrin, N. H. *The token economy: a motivational system for therapy and rehabilitation.* New York: Appleton-Century-Crofts, 1968. © 1968. Adapted by permission of Prentice-Hall, Inc. Englewood Cliffs, N.J.

17. Davison, G. C. Elimination of a sadistic fantasy by a client-controlled counterconditioning technique. *Journal of Abnormal Psychology,* 1968, **73,** 84–90.

18. Marks, I. M. Aversion therapy. *British Journal of Medical Psychology,* 1968, **41,** 47–52.

19. Wilkins, W. Desensitization: social and cognitive factors underlying the effectiveness of Wolpe's procedure. *Psychological Bulletin,* 1971, **76,** 311–17.

20. Paul, G. L. Two-year follow-up of systematic desensitization in therapy groups. *Journal of Abnormal Psychology,* 1968, **73,** 119–30.

21. Bandura, A., Blanchard, E. B., and Ritter, B. Relative efficacy of desensitization and modeling approaches for inducing behavioral, affective, and attitudinal changes. *Journal of Personality and Social Psychology,* 1969, **13,** 173–99. Copyright 1969 by the American Psychological Association. Reprinted with permission.

22. See, for example, Lamberd, W. G. The treatment of homosexuality as a monosymptomatic phobia. *American Journal of Psychiatry,* 1969, **126,** 94–100.

23. Zweben, J. E., and Miller, R. L. The systems game: teaching, training, psychotherapy. *Psychotherapy,* 1968, **5,** 73–76.

24. Bernal, M. E., et al. Behavior modification and the brat syndrome. *Journal of Consulting and Clinical Psychology,* 1968, **32,** 447–55.

25. Luborsky, L., et al. Factors influencing the outcome of psychotherapy: a review of quantitative research. *Psychological Bulletin,* 1971, **75,** 145–61.

26. Alexander, F. G., and Selesnick, S. T. *The history of psychiatry.* New York: Harper & Row, 1966.

27. See, for example, Eysenck, H. J. The effects of psychotherapy: an evaluation. *Journal of Consulting and Clinical Psychology,* 1952, **16,** 319–24.

28. See, for example, Meltzoff, J., and Kornreich, M. It works. *Psychology Today,* 1971, **5,** 57–61.

29. Luborsky, L., et al. Factors influencing the outcome of psychotherapy: a review of quantitative research. *Psychological Bulletin,* 1971, **75,** 145–61.

30. Luborsky, L., et al. See immediately above.

31. Bergin, A. E. Some implications of psychotherapy research for therapeutic practice. *Journal of Abnormal Psychology,* 1966, **71,** 235–46.

32. Luborsky, L., et al. Factors influencing the outcome of psychotherapy: a review of quantitative research. *Psychological Bulletin,* 1971, **75,** 145–61.

33. Miller, N. E. From the brain to behavior. Invited lecture at XII Interamerican Congress of Psychology, Montevideo, Uruguay, March 30 to April 6, 1969.

34. Janowsky, D. S., Khaled El-Yousef, M., and Davis, J. M. Acetylcholine and depression. *Psychosomatic Medicine,* 1974, **36,** 248–57.

35. Kety, S. S., et al. A sustained effect of electroconvulsive shock on the turnover of norepinephrine in the central nervous system of the rat. *Publication of the Proceedings of the National Academy of Science,* 1967, **58,** 1249–54.

36. Zung, W. W. K. Evaluating treatment methods for depressive disorders. *American Journal of Psychiatry,* May, 1968 supp., **124,** 40–48.

Chapter 12
Tests of intelligence and personality

1. Doyle, K. O. Theory and practice of ability testing in ancient Greece. *Journal of the History of the Behavioral Sciences,* 1974, **10,** 202–12.

2. Copyright (1967) by Harcourt Brace Jovanovich, Inc. Reproduced by special permission of the publisher.

3. Terman, L. M., and Merrill, M. A. *Stanford-Binet intelligence scale: manual for the third revision, form L-M.* Reprinted by permission of the Houghton Mifflin Company.

4. See, for example, McClelland, D. C., Testing for competence rather than intelligence. *American Psychologist,* 1973, **28,** 1–14. Also Carver, R. P. Two dimensions of tests: psychometric and edumetric. *American Psychologist,* 1974, **29,** 512–18.

5. Ferguson, G. A. *Statistical analysis in psychology and education.* New York: McGraw-Hill, 1959. Copyright © 1959 by McGraw-Hill Book Company. Used with permission of McGraw-Hill Book Company.

6. Jencks, C. *Inequality: A reassessment of the effect of family and schooling in America.* New York: Basic Books, 1972.

7. Cronbach, L. J. *Essentials of psychological testing.* New York: Harper, 1949.

8. Terman, L. M., and Merrill, M. A. *The Stanford-Binet intelligence scale, 3rd revision, form L-M.* Boston: Houghton Mifflin, 1973.

9. Reproduced from the Pinter-Cunningham Primary Test, Copyright © 1938, 1964, 1965 by Harcourt Brace Jovanovich, Inc. Reproduced by special permission of the publisher.

10. Tyler, L. E. *The psychology of human differences,* 2nd ed. New York: Appleton-Century-Crofts, 1956.

11. Bond, E. A. *Tenth-grade abilities and achievements.* New York: Columbia University, Teachers College, 1940.

12. Wrenn, C. G. Potential research talent in the sciences based on intelligence quotients of Ph.D.'s. *Educational Record,* 1949, **30,** 5–22.

13. Sattler, J. M. *The assessment of children's intelligence.* Philadelphia: Saunders, 1974.

14. Janke, L. L., and Havighurst, R. J. Relation between ability and social-status in a midwestern community. II. Sixteen-year-old boys and girls. *Journal of Educational Psychology,* 1945, **36,** 499–509.

15. McNemar, Q. *The revision of the Stanford-Binet scale.* Boston: Houghton Mifflin, 1942.

16. Kennedy, W. A., Van de Riet, V., and White, J. C. A normative sample of intelligence and achievement of Negro elementary school children in the southeastern United States. *Monographs of the Society for Research in Child Development,* 1963, **28**(No. 6).

17. Jensen, A. R. How much can we boost I.Q. and scholastic achievement? *Harvard Educational Review,* 1969, **39,** 1–123.

18. Herzog, E., and Lewis, H. Children in poor families. *American Journal of Orthopsychiatry,* 1970, **40,** 375–87.

19. Tiedman, D. V. *Righting the balance: report of Commission on Tests.* 2 vols.

New York: College Entrance Examination Board, 1970.

20. Thurstone, L. L., and Thurstone, T. G. Factorial studies of intelligence. *Psychometric Monographs,* Chicago: University of Chicago Press, 1941, No. 2.

21. Stevenson, H. W., Friedrichs, A. G., and Simpson, W. E. Inter-relations and correlates over time in children's learning. *Child Development,* 1970, **41,** 625–37. Also Stevenson, H. W., et al. Inter-relations and correlates in children's learning and problem solving. *Monographs of the Society for Research in Child Development,* 1968, **33**(No. 7, Series no. 123).

22. Guilford, J. P. *The nature of human intelligence.* New York: McGraw-Hill, 1967.

23. Burt, C. The inheritance of mental ability. *American Psychologist,* 1958, **13,** 1–15, Table I.

24. Jencks, C. *Inequality: a reassessment of the effect of family and schooling in America.* New York: Basic Books, 1972.

25. Newman, H. H., Freeman, F. N., and Holzinger, K. J. *Twins: a study of heredity and environment.* Chicago: University of Chicago Press, 1937.

26. See, for example, Kennedy, W. A. A follow up normative study of Negro intelligence and achievement. *Monographs of the Society for Research in Child Development,* 1969, **34**(No. 2).

27. Kagan, J. Inadequate evidence and illogical conclusions. *Harvard Educational Review,* 1969, **39,** 274–77.

28. Pearson, C. Intelligence of Honolulu preschool children in relation to parents' education. *Child Development,* 1969, **40,** 647–50.

29. Wolf, R. M. The identification and measurement of environmental process variables related to intelligence. Unpublished Ph.D. dissertation, University of Chicago, 1963.

30. Skeels, H. M. Adult status of children with contrasting early life experiences: a follow-up study. *Monographs of the Society for Research in Child Development,* 1966, **31**(No. 3).

31. Speer, G. S. The mental development of children of feebleminded and normal mothers. *Thirty-ninth Yearbook of the National Society for the Study of Education,* Blooming-ton, Ill.: Public School Publishing Co., 1940, Part II, pp. 309–14.

32. Willerman, L., Broman, S. H., and Fiedler, M. Infant development, preschool IQ, and social class. *Child Development,* 1970, **41,** 69–77.

33. See, for example, Jensen, A. R. How much can we boost I.Q. and scholastic achievement? *Harvard Educational Review,* 1969, **39,** 1–123.

34. For rebuttal to the Jensen argument (above) see, for example, Cronbach, L. J. Heredity, environment, and educational policy. *Harvard Educational Review,* 1969, **39,** 338–47.

35. Gottesman, I. I. Biogenetics of race and class. In Deutsch, M., Katz, I., and Jensen, A. B., eds. *Social class, race, and psychological development.* New York: Holt, Rinehart and Winston, 1968, pp. 25–51.

36. Layzer, D. Heritability analyses of IQ scores: science or numerology? *Science,* 1974, **183,** 1259–66.

37. Sontag, L. W., Baker, C. T., and Nelson, V. L. Mental growth and personality development: a longitudinal study. *Monographs of the Society for Research in Child Development,* 1958, **23**(No. 2). By permission of the Society for Research in Child Development, Inc.

38. Tuddenham, R. D. Soldier intelligence in World Wars I and II. *American Psychologist,* 1948, **3,** 54–56.

39. Maxwell, J. Intelligence, fertility, and the future. *Eugenics Quarterly,* 1954, **1,** 244–74.

40. Cattell, R. B. The fate of national intelligence: test of a thirteen-year prediction. *Eugenics Review,* 1951, **42,** 136–48.

41. Reproduced by permission. Copyright ©, 1955 by the Psychological Corporation, New York, N.Y. All rights reserved.

42. Owens, W. A., Jr. Age and mental abilities: a second adult follow-up. *Journal of Educational Psychology,* 1966, **57,** 311–25. Copyright 1966 by the American Psychological Association. Reprinted with permission.

43. Harrell, T. W., and Harrell, M. S. Army general classification test scores for civilian occupations. *Educational & Psychological Measurement,* 1945, **5,** 229–39.

44. Duncan, O. D., Featherman, D. L., and Duncan, B. *Socioeconomic background and achievement.* New York: Seminar Press, 1972.

45. Wyatt, S., and Langdon, J. N. Fatigue and boredom in repetitive work. Industrial Health Research Board. London: Her Majesty's Stationery Office, 1937, No. 77.

46. Ryan, T. A. *Work and effort.* New York: Ronald Press, 1947.

47. *Differential aptitude tests.* New York: Psychological Corp.

48. Reproduced by permission. Copyright 1943, renewed 1970 by the University of Minnesota. Published by The Psychological Corporation, New York, N.Y. All rights reserved.

49. U.S. Office of Strategic Services, Assessment Staff. *Assessment of men: selection of personnel for the office of strategic services.* New York: Holt, Rinehart and Winston, 1948.

50. Mackinnon, D. W. Stress interview. In Jackson, D. N., and Messick, S., eds. *Problems in human assessment.* New York: McGraw-Hill, 1967, pp. 669–76.

51. Reprinted by permission of the publishers from Henry Alexander Murray, *Thematic Apperception Test.* Cambridge, Mass.: Harvard University Press; copyright, 1943, by the President and Fellows of Harvard College.

52. McClelland, D. C., Clark, R. A., and Lowell, E. L. *The achievement motive.* New York: Appleton-Century-Crofts, 1953.

53. French, E. G. Development of a measure of complex motivation. In Atkinson, J. W., ed. *Motives in fantasy, action, and society.* Princeton, N.J.: Van Nostrand, 1958.

54. DeCharms, R. C., et al. Behavioral correlates of directly measured achievement motivation. In McClelland, D. C., ed. *Studies in motivation.* New York: Appleton-Century-Crofts, 1955.

55. From *The Rorschach technique: an introductory manual* by Bruno Klopfer and Helen H. Davidson, © 1962 by Harcourt Brace Jovanovich, Inc., and reproduced with their permission.

56. Garfield, S. L. *Clinical psychology.* Chicago: Aldine, 1974.

Chapter 13
Developmental psychology

1. Mussen, P. H., Conger, J. J., and Kagan, J. *Child development and personality,* 2nd ed. New York: Harper & Row, 1963.

2. Mussen, P. H., Conger, J. J., and Kagan, J. *Child development and personality,* 4th ed. New York: Harper & Row, 1974.

3. Lipsitt, L. P., and Levy, N. Pain threshold in the human neonate. *Child Development,* 1959, **30,** 547–54.

4. Bridger, W. N. Sensory habituation and discrimination in the human neonate. *American Journal of Psychiatry,* 1961, **117,** 991–96.

5. Kagan, J. *Change and continuity in infancy.* New York: John Wiley, 1971.

6. Irwin, O. C. The amount and nature of activities of newborn infants under constant external stimulating conditions during the first ten days of life. *Genetic Psychology Monographs,* 1930, **8.** Also Wolff, P. H. Observations on newborn infants. *Psychosomatic Medicine,* 1959, **21,** 110–18.

7. Kagan, J. Personality development. In Janis, I. L., ed. *Personality: dynamics, development, and assessment.* New York: Harcourt Brace Jovanovich, 1969.

8. Thomas, A., Chess, S., and Birch, H. G. The origin of personality. *Scientific American,* 1970, **223,** 106–07.

9. Adapted from *Morris' Human Anatomy,* 12th ed., edited by Barry J. Anson. Copyright © 1966 by McGraw-Hill, Inc. By permission of McGraw-Hill Book Co.

10. Shirley, M. M. *The first two years, vol. II.* University of Minnesota Press, Minneapolis, © 1933, 1961 University of Minnesota.

11. White, B. L., Castle, P., and Held, R. Observations on the development of visually directed reaching. *Child Development,* 1964, **35,** 349–64.

12. Halverson, H. M. An experimental study of prehension in infants by means of systematic cinema records. *Genetic Psychology Monographs,* 1931, **10,** 107–286.

13. McGraw, M. B. *The neuromuscular maturation of the human infant.* New York: Columbia University Press, 1943.

14. Kagan, J., and Klein, R. E. Cross-cultural perspectives on early development. *American Psychologist,* 1973, **28,** 947–61.

15. Harlow, H. F., and Harlow, M. K. Learning to love. *American Scientist,* 1966, **54,** 244–72.

16. Spitz, R. A. Hospitalism: a follow-up report. In Eissler, R. S., et al., eds. *Psychoanalytic study of the child.* Vol. II. New York: International Universities Press, 1946.

17. Goldfarb, W. Effects of early institutional care on adolescent personality: Rorschach data. *American Journal of Orthopsychiatry,* 1944, **14,** 441–47.

18. Suomi, S. J., and Harlow, H. F. Social rehabilitation of isolate-reared monkeys. *Developmental Psychology,* 1972, **6,** 487–96.

19. Koluchova, J. Severe deprivation in twins: a case study. *Journal of Child Psychology and Psychiatry,* 1972, **13,** 107–14.

20. Hasher, L., and Thomas, H. A developmental study of retention. *Developmental Psychology,* 1973, **9,** 281.

21. Kagan, J. The effect of day care on psychological development. *Progress report,* Harvard University, 1975.

22. Zinchenko, V. P., van Chzhi-Tsin, and Tarakonov, V. V. The formation and development of perceptual activity. *Soviet Psychology and Psychiatry,* 1963, **2,** 3–12. By permission of International Arts and Sciences Press, Inc. White Plains, New York.

23. Gibson, E. J. *Principles of perceptual learning and development.* New York: Appleton-Century-Crofts, 1969.

24. Neimark, E., Slotnick, N. S., and Ulrich, T. The development of memorization strategies. *Developmental Psychology,* 1971, **5,** 427–32.

25. See, for example, Neimark, E., and Lewis, N. Development of logical problem solving: a one-year retest. *Child Development,* 1968, **39,** 527–36.

26. See, for example, Leskow, S., and Smock, C. D. Developmental changes in problem solving strategies: permutation. *Developmental Psychology,* 1970; **2,** 412–22.

27. Piaget, J. *The origins of intelligence in children.* New York: International Universities Press, 1952.

28. Stevenson, H. W., and Bitterman, M. E. The distance effect in the transposition of intermediate size by children. *American Journal of Psychology,* 1955, **68,** 274–79.

29. Goodnow, J. J., and Bethon, G. Piaget's tasks: the effects of schooling and intelligence. *Child Development,* 1966, **37,** 573–82.

30. Brown, R. W. *Social psychology.* New York: Free Press, 1965.

31. Harlow, H. F. The development of affectional patterns in infant monkeys. In Foss, B. M., ed. *Determinants of infant behaviour.* London: Methuen, 1961, pp. 75–97.

32. Kagan, J. The effect of day care on the child's development. *Progress report.* Office of Child Development, August, 1975.

33. Hamburg, D. A. Evolution of emotional responses: evidence from recent research on non-human primates. In Masserman, J., ed. *Science and psychoanalysis.* Vol. 12. New York: Grune & Stratton, 1968, pp. 39–52.

34. Ainsworth, M. D. S., and Bell, S. M. Attachment, exploration, and separation: Illustrated by the behavior of one-year-olds in a strange situation. *Child Development,* 1970, **41,** 49–68.

35. Littenberg, R., Tulkin, S., and Kagan, J. Cognitive components of separation anxiety. *Developmental Psychology,* 1971, **4,** 387–88.

36. Kearsley, R. B., et al. Separation protest in day care and home reared infants. *Pediatrics,* in press.

37. Maccoby, E. E., and Feld, S. S. Mother attachment and stranger reactions in the third year of life. *Monograph of the Society for Research in Child Development,* 1972, **37,** Serial No. 146.

38. Bowlby, J. Childhood mourning and its implications for psychiatry. Adapted from the *American Journal of Psychiatry,* 1961, **118,** 481–98. Reprinted by permission of the University of Illinois Press.

39. D'Andrade, R. G. Sex differences and cultural institutions. In Maccoby, E. E., ed. *The development of sex differences.* Stanford, Calif.: Stanford University Press, 1966.

40. Sternglanz, S. H., and Serbin, L. A. Sex role stereotyping in children's television programs. *Developmental Psychology,* 1974, **10,** 710–15.

41. Serbin, L. A., et al. A comparison of teacher response to the preacademic and problem behavior of boys and girls. *Child Development,* 1973, **44,** 796–804.

42. Brown, D. G. Sex-role preference in young children. *Psychological Monographs,* 1956, **70**(No. 421), 1–19. Also Fauls, L., and Smith, W. D. Sex-role learning of five-year-olds. *Journal of Genetic Psychology,* 1956, **89,** 105–17. Also Hartup, W. W., and Zook, E. Sex role preferences in three- and four-year-old children. *Journal of Consulting Psychology,* 1960, **24,** 420–26.

43. Nadelman, L. Sex identity in American children: memory, knowledge,

and preference tests. *Developmental Psychology*, 1974, **10**, 413–17.

44. Bronfenbrenner, U. Reaction to social pressure from adults versus peers among Soviet day school and boarding school pupils in the perspective of an American sample. *Journal of Personality and Social Psychology*, 1970, **15**, 179–89.

45. Kagan, J., and Moss, H. A. *Birth to maturity*. New York: John Wiley, 1962.

46. Weatherly, D. Self-perceived rate of physical maturation and personality in late adolescence. *Child Development*, 1964, **35**, 1197–1210.

47. Jones, M. C., and Bayley, N. Physical maturity among boys as related to behavior. *Journal of Educational Psychology*, 1950, **41**, 129–48.

48. Breed, W. Sex, class and socialization in dating. *Marriage and Family Living*, 1956, **18**, 137–44.

49. Williams, M. J. Personal and family problems of high school youth and their bearing upon family education needs. *Social Forces*, 1949, **27**, 279–85.

50. Kinsey, A. C., Pomeroy, W. B., and Martin, C. E. *Sexual behavior in the human male*. Philadelphia: Saunders, 1948.

51. Kinsey, A. C., et al. *Sexual behavior in the human female*. Philadelphia: Saunders, 1953.

52. Sorenson, R. C. *Adolescent sexuality in contemporary America*. New York: World, 1973.

53. Based on Kohlberg, L. Moral and religious education and the public schools: a developmental view. In Sizer, T., ed. *Religion and public education*. Boston: Houghton Mifflin, 1967.

54. Kohlberg, L. The development of children's orientations toward a moral order. I. Sequence in the development of moral thought. *Vita Humana*, 1963, **6**, 11–33. (S. Karger, Basel, 1963)

55. Kohlberg, L., and Kramer, R. Continuities and discontinuities in child and adult moral development. *Human Development*, 1969, **12**, 93–120.

56. Hall, G. S. *Adolescence: its psychology and its relations to physiology, anthropology, sex, crime, religion, and education*. Vol. I. New York: Appleton, 1904.

57. Macfarlane, J. W. Perspectives on personality consistency and change from the guidance study. *Vita Humana*, 1964, **7**, 115–26.

58. Sorenson, R. C. *Adolescent sexuality in contemporary America*. New York: World, 1973.

59. See, for example, Offer, D. *The psychological world of the teen-ager: a study of normal adolescent boys*. New York: Basic Books, 1969.

60. Macfarlane, J. W. From infancy to adulthood. *Childhood Education*, 1963, **39**, 336–42.

61. Macfarlane, J. W. Perspectives on personality consistency and change from the guidance study. *Vita Humana*, 1964, **7**, 115–26.

62. Adapted from Erikson, E. H. *Childhood and society*, 2nd ed. New York: Norton, 1963.

Chapter 14
Social psychology

1. Lefkowitz, M., Blake, R. R., and Mouton, J. S. Status factors in pedestrian violation of traffic signals. *Journal of Abnormal and Social Psychology*, 1955, **51**, 704–06.

2. Freed, A., et al. Stimulus and background factors in sign violation. *Journal of Personality*, 1955, **23**, 499.

3. Milgram, S., Bickman, L., and Berkowitz, L. Note on the drawing power of crowds of different size. *Journal of Personality and Social Psychology*, 1969, **13**, 79–82. Copyright 1969 by the American Psychological Association. Reprinted with permission.

4. Aronson, E. *The social animal*. San Francisco: Freeman, 1972.

5. Secord, P. F., and Backman, C. W. *Social psychology*. New York: McGraw-Hill, 1964.

6. Benedict, R. *Patterns of culture*, 2nd ed. Boston: Houghton Mifflin, 1959.

7. Mead, M. *Sex and temperament*. New York: Morrow, 1935.

8. McGrath, J. W. *Social psychology: a brief introduction*. New York: Holt, Rinehart and Winston, 1964.

9. See, for example, Bem, D. J. *Beliefs, attitudes, and human affairs*. Belmont, Calif.: Brooks/Cole, 1970.

10. Horowitz, E. L., and Horowitz, R. E. Development of social attitudes in children. *Sociometry*, 1938, **1**, 301–38.

11. Hess, R., and Torney, J. *The development of political attitudes in children*. Chicago: Aldine, 1967.

12. Jennings, M., and Niemi, R. The transmission of political values from parent to child. *American Political Science Review*, 1968, **62**, 169–84.

13. Goldsen, R., et al. *What college students think*. Princeton, N.J.: Van Nostrand, 1960.

14. Bem, D. *Beliefs, attitudes, and human affairs*. Belmont, Calif.: Brooks/Cole, 1970.

15. Freedman, J. L., Carlsmith, J. M., and Sears, D. O. *Social psychology*. Englewood Cliffs, N.J.: Prentice-Hall, 1970.

16. Yankelovich, D. *Changing youth values in the 70's: a study of American youth*. The JDR 3rd Fund, 1974.

17. Hochreich, D. J., and Rotter, J. B. Have college students become less trusting? *Journal of Personality and Social Psychology*, 1970, **15**, 211–14.

18. Newcomb, T. M. Persistence and regression of changed attitudes: long range studies. *Journal of Social Issues*, 1963, **19**, 3–14.

19. Mann, L., and Janis, I. L. A follow-up study on the long-term effects of emotional role playing. *Journal of Personality and Social Psychology*, 1968, **8**, 339–42.

20. Festinger, L., and Carlsmith, J. M. Cognitive consequences of forced compliance. *Journal of Abnormal and Social Psychology*, 1959, **58**, 203–10. Copyright 1959 by the American Psychological Association. Reprinted with permission.

21. Brehm, J. Postdecision changes in the desirability of alternatives. *Journal of Abnormal and Social Psychology*, 1956, **52**, 384–89.

22. Ehrlich, D., et al. Postdecision exposure to relevant information. *Journal of Abnormal and Social Psychology*, 1957, **54**, 98–102.

23. Mills, J. Changes in moral attitudes following temptation. *Journal of Personality*, 1958, **8**, 319–23.

24. Aronson, E. *The social animal*. San Francisco: Freeman, 1972.

25. Pettigrew, T. F. Racially separate or together? *Journal of Social Issues*, 1969, **25**, 43–69.

26. Deutsch, M., and Collins, M. E. *Interracial housing: a psychological evaluation of a social experiment*. Minneapolis: University of Minnesota Press, 1951.

27. Middlebrook, P. N. *Social psychology and modern life*. New York: Knopf, 1974.

28. Jones, E. E., and Harris, V. A. The attribution of attitudes. *Journal of*

Experimental Social Psychology, 1967, **3**, 1–24.

29. Bem, D. J. Self-perception theory. In Berkowitz, L. (ed.) *Advances in experimental social psychology,* Vol. VI. New York: Academic Press, 1972.

30. Jones, E. E., and Nisbett, R. E. The actor and the observer: divergent perceptions of the causes of behavior. In Jones, E. E., et al., eds. *Attribution: perceiving the causes of behavior.* Morristown, N.J.: General Learning Press, 1972.

31. Nisbett, R. E., and Valins, S. Perceiving the causes of one's own behavior. In Jones, E. E., et al., eds. *Attribution: perceiving the causes of behavior.* Morristown, N.J.: General Learning Press, 1972.

32. Festinger, L. *A theory of cognitive dissonance.* Stanford, Calif.: Stanford University Press, 1957.

33. Ehrlich, D., et al. Postdecision exposure to relevant information. *Journal of Abnormal and Social Psychology,* 1957, **54**, 98–102.

34. See, for example, Freedman, J. L. Preference for dissonance information. *Journal of Personality and Social Psychology,* 1965, **2**, 287–89.

35. Benham, T. W. Polling for a presidential candidate: some observations of the 1964 campaign. *Public Opinion Quarterly,* 1965, **29**, 185–99.

36. Hovland, C., and Weiss, W. The influence of source credibility. *Public Opinion Quarterly,* 1951, **15**, 635–50.

37. Mills, J., and Aronson, E. Opinion change as a function of communicator's attractiveness and desire to influence. *Journal of Personality and Social Psychology,* 1965, **1**, 135–46.

38. Walster, E., Aronson, E., and Abrahams, D. On increasing the persuasiveness of a low prestige communicator. *Journal of Experimental Social Psychology,* 1966, **2**, 325–42.

39. Weiss, W., and Fine, B. J. The effect of induced aggressiveness on opinion change. In Maccoby, E. E., Newcomb, T. M., and Hartley, E. L., eds. *Readings in social psychology,* 3rd ed. New York: Holt, Rinehart and Winston, 1958, pp. 149–55.

40. Hartman, G. A field experiment on the comparative effectiveness of "emotional" and "rational" political leaflets in determining electional results. *Journal of Abnormal and Social Psychology,* 1936, **31**, 336–52.

41. Janis, I. L., and Feshbach, S. Effects of fear-arousing communications. *Journal of Abnormal and Social Psychology,* 1953, **48**, 78–92.

42. Hovland, C. I., Lumsdaine, A. A., and Sheffield, F. C. *Experiments on mass communication.* Princeton, N.J.: Princeton University Press, 1949.

43. Aronson, E. *The social animal.* San Francisco: Freeman, 1972.

44. Hovland, C. I., Lumsdaine, A. A., and Sheffield, F. C. *Experiments on mass communication.* Princeton, N.J.: Princeton University Press, 1949.

45. Hovland, C. I., and Janis, I. L., eds. *Personality and persuasibility.* New Haven, Conn.: Yale University Press, 1959.

46. Cohen, A. R. Some implications of self-esteem for social influence. In Hovland, C. I., and Janis, I. L., eds. *Personality and persuasibility.* New Haven, Conn.: Yale University Press, 1959, pp. 102–20.

47. Sears, D. O. Social anxiety, opinion structure, and opinion change. *Journal of Personality and Social Psychology,* 1967, **7**, 142–51.

48. Levy, L. H., and House, W. C. Perceived origins of belief as determinants of expectancy for their change. *Journal of Personality and Social Psychology,* 1970, **14**, 329–34.

49. Asch, S. E. Studies of independence and submission to group pressure. I. A minority of one against a unanimous majority. *Psychological Monographs,* 1956, **70**(No. 416), Fig. 2, p. 7. Also Asch, S. E. Opinions and social pressure. *Scientific American,* 1955, **193**, 32. Copyright © 1955 by Scientific American, Inc. All rights reserved.

50. Milgram, S. Group pressure and action against a person. *Journal of Abnormal and Social Psychology,* 1964, **69**, 137–43.

51. Milgram, S. Some conditions of obedience and disobedience to authority. *Human Relations,* 1965, **18**, 57–76.

52. Milgram, S. *Obedience to authority.* New York: Harper & Row, 1974.

53. Aronson, E. *The social animal.* San Francisco: Freeman, 1972.

54. Malof, M., and Lott, A. J. Ethnocentrism and the acceptance of Negro support in a group pressure situation. *Journal of Abnormal and Social Psychology,* 1962, **65**, 254–58.

55. Festinger, L. A theory of social comparison processes. *Human Relations,* 1954, **7**, 117–140.

56. Gordon, C. Influence and social comparison as motives for affiliation. *Journal of Experimental Social Psychology Supplement,* 1966, **1**, 55–65.

57. Radloff, R. Opinion and affiliation. Unpublished doctoral dissertation, University of Minnesota, 1959.

58. Berscheid, E. Personal communication, 1974.

59. Ross, L., Lepper, M. R., and Hubbard, M. Perseverance in self-perception and social perception: biased attributional processes in the debriefing paradigm. Stanford, Calif.: Stanford University. *Journal of Personality and Social Psychology,* 1975, **32**, 880–92. Copyright 1975 by the American Psychological Association. Reprinted by permission.

60. Berscheid, E., and Walster, E. Physical attractiveness. In Berkowitz, L., ed. *Advances in experimental social psychology,* Vol. 7. New York: Academic Press, 1974.

61. Tesser, A., and Brodie, M. A note on the evaluation of a "computer date." *Psychonomic Science,* 1971, **23**, 300.

62. Dion, K. K., and Berscheid, E. Physical attractiveness and social perception of peers in preschool children. Unpublished research report, 1972.

63. Dion, K. K. Physical attractiveness and evaluations of children's aggressions. *Journal of Personality and Social Psychology,* 1972, **24**, 207–13.

64. Landy, D., and Sigall, H. Beauty is talent: task evaluation as a function of the performer's physical attractiveness. *Journal of Personality and Social Psychology,* 1974, **29**, 299–304.

65. Sigall, H., and Landy, D. Radiating beauty: the effects of having a physically attractive partner on person perception. *Journal of Personality and Social Psychology,* 1973, **28**, 218–24.

66. Cross, J. F., and Cross, J. Age, sex,

race and the perception of facial beauty. *Developmental Psychology,* 1971, **5**, 433–39.

67. See, for example, Murstein, B. I. Physical attractiveness and marital choice. *Journal of Personality and Social Psychology,* 1972, **22**, 8–12.

68. Feldman, S. D. The presentation of shortness in everyday life—height and heightism in American society: toward a sociology of stature. Presented before a meeting of the American Sociological Association, 1971.

69. Wilson, P. R. Perceptual distortion of height as a function of ascribed academic status. *Journal of Social Psychology,* 1968, **74**, 97–102.

70. Dion, K. K., Berscheid, E., and Walster, E. What is beautiful is good. *Journal of Personality and Social Psychology,* 1972, **24**, 285–90.

71. Newcomb, T. M. *The acquaintance process.* New York: Holt, Rinehart and Winston, 1961.

72. Byrne, D. Attitudes and attraction. In Berkowitz, L., ed. *Advances in experimental social psychology,* Vol. IV. New York: Academic Press, 1969.

73. Walster, E. Did you ever see a beautiful conservative? Unpublished research report, 1971.

74. See, for example, Cavior, N., and Dokecki, P. R. Physical attractiveness, perceived attitude similarity, and academic achievement as contributors to interpersonal attraction (popularity) among fifth and eleventh grade boys and girls. Unpublished research report, 1972.

75. See, for example, Bales, R., and Slater, P. Role differentiation in small decision-making groups. In Parsons, T., and Bales, R., eds. *The family, socialization, and interaction process.* Glencoe, Ill.: Free Press, 1955.

76. Aronson, E., Willerman, B., and Floyd, J. The effect of a pratfall on increasing interpersonal attractiveness. *Psychonomic Science,* 1966, **4**, 227–28.

77. Freedman, J. L., Carlsmith, J. M., and Suomi, S. Unpublished study, 1967, cited in Freedman, J. L., Carlsmith, J. M., and Sears, D. O. *Social psychology.* Englewood Cliffs, N.J.: Prentice-Hall, 1970, p. 72.

78. Zajonc, R. B. Attitudinal effects of mere exposure. *Journal of Personality and Social Psychology,* 1968, **8**, 18. Copyright 1968 by the American Psychological Association. Reprinted with permission.

79. Darley, J. M., and Berscheid, E. Increased liking caused by anticipation of social contact. *Human Relations,* 1967, **20**, 29–40.

80. See, for example, Festinger, L., Schachter, S., and Back, K. *Social pressures in informal groups: a study of human factors in housing.* New York: Harper & Row, 1950. Also Whyte, W. H., Jr. *The organization man.* New York: Simon & Schuster, 1956.

81. See, for example, Tagiuri, R. Social preference and its perception. In Tagiuri, R., and Petrullo, L., eds. *Person perception and interpersonal behavior.* Stanford, Calif.: Stanford University Press, 1958, pp. 316–36.

82. See, for example, Worchel, P. Self-enhancement and interpersonal attraction. Paper read at the American Psychological Association, New York, August, 1961. Also Deutsch, M., and Solomon, L. Reactions to evaluations by others as influenced by self evaluations. *Sociometry,* 1959, **22**, 93–112.

83. Aronson, E., and Linder, D. Gain and loss of esteem as determinants of interpersonal attractiveness. *Journal of Experimental Social Psychology,* 1965, **1**, 156–71.

84. Freedman, J. L., and Suomi, S. Unpublished study, 1967, cited in Freedman, J. L., Carlsmith, J. M., and Sears, D. O. *Social psychology.* Englewood Cliffs, N.J.: Prentice-Hall, 1970, pp. 72–73.

85. Jones, E. E., et al. Pattern performance and ability attribution: an unexpected primacy effect. *Journal of Personality and Social Psychology,* 1968, **10**, 317–41.

86. Kelley, H. H. The warm-cold variable in the first impressions of persons. *Journal of Personality,* 1950, **18**, 431–39.

87. Altman, Doris, et al. Trust of the stranger in the city and the small town. Unpublished research, Graduate Center, City University of New York, 1969.

88. Darley, J. M., and Batson, C. D. From Jerusalem to Jericho: a study of situational and dispositional variables in helping behavior. Unpublished study, 1971.

89. Piliavin, I. M., Rodin, J., and Piliavin, J. A. Good Samaritanism: an underground phenomenon? *Journal of Personality and Social Psychology,* 1969, **13**, 289–99.

90. Adapted from *The unresponsive bystander: why doesn't he help?* Bibb Latané and John M. Darley. Copyright © 1970 by Prentice-Hall, Inc. Used by permission of Prentice-Hall, Inc. Englewood Cliffs, N.J.

91. Bandura, A. *Aggression: a social learning analysis.* Englewood Cliffs, N.J.: Prentice-Hall, 1973.

92 and 92a. Lorenz, K. *On aggression.* New York: Harcourt Brace Jovanovich, 1966.

93. Eibl-Eibesfeldt, I. Aggressive behavior and ritualized fighting in animals. In Masserman, J. H., ed. *Science and psychoanalysis, Vol. VI (Violence and war).* New York: Grune & Stratton, 1963.

94. Eiseley, L. *The immense journey.* New York: Random House, 1946.

95. Nissen, H., and Crawford, M. A preliminary study of food-sharing behavior in young chimpanzees. *Journal of Comparative Psychology,* 1936, **22**, 383–419.

96. Hebb, D., and Thompson, W. The social significance of animal studies. In Lindzey, G., and Aronson, E., eds. *The handbook of social psychology, 2nd ed., Vol. 2 (Research methods).* Reading, Mass.: Addison-Wesley, 1968.

97. Campbell, D. Ethnocentrism and other altruistic motives. In Levine, D., ed. *Nebraska symposium on motivation, 1965.* Lincoln: University of Nebraska Press, 1965.

98. Berkowitz, L. The self, selfishness, and altruism. In Macauley, J., and Berkowitz, L., eds. *Altruism and helping behavior: social psychological studies of some antecedents and consequences.* New York: Academic Press, 1970.

99. Schwartz, S. Moral decision making and behavior. In Macauley, J., and Berkowitz, L., eds. *Altruism and helping behavior: social psychological studies of some antecedents and consequences.* New York: Academic Press, 1970.

100. Aronfreed, J. The socialization of altruistic and sympathetic behavior: some theoretical and experimental analyses. In Macauley, J., and Berkowitz, L., eds. *Altruism and helping behavior: social psycho-*

logical studies of some antecedents and consequences. New York: Academic Press, 1970.

101. Rutherford, E., and Mussen, P. Generosity in nursery school boys. *Child Development,* 1968, **39,** 755–65.

102. Rosenhan, D. The natural socialization of altruistic autonomy. In Macauley, J., and Berkowitz, L., eds. *Altruism and helping behavior: social psychological studies of some antecedents and consequences.* New York: Academic Press, 1970.

Appendix:
Statistical methods

1. Hebb, D. O. *A textbook of psychology.* Philadelphia: Saunders, 1958.
2. Garrett, H. *Statistics in psychology and education,* 6th ed. New York: David McKay Company Inc., 1966. By permission of the publisher.
3. Gallup, G. *The sophisticated poll watcher's guide.* Princeton, N.J.: Princeton Opinion Press, 1972.
4. Ferguson, G. A. *Statistical analysis in psychology and education.* New York: McGraw-Hill, 1959. Copyright © 1959 by McGraw-Hill Book Company.

Picture credits

Reproduced with the permission of Edmund Engelman and Basic Books. All reproduction rights to these photographs are the property of Basic Books, Inc.   p. 6 (1-1)
Con Keyes, Image, Inc.   p. 6 (1-2)
Dr. Jose M. R. Delgado   p. 7 (1-3)
Harbrace   pp. 10 (1-4), 95 (3-7), 148 (4-11), 150 (4-12), 491, 518 (14-11)
Marcia Weinstein   pp. 16 (1-6), 477 (both)
Institute for Sex Research, Indiana University, photo by Dellenback   p. 17
Shackman, Monkmeyer Press Photo   p. 19 (top)
Wide World Photos   p. 19 (bottom), 89 (middle), 254 (left), 284, 285, 296 (right, top and bottom), 323 (top right, bottom far left), 366, 506
Harvey Stein   pp. 20, 33, 56, 203, 210 (6-14), 344, 372, 499
National Library of Medicine   pp. 21 (top), 183, 251, 399
Culver Pictures, Inc.   pp. 21, 26, 389 (11-2, middle), 452 (top)

Historical Picture Services   p. 22
Ken Heyman   pp. 23, 49, 396 (11-6)
Dr. Carl Rogers   p. 26 (top)
Bettmann Archive   pp. 29, 34, 98, 105, 384 (top), 397
Sovfoto   pp. 43, 233 (top)
Will Rapport, Harvard University   p. 47 (2-3)
H. S. Terrace   p. 48 (2-4)
Godsey, Monkmeyer Press Photo   p. 49 (2-5, top left)
UPI   pp. 49 (bottom left and top right), 246 (7-10),   323 (top left; bottom, second from left), 480 (13-17)
Lou Merrim, Monkmeyer Press Photo   p. 49 (bottom right)
Yerkes Regional Primate Center of Emory University   pp. 50 (2-6), 145 (4-8)
Van Bucher, Photo Researchers, Inc.   pp. 52, 261
Dr. Albert Bandura   pp. 59 (2-12), 60, 394 (11-4)
Lynda Gordon   pp. 62, 102, 212 (6-15), 294 (middle)
Sid Greenberg, DPI   p. 65
Dr. R. N. Haber and Dr. M. H. Erdelgi   p. 73 (2-18)
Manning Studios for Republic Steel   p. 88
Ken Regan, Camera Five   p. 89 (top)
Guidance Associates   p. 89 (bottom left)
Lee Romero   pp. 89 (bottom), 92, 320, 524
NASA   p. 113
Dr. Harry Harlow   p. 116 (3-21)
Photo Trends   p. 121 (bottom)
Bernard Gotfryd, DPI   p. 127
Dr. David Premack   p. 128 (4-2)
Drs. R. A. and B. T. Gardner   p. 129 (4-3)
Wil Blanche, DPI   p. 130
Dr. N. Pastore   p. 130 (4-4)
Sandi Nero, DPI   p. 131
Vance Henry, Photo Researchers, Inc.   p. 142
Three Lions, Inc.   pp. 145 (4-7), 240 (7-5)
Brent Jones   pp. 150 (middle), 294 (top)
Suzanne Szasz   pp. 150 (bottom), 296 (top left), 400, 460, 465 (bottom), 472
Detail of *Enraged Musician* by William Hogarth   p. 159
Manfred Kage from Peter Arnold   p. 165
Dior Perfumes, Inc., Harbrace Photo   p. 167 (top)
Bert Helfrich   p. 167 (bottom)
Hewlett Packard   p. 170 (5-4)
Charles Gatewood   p. 170, 173, 357
Lineback   p. 172 (5-8)

Dr. James Maas, Cornell University   p. 173 (5-9)
Bibliothèque publique et universitaire, Genève   p. 176
A. L. Yarbus   p. 185 (5-14)
Joel Gordon   pp. 186, 370
Photograph by Harry Putney from the Collection of David R. Phillips   p. 187
Private Collection, U.S.A.   p. 194
Pictorial Parade   pp. 196 (6-2), 323 (top middle, bottom far right), 328 (top left), 379, 383, 384 (bottom), 452 (middle and bottom)
American Museum of Natural History   p. 199
Rapho Guillumette/PRI   p. 200
Library of Congress   p. 205 (6-7)
Philadelphia Museum of Art: The Louise and Walter Arensberg Collection   p. 206
Haags Gemeentemuseum, The Hague   p. 207
Marian Stanley   p. 208 (left)
Marjorie Burren   p. 208 (right)
Irving Biederman   p. 210 (6-13)
Elliot Erwitt, Magnum Photos   pp. 215 (6-18), 306 (bottom left)
United Nations Photo   pp. 216, 328 (top right)
Photos by William Vandivert; from Gibson, E. J., and Walk, R. D., The "Visual Cliff." *Scientific American,* 1960, **202,** 64–71.   p. 217 (6-21)
Ted Polumbaum   pp. 222 (6-25), 327
Marshall Cavandish   p. 224
Leonard Freed, Magnum Photos   p. 233 (bottom)
Courtesy Landrum B. Shettles, M.D.   p. 234 (top)
Dr. J. H. Tjio   p. 234 (7-1)
Dr. Larne MacHattie   p. 235 (7-2)
Bruce Gilden   pp. 236, 519 (top)
Ken Karp   p. 239
Bill Peery, Photo Researchers, Inc.   p. 241
Medichrome Service, Clay Adams, Division of Becton, Dickinson and Company   p. 243
Stan Levy, Photo Researchers, Inc.   pp. 254 (right), 296 (bottom left)
R. W. Sperry   p. 258 (7-16, 7-17)
Photos by Arthur Liepzig   p. 259 (7-18)
Dr. Peter Hauri, Dartmouth Sleep Laboratory   p. 262
Bob Combs, Rapho Guillumette/PRI   p. 266 (top)
Ralph Crane, Time/Life Picture Agency   p. 266 (bottom)
National Institute on Alcohol Abuse and Alcoholism   p. 267
Sandoz Pharmaceuticals   p. 269

Mike Keating, Image, Inc.   p. 279

Lafayette Instrument Company   p. 281 (8-1)

Edward Gallub   p. 282 (8-2)

Costa Manos, Magnum Photos   p. 289

Burt Glinn, Magnum Photos   p. 294 (bottom)

Sepp Seitz, Magnum Photos   p. 306 (top)

Charles Harbutt, Magnum Photos   p. 306 (bottom right)

John Wolcott   p. 309

Henri Cartier-Bresson, Magnum Photos   p. 310

Janine Niepce, Rapho Guillumette/ PRI   p. 314

Bell Laboratories   p. 316 (9-3)

Fred Sponholz, Rochester Institute of Technology   pp. 317 (9-5, 9-6), 461 (bottom), 469 (13-13)

James Foote, Photo Researchers, Inc.   p. 318

Michael Hayman, Image, Inc.   p. 319

N.Y. Knicks   p. 323 (bottom, second from right)

Dennis Connor, UPI   p. 324

Randy Dieter, Image, Inc.   p. 325

Virginia Hamilton   pp. 326, 466, 476 (top)

American Foundation for the Blind   p. 328 (bottom left)

Copyright by Philippe Halsman   p. 328 (bottom right)

Arthur Tress   pp. 341, 365

Marjorie Pickens   pp. 342, 351

Dr. Michael Lewis   p. 350 (10-3)

Luke Black, Image, Inc.   p. 353

Jules H. Masserman, M.D.   p. 354 (10-5)

Bruce Roberts, Rapho Guillumette/ PRI   p. 367

Copyright 1947 Time, Inc. Reproduced by permission of the estate of Boris Artzybasheff   p. 369

Gary Schwartz, Ph.D., Harvard University   p. 371 (10-7)

Reprinted by permission of Newsweek and Joseph Farris   p. 376

Myron Wood, Photo Researchers, Inc.   p. 380

Clark University   p. 382

Michael Rougier, Time/Life Picture Agency   p. 387

Museo del Prado   p. 389 (11-2, left)

New York Public Library   p. 389 (11-2, right)

Psychological Corporation   p. 413 (12-2)

Courtesy of Georgette and Géraldine Binet   p. 418

Courtesy of Houghton Mifflin Co.   p. 419 (12-3)

Nancy Hays, Monkmeyer Press Photo   p. 421

U.S. Signal Corps in the National Archive   p. 431

Joseph Consentino   p. 437 (12-15)

David Strickler, Monkmeyer Press Photo   p. 437 (bottom left)

City of New York, Department of Sanitation   p. 437 (bottom right)

Reprinted by permission of the publishers from Henry A. Murry, *Thematic apperception test,* Cambridge, Mass.: Harvard University Press. Copyright 1943 by the President and Fellows of Harvard College, 1971 by Henry A. Murry   p. 440 (12-17)

From H. Prechtl and D. Beintema. *The neurological examination of the full term newborn infant.* Little Club Clinics in Developmental Medicine, no. 12. London: Spastics Society Medical Information Unit and J.B. Lippincott, 1964. By permission (pp. 400-401)   p. 453 (13-1, 13-2)

Drs. Lillian and Edwin Robbins   p. 455 (13-4)

Bill Ray, Time/Life Picture Agency   p. 457

Courtesy of Dr. Burton L. White. From White, Burton L., Castle, Peter, and Held, Richard. Observations of the development of visually directed reading. *Child Development,* 1964, **35,** 349–364 (figures 2, 3, 4, and 6 on tip-in between pp. 352-353)   p. 459 (13-7)

Ernest Havemann   p. 461 (13-9)

Ben Martin, Time/Life Picture Agency   p. 465

Jerome Kagan   pp. 466 (13-12), 471 (13-14)

Miriam Austerman, Animals, Animals   p. 469

Esther Bubley   p. 473

Jack Corn, Image, Inc.   p. 476 (bottom)

Bob Adelman, Magnum Photos   p. 478

Alex Webb, Magnum Photos   p. 482

Arthur Sirdofsky, copyright 1975   p. 485

Ted Streshinsky, Time/Life Picture Agency   p. 487

Berry's World Cartoon "Reprinted by permission of Newspaper Enterprise Association of (NEA)."   p. 497

William Vandivert   pp. 510 (14-6), 511 (14-9)

Curtis Roseman   p. 519 (bottom)

Ed Lallo, Image, Inc.   p. 521

Dr. John Darley   p. 526 (14-16)

Jan Lukas, Rapho Guillumette/PRI   p. 526

James Karantes, DPI   p. 528

Action   p. 530

Name and reference index

Where full name is given (as Adler, Alfred), the individual is discussed in the text. In addition, this index includes in short form all the studies cited; full information is provided in the end-of-book Reference list. For example, "Adler (1928), 323, 576" means that the study is cited on page 323 and that its full bibliographical particulars may be found on page 576.

Subject index

(Page numbers in *italics* refer to illustrations.)